THE GREEN GUIDE

Chennai and Tamil Nadu

Entrance to the sanctum sanctorum, Brihadisvara Temple, Thanjavur
Photo: © Claude Renault/age fotostock

THEGREENGUIDE **Chennai and Tamil Nadu**

Editorial Director	Cynthia Ochterbeck
Editor	Rachel Mills
Principal Writers	Anurag Mallick, Priya Ganapathy
Contributing Writers	Kamini Dandapani, George Michell
Production Manager	Natasha G. George
Cartography	TTK Maps, Michèle Cana, Thierry Lemasson, Stéphane Anton
Photo Editor	Yoshimi Kanazawa
Proofreader	Liz Jones
Interior Design	Chris Bell, Yoshimi Kanazawa, Rachel Mills
Cover Design	Chris Bell, Christelle Le Déan
Layout	Yoshimi Kanazawa, Rachel Mills, Natasha G. George
Cover Layout	Natasha G. George

Contact Us

Michelin India Tyres Private. Limited
7th Floor, The Pinnacle Business Tower
Shooting Range Road
Surajkund
Faridabad - 121001
+91 - 129 3097777
www.michelin.in

Special Sales

For information regarding bulk sales, customized editions and premium sales, please contact us at:
travel.lifestyle@us.michelin.com
www.michelintravel.com

HOW TO USE THIS GUIDE

PLANNING YOUR TRIP

The blue-tabbed PLANNING YOUR TRIP section at the front of the guide gives you **ideas for your trip** and **practical information** to help you organise it. You'll find tours, practical information, a host of outdoor activities, a calendar of events, information on shopping, sightseeing, kids' activities and more.

INTRODUCTION

The orange-tabbed INTRODUCTION section explores **Tamil Nadu Today** through religion, language, government, economy and cuisine. The **History** section spans various dynasties and empires, the Colonial period and post-Independence today. **Architecture**, **Art, Literature, Cinema**, **Music** and **Dance** are all covered, while **Nature** delves into the natural landscape.

DISCOVERING

The green-tabbed DISCOVERING section is ordered by theme, featuring the most interesting local **Sights**, **Walking Tours**, nearby **Excursions**, and detailed **Driving Tours**. Admission prices shown are for a single adult.

ADDRESSES

We've selected the best hotels, restaurants, cafes, shops, nightlife and entertainment to fit all budgets. See the Legend on the cover flap for an explanation of the price categories. See the back of the guide for an index of where to find hotel and restaurant listings in this guide.

Sidebars

Throughout the guide you will find blue, peach and green-coloured text boxes with lively anecdotes, detailed history and background information.

A Bit of Advice

Green advice boxes found in this guide contain practical tips and handy information relevant to your visit or to a sight in the Discovering section.

STAR RATINGS★★★

Michelin has given star ratings for more than 100 years. If you're pressed for time, we recommend you visit the ★★★, or ★★ sights first:

- ★★★ **Highly recommended**
- ★★ **Recommended**
- ★ **Interesting**

MAPS

- Principal Sights map.
- Region maps.
- Maps for major cities and villages.
- Local tour maps.

All maps in this guide are oriented north, unless otherwise indicated by a directional arrow. The term "Local Map" refers to a map within the chapter or Tourism Region. A complete list of the maps found in the guide appears at the back of this book.

© Konrad Wothe/Look/Photononstop

PLANNING YOUR TRIP

When and Where to Go 10
When to Go 10
Where to Go 10
Themed Tours 11
What to See and Do 14
Outdoor Fun 14
Fishing 14
Golf 14
Hiking 15
Horse riding 15
Birdwatching 16
Organised Sightseeing Tours 16
Indoor Fun 17
Courses 17
Volunteering 18
Activities for Kids 18
Shopping 19
Opening Hours 19
What to Buy 19
Emporiums 21
Books and Films 22
Books 22
Films 23
Calendar of Events 24
Know Before You Go 28
Useful Websites 28
Tourist Offices 28
India Tourist Offices Abroad 29
International Visitors 29
Entry Requirements 29
Customs Regulations 30
Health 30
Accessibility 30
Getting There and Getting Around 31
By Plane 31
By Boat 32
By Train 32
By Coach/Bus 34
By Car 34
By Motorcycle 34
Local Transport 35
Where to Stay and Eat 36
Where to Stay 36
Where to Eat 38
Basic Information 39
Useful Words and Phrases 43

INTRODUCTION TO TAMIL NADU

© Frederic Soltan/Sygma/Corbis

Tamil Nadu Today 48
Lifestyle 48
Population 48
Religion 50
Language 52
Government 54
Economy 54
Media 56
Sport 57
Cuisine 58
History 61
Timeline 61
Architecture 72
The Tamil Style 72
Pallava Temples 73
Chola Temples 74

Nayaka Temples 74
Nayaka Strongholds and Palaces ... 75
The European Impact.............. 77

Art 78
Early Stone Reliefs................ 78
Wall Carvings 79
Column Sculptures 79
Bronzes........................... 80
Ceiling Paintings and Textiles 80
Tanjore Painting................... 81
Ivories and Weapons 81

Literature 82

Cinema 86

Music 89
Carnatic Music 89
Folk Music 90
Light Music 91

Dance 92
Bharata Natyam................... 92
Folk Dances....................... 93

Nature 94
Mountains: Kurinji................. 94
Forests: Mullai.................... 95
Croplands and Plains: Marudham... 96
Seashore: Neidhal 97
Wasteland or Scrubland: Palai...... 99

DISCOVERING TAMIL NADU

© Susan Gibson/Alamy

Chennai and Around 102
Religious and Spiritual Sights 108
Historical Sights.................. 111
Museums and Art Galleries........ 115
National Parks and Wildlife Sanctuaries 116
Beaches.......................... 119

Pondicherry 132
Religious and Spiritual Sights 136
Historical Sights.................. 143
Museums and Art Galleries........ 145
Beaches.......................... 147

Coromandel Coast 156
Religious and Spiritual Sights 163
Historical Sights.................. 174
Museums and Art Galleries........ 181
National Parks and Wildlife Sanctuaries 183
Beaches.......................... 186

Chettinad 194
Religious and Spiritual Sights 198
Historical Sights..................200

Southern Tamil Nadu 204
Religious and Spiritual Sights 210
Historical Sights.................. 218
Museums and Art Galleries........ 221
National Parks and Wildlife Sanctuaries 223
Beaches..........................225

Central Tamil Nadu 232
Religious and Spiritual Sights 238
Historical Sights..................248
National Parks and Wildlife Sanctuaries 250
Hill Stations......................251

Western Ghats 260
Religious and Spiritual Sights 265
National Parks and Wildlife Sanctuaries 267
Hill Stations......................270

Index 290
Maps and Plans.................296
Map Legend 297

Welcome to Tamil Nadu

The southern state of Tamil Nadu spreads to the very tip of the Indian peninsula. Set against the backdrop of ancient signatures in art, sculpture, palaces, forts and temples of epic dynasties are seaside villages, English bungalows and chic French quarters with landscapes shifting from hills and plantations to iridescent paddy fields and soft sandy beaches. As a cultural capital with a thriving music and movie industry, Tamil Nadu is a heady fusion of tradition and commerce.

Museum Theatre, Chennai

CHENNAI AND AROUND

(pp102–131)

The lively metropolis of Chennai, formerly Madras, holds a mirror to the city's evolution from a small fishing village to a major British stronghold before finally transforming into the prosperous state capital. Iconic landmarks like Fort St George, monuments around Marina Beach and museums reveal Chennai's illustrious history. The lasting presence of esteemed institutions, old temples, churches and mosques, local music and dance *sabhas*, illustrate the city's secular temperament and robust cultural ethos. Chennai also boasts ecological oases like Guindy National Park, Vandalur Zoo, Pulicat Lake and Crocodile Bank nearby.

PONDICHERRY *(pp132–155)*

Pondicherry (Puducherry) is a place that blends the finer things in life and all things French with the richness of traditional Tamil culture. Its unique *laissez faire* charm draws people to experience unifying peace at Aurobindo Ashram and Auroville, indulge at a quaint cafe or *patisserie* or browse the many fashionable boutiques selling clothes, jewellery and organic arty products. Creole cuisine and the comforts of villas in the French Quarter and Franco-Tamil homes make Pondicherry an irresistible getaway.

COROMANDEL COAST

(pp156–193)

Mighty dynasties like Pallavas and Cholas and European powers like the Portuguese, Danes, Dutch, French and English have ensured the Coromandel Coast a chequered history. The area triggered trade, inspired the creation of great temples and evoked poetry in kings and ordinary folk. The exhilarating coastal journey takes in historic ports Mamallapuram and Poompuhar, to temple-towns Kanchipuram and Chidambaram, past Pichavaram's mangrove forests, the Danish outpost Tranquebar and the French colony of Karaikal to the final frontier of south-east India at magical Rameswaram.

Varadaraja Perumal Temple, Kanchipuram, Coromandel Coast

CHETTINAD *(pp194–203)*

The industrious community of Nattukottai Chettiars chose a hot dry area of central Tamil Nadu and carved for themselves a unique territory called Chettinad. Their impact is seen in the colossal mansions of Karaikudi, Kanadukathan and Kothamangalam, the nine clan temples and Athangudi's stunning floor tiles. In textiles, the bold checks and stripes of the Chettinad cotton sari has been a fashion statement for over a century while Chettinad's delectably spicy and elaborate cuisine has a permanent place on Indian menus.

SOUTHERN TAMIL NADU *(pp204–231)*

A trip to Southern Tamil Nadu opens windows to many worlds. The journey begins from the regal city of Madurai and takes in revered temples at Tirunelveli, Tiruchendur and Tenkasi. Wildlife trails can be enjoyed in Mundanthurai, alongside therapeutic baths under Courtallam's waterfalls and relaxation in luxury resorts. The magical Land's End at Kanyakumari should not be missed. Discover the splendour of royal palaces, architectural marvels and historic relics in museums and repositories of knowledge or enjoy a splendid sunset while meditating on sacred beaches.

CENTRAL TAMIL NADU *(pp232–259)*

Central Tamil Nadu shines like a gilded Tanjore painting studded with gems of architecture, sculpture, metalcraft, literature and art. The unparalleled beauty of UNESCO World Heritage sites and magnificent temples in Thanjavur, Gangaikondacholapuram and Darasuram, the pilgrim town of Kumbakonam, Trichy's Rock Fort and the massive reclining Ranganatha

Maratha Darbar Hall, Thanjavur Palace, Central Tamil Nadu

idol at Srirangam all showcase the brilliance of artisans of yore and genius of visionary kings – the Cholas, Nayaks and Marathas. Enjoy pastoral views and the beauty of the meandering Kaveri River or relish the hilly charms of misty Yercaud.

WESTERN GHATS *(pp260–289)*

As one of the richest biodiversity hotspots in the world, the hill tracts of the Western Ghats nurture a fabulous treasure-trove of animal, bird and plant species, luring nature lovers to its forests at Mudumalai, Mukurthi and Anamalai. Erstwhile Colonial retreats like Ooty, Coonoor and Kotagiri in the blue hills of the Nilgiris and Kodaikanal in the sacred Palani Hills are scenic and historic locales. Stunning drives on ghat roads and the century-old Nilgiri Mountain Railway hold the promise of journeys that will never be forgotten.

Tea plantation in the Nilgiris, Western Ghats

Fishing boats on Marina Beach, Chennai

PLANNING YOUR TRIP

When and Where to Go

WHEN TO GO

SEASONS

Tamil Nadu is essentially a tropical region and shows slight seasonal variations. The dry season stretches from January to May. Rainfall occurs twice a year. June to September witnesses the south-west monsoons accompanied by strong south-west winds, while the north-east monsoon kicks in from October to December with thunder, lightning and forceful north-east winds.

Sporadic depressions in the Bay of Bengal tend to cause cyclonic storms and heavy rainfall across the year. With several agricultural zones, the area relies heavily on the monsoons to replenish its water resources for crop production; the absence of rain results in severe water scarcity and drought. Lightweight cotton wear is ideal for most parts of the year, though warm woollen clothes are recommended in hill stations as mornings and winters are pretty chilly. An umbrella offers good protection from the harsh sun or rain. November to March is the ideal time to visit as it is cooler and rainfall is lower.

CLIMATE

The climate can vary greatly from the plains to the hills. Temperatures tend to remain on the higher side throughout the year on the plains with dry sub-humid or semi arid climate while coastal regions experience high temperatures and high humidity. The maximum temperature on the plains is around 43°C and the minimum temperature remains around 23°C. The hottest months are usually April–June. However, in the hills, the maximum temperature can average around 22°C–32°C or sink to a minimum low of 12°C–0°C. On the coast, the cool sea breeze provides some respite in the evenings through the night.

WHERE TO GO

WEEKEND BREAKS

Depending on how far one wishes to travel, there are many interesting places just short drives away from Chennai. The historic town of Mamallapuram via Kovalam and Muthukadu along the East Coast Road is an ideal weekend getaway besides the temple town of Kanchipuram with its ubiquitous silk weaving units. Both places are under 75km from Chennai. Within a 200km radius from Chennai, one can dock at the beach town of Pondicherry with peaceful Auroville nearby or if one prefers a more quiet, off-beat place, Tranquebar has some wonderful beach bungalows to put one's feet up.

ONE WEEK

The 8-Day Tamil Nadu Tour offered by TTDC leaves Chennai at 7am every Saturday and returns at 6pm the following Saturday. It covers Pondicherry, Pichavaram, Chidambaram*, Vaitheeswaran Kovil, Nagore, Vellankanni, Mannargudi, Thanjavur*, Rameswaram*, Kanyakumari*, Suchindram, Madurai*, Kodaikanal* and Trichy*. (*Night halts). Another 8-day option, the East West Coast Tour by TTDC, leaves Chennai every Wednesday at 7am and returns the following Wednesday at 6pm, covering regions of Tamil Nadu and Kerala.

For a leisurely one-week independent trip, one can devote three days for Chennai and around, two days for Kanchipuram and two days for Mamallapuram.

SECOND WEEK

For the second week fly or take a train to Coimbatore and cover the Nilgiris. Spend at least five days exploring Ooty, Coonoor and Kotagiri, which have some great homestays, resorts and sights. Don't miss the delightful Nilgiri Mountain Railway Tour, a great way to savour this scenic region. Drive from Ooty to Mudumalai for a wildlife adventure and safari at the sanctuary. One can easily spend two days at Mudumalai and drive down to Bangalore or Cochin thereafter to take a flight back. Another tour option is to take a train from Chennai to Kumbakonam and cover central Tamil Nadu's famous temple circuit of Kumbakonam, Thanjavur and Trichy from where one can fly out. A good 2-day extension from here would be a halt at Karaikudi or Kanadukathan to explore the unique region of Chettinad.

THEMED TOURS

The geographical, ecological, cultural and spiritual diversity of Tamil Nadu makes it a great place to design or customise tours as per the interest of its visitors. In most places, archaeological remains, heritage structures and monuments exhibit their political, social and regional history, despite being weathered by time.

TEMPLES AND PILGRIMAGES

From mystic mountains like Tiruvannamalai and Velliangiri to hoary temple towns like Kumbakonam and Kanchipuram and the banks of holy rivers to sacred hot spots like Kanyakumari and Rameshwaram, Tamil Nadu in many ways is a celebration of the divine. In the hill shrines of Trichy and Palani and cave temples in Swamimalai and Sittanavasal, legends recall how gods claimed these abodes and reveal art fashioned by the hands of men. Hailed in scriptures, deified through majestic shrines and worshipped by kings and sages, these hallowed spots reverberate with a primordial energy that can drown out the noise and hubbub of pilgrim traffic.

HILL STATIONS

Home to wildlife and old tribes for centuries past, the mountains of Tamil Nadu wooed early explorers and British officers to establish townships and sanatoria on higher ground to escape the heat of the plains. Later, Christian missionaries also moved in to spread the gospel and set up elite residential educational institutions that have added another dimension to the region's popularity. Today, panoramic views from well-known vantage points in Ooty, Coonoor and Kotagiri and the beauty of its tea gardens, horticultural parks, lakes, forests and unique Mountain Railway, make the Nilgiris one of the most sought-after tourist destinations and filming locales. People drive up the serpentine ghat roads to savour the Colonial heritage and plantation lifestyle in these hills. The heady spirit of the hills can also be captured in smaller hill stations. Yercaud, an erstwhile Colonial outpost known for coffee and citrus plantations, Kodaikanal with its breathtaking rocks and caves,

Pilgrims having a ritual bath at Agni Theertham on the seashore, Rameswaram

valley views and landmark schools and Yelagiri are also charming getaways.

WILDLIFE

From Chennai's Guindy National Park and Crocodile Bank to the sholas and densely forested Western Ghats, Tamil Nadu is blessed with excellent biodiversity. Several areas and former hunting grounds were amongst the earliest notified national parks and wildlife sanctuaries of the country. Famous forests like Mudumalai, Mukkurthi, Mundanthurai and Anamalai are the terrain of tigers, gaurs, elephants, reptiles, birds and insects. Numerous rare, endemic and endangered species including the Nilgiri tahr, Nilgiri langur, Nilgiri laughing thrush, lion-tailed macaque and Ceylon frogmouth can be found here. Herds of blackbuck roam the central and southern scrub forests while coastal swamps witness massive flocks of migratory birds in season. Water birds come to roost at Vedanthangal, Point Calimere's mudflats are renowned for fantastic flamingo and pelican congregations and Viralimalai is a peacock haven.

BEACHES AND RESORTS

Stretching for miles along the eastern and southern edges of the subcontinent, the Coromandel Coast displays numerous sunkissed famous and lesser-known beaches overlooking vast open waters. The long curve of Marina and Elliot's Beach at Chennai, the sandy strips of Kovalam (Covelong), Mamallapuram and Pondicherry present stunning seascapes at dawn or dusk and remain the most popular beaches. Each possesses all the trappings of a leisure holiday with luxury beach resorts, food stalls and curio shops in the vicinity. Further south in Tiruchendur, Rameswaram and Kanyakumari, the beaches are located beside famous temples and witness heavy pilgrim traffic. Tranquebar is a good off-beat beach destination while Dhanushkodi's remarkably unusual shoreline is an adventurous drive. Although the sea tends to be rough on the East Coast, certain locations encourage water sports in the safer zones.

CULTURAL HERITAGE

In a land synonymous with classical arts like Bharatanatyam and Carnatic music, vibrant folk dance forms like Kummi, Koravanji and Kuthu, exquisite bronze and stone sculptures and paintings, signature cuisines and a silken textile tradition of Kanjeevarams that turn into heirlooms, Tamil Nadu's cultural foundation is very solid.
The Tamil people are known to be a passionate lot who have guarded their cultural traditions with fierce pride and woven it inextricably into their social fabric. Yet, travelling across the state reveals how foreign cultures like the British, Danish and French or rulers from bordering states like the Telugu Nayaks, Marathas and Kerala kings managed to leave an indelible influence upon the region's landscape.

NATURAL SITES

Mighty mountains, undulating meadows, glittering lakes, healing waterfalls, mysterious forests and caverns: this southern state is a veritable paradise. Many of these spectacular natural sights have unusual names and fascinating stories that recall a bygone era.
Waterfalls like Silver Cascade and Bear Shola in Kodaikanal, the cluster of falls acting as a natural spa in Courtallam, Catherine Falls in Kotagiri, vantage points and extraordinarily shaped cliffs like Pillar Rocks in Kodaikanal, Dolphin's Nose, Lamb's Rock in Coonoor, and Pagoda Point and Lady's Seat in Yercaud are major tourist spots. The web of rivers and tributaries nourishing the state, like the mighty Kaveri, Bhavani, Tambaraparani, Gadana, Chittar, Ponnaiyar and Vaigai present lovely glimpses of pastoral life. Poompuhar's lush delta has been eulogised for eons, while the confluence of rivers and the sea has evoked reverence in men. Another

Spiritual Circuits

To the spiritually inclined, there's no dearth of places where one can find inner peace. What makes Tamil Nadu truly special is not just the plethora of temples related to the legends or feats of gods, but the thematic spiritual circuits that criss-cross the land. **Divya desams** are 108 temples of Lord Vishnu glorified in the *Divya Prabandham* or poems of the 12 Alvars (Tamil poet saints) of the Vaishnava tradition. Among these, the Nava-Tirupathi or nine Vishnu temples form an important circuit along the banks of the Thamirabarani (Tamraparni) between Tirunelveli and Tiruchendur.

Paadal Petra Sthalam are 275 Shiva temples revered in the verses of the 63 Nayanmars or Shaiva saints who lived between the 6C and the 9C, chiefly Sambandhar, Sundarar, Appar and Manickavasagar. **Pancha Bhoota Sthalams** are five temples where Shiva is worshipped as the five elements – as earth *(prithvi lingam)* at Ekambareswarar Temple in Kanchipuram, as fire *(agni lingam)* at Arunachaleshwara in Tiruvannamalai, as ether *(aakash lingam)* in Chidambaram, as water *(appu lingam)* at Thiruvanaikaval near Trichy and as air *(vayu lingam)* at Srikalahasti in Andhra Pradesh. Pancha Sabha are the five dancing halls where Lord Shiva performed the cosmic dance of Taandav – *kanaka sabha* or Hall of Gold at Chidambaram, *velli sabha* or Hall of Silver at Madurai, *tamra sabha* or Hall of Copper at Tirunelveli, *ratna sabha* or Hall of Ruby at Tiruvalangadu north of Kanchipuram and *chitra sabha* or Hall of pictures at Kutralam (Courtallam).

Another important circuit is the **Arupadai Veedu** or six abodes of Lord Murugan at Palani, Swamimalai, Tiruchendur, Tiruttani (near Chennai) and Thirupparankundram and Pazhamudircholai near Madurai. Lord Ganesha too occupies a prominent place with temples dedicated to his various forms – Uchhipillaiyar at Trichy, Manakula Vinayagar at Pondicherry, Mukkurunu Vinayagar at Madurai Meenakshi Temple and the sacred Karpaga Vinayakar Temple at Pillaiyarpatti, one of the **nine clan temples** of the Chettiars. In a rough triangle between Kumbakonam, Sirkazhi and Karaikal are the **Navagraha temples** dedicated to the nine planetary bodies, where many devotees offer prayers for merit and perform *pujas* for removal of ill-effects of planets.

Thillai Nataraja Temple, Chidambaram – where Shiva is worshipped as akash lingamram

© Anurag Mallick, Priya Ganapathy/MICHELIN

geographical feature, the natural caves found around Madurai, Trichy and South Arcot, lured Jain monks to silent isolation. The caves contain early epigraphical records of Jainism from the 2C BC to the 3C AD.

What to See and Do

OUTDOOR FUN

CYCLING

Heritage towns like Pondicherry, Mamallapuram and Kanadukathan (in Chettinad) are a delight to explore by bike. For those who love mountain biking, there's no better playground than the Nilgiris and the Palani Hills. The state hosts two excellent week-long cycling events – the Tour of Nilgiris (16–23 Dec) and the BSA Tour of Tamil Nadu (25–31 Dec), an 800km theme-based tour (previous years have included 'mountains' and 'cuisine').

USEFUL ADDRESSES

- **Tour of Nilgiris**
  Organised by Bangalore-based Ride a Cycle Foundation, the seven stage tour of the Western Ghats in three South Indian states covers 860km with a total elevation gain of 17,000m/155,800ft. ☏9900158768. www.tourofnilgiris.com.
- **Tamil Nadu Cycling Association**
  A non-governmental association of district-level cycling associations that regularly organises cycling tournaments. ☏044 24340252, 9381712008. www.tncycling.org.
- **Tamil Nadu Cycling Club**
  Formed in 2010, the club organises regular road and track, mountain biking and social rides. ☏9840126666.

FISHING

Though fishing and pearl culture have been hereditary occupations in the coastal and riverside villages of Tamil Nadu, modern fisheries were courtesy of the British. The Madras Fisheries Department was founded and fish farms were introduced in the Nilgiris, where streams and lakes are great haunts for carp and trout. At Hogenakkal Falls, fish on the Kaveri River on a coracle or standing on wet rocks next to a raging waterfall.

Or hit the high seas for some marine adventure for giant trevally, king mackerel, wahoo, barracuda, barramundi, yellowfin tuna and sailfish. A few angling operators in Chennai offer 2hr, 4hr and 8hr packages to estuarine sanctuaries, large breakwaters, wrecks and deep offshore ledges.

USEFUL ADDRESSES

- **Blue Waters**
  Pioneering angling tour operator off the coast of Chennai, organise sportfishing trips aboard their 8.5m/28ft-long state-of-the art craft, *Sea Hawk*. ☏044 42102287, 9500032662/9. www.chennaisportfishing.com.
- **Barracuda Bay Sportfishing**
  Saltwater Sport fishing and boat charters off the coast of Chennai in an 8m/27ft 120 hp boat *Mako Polo*. ☏9841072072. www.barracudabay.in.
- **Tamil Nadu Fisheries Department**
  The nodal state agency that grants permits for fishing in streams, reservoirs and lakes in popular tourist spots like the Nilgiris. ☏0423 2443946. www.tn.gov.in/fisheries/department5.html.

GOLF

Tamil Nadu can surprise any golfing enthusiast by the number of elite courses founded over a century ago. From high in the hills to down on the plains, clubs come with attached rooms, clubhouses, dining, recreation facilities and a code of conduct. Open to members and their guests, each course has its own set of challenges.

USEFUL ADDRESSES

- **Cosmopolitan Club Chennai**
  Founded in 1873, the 18-hole course is spread over 57ha/87 acres at Guindy. ☏044 28525836/ 141, 28413853 55, 28584353 55. www.cosmoclubchennai.com.
- **Madras Gymkhana Club**
  Set up in 1877 abutting the

racetrack, the 18-hole course (5,722m/6,258yd, Par 70) is tricky because of strong winds. ✆044 25368160/8/9. www.madrasgymkhanaclub.com.

- **Ootacamund Gymkhana Club**
  Besides the Wellington Gymkhana Club *(✆0423 2202040)*, golf at 2,100m/7,000ft in Ooty at an undulating 18-hole course built in 1889 (5,701m/6,235yd, Par 70). ✆0423 2448497. www.ootygolfclub.org.
- **Kodaikanal Golf Club**
  Established in 1895, the golf course (Par 71) high in the forested Palani Hills holds surprises like barking deer at the fourth fairway or bison at the 15th and 16th holes. ✆04542 293323. www.kodaigolf.com
- **Coimbatore Golf Club**
  A private-owned 18-hole course in Chettipalayam. ✆0422 3293949, 2655258/363. www.coimbatoregolfclub.com.

HIKING

The best hikes in the state are in the Western Ghats – plantation walks, day hikes to viewpoints or multi-day adventures. There are 17 treks around Kodaikanal outlined in 'Sholas for Survival', available at the DFO Office. Coimbatore is a good base for hikes to Siruvani, Anaikatti and Velliangiri. In the Nilgiris, do the historic John Sullivan Trail, trek from Kotagiri to Longwood Shola, Catherine Falls or Kodanad, walk from Coonoor to Lambs Rock or reach Droog Fort from Law's Falls, trek from Ooty to Mukurthi Lake via Porthimund or hike to the lakes of Emerald and Avalanche.

USEFUL ADDRESSES

- **Chennai Trekking Club**
  The largest and most active trekking community in South India with 13,000+ members, they organise easy treks, extreme survival trips, workshops and periodic seniors'/ladies' treks. www.chennaitrekkers.org.
- **Environment Conservation Group**
  Coimbatore-based group that organises treks in Nilgiris and other areas, camping, wildlife and photography workshops. ✆9787878910. www.ecgindia.org.
- **Nilgiri Wildlife and Environment Association (NWEA)**
  Ooty-based wildlife conservation group with good knowledge of local trails, apart from the Nilgiri Trekking Association. ✆0423 2447167. http://nwea.in.

HORSE RIDING

Popular hill stations like Ooty and Kodaikanal offer touristy horse rides around the lake that cost Rs.50–200, depending on the distance.
A few farms and tea estates offer the charms of more leisurely rides around plantations.

USEFUL ADDRESSES

- **Destiny Farmstay**
  Ride through the Nilgiris with a choice of 10 well-groomed horses while staying at a farm near Ooty. ✆0423 2224545, 9487000111, 9487000222. www.destinyfarmstay.com.
- **High Field Horse Riding School**
  High Field Tea Estate in Coonoor has nine retired racehorses with lessons from trainers for Rs.50/half-hour. ✆9095567811.
- **Elephant Valley**
  A 40ha/100-acre organic farm near Kodaikanal with horse riding in an arena or on scenic riding tracks. ✆0454 2230399. www.elephantvalleyhotel.com.
- **Red Earth Riding School**
  A 9ha/22-acre riding school near Auroville offering guided walkouts, riding lessons and workshops by qualified teachers in arenas and cross-country courses (closed Mon). ✆9629312071. anngallopaway@yahoo.com.

BIRDWATCHING

With over 340 bird species, Tamil Nadu has several birding hot spots like Pulicat Lake and Vedanthangal bird sanctuary, ideal for aquatic species. Chennai is dotted with numerous habitats including Guindy National Park, IIT Madras and Theosophical Society campus, Pallikaranai Marsh, Adyar Estuary and Muttukadu, besides Vandalur Zoo. The city also hosts the annual Chennai Bird Race, a dawn-to-dusk birdwatching race for four-member teams. Prakriti, the IIT Madras Wildlife Club and Madras Natural History Society organise regular field trips. The Western Ghats are ideal for longer explorations and endemic species; particularly good locations for birdwatching include Mudumalai and Longwood Shola in the Nilgiris.

USEFUL ADDRESSES

- **Madras Natural History Society**
  Madras Naturalists' Society, 8, Janaki Avenue, Abhirampuram, Chennai 18. ✆044 24995833.
- **Prakriti, IIT Madras**
  prakriti@iitm.ac.in. IIT Madras Wildlife Club. Walkers' passes are issued by the security section on request.

ORGANISED SIGHTSEEING TOURS

BY COACH

The Tamil Nadu Tourist Development Corporation runs a fleet of 22 coaches (four air-conditioned) with sightseeing tours of Chennai and Pondicherry, hop-on, hop-off tours from Chennai to Mamallapuram, 1-day trips to Mamallapuram, Tirupati, Sripuram and Tiruvannamalai, besides longer road trips like the 3-day Navagraha temple tour, 4-day Arupadai Veedu tour, 8-day Tamil Nadu tour or inter-state South India tours (6, 8 or 14 days).

USEFUL ADDRESSES

- **TTDC**
  Wallajah Road, Chennai ✆044 25383333, 25367850. www.ttdconline.com.

ON FOOT

Chennai is the perfect starting point with a wide choice of guided walking trails – Fort St George, Mylapore, Marina Beach, San Thome, Mount Road and Tree Walks (see p113). INTACH organises heritage walks in Pondicherry and Tranquebar, while Mamallapuram, with its closely clustered monuments, is also best explored on foot.

USEFUL ADDRESSES

- **INTACH**
  ✆044 24918479, 28415474. www.intach.org.
- **Madras Heritage Walks**
  ✆9841049155. www.madraswalks.com.
- **Story Trails**
  ✆044 42124214, 9940040215. www.storytrails.in.

WATER SPORTS

TTDC operates several boathouses across the state with boating, windsurfing and other water sports – Muttukadu on East Coast Road *(✆044 27472369)*, Chunnambar near Pondicherry *(✆0413 2356816)* and tourist hot spots like Ooty, Yercaud and Kodaikanal. Tourists have a choice of boats – rowboat *(Rs.130/30min)*, powerboat *(Rs.300)* and speedboat *(Rs.450/10min)*. The Madras Boat Club, set up in 1867, is one of the oldest rowing centres in India with regular regattas. A few adventure outfits organise scuba and surfing *(Rs.800/3hr)* with bodyboards, surfboards and equipment on hire.

USEFUL ADDRESSES

- **Temple Adventures**
  PADI-certified scuba diving outfit on Covelong Road, Mamallapuram ✆9789844191, 9940219449. www.templeadventures.com.
- **Madras Boat Club**
  ✆044 24354751, 24339289. www.madrasboatclub.in.
- **Kallialay Surf Club**
  ✆9442992874, 9787306376. kallialaysurfschool@hotmail.com.

INDOOR FUN

SPAS

Plush resort hotels run boutique spas offering Oriental and European massage and rejuvenation treatments. Taj Hotels' Jiva Spa at Chennai, Kovalam and Coonoor *(www.tajhotels.com)*, Radisson Blu Temple Bay at Mamallapuram *(www.radissonblu.com)* and Heritage Madurai *(www.heritagemadurai.com)* are great places to pamper the senses. For Ayurvedic spa treatments, try Mantra Veppathur *(www.mantraveppathur.com)* and Paradise Resort *(www.paradiseresortindia.com)* around Kumbakonam, with traditional massage techniques at Mamallapuram, the Nilgiris and Courtallam (dubbed the Spa of the South), besides a few specialised wellness centres.

USEFUL ADDRESSES

- **Sowkhya**
  Sowkhya Way2Health has an Ayurvedic therapy centre in Chennai *(✆044 42059797)* and spa and wellness centres at Hill Country Resorts in Kodaikanal *(✆04542 240953/4)* and Ooty *(✆0423 2445962)*.
- **Ayurveda Retreat**
  Set amidst a 4ha/10-acre tea plantation in Coonoor, the retreat offers a range of rejuvenative and therapeutic programmes. ✆0423 2231912, 2233161, 2201253. www.ayurveda.org.

COURSES

COOKERY

Tamil Nadu offers a diverse choice of cuisines – exciting seafood along the coast best enjoyed at Chennai, Mamallapuram and Tranquebar, Creole or Franco-Tamil cuisine in Pondicherry, tribal cuisine of the Badaga tribe in the Nilgiris and Kodaikanal, which also exhibit a Colonial touch with bakes and continental dishes. However, the ultimate experience is Tamil Nadu's signature cuisine from Chettinad. A few homestays and hotels organise cooking lessons for interested guests.

USEFUL ADDRESSES

- **Great Grandfather's Holiday Homestay**
  Stay in a century-old Colonial villa in Coonoor and learn Parsi cuisine from Diana Bharucha. ✆9880433711.
- **Banyan Tree Farm Stay**
  Experience life on a farm at Sethumadai near Pollachi while picking up nuances of Indian cuisine from Mr V.M. Prabhu. ✆0422 2573329, 9842375524. www.banyantreefarm.com.
- **Visalam**
  A heritage hotel in Kanadukathan with live kitchen counters, neatly labelled Chettinad spices in an interactive kitchen and cooking demos for house guests. ✆04565 273301. www.cghearth.com.

MEDITATION

In a land where kings and sages have performed austerities and even the gods have undertaken penance to redeem their curses, the very air is charged with mysticism. Mahatma Gandhi adopted the loincloth in Madurai. At Kanyakumari Swami Vivekananda meditated for three days before attaining divinity. Sri Ramana Maharishi chose the holy shade of the Arunachaleshwara mountain in Tiruvannamalai for his ashram. Pondicherry was the sacred ground of Sri Aurobindo. The southern branch of Ramakrishna Mission was set up first in Chennai while the Theosophical Society found sanctuary in Adyar. Each of these places occupies a special place in the spiritual landscape of the land with other specialised retreats dedicated to meditation and inner growth.

USEFUL ADDRESSES

- **Sahaja Yoga Meditation Centre**
  Started by Shri Mataji Nirmala Devi in 1970, Sahaja Yoga is a unique method of meditation based on Kundalini awakening and self-realisation. www.sahajayoga.org.in.

- **Sri Ramana Asramam**
  A serene ashram where guests are welcome to stay for meditation for a maximum of 3 days by prior appointment. There are no charges though donations are accepted. ✆04175 237200, 9244937292. www.sriramanamaharishi.org.

YOGA

Sage Patanjali, who compiled the epic treatise *Yoga Sutra*, spent considerable time in the present state of Tamil Nadu, where he witnessed the divine dance Tandav at Thillai Vanam (Chidambaram). Lord Shiva's 108 dance postures form the basis of Natya yoga. Not surprisingly, the region has several yoga schools and retreats, which embody this rich tradition.

USEFUL ADDRESSES

- **Isha Yoga Centre**
  Short residential programmes in Hatha Yoga and Inner Engineering at Chennai, ✆044 24333185; a 60ha/150-acre campus near Coimbatore, ✆0422 2515345; besides regular 3–7 day retreats in India and abroad. www.ishafoundation.org.
- **Sivananda Yoga Vedanta Centre**
  Well-known yoga school with many centres overseas, it has retreats in Chennai *(✆044 24511626)* and Madurai *(✆0452 2912950)*. www.sivananda.org.
- **Kodaikanal Yoga Center**
  Yoga and meditation taught by an Israeli couple at the serene Karuna Farm, 14km from Kodaikanal. www.kodaikanalyoga.com.

VOLUNTEERING

There are many areas where socially aware tourists can contribute in the field of voluntourism. Be it economically backward zones, rural hinterlands, urban sprawls or disaster-affected areas, one can volunteer in education, women's and children's welfare or the environment.

USEFUL ADDRESSES

- **Unity Charitable Trust**
  Teach English, music, dance or computer training to poor girls or aid women's self-help groups. ✆04562 420290, 654221. www.unitycharity.org.
- **Tsunamika**
  Participate in tsunami-relief livelihood projects across Tamil Nadu conceived by Upasana Design Studio of Auroville. www.tsunamika.org.
- **Asha for Education**
  Spend 6 weeks to a year at an Asha sponsored project in India for about US$100 a month to support the cost of food, board and lodging. www.ashanet.org.
- **Heal The Soil**
  Do your bit for community-supported agriculture via 'Village Kitchen Garden Project' (on Sundays) and 'Permaculture Introduction Workshop' at Sapney Organic Farm in Kottakarai village, Auroville. ✆04132 623454. www.healthesoilcsa.org.

ACTIVITIES FOR KIDS

Hill stations like Ooty, Kodaikanal and Yercaud offer boating and horse riding. TTDC's boathouses at Muttukadu and Chunnambar are equally popular. Besides the Snake Park and Crocodile Bank, Chennai has a profusion of amusement parks like Kishkinta and VGP Golden Beach Resort, MGM Dizzee World and MayaJaal on the ECR. The Wax Museum and Baywatch Theme Park at Kanyakumari and the seaside Mandapam Beach Park near Rameswaram are also child-friendly.

HIGHLIGHTS

- MGM Dizzee World, Chennai (*see p105*).
- Athisayam Theme Park, Madurai (*see p230*).
- Baywatch Water Amusement Park, Kanyakumari (*see p230*).
- Black Thunder, Mettupalayam (*see p288*).

Shopping

Shopping for souvenirs, traditional Tamil items, handicrafts, home decor, a personal wardrobe or accessories in Tamil Nadu can be quite an adventure. Several of these items are available at bargain prices off the street in atmospheric bazaars, flea markets and street and pavement stalls. However, Government emporia, glitzy malls, boutiques and showrooms selling branded items in the main cities assure quality products for a higher price.

OPENING HOURS

As early risers, Tamil people enjoy brisk business from morning to night. Street shops and stalls clustered around major tourist sights, often start as early as 8am and close at 8 or 9pm. However, most retail shops and boutiques remain open from 10am to 8.30pm with a 1hr lunch break in between. Government showrooms or emporia tend to pull down their shutters a little sooner.

WHAT TO BUY

CRAFTS

Apart from genuine antiques like Chola bronzes and Tanjore art, many age-old traditional crafts are still practised. Exquisite sculptures and statues can be bought directly from stone-carvers in Mamallapuram or bronze artisans in Swamimalai and Kumbakonam. Beautiful artefacts in brass and copper like lamps, ashtrays and wall plaques are on sale at various curio shops. Wooden carved dolls and Tanjore's famous bobble-head dancing dolls are the rage with tourists. Simple basket makers and cane weavers churn out interesting utility and home decor items. Tourists can bargain for Chettinad's vintage carved doorways, windows and pillars, sometimes sold on the wayside!

LEATHERWORK

The state's booming leather industry accounts for 70 percent of India's tanning capacity and 38 percent of leather footwear and components. Chennai is a major production centre and Vellore District leads the finished leather exports market. Nearby towns like Ranipet, Ambur and Vaniyambadi have helped Tamil Nadu become a market leader. With leather exports clocking around US$762 million, the region accounts for nearly 42 percent of Indian leather exports. Famous for its fashionable high-quality leather crafts that meet international standards and style, Pondicherry is a shopping haven. From exporting raw materials in the 1960s to creating value-added products such as shoes, jackets, gloves, handbags, wallets, rucksacks, folios, briefcases, travelware, belts, sports goods, upholstery and saddlery goods in the last two

Bronze caster at work, Kumbakonam

decades, shopping for leather has only got better.

JEWELLERY

Gold occupies a prominent place in South Indian culture. Tamil people have used gold not only as an ornament but have also woven it inextricably into their art and textile tradition. Be it a festive season or wedding, people throng the streets around Mylapore in Chennai, where a community of jewellers create timeless traditional designs. Prominent showrooms like GRT Jewellers, Arc Jewellers, Art Karat and Bapalal have eye-catching collections in gold, silver and diamond. Precious gems and semi-precious stones are set in 22-carat gold and sold by weight. However, silver is more popular with tourists. Contemporary designs are found everywhere but the rare, intricately carved, heavy silver jewellery of ethnic tribes like Todas in the Nilgiris are becoming collectors' items.

TEXTILES

Home to 'Madras checks', Kanjeevaram silks, Kanchi and Coimbatore cotton, handloom and khadi, Tirupur hosiery and knitwear, Ooty's petit point and Toda tribal embroidery, Tamil Nadu's textile trade has flourished since the days of the Pandyas, Cheras and Cholas. Today Kanchipuram, Darasuram, Arni, Kumbakonam, Swamimalai, Coimbatore, Salem, Chettinad and Madurai are legendary for their distinct silk- and cotton-weaving rural industry. Tirupur, Erode and Coimbatore are India's largest exporters of knitwear, with Tirupur grabbing 56 percent of total knitwear exports! The cotton fields near Madurai and Karur feed the Sungudi sari and home linen industry. Trousseau and festive shopping for Kanjeevaram silks, exotic brocades and ethnic wear and the year-round demand for saris, stoles, scarves, ties, zari dhotis, casual T-shirts and hip knitwear, fuels the growth of the industry. To top it, shopping is easy and economical as there are many tailors who stitch made-to-measure garments in a jiffy! Tamil Nadu Handloom Weaver's Co-operative Society Co-optex Showrooms, Weaver's Co-operative Society and Khadi Gram Udyog are reliable outlets with a wide range of affordable products. Big brands like Nalli, India Silk House, Handloom House and Radha Silk House showcase exquisite cottons and silks.

Listings

Free fortnightly booklets (*CityInfo* Chennai, Madurai, Pondicherry) available in some stores are a great resource for shopping, nightlife and events. Newspapers often carry listings of discounts and exhibitions around town.

MUSICAL INSTRUMENTS

Vibrant classical and folk traditions are preserved across the state of Tamil Nadu through music, dance and theatre. For a musician, Chennai is the ideal place to pick up Carnatic musical instruments like the stringed *thanjavur veena* and *tambura*. Unique percussion instruments like *mridangam*, *khol*, *tabla* and *ghatam* (a specially designed clay pot) are also available. Bamboo flutes can be bought for a song besides the harmonium, *nadaswaram* (a typical nasal-sounding ceremonial pipe), electronic instruments or dance accompaniments like *salangai* (bell anklets). Sruthilaya in Mylapore is a good place to shop *(044 24994045, www.thesruthilaya.com)*. Sitars, drums and flutes can be bought at Musee Musical *(67 Anna Salai)* or AR Dawood & Sons *(286 Quaide Milleth Salai, Triplicane High Road)*.

TEA AND COFFEE

Hill towns Ooty, Coonoor and Kotagiri specialise in marketing leaf tea which is plucked, hand sorted and processed within a day, and the lush plantations are dotted by tea pickers at work. Production follows the Crush, Tear and

Unique to Tamil Nadu

Here's a ready reckoner for traditional shopping in Tamil Nadu: stone carvings of Mamallapuram and Madurai, handcrafted *pattamara* mats and Palmyra handicrafts from Tirunelveli, traditional jewellery, bronze and brass statues and curios from Kumbakonam, metal sculptures, wall plates, exquisite gilded Tanjore paintings and painted bobble-head dolls from Thanjavur, dazzling silk saris, scarves and stoles, khadi and cotton textiles, ready-made garments from Kanchipuram, Chennai, Darasuram and Chettinad, Madurai, Coimbatore and Kumbakonam, unique arty handmade paper crafts, glazed pottery and leather items from Pondicherry and Auroville and shell handicrafts and beads from beach stalls.

Curl (CTC) process of manufacture. Of the seven grades of tea produced here, Orange Pekoe (OP) is the best and most expensive and is highly sought after in the international market while the lowest grade, a dry tea dust, is used to make chai. Broken Orange Pekoe is a machine-sorted less expensive semi-full leaf variety. Korakundah Organic Tea from The United Nilgiri Tea Estates Co. Ltd is a well-known brand from the region. Tea-tasting programmes are organised by Tranquilitea. Coffee is grown in several regions of the Western Ghats. In Tamil Nadu, the slopes of Yercaud and Valparai abound with plantations. South Indian Coffee is synonymous with Kumbakonam's degree coffee with big brands like Narasu's. To visit a tea or coffee plantation contact UPASI *(United Planter's Association of Southern India, www.upasi.org)*.

SPICES

The spice trade in Southern India has flourished for eons. Black pepper, cinnamon, cloves, cardamom, red chilli, turmeric, vanilla, ginger, nutmeg, mace, herbs and other exotic spices are grown in various parts of Tamil Nadu and can be bought in cities including Ooty, Coonoor, Kodaikanal, Yercaud, Courtallam.

EMPORIUMS

The State Government runs various emporia to showcase the wealth of Tamil Nadu's culture, especially handicrafts and clothing. Central Cottage Industries Emporium also offers a wide range of products under one roof. While the quality of items is usually better and more reliable here, prices are fixed and much higher than those one can buy on the street. Yet it is worth a visit for the sheer range of crafts and to get an idea of prices.

MAIN EMPORIUMS IN THE STATE

- **Poompuhar**
  16 showrooms across the state and in three major metros, Poompuhar is run by Tamilnadu Handicrafts Development Corporation Ltd. Open daily. ✆044 28521271/798/325. www.poompuhar.org.
- **Maroma/Kalki Auroville**
  Auroville's boutique outlets Maroma and Kalki in Chennai, Pondicherry and Auroville sell a range of interesting Auro products. Open daily 10am–6pm. ✆0413 2623450. www.maroma.com.
- **Fabindia**
  Block-printed cotton, khadi and tussar garments, home furnishings, personal care, organics and gifts with outlets in Coimbatore, Trichy, Vellore and nine in Chennai. Open daily 10.30am–8.30pm. ✆044 42151892/3, 42150975. www.fabindia.com.
- **Nalli**
  A renowned name in silk saris, Nalli has seven outlets in Chennai, besides Kanchipuram, Madurai, Trichy, Coimbatore and Tirunelveli. www.nallisilks.com.

Books and Films

Being an erudite and culturally rich society, Tamil Nadu prides itself on its treasure-house of literature, sacred texts, traditional forms of dance and music, folk arts and films. The Tamil film industry, centred around the Kodambakkam area in Chennai, is dubbed Kollywood and churns out more movies than any other film fraternity.

BOOKS

Entire tomes, coffee table books, guides and research papers have been written on Tamil Nadu's art and culture, temples and architecture, and craft and cuisine. Here's a small selection of interesting titles that is a good primer to the region.

Reference/Biography

The Province of the Book – Scholars, Scribes, and Scribblers in Colonial Tamilnadu by A. R. Venkatachalapathy, Permanent Black (2011). Scholarly work focusing on books, book publishing and book reading in Tamil Nadu from the time of parchment to present-day Pagemaker. Considering the first Indian-language book ever to be printed was in Tamil in 1577, this superb documentation of Indian culture and history reveals the little known world of the Tamil book.

Silk Sarees of Tamil Nadu by Nesa Arumugam, Abhinav Publications (2011). Printed on art paper with beautiful pictures, the book traces the rich silk weaving tradition of Kanchipuram in Tamil Nadu and the transformation of a silkworm's cocoon to yarn and sari with insights into the dyeing process, designers and weavers. A treat for those fascinated by Indian textiles and art and culture.

Eternal Romantic, My Father, Gemini Ganesan, by Narayani Ganesh, Roli Books (2010). The book is a tribute to the larger-than-life Tamil star by his daughter and includes a glowing foreword by movie icon Kamal Hassan.

Tamil Cinema: The Cultural Politics of India's other Film Industry, edited by Selvaraj Velayutham, Routledge (2009). An academic study of Tamil cinema in a wider social, political and cultural context.

Travel

Temple Towns of Tamil Nadu, by George Michell with photos by Bharath Ramamrutham, Marg Publications (2006). An insightful treatise on sacred spaces like Kanchipuram, Tiruvannamalai, Chidambaram, Srirangam, Madurai and Mylapore (Chennai) by renowned architect and historian George Michell.

Madras: The Architectural Heritage, by K Kalpana and Frank Schiffer, INTACH Guide, Tamil Nadu Chapter (2003). This vivid documentation of the living heritage and history behind Chennai's old buildings features 254 heritage structures.

The Smile of Murugan, by Michael Wood, John Murray Publishers Ltd (2002). A wonderfully written travelogue based on the author's journeys to Tamil Nadu in the 1980s and 1990s.

Fiction

The Blaft Anthology of Tamil Pulp Fiction, edited by Rakesh Khanna and translated by Pritham K. Chakravarthy, Blaft Publication (2008). This collection of stories by 10 of India's best-selling Tamil authors revolves around mad scientists, hard-boiled detectives, vengeful goddesses, murderous robots, scandalous starlets and drug-fuelled love affairs! Translated into English for the first time, with an equally interesting follow-up book.

A Place to Live: Contemporary Tamil Short Fiction, edited by Dilip Kumar and translated by Vasantha Surya, Penguin India (2004).
The anthology features 29 short stories by some of the best-known contemporary Tamil writers from 1960–90.

Where Are You Going, You Monkeys?, K Rajanarayanan, translated by Pritham K. Chakravarthy, illustrations by Trotsky Marudu, Blaft Publications (2009).
Folk tales, fiction and anecdotes from Tamil Nadu.

Gastronomy

Flavours of Chettinad, by Mrs. Seetha Muthiah, Standard Press.
A compilation of about 280 classic Chettinad recipes, including palakarams (snacks), chutneys, pickles, dessert besides veg and non-veg main courses and side dishes.

Classic Tamil Brahmin Cuisine by Viji Varadarajan and Padmini Natarajan (2008). The book is dedicated to pure vegetarian South Indian *samayal* (cuisine) with 70 classic recipes. Winner of the Gourmand World Cookbook Award.

Festival Samayal: An offering to the Gods, by Viji Varadarajan, Orient Enterprises (August 2009).
A brilliant short story of temples of India that prepare specialised food, always offered untasted to the Divine.

FILMS

Today, the Tamil cinema industry is among the largest in the world. The earliest movies were based on mythology, folklore, pseudo historical or stage plays with 30 songs! Contemporary Tamil films continue to inspire and entertain the masses with complex issues, groundbreaking themes, realistic dialogues and earthy humour. Fresh talent in acting, music and direction has prompted remakes in other languages.

Chandralekha (1948).
S.S. Vasan's *magnum opus* about a beautiful dancer and two princes. Lavish sets, elaborate dances, fights and circus scenes picturised in Gemini Studio resulted in the formation of Gemini Circus. The most expensive Tamil film till then, it was released across the world with subtitles, and was the widest released Indian film of the time (609 theatres).

Veerapandiya Kattabomman (1959).
All-time classic with Sivaji Ganesan as the fearless 18C chieftain who fought the British. Memorable lines, grand sets, elaborate war sequences, evergreen music and great lyrics.

Uthiri Pookal (1979).
A groundbreaking film by J. Mahendran, acclaimed for its non-mainstream approach. It had one of the most quoted climax scenes, powerful dialogues and Ilayaraja's music.

Nayakan (1987).
A film by Maniratnam based on the true story of a Tamil gangster, stellar role by Kamal Haasan and brilliant music by Ilayaraja. In 2005, it made it to *Time* magazine's list of All Time 100 Best Films.

Iruvar (1997).
A Mani Ratnam classic retelling Tamil Nadu's most famous modern political saga with career-best roles by Mohanlal and Prakashraj with A.R. Rahman's music and cinematography by Santhosh Sivan.

Endhiran (2010).
The most expensive Asian movie ever and India's biggest blockbuster with Rajinikanth in a stellar double role, director S. Shankar's vision, mind-numbing SFX, Aishwarya Rai dancing to A.R. Rahman's music and the longest final action sequence (45 minutes!).

Calendar of Events

Tamil Nadu's calendar is peppered with music, dance and theatre performances, spiritual events, theme festivals and all-year-round temple festivities that range from grand celebrations like *ther* (chariot or car festivals), *theppotsava* (float festivals in temple tanks), *abhishekams* (ritualistic anointing ceremonies) to devotional songs and performances.

FESTIVALS AND PUBLIC HOLIDAYS

JANUARY

Pongal – One of the most widely celebrated festivals across Tamil Nadu, the 4-day festival marks the end of the south-east monsoon and reaping of the harvest. The name is derived from the rice dish prepared to mark the occasion.

Jallikattu – A bull taming/racing sport played on Mattu Pongal day as part of the Pongal celebrations, the ancient tradition gets its name from *salli kaasu* (coins) and *kattu* (package) tied to the bulls' horns as prize money.

Mamallapuram Dance Festival – Open-air festival against the backdrop of Arjuna's Penance in Mamallapuram with traditional dance performances of Bharatanatyam, Kuchipudi, Kathakali and Odissi.

Thyagaraja Aradhana Festival – A music festival in honour of legendary 18C composer Thyagaraja held at Thiruvaiyur (13km from Thanjavur) on the banks of the sacred Kaveri where leading exponents of Carnatic music converge to perform at his memorial.

FEBRUARY

Hamara Shakespeare – A unique showcase of Shakespearean plays presented in Indian languages at Chennai. ✆044 45904707. www.hamarashakespeare.com.

Natyanjali Classical Dance Festival – A 5-day festival dedicated to the Lord of Dance held against the stunning backdrop of the Nataraja Temple in Chidambaram. Starts on Mahashivratri.

MARCH

Festival of Sacred Music – A 3-day festival between 4–6 Mar on the banks of the Kaveri at Thiruvaiyur at the memorial of poet-saint Thyagaraja. ✆044 66848484. www.prakritifoundation.com.

Gharana Festival – Annual festival of Hindustani classical music held in Chennai. ✆044 45904707. www.gharanafestival.com.

MAY

Summer Festival – Celebrated at various hill stations with boat races, pageants, flower and fruit shows, sporting events and dog shows spread across a week in each location. Starting off in the second week of May at Yercaud and Ooty with rose shows at the Government Rose Garden, flower shows at the Botanical Gardens and fruit shows at Sim's Park in Coonoor, celebrations continue in Kodaikanal towards the month end.

JULY

Short+Sweet Theatre Festival – The world's largest '10-minute play' festival came to Chennai in July 2011, organised by the Prakriti Foundation and The Blu Lotus Company. ✆044 45904707. www.shortandsweet.org/shortsweet-theatre/chennai.

AUGUST

Saral Vizha – A 3-day festival held at Courtallam waterfalls celebrated with a ritual bath in the therapeutic waters plunging down the mountainside, full of herbs and medicinal plants.

Cave Temple Festival – Held at the Jain cave shrine of Chitharal, 7km from Marthandam and 45km from Kanyakumari, with cultural programmes.

OCTOBER

Kanyakumari Cape Festival – A 3-day festival with cultural programmes, music and dance performances at Kanyakumari.

DECEMBER

Madurai Film Festival – Organised since 1998, the film festival in Madurai is held between 7–9 Dec (10am–8pm). ✆8695279353, 9344479353. www.madurai filmfest.blogspot.com.

Parks New Festival – A festival showcasing new and emerging work in the fields of music, dance and theatre. ✆044 45904707. www.theparksnewfestival.com.

Chennai Dance & Music Festival – Month-long extravaganza that began in 1927 as the Margazhi Festival, takes place in Dec–Jan across multiple locations in Chennai – halls, temples and auditoriums.

One Billion Eyes – Indian documentary film festival held in Chennai with annual themes (Divinity, Ecology, Festivals, Gandhi…) representing a billion points of view. www.abillioneyes.in.

Poetry with Prakriti – A 2-week poetry festival, usually 15–30 Dec with 25 poets and about 100 readings at different venues across Chennai – halls, temples and auditoriums. ✆044 66848506. www.poetrywithprakriti.in

RELIGIOUS FESTIVALS

JANUARY

Thaipusam – Held in the Tamil month of Thai when the star Pusam is at its highest point, the festival marks the gifting of the *vel* (spear) to Lord Murugan by Parvati to vanquish evil. Devotees carry *kavadis* (burdens) and pierce their bodies with spears or skewers to fulfil vows. Thaipusam is celebrated with great fervour at Palani and Thanjavur, besides Malaysia, Singapore and Mauritius.

FEBRUARY–MARCH

Kamakshi Brahmotsavam, Kanchipuram – The annual temple festival of Kanchi Kamakshi Amman Temple marked by *ther* (chariot) and *theppam* (float) festivals in the streets and temple tank.

Kumbeswara Festival, Kumbakonam – The image of Lord Kumbeswara is taken out in a procession during the 10-day festival in Maasi. The Theppam festival is held during Panguni

Rare Festivals

Festivals are celebrated nearly every fortnight in Tamil Nadu. However, a few major religious festivals are rare events. Considered as the Mahakumbh Mela of the south, the **Mahamagam Festival** of Kumbakonam happens once in 12 years. Lakhs of devotees congregate to take a holy bath at the sacred tank of Adi Kumbeswara Temple. Celebrated when planet Jupiter enters Leo, the Mamagam marks the auspicious time when all the holy rivers of India come to bathe in the sacred tank and rid the accumulated sins of people who took a dip in their waters. The last festival took place in 2004 and the next will take place in 2016.

The ancient **Varadaraja Perumal Temple** at Kanchipuram witnesses another rare festival. The original idol Athi Varadan, made of wood from the Athi tree, lies at the bottom of the temple tank. Once in 40 years, the idol is removed and placed outside for 10 days of public worship. The last event took place in 1979 and the next one is slated for 2019.

(Mar–Apr) and the marriage of Lord Adikumbeswarar and Goddess Mangalambigai is conducted in Vaikasi (May–Jun).

MARCH

Float Festival, Trichy – The Rock Fort temple in Trichy celebrates the *theppotsavam* or float festival in the temple tank at the base of the hill shrine.

Arupath Moovar Festival, Chennai (Mar–Apr) – A popular festival where the bronze statues of the 63 Shaiva saints at Kapaleeswarar Temple in Chennai are taken in a procession around the streets of Mylapore.

APRIL

Chithirai Festival, Madurai (Apr–May) – The grand reenactment of Meenakshi Thiru Kalyanam, or the marriage between Lord Sundareswar and Meenakshi. Lord Vishnu, her brother, is taken in a procession from Azhagar Kovil on a golden horse-drawn chariot to attend the wedding rituals. Unmarried girls pray for suitable grooms while women renew their wedding vows with the symbolic tying of the *mangalsutra* (wedding thread).

Sapthathanam Festival, Kumbakonam – Held at the Adi Kumbeswara Temple, the lord's idol is carried in a palanquin to nearby villages. During the Cradle Festival the deities are placed on a swing for 9 days. The massive ritual anointing ceremony, Kumbha Abhishekham, is conducted at the temple once in 12 years. The last ceremony took place in 2009.

Kavadi Festival, Palani – Devotees of Lord Murugan carry the *kavadi*, a flower-bedecked decoration, with body piercings in a hypnotic trance to the hill shrine at Palani.

Kanthuri Festival, Nagore – A 10-day festival in memory of the Sufi saint at the Qadirwali Shrine at Nagore, marked by lofty pennants and prayer. On the tenth day, the Saint's tomb is anointed with sandalwood – and later the holy sandal paste, known for its healing powers, is distributed to everyone.

MAY–JUNE

Ramalinga Pratishtha Festival, Rameswaram – After Ravanavadham at Thittakudi in Rameswaram bazaar, the festive idol of Lord Rama is brought in a golden chariot to Kothandarama Temple for Vibheeshan's coronation the next day. The following day, the main festival is celebrated at Rameswaram.

April: Chithirai Festival, Madurai

JUNE–JULY

Aani Thirumanjanam, Chidambaram – A 10-day festival at the Nataraja Temple, where *abhishekam* is performed for the Lord on the day of Uthiram Nakshatra. The deity is brought outside in a procession followed by the anointing ceremony. Thousands flock to see the ritualistic dance of the Lord when he is taken back to the sanctum sanctorum.

AUGUST–SEPTEMBER

Krishna Jayanti – The birthday of Lord Krishna is celebrated with pomp at all Vaishnava shrines and divya desams across Tamil Nadu.

Avani Moola Utsavam, Madurai – A 10-day festival for the coronation of Lord Sundareshwar. Priests recite and reenact the Tiruvilaiyadal (sacred games) or the 64 miracles of Lord Shiva.

Velankanni Festival – The 11-day (29 Aug–8 Sep) annual feast of Our Lady of Good Health attended by thousands of orange-robed pilgrims on foot. It commences with the hoisting of the flag on the first day and ends with the feast on 8 Sep and lowering of the flag.

Vinayagar Chaturthi – Celebrated in the Hindu calendar month of Bhaadrapada or Tamil Aavani, starting on the *shukla chaturthi* (fourth day of the waxing moon period). The festival usually falls 19 Aug–15 Sept and lasts for 10–12 days, ending on Anant Chaturdashi. Devotees install clay idols, offer prayers, maintain vows and make sweet preparations like *vella kozhukkattai* (sweet modak), dear to the Elephant god.

OCTOBER

Deepavali – The Festival of Lights, where people illuminate their houses with oil lamps and lights to welcome the goddess Lakshmi, burst crackers and make various festival sweets and preparations.

NOVEMBER

Dasara/Vijaya Dasami – Dasara is celebrated across Tamil Nadu and the festival incorporates worship of Lakshmi, Saraswati and Shakti. The Dasara festival at Kulasekarapatinam *(20km from Tiruchendur)* is unique as in the Mutharamman temple, Shiva and Shakti are in the same shrine and lakhs of devotees converge to seek their blessings.

Karthigai Deepam, Tiruvannamalai (Nov–Dec) – A great spectacle on the full moon day of Karthigai month, wherein a huge fire lamp (mahabharani deepam) is lit up on the sacred Arunachaleshwara hill, visible for several kilometres all around.

DECEMBER

Kal Garuda Sevai, Nachiyar Kovil – At the Nachiyar Temple celebrations, during Purapaadu, the idol of Garuda is carried out in a procession, which starts with four people lifting the idol from the sanctum. As the procession continues Garuda increases in weight and the number of people required to lift the idol keeps on doubling with each step.

Marghazhi Thiruvaadhirai, Chidambaram (Dec–Jan) – Held under Marghazhi, the star of Lord Nataraj, the chariot festival is held in winter as Marghazhi Thiruvaadhirai and a second time in summer as Aani Thirumanjanam (Jun–Jul).

Vaikuntha Ekadesi, Srirangam – The most important festival celebrated for 21 days during margazhi (Dec–Jan), divided into two 10-day periods. On Vaikuntha Ekadesi day, Lord Ranganatha is dressed in splendid garments and paraded through Paramapada Vasal to arrive at Thirumamani Mandapam in the thousand-pillared hall. As Sri Rangaraja, he holds his Divine Durbar like a king before returning to the temple late in the night.

Know Before You Go

USEFUL WEBSITES

www.tamilnadutourism.org
A comprehensive website of the Department of Tourism on destinations and sights by theme. Hill Stations, Wildlife, Temples, Astrology, Fine Arts and Cuisine, as well as tours, stay options, tourist offices, info centres, consulates and links to railways and roadways.

www.ttdconline.com
Tamil Nadu Tourist Development Corporation (TTDC) provides tourism infrastructure facilities like transport and accommodation through its chain of hotels, youth hostels, boathouses, restaurants, snack bars and rail-cum-road tour packages. Contact and tariff details for all these can be found here.

www.tn.gov.in
Official website of the Government of Tamil Nadu with useful links to various district websites that have detailed info on the history of each district, tourist destinations in the region and main festivals.

www.forests.tn.nic.in
Official website of Tamil Nadu Forest Department, an excellent resource for info on national parks, sanctuaries, eco-tourism destinations, natural resources and relevant contact details for entry permissions and booking Forest Rest Houses.

www.tnarch.gov.in
Official website of the Department of Archaeology that maintains 85 protected monuments, 14 site museums and eight district archaeological offices.

TOURIST OFFICES

Information on the following tourist offices can be found online at www.tamilnadutourism.org.

- **Chennai**
  Tamil Nadu Tourism Complex, 2, Wallajah Road, Chennai 600002.
  ☎ 044 25368358.
- **Kanyakumari**
  Beach Road,
  Kanniyakumari 629702.
  ☎ 04652 246276.
- **Kodaikanal**
  Municipal Bus Stand Rest House, Kodaikanal 624101.
  ☎ 04542 241675.
- **Madurai**
  1, West Veli Street,
  Madurai 625001.
  ☎ 0452 2334757.
- **Mamallapuram**
  Kancheepuram District,
  Mamallapuram 603104.
  ☎ 04114 242232.
- **Thanjavur**
  Hotel Tamil Nadu Complex,
  Thanjavur 613001.
  ☎ 04362 230984.
- **Ooty**
  Wenlock Road,
  Udhagamandalam 643001.
  ☎ 0423 2443977.
- **Bangalore**
  Tourist Information Centre,
  Bangalore City Railway Station,
  Bangalore 560023.
  ☎ 080 2286181.
- **Delhi**
  C-1, State Emporia Complex,
  Babha Kharak Singh Marg,
  New Delhi 110001.
  ☎ 011 23745427.
- **Mumbai**
  G.2A, Royal Grace, Lokmanya Tilak Colony, Marg No.2, Dadar East,
  Mumbai 400014.
  ☎ 022 2411018.
- **Thiruvananthapuram**
  Tourist Information Centre,
  TC 25/1641, Thambanoor,
  Trivandrum 695001.
  ☎ 0471 2327310.

INDIA TOURIST OFFICES ABROAD

For information, brochures, maps and assistance in planning a trip to India travellers should apply to the official Indian Tourist Office in their own country:

Malaysia

Kuala Lumpur – Wisma HLA, Lot 203, 2nd Floor, Jalan Raja Chulan, Kuala Lumpur 50200.
☎00 60 3 2425285.

Singapore

Singapore – 20, Kramat Lane, 01–01 United House, Singapore 228773. ☎00 65 62353800.
indtour.sing@pacific.net.sg.

United Kingdom

London – 7 Cork Street, London WIS 3LH.
☎0044 207 4373677, 7346613.
www.indiatouristoffice.org.

United States

East Coast
1270, Avenue of the Americas, Suite 1808, 18th Floor, New York 10020.
☎001 212 586 4901/4902/3.
ny@tourisminindia.com

West Coast
3550 Wilshire Boulevard, Suite 204, Los Angeles, California 90010 2485.
☎001 213 380 8855.
la@tourisminindia.com

INTERNATIONAL VISITORS

EMBASSIES AND CONSULATES

British Deputy High Commission
20 Anderson Road, Chennai 600006.
☎044 42192151.
www.ukinindia.fco.gov.uk.

Malaysian Consulate General
No. 7, (Old No. 3), Cenotaph Road, 1st Street, Teynampet, Chennai 600018.
☎044 24334434 36.
www.kln.gov.my.

Singapore Consulate General
17-A North Boag Road, T Nagar, Chennai 600017.
☎044 28158207/8.
www.mfa.gov.sg/chennai/.

Sri Lanka Deputy High Commission
196, TTK Road, Alwarpet, Chennai 600018.
☎044 24987896, 24987612.
www.sldhcchennai.org.

US Consulate General
Gemini Circle, Chennai 600006.
☎044 28574000.
http://chennai.usconsulate.gov.

ENTRY REQUIREMENTS

PASSPORT

Foreign tourists require a passport that is valid for 6 months, besides accredited travel documents and a valid visa, which is granted by the Indian embassy or consulate in their respective countries. Make multiple copies of relevant pages of your travel documents and keep passport-size photographs handy for various forms. Keep a soft copy of your scanned documents on your mail as back-up. For detailed travel information visit the websites of the Ministry of External Affairs *(www.mea.gov.in)* and Ministry of Tourism *(www.incredibleindia.org)*.

VISA

A multiple-entry visa for tourists is valid for 6 months (from the date of issue) and is issued by the Indian Embassy/High Commission in one's country of residence. To obtain a visa, an applicant must present a valid passport, signed non-immigration visa application form, recent passport-size photographs, proof of intent to return, documentation to prove bona fide purpose and appropriate visa fee. Fee for tourist visa with six months' validity is US$30, one year validity is US$50 and 1–5 year validity is US$100. If the visa is valid for over 180 days, one must register within 14 days of arrival in India at the Superintendent of Police Office or The Foreigner Regional Registration Office in Chennai *(26, Haddows Road; ✆044 23454970; frrochn@nic.in).*

CUSTOMS REGULATIONS

Every passenger entering or leaving the Indian border has to pass through customs check. A Disembarkation Card must be filled in, clearly mentioning the quantity and value of goods brought. If dutiable goods are carried, passengers must go through the red channel and pay the required duty. The green channel is for those who have nothing to declare. High-value items and jewellery require an export certificate from customs. Trafficking of narcotics and psychotropic substances, wildlife articles and antiquities is a serious and punishable offence. For more information on baggage rules, visit the website of the Central Board of Excise and Customs, www.cbec.gov.in.

HEALTH

The quality of health care facilities is excellent in Tamil Nadu with 24hr chemist shops and very good hospitals in Chennai, Vellore, Madurai and Coimbatore. It is advisable to carry your medical prescription while buying medicines. Tamil Nadu can be hot and humid in summers so adequate protection like sun block, umbrellas and sufficient water intake is advisable to prevent heat stroke. Most decent restaurants serve purified Reverse Osmosis (RO) water but to be safe avoid tap water and ice and stick to bottled mineral water. Traveller's diarrhoea is the most common ailment so avoid street food and oily preparations, raw salads and cut fruits unless from a trustworthy source. Mosquitoes can be a menace in riverside, forest or coastal areas so use insect repellent and if possible, sleep under a mosquito net.

INSURANCE

It is important to have proper travel insurance that covers theft or loss of baggage, tickets and money (cash or cheques up to a certain limit), besides cancellation or curtailment of journey. Sometimes, additional health insurance may be required that covers medical expenses abroad. Any existing medical conditions must be declared. Insurance companies check if the problem was pre-existing and if undeclared, they offer no cover.

VACCINATIONS

It is not mandatory to get an inoculation before visiting unless arriving from a country infected with yellow fever. As a precautionary measure, it's recommended to get inoculated against hepatitis A/B, typhoid and meningitis, besides pre-exposure rabies vaccination and anti-malaria. As vaccinations for recent outbreaks like dengue fever, Japanese encephalitis and chikungunya are still being developed, protection from mosquitoes is the best form of prevention. Vaccinations for all major illnesses are available in Chennai and at all points of entry.

ACCESSIBILITY

Most of the temples and monuments in Tamil Nadu have stepped doorways or high steps leading to the inner shrine, making it tough to explore for the physically challenged. However, the sites, hotels and restaurants described in this guide that are easily accessible to people of reduced mobility are indicated in the admission times and charges information by the symbol ♿ *(see Discovering section).*

Getting There and Getting Around

BY PLANE

Chennai Airport is the third-largest/busiest international airport in the country after Delhi and Mumbai. The Kamaraj Terminal handles domestic flights to over 20 destinations across the country, including Coimbatore, Madurai, Trichy and Tuticorin within Tamil Nadu and Port Blair in the Andamans. Barely a minute's walk, in an adjoining building is the International Anna Terminal connecting Chennai to London, Frankfurt, Singapore, Kuala Lumpur and several destinations in the Middle East.

International airlines to Tamil Nadu include:

- **British Airways**
  www.ba.com. Direct flights from London Heathrow to Chennai 5 days a week *(except Thu, Fri)*, daily flight to Bangalore and twice a day to Delhi and Mumbai. ✆1800 102 3592.
- **Lufthansa**
  www.lufthansa.com. Daily direct flights from Frankfurt to Chennai *(10hr)*. Airport Office ✆044 22569393, 1800 102 5838 (toll-free).
- **Emirates**
  www.emirates.com. Two daily direct flights from Dubai to Chennai *(3hr45min)*. ✆044 66834444.
- **Malaysia Airlines**
  www.malaysiaairlines.com. Daily direct flight from Kuala Lumpur to Chennai *(3hr40min)* and Bangalore *(4hr)*. ✆044 4219 9999/1919.
- **Singapore Airlines**
  www.singaporeair.com. Two daily flights from Changi Singapore to Chennai *(4hr)*, besides two flights by SilkAir, its sister concern, which also flies to Coimbatore. ✆044 28473976, 22560409.
- **SriLankan Airlines**
  www.srilankan.lk. Two flights from Colombo to Chennai *(1hr20min)* and Trichy *(1hr)* everyday. ✆044 22560551/77, 22561279.

Internal airlines within Tamil Nadu include:

- **Indian Airlines**
  Daily flights to Chennai, Madurai and Trichy. Egmore Office ✆ 044 25453301, Helpline 022 27580777, 1800 180 1407. www.airindia.in.
- **GoAir**
  Chennai Airport Office. ✆ 044 28554488, Helpline 9223222111, 1800 222 111. www.goair.in.
- **IndiGo**
  Daily flight between Chennai and Coimbatore, besides several destinations across the country. ✆044 65272262, 9910383838. www.goindigo.in.
- **Jet Airways**
  Three daily flights from Chennai to Madurai and Coimbatore besides other cities. ✆044 39893333. www.jetairways.com.
- **Kingfisher Airlines**
  Flights to Chennai, Coimbatore, Trichy and Port Blair. Meenambakkam Airport Office. ✆044 22561827 8. Helpline ✆1 860 266 9000, 1 800 200 9000. www.flykingfisher.com.
- **SpiceJet**
  Daily flights connecting Chennai, Madurai, Coimbatore and Trichy. ✆9871803333, 1800 180 3333. www.spicejet.com.

As a main entry point into India, Chennai's International Airport is well equipped to handle heavy inflow of passengers. Decent facilities like free luggage trolley, pre-paid taxi counter, bookshop, snack bar, cyber cafe and international money exchange, ground transport and information booths are easily accessible. Delays due to increased security measures may occur, so make sure you arrive early enough to check in on time.

The main international airports in the region are:

- **Anna International Airport, Chennai**
  7km south-west of the city at Meenambakkam/Tirusulam. Chennai 600027. ✆044 22560551.
- **Trichy Airport**
  5km south of the city, Tiruchirapalli (Trichy). ✆0431 2340551, 2341810, 9443334189.

Other airports in the region are:

- **Madurai**
  12km from Madurai Railway station in the city. Madurai 625022. ✆0452 2690717.
- **Coimbatore**
  11km from the city at Peelamedu. Civil Aerodrome, Coimbatore 641014. ✆0422 2592155.
- **Tuticorin**
  20km from the city. Tuticorin 628103. ✆0461 2271863.

GETTING TO AND FROM THE INTERNATIONAL AIRPORT

There are pre-paid minibus and cab counters near the exit in the international arrival halls. Taxis cost around Rs.300 to the city centre and railway stations. Auto rickshaws charge Rs.150–200 but must be hailed from the main road as they are not permitted inside the airport parking area.

BY BOAT

The city has two major ports – Ennore Port for rock minerals and bulk cargo and Chennai Port, one of the largest ports in the Bay of Bengal and India's second busiest container hub. A smaller harbour at Royapuram is used by fishing boats and trawlers. A few cruises dock at Chennai, including Princess Cruises and Azamara Club Cruises via Mumbai–Goa–Kochi–Maldives–Sri Lanka or connecting Chennai to Burma–Thailand–Singapore. Chennai is also a staging point for passenger ships to Port Blair *(60hr)* in the Andamans, four a month either way.

- **Shipping Corporation of India**
  Jawahar Building, 17 Rajaji Salai. Chennai 600001. ✆044 25231401. www.shipindia.com.
- **The Deputy Director of Shipping Services**
  Andaman & Nicobar Administration. 6 Rajaji Salai, Chennai 600001. ✆044 25220841, 25226873. http://tourism.andaman.nic.in/traveltips.htm

BY TRAIN

The headquarters of Southern Railways, Chennai has two main rail terminals. Chennai Central *(✆044 25350586)* on Poonamallee High Road is linked to many major cities and smaller towns across India. It has a pre-paid auto rickshaw booth. Egmore Station *(✆044 28194579)* 1.5km away on Gandhi Irwin Road, handles trains mostly within Tamil Nadu besides a few inter-state trains. Southern Railways runs a computerised ticket reservation counter outside the domestic terminal of Chennai Airport. The city's suburban train network, one of the oldest in the country, has four broad-gauge sections – Chennai Central to Arakkonam/Gummidipoondi and Chennai Beach to Thiruvanmiyur/ Tambaram.

- **Indian Railways Catering and Tourism Corporation**
  For booking railway tickets.
  ✆044 28363453.
  www.irctc.co.in.

- **Indian Railways (official website)**
  For train timings, PNR status, fare enquiry, routes and other details.
  ✆044 25353351 (Chennai Central), 28192165 (Egmore Station).
  www.indianrail.gov.in.

CLASS

Accommodation in Indian trains is of three types – berths, seats or chair cars. The classes for long distance trains are Sleeper (non-AC), AC 3-tier, AC 2-tier and AC First Class or Second Sitting (non-AC) and AC Chair Car for day trains. Premier trains like the daytime Shatabdi Express and the overnight Rajdhani Express have special fares, with meals included.

A limited number of seats are released as per a special emergency quota called Tatkal (Instant) 2 days before the train journey for a premium of 30 percent of basic fare (non-refundable, non-transferable). There's also a limited Foreign Tourist Quota, which can only be booked at reservation offices through foreign currency or Indian currency by showing an encashment certificate or ATM receipt, besides the passport. Chennai has an International Tourist Bureau at the railway station. Indrail passes for short-term unrestricted travel across the Indian Railways network are also sold at General Sales Agents abroad.

RESERVATIONS

Seat/berth reservations for all long-distance trains must be made in advance as there's a lot of demand, especially during festivals and summer holidays. Bookings open 90 days before departure (30 days for short distance trains) and can be made online or at railway reservation counters. Once a train is fully booked, a few tickets are sold in each class as Reservation Against Cancellation (RAC), after which further prospective passengers are waitlisted (WL). Often an RAC or WL ticket will be confirmed (CNF). Passengers can track the status of their RAC/WL tickets at www. indianrail.gov.using the PNR, a 10-digit number on the top left of the ticket or top right of an e-ticket. Passengers with WL tickets cannot board the train while those with RAC tickets are allotted shared seats and a berth is confirmed during the journey. The final chart is prepared three hours before the departure of the train.

DISCOUNTS

The Indian Railways offer a 50 percent discount on base fare to women over 58 years of age and a 40 percent discount on base fare to men over 60 years. To avail of the discount, select the Senior Citizen option under Quota and carry a proof of age along with the e-ticket. Children aged 0 to 4 travel free of charge, children aged 5 to 11 travel at half the fare while those aged 12 and above are charged the full fare.

SCAMS

Touts outside railway stations or unauthorised persons near computerised reservation offices often sell illegally procured tickets booked on another name or false aliases, while instructing prospective passengers to use the name of the original passenger. Often such tickets are sold at a considerable premium, usually 75–100 percent of the original ticket fare. A person found travelling on transferred tickets is liable to be fined.

BY COACH/BUS

Public transport like buses, though less comfortable, are a lot more economical on the pocket than cabs and auto rickshaws. Apart from several private bus operators like KPN, Parveen Travels, Sangita Travels and RathiMeena, the State Express Transport Corporation runs an efficient network with semi- super- and ultra-deluxe buses and video coaches to several destinations across the state. Ordinary buses plying across the cities are usually overcrowded while long distance private buses and coaches offer more leg room and lean-back seats. Luggage is usually stowed in a separate hatch.

- **Tamil Nadu State Express Transport Corporation**
  Runs semi- super- and ultra-deluxe buses and video coaches to several destinations across the state.
  ✆044 25364656. www.tnstc.in.

- **Red Bus**
  Online bus tickets booking service with no extra charges for over 10,000 routes across India and a choice of 700 bus operators.
  ✆044 39412345 *(7.30am–11pm)*. www.redbus.in.

BY CAR

Travelling by car in Tamil Nadu is a pleasurable experience especially along the East Coast Road. Domestic travellers need to have a valid license and foreign tourists require an international driving licence. However, most tourists prefer to hire a cab with a driver rather than self-drive. Unfamiliarity with the roads and road signals, the fact that nearly all vehicles are right-hand drive, honk a lot and drive in very close proximity could make self-drives rather daunting for a foreign tourist. Road rules are often ignored by commuters and one's ignorance of Tamil, the dominant regional language, puts drivers at a clear disadvantage. Ask locals for directions and stick to the main highways wherever possible. Night driving is dangerous as heavy trucks without lights, drunken drivers and errant cows or tractors may cause accidents.

HIRING A CAR AND DRIVER

It is always better to book a car and driver from a recognised or reputed car rental company in advance. This can also be arranged through the local tourist office or hotel. Compare prices with a couple of operators before booking. Depending on the choice of car, local journeys generally costs Rs.1,300–1,800 for 10hr/100km and Rs.130/extra hour and Rs.8–14/km thereafter. Minimum distance for outstation trips is 250km/day. There is a separate driver fee called *bata* that is Rs.200–300/day and Rs.100 for night halts during outstation trips. Inter-state permits, parking and toll charges are extra.

- **Avis Rent-a-Car**
  1/24, GST Road, Chennai 600027.
  ✆044 42212800205, 42148047, 1800 103 2847 (toll-free).
  www.avis.com.

- **Hertz**
  18, Anna Salai, Chennai 600015.
  ✆044 2235112.
  www.hertz.com.

- **Fast Track Call Taxi**
  A 24hr service with airport and central pick-up.
  ✆044 24732020, 28889999.

- **B B Travels**
  22, Damodharan Street, Gopalapuram, Chennai 600086.
  ✆9789097070, 9043871710, 8925538855.

BY MOTORCYCLE

Travelling by a motorbike is a great way of exploring the state with the added advantage of transporting the bike in the luggage compartment of a train over long distances for a nominal fare. Though bikes can be brought overland from Europe, it is better to hire or purchase one locally as Tamil Nadu lies in the far south-east of the Indian subcontinent. It is possible to find shops that rent bikes for local use in many places across the state, though some consider buying a bike to be a reasonable choice. While there are several motorcycle brands and models to choose from, cheaper options like mopeds, scooters and cycles are also available.

HIRE

Motorbike rental is concentrated around tourist spots like Mamallapuram and Pondicherry and can be arranged in most cities on producing your driver's licence/ identity proof and leaving some kind of security – either an important document or cash deposit. Prices range from Rs.175/day for a Scooty or moped to Rs.350–400/day for bigger 100cc bikes and 350cc Enfield Bullets. A better rate can be negotiated for a longer trip.

PURCHASE

The Royal Enfield factory at Tiruvottiyur near Chennai *(✆044 42230400; www.royalenfield.com)* is a must-stop for motorbike enthusiasts. The Classic 350cc comes for about Rs.74,000 and the 500cc model is available for nearly Rs.1.3 lakh. There are several showrooms in nearly two dozen cities across Tamil Nadu though the best prices can be found in the Union Territory of Pondicherry. Second-hand bikes are also available for anything between Rs.20,000–55,000 depending on the bike's condition, though the paperwork is often simpler than buying a new machine.

INSURANCE

A comprehensive motor insurance policy for your two-wheeler ranges between Rs.500–2,000 per year and keeps it safe from damage caused by natural or man-made calamities, including acts of terrorism. Several insurance companies offer an online all-in-one policy that covers Own Damage, Personal Accident and Liability with access to over 2,700 network garages across India.

Ownership Papers

Owning a motorbike requires a fair amount of paperwork and the process can take up to 2 weeks before you finally hit the road. When the bike is first sold, the local registration authority issues registration papers, which are required when buying a second-hand bike. Foreign nationals cannot change the name on the registration; only a change of ownership and transfer of insurance is possible. While buying a new bike, the company selling it does the registration for a small cost. For all bikes, registration has to be renewed every 15 years and costs around Rs.5–6,000.

LOCAL TRANSPORT

There are various forms of local city transport, metropolitan buses being the most popular and cost-effective mode. Chennai has a suburban train network called the Mass Rapid Transit System (MRTS). For covering multiple sights within a city it is best to hire an auto rickshaw or cab for the day at a pre-negotiated price.

AUTO RICKSHAWS

The ubiquitous three-wheeler on any Indian road, the yellow and black auto rickshaw is another convenient local mode. The only hitch is that these contraptions are notorious for driving recklessly through chaotic traffic. Although auto rickshaws have meters, they are often manipulated or not in use. So drivers may inflate the price if you are an outsider. It is better to ask a local for the approximate cost to your destination and fix the price earlier with the driver to avoid being taken for a ride.

Where to Stay and Eat

WHERE TO STAY

The choice of accommodation options in Tamil Nadu covers the entire spectrum from 5-star luxury to intimate homestays. Choose from boutique or business hotels, service apartments, guesthouses, plush resorts, heritage bungalows, quaint homestays, Colonial bungalows and spiritual retreats. Several temples run *dharamsalas* and *choultries* or budget accommodation options for pilgrims free of cost or at a nominal charge.

SELECTION

The Addresses in this guide provide a selection of hotels, resorts and homestays across Tamil Nadu, classified according to the price of a standard double room in high season. We have reported the prices (double occupancy) and conditions as we observed them, but of course changes in management and other factors may mean that you will find some discrepancies. Please feel free to keep us informed of any major differences you might encounter. Some hotels have a lower tariff on weekdays, nearly 20 percent discount in off-season (1 May–30 June) and a higher rate for peak season (Christmas to New Year). Most hotels are air-conditioned and accept credit cards unless indicated otherwise. The Legend on the cover flap explains the symbols and abbreviations used in this guide.

BOOKING

Rack rates (published rates) are usually higher than online reservations, which offer much cheaper deals. Rates often fluctuate across the year so it's best to enquire before booking, which should be done well in advance. In most top-star hotels guests have to pay an additional luxury tax, 12.5–20 percent of the room tariff. Most homestays do not accept cards and prefer cash settlements with confirmation of a reservation only after receiving an advance payment through transfer to a bank account.

HOSTELS

The Madras YMCA was established in 1890 and its centrally located Youth Centre on Ritherdon Road in Vepery was the first hostel in India with centralised AC rooms, swimming pool, restaurant and games facilities. Over 50 rooms of various types are available for Rs.1,000–1,700/day *(℘044 25322628 32; www.ymcamadras.org)*. The Youth Hostels Association of India too offers dorms for Rs.150–200 and rooms for Rs.900–1,200 at its hostels in Ooty, Madurai and Tiruvannamalai *(www.yhaindia.org)*.

ECONOMY CHAIN HOTELS

The no-frills TTDC-run Tamil Nadu Hotels offer the most affordable choice of single, double or triple rooms, either non-AC or AC, for as little as Rs.500–1,500. Though not always in the best of condition, they usually have the ideal location. The state also has its fair share of hotel chains from economy to more luxurious options.

- **Hotel Tamil Nadu**
  Chain of 20 Government hotels at prominent tourist locations across the state.
  ℘044 25383333.
  www.ttdconline.com.

- **Ginger**
  A first-of-its-kind chain of 'Smart Basics' hotels with branches in Chennai, Pondicherry and Tirupur.
  ℘1800 2093333.
  www.gingerhotels.com.

- **Vinayaga**
  Chain of reasonably priced business hotels with branches in Rameswaram, Pollachi, Ooty and three in Tirupur.
  ℘04296 304300/272101, 04573 222361.
  www.vinayagahotel.com.

Some more expensive chain hotels include:

- **GRT Hotels**
  Tamil Nadu's most prominent chain of hotels with modern facilities, great food and efficient staff at 10 destinations.
  ✆1800 425 5500 (toll-free).
  www.grthotels.com.

- **Sangam Hotels**
  Chain of 3/4-star hotels in Madurai, Trichy and Thanjavur.
  ✆0452 4244526, 2537531.
  www.hotelsangam.com.

- **Residency Group**
  A mix of business, boutique and luxury hotels in Chennai, Pondicherry, Coimbatore and Karur.
  ✆044 28156363, 28253434.
  www.theresidency.com.

- **Fortune Hotels**
  National chain affiliated to the ITC Group with hotels in Chennai, Ooty and Madurai.
  ✆0124 4171717, 1 800 102 2333.
  www.fortunehotels.in.

RAILWAY RETIRING ROOMS

Most important railway stations have AC and non-AC retiring rooms and dormitories, which serve as transit accommodation for rail passengers at a reasonable cost. Only those holding a valid ticket for an inward/outward journey are eligible to apply.
The completed application form along with the journey ticket must be presented to the station manager/ matron-in-charge to book rooms/beds, which are allotted for a maximum of 12–24hr based on availability.

HOMESTAYS

Staying with knowledgeable hosts in Colonial-era homesteads, tea estate bungalows and organic farms is a great way of understanding local culture and cuisine. While Pondicherry has several boutique French guesthouses, most of the British Colonial bungalows and farmstays are concentrated in the Nilgiris, Palani Hills and Kamarajar Valley (*see Western Ghats*). Unless specified, meals are usually included in the price, which can range from Rs.3,000 to Rs.7–8,000 for more fancy ones.

HERITAGE HOTELS

Traditional heritage bungalows around Kumbakonam, the mansions of Chettinad, French villas in Pondicherry, Art Deco buildings and erstwhile summer palaces – Tamil Nadu has its fair share of heritage hotels. Colonial-era bungalows can be found mostly in hill stations like Ooty, Coonor, Kotagiri and Kodaikanal.

- **CGH Earth**
  South India's leading heritage hotel chain with stunning Chettiar mansions in Pondicherry and Chettinad.
  ✆0484 3011711, 3011712.
  www.cghearth.com.

- **Neemrana**
  Popular chain of heritage hotels across India with stunning properties in Coonoor, Pondicherry and three in Tranquebar.
  ✆011 40778131, 9786100436.
  www.neemranahotels.com.

- **Indeco Hotels**
  Unique 'museum' hotels set up by Indologist Steve Borgia at Mamallapuram, Swamimalai and Yercaud with upcoming projects in Madurai and Chettinad.
  ✆9444410394.
  www.indecohotels.com.

NATURE LODGES

The Tamil Nadu Forest Department *(www.forests.tn.nic.in)* runs several forest rest houses at various wildlife and bird sanctuaries like Vedanthangal, Mudumalai, Mundanthurai, Mukurthi, Point Calimere and Indira Gandhi national parks. Popular destinations like Masinagudi near Mudumalai

Street and Railway Platform Food

Tamil Nadu's streets are packed with eateries and roadside stalls serving a wide choice of economical street food like *dosas* and parottas. *Idlis* with *sambar* and chutney are usually the safest bet as they are steamed, hygienic and prepared using very little oil. An assortment of *vadas* made out of gram flour and *bajjis* or fried savouries made of raw banana, long green chillies, potato or onion are equally popular. At lunch hour, several stalls serve *sambar*-rice, tamarind rice and *biryanis*. Many shops along the coast sell a wide variety of seafood and fried fish while in the forests and hill tracts, local fruits, berries and raw mango slices are sold on push carts and pavements.

IRCTC runs food stalls at various railway platforms across Tamil Nadu. The South Indian staples of *idli*, *dosa*, *vada* and *upma* are most commonly sold by hawkers in pre-packaged boxes or served fresh on banana leaf or makeshift newspaper plates. Many food stalls also dish out the ubiquitous bread-omelette and *bajjis*. There's a regular procession of vendors selling tea, coffee, milk, soup and cool drinks. Large railway stations like Chennai Central, Egmore, Madurai, Trichy, etc have a wider choice of eateries and coffee shops.

and Sethumadai near Top Slip have a profusion of privately owned wildlife lodges (*see Western Ghats*).

TOP-END HOTELS

Most 5-star hotels come equipped with a choice of speciality restaurants, all modern amenities, spa and fitness centre, swimming pool, boutiques, travel desk, money exchange and other facilities. Some even offer free pick-up and drop to/from the airport or railway station.

- **Taj Hotels**
  Leading chain that operates the Taj, Vivanta by Taj and Gateway brands with hotels at Chennai, Covelong, Madurai, Ooty, Coonoor and Coimbatore.
  ✆044 28222827.
  www.tajhotels.com.

- **ITC Hotels**
  Leading high-end chain running the ITC Grand Chola and Sheraton Chola Hotels.
  ✆1 800 102 2333.
  www.itchotels.in.

WHERE TO EAT

Eating out can be a lot spicier when you can choose from typical South Indian fare rather than Punjabi, Bengali, Mediterranean, Vietnamese, Chinese, Japanese, Thai, Italian, Mexican or French cuisine.

RESTAURANTS

Almost every nook and cranny of Tamil Nadu has meal joints, tiffin rooms or eateries that serve an array of 'high class vegetarian cuisine', from South Indian snacks to meals or *thalis* at lunch time. Sri Saravana Bhavan, Meenakshi Bhavan, Sri Annapoorna, Sangeetha's Restaurant and Murugan Idli Shop are some prominent names in the category. Restaurant chains like Anjappar Heritage and Madurai Appu serve excellent non-veg Chettinad fare. Pondicherry is dotted with little cafes and boutique restaurants serving Franco-Tamil and French-inspired cuisine. Most 5-star hotels serve a wide choice of South Indian, North Indian, frontier, Chinese and continental fare, with the maximum diversity found in Chennai.

Basic Information

BARTERING

Notice boards at popular lodges, restaurants, eateries and cafes at Pondicherry, Auroville, Mamallapuram and other tourist spots have interesting deals for sale/exchange of motorbikes, bicycles, phones, cameras, books, travel equipment to accessories. With the rise of social networking and Internet exchange, one can even barter things online on travel communities like India Mike or Thorn Tree and dedicated sites like eBay, Booksvilla or Locanto.

BUSINESS HOURS

Most businesses operate from Monday to Saturday 9am–6pm, though Government shops and monuments open and close half an hour later/earlier in winters. Malls remain open till 10–11pm, while privately owned shops usually stay open till 8 or 9pm. Various shops, restaurants and eateries have different weekly holidays *(indicated in the Addresses of the Discovering sections)*, so it's best to enquire in advance.

COMMUNICATIONS

Phone, postal services, video conferencing, Internet facilities, courier services and all forms of telecommunication are possible across India. Tamil Nadu is well networked with Internet parlours and cyber cafes in all major towns and cities. Privately run phone services in shops and booths are available even in the remotest villages, where one can make local, national or international calls.

NATIONAL CALLS

A board that boldly announces STD/ISD indicates the presence of a privately run phone service. Standard Trunk Dialling, or STD, is a quick and easy way to make any calls within India. Just punch in the area code and dial the number directly. An automated bill is generated once you disconnect the call.

INTERNATIONAL CALLS

International Subscriber Dialling, or ISD, phone booths allow you to make calls to other countries. Just dial the country code followed by the number and your call will go through with a ticker indicating the number of minutes. It works in the same manner as STD calls, and a bill is generated once you disconnect. Most phone booths charge according to Government rates which is about Rs.10 per minute to most Western countries. Call-back is also possible, usually at a fee of Rs.3–5 per minute. Avoid calling from hotel rooms as it is always more expensive. Internet parlours offer Net2Phone (or NetPhone) eg. iWay, which allows online telephonic calls for as low as Rs.2–3 to the UK or US.

MOBILE PHONES

The mobile phone industry is booming in India. Service providers and networks have penetrated the urban sector and rural market even in the farthest corners of the country. With mobile phones available at throwaway prices and call charges much lower than in Western countries, the use of mobile phones cuts across all strata of society. Foreign tourists can buy a local SIM card for around Rs.300 from a mobile phone shop, pick up a top-up or pre-paid card for Rs.200-300 and use it on a mobile phone. Check the rates for outgoing, incoming, texting and roaming facilities. If you are away from the local coverage area, you automatically pay roaming charges. Seek local advice to choose a good service provider. BSNL, Airtel, Vodafone and Idea are some of the main players. Indian mobile numbers have 10 digits.

EMERGENCY NUMBERS	
Police	℘**100** (city) 103 (traffic) ℘**106** (outside city limits)
Fire	℘101
Ambulance	℘102

INTERNET

All large cities and tourist spots have cyber cafes or Internet parlours that usually charge Rs.20–30 for half an hour of browsing. It's safer not to transmit personal or sensitive details on unsecured networks. Most 5-star hotels have Wi-Fi connectivity that is free in the lobby, lounge and common areas, but chargeable in the room. Some business hotels offer free Wi-Fi but it's best to check the hotel policy.

DISCOUNTS

Many hotels offer good discounts on rack rates for booking online in advance or for group travel. Some establishments offer lesser rates for booking on weekdays, longer stays and discounts of up to 20–25 percent in the off-season. TTDC offers a 10 per-cent discount for hotels and package tours on special days like Valentines Day, Women's Day, Children's Day, Family Day, World Tourism Day, etc. One can also avail 15 percent discount upon continuous stay in a minimum of three Tamil Nadu Hotels and reimbursement of one-way auto fare for 1-day stay and two-way auto fare for 2 or more days' stay at any of the TTDC hotels.

ELECTRICITY

Tamil Nadu was the first state in the country to achieve 100 percent electrification of all villages as early as 1992. However, power cuts and voltage fluctuations are common and the Tamil Nadu Generation and Distribution Corporation (TANGEDCO) publish a load-shedding schedule for various circles, helping people work around it. Most 5-star hotels have complete power back-up while smaller entities use inverters. Electricity in Tamil Nadu is generally 240 Volts, which alternates at 50 cycles per second. For non-compatible devices, it's better to carry a voltage converter or a surge protector.

LAUNDRY

There are no self-service launderettes in Tamil Nadu. Hotels and resorts offer laundry services at a cost. City folk have the option of washing machines or maids at home and *dhobis* (washermen) to do the job. Villagers are often seen washing their clothes by tanks and riversides. Tourists can request for a *dhobi* to collect, wash, iron and return dirty linen. Clothes are washed in a traditional manner – soaped, scrubbed vigorously and thrashed on granite slabs in a public washing area *(dhobi ghat)*. Avoid giving expensive clothes or those that need gentle washing. Send them only to trusted dry cleaners if you are in a city or major town.

LIQUOR LAW

The state has a long history of prohibition and after 1983 all wholesale liquor sales came under the Tamil Nadu State Marketing Corporation. Owned by the Government of Tamil Nadu, TASMAC has a monopoly over wholesale and retail vending of alcohol in the state, including Indian Made Foreign Liquor (IMFL). The lack of a wide range of choices at these state-run 'wine shops' and high retail prices due to higher taxation have led to a thriving alcohol tourism industry in the union territory of Pondicherry, where alcohol prices are low and different brands are available.

MAIL/POST

The Tamil Nadu Postal Circle has a vast network of 12,180 post offices across the state and Pondicherry. Mail is transported over a length of more than one lakh kilometres per day by rail, road and waterways.

Sending parcels abroad needs to be cleared by customs at the post office. Stamps, postcards and aerograms are not expensive. Letter-post items and parcel post can be sent by surface mail, Surface Air Lifted (SAL) or airmail, which vary in rate and transit speed. EMS Speed Post is a premium service that reaches faster and there's also an efficient Railway Mail Service (RMS). For more details on services, postal rates, pin codes, etc visit www.tamilnadupost.nic.in.

MONEY

Any foreign traveller arriving on Indian soil can bring in any amount of currency he wishes to, including traveller's cheques, but this must be officially declared at the time of arrival in India. If entering the country with more than US$10,000, a currency declaration form has to be filled out. While leaving, no more than the amount already declared while entering the country, can be taken out. There is a good network of banks, ATMs and foreign exchange facilities at almost all cities, airports and tourist spots. US dollars are the easiest currency to convert, besides euros and pounds sterling.

CURRENCY

Regulated by the Reserve Bank of India and recently abbreviated from *Rs.* to ₹, the Indian rupee is the currency across Tamil Nadu, as with the rest of India. A hundred paise make one rupee. Notes of 5, 10, 20, 50, 100, 500 and 1,000 rupees and coins of 1, 2, 5 and 10 rupees are in common circulation. While travelling, be careful of people trying to palm off patched-up banknotes, which often get worn out after changing many hands. Do not accept torn or damaged notes, as no one is prepared to take them. They can however be changed at the Reserve Bank of India or large branches of other big banks.

BANKS

With over 800 co-operative banks and numerous commercial banks, Tamil Nadu has a well-developed banking system with good penetration of banks in the smallest of places. Chennai is an important centre for banking and finance; home to three large national-level commercial banks and many state-level co-operative banks. Many

American Express ✆+91 124 2801800 /666

VISA ✆000 800 100 1219

MasterCard/Eurocard ✆000 800 100 1087 (India only)

Diners Club ✆044 2852 2484

Indian banks, multi-national banks and the World Bank have located their back-office operations in the city. All the main branches of top banks across Tamil Nadu offer currency exchange.

TRAVELLER'S CHEQUES

Besides carrying cash and plastic money, it's good to have some back-up in the form of traveller's cheques. The advantage over cash is that if lost or stolen, they can be replaced. You pay a small commission (usually 1 percent) to buy these with cash in the same currency and a little more to convert from a different currency. Thomas Cook and American Express are widely accepted by most leading banks.

CREDIT AND DEBIT CARDS

International credit and debit cards like Visa, MasterCard and American Express are accepted for payment at major hotels, top restaurants, shops and airline offices. For cash withdrawals at ATMS, the card issuer adds a foreign transaction fee and the Indian bank also charges a fee of about Rs.25.

ATMS

ATMs can be found at main banks and as separate kiosks in business districts and markets in all major towns and tourist spots. An international ATM card will work in any of the nationalised bank ATMs across Tamil Nadu and banks like HDFC, Axis, ICICI, Citibank, Standard Chartered, etc. The limit on ATM cash withdrawals is usually Rs.15,000 with a daily cap that can vary. India's largest bank, The State Bank of India, and its associated banks offer access to over 26,000 ATMs across India and 40,000 ATMs of other banks under multi lateral sharing. All national and international debit/credit cards displaying Maestro, MasterCard, Cirrus, VISA and VISA Electron logos are accepted.

NEWSPAPERS AND MAGAZINES

Chennai has six major print media groups that publish about eight major newspapers and magazines. The *Hindu* is a Tamil Nadu institution and the other English dailies are the *Times of India*, the *New Indian Express* and the *Deccan Chronicle* and evening dailies like the *Trinity Mirror* and the *News Today*. The major business dailies include the *Economic Times*, the *Hindu Business Line*, *Business Standard* and the *Financial Express*. Tamil dailies like *Dinakaran* and local magazines are read widely. The state also has pioneering magazines like *Frontline* and *Sportstar*, which are published from the city, besides popular national English magazines like *Outlook*, *India Today*, *Time Out* and *The Week*.

PUBLIC HOLIDAYS

The English New Year and Tamil New Year or Pongal on the first of Tamil month Thai (mid-Jan) are Government holidays, as are Thiruvalluvar Day (16 Jan), Republic day (26 Jan), Independence Day (15 Aug) and birthdays of notable personalities and deities – Ambedkar Jayanti (14 Apr), Mahaveera Jayanti (16 Apr), Krishna Jayanti (Aug) and Gandhi Jayanti (2 Oct). Religious festivals like Milad Nabi (mid-Feb), Good Friday (Apr), Ramzan (Aug), Vinayaka/Ganesh Chaturthi (Aug–Sep), Sarasvati/Ayutha Pooja, Vijaya Dashmi and Deepavali (Oct), Bakrid (Nov), Moharram and Christmas (Dec) are also public holidays, when all Government shops and offices remain closed.

SMOKING

A Prohibition of Smoking in Public Places was issued in 2008 by the health ministry, banning smoking in all public places across Tamil Nadu, including railway premises, hotels, bars and restaurants. Some hotels and airports have designated smoking zones. Though some passengers smoke on the sly at platforms and near doors of compartments, Train Ticket Examiners (TTEs) and Railway Protection Force (RPF) officers are authorised to take action against offenders, usually a fine of Rs.200.

TIME

Tamil Nadu is ahead of GMT in London and the US and behind Singapore/ Hong Kong and 5.5hr ahead of Sydney.

TIPPING AND BAKSHEESH

Tipping is a common practice across Tamil Nadu and varies depending on the quality of service rendered. While local cabs are to be paid the requisite fare, it's always good to tip the driver of a car hired for a long road trip, besides the tour guide. Tips should also be given to the porter and room service personnel at the time of departure. Parking attendants and ushers too expect a small tip. At hotels and restaurants, 10 percent of the bill is standard practice, but for an average eatery, Rs.10 and/or any loose change is acceptable. It's always good to tip low-paid forest department guides and boatmen who augment your overall experience. Often, temple attendants or priests double up as guides, help you a jump a queue or show you special facets of a temple for a small fee, though it's better to discuss any financial expectations at the beginning. At homestays and estate bungalows, one is expected to tip the domestic help or caretakers before saying goodbye. In some places, a common tip box is maintained for distribution among all, including backend staff, so tipping is best done in consultation with the host.

VAT

The Tamil Nadu Value Added Tax Act 2006 governs VAT rules. For more details, visit www.tnvat.gov.in.

Useful Words and Phrases

TAMIL

On The Road

	Translation
Car park	Vandi parking
Centre/Middle	Nadu/Matthiyil
Direction	Dhisaigal
East	Kizhakku
In	Ulle
In front	Munnaal/Munpuram
At the back	Pinnaal/Pinpuram
Left	Idadu
North	Vadakku
Out	Veliye
Right	Valadu
Side	Pakkam
South	Yhekku
West	Maerku
I want to go to xxx	Naan xxxsella Virumbugiren
I have lost my way	Naan en vazhiye thavari vitten / Enakku vazhi theriyala
Straight ahead	Neragha sellavum
Opposite	Ethir pakkam seallavum
Drive slowly	Meduva ottu

Time

	Translation
Time	neram
Early morning	vidiyarkaalai
Morning	kaalai
Noon	nannpagal
Afternoon	pirpaghal
Evening	maalai
Night	iravu
Daily	dinamum

Sights

Aar River

Amavasya New moon

Anicut Irrigation dam

Aruvi Waterfall

Ashram/asramam Centre for spiritual learning and practice

Choultry Lodging for pilgrims

Dham Important religious site

Dhwajastambham Flagpole

Dwarapalaka Doorkeeper

Garbha griham Sanctum sanctorum

Giri valam Circumambulation of a holy mountain

Gopuram Towered temple gateway

Ilam House

Kaad Forest

Kal Rock

Kalyana mandapam Marriage hall

Koil/kovil Temple

Kolam Geometric floor decoration done with rice powder

Kottai Fort

Kunram Hill

Makara Mythical crocodile like creature flanking temple doorways

Malai Mountain

Mandapam Hall or porch with pillars

Nandi Bull, the mount of lord shiva

Nataraja Shiva as lord of dance

Patnam Port

Poornima Full moon

Pradakshina Circumambulation path around a temple

Prakaram Enclosure or compound

Ratha Chariot

Sangam Confluence

Sannidhi Shrine

Shola Clumps of rainforest surrounded by grasslands

Surya Sun or sun god

Taandav Shiva's cosmic dance

Theppam Tank

Thiru Holy/sacred

Tirtha Sacred water or holy river crossing

Trimurti Divine hindu trinity

Utsava murti Festive deity

Vahana Vehicle of a deity, typically an animal or mythical entity

Vigraha Idol

Vimanam Tower over sanctum

Yali Mythical creature with lion's body and elephant's head

Yantra Sacred geometric design for concentration

Tomorrow	naalai
Today	inndru
Yesterday	neytru
Day before yesterday	mundhanaal
Day after tomorrow	naalai marunaal
Season	kaalangal
Winter	kulirkaalam
Spring	vasanthakaalam
Summer	kodaikkaalam
Autumn/fall	illaiudirkaalam
Monsoon/rain	mazhaikaalam
Week	vaaram
Monday	thingal
Tuesday	sevvaai
Wednesday	budhan
Thursday	viyaazhan
Friday	velli
Saturday	sani
Sunday	gnayiru

Numbers

	Translation
Numbers	enngal
1	Ondru
2	Erandu
3	Moondru
4	Naangu
5	Aindhu
6	Aaru
7	Aezhu
8	Ettu
9	Onbadhu
10	Paththu
11	Pathinondru
12	Pannirandu
13	Pathimoondru
14	Pathinaangu
15	Pathinaindhu
16	Pathinaaru
17	Pathinezhu
18	Pathinettu
19	Pattonbadu
20	Irubadhu
30	Muppadhu
40	Naapadhu
50	Ayimbathu
60	Aruvathu
70	Ezhuvathu
80	Enbathu
90	Thonnooru
100	Nooru
1000	Aayiram

Tamil Months

Thai	15 Jan–15 Feb
Maasi	15 Feb–15 Mar
Panguni	15 Mar–15 Apr
Chiththirai	15 Apr–15 May
Vaikasi	15 May–15 Jun
Aani	15 Jun–15 Jul
Aadi	15 Jul–15 Aug
Aavani	15 Aug–15 Sep
Purattasi	15 Sep–15 Oct
Aippasi	15 Oct–15 Nov
Kaarthikai	15 Nov–15 Dec
Margazhi	15 Dec–15 Jan

The year starts on the first day of the month of Chiththirai, usually 15 April.

Shopping

	Translation
Closed	mudu
Open	thera
Small	chinna
Big	periya/perasu

Food and drink

	Translation
Bar	mathu arunthum iddam
Breakfast	kalai tiffin
Dessert	inippu vagaigal/ dessert
Dinner	night saapadu
Drinks	kudikka
Fork	mulkarandi
Glass	lota, tumbler
Hotel	thangum veduthi
Knife	kaththi
Lunch	madhiyam saapadu
Plate	thattu
Restaurant	unnavagam
Salt	uppu
Snacks	norukkutheeni
Spoon	karanti/chamcha
Sugar	akkaram
Water	thanni

Personal documents and travel

	Translation
Airport	vimana nilaya
Bus station	perunthu nilayam
Credit card	credit card
Customs	customs
Passport	passport

MENU READER

Kozhi kunju	chicken
Maatirachi	beef
Aatukari	mutton
Meen	fish
Meen vagaigal	seafood
Nandu	crab
Kaadai	quail
Vaatthu	duck
Muttai vagaigal	egg
Vennai	cheese
Bread/Bannu	bread
Muru murunu	toast
Pazhangal	fruit
Salad/ Pachai kaikari	mixed salad
Kaaikarigal	vegetables
Poriyal/varuv	
Thair saadam	
Thayir	
Kuzhambu	spicy sauce
Sambar	thick stew with vegetables and dal
Rasam	thin spicy soup made with tomato or tamarind
Kootu	lentil-based curries
Saadam vagaigal	rice dishes
Tiffin	breakfast or snack
Nattu kozhi curry	country chicken curry
Kozhi varthadu	chicken fry
Nandu masala	crab curry
Eral masala	prawn masala

Railway station	pugai vandi nilayam
Suitcase	paiyai
Train/plane ticket	pugai vandi/ vimana ticket
Wallet	pana paiyai

Commonly used words

	Translation
Goodbye	nalladu, varugiren or poittu varen
Hello/good morning	vannakam
How are you	neengal eppadi irukirergal
Good, so so	seri
Fine, thanks	nallam, nanri/nandri
Thank you	unnaku migavum nanri
Don't mention it/ you are welcome	paravaa illai
Yes	aamam
No	illai
Excuse me	mannichu viddungal
Sorry	varundhukiren
Sorry, i'm late	naan neram kazhithu varundhukiren
See you later	apram paarkalame
Why	yae
When	eppo
Please	thayavu saidu

Useful phrases

Do you speak English? Nienga english paesuviengala?

I don't understand enakku puriyala

Talk slowly porumaiya pésunga

Where's...? Enge..?

How much time will it take? Etharke evvalu neram tedukkum

How far / what is the distance i must go? Evalavu thooram poakanum

Whom should I contact? Yeara santhikanum?

When does the... Arrive? Eppo ....Vanthu saerum?

When does the museum open? Museum eppo therakum?

What does it cost?/ How much? Yidhan vilai enna / evvalu?

Where is the nearest petrol/gas station? Kaaval nilayam arugil engu irukiradu?

Where can I change traveller's cheques? Payanikal check-a ennala engae maattha mudiyum?

Where are the toilets? Toilet/kazhivarai engae irukiradu?

Do you accept credit cards? Neenga credit carda yetrukkolveergala?

Please translate this into English? Edai angilathil mathungal?

Where can I go shopping? Naan porutkal vaanga engu selvadu?

What are you doing? Neengal enna seigireergal?

What is your name? Ungala paeru enna?

Will you join me for lunch? Madhya unavu sappida varuveergala?

Gangaikondacholapuram Temple near Kumbakonam, Central Tamil Nadu

INTRODUCTION TO TAMIL NADU

Tamil Nadu Today

Tamil Nadu has a reputation for being a tradition-loving, religious, gentle and courteous place, that moves at a calm, unhurried pace, its people following customs and a way of life that have endured for a long time. All of this is true, but it fails to acknowledge a whole other side: that of a forward-thinking, far-sighted place that is a leader in industry and technology, and a cutting-edge innovator and pioneer in many areas. Tamil Nadu has succeeded in achieving a happy balance of the modern and the traditional, the spiritual and the commercial, the old and the new, which makes this southernmost state of India unique and special.

LIFESTYLE

Life in Tamil Nadu revolves around family, religious festivals and age-old rituals and traditions, while also embracing the modern world.

There are festivals and celebrations throughout the year, some religious, some not, and all with delicious food to make them all the more special. There is Pongal, the harvest festival that falls in mid-January, that celebrates the successful harvest of rice, turmeric and sugar cane by cooking dishes with these ingredients and also thanking the cattle that worked hard in the fields to make the harvest happen. In rural Tamil Nadu, *jallikattu* or bull-fighting is a popular sport during Pongal, with the entire village participating or observing the raucous fun.

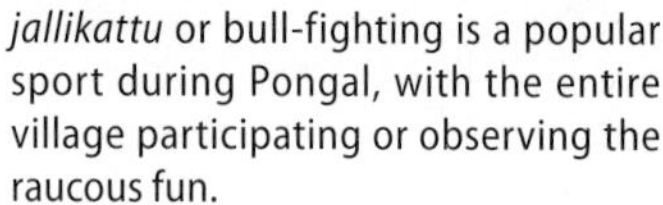

Three Seasons

The state is often said to have three seasons: hot, hotter and hottest. Of course, this is not really true; the winter months of December, January and February are wonderfully pleasant, a welcome respite from the searing heat of May and June, and the drenching monsoon rains of October and November.

The hot summer months are also the season for marriages, and marriage halls around the state echo to the sounds of joyous celebration. Navarathri, the 9-day festival, falls in the cooler autumn months. Many homes are decorated with a *golu*, an arrangement of dolls that is often breathtakingly elaborate, and women visit each other's homes to admire the *golu* and sing songs.

Karthigai Deepam, the Tamil festival of lights, comes later in the year, usually in November, and homes are aglow with the flickering light of candles and lamps.

Music and dance are a very important part of Tamil Nadu's heritage, and there are concerts throughout the year, but during the months of December and January, the city of Chennai is transformed into something else altogether as the Music Season descends upon the city and concerts and performances take place in hundreds of venues throughout the city *(see sidebar p90)*.

POPULATION

According to the latest provisional figures released by the 2011 Census of India, the population of Tamil Nadu is 72 million, making it India's seventh most populous state. It is also the state with the highest level of urbanisation, with around half the population living in towns and cities; this number is projected to increase to 75 percent in the next couple of decades. Tamil Nadu's literacy rate of 80 percent puts it among the top 10 states in India, and its ratio of females to males is a healthy 995 females to every 1,000 males.

Two interesting population trends can be seen in Tamil Nadu. As a result of the state's healthy economic growth, there has been an influx of people from all over India, including from as far away as Jharkhand and Bihar, who come here seeking economic advancement. This is very evident in a large city like Chennai, where a good number of the workforce in restaurants, security agencies and construction sites, to name a few, are from out of state. Almost half of the increase in population over the last 10 years has been as a result of this immigrant movement. At the same time, large numbers of Tamils have left the state, seeing better and bigger opportunities in foreign lands.

BIRTH AND DEATH

Tamil Nadu today ranks among the top states in India for various parameters of good health, like life expectancy, and birth and death rates. Male life expectancy is around 67 years for males, and 69 years for females, a quantum leap from the figures of just a few decades ago. Much of this improvement is thanks to the state's goal of health and health care for all, and its active role in immunisation, disease control and maternal and child health programmes.

The latest that modern medicine has to offer goes hand in hand with traditional pregnancy and birth rituals and customs, of which there are several in Tamil Nadu. An important ceremony is the Seemantham, which takes place dur-

Kolams and Mathematics

All over Tamil Nadu – urban or rural, at the homes of the poor or rich, highly educated or illiterate, an almost identical ritual takes place early every morning. The threshold of the home is swept, washed clean with a sprinkling of water and, with a handful of white powdered rice (or more commonly these days, stone), a beautiful pattern is drawn out by hand. It is always done by a woman, and is a wonderful way to showcase her artistry, skill and imagination. The *kolam* may be a small, simple, hastily drawn lotus, or a plain and straightforward six-pronged star, but on festival days, particularly Pongal, the displays are mind-boggling in their colourfulness, complexity and size.

It is heart-warming to see that in this age of hustle and bustle, of high-tech gadgets and instant meals, people still take the time and effort to create these works of art. However, *kolams* are so much more than pretty drawings. They are a cultural and artistic expression of a whole array of mathematical ideas and concepts. *Kolams* have symmetry, patterned repetition, closed continuous curves and curve families, all of which have applications and meaning in mathematics and computer science. With their impeccably logical building up of patterns – their algorithmic nature – they have attracted the attention of computer scientists who have used *kolams* to study picture languages.

ing the sixth or eighth month of pregnancy. Specific verses are recited, which are believed to aid in the baby's mental development. Valaikkapu, or the bangle ceremony, is also popular, and the mother-to-be is decked with an armful of tinkling glass bangles. Once the baby is born, he or she is often adorned with amulets or talismans to chase away bad spirits and the evil eye. It is common that the hair from the baby's first haircut is offered to a temple as a way of thanking the deity.

There are traditional death rituals as well, that vary by caste and community, all geared towards ensuring that the departed person's body and soul are put properly to rest.

MARRIAGE

Although there is no such thing as a 'typical' Tamil wedding, the word conjures up images of fragrant jasmine garlands, rustling Kanchivaram silk saris, all manner of delicacies served on generously-sized banana leaves, and the noisy celebratory music of the *nadaswaram*. The actual rituals vary according to the religion, caste and socio-economic status of the families.

Weddings in Tamil Nadu are generally deeply religious, traditional affairs, and while they are colourful and festive, they tend to be calmer, quieter affairs than the more boisterous weddings of north India. Caste still plays an important role in marriages in Tamil Nadu, and arranged marriages are still very much the norm. The parents of the bride and groom are deeply involved in every stage: from the exchanging and scrutinising of the horoscopes, the meeting of the families, the arrangements and the actual ceremonies during and after the wedding every step involves multiple family members. It is a union not only of the bride and the groom, but of their entire families as well. Modern-day weddings in Tamil Nadu use the age-old networks of families and friends to find alliances, and have also embraced newer sources like matrimonial advertisements placed in newspapers and online sites.

Great importance is placed on selecting a 'good' day and time for the wedding; certain months considered particularly auspicious, including the Tamil months of Thai (mid-January to mid-February) and Avani (mid-August to mid-September), during which time the majority of weddings take place. Nothing is left to chance, and astrologers and almanacs are consulted to help fine-tune the details.

Sari and jewellery shopping are important and much-enjoyed activities, and a Tamil wedding is a showcase for the beautiful, brightly coloured woven silk saris from the temple town of Kanchipuram as well as traditional jewellery, with the bride aglitter with gold and diamonds.

The wedding feast is an elaborate affair, and generally spans several meals. The food is often served on that ultimate eco-friendly plate, the banana leaf, and includes traditional items like rice with *sambar*, *rasam* and yoghurt, with crunchy papadams, a variety of vegetables, spicy pickles and dessert. The food, which is eaten with the fingers, is served out of gleaming buckets with warmth, generosity and assembly-line efficiency. Many weddings feature the music of the *nadaswaram* and *tavil*, a wind instrument-and-percussion ensemble whose joyously raucous sounds add to the festive atmosphere.

Most weddings are followed by a reception, which is another occasion for the guests to bless and wish the couple, to socialise, and enjoy another delicious meal, while often also enjoying a performance of classical or semi-classical music and dance.

RELIGION

Tamil Nadu is home to people who follow a diversity of religions: Hindu, Muslim, Christian and Jain, as well as a small number of Buddhists and Sikhs. The state has enjoyed admirable communal harmony, and has been fortunate in that it has not had the friction or riots that have plagued other states.

HINDUISM

Hinduism is followed by approximately 85 percent of the population of Tamil Nadu. Its roots in Tamil Nadu are ancient, and to this day, it permeates the daily life and rituals of many of its followers. Tamil Hindus are deeply religious; centuries-old temples are alive with people who throng to them to worship there, following customs and practices that are timeless and evergreen. This is a state filled with some of the most stunning temples that are not merely architectural wonders, but also carriers of traditions and beliefs that go back hundreds of years. Among the best-known and most venerated temples of Tamil Nadu are those of Madurai, Thanjavur, Kanchipuram, Thiruvannamalai, Chidambaram, Srirangam, Kanyakumari and Chennai, to name just a few.

Many of these temples were built during the golden years of the great Tamil empires of the Pallavas, Pandavas and Cholas, and later, the Vijayanagar emperors and the Nayaks, when the kings lavished extravagant sums of money to build edifices worthy of the greatness of their gods. The temple was the centre of not just religious life, but also of the social and economic activity of the town. Thus, the temple was a crucial factor in the life and development of the town. In these temple towns, the temple formed the core of the urban space, with crowded streets and shops in the immediate periphery.

The festivals and celebrations associated with the temples and their deities are major events in the lives of temple towns. The life and rituals of the temple spill out onto the streets with the gods, decked in colourful silks and dazzling jewels, taken out in procession on grand temple chariots. The air is thick with the scent of jasmine and incense, the piety and excitement of the devotees, the chanting of the priests, the music of the *nadaswaram* ensemble and the trumpeting of the temple elephant. It is a feast for all the senses.

There are countless Hindu festivals that are celebrated throughout Tamil Nadu. Some are followed by all Hindus, others are specific to a particular caste, community, region or even family. Almost all involve the preparation of special foods that have one thing in common: they are all delicious. Religious sentiment is sometimes followed quietly and simply, and sometimes extravagantly and exuberantly; it is woven into the very warp and the weft of life in Tamil Nadu.

CHRISTIANITY

Christians, who form just over 6 percent of the population in Tamil Nadu, are its second-largest religious group. There is a large population of Christians in the southern districts, particularly Kanyakumari.

The origins of Christianity in Tamil Nadu can be traced to the 1C, when the Apostle Thomas arrived in India around AD 52, and soon after established a settlement of Tamils converted and baptised by him in present-day Chennai. This area came to be known as San Thome, and is home to the San Thome Basilica which was built (originally by the Portuguese in the 16C, and then rebuilt as a cathedral by the British in the 18C) on the site where his remains are interred.

A wave of conversion to Christianity in Tamil Nadu took place before and during the Colonial era, when missionaries accompanied the traders and merchants, in their quest to get 'souls and spices'. In the 15C, the Paravars, who were deep-sea fishermen and pearl divers along the Pearl Fishery Coast from Rameshwaram to Kanyakumari, were among the first large-scale converts to Christianity in that area. Soon after, the Society of Jesus (commonly known as the Jesuits) was founded in Spain under the leadership of Ignatius Loyola, who determined that India would be a major province for his Society. The person who introduced the Jesuit doctrine to India was Francis Xavier, who arrived in India in 1542, and went on to convert large numbers of the fisherfolk of the Pearl Fishery Coast. He had a prayer instruction book translated into Tamil and learnt by heart a couple of sermons in Tamil, thus hugely enhancing his appeal. Besides helping the fishing community, he ensured that they were properly instructed in their new faith. Today, India is home to the largest Jesuit population in the world.

Proselytising by Protestant missionaries began with the Dutch and the English, who came to India in the 17C. Bartholomaeus Zeigenbalg was one of those earlier missionaries, who made important contributions to Tamil by preparing a catalogue, with notes, of Tamil literary works.

The first Bible of India was published in Tamil Nadu in 1715 by the Lutheran Mission; it was the Tamil New Testament. The first full Tamil Bible was published in 1726. Other parts of the Bible, including the Gospel of Mathew, had been translated earlier.

Christianity spread through Tamil Nadu largely thanks to the efforts of the missionaries, who converted large numbers of lower-caste people. These missionaries have done excellent work in the fields of education and social work.

Today, one of the most visited religious sites in India is the Basilica of Our Lady of Good Health, known as the Lourdes of the East, in the small town of Velankanni in the district of Nagapattinam.

ISLAM

Muslims form nearly 6 percent of the population of Tamil Nadu, and are the third-largest religious group in the state. Islam came to Tamil Nadu largely because of trade and traders, and not conquest. Over 2,000 years ago, South India was an important part of the maritime trade routes that connected Europe with pre-Islamic Arab lands. Trade with these lands continued after Islam swept through many of these countries, and there are accounts of Muslim traders in Tamil lands from as early as the 10C. Famous travellers like Marco Polo of the 13C and Ibn Battuta of the 14C have written about the presence of Muslim traders in Tamil country. Marco Polo wrote that the butchery of animals for food was done by the Saracens, who were almost certainly Muslims. There was a thriving trade in horses with the kings, who were highly taken up by the horses, and imported them by the thousands. Ibn Battuta and other travellers wrote of how it was possible to buy slave girls and how hospitable the Tamil kings were to the traders; they exercised a growing influence on the kings, who even appointed some of them as officials in their courts. Some of these traders and merchants might have formed families with the slave girls, and thus established their presence, which eventually grew into a strong community.

In the 14C, Madurai came briefly under the influence of the Delhi Sultans. The local Muslim community might have grown quite a bit by then, and what is interesting is that the Muslims of Tamil lands maintained strong roots with the ways and customs of the community. They converted to Islam without abandoning other aspects of their identity like language, dress, food and habits. To this day, Tamil Muslims consider themselves as Tamil are they are Muslim, a vital factor in preserving peace and harmony in the community.

From the 17C and 18C, Tamil Muslims started producing their own literature, a genre that is now known as Tamil Muslim Literature. The epic *Seerapuranam* by Umaru Pulavar of the 17C is a highlight of Tamil Muslim literature. Today, the University of Madras has a department of Tamil Islamic Literature; the first Tamil Islamic Literature Conference was held in Trichy in 1973. There is a journal called *Samarasam* that is geared towards addressing issues specific to the Tamil Muslim community.

The Tamil Muslims of today belong to multiple ethnicities and thus follow a variety of customs. There is a large Tamil Muslim diaspora in South-east Asia, particularly Malaysia. One of India's most beloved presidents, Abdul Kalam, is a Muslim from Madras.

LANGUAGE

The language of Tamil Nadu is, quite obviously, Tamil. This Dravidian language is one of India's 22 official languages, and was the first Indian language to be pronounced a classical language by the Government of India.

Chennai Wall Art

Among the many things that strike people about Chennai are its walls. They are riotously colourful, wonderfully imaginative, often hilarious representations of the city's political and entertainment landscape.

The Chennai Corporation, in an effort to beautify the city and elevate it to the pantheon of great world cities, decreed that most of these posters and graffiti are illegal. And, in order to further beautify the place, one of the steps that has been taken is to paint many stretches of its walls with scenes depicting Tamil culture, traditions, tourist sights and scenery. There are walls depicting the beautiful temples of Tamil Nadu; others showing rural and agricultural scenes; there are scenes from the great Tamil epics and the faces of eminent Tamilians painted on walls around the city. Some of them are quite lovely, and added to all the posters and graffiti that they have not quite succeeded in eliminating, they add yet another layer of colour and life to this bustling city.

Tamil is one of the oldest surviving classical languages of the world, with a known literature that dates from over 2,000 years ago. Some of the finest poetry in the world is the Tamil poetry of the Sangam era that flourished in the years surrounding the beginning of the second millennium.

The oldest extant grammar of the Tamil language is the *Tolkappiam*. It is uncertain as to when exactly it was written; it may have come about over several centuries, but the oldest parts of it are at least 2,000 years old. The rules of Tamil grammar laid out in the Tolkappiam all those years back form the backbone of modern Tamil.

The evolution of Tamil is generally divided into three phrases: old, middle and modern. Old Tamil is the language of the Sangam era, based almost entirely on the *Tolkappiam*, and written with letters based on the Brahmi script. An important feature of Old Tamil was that it lacked a distinctive present tense.

As the history of the Tamil lands unfolded and new influences made themselves felt, Tamil evolved into what we today call Middle Tamil, around the 8C. This period saw the emergence of a present tense, and most importantly, the Pallavas, and later, the Cholas, dropped the old Brahmi-based script for one based on the Grantha script. It was this that developed into the modern Tamil script. A certain amount of Sanskritisation crept in. The *Tevarams* and *Divya Prabandams* of the Bhakti saints and the *Ramayana* of the poet Kambar date from this period. The *Nannul*, the grammar book of literary Tamil that is followed to this day, was written in the 12C.

Modern Tamil can almost be said to consist of two separate languages: Sentamil, or formal, literary Tamil, which is the language of academic writing, public speaking and news broadcasts; and Kotuntamil, or spoken, or colloquial Tamil which is the language of everyday conversation. The two Tamils have different grammatical structures and vocabularies. Sentamil is based on the Middle Tamil grammar book, Nannul. This is a trans-regional Tamil; regardless of district, caste or community, this is

Tamil palm leaf manuscripts, Sarasvathi Mahal Library Museum, Thanjavur Palace

the language of formal communication. Colloquial Tamil, on the other hand, has endless variations in vocabulary, sentence structure, intonation and pronunciation. Some of this has come about because of contact with other Indian languages and even European languages.

With the emergence of the Dravidian movement in the first half of the last century, an emphasis on linguistic purity has emerged, with a push to rid the language of Sanskrit and other foreign elements. Tamils are fiercely proud of their culture and heritage, and view their language as one of the primary means of preserving and promoting them.

GOVERNMENT

The headquarters of the Government of Tamil Nadu is in Fort St George in the capital city of Chennai. The government is headed by the Governor of the state, who is the constitutional head, and run by the Chief Minister, who leads and controls the Council of Ministers. The Governor is nominated by the President of India for a five-year term. The Chief Minister is selected by the legislators from the party that won the right to form a government and can remain in position as long as he or she enjoys the confidence of the legislative assembly. The Governor, Chief Minister and Council of Ministers form the executive branch of the Government.

The Chief Justice of the Madras High Court is the head of the Judicial branch of the Government.

The Governor is also part of the legislative branch, which also includes the unicameral Tamil Nadu Legislative Assembly. The Legislative Assembly consists of 235 members, of whom 234 are democratically elected every 5 years; the remaining one candidate is a nominated representative of the Anglo-Indian community.

The Council of Ministers is responsible for a variety of portfolios, like Finance, Agriculture, Rural Industries, Taxes, Forests, Education and Highways, to name a few.

Administratively, Tamil Nadu is divided into 32 districts, as well as numerous revenue divisions, *taluks*, municipal corporations, municipalities, *panchayat* unions, town *panchayats* and village *panchayats*.

The Corporation of Chennai, which is the body that runs the city of Chennai, was established in 1688, and is the oldest municipal corporation in India, and also the oldest among the Commonwealth nations outside the UK.

The Government of Tamil Nadu has been a pioneer in e-governance. Land ownership records have been digitised and many government departments are now accessible online.

ECONOMY

Tamil Nadu boasts an impressive set of facts and figures that make it one of the most economically vibrant and healthy states in the country. It tops the country in the Economic Freedom Rankings for the States of India, where economic freedom has been defined as 'the absence of government coercion or constraint on the production, distribution or consumption of goods and services beyond the extent necessary for citizens to protect and maintain liberty itself'. This industrialised state ranks high in areas like per capita income and total Foreign Direct Investment (FDI). Tamil Nadu has the highest number of small and medium enterprises in the country. Its high level of urbanisation ensures that its assets and infrastructure are spread throughout the state and not clustered in a few areas.

The government has made it a policy to be industry-friendly, and has invested major resources in setting up state-of-the-art industrial as well as social infrastructure. There are over one hundred industrial parks in the state supporting the information technology, biotechnology, rubber and apparel sectors, to name a few. This has attracted large numbers of foreign and domestic business into the state.

AGRICULTURE

Agriculture has historically been the backbone of Tamil Nadu's economy, and over half of its population works in this sector. The verdant countryside, with paddy fields, and mango, banana and coconut groves stretching in every direction, is a sight to behold. However, with the growth of the non-agriculture sector, the share of the state's domestic product from agriculture has declined steadily. In 1950, over half of the net state domestic product came from agriculture; 50 years later, that number dropped to 16 percent.

Even with Tamil Nadu's aggressive and successful push into developing the non-agricultural sphere, it still remains an agricultural powerhouse, and is a leading producer of a variety of products like rice, pearl millet, corn, rye, sugar, coffee, tea, bananas, mangoes, coconuts and seeds. The region around the delta of the River Kaveri is called the Rice Bowl of India. Tamil Nadu has also invested in research and development of new crop varieties and technologies through the Tamil Nadu Agricultural University, which has colleges throughout the state. Tamil Nadu is also a leading state in livestock, poultry, egg and fish farming.

INDUSTRY

Tamil Nadu is one of the most highly industrialised states in the country today. The area around Chennai has been called the 'Detroit of Asia', and the Coimbatore region has earned the moniker 'Manchester of India', thanks to the thriving automobile and textile industries, respectively.

Tamil Nadu has been a leading manufacturer of automobiles and automobile parts, producing cars, rail coaches, tractors, motorbikes, spare parts and tyres. In recent years, its industry- and investment-friendly policies, skilled and educated workforce, and excellent port facilities have taken this sector to dizzy new heights, and have opened the doors to many foreign automobile companies, including BMW, Ford, Renault-Nissan, Caterpillar, Hyundai and Mitsubishi, who have set up state-of-the-art manufacturing plants around Chennai. In 2010, over one million cars were produced in these factories, with around a third

Energy Sources

This is another area in which Tamil Nadu has shown itself to be at the vanguard of the latest and best in trends and innovations. It has invested major resources in researching and developing renewable energy sources, and is a pioneer in the country in the building up of wind power. In 1985, the government of Tamil Nadu set up the Tamil Nadu Energy Development Agency, which was invested with the specific mandate to promote the awareness and use of renewable energy sources. It has succeeded admirably, and today, approximately one-third of the state's grid capacity is from renewable sources like wind, solar and biomass energy. Tamil Nadu is the top state for generation of power from renewable sources.

The bulk of Tamil Nadu's energy production still comes from 'traditional' sources, its nuclear and thermal plants. Important among these are the Kalpakkam Nuclear Plant, the Ennore Thermal Plant and the Neyveli Lignite Power Plant. The Tamil Nadu Electricity Board (TNEB), which was established in 1957, is responsible for the generation, distribution and regulation of power to the state, and has performed admirably under difficult conditions. Currently, all villages and towns in Tamil Nadu have been electrified, and the TNEB is now working on ensuring that every household in the state is supplied with electric power.

Around one-fifth of the power supply of Tamil Nadu comes from hydroelectricity. The Mettur Dam, one of the oldest and largest in India, and the associated hydroelectric plant, are a major source of power. Tamil Nadu has also been a pioneer in biofuels as a source of energy.

of them exported to countries in Asia, Africa and Europe.

The state's far-sighted and savvy measures like tax incentives, easing stultifying red-tape procedures and allowing easy land acquisition have resulted in millions of dollars pouring in. It is not just the foreign automobile companies who have taken advantage of Tamil Nadu's friendly environment; many domestic automobile and automobile parts companies have set up shop in the state, including Ashok Leyland, Hindustan Motors, TVS, Royal Enfield and MRF.

The area around Coimbatore, including Tiruppur, is home to a number of textile mills and factories. Over half of India's knitwear exports come from this area.

Many heavy electrical and metal manufacturing companies have plants in Tamil Nadu, including Bharat Heavy Electrics (BHEL) and the Steel Authority of India (SAIL).

Another area where Tamil Nadu has historically had the lead, and continues to do so, is the leather industry, particularly tanning. There are hundreds of tanneries around Vellore and its environs. The Central Leather Research Institute (CLRI) in Chennai is the largest of its kind in the world, and links academic research with industrial production.

Sivakasi, an ancient town in the middle of Tamil Nadu, is the country's leading producer of fireworks and matches. It was once notorious for employing children in this industry; however, it responded to the outrage that erupted around this practice and completely eradicated the use of child labour. This town also has the world's second-highest number of offset printing presses - second only to Gutenberg, in Germany; this is the place from where many of the colourful calendars and posters that are seen around India come from.

Taking advantage of all the incentives and policies of the State Government, many of the world's leading electronics manufacturers have set up manufacturing hubs in Tamil Nadu. These include Nokia, Motorola, Sony-Ericsson, Foxxcon, Cisco, Samsung, Moser Baer and Dell.

Perhaps the most remarkable growth of all has taken place in the Information Technology (IT) sector, thanks in large part to the Government's policy and efforts to make Tamil Nadu a destination of choice for IT investments and to develop it as a global centre for business process outsourcing. The IT 'parks' that have sprouted around the state, particularly in Chennai, are to be seen to be believed; they are as modern and well setup as the best in the world, and employ a highly educated, motivated and savvy workforce. The state is second only to Karnataka in software exports, which have seen galloping growth figures in the last decade. The world's and the nation's Who's Who of IT companies have offices in Tamil Nadu. These include Infosys, Wipro, Cognizant, Mahindra Satyam, Amazon, Hewlett Packard, Verizon and IBM, to name just a few.

Tamil Nadu has been truly far-sighted in its approach to developing its industries, and this has paid off brilliantly.

MEDIA

The newspaper, television and radio industries are thriving in Tamil Nadu, helped in big part by its literate and highly engaged, opinionated and curious population.

There are many newspapers and magazines, published daily and weekly, in both Tamil and English, all with loyal and committed followings.

In English, the grandfather of all the papers is the venerable *Hindu*, which was founded in, and has been published continuously since, in 1878. The *Hindu*'s headquarters are in Chennai, and it is one of the most widely read newspapers in all of South India. It has been a pioneer in many areas: it was the first to offer colour, to own a fleet of aircraft for distribution, to use computer-aided photo editing and composing, and to offer an Internet version. Nipping at the *Hindu*'s heels are the *Times of India*, the *New Indian Express* and the *Deccan Chronicle*, all of which are enjoying growing readership numbers. There are also several business dailies published out of Chennai. English-language magazines published from Tamil Nadu include *Frontline* and *Sportstar*.

The Tamil newspaper and magazine industry is also thriving. Most popular among the newspapers is the *Dina Thanthi*, which was started in Madurai in 1942 and now has multiple editions. This is a paper aimed at the common man, with an easy-to-read format and content that appeals to all.

There are several hugely popular Tamil magazines, some of which rose to fame with their serialised stories that kept loyal readers in thrall. These include the *Ananda Vikatan*, *Kumudam* and *Kalki*.

Television is another enormously popular source of news and entertainment. There are many private Tamil satellite networks, like Sun TV, Raj TV, Vijay TV, Makkal TV and Jaya TV, that broadcast out of Chennai. These networks broadcast drama serials, news, concerts and educational content among other things, and have been lapped up by the population. The Sun TV Network, a multi-thousand crore firm, is India's second-largest broadcasting company in terms of viewership, and some of its shows have enjoyed top rating points. Chennai has been a pioneer in India in implementing the Conditional Access System for cable television.

The radio is another popular medium in Tamil Nadu, with radio stations broadcasting in Tamil and English, and in Hindi as well, to cater to the growing Hindi-speaking immigrant population. FM radio stations are widely listened to in big cities like Chennai and Coimbatore. Many colleges have also set up radio broadcasting stations.

SPORT

Like the rest of India, Tamil Nadu is cricket-crazy. On streets and fields in cities, towns and villages, teams of people, young and not-so-young, can be seen playing the game, often using the crudest of equipment, but with the spirit of the game intact. This just intensifies when a 'real' match is in progress, as the lads imagine themselves to be playing to a packed stadium in Chepauk, or any of the other great stadia of the world.

Rachel Mills/MICHELIN

2011 ICC Cricket World Cup, M. A. Chidambaram Stadium, Chennai

Chennai is one of the Indian cities that is featured in the Indian Premier League, with the Chennai Super Kings team enjoying massive support and adulation from all over the state.

Car racing is also popular here, on the motor racing tracks in Sholavaram, Kari Motor Speedway (near Coimbatore), and Irungattukottai (near Sriperumbudur). Narain Karthikeyan, the first Indian to participate in Formula One racing events, is from Chennai.

Tennis, while an elitist sport, is also well liked and widely followed in Tamil Nadu. Chennai is home to the ATP Chennai Open Tournament that is held early every January, and which has hosted the likes of Rafael Nadal and Carlos Moya.

The Sports Development Authority of Tamil Nadu, a Government entity, has played an important role in developing sports and sports facilities, and Tamil Nadu can boast of world-class stadiums. The Mayor Radhakrishnan Stadium hosts hockey tournaments, and has been recognized by the International Hockey Federation as one of the best in the world in terms of infrastructure. The Indian Triathlon Federation as well as the Indian Volleyball Federation have their headquarters in Chennai.

The state sport of Tamil Nadu is kabbadi, known locally as *sadugudu*.

Meal with dosa

© Anurag Mallick, Priya Ganapathy/MICHELIN

Other sports are played here as well: golf, squash, boating and horse racing all have excellent facilities.

Thanks to the great success enjoyed by the chess Grand Master Vishwanathan Anand, this mental 'sport' has seen a surge in popularity.

Tamil Nadu has produced world-renowned athletes in a range of sports. Here are some names: K. Srikanth and S. Venkataraghavan for cricket; the Amritraj brothers, Ramanathan and Ramesh Krishnan, and Mahesh Bhupathi for tennis; and Narain Karthikeyan and Sundaram Karivardhan for motor racing.

CUISINE

For the longest time, alas, the notion of Tamil Cuisine was confined to a handful of items: *idli*, *dosa*, and *vadai*, accompanied by searingly hot and mouth-puckeringly tart curries. That was it. These were the dishes that Tamilians who travelled away from home had to limit themselves to, absent all their locally available vegetables and spices and masalas and the heat, soil and water that had such magical, alchemical properties. Luckily that has changed. With the opening of food borders and a growing appreciation for the subtleties and varieties of regional specialities, the world has had its eyes (and taste buds) opened to the infinite nuances, the range of dishes, the absolute deliciousness of Tamil cuisine.

Food is traditionally eaten with the fingers, and is often served, particularly at weddings and other feasts, on banana leaves.

REGIONAL VARIATIONS

Of course, there is no such thing as one Tamil cuisine. For sure, certain dishes can be found all over the state: the afore mentioned *idli* (feather-light steamed cakes of fermented rice-and-legume batter) *dosa* (crispy pancakes, also made from a fermented rice-and-legume batter, but with different proportions), *sambar* (a fiery-hot and tart liquid curry with legumes and vegetables) and *vadai* (deep-fried legume balls) and many others, but even among these there are variations depending on the region, the caste, the community and the religion, of the cook. There are both vegetarian and non-vegetarian dishes that are specialities of different communities in the state.

Rice, lentils and legumes – of which there are many varieties – are the staples of Tamil food. There is *idli* rice and *dosa* rice and tamarind-rice rice, and all sorts of other varieties, each of which shines in particular recipes, and most of which is grown in the state itself. Spices and flavourings that give the food its distinctive flavour and aroma include curry leaves, mustard seeds, tamarind, coconut, sesame, coriander, ginger, garlic, pepper, asafoetida and cumin, most of

Chettinad Cuisine

Chettinad's most famous export is its cuisine, and Chicken Chettinad is its legendary brand ambassador. Like the ubiquitous Udupi restaurants from Karnataka's west coast, Chettinad restaurants dot every city in Tamil Nadu and as far as Canada, US and the Far East. The traditional *set-samayalkarar* (team of cooks) learnt their skills from *aachis* (older ladies of the house) while working at Chettiar marriages and functions. Though *kalyan sappad* (wedding feasts) are primarily vegetarian affairs, Chettinad cooking includes a variety of sun-dried meats and salted vegetables, adapting to the region's dry environment. In the inhospitable parched terrain where little grew, Chettiars extended their repertoire to wild game like *kaada* (quail), *muyal* (rabbit), *pura* (pigeon) and *pitta* (turkey). Using a variety of dry-roasted *masalas*, including exotic spices like *marathi mokku* (dried flower pods), *anasipoo* (star aniseed) and *kalpasi* (a lichen called black stone flower), Chettinad cuisine boasts an extensive menu.

Meals are traditionally served on banana leaf with the tip pointing left. There's a designated space for every dish and a particular sequence of serving them. Starting at the top left from salt, pickle and *mor milagai* (chilli dipped in salty yoghurt and fried) to *varuval* (dry dish), *kootu* (lentil curry), *urundai* (fried lentil balls), *poriyal* (side dish) mostly cabbage or beetroot and *masiyal* (mash), either potato, *keerai* (spinach) or *senai kilangu* (yam). The bottom left is for fries like *appalam* (papad) and *vadai*, and the centre for chapatti followed by a succession of rice dishes. White rice is served with *sambar* or *rasam*, then lemon rice, vegetable *pulav* with *kuzhambu* (veg or non veg gravy) and finally the clincher, curd rice. The bottom right is reserved for sweets like *kavuni arisi* (black sticky rice pudding), an influence picked up from Burma, rhubarb cheesecake, a British Colonial touch, or the traditional *halwas* and *payasams*.

Example of a Chettinad meal

Despite its inland location, Chettinad dishes include a lot of seafood like *nandu* (crab) *masala*, *sora puttu* (shark curry), *eral* (prawn) *masala* and *meen kuzhambu* (fish curry), which points to its earlier proximity to the sea. The *vaalai yaley meen* (banana wrap fish) and Masala Fish Fry are not to be missed.

Snack dishes constitute another category with a variety of *murukku* and *paniyarams* (fluffy balls made in moulds out of batter). Breakfast too has its own ensemble with soft *idlis*, *dosa*, *adai*, *appam* and *idiappam* (string hoppers) served with a host of chutneys. A typical Chettinad dish is the *kozha kattai* (steamed rice dumplings), one sweet with sesame and jaggery, the other salted with lentil, coriander and grated coconut.

More than the meal itself, it is the gracious manner in which it is served and the host's *upachaaram* (constant enquiry) that's the trademark of Chettinad hospitality. Many an *aachi* will scoff at the plethora of 'authentic' Chettinad restaurants today. For them, unless *masalas* are prepared in stone grinders, an *aruamanai* (iron blade) is used to cut vegetables and particular firewood is used to cook specific dishes, it is not authentic Chettinad cuisine!

them items that sparked the spice trade and the colonisations that have had such a major and lasting impact on the history of India.

The different regions of Tamil Nadu are well known for certain dishes and flavours. **Chettinad** food (*see Feature Box, opposite*) is known for its peppery heat, and dishes like *appam*, *iddiappam* and *uthapam*, and Chettinad chicken curry, are now popular well beyond the boundaries of Chettinad.

In the southern districts of Tamil Nadu including **Madurai** and **Tirunelveli**, mutton, and chicken-based non-vegetarian curries are a staple, often eaten with a *parotta*, a type of layered flat bread made with plain flour or maida. Perhaps greater Christian and Muslim influences in these parts were responsible for this.

Kanyakumari, at the very tip of Tamil Nadu and India's Land's End, makes use of the abundant seafood present in the three seas that lap at its shores, and is known for its fish curries and coconut-based cuisine.

And in the west of the state, near and around **Coimbatore**, locally grown crops have given birth to local delicacies like sweet balls made of ground seeds and jaggery (an unrefined sugar), and dishes based on the grains, coconut, sugar and seeds that are grown there.

ON THE MENU

The day might start with a tiffin with *idlis*, *dosa* or *pongal* (a mildly-spiced mixture of rice and lentils, flavoured with ghee, cumin and peppercorns), accompanied by a coconut chutney and sambhar, and washed down with hot, milky coffee. Lunch is almost always rice based, with freshly cooked rice served with *sambar*, *rasam* (a spicy soup-like dish prepared with the water used to boil the *sambar* lentils) and *poriyal*, a dry vegetable dish flavoured with mustard seeds, chillies, curry leaves and coconut; all that spiciness is tamed with a helping of curd rice, a dish beloved across all regions and communities in Tamil Nadu.

Often, there is an evening tiffin as well, with any of the infinite variety of snack dishes that the state is so famous for: many varieties of *vadais* (utterly delicious deep-fried lentil balls), *sevai* (rice noodles), bondas, *samosas*, *pakodas* (all deep-fried goodies with a range of stuffings or flavourings) or one of many flavoured rice preparations with lemon, tomato, tamarind, coconut, mustard or sesame seed.

Tamilians love their sweets, and their *payasams*, liquid concoctions made with milk, coconut milk, rice or lentils, are well known, especially during festivals and weddings.

DRINK

Coffee is the most favoured drink throughout the state. Tamilians take great care and pride in how they make their coffee. Nothing but freshly roasted and ground coffee beans will do, along with just-boiled milk and a generous quantity of sugar. The aroma is indescribably good; the taste, divine. Coffee and tea are also served in little roadside stalls all over the state. It is quite a sight to see how the steaming hot beverage is cooled, and a bubbly froth produced, by pouring it from one container to another that is a good distance away! Not a drop is spilled during this extraordinary performance. The coffee is traditionally served in a stainless tumbler along with a *dabarah*, a kind of bowl into which the hot coffee is poured to cool it down.

Tea is also well liked, and tea stalls throughout the state prepare and serve strong, sweet, milky tea.

Coffee served in a typical way

History

PREHISTORY IN TAMIL NADU

The history of Tamil Nadu stretches far, far back to the shadowy period when humankind was in its earliest stages of development, when the first stirrings of civilisation were developing and the story of mankind was still in its infancy. There is evidence that the area today known as Tamil Nadu has had continuous human habitation since Paleolithic times, making this one of the oldest civilisations in the world.

OLD STONE AGE: 1,000,000 BC TO 3,000 BC

In 1863, a British geologist, Robert Bruce, found a rich lode of stone-age implements including spears, axes and blades around the shale gullies near the Attirampakkam Canal, an area that is on the fringes of present-day Chennai. His discovery triggered the birth of the study of the paleolithic history of Tamil Nadu. More recently, an international team led by Dr Shanti Pappu conducted a detailed and lengthy excavation of the site, and found that many of the artefacts date from over a million years ago, an astounding fact that has resulted in the complete re-evaluation and rethinking of everything that was formerly believed to be true about when humans arrived in India. The Attirampakkam site spans a vast period of time, making it an invaluable resource to study the life of stone-age humans and how they adapted and evolved over the earliest stages of human life.

LATER STONE AGE AND IRON AGE: 3,000 BC TO 300 BC

Sites from this broad span of time are widespread in Tamil Nadu, from inland to coastal regions, hilly terrain, river basins, and cave and rock shelters, and include Kodumanal, Salem, Periyar, Dharmapuri, North Arcot, Madurai and Tirunelveli. A large number and wide variety of relics have been found, and these show the progress from crude stone tools to well-shaped and decorated objects made from ceramics, clay and a variety of metals. Archaeological explorations have unearthed agricultural tools, weapons and decorative objects and jewellery. However, the most interesting and significant finds are hundreds of mortuary sites, with burial urns, cairns and pits, underground and above-ground stone chambers and cemeteries. Graffiti and other markings have been found on some of the artefacts, suggesting the existence of social groups and rituals in those long-ago times. By the end of the prehistoric period of Tamil Nadu's history, people were living in tribal groups, had mastered the rudiments of agriculture and may have conducted trade with nearby tribes and settlements.

1,000,000 BC-50,000 BC Remains found of earliest humans in Attirampakkam Canal. Paleolithic humans lived near river basins.

50,000 BC-6,000 BC A variety of flake tools and blade-like tools found.

6,000 BC-3,000 BC The age of microlithic tools made of jasper, agate, flint and quartz, found in abundance around Tirunelveli District.

2,500 BC-1,000 BC Neolithic period with more finely crafted tools. The dead were buried in urns or pits.

1,000 BC-300 BC The Iron Age. Hundreds of megalithic burial sites found from this period.

SANGAM PERIOD: 300 BC TO 300 AD

Tamil history and identity, as we conceive of it today, began around the 3C BC. The 600 years that followed are considered the classical period of Tamil antiquity. It spanned an area that is referred to as 'Tamilakam', or Tamil country, that covers today's Tamil Nadu, Kerala, parts of Karnataka, Andhra Pradesh, Sri Lanka and the Laccadive Islands.

As the area emerged out of the prehistoric Iron Age, the rudiments of society developed with the establishment of agriculture, particularly around river basins. Social hierarchies came into being with *vellalars*, or agricultural landlords and *velalas*, or peasants, who worked under them Other specialised professions, like weaving, carpentry and that of the blacksmith, gained in importance as life in the tribal groups settled and expanded. Slowly, these groups coalesced and village life evolved with a combination of local tribal practices and Brahminical customs that came from further north.

Dravidian Culture

Tamil Nadu is the home of Dravidian culture, a name that evokes many emotions and interpretations. Historians believe that Dravidians came into India over 6,000 years ago, a branch of a family that had its early roots in the Mediterranean region. Today, the term Dravidian is used for the part of the country where Tamil is spoken as well as for its inhabitants. The term is believed to originate from the word *Dravida*, *Dramida* or *Dramila* (or *Damila* in Pali), from which the word Tamil is derived. The name Termilai, which is what Herodotus called the inhabitants of ancient Greece, is probably the same as *Dramila*, lending support to the Mediterranean theory. The Dravidians are thought to be the creators of the great Indus Valley civilisation. Aryan invasions of northern India pushed the Dravidians far south, where the distance from the Aryans helped them to maintain and develop a distinct culture while also imbibing elements of the ways of the invaders. Also, the people of the south were anything but isolated from the world at large: there is plenty of evidence to show that extensive trade was conducted, as long as 4,000 years ago, with Egypt, Babylon, Arabia and Palestine. During the years of the first century AD, there was large-scale trade with the Roman Empire, mainly in pearls, pepper and precious stones, and there was a fairly large population of Greeks and Romans in the cities of the time.

EARLY KINGDOMS: 200 BC TO 300 AD

While large stretches of northern India and parts of the Deccan were ruled by the Maurya Empire, Tamilakam in the centuries before and after the second millennium was under the control of three dynasties: the Chola, Chera and Pandya, who between them ruled the area stretching from Kanyakumari to the hills of Tirupathi. This era, called the Sangam Period, is named after the poetic academies, or Sangams, that were important parts of the socio-cultural landscape of the time. There were three Sangams, each lasting many centuries, and each consisting of large numbers of poets. The works of the first two Sangams have all but disappeared; one of the oldest extant works of literature in Tamil, the *Tolkappiam*, dates from 200 BC. Some of the most important works of Tamil literature, the epic poems *Silappathikaram* and *Manimekalai*, date from the third Sangam, which ended around 2,000 years ago. The works of the third Sangam are invaluable resources that provide glimpses into the political, social, economic and cultural ways of the time. Ample mention is made of the Pandyas, Cheras and Cholas in the literature of the time. In addition, they are mentioned in the edicts of Emperor Ashoka, the outer borders of whose kingdom adjoined theirs.

EARLY PANDYA DYNASTY: C. 500 BC TO AD 300

The Pandyas were the most ancient of the Tamil dynasties. They ruled over the extreme south of Tamilakam, including the districts of Kanyakumari, Tirunelveli, Ramnad, and Madurai. The first Pandyan king that we have any substantial information about was Nedunchezhian I, who, through fighting and conquest, expanded his kingdom and moved the capital city from Korkai to Madurai. The greatest of the early Pandyan kings was Nedunchezhian III of the 3C AD. He ruled over a considerably larger kingdom than his predecessors, after making sizeable inroads into the territories of his enemies, the Cholas and the Cheras. His most celebrated victory and crowning achievement was at a fiercely fought battle at Talaialanganam (in present-day Thanjavur).

EARLY CHERA DYNASTY: C. 400 BC TO 12C AD

The Chera dominion was the western part of Tamilakam, in present-day Kerala. Muziris, a seaport that was well-known in Antiquity, was in the Chera kingdom; from here and other Chera seaports precious spices, pearls, ivory and timber made their way to the Middle East and beyond, and brought great prosperity to the kingdom. King Senguttavan, who ruled in the early years of the new millennium, was the best known of the early Chera kings. He is believed to be the brother of the Jain monk Ilango Adigal, who wrote one of the best-known and most beloved works of Tamil literature, the *Silappathikaram*. At this time, the people of the Chera region spoke the same language as the other people of Tamilakam. It was only several centuries later that, with the growing influence of Sanskrit, a new language, Malayalam, began to evolve in that region.

EARLY CHOLA DYNASTY: C. 300 BC TO 13C AD

The Cholas ruled over the eastern parts of Tamilakam, including the delta of the great Kaveri River and the fertile plains between the Kaveri and the Vellar rivers. Poompuhar was its capital, and Karikala Chola, who ruled in the 3C BC., was its best-known ruler. Truth and fantastic legend are inextricably mixed together in the retelling of the life of this great king, and many extravagant tales have been told about his exploits, very little of which can be actually substantiated by historical fact.

Towards the end of this period, another dynasty, the Pallavas, who would conquer the northern parts of Tamilakam, began their rise. Their real efflorescence, however, took place several centuries later.

The three kingdoms were in constant conflict with each other, and this glorious period came to an end in the third century AD, when the conquering Kalabhras displaced these kingdoms and established their rule.

C. 270 BC Rule of King Karikala Chola
C. 200 BC The Tolkappiam, the oldest extant work of Tamil literature, is written
C. 150 AD Rule of King Senguttavan of the early Cheras.
C. 210 AD Pandya King Nedunchezhian of Madurai victorious in the battle at Talaiarangam.
C. 300 AD The Kalabhras invade Tamil country.

THE KALABHRAS INTERREGNUM: AD 300 TO AD 600

Very little is known about this period in Tamil Nadu's history. The Kalabhras, a group who may have originated in modern-day Karnataka to the immediate north, invaded the lands of the Pandyas, Cheras and Cholas, causing a good deal of political upheaval and turmoil in the region. This dynasty was more overtly religious than its predecessors, and Jainism and Buddhism strengthened their roots during their reign, as they were practised and favoured by the rulers. Literature and education, the latter in good part due to the efforts of Buddhist and Jain monks, flourished. Towards the end, Saivism emerged as a dominant religion as some of the later Kalabhras rulers embraced it. Thus the stage was set for the flowering of the great Bhakti movement of the following centuries.

Three centuries after they came to power, they were defeated by the Pandyas, Chalukyas and Pallavas, who mobilised their forces and overthrew this dynasty. The Kalabhras slipped into history's shadows, with nary a monument or any artefacts to show for their years in power.

THE AGE OF EMPIRE: AD 600 TO AD 1300

This period saw the rise and fall of several empires, each of which left behind monuments, and even rituals, customs and beliefs that are alive and present to this day. The three dynasties of the Sangam Period – the Pandyas, Cheras and Cholas – rose to prominence again, and were now joined by a fourth one, the Pallavas. They reached amazing heights, and their beautiful works of art, literature and temples are testament to their achievements.

THE PALLAVA DYNASTY: 3C-9C

The Pallavas may have started their reign in the northern reaches of Tamilakam as early as the 3C, but they reached their peak in the 7C–8C. Their origins are the subject of much controversy, and prevailing theory links them to the Satavahanas of western India (parts of present-day Maharashtra and Andhra Pradesh). Their capital was the temple city of Kanchipuram; the seaport of Mahabalipuram was also of vital importance.

King Simhavarman of the late 6C was the first of the great rulers of this dynasty, who made his mark by vanquishing the Kalabhras and subduing the Pandyas, Cheras and Cholas. His son, Mahendravarman, who ruled in the early 7C, involved himself in both warfare and artistic endeavours. Alas, his attempt to attack the Chalukyas did not pan out, but where he succeeded magnificently was in the building of the stunning monolithic rock temples and some of the sculpted caves of Mamallapuram. In addition, he was a keen musician and writer. He converted to Saivism during his reign, and this sparked the renewal of Saivite (and Vaishnavite) Hinduism, and the decline of Jainism and Buddhism in the area. Another great king of this dynasty was Mahendravarman's son, Narasimhavarman. Where his father had been unable to defeat the Chalukyas, Narasimhavarman succeeded not once but several times. He captured Badami, the Chalukya capital, and expanded his kingdom to as far as Sri Lanka. While doing all this, he nurtured his artistic side as well: the lovely monolithic *rathas* of Mamallapuram are attributed to his time.

The next king of note in the Pallava dynasty was Narasimhavarman II, the great-grandson of the first Narasimhavarman. During his largely peaceful reign, the beautiful Shore Temple of Mamallapuram and Kailasanatha Temple of Kanchipuram were built. He pioneered the use of stone in architecture and laid and strengthened the foundations of South Indian temple design and construction.

The Pallava dynasty went into decline after this, as its rulers suffered a string

Shore Temple (8C) in Mamallapuram, built during the reign of Narasimhavarman II, the Pallava Dynasty

of defeats at the hands of their old enemies, the Chalukyas, as well as the Pandyas and others. The sun set on this glorious empire in the 9C as the last emperor, Aparajita, suffered total defeat by the reigning Chola ruler.

There was religious tolerance under the Pallavas. At the same time a Hindu religious movement called the Bhakti movement developed, and the words of the great Saivite and Vaishnavite saints of this age, the Nayanmars and the Alwars, can be heard to this day. Cultural and educational institutions thrived. The great city of Kanchipuram was a major cultural centre. Their loveliest and most lasting legacy is their stunningly beautiful architecture.

560-580 King Simhavarman overthrows the Kalabhras at Tondaimandala and re-establishes Pallava dominance.

590-630 Reign of King Mahendravarma; several monolithic rock temples and cave temples built in Mamallapuram.

630-668 Reign of King Narasimhavarman I.

700-728 Reign of King Narasimhavarman II; Kailasanatha Temple in Kanchipuram and Shore Temple in Mamallapuram built.

903 King Aparajita, the last of the Pallava emperors, defeated by King Aditya Chola.

LATER CHOLA DYNASTY: 9C TO 13C

The heartland of the Chola Empire was the verdant and fertile plain watered by the Kaveri River, and its capital was Thanjavur, which lay along its banks. At its height, the Chola empire's power and influence extended overseas to South and South-east Asia, and as far north as the River Godavari in Andhra Pradesh.

The most famous of the Chola Emperors was Rajaraja Cholan of the 11C. He inherited an emaciated empire, and expanded it greatly, annexing vast portions of Chera, Pandya and Pallava territory. His supreme legacy is the magnificent temple to Lord Shiva, the 1,000-year-old Brihadeeswara Temple in Thanjavur. Rajaraja Cholan's son, Rajendra Cholan, was a worthy successor. He consolidated his father's conquests and pushed the borders of his empire further north. His victorious soldiers brought back holy water from the River Ganga, and this was used to consecrate another magnificent Shiva temple, this one at Gangaikondacholapuram. He was ambitious, Rajendra Cholan. He sent his armies across the sea in a successful

A Fearless Freedom Fighter

18C India saw large parts of the country fighting against the British, surrendering to them, or making deals with them. At this time, deep in rural Tamil Nadu, a little hamlet called Panchalamkurichi that lay 75km south of Madurai was ruled by local chieftain **Veerapandya Kattabomman**. Kattabomman was a strong and daring leader who remained defiant against the British, refusing to bow down to their demands for taxes which he felt was an unfair imposition.

Kattabomman, fierce, fearless and unwavering in his loathing for the British and his burning desire to preserve his independence and territory, engaged in many fights against the British, earning him no small measure of admiration and fear for his bravery and refusal to give up. In his final battle, his fort at Panchalamkurichi was ravaged by gunfire. Realising that he would not survive the intense, ceaseless attack by superior firepower, Kattabomman escaped to the forests around Pudukottai where, alas, he was betrayed by his own countrymen, handed over to the British, and hanged.

quest to conquer Sri Lanka and several kingdoms of South-east Asia.

After Rajendra Cholan, succeeding kings continued to conquer and reign. However, the later Chola rulers were highly intolerant of non-worshippers of Shiva, and persecuted many Vaishnavites, including the famous philosopher Ramanuja, who had to flee to another state.

There was a well-organised system of government, and local officials were elected into power. In the Chola kingdom, and elsewhere in Tamilakam as well, the temple was the heart of social, cultural, religious and economic life. The temple organisation was huge, in order to cater to all this activity. Tamil literature thrived in Chola times. Their most exquisite legacy is their bronze sculptures. Their perfect form and symmetry make them among the most beautiful in the world.

The Cholas were responsible for the downfall of the Pallavas; in turn, their demise came at the hands of their arch-rivals, the Pandyas, in the 13C.

985 Rajaraja Cholan becomes king.
993 Invasion of Sri Lanka by Rajaraja Cholan's forces.
1010 Brihadeeswara Temple completed In Thanjavur during reign of Rajaraja Cholan.

Seated Four-Armed Vishnu (8C-9C), Pandya Dynasty, The Metropolitan Museum of Art, New York

1012 Rajendra Chola becomes king.
1023 Rajendra Chola sends forces to North India, including to the River Ganges.
1025 Gangaikondacholapuram becomes Rajendra Chola's capital.
1246-1279 Reign of Rajendra Chola III, last of the Cholas.

LATER PANDYA DYNASTY: 6C TO 15C

This most ancient of the Tamil dynasties, celebrated in song and legend, roared back into power after breaking free of the Kalabhras in the 6C under the leadership of King Kadungon. The Pandya Empire grew in size and prosperity, through conquest and trade, in the centuries that followed, and reports of its wealth and power made their way to the Western world. Marco Polo wrote admiringly of its immense riches, and the Greek geographer Megasthenes wrote about its pearl fisheries, another source of fortune.

In the early years of the re-ascendancy of the Pandyas, the Cholas remained in relative obscurity, and the Pallavas were their main rivals. The victories and defeats went back and forth between the two powers. Then, in the 10C the Chola king Parantaka I invaded the Pandya country and the Pandyas were forced to accept Chola domination over their lands. This state of affairs continued until King Mahavarman Sundara Pandyan reestablished Pandya power in the 13C. This Pandya resurgence coincided with the decline of the Chola Empire. Mahavarman Sundara Pandyan's successor, the revenge-hungry and war-loving Jatavarman Sundara Pandyan, was determined to wipe out the Cholas as well as another dynasty, the Hoysala, that was attempting to establish a foothold in Pandya territory. To a large extent, he succeeded. His actions sounded the death knell for the Chola Empire.

In the 14C, the great Pandya capital of Madurai fell to the invading forces of Alaudin Khilji of the Delhi Sultanate. For a short four decades, Madurai became a

Sultanate under Muslim rule. The Vijayanagar rulers from further north in the Andhra region defeated the Sultanate in 1371, and established their rule in Madurai and eventually spread their power over much of Tamilakam.

1216 Mahavarman Sundara Pandya becomes king and reignites the glory of the Pandyas.
1251 Jatavarman Sundara Pandyan becomes king.
1268-1310 Reign of Kulasekara Pandya.
1311 Delhi Sultanate forces invade and attack Pandya territory
1327-1370 Period of the Madurai Sultanate.

VIJAYANAGAR, NAYAKS & MARATHAS: 14C TO 19C

THE VIJAYANAGAR EMPIRE: 14C TO 16C

As the Islamic invasions of and influence in northern India gained in strength, five brothers, who had fled the Telugu lands, established the beginnings of an empire on the banks of the Tungabhadra River in modern Karnataka in the early 14C. Their aim: to protect and defend the Hindu religion and way of life from the Muslims and other foreign influences.

Their empire grew rapidly, extending its power over the Hoysala lands, and successfully holding in check the Delhi sultans and the Muslim Bahmani kingdom in Hyderabad to the south.

Its history is one of a succession of wars, and the eminent historian, Nilakanta Sastri, describes the empire as essentially a 'war-state', with its military needs controlling and guiding its actions. Many defeats were suffered, but there were also numerous victories, and the Vijayanagar Empire spread over most of South India. Local governors, called Nayaks, were appointed to administer the various territories. Tamil country had three 'Nayakships', in Thanjavur, Madurai and Gingee. The empire reached its peak during the early-16C reign of Krishnadevaraya, who enjoyed a great many military victories, and during whose reign the arts and literature blossomed.

Travellers from Italy, Persia and Portugal to the city of Vijayanagara have left wonder-struck descriptions of the wealth and power of the empire. Cultural and economic life was lived at the highest standards. Large numbers of seaports conducted and controlled trade with many nations, both to the east and the west.

The constant warring eventually took its toll; the empire suffered a crushing defeat at the hands of the Delhi Sultans at the battle of Talikota in 1564. In Tamil country, the local Nayaks declared their independence, and took over the rule of their territories.

THE NAYAKS: 16C TO 17C

The best known of these were the Thanjavur and the Madurai Nayaks. The first of the Thanjavur Nayaks was Sevappa Nayak, who had had a distinguished career under Krishnadevaraya. His son was Achyutta Nayak, under whose reign the Srirangam Temple in Tiruchirapalli, widely regarded as the largest functioning Hindu temple, benefited greatly from his largesse. The most well-known was Raghunatha Nayak, who ruled in the first decades of the 17C, and who was well-renowned for his patronage of music and literature. He established a library in Thanjavur, Saraswathi Bandar, where the works of his court scholars was stored. This library went on to become, under a future ruler, the Saraswathi Mahal Library, one of the finest in the world, with its priceless collection of rare and ancient art. Raghunatha Nayak was instrumental in setting the stage for the European presence in India, by allowing the Danish to establish a settlement in Tarangambadi (Tranquebar).

The Nayak rulers of Thanjavur and Madurai were not on particularly friendly terms. They had differing opinions on what the terms of their allegiance to their old masters, the now-weakened Vijayanagar rulers, should be. In Madurai, the Nayaks worked hard to restore the temples sacked by the Delhi Sultans, and were also known for their support of art, architecture, literature and music. There were 13 rulers in this regime, of which Tirumala Nayak was the most eminent. A good part of his reign (1623-59) was spent fending off the armies of the Delhi Sultanate, in which he was successful. There was also tension with the rulers of Vijayanagar and Mysore, and there was dissension within his own kingdom. Yet through all this turmoil he saw to the construction of many marvels of architecture in Madurai. An example is his palace, the Tirumalai Nayak Palace, a stunning building that is a fusion of Dravidian, European and Islamic styles.

The decline of the Madurai Nayaks began after the death of Tirumala Nayak; the end of the Thanjavur Nayaks came at the hands of the Madurai Nayak Chokkanatha. In the chaos and disarray that presided over these crumbling regimes, the Marathas of western India entered and took control over Thanjavur.

THE MARATHAS: 17C TO 19C

Eight Maratha kings ruled over Thanjavur and its surrounding areas. Of these, the best and most admired was Serfoji II, who ruled in the late 18C to early 19C. His court was renowned for the high quality of the arts it embraced. Eminent musicians and dancers vied for positions in his court. The reign of Serfoji II coincided with the lives of the most venerated Carnatic music composers: Thyagaraja, Muthuswami Dikshithar and Syama Sastry. Sanskrit and Telugu were favoured over Tamil, and a lot of the music and literature of the day was composed in these languages. Serfoji II expanded the Saraswathi Bandar library that had been established by the preceding Nayak dynasty, and developed it into the Saraswathi Mahal Library, a source of awe and wonder to this day.

By this time, the British and other European powers were establishing themselves all over India, and were part of the mix of powers vying for land and control. In the chaos of rival rulers and dynasties, one was played against the other, once-powerful empires were weakened, and the stage was set for the foreign domination of the land. The Maratha Empire in Tamil Nadu came to an end when British annexed their kingdom after the death of the last ruler Shivaji II, a weak and ineffectual man who died childless.

1336 The Vijayanagar Empire is established.

1370 Tamil country is captured by the Vijayanagar ruler Bukka Raya I

1424-1446 Reign of Krishna Deva Raya II, one the great Vijayanagar emperors

1535-1590 Sevappa Nayak is appointed and rules as the first independent Nayak of Thanjavur

1600-1645 Reign of Raghunatha Nayak, the greatest of the Thanjavur Nayaks

1609 AD Dutch settlement established at Pulicat

1623-1659 Reign of Tirumalai Nayak in Madurai

1675 Maratha rule established in Thanjavur

1777 -1832 Reign of Serfoji, the greatest of the Thanjavur Marathas

1832-1855 Reign of Shivaji II, the last of the Thanjavur Marathas

1855 Thanjavur annexed by the British

THE COLONIAL PERIOD: 17C TO 1947

THE ENGLISH EAST INDIA COMPANY: 1600 TO 1857

When several European nations, starting with Portugal, discovered that they could make their way by sea to India and thus dispense with the middlemen they had been dealing with for several centuries, a new chapter began in the history of India, that of the Colonial era. In the Tamil lands, the power struggle boiled down to the French and the British, with the Dutch and the Danish left with small settlements that were of minor consequence.

The British presence in India began with the English East India Company, a

Key Figures in History

From very early times, Tamil history has been influenced by many extraordinary people. Here are a few details about some of them.

Karikala Chola (3C BC): one of the great emperors of Tamil antiquity, he is said to have been a fair and just ruler, and a great warrior. His name and tales of his life have become part of Tamil lore and legend.

Narasimhavarman II (6C AD): this multifaceted king was successful at war, expanding his kingdom greatly, and was also a great patron of the arts, literature and architecture. The Kailasanatha Temple in Kanchipuram, and the Shore Temple of Mamallapuram, were among the monuments built during his reign.

Rajaraja Chola (11C AD): he presided over the golden period of the Chola Empire, expanding his kingdom, and accomplishing the construction of one of the most glorious temples of South India, the Brihadeeswara Temple in Thanjavur.

Mahavarman Sundara Pandyan (13C AD): he re-established the power of the mighty Pandyan Empire after it was decimated by the Pallavas the Cholas.

Serfoji II (18C-19C): one of the greatest of the Maratha rulers of Thanjavur, he presided over a court that enjoyed the best musicians and dancers of the day, and completed the Saraswathi Mahal Library, an indispensable and priceless collection of literature and art.

Francis Day and **Andrew Cogan** (17C): they were responsible for the establishment and construction of Fort St George, which lay the foundation for the city of Madras (Chennai), Tamil Nadu's capital city.

Veerapandya Kattabomman (18C): this Tamil chieftain and king bitterly opposed British rule; he paid for his views and his actions against the British with his life, when he was captured and hung, his fort wrecked and his possessions looted *(see sidebar p65)*.

Subramanya Bharathi (19C-20C): one of the most beloved poets of Tamil Nadu, his simple yet affecting words galvanised the Independence movement in Tamil Nadu. He was also a social reformer whose views were extraordinarily far-sighted and forward-thinking for his time.

C. Rajagopalachari (19C-20C): he was a brilliant lawyer, statesman and writer, and an independence activist who was one of Gandhi's closest confidantes. He was the last Governor General of India and the Chief Minister of Madras State. He was awarded the Bharat Ratna, India's highest civilian honour, for his myriad contributions to his country.

Periyar E.V. Ramasamy (19-20C): he was an Independence and social activist among other things, and he started the Self-Respect movement and the Dravida Kazhagam organisation. He was an avid proponent of rationalism and he promoted awareness of and pride in Tamil identity, while also being extremely critical of Brahmins and their role in marginalising and discriminating against the non-Brahmins whom he considered indigenous to Tamil Nadu.

C.N. Annadurai (20C): founder of the Dravida Munetra Kazhagam (DMK), he was the first Chief Minister of Madras State elected from this party that revolutionised the political landscape of the state. He fought for the rights of the lower castes and classes and gained immense popular support.

joint-stock company that was founded in 1600 and whose primary activity was trading with India as well as with China. It traded mainly in cotton, silk, indigo, saltpetre, tea and opium, and gradually, its trading pursuits became secondary to its broader ambitions of acquisition of land, power and administrative authority. They took advantage of the rivalries between dynasties, playing one side against the other, and thus achieving more domination and influence.

On 22 August 1639, Francis Day, an English East India Company employee working under the guidance of his boss Andrew Cogan, obtained the rights from local leaders to a narrow stretch of land on the Coromandel Coast. On that day, on that piece of land, began the history of the city of Madras, the capital of Tamil Nadu that is today called Chennai. Until that point the area had been a collection of villages separated by tracts of paddy fields and forests, overseen by a local Nayak. Soon, the construction of a fort and other buildings was underway; this was British India's first real seaside settlement, built right on the beach. On 23 April 1640, the first stage of this British outpost was completed. It was St George's day, and thus, the fort was named Fort St George, a name which stands to this day. The fort complex grew, and within its walls were stately mansions, army barracks, traders' homes, well-swept streets, a church, a stock exchange… in short, a fully-functioning, bustling township.

The British were in frequent conflict with the French, who arrived in India in the 1660s. They established a trading post in Pondicherry, further south along the Coromandel Coast from the British Fort St George. Events in faraway Europe had their repercussions in these outposts: the War of the Austrian Succession began in 1740, in which Britain and France were soon embroiled. The navies of these two countries were engaged in numerous battles along the coast, and in 1746 the French in Pondicherry, under the governorship of Joseph François Dupleix, attacked and occupied Fort St George. Two years later, when the war in Europe ended, the Treaty of Aix-la-Chapelle restored the fort to the British. In the decades that followed, the British control over Tamil territories increased rapidly. After the long and bitterly fought Polygar Wars (against the Madurai kingdom) of the late 1700s and early 1800s, the British domination over Tamil territory was nearly complete. Under the leadership of Lord Wellesley, the Madras Presidency was established so that the territory under the East India Company's control could be better administered. In the meantime, as the various royal dynasties weakened and crumbled, the city of Madras grew in importance as an economic and cultural centre.

Engraving (1794) by I Van Ryne showing East India Company's Fort St George in Madras on the Coromandel Coast

BRITISH COLONIAL RULE: 1858 TO 1947

After the Sepoy Mutiny or the First Indian War of Independence in 1857, the British Crown took control and established Colonial rule over large parts of India. As resentment and outrage over this state of affairs grew, the independence movement took root all over India, including in Tamil Nadu. Many freedom fighters from the state joined hands with others from around the country to fight the British rule. Prominent among these were C. Rajagopalachari, Tiruppur Kumaran, Kattaboman, V.O. Chidambaram Pillai, Dheeran Chinnamalai, E.V. Ramasamy and S. Subramania Iyer. The beloved Tamil poet, Subramania Bharati, wrote many stirring songs and poems urging revolution and Independence. Many Tamils joined the Indian National Army, a non-pacifist set-up to fight the British occupation of India.

While many people in Tamil Nadu were involved in issues of national significance, there were also many people active in causes and concerns that were specific to the region. In 1916, the anti-Brahmin movement took root with the publication of the anti-Brahmin manifesto. The Justice Party, which came into being in the 1920s, focused on strictly local issues, like reservations for backward classes, and won legislative elections on this platform. At around the same time, **E.V. Ramasamy**, known popularly as Periyar, started an anti-Brahmin, anti-religious movement whose impact on the politics and social life of Tamil Nadu is felt to this day. Leaders like Periyar and his follower **C.N. Annadurai** inculcated a strong sense of Tamil identity and pride in the population.

1639 Fort St George established; the birth of the city of Madras.
1746 The French army captures Fort St George.
1749 The British regain control of Fort St George thanks to the Treaty of Aix-la-Chapelle.
1800-1805 The Polygar Wars.
1909 The Madras Legislative Council is formed.
1921 The first regional elections are held in Madras; the victorious newly formed Justice Party forms the government.
1944 Periyar and C.N. Annadurai establish the Dravida Kazhagam.

POST-INDEPENDENCE TAMIL NADU: 1947 TO TODAY

While large stretches of India reeled under the violence that was unleashed in the years after Independence, Tamil Nadu remained calm, and communal relations were harmonious.

The first Chief Minister of the independent Madras Presidency was the highly respected and brilliant lawyer, writer and statesman **C. Rajagopalachari** (Rajaji) who had served as the last Governor General of India. The area covered by the Madras Presidency right after Independence was the same as before, comprising present-day Tamil Nadu, parts of Andhra Pradesh, Karnataka and Kerala. However, there was heavy agitation to reorganise state territories on linguistic lines, and the Madras Presidency became Madras State while losing parts of Telugu-speaking areas to the newly formed state of Andhra Pradesh, and Malayalam-speaking areas to Kerala, and gaining other areas (like Kanyakumari and Shencottah, parts of Chingleput and Salem districts).

In 1956, all exchanges and transfers of land were complete, and the state assumed its present borders. Madras was retained as the capital. Madras State was renamed Tamil Nadu in 1968, and Madras was renamed Chennai in 1996.

1953 Madras State is established along linguistic lines.
Mid-1960s Anti-Hindi agitation and movement.
1968 Madras State is renamed Tamil Nadu.
1996 The city of Madras is renamed Chennai.
2004 Tsunami significantly affects coastal regions of Tamil Nadu.

Architecture

Tamil Nadu's varied architectural history is immediately apparent in Chennai. Now a bustling modern metropolis, with clusters of concrete and glass-clad high-rises crowding the central business district, Hindu temples dating back more than 1,000 years can be visited in the southern part of the city; Fort St George with its ramparts and steepled church near to the seashore testifies to the British Colonial era. Hindu religious monuments with soaring towered gateways dominate most towns of Tamil Nadu, while traditional mud and thatch houses can still be seen in many villages.

THE TAMIL STYLE

The earliest examples of monumental architecture in Tamil Nadu are modestly scaled Hindu temples cut into solid granite as artificial caves, or constructed out of chiselled granite blocks laid without any mortar, associated with the Pallavas in the 7C-8C. The pioneering efforts of these early rulers to create a distinctive Tamil architectural style developed over time, reaching a dramatic climax in the magnificent religious edifices commissioned by the Cholas in the Kaveri delta region during the 11C-12C. Temple building was interrupted at the end of the 13C with the invasion of Tamil Nadu by the troops of the Delhi sultans. The conquerors were soon expelled by the Vijayanagara rulers, but these overlords made little effort to promote temple construction in the Tamil province of their domains. After 1565, when the Vijayanagara capital in Karnataka was abandoned, local governors, known as Nayakas, based in Vellore, Gingee, Thanjavur and Madurai, began to sponsor ambitious projects, as represented by gigantic religious and royal complexes that assumed an almost urban dimension.

The Muslim presence in Tamil Nadu is attested to by mosques and shrines, but except for the 18C *dargah* at Nagore, with its unusual group of five minaret-like towers, these are of little distinction. In the course of the 17C, English and Danish merchants established themselves on the Tamil coast, fortifying their settlements at Madras (Chennai) and Tranquebar (Tarangambadi) respectively. These Europeans were responsible for erecting Protestant churches at their trading ports and wherever Christian missionaries were active; at the same time the French, who had also arrived on the coast, built Catholic cathedrals in Pondicherry (Pudicherry). Imposing residences in the European manner were raised by colonial governors at all these centres. As the capital of a British Presidency, Madras was enhanced with a series of handsome, Neoclassical civic buildings; some were even built in the curious Indo-Saracenic style invented by local British architects towards the end of the 19C.

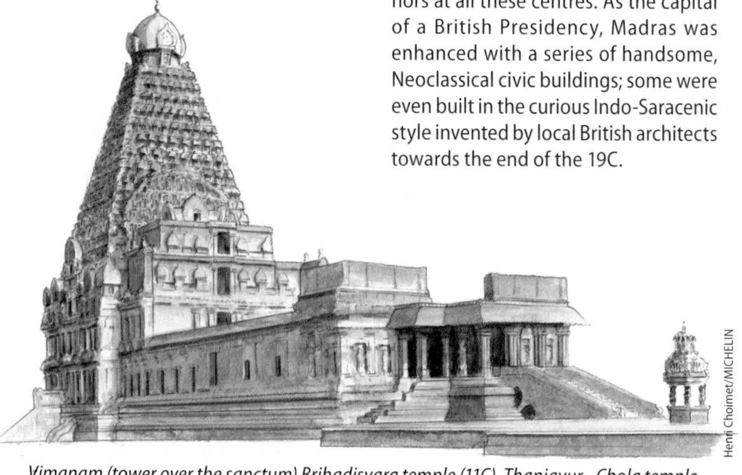
Henri Choimet/MICHELIN

Vimanam (tower over the sanctum) Brihadisvara temple (11C), Thanjavur - Chola temple

Pancha Rathas at Mamallapuram (7C) - Pallava temple

PALLAVA TEMPLES

Hindu sanctuaries at Mamallapuram and Tiruchirapalli are excavated into granite cliffs to create artificial caves with pillared halls open on one side. Columns have bases fashioned as seated fantastic leonine beasts called *yalis*, while shafts are circular or polygonal with prominent square projecting capitals. Small cells, generally for Shiva *lingas*, are set into the rear or side walls. No doubt there was a tradition of free-standing architecture at the time, but since this was in perishable materials nothing now remains. An idea of how such building might have appeared may be had from the so-called *rathas* at Mamallapuram. Hewn out of boulders, these monoliths were never completed and are of no obvious purpose. But they are of considerable architectural interest since they imitate thatch roofs carried on curved, flexible bamboo frameworks. Two *rathas* have multi-storeyed towers that rise in pyramidal fashion, to be crowned with octagonal domed roofs. This multi-storeyed, towered scheme was to remain a permanent feature of Tamil Nadu's temple architecture, testifying to an inherently conservative building tradition.

The transition from rock-cut to structural building techniques occurred during the reign of Rajasimha in the early 8C. The first free-standing example is the 'shore' temple overlooking the Bay of Bengal at Mamallapuram, the main Pallava port. This has a pair of small sanctuaries with steeply pyramidal towers built out of granite blocks. The sanctuaries are unusually disposed in diagonal formation, and encased on three sides by an outer wall that creates a narrow passageway open to the sky. This scheme was further developed at Kanchipuram, the Pallava capital. In the Kailasanatha Temple a single towered sanctuary becomes the ritual focus of a formally planned complex. Its outer walls have projections with deep niches accommodating sculpted panels framed by pilasters with leaping *yalis* at the bases. The sanctuary stands in a paved compound surrounded by an enclosure wall lined with tiny subsidiary shrines, entered at one end through a gate roofed with a masonry barrel vault.

Vernacular Traditions

Though no wooden structures with thatch or tiled roofs of any antiquity have survived Tamil Nadu's severe monsoons, it is worth noting the hut-like sanctuary for the god Nataraja at the core of the temple at Chidambaram (*see p158*). Rising on a stone base, this consists of a timber framework encased by metal-clad timber screens; its curved roof is clad in gilded metallic shingles that recall tiles. Such timber-tiled buildings can still be seen today, but generally only in remote villages.

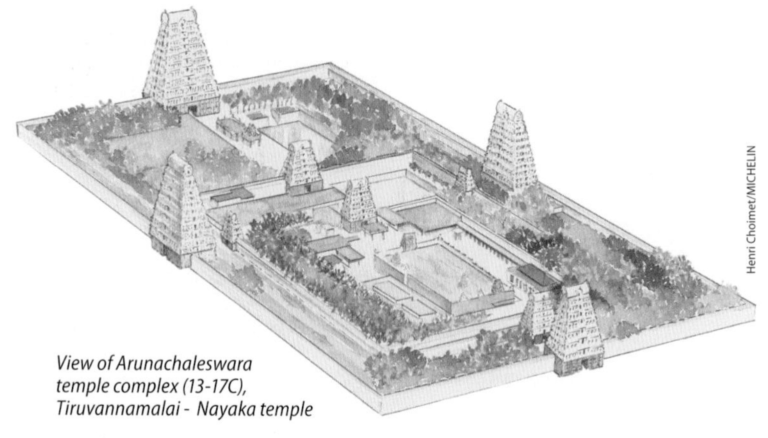
Henri Choimet/MICHELIN

View of Arunachaleswara temple complex (13-17C), Tiruvannamalai - Nayaka temple

CHOLA TEMPLES

Multi-storeyed, towered sanctuaries continued to be developed by architects in the service of the Chola kings, as dramatically illustrated in the Brihadishvara Temple at Thanjavur, capital of Rajaraja I at the turn of the 11C. The *linga* sanctuary of this stupendous edifice is surmounted by a steeply pyramidal, hollow granite tower composed of 11 diminishing tiers, each with a parapet of model roof forms of different shapes. Soaring more than 65m/213ft high, the Thanjavur tower remained the highest structure in Tamil Nadu until recent times. The double-storeyed walls on which the tower rises are rhythmically divided into pilastered projections alternating with recesses, both filled with sculpted panels depicting different aspects of Shiva. Huge, fierce guardian figures flank the doorways and window openings. The chamber at the core of the monument, which houses a gigantic polished stone *linga*, is surrounded by a narrow passageway lined with murals; two interconnecting halls with pillared aisles extend in front. The Nandi pavilion that stands freely a short distance away from the main temple is a later, Nayaka-period addition, but probably replaces an earlier structure. The temple stands in a vast paved rectangular compound with a towered entrance gate in the middle of one side.

Rajaraja I's son and successor Rajendra I abandoned Thanjavur, shifting to Gangaikondacholapuram, where he commissioned an imitation of his father's great monument, compete in almost every detail. Subsequent Chola religious projects are generally smaller in scale and lower in height, but more elaborate in detail. The Airavateshvara Temple at Darasuram, erected by Rajaraja II in the mid-12C, is entered through an ornate pillared porch conceived as a festival chariot, complete with great wheels and prancing horses carved on its basement. Instead of being built of granite, the pyramidal tower above the sanctuary is of plaster-covered brickwork. As time passed sanctuary towers came to be superseded in height by towered gates known as *gopuras*, as in the quartet of matching entryways at Chidambaram dating from the 13C. These soaring structures have granite lower walls penetrated by passageways with lofty stone ceilings that give access to the temple compound from four sides. Their pyramidal towers, built of plaster-covered brickwork on timber frameworks, served as models for the later *gopuras*.

NAYAKA TEMPLES

From the second half of the 16C onwards all of the major Hindu monuments in Tamil Nadu were subjected to modification and expansion as a consequence of renewed investment in religious monuments and ceremonies on the part of Nayaka kings and their ministers. Shrines founded in Pallava or Chola times came to be concealed within labyrinths of pillared corridors, great halls, courtyards with tanks, and countless minor shrines consecrated to subsidiary divinities and their consorts. These components were contained within high walls that defined square or rectangular enclosures, generally arranged in concentric formation, as in the temple at Srirangam which employs seven such enclosures, one within the other, with the original core shrine in the middle. Here, as elsewhere, the complex expanded over many years, with the outermost portions being added last. In Madurai, two compounds are arranged side by side so as to define separate shrines for Shiva and his divine consort Minakshi to whom the monument is dedicated. The approach to each shrine is punctuated by gopuras set into the peripheral walls. At Tiruvannamalai, the compounds are extended so as to emphasize the principal axis of the monument, with Shiva's sacred mountain providing a scenic background to the rear.

Nayaka temples are surrounded on four sides by broad streets along which chariots were pulled during the festivals that attracted huge crows of devotees, as they continue to do so to this day. Access to the temple from the streets, and even from one part of the religious complex to another, was through *gopuras* aligned with the sanctuary within. Their steeply pyramidal towers were covered with ascending tiers populated by plaster figures of gods and goddesses, attendants and guardians, all painted in vivid colours. At Madurai such sculptures entirely cloak towers that rise more than 50m/164ft high. *Gopuras* are topped with curved, masonry vaults with horseshoe-shaped ends inhabited by auspicious monster heads with bulging eyes and tusks. Gilded pot finials line the ridges of these curving roofs, providing gleaming highlights to Tamil Nadu's most obvious urban markers.

NAYAKA STRONGHOLDS AND PALACES

Wars between the different Nayaka kingdoms of Tamil Nadu and threats of invasion from outside the region meant that security was a constant concern. In addition to temples, the Nayakas also erected mighty citadels to protect their residences. The ramparts at Vellore are reinforced by part-circular bastions topped with curving battlements to shield gunners, and surrounded by a deep moat. The stronghold at Gingee comprises three separate hill forts linked by colossal walls to defend an extensive, triangular zone. The

Henri Choimet/MICHELIN

Audience Hall of Nayakar Palace (17C), Madurai

Chettinad Mansions

Extending over thousands of square feet, Chettinad houses are built on a rectangular plot that stretches across two streets. If all doors facing the main threshold are open, the eye travels in a straight line across a series of inner courtyards, each a diminishing rectangle of light, leading out to the back door that opens onto the second street. Chettiars believe that it ensures an easy exit for evil spirits lurking around.

An outer gate on the street front leads past the *mugappu* (central façade) to the reception area with ornate pillars capped by carved capitals and brackets. On either side of the main door is the *thinnai* (raised platform) where the host entertained male guests and went about his business of money-lending. The *kallapetti* (desk) was the quintessential sign of a prosperous Chettiar. Flanking the *thinnai* are storerooms and the office of the *kanakupillai* or accountant. Traditionally, *navaratna* (nine precious gems) were buried under the *vasapadi* (threshold) for luck and a richly carved panel bearing an image of Lakshmi, the Goddess of Wealth, crowned the elaborate front door. The intricacy of the wood indicated the family status.

The private area, beyond the main door, is dominated by the *mudhal kattu* (first courtyard) and a *paadsalai* where children were tutored. Adult males slept in the verandah while individual rooms for married sons lined the *valavu* (pillared corridors). Beyond the male quarter is the second courtyard, used for ceremonies and social gatherings with large dining spaces on either side. The third courtyard, with rooms reserved for womenfolk and kids, was where pickles and papads were dried. The *nalankattai* (fourth courtyard) comprising the kitchens with grindstones, stone vats for storing water and wooden bins for firewood, led out to the backyard.

Procuring the best from their sojourns, Chettiars lavishly used Burma teak, Ceylon satinwood, Italian marble, Swedish enamelware, Belgian chandeliers, English crockery and ceramic tiles imported from Japan. An incredible pastiche, the decorative carvings, friezes and murals depict not only Hindu gods and goddesses but also British soldiers, Victorian women and scenes from the Raj. Most of the larger mansions were built between 1880 and 1920, when Chettiar business power was at its peak. Today, their houses stand like proud symbols of the community's enterprise.

SARM House

palaces within are now mostly reduced to stone basements with footing blocks showing the location of timber columns. Overlooking these vestiges is a tall square tower with arched openings at each level, crowned by a small chamber that probably functioned as a lookout. Nearby lofty structures with pointed masonry vaults served as granaries. The palace at Madurai erected by Tirumala Nayaka in the mid-17C has a huge domed chamber with a throne for formal audiences that looks onto a spacious courtyard surrounded by massive circular columns. A small doorway leads to a hall for music and dance performances, roofed with a lofty pointed vault carried on transverse arches. The Nayaka palace in Thanjavur has a similar courtyard overlooked by a domed audience chamber. A massive square watchtower nearby overlooks the surrounding streets of the city. All these royal complexes employ Islamic-style domes, vaults and arches decorated with exuberant plaster ornament. Deriving from the architecture of the sultanate kingdoms to the north, these features testify to cultural contacts between Tamil Nadu and the Muslim Deccan courts.

THE EUROPEAN IMPACT

Little survives of the fortified settlements founded by Europeans in Tamil Nadu, an exception being Fort St George in Chennai. Its ramparts, which form an arc fanning away from the Bay of Bengal shore, are reinforced with triangular bastions that protrude outwards to create a star-shaped plan. This scheme reflected contemporary European developments in military engineering and the introduction into Tamil Nadu of cannon warfare. Within Fort St George are the Public Exchange Hall and Admiralty House, both with elegant colonnaded verandas in an elegant Neoclassical manner. Nearby St Mary's church is recognized by its slender steeple, which rises above a pedimented entrance porch. Among the other Neoclassical erected in the rapidly expanding port city of Madras are the Banqueting Hall, with its commanding staircase ascending to a facade with Doric columns, and St Andrews Kirk, with its colonnaded porch topped by the usual tapering, octagonal spire leading to an unusual circular nave ringed by Corinthian columns supporting an impressive dome. That Neo-Classical architecture was the preferred idiom for other Europeans in Tamil Nadu is borne out by the residence of the French Governor of Pondicherry.

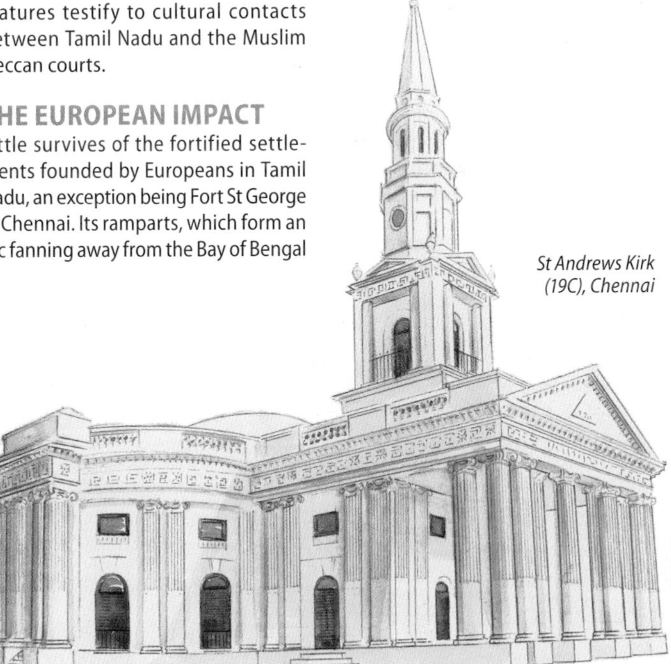

St Andrews Kirk (19C), Chennai

Henri Choimet/MICHELIN

Art

For more than 1,500 years Tamil Nadu's art has responded to the requirements of Hindu devotional practice by fashioning images of gods, goddesses and saints in stone and metal, and painting popular legends associated with particular Hindu shrines on walls and ceilings. The sponsors of this predominantly religious art were kings and queens, their ministers and commanders, all of whom embellished shrines and pilgrimage temples in order to promote temporal power and win divine support. Stone Hindu art dates back to the Pallava period, but associated metallic arts, especially bronze statues, only attained perfection under the Cholas. Patronage during Nayaka and Maratha times focused on granite column sculptures and paintings on ceilings, as well as printed cotton hangings, ivory furniture and ceremonial steel weapons. These arts adorned the interiors of temples as well as those of palaces and grand mansions.

Crafts in Tamil Nadu continue to flourish, as can be seen from the gorgeous silk saris with gold and silver borders woven in household looms in Kanchipuram. Tamil potters fire impressive vessels for domestic use, as well as the hollow terracotta figures of deities and horses set up in village shrines. That there is now a widespread revival of Tamil crafts is evident from the diverse wares displayed in the artists' colony of Cholamandal on the outskirts of Chennai, as well as from the many busy-stone carving workshops at Mamallapuram. A thriving contemporary scene is now well established, with up-and-coming Tamil artists, many trained in Chennai's School of Art, exhibiting their paintings and sculptures in the city's many new galleries.

EARLY STONE RELIEFS

The oldest carvings of Tamil Nadu display an astonishing naturalism, in spite of the fact that statues of gods, goddesses and humans as well as of animals were all fashioned out of roughly grained granite with only the simplest iron chisels. Early Pallava art is characterised by figures with gently modelled bodies and delicate, other-worldly expressions. This is well illustrated in the two wall panels in the Mahisharamardini cave-temple at Mamallapuram. These depict Vishnu sleeping on the coils of the cosmic serpent Ananta; and Durga riding on the lion, advancing towards Mahisha, the buffalo-headed demon, clutching a vicious club. Among the deities depicted in the nearby Adi Varaha cave-temple are boar-headed Varaha rescuing the earth-goddess Bhu; Lakshmi being bathed by

Mahishasuramardini cave-temple, Mamallapuram showing Durga riding on the lion, advancing towards Mahisha

elephants; and Durga standing on the severed Mahisha's severed head. The extensive, outdoor rock carving a short distance away is entirely devoted to a legend which enjoyed particular popularity in Tamil Nadu. This relates the story of the hero Arjuna who performed austerItles beside the Ganga River in order to earn Shiva's magical axe. The relief shows flying gods, goddesses and semidivine figures, together with elephants and other animals, all converging on a central cleft. The gap is filled with a slab sculpted with male and female snake deities, over which water was once made to flow from a cistern cut into the top of the boulder, so as to suggest the Ganga itself. Arjuna appears to the left of the cleft, standing on one foot, in the presence of four-armed Shiva. A few metres away is another rock relief, originally open to the skya, but later sheltered in a pillared veranda. This portrays youthful Krishna lifting up the legendary Govardhana mountain in order to shield a herd of cows and their attendants from Indra's storm.

WALL CARVINGS

The following phases of Hindu sculpture in Tamil Nadu are generally less concerned with illustrating popular legends, so as to concentrate on the many different gods and goddesses that received worship in temple sanctuaries. Panels on the Kailasanatha Temple at Kanchipuram each portray a range of Shiva's aspects, especially those showing the god killing one or other enemy, and then dancing in triumph. A polished black stone *linga* serves as the principal cult object within the sanctuary, but the panel set into the wall behind depicts Shiva together with Parvati, his consort. Common representations of Shiva in Chola temples include Dakshinamurti, the Southern Form, with the god seated as a yogi beneath a tree. But there are also icons of the god emerging from out of a fiery *linga*, and the god combined with Parvati in a single figure in a form known as Ardhanarishvara. Even Brahma and Durga are found in Shiva temples. At Thanjavur and Chidambaram, Shiva assumes a host of further appearances, including that of the dancer, Nataraja, as well as the fearful Bhairava, and the ascetic Bhikshatana accompanied by a prancing dog. A panel from Darasuram portraying Shiva dancing within the skin of the elephant demon that he has slain, now displayed in the Thanjavur Art Gallery, is remarkable for its vigorous dynamism. The Darasuram monument is also of interest for its portrayal of scenes from the stories of all the 64 Tamil Shaiva saints, known as Nayanmars, as well as the naturalistic depiction of massive, striding elephants beside the entrance steps to the porch.

COLUMN SCULPTURES

Stone carving in Nayaka temples reprises all the subjects just noticed, but adds topics specific to particular temples, thereby emphasising the legendary underpinning of particular religious monuments and their deities which received sponsorship from local patrons. In the temple at Madurai, the marriage ceremony of Shiva and Minakshi as well as multiple aspects of Shiva are sculpted at a huge scale onto the pillars in corridors and halls. Fashioned almost in three dimensions, as if to spring away from their supports, these gigantic figures manifest outwards spreading arms and vivid facial expressions. Sacred themes are supplemented by new topics, such as ferocious, fantastic beasts. These are carved onto columns that line the aisles leading to temple sanctuaries, providing magical protection for the deities enshrined within, as well as the royal patrons who came there to worship. A related theme is that of leaping, richly caparisoned horses ridden by armed riders who battle tigers or human adversaries. Animating the halls of temples at Vellore and Srirangam, such animals and warriors are depicted with a naturalism that conveys the martial spirit of the Nayaka age. Another innovative aspect of stone art at this time is the emphasis on portraiture, with kings shown with their hands held together, paying respect to temple deities. The figures wear elaborate crowns and bear daggers, maces, swords and other emblems of temporal power. Like the sculptures, the kings are carved almost in the round in an unmistakable lifelike manner, best seen in the Pudu Mandapa at Madurai.

BRONZES

As perfected under the Cholas, the metal art of Tamil Nadu specialised in bronze figures cast by the lost-wax technique. According to this method, a wax effigy was set into a clay mass, and then heated so as to melt and remove the wax by means of a small outlet. The resulting hollow interior was then filled with molten metal. After cooling, the image was carefully chiselled to create a final finish. Many bronze figures are set on bases with holes to take wooden poles, so that they could be carried in procession at festival time, thereby substituting for the immoveable stone images within the sanctuary. To this day such bronze figures, richly decked in cloths and flowers, proceed through the streets of Tamil Nadu's towns. Numerous Chola bronzes continue to receive worship in this manner, but numerous examples have now been removed to the Government Museum in Chennai and Thanjavur Art Gallery, where they can be more easily appreciated. Bronze figures depict a similar range of Hindu deities to stone art, with virtually the same bodily poses and costumes, and emblems and weapons held in the hands. However, Chola metal icons may be distinguished from their stone counterparts by an exceptional elegance achieved through the rounded modelling of torsos and limbs, intricately cut facial features and costume details, and overall poise. In the remarkable Ardhanarishvara in the Madras collection, the figure of the god miraculously combines a two-armed, half-masculine torso with a one-armed, half-female torso with a single breast and curvaceous female hip. A bronze invested with unusual tenderness is that of Shiva and Parvati seated in the company of Skanda, their infant child. Nayaka bronzes faithfully imitate their Chola predecessors in all essential details, but there is a noticeable loss of quality.

CEILING PAINTINGS AND TEXTILES

That the art of painting was also perfected by the Cholas is confirmed by the murals in the passageway of the Thanjavur Temple (best seen in photographic reproductions in the temple museum). Panels here depict seated Shiva as Dakshinamurti, surrounded by forest sages; and the same god riding in a wheeled chariot, energetically aiming arrows at the demons of the triple cities. The composition showing Rajaraja I with his three queens visiting the temple at Chidambaram may be regarded as the first extant royal portrait in Indian painting. The paintings are charcterised by fluid brushwork and a vivid palette derived from natural pigments such as ochres, terre verte and lampblack, all applied to a background of plaster that had already dried. Temple painting in Nayaka times is mostly confined to ceilings. Scenes disposed in long strips with identifying labels on the borders illustrate legendary narratives in recognisable local settings. They include the story of Shiva as Bhikshatana in the Shivakamasundari shrine at Chidambaram, in which the god appears as a white-skinned, naked beggar holding a parasol. He is accompanied by the beautiful, scantily clad Mohini, a delusory female form of Vishnu, who creates havoc among the forest sages.

Mythological topics also appear in the cotton hangings displayed in temple halls, manufactured at workshops on the Bay of Bengal (Coromandel) coast. Known as *kalamkaris*, these textiles were produced by a laborious combination of printing and dyeing techniques. The indigo, cochineal, turmeric and various plant seeds used as dyes guaranteed vivid, permanent colours, which made these cottons much prized by the Dutch and English who shipped them in bulk to Europe and South-east Asia. Export textiles, however, tended to be non-figurative, specialising in decorative themes such as stylised trees and bushes sprouting brightly tinted flowers.

Nataraja

Chola bronze of Nataraja - dancing Shiva, Thanjavur Palace Art Gallery

© Anurag Mallick, Priya Ganapathy/MICHELIN

Probably the most celebrated image in all of Tamil Nadu art is that of Shiva as Nataraja, Lord of the Dance, an icon that was invented by stone carvers and metal casters in the employ of Chola patrons. This particular form of Nataraja is linked with the cult celebrated in the temple at Chidambaram, where the legendary dance competition between Shiva and Parvati is believed to have taken place (*see p170*). The god appears in the actual act of dancing, one leg slightly bent with the foot raised up, the other foot pressed firmly down on a squirming dwarf, a posture imbued with amazing balance. His two rear hands hold a tiny drum and flame; one of the front two hands is held up in the gesture of protection; the other points to the uplifted foot. Nataraja's dance is further emphasised by long, flying tresses; they contain a crescent moon and the tiny figure of the goddess Ganga (who was received in Shiva's hair on her descent to earth).

TANJORE PAINTING

Patrons at the Thanjavur Maratha court were responsible for fostering a school of painting that survives to this day. The typical Tanjore (Thanjavur) painting is executed in thick watercolour pigment on cloth or board, and encrusted with mirrored pieces, sometimes even semi-precious gems. The resulting glittering, brightly toned compositions are set in European-inspired gilded frames.

Cotton cloth is stuck onto a plank of jackfruit wood with the gum of the drumstick tree. An outline is drawn with pencil. Then a paste of *puli* (tamarind) seeds and *chunnam* (limestone) is used to make an embossed design, on which gemstones (or semi-precious stones) are pressed. The painting is sun-dried for two days and gold leaf is pressed on it to accentuate the embossed design and finished with a detailed paint job. Traditionally, only natural colours were used – *sembarti* (hibiscus) for blue, *gundumani* (crimson seed with black dot) for red, *manjal* (turmeric) for yellow, *manjal* mixed with *chunnam* (lime) for saffron, *marudani* (henna leaves) for orange and eggshell and milk for white. Since natural colours are more expensive, artists have switched to watercolours.

Mostly intended for shrines in palaces and private houses, Tanjore paintings portray popular Hindu deities, especially the much-adored infant Krishna held by his foster-mother; or the enthronement of Rama together with Sita in the company of Hanuman and the monkey warriors. Such paintings are occasionally on a larger scale in architectural settings, such as the mirrored, plaster Rama scenes on the walls behind the thrones in the palace at Thanjavur.

IVORIES AND WEAPONS

Ivory carving represents yet another facet of Tamil Nadu's art traditions. Doors in palaces and mansions were clad with ivory panels, as were royal wooden seats and caskets. Surviving ivories are of interest for their courtly subjects, many showing a royal figure within a palace setting in the company of a female companion whom he affectionately embraces. Other artefacts coming from Tamil Nadu's palaces include steel weapons, such as those displayed in the Chennai Government Museum. The finest are the exquisitely chiselled elephant goads, or *ankushas*; the daggers with perforated hand-guards; and the swords with polished curving blades.

Literature

The literature of Tamil Nadu is as ancient as it is vast. The oldest literary works that are available to us today are at least 2,000 years old; they display a level of sophistication, maturity and finesse that indicate that they are part of the continuum of a literary heritage that goes much further back in time. The literature of Tamil Nadu provides a detailed view of many aspects of Tamil society, culture and politics. Love and war, religion and philosophy, science and medicine, grammar and critical analyses; all form part of the rich tapestry of Tamil literature.

Tracing the history of this distinctive, voluminous and glorious heritage, its development can be divided chronologically into several segments: the Sangam period; the Buddhist and Jain period; the age of Bhakti or religious literature; the period of literary flowering under the Tamil empires; the literature of Mutts or religious monasteries; the Colonial era and the modern age.

SANGAM PERIOD: UNTIL AROUND AD 300

Tamil tradition and belief holds that there were three great Sangams, or literary academies, that were responsible for some of the most prolific and glorious periods of Tamil literature. Almost nothing is known about the first two Sangams, other than that they existed; all the works from these epochs are lost to us. From the Third Sangam, which is said to have lasted 1,850 years and ended in the 3C, however, a fair amount of literature has survived, which provides tantalising glimpses of the life and times of Tamil Antiquity, and the advanced form and structure of the language itself. A lot what was written about in these finely nuanced, vividly detailed, metaphor-rich poems – love, longing, war, governing, morality, grief, trade – is as fresh and as relevant as if it were written just yesterday. Among the best known – and best – of the Sangam works are the Eight Anthologies and the Ten Idylls. And one of the most remarkable works of this period, the *Tholkappiam*, is still respected, studied and valid today.

THOLKAPPIAM

It is difficult to describe the *Tholkappiam* in a way that does it justice. It dates from around 2,000 years ago, and is most often referred to as a book of Tamil grammar. It is that, yes, but that is merely the tip of an iceberg that runs deep and wide. Divided into several sections, it expounds in masterly detail about the letters of the alphabet, and about vocabulary and structure and grammar. But then it also provides an in-depth commentary about the substance or matter of literature itself. Drawing upon the literary culture that preceded it, it lays down rules for different types of literary compositions, providing examples from writers whose works are now lost to us. The *Tholkappiam* tells us that poems can be about inner subjects like love; these are called Akam poems. Those that deal with outer subjects, like war, ethics, or valour, are called Puram poems. There is a detailed and systematic classification of various landscapes that are associated with certain emotions and actions. In its exhaustive coverage of semantics, phonology, orthography, prosody and so much more, the *Tholkappiam* is one of the most valuable works of not just ancient, but any Tamil literature.

BUDDHIST AND JAIN PERIOD: AD 100 TO AD 600

As the Sangam era drew to a close, Tamil lands came increasingly under the influence of the Buddhist and Jain religions. In around AD 300, the Kalabhras, who were mostly Buddhists, ruled over Tamil Nadu, and Buddhism, along with Jainism, flourished. This period saw a large number of literary works by Jains and Buddhists, most of them dealing with morality and ethics. Perhaps the best known and the most beloved of these, taught even today all these centuries later to school children all over Tamil Nadu, is the *Thirukkural*. Two of the

The Miracle Yogis

Yogi depicted in 8C Arjuna's Penance rock carving, Mamallapuram

© Anurag Mallick, Priya Ganapathy/MICHELIN

The Siddhas are devotees of Shiva and yogis who claim to be endowed with eight types of miraculous powers. These are: the power to make one's way into solid rock; to ascend to the sun upon a sunbeam; to swell oneself up to any size to occupy any space; to reach and touch the moon with a fingertip; to float and dive on land as if in water; to master and conquer the elements; and to command inanimate objects and transform them into anything one wishes. In attempting to achieve a complete mastery over body and mind, the Siddhas have conducted deep studies into the workings of the human body and mind, and the elements and nature as well. They were believed to be experts at alchemy and at transmuting base metals into gold. They have written detailed works that are the fruits of their studies and observations. Their books on the human body and its workings, its diseases and cures, are a mine of information that people tap into to this day. They span a broad range of time, covering over one thousand years from the first millennium to the second. Their verses are written in colloquial Tamil that is simple and easy to follow, and it is the rare Tamilian who has not committed at least a few verses of Siddha poetry to memory, for the betterment of his body and soul.

greatest epics of Tamil literature were also written around this time: *Silappathikaram* and *Manimekalai*.

THIRUKKURAL

The *Thirukkural*, one of the world's gems of wisdom about virtue, wealth and love, was written as 1,330 couplets (or *Kural*) by Thiruvalluvar, a poet who might have lived any time between the 2C and 6C. Often, his work is classified as belonging to the Sangam period, but on its literary merits, the beautiful simplicity of the language, the straightforward practicality of its advice and the far-ranging variety of matter it deals with, it stands and shines alone. Through its words, the *Thirukkural* reveals the power and richness of the Tamil language.

SILAPPATHIKARAM

The story of *Silappathikaram*, the Tale of the Ankle Bracelet, is hugely popular with children and grown-ups alike. It was written, perhaps around the 3C, by a Jain monk who was the brother of the Chera king Senguttavan. Growing up, Ilango Adigal had ample time to indulge and cultivate his passion for literature and music. These he employed in full measure in his magnificent epic that is a masterpiece of a combination of different metres, love songs, dramatic scenes and religious hymns. It is an engrossing story, but it is also an invaluable source of information about the daily life, customs, arts, religious life, philosophy and politics of the Chera, Chola and Pandya kingdoms of antiquity.

OTHER JAIN AND BUDDHIST WRITERS

Cheethalai Sattanar, a corn merchant and a perfectionist who struck his head with an iron stylus if he felt his work was not up to the mark, wrote one of the earliest of the Tamil epic stories, the *Manimekalai*. The book is a mine of information on Buddhism and is written in a simple and elegant style with exquisite descriptions of nature's beauty. Thiruthakka Thevar, a Jain writer, wrote the *Jivaka Chintamani*, which, with lovely poetry and chaste diction, brimming with religious sentiment and reflections on human nature, is an exposition of Jain doctrines and beliefs.

THE BHAKTI PERIOD: HINDU REVIVAL LITERATURE: AD 600 TO AD 1100

The reign of the Kalabhras was relatively short-lived, and while they were largely tolerant of all religions and did not force their faith on their subjects, a movement rose once they were deposed, to suppress the growing popularity of the Jain and Buddhist religions. During this Hindu revival movement that took place around the 7C, a large number of Saivite and Vaishnavite poets wrote meltingly beautiful and soul-stirring songs and poems. Between them, they composed thousands of verses that are a major part of Tamil devotional literature.

THE NAYANMARS

The poet-devotees of the god Shiva were called Nayanmars. They came from a variety of backgrounds, including royal, military and untouchable. Around the 11C, the hymns and poems of the Nayanmars were collected into a group of works called the Thirumurais. Of these, the first seven, by some of the most well-known of the Nayanmars - including Appar, Jnana Sambandar and Sundarar, form the Thevaram or Garland to the Deity.

The Nayanmars are venerated as practically holy themselves, and beautiful sculptures have been made of their images. One of the earliest prominent Nayanmars was Manikkavasar, whose words have been likened to a cascade of rubies. He composed the *Thiruvasakam* and *Thirukovaiyar*, in which can be seen the early beginnings of the fusing of the mythologies of the Aryans with those of the Tamils. Full of devotion and piety, it is also lively and interesting enough to be palatable to a youthful audience. Other legendary Nayanmars are Appar (the Father) who, early in life, converted to Jainism and then reconverted back to Hinduism; Jnana Sambandar, the boy wonder, and Sundarar.

The lives of the 63 most acclaimed Nayamars were immortalised in the 12C epic by Sekkizhar, the *Periya Puranam* (Big Work or Epic).

THE ALWARS

Singing the praises of Vishnu were the Alwars, who also composed thousands of verses, hymns and prayers in praise of the multiple forms of the lord. Twelve of them stand out and shine brightly and are even worshipped. They include Nammalvar, the Lord's Chosen One, from whom devotional poetry is said to have burst forth spontaneously when he was a mere boy, and Andal, a pretty lass and the only female among the 12, whose passionate love and longing for unison with Vishnu are immortalised in her work, the *Thiruppavai*. A Tamil scholar, Nathamuni, compiled the beautiful words of the 12 Alwars into an anthology called the *Divya Prabandam*, which remains a source of inspiration for devotees, scholars, musicians and dancers.

LITERATURE IN THE AGE OF TAMIL EMPIRES: 1100-1400

During this golden era when the Cholas and Pandyas held sway over Tamil lands, literature flourished as well. Aryan ideas and religious literature in Sanskrit were eagerly studied, and had an impact on the writing of this age.

KAMBAR

This poet's poet, another among Tamil literature's most beloved, Kambar is best known for his adaptation of the Indian epic, the *Ramayana*. Tapping into the rich vein of Tamil literature of the preceding centuries, Kambar's *Ramayana* is a true gem. With its melodious, jewelled stream of verse, powerful descriptions, harmony of sound and meaning, and fantastic metaphors and similes strewn lavishly through the text, it is an absolute delight to read. Kambar has used Valmiki's original version as a stepping stone from which he has taken literary flight, expanding on some sections, adding drama, elaborations and his own versions, making his *Ramayana* a worthy work on its own merit, not a mere modification and variation of an earlier piece.

COMMENTARIES AND ANALYSES

A lot of Tamil literature is dense and difficult to understand. The reader can miss the deeper meanings present, and in order to address this, many writers took up the task of writing detailed commentaries and analyses. Two forms of these can be found: one that explains the text, and the second that includes critical analysis, comments on other commentaries, and supplements. These works are invaluable to help grasp and appreciate the literature more thoroughly. One of the best known of the commentators was Nacchinarkiniyar, who has penned elaborate, well-written treatises on the *Tholkappiam* and the *Jivaka Chintamani* among others. His erudition and clear, analytical mind make his works a real treasure.

MUTTS: THE LITERATURE OF THE MONASTERIES

Around the 1400s, a number of religious monasteries, called *mutts*, or *Madums*, were established throughout the Tamil lands, largely for the diffusion of knowledge of Tamil and the Hindu (mostly Saivite) religion. These places were great repositories of learning, and played an invaluable role in preserving the palm-leaf manuscripts of the Siddhi yogis (who wrote detailed medical treatises). Many of the *mutts* had their own poets, from whom came an outpouring of poetry that was religious or philosophical in nature. Many other writers were inspired by this and penned their own religious and philosophical works. Arunagirinathar was one of them; this 15C poet is best-known for his *Thirupuggazh*, a book of beautifully lyrical and rhythmically complex verses about the god Muruga.

THE COLONIAL ERA: 1700-1900

As sea-routes to India were explored by a variety of nations, the country saw an influx of people from several European nations. These included traders, administrators, travellers and missionaries, and many of them made their way to Tamil country, where they were influenced by, and had an influence on, the language and literature of the place. This period saw the development of vernacular journalism, and a revival and renaissance of old Tamil prose, which was translated into both Western languages like English, as well as into the Tamil of the time. Old classics were printed in book form, and Tamil drama was born.

One of the Europeans who had a big impact upon the Tamil literary world was Constanzo Beschi, an Italian Jesuit missionary, who arrived in Tamil Nadu around 1710. He is also known as Virama Muniyar, and is remarkable in how completely he adapted to and adopted local habits. He became a scholar of Tamil, and wrote *Thembavani*, a beautiful epic poem on the life of Saint Joseph. He also wrote a grammar of the Tamil language in Latin, a dictionary, modelled after the Western version, of the language, as well as on Christian theology, in Tamil, for the local population. The political, social and cultural changes that roiled life in Tamil Nadu were reflected in its literary output. Pride in their heritage prompted the revival and study of ancient Tamil works. Poets like Gopalakrishna Bharati and Bharati Dasan wrote beautiful works, touching upon social issues like caste and inequality. Gopalakrishna Bharati's Nandan Charitam, about the life of a lower-caste man, was considered quite revolutionary for its time.

Exposure to English novels might have given birth to the Tamil novel. In 1879, Mayuram Vedanagam Pillai wrote the first Tamil novel, *Prathapa Mudaliar Charitram*. This was meant for pure entertainment, with its mix of fables and folk tales.

The Tamil Muslim population also contributed many literary works that covered a broad range of topics from fiction to politics, mysticism to medicine, and law and philosophy; foremost among these is the Seerapuranam, on the life of the prophet Mohammed Nabi.

MODERN TAMIL LITERATURE: 1900 TO TODAY

With the Independence movement gaining strength, Tamil literature echoed the concerns and issues of the times. **Subramanya Bharathi** was a poet who lived in the 19C-20C, and is probably the greatest modern poet of Tamil literature. His ideas and thoughts were way ahead of their time, and he wrote, in simple, yet stirring and passionate language, on a variety of issues including women's rights and freedom. He broke free of the rigid constraints dictated by the *Tholkappiam*, and opened the doors to a looser, more accessible form of poetry that was powerful in its simplicity.

Another towering figure in modern Tamil literature was **U.V. Swaminatha Iyer**, who was single-handedly responsible for the revival of many long-forgotten treasures of Tamil literature, in addition to writing dozens of books on it.

Today, the great Tamil literary tradition lives on in numerous journals, newspapers and magazines, in the ever-popular crime and detective novels, and drama. Writers like Tamilvanan, Subha, Pattukottai Prabhakar and Indra Sounder Rajan continue to thrill and entertain.

Cinema

Tamil Nadu – particularly the capital city of Chennai – is home to one of the largest and most prolific cinema industries in India, indeed, in the world. It is impossible to overstate the influence that cinema has had on almost every aspect of life in the state. The catchy songs and tunes are on the lips of the auto rickshaw driver, the socialite, the vegetable vendor, the business tycoon. Film heroes and heroines are venerated like gods and goddesses and the storylines are always a hot topic of conversation. If there is one thread that links the rich and poor, the rural and urban, the college student and the household help, it is the cinema of Tamil Nadu.

Today, the film industry of Tamil Nadu is a multi-million-dollar industry, churning out around 200 movies every year. Many movie studios are located in a part of Chennai called Kodambakkam; marry together Kodambakkam with Hollywood, and you get Kollywood, the moniker for the Tamil cinema industry today *(see feature box, opposite)*.

Cinema first came to India in the 1890s, during the British Colonial years. It took root in the three most 'British' cities of the time: Bombay, Calcutta and Madras. Several film halls opened so that people could view these new wonders, and it was only a matter of time before this Indians started making their own films.

The first movie made in Tamil Nadu was a silent film called *Keechaka Vadham*, which was produced in 1918 by a London-educated automobile dealer called Nataraja Mudaliar, who built South India's first movie studio to bring his new and latest passion to fruition. Many others entered this newly born industry and there was a spate of silent films in the early decades of the 20C. These silent films were often accompanied by live background music and dance, along with title cards written in English, Tamil, Hindi and Telugu, which meant that these movies could be screened across India, in addition to in the neighbouring colonies like Burma and Ceylon (Sri Lanka). The industry grew rapidly as the infrastructure (film studios) developed, and Madras was soon a centre in its own right. The first feature film with sound was produced in Madras in 1931. It was called *Kalidasa*, and told the story of the

© NATHAN G./epa/Corbis

Fans gathered outside a cinema in Chennai for the opening of Enthiran-Robot *(2010) starring Rajnikant*

Kollywood

For many decades, Bollywood and Kollywood ran as parallel industries, not having much connection with each other. Tamil movies were considered to be more realistic, in contrast to the outrageously extravagant fantasies put out by Bollywood. Socially conscious movies were more popular in Tamil cinema.

Kollywood relies heavily on star power to sell its movies and in the south fan groups of the different stars take their rivalries very seriously. Several times, cinemas in Chennai have witnessed 'the clash of the superstars', as movies with rival stars compete with each other and eat into overall ticket sales. Serious fans of one movie star will not see – and even discourage others from seeing – movies of a competing superstar! This is not so much the case in Bollywood, which relies on other mediums, like the television, radio, news media, the Internet and preview showings to promote its movies. However sophisticated Bollywood might be in advertising its movies, it is widely accepted that Kollywood is technologically superior, with better infrastructure, cinematography and computer graphics.

Today, Bollywood and Kollywood are no longer strangers to each other. Actors and actresses who make their names in one industry capitalise on that to succeed in the other. Often, Hindi and Tamil versions of the same movie are released, to capture audiences countrywide.

great Sanskrit poet and playwright with dialogue in Tamil and Telugu. The fate and bright future of the Tamil film industry were sealed. It was poised to grow, and grow it did, with giant strides. Music became an integral part of the movies as the best singers and composers of the day were recruited to add their musical input to the movies. The songs played a huge role in enhancing the appeal of both the movies and the musicians who became the rock stars of the age.

As the industry and its popularity grew by leaps and bounds, movies became an important means for communication to the masses. Social issues like caste discrimination and family problems were explored; in the heady days of the Independence movement, patriotic movies, with soul-stirring songs, were enormously popular, and even the British tried to influence public opinion by encouraging the production of films that showed the Japanese – who had made alarming inroads into South-east Asia – in a bad light.

In the post-World War II and Independence years, Dravidian issues and con-

Kamal Hasan

© Piyal Adhikary/epa/Corbis

cerns of Tamil identity were major factors in the political, social and cultural milieu of Tamil Nadu; cinema echoed these topics and was an important medium in the development of Tamilness. From mythological and historical themes, movies now brought in anti-Brahmin, anti-North themes, and rang to the glories of the great Tamil empires and kings of yore. The importance of its role in propagating a certain political and cultural message cannot be stressed enough: Tamil cinema played a major role in the rise of the Dravida Munetra Kazhagam party and its landslide victory in 1967, which changed the nature and tenor of Tamil Nadu politics forever after. Cinema in Tamil Nadu is an integral part of life here, not an abstract, distant entity that is mere entertainment. Here the line between politics and entertainment, between real life and celluloid, is blurry, and often non-existent.

It was during this period that some of the greatest and most beloved of Tamil cinema heroes and heroines embarked upon their careers. Stars like **M.G. Ramachandran**, **Sivaji Ganesan**, **Gemini Ganesan**, **Savitri** and **Bhanumathi** are household names all over the state and beyond, and command the kind of adoration and worship that would be the envy of anyone anywhere. As these actors and actresses faded into the twilight of their careers, Tamil cinema remained invigorated and fresh as new faces entered the pantheon of venerated and idolised movie stars: **Rajnikant**, **Kamal Hasan**, **Sridevi** and **Smitha**, along with highly respected movie directors like **Bharatiraja** and **Mani Ratnam**.

From rural and rustic themes, Tamil cinema has kept apace with modern sensibilities and tastes. Aware of the economic liberalisation sweeping through the country and the rise of the middle class, the new wave of movies are set in cities and deal with modernity, consumerism, college romance and the underworld. Family relationships and social themes remain popular. Now, smaller-budget independent movies and realistic documentaries are enjoyed by urban audiences who want something more than the overblown romances and song-and-dance sequences that are so dear to movie audiences around India.

Today, Tamil films employ the most people in this industry, and its studios and infrastructure are respected as being the best and most advanced in the country. Tamil films have been dubbed into Hindi and other regional languages and Tamil actors and actresses are in demand and famous around the country. Enormous hoardings, billboards and posters form a vital part of the cityscape. Many of these border on the obscene, with buxom, doe-eyed heroines and fiercely moustachioed, red-eyed villains splashed across enormous banners.

Kollywood is often called Bollywood's little sister, but this is a little sister who is fast catching up with its bigger, better-known sibling. For a medium that does not have the ancient heritage and storied past of Tamil dance and music, Tamil cinema has grown in a fashion that is nothing short of remarkable. In just one century, which, in the history of this state is the mere blink of an eye, it has achieved a reach, relevance and influence that is truly amazing.

Music

Tamil Nadu is the birthplace and home of several musical forms that span the ancient to the modern, the rigorously classical to the light and catchy, the deeply spiritual and devotional to the worldly and frivolous. Music suffuses the air; it wafts from temples, blares from tea shops and cavorts through paddy fields. It is everywhere. The music of Tamil Nadu falls into three broad categories: Carnatic, or classical; folk and light, or pop, music. The three are distinct and discrete, but all draw from and influence each other.

CARNATIC MUSIC

Carnatic music is the devotion-laden, soulfully melodic and rigorously rhythmic classical music of South India. It shares certain common characteristics with Hindustani music of North India, like *raga*-based songs and *tala*-based rhythms, but is a distinct and unique style of music in itself. Its roots go back several thousand years to the Sama Veda, an ancient Hindu scripture. The literature of the Sangam period of 2,000 years ago, including the *Silappathikaram* and *Tolkappiam*, describes well-developed systems of music and performances in royal courts and temples. In the 7C-10C, the Bhakti movement took root in Tamil Nadu, with the Tevarams of the great Saivite saints, and the Divya Prabandams of the Vaishnavites; several of these sacred hymns are still performed today in dance and music concerts – possibly, this is the oldest extant music of the Carnatic music canon. In their time, they were performed as part of temple rituals and festivals.

The flowering of the great city of Thanjavur as a major centre for the patronage of music and dance took place in the 17C-19C, and this period saw the blossoming of this wonderful music, as its shape, form and repertory evolved, and are recognisable and in use to this day. Some of the greatest composers of this genre, including the revered trinity of Thyagaraja, Muthuswami Dikshithar and Syama Shastri, lived and composed in this time. The kings who ruled the Tamil lands were great patrons of music, and the best musicians of the day vied for positions of power and privilege in their courts.

With the decline of the great Tamil empires, and the rise of British power and rule, the city of Madras became the centre of the Carnatic music universe, which position it retains to this day. The early decades of the 20C saw the establishment of *sabhas*, cultural organisations that arranged music and dance performances that the general public could attend by buying tickets. There were a handful of *sabhas* to begin with; the last few decades have seen burgeoning growth in *sabhas* throughout the city, many of which host performances around the year.

Every year in December and January Chennai plays host to a unique festival of music and dance (*see sidebar p90*). Every neighbourhood, from the most humble to the abodes of the rich and famous, hosts a series of performances, lasting for anything from a few days to the entire period and beyond of the Tamil month of Margazhi. The city basks in the happy confluence of Margazhi, a holy and blessed month considered to be the dawn of auspicious times.

The audiences at Carnatic music recitals are remarkably well-informed about this genre and its musicians. They can instantly identify a false note in a *raga*, they can keep to complex rhythmic patterns, they can identify several dozen *ragas* within a few seconds of their being sung, and they know the strengths and weaknesses of a large number of musicians. They are a strongly opinionated lot and expect uncompromisingly high standards from performers.

There is tremendous scope for a Carnatic musician to display his or her skills of improvisation, innovation and imagination. A Carnatic music concert is never a sedate, stiffly dignified affair. Everyone is involved, wholeheartedly, openly, with the music. The music is never performed in a social vacuum. Communication flows in every direction – between the performers, from the performers to the audience, between the audience members, and from the audience to the performers. The experience spans many dimensions, and a great deal of variety is provided in the course of the concert from the different *ragas*, composers, *talas*, speeds, length, complexity, forms and languages of the songs. It is a glorious embarrassment of riches, and there is nothing quite like it anywhere in the world.

FOLK MUSIC

Folk music traditions in Tamil Nadu also go back many hundreds of years. This music is catchy, with lilting melodies and snappy rhythms. A lot of the raw material for Carnatic music has roots in folk music, which, with its lively (and often very intricate) rhythms and sinuous melodies, enjoys a much wider following, particularly in rural and agricultural areas. Often a variety of instruments, both melodic and percussive, like drums and cymbals, are used.

There are folk songs for a variety of occasions. There are songs sung on the fields while planting seeds or weeding or irrigating or doing any of the laborious chores that are made more bearable and more fun when accompanied by music. These songs are sung in groups, sometimes in call-and-response fashion, to the rhythms and pace of the work being done. Another very popular variety of Tamil folk music is the Chindu; this music is sung to keep pace with walking.

The Music Season of Chennai

The city of Chennai is magical in the months of December and January. The blazing heat of the summer is but a dim memory, and the monsoon-lashed skies have calmed into a brilliant blue. The days are perfect, mild and sunny, and the city goes about its business with a cheery spirit that is infectious.

But best of all, this is the Season. That's what the locals call it, and it is a weeks-long extravaganza of music and dance performances that encompasses even the most far-flung parts of the city. Chennai puts forth a lavish banquet of music, dance and theatre where performers, from superstars to those struggling to make a name for themselves, vie for the approval and appreciation.

Chennai Sangamam

© Arvind Balaraman/Bigstockphoto.com

There are both vocal and instrumental performances, and most of these are solos; instruments include the violin, flute and *veena*, and all are accompanied by percussion instruments like the *mridangam* and *ghatam*.

The type of performance venue varies widely, from small, humble, open-air halls with primitive sound systems to plush upholstered air-conditioned auditoriums with state-of-the art audio equipment. Some places charge no fee, and the performers at these venues are usually the young, up-and-coming musicians who hope to start on the long road to fame by attracting neighbourhood music-lovers. Performances by well-established musicians are almost always fee-based, but even there, the rates are rarely exorbitant.

The Kavadi Chindu is one of the best-known of the Chindus. These songs are generally in praise of Lord Muruga, the son of Shiva, and are sung by groups of pilgrims as they make their way to a Murugan temple with a *kavadi*, or a pole with offerings tied to either end, slung over their shoulders. The song, sung with intense devotion and joy, makes the arduous trek with the heavy *kavadi* easier to bear.

Other types of Chindus are the Nondi Chindu and Vazhi Nadai Chindu, both beautifully evocative of long treks in the countryside, blending fun and hard work, devotion and companionship in their catchy tunes and rhythms.

Lullabies are another form of folk music, and can be hauntingly soporific with their slow and sedate pace. There is also a tradition of grief-stricken songs of lamentation that are sung at funerals.

One very popular type of Tamil folk music is the *villu pattu* or bow music, so-named because it is sung to the accompaniment of a bow-shaped instrument that is embellished with bells and cymbals. Wandering minstrels sing beloved tales from ancient myths or stories about the triumph of good over evil, or about social themes, to large audiences of villagers. *Villu pattu* performances generally take place near temples and at village fairs during the cooler months of the year. Often, audience participation is encouraged with a call-and-response format.

LIGHT MUSIC

Light music in Tamil Nadu refers mostly to the music of its prolific cinema industry. The early decades of the 20C saw the dawn of Tamil cinema, and with it, the birth and exploding popularity of cinema music. This music, which enjoys immense adulation across Tamil Nadu and beyond, is a happy amalgam of a whole assortment of musical styles: Carnatic, Hindustani, folk, Western classical and Western pop. Free of the rigours and restrictions of Carnatic music, cinema music, with its cheery orchestration, dulcet melodies and toe-tapping tempo, is easily accessible to one and all.

In the early days, Tamil cinema music had a distinctly classical flavour. Indeed, many great classical musicians sang and performed for the cinema, thus enhancing both their and the movie's appeal. Tamil cinema recruited artistes who could sing Carnatic music, and became synonymous with good music. Classical music was made accessible to the masses through the medium of the cinema. Songs were composed in 'easy' *ragas* and were made shorter and less embellished, making them much easier on the ears than 'pure' Carnatic music. The themes of Tamil cinema music are generally fun and light, often dealing with love and romance. During the years of the freedom movement, patriotic songs were popular.

In 1934 the first sound studio in Madras, Srinivasa Cinetone, opened. This simple event opened the floodgates to a whole new world: the mass commercialisation and availability of the music and the birth of the film music industry. Early Tamil movies had dozens of songs; that number has decreased, but only slightly. Today, Tamil cinema music is perhaps its largest cultural product: stand on a street anywhere in Tamil Nadu, and you will hear the music – from tea shops, auto rickshaws, buses, homes, radios, Internet cafes, roadside megaphones. The depth and breadth of the penetration of this music is breathtaking.

Tamil cinema songs are so catchy that they enjoy a robust life outside the context of the movie. Music directors are constantly innovating, trying new rhythms and incorporating other styles, experimenting with new instruments, to keep this music alive and fresh. Its enduring popularity is proof of its success.

Another type of light music is devotional music, or light classical music. This is often sung in groups, in homes and in temples, again with catchy rhythms and simple, easy-to-sing tunes.

To say that music is everywhere in Tamil Nadu is no exaggeration. The variety of styles, forms, instruments and themes is simply staggering.

Dance

Tamil Nadu has been the crucible for one of the oldest and loveliest dance forms alive today, the invigorating, spiritual, rigorous and visually stunning Bharata Natyam; it is also home to a whole range of colourful and spirited folk dances. Dance is a celebration of the joys and important occasions of life, and it embraces the spiritual as well as the fun.

BHARATA NATYAM

Born 2,000 years ago, Bharata Natyam, the classical dance of Tamil Nadu, has had a fascinating evolution. The story goes that many, many aeons ago, when the world was filled with bitterness, greed, jealousy and ugliness, the people of the Earth yearned for something beautiful and enchanting that would take their minds off the wretchedness and misery of their lives. They approached Brahma, the Supreme Creator, and begged him to do something to mitigate their pain and suffering.

Brahma went into a deep and lengthy meditation, and from this was born the *Natya Veda*, the holy scripture of dance, music and drama. Drawing inspiration directly from this *Natya Veda*, Bharata, an ancient Indian sage, wrote the *Natya Shastra* 2,000 years ago, a veritable encyclopedia that covers every aspect of dance, all haloed with the sheen of the divine and the spiritual.

The rules of Bharata Natyam are laid out in staggering and mind-boggling detail in the *Natya Shastra*. Blending all the ingredients of drama, music and literature, Bharata Natyam – and all classical Indian dance – has three components: *nritta*, or pure dance, *natya*, the dramatic element, and *nritya*, the histrionic element, also known as *abhinaya*.

Until the early years of the 20C, what is known as Bharata Natyam today was called Sadir, Dasi Attam, or Thanjavur Natyam. It was performed in a milieu that is vastly different from today's world. The earliest exponents of this dance were temple and court dancers. These dancers were called *devadasis*, and they formed part of a 2,000-year-old temple dancing tradition. The grandeur of the king was expressed in his courts and his temples, and what better way to showcase his enlightenment and learning, his refinement and taste, than by having the best and greatest number of dancers, the most venerated dance teachers and musicians?

Nothing lasts forever. The world of the *devadasis* collided head-on with the British Colonialists and their ideas of morality and seemliness, and in the end, it was the devadasi world that lay in the dust. The official death knell was struck in 1947 with the Madras Devadasi Act, which abolished all temple dedications and effectively killed this tradition.

The story of Bharata Natyam after the

Bharata Natyam Today

There are people experimenting with using the language of Bharata Natyam to explore new themes like dowry deaths, women's issues, poverty, AIDS, the environment and war; there are those who throw themes and narrative to the winds and rejoice in the framework of Bharata Natyam to highlight the excitement and visual stimulation of abstract dance; there are some who have chafed at the rigid outlines of Bharata Natyam, and have incorporated elements of modern and other dance styles to enable them to best express their ideas and ideals. Some dancers have eschewed the whole devotional element; others vigorously oppose this viewpoint and are uncompromising in their belief that Bharata Natyam is a spiritual experience, not just another means to express modern life and its dilemmas. There has been experimentation in music; there has been venturing into a variety of different musical genres. Ancient texts and scripts have been revived; brand new words and music have been written to express something new, something unique, something original and utterly personal.

Bharata Natyam dancer performing at a festival in Mamallapuram

© Yan Liao/Alamy

fall of the *devadasi* system is one of unremitting, untiring effort and devotion by a group of pioneers, including **Rukmini Devi Arundale**, **E. Krishna Iyer**, **Balasaraswati** and **V. Raghavan**, who have ensured that this ancient tradition has not died. Today Bharata Natyam enjoys enormous popularity not only in its birthplace, but all over India, and increasingly, the world.

FOLK DANCES

Like folk music, folk dances are also a beloved part of Tamil Nadu's cultural heritage, and are particularly popular in the rural areas. These dances do not require the rigorous footwork or years of training that Bharata Natyam does and therefore enjoy great popular support and participation. As in the case of folk music, there are dozens of folk dances for a variety of occasions. A few are explained briefly below.

KOLATTAM

This is a charming and lively dance performed by groups of young girls, who use *kols* (sticks) to keep rhythm to their *aattam*, or dance. Popular in villages throughout the state, this dance is mentioned in several ancient texts.

KAVADI

This is the dance of pilgrims, who perform it to relieve the tedium of long journeys on foot and to keep alive and enhance the spiritual nature of their travel. They carry their offerings to the Lord and their belongings in pouches tied to long poles that are slung over their shoulders. Very often, the music accompanying the Kavadi dance is in praise of Lord Muruga. Some devotees take things to an extreme, putting themselves through great pain and austerities, to show the depth of their faith. Drums and pipes often accompany the lilting music, making the Kavadi dances a real feast for the eyes, ears and soul.

PURAVAI ATTAM

Puravai Attam, which is also called Poikkal Kuthirai, is another spectacle for the senses. The dancers perform with a richly and colourfully decorated dummy horse. The dance, performed by a pair of dancers who impersonate a king and queen, is often done on stilts, which takes a great deal of time and practice to master.

KUMMI

Another popular village dance, Kummi is performed by groups of women to no accompaniment other than the clapping of their hands and their own singing. There are many varieties of Kummi that are performed during various festivals and ceremonies: Pongal (the harvest festival), temple festivals and family celebrations. The singing is of the call-and-response type: the leading lady sings the first line, which is then taken up and repeated by the rest of the group.

Nature

Covering an area of over 130,000 square kilometres, India's southernmost state has a variety of landscapes, terrains and habitats. There are beautiful, wave-lapped golden beaches and emerald-green paddy fields; lush tropical forests and cool mountain ranges. There is a staggering variety of wildlife; a nature-made counterpoint to the cultural and historical riches of the state. It is mineral-rich, with abundant reserves of lignite, quartz, feldspar, bauxite, limestone, graphite and granite.

Tamil Nadu's northernmost point is Lake Pulicat, a brackish lake or lagoon that is home to a large variety of birds. The southern extremity of the state is also India's Land's End, Cape Comorin, or Kanyakumari. The Mudumalai National Park, the densely forested, flora-and-fauna rich part of the Nilgiri Biosphere Reserve, is at the western end, and Point Calimere, bulging out gently into the Bay of Bengal, is at Tamil Nadu's eastern limit.

Tamil Nadu has a rich diversity of plants, animals, birds, insects and aquatic life, a good proportion of it native to the state. It has taken an active role in the conservation of this natural heritage, and has set up and developed active eco-tourism and management programmes. Ancient Tamil poetry describes five geographical landscapes in Tamil country, each evoking a particular emotional state and imagery. These are *kurinji*, or mountainous regions; *mullai*, or forests; *marudham*, the fertile croplands and plains; *neidhal*, or the seashore and *palai*, the desert or wasteland. All of these exist in Tamil Nadu, and provide a lovely framework to explore the natural landscape of the state.

MOUNTAINS: KURINJI

There are several mountain and hill ranges in Tamil Nadu. Foremost among these are the Anamalais, or the **Elephant Hills**, that rise sharply from the plains past Coimbatore. Geologically, they are formed from metamorphic gneiss, with veins of feldspar and quartz, and a scattering of reddish porphyrite. The Anamudi Mountain, at over 2,600m/8,530ft high, is the tallest point in all of South India. The Anamalais are part of the **Western Ghats**, the ridged edge of the Deccan Plateau, that run along India's western flank. This is one of the most biodiverse spots in the world, the habitat for a staggering variety of flora and fauna. The **Indira Gandhi National Park**, Tamil Nadu's largest wildlife sanctuary, is in the Anamalais. It is a birder's dream come true with over 300 bird species, including the great pied hornbill and the extremely rare frogmouth. Animals include tigers, leopards, elephants, Nilgiri tahr and flying squirrels.

Further north, and also part of the Western Ghats at the meeting point of three states – Karnataka, Kerala and Tamil Nadu – are **The Nilgiris**, or the Blue Mountains. With at least two dozen peaks that rise above 2,000m/6,500ft, they are probably best known as the home of the hill stations of **Ooty** (Ootacamund or Uthagamandalam) and **Coonoor**, that are popular retreats from the searing summer heat for people from all over Tamil Nadu and beyond. One of the first wildlife sanctuaries to be established in India, the **Mudumalai National Park**, is in the Nilgiris, and is home to several threatened and endangered species like elephants, chital, gaur, tigers and leopards. Like the Indira Gandhi Park, the Mudumalai Park is also a tiger reserve, and the Government is active in protecting and conserving the habitat and lives of the tigers in these reserves. The Western Ghats receive abundant rainfall and provide fertile ground for the coffee, tea and spice plantations that thrive on the hillsides.

In addition to the Western Ghats, Tamil Nadu also includes the tail-end of the Eastern Ghats, an irregular and broken chain of hills and mountains running along eastern India. The Eastern Ghats end, somewhat tamely, near the Vaigai River in Tamil Nadu. The Shevaroy Hills and the hill-station of **Yercaud** in the northern part of the state, are perhaps the best-known of the Eastern Ghat ranges in Tamil Nadu.

FORESTS: MULLAI

Roughly one-sixth of Tamil Nadu is forested land. Variations in climate, altitude, soil, water, topography and other factors result in the different forest types that are found in the state. There are wet evergreen forests and moist deciduous forests, dry deciduous and shola, grasslands, scrub forests and even mangrove forests. Precious trees like sandalwood, teak and rosewood grow in these forests, and are a vital part of the state's natural heritage.

Within these forests is a stunning variety of flora, and with well over 5,000 species of plants, Tamil Nadu ranks first in India in floral diversity. These include endemic species, endangered species, medicinal plants and wild relatives of cultivated plants. The forests are also home to a variety of aquatic habitats that harbour hundreds of fish, amphibian, reptile, insect and bird species.

With such a wealth of natural riches, Tamil Nadu has established many sanctuaries and parks to protect, conserve and manage the life within them. The state has 10 wildlife sanctuaries, largest among which are the **Indira Gandhi National Park** and **Mudumalai National Park**. Others include the **Point Calimere Sanctuary** in Nagapattinam District, where the endangered blackbuck lives, and whose swamps are home to many avian species; and the Srivilliputhur Grizzled Squirrel Wildlife Sanctuary in the southern part of the state. There are five National Parks, including **Guindy National Park** that lies smack in the city of Chennai, and has the rarest vegetation type of the Tamil Nadu forests, the tropical dry evergreen variety. Among the smallest of the National Parks, it plays a huge role in nature conservation and education.

The forests of Tamil Nadu, teeming with a variety of wildlife, boast three tiger reserves: the **Anamalai Tiger Reserve**, the **Mudumalai Tiger Reserve** and the **Kalakad-Mundanthurai Tiger Reserve**, all within the Western Ghat mountain ranges. These mountains and forests are home to some of India's oldest tribal communities who have lived there for generations and subsisted through gathering and hunting the forest's offerings. Now that these areas are protected, and that any hunting is forbidden, the government has handled what could have been a potentially difficult situation by involving the tribal people in their education and conservation efforts. Taking advantage of their immense wealth of knowledge about the life of the forest, the forest officials enlisted their support to help protect the very things they had hunted. They are now employed in surveying, habitat

Shola Forests

The Western Ghats are known for their shola forests. The name for these evergreen forests comes from the Tamil word 'solai', meaning luxuriant growth of trees. The sholas of South India are part of the Indo-Malay tropical forest belt. The trees here are short, compared to those in other tropical forests. A unique feature of this shola is that it occurs amidst stretches of open grassland. This juxtaposition has intrigued and fascinated scientists, as it forms a unique ecosystem not seen anywhere else. It harbours an exceptional variety of fauna, including the Nilgiri langur, the hornbill, and the Nilgiri tahr, an endangered mountain goat. Alas, this shola, which once stretched continuously for mile after mile through the Western Ghats, was exploited and destroyed, with tea, cardamom and teak displacing much of the indigenous flora. Large swathes of the shola have been wiped out. The parks and sanctuaries here are some of the few remaining areas where the original shola-grassland ecosystem remains intact.

Hogenakkal Falls

improvement, tourism work and monitoring of nesting trees.

CROPLANDS AND PLAINS: MARUDHAM

Much of eastern Tamil Nadu is fertile cropland. Emerald-green paddy fields ripple gently into the horizon, interspersed with dense groves of banana, coconut and mango. The tropical lushness everywhere is one of the most soothing, loveliest sights anywhere. The heartland of this agricultural luxuriance are the plains and delta of the great **Kaveri River**.

Originating from the forested heights of the Brahmagiri Hills of Karnataka, the Kaveri, south India's most sacred river, flows south-eastwards across Karnataka and Tamil Nadu, across lush vegetation and through twisted gorges, cascading in a series of spectacular waterfalls, for over 700km before emptying itself into the Bay of Bengal south of Cuddalore in Tamil Nadu. Once it descends into the plains, it spreads its largesse through several tributaries, forming a vast and fertile delta, the Rice Bowl of India. Ancient systems of irrigation and modern hydroelectric dams combine to make the over 72,000sq km of the Kaveri basin one of the most bountiful areas of India.

The Kaveri River enters Tamil Nadu in the district of Dharmapuri and makes its presence felt in the most spectacular way in the **Hogenakkal Falls**, India's Niagara. Here, a drop in the elevation of the land, combined with the growing volume of the river, results in these breathtaking falls with their huge plume of mist and booming roar. The waters here are thought to have healing properties, as the river has flowed through forests filled with medicinal plants. The richly wooded forest all around, the towering trees, the rocky outcrops in the river and the exhilarating mist make this one of the most beautiful places in Tamil Nadu. The carbonatite rocks in the area are believed to be among the oldest of their kind in the world.

The wild river is tamed after its thunderous incarnation at Hogenakkal. The dam at Mettur, an engineering marvel that harnesses the Kaveri's waters for irrigation and electricity purposes, subdues and tempers the river as it widens and grows in its journey through the plains, joined by the rivers Bhavani, Noyyal, and others. After sweeping past Thiruchirappalli, the river divides itself as it flows around the sacred island of Srirangam. Near here is the Kallanai, also called the Grand Anicut, an ancient dam built on the river around 2,000 years ago by the Chola king Karikalan. And a little further downstream, near the majestic temple city of Thanjavur, the now-expansive river breaks up into innumerable channels that wend their way through the fertile paddy fields of the plains, forming a massive delta. Here, the lovely Kaveri has been a silent witness and spectator to the rise and fall of the great Chola Empire *(see p63-66)* and the ebb and flow of centuries of life.

SEASHORE: NEIDHAL

Tamil Nadu has approximately 1,000km of coastline, the third longest in India. Most of it runs along the Bay of Bengal, and a small portion, at the southern extremity of the country, touches the Indian Ocean as well as the Arabian Sea. It is a beautiful coastline, with golden sands, and groves of wispy casuarina as well as mango, coconut and banana. There are beautiful temples and abandoned forts along the coast, but the natural beauty and coastal ecosystems are fascinating and lovely in their own right. There are lagoons, mangroves and coral reefs, in addition to the beaches and estuaries. Some of the most important coastal areas from an ecological and nature standpoint include **Pulicat**, with its lagoon, the mangrove forests of **Pichavaram** and **Nagapattinam** and the **Gulf of Mannar** in Ramnad District with its coral reefs.

Pulicat Lake, India's second-largest brackish-water lake or lagoon, is at the northern limit of Tamil Nadu, straddling both this state and Andhra Pradesh to the north. The lagoon, with its varying degrees of salinity, has a stunningly rich biodiversity. The **Pulicat Lake Bird Sanctuary** lies here, a welcoming home to many species of aquatic and terrestrial birds. To its waters, teeming with phytoplankton and zooplankton, flock over 15,000 greater flamingos every year. The sight and sound of the vast numbers these pink-tinged beauties is simply unforgettable. Pelicans, kingfishers, herons and painted storks are just a few of the other bird species that can be found in Pulicat.

With its abundant marine life, fishing and fisheries are the main commercial occupations in the area. There are over three dozen marine species here, including a teeming population of prawns, crabs, catfish and mullet.

Around 250km south of Chennai, in the district of Cuddalore, is the Pichavaram Mangrove Forest, the world's second largest *(see Feature Box p98)*.

Further down the coast are the **coastal wetlands of Vedaranyam** in Nagapattinam District. With tidal flats, salt pans, salt marshes and mangroves, it is another area of biological complexity. It is an important wintering ground for migratory birds from northern India and other parts of Asia, and even from as far away as Europe and Africa. In addition, animals like the blackbuck, spotted deer, wild boar and civet cat can be found here. Salt manufacturing, fishing and saltwater prawn culture are the main businesses here.

Coromandel's Tumultuous Coast

There have been many cyclones, and several tsunamis, or gigantic tidal waves, that have wrought destruction on this lovely, largely low-lying coast. Poompuhar was once the capital of the ancient Chola Empire, with streets alive with the sound of traders from as far away as Greece, Egypt and Rome. Around 1,500 years ago, there came a mighty flood – possibly a tsunami – that roared up the ocean and tore through the coast, destroying this great city, which never regained its former glory. Ancient Tamil texts and stories speak of the flood, and marine archaeological expeditions have proven that the legend of Poompuhar and the great flood that washed over it were true.

Most recently the terrible tsunami of December 2004 caused a trail of devastation along the length and breadth of the coast. A fascinating thing that came to light during this tsunami was that as the sea receded almost half a kilometre before roaring back inland, rocks and what looked like the remnants and ruins of a lost city were revealed at Mamallapuram. Another instance where myth and legend might be proven right after all!

The Pichavaram Mangrove Forest

The Pichavaram mangrove forest is a magical place. Nestled between the Vellar River to the north and the Coleroon River to the south, separated from the Bay of Bengal by a solid band of sand, this coastal ecosystem is like no other place on earth. There are thousands of islands – it is impossible to keep count as the numbers shift with the tides – that dot the many channels, canals and creeks that flow around and over them. The only way into the forest is by boat, or, on the shallower waterways, by foot. The place is a veritable maze, and only the local boatmen know their way around some of the parts of the forest, and are intimately acquainted with the ebb and flow of the tides. They will take you around, and are happy to point out the wealth of bird, marine and floral life.

This is a forest unlike any other. The roots of the trees burrow into several feet of saline water and are visible above the water as well. The canopy is dense and deep inside the forest; it is a zone of permanent twilight with the sunlight barely making it through the thick leafy cover overhead. It has a unique ecosystem that includes trees, seaweeds and seagrasses, rare varieties of aquatic life, and a healthy population of birds of over 200 varieties, including waterfowl, cormorants, egrets, storks, herons, spoonbills and pelicans. The birding season is from September until April, with the cooler months of November to January being the peak period for birdwatching.

This mangrove forest is vibrantly healthy. During the terrible tsunami of 2004 (*see p97*), it was the Pichavaram mangroves that saved the coast to its west. The thick forest absorbed much of the force of the water as it slammed into land; its strength and impact were further weakened as the water was channelled into the network of waterways. Had the mangrove forest been any less healthy and dense, the coastal communities behind it would have suffered the same devastation as those with no natural protection.

This is a popular place for water sports, as well as canoeing, kayaking and rowing. The tourism department of Tamil Nadu and the administration of the District of Cuddalore have established a Dawn Fest, or Vidiyal Vizha. Promoted as an eco-tourism event, it includes activities like boat rides through the backwaters and watching the local Irula tribals catch prawns and crabs; enjoying music performed on a floating platform on the water; watching the spectacular sunrise from one of the many islets in the forest; yoga on the beach to the accompaniment of traditional music; and a seafood fest. For information about visiting Pichavaram, see p184.

Pichavaram mangrove forest

Going still further south is the area around the **Gulf of Mannar**, extending from Rameshwaram down to Kanyakumari. This area is in South-east Asia's first marine Biosphere Reserve, and encompasses nearly two dozen islands and a variety of ecosystems and terrains including estuaries, mudflats, mangroves, beaches, rocky shores, seagrass beds and coral reefs. Marine creatures like sea cows, dolphins, sea cucumbers and sea anemones thrive in the nutrient-rich waters. It is also rich in bird life, and is another stopping point for migratory birds.

Of course, the most popular of the seaside attractions are the beaches, of which there are many in Tamil Nadu, given the length of its coastline. **Marina Beach**, right in the capital, Chennai, is, at 12km in length, India's longest urban beach. Gazing out to sea, it is almost possible to forget the vibrant, noisy city to the west; almost, but not completely, for the beach is an urban one after all, with all the urban trappings and charms of countless vendors, kite fliers, screaming children, cooing couples, elderly walkers and boisterous students.

Just 40km south of Chennai, a world away from the hustle and bustle of the city, is **Covelong Beach**, with its endless expanse of pristine sand, with the tropical allure of coconut and palm trees.

A little further south is the ancient Pallava port town of **Mamallapuram**, with its Shore Temple and beautiful monuments scattered along the sands and the beach. It is breathtaking there, a meeting place of natural beauty and history, a sight very few places in the world can match.

And all the way down, to the very end of India where the coast is lapped by the waters of three oceans that merge there – the Bay of Bengal, the Arabian Sea and the Indian Ocean – is the multi coloured sand of **Kanyakumari**, the ancient temple town of the Virgin Goddess. Another place where mythology, history, religions and nature have converged and lived together.

WASTELAND OR SCRUBLAND: PALAI

The scrub or thorn lands of Tamil Nadu occupy a small area of the state, primarily around Tirunelveli, which lies on the leeward side of the mighty Agasthiyar Mountains of the Western Ghats. Here, the relatively scanty rainfall has resulted in a type of landscape that comes close to the barren wastelands described as Palai in Tamil poetry.

Only small patches of this scrubland remain, as most of it has been cleared for grazing and other activities. Environmentalists have been crying themselves hoarse, trying to stress the importance of this landscape and its ecosystem and the wealth of flora and fauna it harbours.

The vegetation of this area used to be primarily dry deciduous forest, but over the centuries has degraded into thorny scrub-like vegetation. In Tamil Nadu, the thorny acacia planiforms are the most common tree type and are often referred to as Carnatic umbrella thorn forests; these have short trunks and low crowns, and the landscape presents itself as one with open, low vegetation.

Arid and barren though this landscape might seem, it is actually rich with a variety of birds and animals, including jackals, rodents, squirrels, blackbuck, slender loris, the great Indian bustard, the yellow-fronted barbet and Ceylon jungle fowl. A large number of rare and potentially valuable medicinal plants grow here. The region once teemed with tigers and elephants; sadly, with the destruction of their habitat, they no longer live here.

It would be a crying shame to destroy what little remains of this landscape. One can only hope that the Palai wasteland does not become a true wasteland, its original ecosystem destroyed forever.

Tea plantation in Valparai, Coimbatore, Western Ghats

DISCOVERING TAMIL

Chennai and around

Highlights

- Spiritual circuit of Mylapore *p108*
- Historic Fort St George *p111*
- Chola Bronzes, Govt. Museum *p115*
- Guindy National Park *p116*

Chennai (formerly Madras), the capital of Tamil Nadu and gateway to the South, is a thriving metropolis that seamlessly fuses tradition and contemporary cultures. Once a small fishing village called Chennaipatinam, it was founded by the British East India Company in 1639 on a strip of land chosen by Francis Day between the Cooum and Adyar rivers. Despite the lack of a natural harbour, Chennai became an active trading post, especially for cotton. After the completion of Fort St George in 1640, the British acquired Triplicane, Egmore and neighbouring regions, until they consolidated most of southern India under the capital of Madras Presidency.

While the city is dotted with fine relics of Colonial architecture, ancient temples, churches and mosques, post Independence it has redefined itself as the nucleus of the Tamil film industry, the hub for Dravidian nationalism, the cradle of Bharatanatyam and the cultural centre for classical music, theatre and art. The infectious passion of Chennai's people for sports, IT, business, eating out, books, silk saris and jewellery tempt cosmopolitan crowds to drop anchor on these shores.

Chariot festival during the month of Pankuni, Kapaleeswarar Temple, Mylapore

CHENNAI

Chennai can be broadly divided into three areas: North, South and Central. **Fort St George**, the old British settlement and **George Town** (formerly 'Black Town'), the traditional Tamil quarter, lie to the north. The upmarket commercial hub of **Central Chennai** is wedged between rivers Cooum and Adyar with the arterial road, Anna Salai, slicing across. The famous shrines, **Kapaleeswarar Temple**★ and **San Thome Basilica**★, are in **Mylapore**★ towards the south. Besides its architectural marvels, the **Government Museum**★★ and **Guindy National Park**★, **Marina Beach**★ and **Elliot's Beach** are popular city attractions.

Fort St George and George Town

Fort St George was the first British structure in Madras and the most lasting symbol of British territorial possession in India. The citadel faces the Bay of Bengal and looms over the state offices on the east corner of Chennai on Rajaji Salai. Built in 1640 and reinforced later, the fort is considered among the finest examples of military architecture in India. Towards the north of the fort is George Town, the trading centre of the East India Company. Originally called Black Town since the area was occupied by native people, it was officially renamed George Town after a visit by the Prince of Wales in 1906.

Exploring the Area – Beyond the daily drone of political activity, the Fort Complex offers historic sights like the **Fort Museum** and **St Mary's Church**★, the oldest Anglican church in Asia. Nearby, the derelict house of Robert Clive now serves as the office of the Archaeological Survey of India (ASI). In the crowded chaos and bazaars of George Town is an architectural collage of churches, Hindu and Jain shrines, mansions and landmark buildings including the General Post Office, High Court, Parry's Corner and Law College.

See Religious and Spiritual Sights, Historical Sights.

Central Chennai and the Marina★

Glitzy malls, high-rise buildings, massive billboards, hoardings emblazoned with movie icons, political posters and colourful wall art (*see sidebar p53*); Central Chennai is the most happening part of town. Once lined by garden bungalows of the elite, Anna Salai (Mount Road) is a lifeline that cuts diagonally across from a corner of Cooum Creek, south of **Fort St George**. Despite rapid

How Mylapore got its name

Among the many legends that enrich the spiritual landscape of Tamil Nadu, is the intriguing story of Lord Shiva and Goddess Parvati in **Mylapore★**. When Parvati, the epitome of devotion, gets distracted briefly by the alluring dance of a peacock (*mayil* in Tamil), her Lord and master Shiva is enraged that she could disregard her responsibilities towards him for even a moment. His angry curse turns her into a peahen. To atone for her sins, Parvati flees to a place called Kapalinagar where she performs the severest penance in a bid to win back his love. Pleased by her utmost dedication, Shiva relents and appears before her to bless and accept her again. The divine couple returned happily to their abode in Kailash and the town came to be known as 'Mayilapore' or Mylapore, meaning 'Land of the peacock'. The shrine under the *punnai* tree at the **Kapaleeswarar Temple★** (*see p108*) portrays this tale with a sculpture of Parvati as a peahen, worshipping a *lingam*.

urbanisation, heritage buildings like Higginbotham's and the exclusive Gymkhana Club near the Army headquarters have survived. Spanning a 14km stretch from the edge of **George Town** to **San Thome Basilica★**, **Marina Beach★** is India's longest, and its fringing esplanade, conceived by a former Governor, adds to its charm.

Exploring the Area – Anna Salai and Chennai Central Railway Station make it easy to navigate Chennai Central, which spans the triangle of Nungambakkam, T Nagar (Thyagaraya Nagar) and Triplicane; an area flush with branded showrooms, bookshops, hotels and restaurants. The Marina brims with people of all ages who play, walk and picnic around the beach, unmindful of fisherfolk nearby. The long esplanade walk from the lighthouse continues north of the Marina past **Vivekanandar House**, Madras University and Chepauk Palace, past statues of luminaries to MGR Memorial and Anna Memorial.

See Religious and Spiritual Sights, Historical Sights, Museums and Art Galleries, Beaches.

Egmore

One of the earliest villages acquired by the British in 1720, Egmore (an anglicised form of Ezhumbur) is located on the northern banks of the Cooum River. In 1796 an asylum for military male orphans was established here, headed by Andrew Bell who conceived the Madras System for schooling. Egmore underwent a sea change under British rule when several enduring monuments were constructed – the **Government Museum★★** (1851) and Connemara Library (1896) in the Pantheon Complex, **St Andrew's Kirk** (*see below*), and Egmore railway station (1908).

Exploring the Area – The prominent public structures in Egmore showcase a melange of styles – from Gothic-Byzantine and Romanesque to Indo-Saracenic. The **Government Museum★★**, one of the oldest in the country, gives glimpses of Tamil Nadu's rich heritage through thematic galleries, ancient stone sculptures and the best collection of South Indian bronzes. **St Andrew's Kirk**, a beautiful Scottish church with a 50m/164ft-high steeple, is north-east of Egmore Railway Station.

See Museums and Art Galleries.

Mylapore★ and South Chennai

Recorded by Ptolemy in the 2C as 'Maillarpha', a thriving ancient port, Mylapore's well-planned streets and tree-lined avenues make it one of Chennai's oldest residential areas. Stretching south of **the Marina★** from Triplicane and Teynampet in the west until the sea, Mylapore is bordered by Royapettah and River Cooum in the north and Adyar in the south. The **San Thome Basilica★** marks the eastern edge. Less than 1km west, a towering *gopuram* signals the famous **Kapaleeswarar Temple★** whose busy market streets lined by flower-sellers and shops sell religious paraphernalia, silk saris and jewellery. As a cultural nerve centre Mylapore is home to distinguished members of performing arts and numerous music *sabhas*, so classical performances are a regular feature.

Exploring the Area – The devout throng Mylapore's main spiritual centres – the 7C **Kapaleeswarar Temple**★, the tranquil compound of **Sri Ramakrishna Math** and the neo-Gothic **San Thome Basilica**★. Further south in the neighbourhoods of Adyar and Besant Nagar, people lead a sedate lifestyle enjoying the quieter charms of the **Theosophical Society**★ and **Elliot's Beach** besides classical dance performances at Kalakshetra *(see Addresses p131)*. **Luz Church**, a 16C landmark dedicated to Our Lady of Light lies west of Kapaleeswarar Temple. Further south-west is **Guindy National Park**★ where the Snake Park and Children's Park are favourite local hangouts.

See Religious and Spiritual Sights, National Parks and Wildlife Sanctuaries, Beaches.

AROUND CHENNAI

Being a major metropolis, Chennai is well connected to several tourist hubs by five national highways. Off NH-5 to the north of town lies **Pulicat Lake Bird Sanctuary** *(60km)*, a large picturesque lagoon and breeding ground for huge congregations of flamingos every winter. From Guindy, the nature trail continues along Grand Southern Trunk (GST) Road or NH-45 to **Arignar Anna Zoological Park**★ at Vandalur *(30km)* and **Vedanthangal Bird Sanctuary**★ *(see Coromandel Coast)*. Also south-west of Chennai, en route to **Kanchipuram**★★ *(see Coromandel Coast)* on NH-4, visit the memorial of former PM the late Rajiv Gandhi at Sriperumbudur.

Exploring the Area – Most attractions around Chennai are located along the scenic **East Coast Road**★ (ECR) dotted with highway restaurants, amusement parks and cultural haunts *(see feature box p120)*. The **Cholamandal Artists' Village** at Injambakkam, entertainment parks like VGP Golden Beach Resorts and MGM's Dizzee World and **DakshinaChitra**★, a sprawling campus showcasing South Indian heritage, are great stop-overs for all ages. Muttukadu *(36km along the ECR)* is a picnic spot with boating and windsurfing options. Beyond **Covelong**'s sandy beaches is the fascinating **Crocodile Bank**★ and **Mamallapuram**★★★, the shore capital of the Pallavas *(see Coromandel Coast)*.

See Museums and Art Galleries, National Parks and Wildlife Sanctuaries.

- **Population:** 4.68 million (2011 Census)(Chennai).
- **Info:** India Tourism Office, 154, Anna Salai *(Mon–Fri 9am–6pm, Sat 9am–1pm, 044 2846 0285)*. Tamil Nadu Tourism Development Corporation (TTDC), 2, Wallajah Road, near Anna Park, Triplicane *(Mon–Sat 10am–5.30pm, 044 2538 3333/2536 8358, www.tamilnadutourism.org)*.
- **Location:** North-eastern corner of Tamil Nadu off the Bay of Bengal.
- **Kids:** The Children's Museum (part of the Government Museum) and Guindy National Park. The ECR also has many attractions for children.
- **Timing:** Chennai's hot tropical weather and high humidity has little seasonal variation. Avoid April–May when the mercury soars above 40°C. The monsoons bring heavy rainfall from mid-Sept–mid-Nov. Dec–Jan is the music season in Chennai *(see sidebar p90)*.
- **Guided Tours:** TTDC organises daily half-day city tours *(1.30–6.30pm)* and Hop On Hop Off Tours from Chennai to Mamallapuram *(9am onwards)* with stops at major tourist spots.

GETTING THERE AND AROUND

See also Planning Your Trip.

GETTING THERE

BY AIR – Chennai International Airport at Meenambakkam *(16km south-west of the city centre)* on NH-45 has two terminals a minute's walk apart. Kamaraj Terminal manages domestic flights from over 20 destinations including Port Blair (Andaman Islands). Anna Terminal handles major international flights. Pre-paid taxi/rental counters are at the arrivals hall *(fare to city centre Rs.300–400)*. Autorickshaws are slightly cheaper but park outside. Shuttle buses *(Rs.50)* ply to Egmore, Central stations and Thiruvalluvar Bus Stand. Suburban trains ply every 10–15min between 4.30am–11pm from Trisulam station *(500m walk from airport)* and cost around Rs.10 for the 30–40min trip to Park, Egmore and North Beach stations. Local bus #70 or #70A goes to the new Mofussil Bus Stand.

BY TRAIN – Long-distance trains arrive daily at Chennai's two main hubs *(north of the city)* Egmore and Central Stations *(1.5km from each other on EVR Periyar High Road)*. Most trains from Tamil Nadu and Kerala arrive at Egmore, while trains from other places halt at Central Station (near George Town) which has a 24hr luggage office, Internet centre, pre-paid auto rickshaw booth plus metred taxis and autos. For train timings and online reservations, visit Indian Railways Catering and Tourism Corporation website http://www.irctc.co.in/.

BY BUS – Chennai's sprawling Mofussil Bus Stand *(✆044 2479 4705)*, one of Asia's largest bus terminals, is located in Koyambedu *(10km west of the city centre)* and caters to long-distance travel with hourly buses (AC and non-AC) to Tirupati, Puducherry (Pondicherry) and Coimbatore. There are two stands – CMBT for State-owned, and Omni for private buses. The old Express and Broadway bus stations in the city cater to local services. Most buses from Mamallapuram, Pondicherry and other southern towns stop at Guindy suburban railway station before entering the city. To save time, catch a train into the city from there.

BY CAR – Five major national highways connect Chennai with Kolkata, Bengaluru (Bangalore) *(5–6hr)*, Trichy (Tiruchirappalli), Madurai, Tiruvallur and Pondicherry.

GETTING AROUND

TAXIS AND AUTOS – A fleet of yellow-top metred taxis are parked at the airport and railway stations daily but drivers haggle and fix their own fares! Radio Taxis *(Fast Track ✆044 2473 2020/2888 9999 and Bharati Call Taxi ✆044 2814 2233)* are more reliable. Auto rickshaws are also popular but drivers are notorious for hiking fares.

BY CAR – Car rentals with drivers can be booked from the airport, hotel or via agents like Welcome Tours and Travels *(150 Anna Salai; ✆044 2846 0908; www.allindiatours.com)*. A local car with driver costs around Rs.1,400–2,000/day.

BY BUS – Chennai's Metropolitan Transport Corporation buses, though regular and cheap, are crowded, especially at rush hours. The Mofussil bus station is linked to the rest of the city from organised platforms outside the main terminal. Buses #15B, #15F, #17E and #27 go to Egmore/Central area and Parry's Corner, #27B goes on to Triplicane while buses #70 and #70A are airport-bound. Anna Salai and major roads have specific bus stops but on smaller streets one must hail them down. When in doubt, seek local help.

BY TRAIN – The city's fast and reliable suburban train network has four routes – Chennai Central to Arakkonam, Chennai Beach to Tambaram and Chengalpet, Chennai Beach to Thiruvanmiyur and Chennai Central to Gummidipoondi. First Class tickets offer more comfort and space.

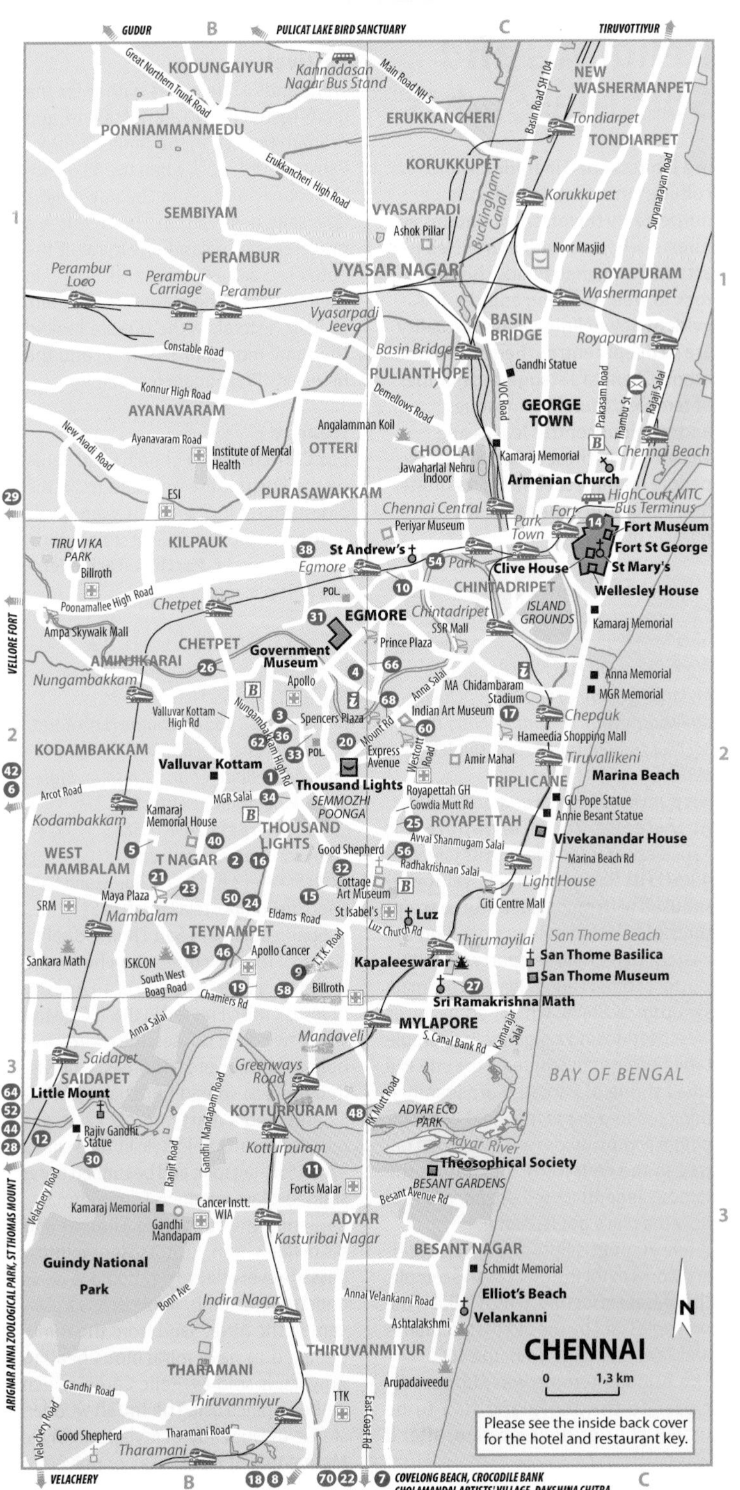

GUDUR
PULICAT LAKE BIRD SANCTUARY
TIRUVOTTIYUR
KODUNGAIYUR
Kannadasan Nagar Bus Stand
NEW WASHERMANPET
ERUKKANCHERI
Tondiarpet
TONDIARPET
PONNIAMMANMEDU
KORUKKUPET
Korukkupet
SEMBIYAM
VYASARPADI
Ashok Pillar
Noor Masjid
PERAMBUR
VYASAR NAGAR
ROYAPURAM
Perambur Loco
Perambur Carriage
Perambur
Washermanpet
Vyasarpadi Jeeva
BASIN BRIDGE
Basin Bridge
Royapuram
PULIANTHOPE
Gandhi Statue
AYANAVARAM
GEORGE TOWN
Angalamman Koil
OTTERI
CHOOLAI
Institute of Mental Health
Jawaharlal Nehru Indoor
Kamaraj Memorial
Chennai Beach
Armenian Church
PURASAWAKKAM
ESI
High Court MTC Bus Terminus
Chennai Central
Fort
Periyar Museum
Park Town
Fort Museum
Fort St George
St Mary's
KILPAUK
TIRU VI KA PARK
Billroth
St Andrew's
Egmore
Park
Clive House
CHINTADRIPET
Wellesley House
Chetpet
EGMORE
Chintadripet
ISLAND GROUNDS
Kamaraj Memorial
Ampa Skywalk Mall
SSR Mall
CHETPET
Government Museum
Prince Plaza
AMINJIKARAI
Nungambakkam
Apollo
MA Chidambaram Stadium
Anna Memorial
MGR Memorial
Spencers Plaza
Indian Art Museum
Chepauk
KODAMBAKKAM
Express Avenue
Hameedia Shopping Mall
Valluvar Kottam
Amir Mahal
Tiruvallikeni
Thousand Lights
TRIPLICANE
Marina Beach
Royapettah GH
SEMMOZHI POONGA
GU Pope Statue
Annie Besant Statue
Kodambakkam
Kamaraj Memorial House
ROYAPETTAH
Vivekanandar House
WEST MAMBALAM
THOUSAND LIGHTS
Good Shepherd
Marina Beach Rd
T NAGAR
Light House
Maya Plaza
Cottage Art Museum
SRM
Mambalam
St Isabel's
Luz
Citi Centre Mall
TEYNAMPET
Thirumayilai
San Thome Beach
Sankara Math
ISKCON
Apollo Cancer
Kapaleeswarar
San Thome Basilica
San Thome Museum
Billroth
Sri Ramakrishna Math
MYLAPORE
Mandaveli
Saidapet
SAIDAPET
BAY OF BENGAL
Little Mount
Greenways Road
KOTTURPURAM
ADYAR ECO PARK
Rajiv Gandhi Statue
Adyar River
Kotturpuram
Theosophical Society
Fortis Malar
BESANT GARDENS
Kamaraj Memorial
Cancer Instt. WIA
ADYAR
Gandhi Mandapam
Kasturibai Nagar
BESANT NAGAR
Guindy National Park
Schmidt Memorial
Elliot's Beach
Indira Nagar
Velankanni
Ashtalakshmi
N
THIRUVANMIYUR
CHENNAI
THARAMANI
Arupadaiveedu
0 1,3 km
Thiruvanmiyur
TTK
Good Shepherd
Tharamani
Please see the inside back cover for the hotel and restaurant key.
VELLORE FORT
ARIGNAR ANNA ZOOLOGICAL PARK, ST THOMAS MOUNT
VELACHERY
COVELONG BEACH, CROCODILE BANK
CHOLAMANDAL ARTISTS' VILLAGE, DAKSHINA CHITRA

Religious and Spiritual Sights

In a land steeped in tradition and culture, where saints and gods purportedly traversed mountains and forests, where royalty patronised the arts and unnamed hands chiselled rock to create soaring edifices, it is evident how religion and spirituality are so deeply entrenched in its very ethos. Chennai's staggering number of temples, churches, mosques and religious centres leaves one awestruck. In these spiritual spaces, people reaffirm their faith, meditate, find peace and experience the miracle of prayer.

KAPALEESWARAR TEMPLE★

1km west of San Thome Basilica, next to Mylapore Tank on Ramakrishna Math Road. Off Kutchery Road, Mylapore, Chennai 600004. Open daily 6am–1pm, 4–8pm. Entry free. . Guided Tours: Local guides available. 044 2464 1670. www.mylaikapaleeswarar.org.

At the epicentre of **Mylapore**★ is Kapaleeswarar Temple with its towering 40m/131ft Rajagopuram (Royal Tower) suffused with multi-hued stucco sculptures of celestial beings signalling the eastern gate. A large courtyard with a cluster of other shrines leads to the main sanctum of Shiva, which, oddly, faces west overlooking a gigantic 18C temple tank. Adding mystique to the site is a small shrine of Parvati (Karpagambal) depicted as a *mayil* (peahen) worshipping a *lingam,* under a *punnai* (dilo oil) tree in the courtyard, illustrating the famous legend (*see sidebar p104*) of how the place got its name.

While 7C poet-saints and several literary works extol the glory of this temple, the present structure, which follows the principles laid by the old texts (*Puranas* and *Tevaram*) dates from the 16C.

The original temple was supposedly closer to the shore and had to be rebuilt at its present location, after it was destroyed.

Festivals

Thousands of devotees gather for the main festivals – Brahmotsavam and Arupath Moovar in the Tamil month of Pankuni *(Mar–Apr)*, when the 63 exquisite bronze statues of the *nayanmars* (Shaivaite devotees) are taken out in a procession of palanquins to meet the bedecked deities, Shiva and Parvati in their chariots; the elaborate Teppam, or float festival, in the temple tank in the Tamil month of Thai *(Feb)* and the bi-weekly Prashodam festival.

Nearby

Luz Church (on Luz Church Road), built by the Portuguese and said to be the oldest church in Chennai, is a short walk from here. Another ancient shrine worth visiting is the 8C **Parthasarathy Temple** in Triplicane.

SAN THOME BASILICA★

Southern end of Marina Beach at the Kutchery Road junction next to St Bedes School. 38 San Thome High Road, Mylapore, Chennai 600004. Open daily 6am–8pm (Church Museum Mon–Sat, 10am–5pm). Entry free. . 044 2498 5455/2498 0758. www.santhomechurch.com.

After St Peter's Basilica in Rome and Santiago de Compostela (Tomb of St James) in Spain, Chennai's San Thome Basilica is one of the only three churches in the world built over the tomb of an Apostle of Jesus Christ. Erected in the 13C on the site of two older shrines, the church was built in honour of St Thomas, who visited India to spread Christianity in AD 52 and died a martyr in AD 72. It was rebuilt in neo-Gothic style in 1896 with a 47m/155ft-tall spire and beautified using stained-glass windows from Germany, depicting the story of St Thomas and his divine vision. Visitors stream into a passage every day to pay homage to his underground tomb, visible below a glass vent in the nave. Sand from the tomb, believed to have miraculous healing powers, is sold as 'Relic Cards' which embed a pinch of it. The 1m/3ft wooden statue of Our Lady of Mylapore (Mylai Matha) that St Francis Xavier prayed to during his visit in 1545 was brought from Portugal. An ancient pipe organ, sundial and the pole of St Thomas near the beach are other highlights. A piece of his bone, the lance-head that killed him and stone inscriptions are among the artefacts kept in **San Thome Museum** (*044 24985454*) behind the church. The Day of St Thomas (3rd of every month), Day of our Lady of Mylapore (2nd Saturday every month) and Mylai Matha Feast in December are celebrated with great pomp.

THEOSOPHICAL SOCIETY★

Access from Besant Avenue Road or Durgabai Deshmukh Road, near Adyar Bridge opp. Malar Hospital. Besant Avenue Road, Adyar, Chennai 600020. Campus open Mon–Sat 8.30–10am, 2–4pm, bookshop open Mon–Sat 9am–12noon, 3–6.30pm. Closed public holidays. Entry free, except full access to library. 044 2491 2474/2491 2815. www.ts-adyar.org.

A serene wooded enclave of gardens and tree-lined avenues alive with birds, the Theosophical Society headquarters in Adyar is one of the most peaceful pockets in suburban Chennai. In 1882, the founders Madame H.P. Blavatsky and Col. H.S. Olcott, shifted their former base from New York to this site, previously called Huddleston Gardens. The estate was expanded by Dr Annie Besant to its present size of 103ha/263 acres with heritage buildings like **Blavatsky Bungalow**, **Leadbeater Chambers**, and **Headquarters Building** (which includes a superb museum and garden of remembrance). Illustrating the concept of Universal Brotherhood, the campus is sprinkled with shrines of various faiths – a Zoroastrian Fire Temple, a Buddhist shrine, Church of St Michael and Bharata Samaja's Temple of Light.

Over the years, the venue became a hive of activity where great thinkers converged to enrich the place with their vision and wisdom.

People gathered under the **banyan tree** to hear the words of Mahatma Gandhi, J. Krishnamurti, the Dalai Lama and Dr Annie Besant. Standing 12.2m/40ft high and spanning 252m/827ft, the 450-year-old tree could seat 3,000 people under it; making it one of the oldest and largest in the country. It even survived a storm in 1989 which uprooted its main trunk. One can easily spend hours in these peaceful environs experiencing oneness with the universe. Browse the Adyar Library *(open 9am–5pm, Tue–Sun)* and bookshop (*044 24463442*) for books on theosophy.

SRI RAMAKRISHNA MATH

1km south of Kapaleeswarar Temple. 31 Ramakrishna Math Road, Mylapore, Chennai 600004. Temple open daily 4.30–11.45am, 3–9.30pm; office open Mon–Sat 9.30am–5.30pm. Entry free. 044 2462 1110. www.chennaimath.org.

Across a busy street in **Mylapore**★, an arresting 18m/60ft-wide gateway designed in Vijayanagar style perfectly frames the Universal Temple of Sri Ramakrishna Paramahamsa, the 19C spiritual master of Vivekananda. The temple embodies Sri Ramakrishna's inclusive spiritual philosophy. As a mystic, he did not restrict himself to Hinduism alone and adopted the doctrines of Christianity, Islam and Sikhism into his spiritual practice.

Set at the far end of a manicured forecourt reminiscent of Mughal gardens, the shrine is a symbol of peace and harmony. Built in 2000, the temple structure blends elements of Jain, Buddhist, Hindu and Christian architecture. A flight of steps leads to a serene prayer hall adorned by a pristine marble statue of Sri Ramakrishna. The first centre of the Ramakrishna Math in South India was started at **Vivekanandar House** (*See p116*) before it was shifted here. The spiritual organisation has 128 centres in India and 43 overseas, and has been involved in social activities for over a century. The Chennai Math organises daily worship, *arti* and *bhajans*, weekly discourses, spiritual retreats, youth programmes, besides publishing over 750 titles on spirituality. The shrine is open to all.

ARMENIAN CHURCH

Near Parry's Corner, opp. High Court. 60/116, Armenian Street, Netaji Subhash Chandra Bose Road, Chennai 600001. Open daily 9.30am–2.30pm. Guided Tours: Caretaker Trevor Alexander. 044 2538 6223.

Hidden behind a row of crummy shoe shops in a marketplace is the old Armenian Church of Virgin Mary, a charming relic of the Armenian traders who came here long before the British.

First built in 1712 near the esplanade on **Marina Beach**★, it was reconstructed in 1772 at its present location after being destroyed in the French Siege of Madras in 1746 (*see History p70*). The silent church, with temple trees in its courtyard, is in complete contrast to the clamour outside. The church is famous for its **belfry** of six bells, counted among the largest and heaviest in Chennai. They were cast at different times in England exclusively for this church. Between the 17C and 18C, the church served about 200 Armenian families in Chennai and their gravestones pave the church corridors. Hanging on a dusty wall in the outer corridor is an interesting collection of pencil sketches of the Armenian Pope and his official seat at Yeravan. They were made by George Gregorian, an artist who lived here for 50 years and died at the age of 91 in 2001, the last of the Armenians in Chennai.

THOUSAND LIGHTS MOSQUE

Near Anna Flyover, at the junction of Mount Road and Peters Road. Thousand Lights, Anna Salai, Chennai 600002. Open daily 5.30am–9pm.

Built by Nawab Umdat-ul-Umrah of Arcot as an old Assembly Hall in 1810, it was converted to a mosque a decade later. Its name is attributed to the thousand oil lamps that used to illumine the assembly hall. A typical medieval-style building with multiple domes and two minarets rising to 20m/64ft, it has a large prayer hall on the ground floor and a separate hall for women. Sayings from the Koran are painted on its walls. The mosque is a famous pilgrim site for Shia Muslims, who throng the area during Muharram. Located on the premises are a library and a burial ground.

Also worth a look is the older **Big Mosque** or Wallajah Masjid in Triplicane constructed by Umdat-ul-Umrah's father, Nawab Mohammed Ali Wallajah.

ST THOMAS MOUNT★

11km south of city centre. St Thomas National Shrine, St Thomas Mount, Chennai 600016. Open daily 6am–8pm. Entry free (Rs.10 camera). Rs.5–50. 044 2231 1925/2234 2028.

St Thomas Mount (Parangimalai) is a hillock near Guindy where St Thomas the Apostle is believed to have been martyred. Known as Calvary of St Thomas, the 100m/330ft hillock is reached by a flight of 135 steps or a steep road past Wesley English Church and St Patrick's Church. Legend has it the Apostle was martyred here while praying to a stone cross, allegedly carved by him. The blood-stained cross was discovered while digging the foundations of the present church built in 1523 by the Portuguese. Dedicated to Our Lady of Expectation, the church altar marks the spot where St Thomas was killed. Every year on 18 December from 1551-1704, the cross oozed blood, hence its popular name, the Bleeding Cross. A picture of Mary painted by St Luke rests above the altar, besides 14 ancient paintings in the hall. In the courtyard, an old banyan tree and a cluster of gilded statues surround a *dhwajasthamba* (flagstaff) crowned by a cross. A benign statue of Pope John Paul II commemorates his visit on 5 February 1986. Visitors flock to enjoy magnificent **views** of the city and the airport nearby but a terse message says 'the holiness of this place does not permit the pairs to misuse this place for their merriment'.

Little Mount

The St Thomas pilgrim trail includes one other prominent shrine in the city. 3km closer to the city centre is Little Mount (Chinnamalai), a cave where St Thomas lived, prayed and preached.

Historical Sights

With stately buildings generously filling its streets, shaded boulevards, churches and a fort, Chennai bears the stamp of a former headquarters of the British Empire without any airs. For it has other histories, dating back more than one thousand years, buried within it – before the English came the Dutch, Portuguese and Armenian traders, and before them, the region was ruled by the Cholas, Pallavas, Pandyas, Deccan Sultans and Vijayanagar kings. The excavated art and relics that litter the museums help us piece together bits of Chennai's amazing past.

FORT ST GEORGE

North of Marina Beach and War Memorial on Rajaji Salai, between Flagstaff Road and North Fort Road, Entrance opp. parking lot. Rajaji Salai, Chennai 600009. Fort Museum open Mon–Thu & Sat–Sun 9am–5pm. Fort Museum Rs.5 (Rs.100 foreigner). Child below 15yr free. ✕. 044 2567 1127. www.asi.nic.in/asi_museums_chennai.asp. Carry identification, avoid Govt. & Military offices.

A Bit of History

The genesis of the modern city of Chennai took shape around the historic Fort St George. Built on a strip of land acquired from the Raja of Chandragiri by Francis Day and Andrew Cogan, two officers of the British East India Company, the fort's construction was completed on 23 April 1640. As the day coincided with St George's Day, the patron saint of England, the fort acquired its name. Overlooking the Bay of Bengal, the massive grey and white citadel is the first seat of British power in India. It was here Governor Elihu Yale hoisted the Union Jack for the first time in India in 1687. The soaring 45m/148ft flagstaff, believed to be the country's tallest, is a replica of the original one in teak. Established as a protected trading post, Fort St George is a marvel of military architecture and considered the birthplace of the modern Indian army. It continues to be a base for the armed forces, besides the State Legislature and Secretariat.

Sights

Beyond the maze of government buildings, in a quiet corner, stands the first Anglican church in India. Designed by Edward Fowle and built by William Dixon in 1680, it was named **St Mary's Church★** as its foundation was laid on the Annunciation Day of Virgin Mary. With 1.2m/4ft-thick walls and a brick roof of 0.6m/2ft-thick masonry, the bombproof structure was built as much for prayer as to withstand bombings, siege, cyclones and other contingencies. The sanctuary, steeple, tower and vestry were later additions and by the time Col. Gent added the church top in 1795, the church was fondly referred to as 'Westminster Abbey of the East'. The tombstones in the courtyard are among the oldest British tombstones in India and house the graves of former governors Lord Pigot and Sir Thomas Munro. The ASI-run **Fort Museum** showcases a treasure-trove of old coins, military regalia, porcelain, paintings, etchings by Thomas Daniell, letters and artefacts from the Colonial era. The statue of Lord Cornwallis in front of the museum was shipped from Britain.

VALLUVAR KOTTAM

On the corner of Kodambakkam High Road and Village Road, opp. Vidyodaya School. Valluvar Kottam High Road, Nungambakkam, Chennai 600034. Open daily 9am–6pm. Rs.3, Rs.2 child. 044 2817 2177.

Without doubt Valluvar Kottam is Nungambakkam's prime landmark and symbol of Tamil culture. The **memorial** is a modern-day ostentatious architectural tribute to the Tamil poet-saint Thiruvalluvar.

Shaped like a colossal temple chariot in Dravidian style, it is a profusely carved granite creation inspired by the famous Thiruvarur temple chariot, claimed to be the biggest in the world. A life-size

WALKING TOUR

AROUND FORT ST GEORGE

One of the best ways to discover Chennai's Colonial heritage is on foot. Set out early on a Sunday as traffic is low and crowds around the State offices are absent.

Fort St George

One can see the parade ground, barracks, fortifications and ramparts. *See also p111.*

North of Marina Beach past the War Memorial, enter the fort from the gate opposite the car park on Rajaji Salai.

Fort Museum

Landscaped by a row of cannons, the three-storey building is a repository of arms and artefacts from the British Raj. Don't miss the fragment of a shell fired at the fort during World War I by German warship *Emden*. A round pavilion to the left serves as a memorial for soldiers who lost their lives in the war.

Located to the right as one enters the compound.

St Mary's Church★

The oldest surviving British church in India makes for a fascinating visit. In front is a memorial to famous Christian missionary Frederick Christian Shwartz (1726-98) and a statue of General Conway. The first marriage to be solemnised in this church was that of former Governor Elihu Yale (after whom the university is named). Yale married Catherine Hynmers on 4 Nov 1680 and donated the altar plate in 1687, now on display at the **Fort Museum**. The altar painting, a copy of the Last Supper by an unknown artist, was brought by the British from Pondicherry in 1761. The baptismal font, made of Pallavaram granite, was shifted here from **St Thomas Mount**★ in 1685; its wooden cover was added two centuries later. The 1894 organ is still played at every church service. Don't miss the floral details on the pulpit, the semicircular stained-glass windows, the intricately carved balustrade made of Burma teak or the Visitors' Book, with records from 1903 to 1947.

Past the Fort Museum, take the narrow left between the Legislature and Secretariat buildings to St Mary's on the southern side.

Clive House

Once an Armenian-owned house on 'Charles Street', this was where Robert Clive lived with his wife for a year after their marriage in 1753. Later, Clive House became the seat of the Admiralty Courts, an entertainment venue of the Governors of Madras (Town House), before becoming a Government office. Today, it houses the Chennai headquarters of the Archaeological Survey of India.

Walk straight from St Mary's Church, to its immediate west.

Wellesley House

Named after Richard Wellesley, Governor General of India, Wellesley House has an old banquet hall on the first floor dating back to 1802, which has paintings of governors and British officials on display.

South-western edge of the fort, a short walk south of Clive's House.

From Fort St George, the road north leads past the High Court, Parry's Corner to GPO. Heading south down **the Marina**★ on San Thome High Road, one can see regal buildings like Madras University, Chepauk Palace, Presidency College and statues of luminaries lining the path.

Chennai Guided Walking Tours

Walks led by local experts are a great way to experience Chennai's rich cultural, architectural and ecological landscape.

Living Statues of Marina Tour
San Thome High Road. ✆9840394282. www.storytellinginstitute.or.
Dramatic reenactments of the six statues of Kannagi, Netaji Subhash Chandra Bose, Thiruvalluvar, George Pope, Bharathidasan and Avvaiyar organised by the World Storytelling Institute. Also on offer are Storytelling by the Sea, a guided tour of the Marina fish market and an 11-day Places of Kannagi Storytelling Tour from Poompuhar to Madurai.

Madras Heritage Walks
San Thome High Road. Contact Vincent D'Souza.
✆9841049155. www.madraswalks.com.
A choice of leisurely historic walks including Mylapore: From Luz Church to Kapaleeswarar; San Thome Walk: Up the Quibble Island Cemetery; Mount Road: Queen of All Roads and Village Settlements of Velachery.

Story Trails
Across Chennai. Walks can be customised for adults or children.
✆044 4212 4214/9940040215. www.storytrails.in.
Rediscover Chennai's neighbourhoods through thematic guided walks and storytelling – Peacock Trail in Mylapore, Bazaar Trail in George Town, Jewellery Trail in craft shops and Steeple Chase covering Chennai's Christian history.

Tree Walks
Across Chennai.
✆9840904621/9884114721. www.nizhaltn.org.
Botanical explorations of the Theosophical Society, Guindy National Park and various shaded alcoves of Chennai organised by local environmental NGO Nizhal (literally, 'shade' in Tamil). Walks are also arranged in My Ladye's Gardens, Valmiki Nagar, Thiruvanmiyur, Adyar, Anna Nagar, Arumbakkam, K.K. Nagar, Kotturpuram and other leafy precincts of the city.

IIT Madras Nature Walk
Starting from Durga Peelaiamman Temple, Delhi Avenue. Prakriti, the Wildlife Club of IIT Madras organises a nature walk twice a month and on prior request for groups of 3–15. Contact prakriti@iitm.ac.in, 6172 (7–10pm). http://hsb.iitm.ac.in/~prakriti/.
Carved out of Guindy National Park, the IIT Madras campus harbours 40 species of butterfly, 100 bird species and 300 species of native and exotic plants.

Madras Musings
Across Chennai.
✆044 2811495. editor@madrasmusings.com.
Discover Chennai Heritage through the Wallajah Trail of the Nawabs of Arcot in Triplicane, Studios of Kollywood in Kodambakkam and Vadalapani, The Magnates of Mount Road and Meandering down Mint Street. Led by Sriram V, Associate Editor of *Madras Musings*, a local magazine.

Vellore Fort

© Simon Reddy/Alamy

statue of the saint has been installed in the 39m/128ft-tall chariot. A bas-relief at the base of the chariot depicts the 133 chapters of Tiruvalluvar's monumental work *Thirukkural* (*see Literature p83*), while the adjoining 4,000-seater auditorium has all 1,330 verses of *Thirukkural* etched on its granite pillars in the corridor.

EXCURSION
Vellore Fort★

125km west from Chennai. Off NH-234, at the junction of Bangalore Road. Entry from Mahatma Gandhi Statue, Arni Road. Fort, Vellore 632004. Open Mon–Fri 10am–5pm. Museum open daily 9am–12.30pm, 2pm–5pm. Museum closed Fri & public holidays. Rs.15. Guided Tours: Tourist Information Centre inside the fort. 041 6221 7974. www.vellore.nic.in/fort_tour.htm.

The impressive 16C fort situated in the heart of the city was the headquarters of later Vijayanagara kings (*see History p67*). The granite fortification with grand ramparts, its meandering wide moat and robust masonry made it one of the strongest forts of its time. Once running 61m/200ft deep with a circumference of 2,438m/8,000ft, the moat was the widest and deepest around any fort in India. Locals contend there were more than 10,000 crocodiles lurking in its depths. Today the waters are shallow and tourists enjoy boat rides around it, often oblivious of the fort's significance. Stone inscriptions suggest the fort was built around 1566 by Chinna Bommi Nayak and Thimma Reddy Nayak, subordinates to Sadasiva Raya of the Vijayanagara Empire. Earlier known as 'Raya Vellore' it included the present-day Chennai region and Tirupati under its domain. The fort's bloody history recounts years of in-fighting between the Raya families. A gruesome massacre of the royal family of Vijayanagar king Sriranga Raya was followed by enemy attacks. The fort changed many hands from the Deccan Sultans to the Marathas, the Nawabs of Arcot and eventually the British, who controlled it until India's Independence (*see sidebar below*). During British rule, Tipu Sultan's family and Vikrama Rajasinha, the last king of Sri Lanka, were imprisoned here. Within the Fort complex is the **ASI Museum**, the lovely old **St John's Church** built in 1846, a mosque and the ancient **Jalakantesvara Temple** (originally Jvarahareshwara). The sunken temple built in 1566 or earlier, has an elaborate *gopuram* leading to the main shrine. The *kalyanamandapa* on the south-west is noteworthy and displays the exemplary finesse of the late Vijayanagar style in its carved pillars, ceiling and regal pedestal.

Vellore Mutiny

The first mass rebellion against British rule took place 50 years before the Sepoy Mutiny of 1857, here at **Vellore Fort★**. In 1806, the brutal Vellore Mutiny witnessed Indian soldiers storming the bastion and killing nearly 200 British troopers in a day-long attack that nearly changed history. Tragically, they were subdued by reinforcements from Arcot, and put to death. Nearly 700 Indian soldiers were shot dead or injured in the attack.

Museums and Art Galleries

Culturally rich and proud of its traditions and heritage, Chennai has excellent showcases of art and history. The Regional Rail Museum near the bus stand offers nostalgic glimpses of old coaches. Lalit Kala Akademi at Thousand Lights and Art World (earlier Sarala's Art Centre, one of India's oldest art galleries) in Ganeshpuram, display riveting contemporary Indian art. Faraway Tree and Artsphere at Nungambakkam, Vinnyasa and Ashvita in Mylapore, Prakrit in RA Puram and Focus in Alwarpet are other noteworthy galleries.

GOVERNMENT MUSEUM★★

Near Don Bosco School, opp. Alsa Mall. Pantheon Road, Egmore, Chennai 600008. Open Sat–Thu 9.30am–5pm. Closed national holidays. Rs.15, Rs.10 child below 12yr (Rs.250 foreigner, Rs.200 camera, Rs.500 video). . 044 2819 3238. www.chennaimuseum.org.

Established in 1851 at **Fort St George** and shifted here in 1854, Chennai's Government Museum is the oldest and second-largest museum in India, after Calcutta. Formerly the Cutchery (Court), the brick-red museum is part of the large Pantheon Complex fronted by the circular-pillared **Museum Theatre** and heritage buildings like the **National Art Gallery** and **Connemara Library**. Perhaps it is this setting that accentuates the beauty of its exhibits. The thematic sections can keep one engaged for hours. The Archaeology section houses inscriptions and stone sculptures from South India in chronological order. The Zoology section's fascinating displays include an 18m/60ft-long skeleton of a sperm whale (washed ashore at Mangalore in 1874). The Numismatics division has 65,000 coins in gold, silver and copper from South India and a Medal Gallery nearby.

The three-storeyed Bronze Gallery keeps one in thrall to the world's best bronzes from the Chola period. Arranged according to Shaiva and Vaishnava styles, besides Pallava, Hoysala and Chalukya dynasties, the alluring images of the Nataraja collection and Ardhanarishwara are particularly dazzling. Marble Buddha statues and Buddhist relics are displayed in the Amaravathi Collection. Other intriguing exhibits include an Ethnography Collection of various tribes by J.W. Breeks, the first Commissioner of Nilgiris, archaeologist Robert Bruce Foote's collection of megalithic stone implements and the Rock and Cave Art Gallery, spanning 50,000 years.

The first to have a Philately section with 45,000 stamps, the museum also houses the only Holographic Gallery in India, with holograms of rare coins and ancient jewellery. The **National Art Gallery**, formerly Victoria Memorial Hall, is a magnificent Indo-Saracenic structure dating to 1906. It houses seven Raja Ravi Varma originals, declared national treasures, including his masterpiece, Sakuntala. The **Gallery of Contemporary Art** showcases 1,200 paintings by Indian artists. The **Children's Museum** is a tour around ancient civilisations, scientific exhibits and a vast doll collection.

Bronze Gallery

Ice Houses

In 1833 a Boston ice merchant, Frederic Tudor, brought ice to India for the first time aboard the *Clipper Tuscany* after a 4-month voyage to Calcutta. When ice reached the ports of Bombay and Madras in 1840, Tudor, the Ice King, built three houses in each of these cities to keep ice under proper insulation for months. His business flourished between 1842 and 1880 but collapsed after the invention of ice-making by steam. The Madras Ice House was later bought by Biligiri Iyengar, a Madras High Court advocate who named it Kernan Castle after his friend, Justice Kernan. He also added the semicircular verandah.

VIVEKANANDAR HOUSE

On San Thome High Road between Annie Besant statue and Bharathi Dasan statue. Kamarajar Salai, Marina Beach, Chennai 600005. Open Thu–Tue 10am–12.30pm, 3–7pm (ticket counter closes 6.30pm). Rs.2, Rs.1 child. 044 2844 6188. www.sriramakrishnamath.org.

Built 170 years ago as an Ice House, the Vivekanandar Illam (House) is the lone survivor of the three built in the 1800s (*see sidebar above*). When Swami Vivekananda made a triumphant return from his lecture tour of the West in 1897, he stayed here and delivered his famous speech for the reconstruction of India. A month later, the first centre of the Ramakrishna Math (*See p109*) in South India was started in this building by Swami Ramakrishnananda, a brother disciple. To commemorate Swami Vivekananda's birth centenary in 1963, Ice House was renamed as Vivekanandar House. The room where he stayed is now a meditation hall.

A 4-minute film is screened for visitors and the permanent exhibition, Vivekananda Cultural Heritage of India, showcases a photo gallery, paintings and history of the house. Cultural activities such as yoga, guided meditation and literary competitions are held here.

National Parks and Wildlife Sanctuaries

Regardless of being a densely populous city, Chennai surprises any visitor by the sheer choice of nature and wildlife options. Watch snake demonstrations at Chennai Snake Park or go on a nature walk at Guindy, one of the few national parks in India located within city limits. Short drives away are Madras Crocodile Bank on ECR *(See feature box p121)* **and Arignar Anna Zoological Park, the largest zoological garden in the country. Migratory birds can be spotted at Pulicat Lake, 60km north of the city.**

GUINDY NATIONAL PARK★

South-west of Chennai near Adyar, entrance next to Adyar Cancer Institute. Sardar Patel Road, Guindy 600032. Open Wed–Mon 9.30am–5.30pm. Rs.10, Rs.2 child. Rs.15. Guided Tours: Contact Superintendent, Children's Park Complex, 044 2230 1328; Wildlife Warden, Teynampet 044 2432 1471. www.forests.tn.nic.in.

Spread over 270ha/668 acres on the south-western edge of the city, Guindy is literally the lung space of Chennai. Originally a private game reserve owned by Englishman Gilbert Rodericks, the park was once part of the Governor's estate. Later, its outer edges were hived off to create a plethora of institutes – IIT, CLRI and Anna University.

Primarily a tropical dry evergreen forest interspersed with scrub jungle and grasslands, the park is dotted with centuries-old banyan trees and numerous water bodies. Of the three ponds, Appalan Kulam is a habitat for water birds, Kathan Kulam is where deer congregate while Bhogi Pond is near the edge. The grassland, Polo Ground, is maintained as a grazing habitat for blackbuck. Thorny scrub is regularly cleared by the forest department and burnt; its ash contains essential minerals beneficial to the 350-strong population of blackbuck. Minimum groups of four, or larger school groups are taken on 1.5hr nature walks accompanied by forest staff. Along the two trails, one can spot nearly 132 bird species and deer, jackal, mongoose and herbivores in a free-ranging habitat.

The complex also houses other popular attractions like the Children's Park and Chennai Snake Park, which have separate entrances and fees.

Snake Park

Open Wed–Mon 8.30am–5.30pm. Rs.10, Rs.1 child (Rs.10 camera, Rs.100 video). www.cspt.in.

The Snake Park was the old site of the Madras Crocodile Bank Trust until it was relocated to a larger site on the **ECR**★. However, small open enclosures with an assortment of crocodiles remain, providing a complete reptilian atmosphere, in addition to the glass enclosures for snakes. Lec-Dems are conducted at the Interpretation Centre as are regular snake demonstrations at 11am, 1pm, 3pm and 4.30pm. The Snake Park conducts free environment education programmes for local schools between 10am and 12noon on weekdays, making it a busy time to visit.

Children's Park

Open daily 9am–5.30pm. Rs.10, child up to 10yr free (Rs.20 camera, Rs.100 video).

Spread over 9ha/22 acres, the adjoining Children's Park is bisected by a long tree-lined pathway leading off into 70 enclosures with caged birds and animals like deer, fox, jackal, hyena and primates. There's a great collection of pelicans, ibis and other water birds in the Vedanthangal Birds enclosure while exotic bird species like cassowary, emu and parakeets get individual cages. Don't miss the 20-million-year-old tree fossil on display between the lion-tailed macaque and the Tower Slide near the playground to the right.

EXCURSIONS

Arignar Anna Zoological Park

31km from Chennai on the Grand Southern Trunk Road, 6km after Tambaram. GST Road, Vandalur, Chennai 600048. Open Wed–Mon 9am–5pm. Rs.15, Rs.10 child 5–12yr (Rs.25 camera, video not allowed).

Gharials in Snake Park

Rs.5–25. Guided Tours: lion safari & zoo safari (Rs.12), elephant safaris also organised. 044 2275 0741/2275 1089/ 2376 6089. www.aazoopark.gov.in.
The Vandalur Zoo, founded in 1855, is India's first public zoo. Also called Arignar Anna Zoological Park, it is hailed as the largest zoo in the country, spilling across an area of 603ha/1,490 acres. Built on the lines of an open-zoo concept, the park has 80 island-type enclosures for captive species in a free-ranging environment surrounded by wet and dry moats, chain-link fences and camouflaged walls. In 2001, a rescue and rehabilitation centre was created for confiscated and abandoned animals. Easily one of the country's most visited zoos, it has clocked up a record 57,000 visitors on a single day! There are more than 170 species of mammals, birds and reptiles, several primates and endangered species including the lion-tailed macaque, Bengal tiger and Muscovy duck. Most of the animals are found along the 2.5km arterial circuit while smaller mammals are located along the three inner roads. The key attractions are the **Lion Safari** across a gently sloping terrain, the snake-shaped **Reptile House**, the **Butterfly House** and the expansive **Otteri Lake**, which is an ideal roost for migratory water birds. An elephant safari was introduced in 2008 and allows visitors to tour the park in the morning *(9.30–11.30am)* or in the evening *(4–5pm).*
The zoo also has a well-stocked library of wildlife books and 24hr medical care facilities available for rescued, wounded or sick animals. Visitors can replenish themselves at the restaurant, ice-cream parlour and soft drinks counter at the entrance. Battery operated vehicles are available for rides throughout the park.

Pulicat Lake Bird Sanctuary

Drive north of Chennai on NH-5 towards Nellore and turn right at Sullurpet for the bird sanctuary. For Pulicat town (60km), turn right onto SH-56 via Ponneri and get on SH-104. Sullurpet, Tiruvallur District, 85km (1.5hr) from Chennai. Open daily 6am–5.30pm. Rs.2 (Rs.400 foreigner). P. *Guided Tours: contact Wildlife Warden, Chennai. Local fishermen offer boat rides for about Rs.200. 044 24321471. www.forests.tn.nic.in.*
The second-largest brackish water lagoon in India after Chilika in Orissa, Pulicat is one of the most important sanctuaries for water birds in South India (*see Nature p94*). Spread over 720sq km across Andhra's Nellore and Tamil Nadu's Tiruvallur districts, only 16 percent of the 60km-long lagoon lies in the state. The vast lake can be accessed from Sullurpet in the north near Sriharikota or Pulicat town to the south.
Ranked as an Important Bird Area (IBA) by BirdLife International and Bombay Natural History Society, Pulicat Lake harbours six vulnerable or near-threatened bird species, including the oriental darter, black-bellied tern, lesser flamingo, spot-billed pelican, black-headed ibis and the painted stork. Nearly 113 bird species have been reported at Pulicat Lake and its adjoining wetlands, including many species of egrets, herons, bitterns, storks, ducks, gulls, plovers, terns and ibis. Pulicat is dotted by 20 islands, of which Sriharikota Island at its eastern edge is the largest. It serves as a base for India's spaceport, the Satish Dhawan Space Centre, and is a high-security area. However, it is the shallow central region between Sriharikota and Kudiri that is of prime interest to a birder. Connected by road, it is the most easily accessible area of the lake and forms an important foraging ground for water birds. A large number of piscivorous (fish-eating) birds and wader species like flamingos throng the many culverts along the Sullurpet-Sriharikota Road. The Greater Flamingo can be seen nearly all year round at Moolah Kuppam on the western edge of Pernadu Island.
Annamalai Cheri, on the southern tip of the lake, is also great for birdwatching. Pulicat town nearby has an old Dutch cemetery and ruins of a fort. November to February is a great time to visit because of the presence of winter migratories.

Beaches

Spectacular sunrises and blazing sunsets, Chennai's beaches are the best seats in the house to catch the drama of the sky and sea. The enchanting coastline is dotted by several beaches, each with its own charm. The 14km-long Marina is ideal for a drive-by while Elliot's is excellent for an evening jaunt. Foreshore Estate beach near the mouth of the Adyar River is where Ganesha idols are immersed every September. Along the ECR, Covelong *(see Coromandel Coast)* **is an idyllic getaway on the way to the sandy shores of Mamallapuram.**

MARINA BEACH★

Off Rajaji Salai, south of Fort St George until San Thome. Rajaji Salai-San Thome High Road.

The Marina was once a sludge strip where mudskippers roamed. After the Madras Harbour was built, the beach accumulated a sandy shore that washed up to the road. It was the vision of Mountstuart Elphinstone Grant Duff, the Governor of Madras (1881-86) to design an esplanade along the beach in 1885 for social interaction. He christened it the Madras Marina. (*see sidebar below*). Today the 14km shoreline is India's longest urban beach, bracketed by **Fort St George** and **San Thome Basilica**★ at its two ends (the southern end of Marina Beach is often referred to as San Thome Beach). The prime location, with heritage landmarks and statues of eminent personalities fringing one side and scenic seascapes on the other, draws crowds to play beach cricket, volleyball, fly kites, jog, walk, romance and romp in the sand and sea. Be warned, the waters are unsafe due to strong undercurrents, whirlpools and rocks; besides swimming and bathing are banned.

ELLIOT'S BEACH

From Besant Nagar, take 5th Avenue to the north or 7th Avenue to the south of the beach. Besant Nagar, near Adyar.

In contrast to the din of **Marina Beach**★, Elliot's Beach – named after former Governor Edward Elliot – is a quieter shore in Besant Nagar, the city's southern suburb. Its mellow ambience makes 'Bessie' (another nickname for Elliot's) a favourite for those seeking a calmer experience by the sea. The lone **Karl Schmidt Memorial** stands in the sand as an ode to the Dutch sailor who drowned while trying to save a swimmer. At sundown, the beach breathes with life as rows of seaside shacks and carts stir up fried fish and a wide array of seafood. The added presence of trendy restaurants makes it a popular youth hangout. It's also a stopover for families and tourists visiting **Velankanni Church** and **Ashtalakshmi Temple** (dedicated to eight forms of Goddess Lakshmi) on the southern end of the beach.

The Marina★

The wide open spaces of the Marina esplanade makes it an ideal venue for high-profile events and public gatherings. The annual Independence Day and Republic Day ceremonial parades and airshows are held along the promenade, with flag hoisting in the Marina. Come Aug–Sept, the yearly festival of Vinayagar Chaturthi culminates here with people parading their Ganesha idols, before immersing them in the sea. In 2008, the Marina hosted India's first International Beach Volleyball Championship. The grand event saw 11 Indian teams along with 60 teams from 21 countries participating in the 6-day event for men and women.

A few years ago, a 4.5km stretch of the Marina underwent a major makeover. Today, there are 14 galleries with seating, a sandy walkway with fountains and impressive lighting to allow visitors to enjoy the seaside at night. This stretch was declared as a plastic-free zone with a fine of Rs.100 imposed on offenders.

East Coast Road (ECR)

Palm-fringed beaches, casuarina groves, quaint fisherman villages, French towns and catamarans bobbing over waves are some highlights of a drive along the 737km stretch of SH-49, or East Coast Road. The two-lane highway fringes the Bay of Bengal and links Chennai to Thoothukudi and Kanyakumari in the south. Dotted with great eateries, drive-in cinemas, unique art and cultural centres, boating options in Muttukadu backwaters, several plush beach resorts, amusement parks, go-karting tracks, adventure zones for water sports and ATVs, the route is a heady mix of food, relaxation and fun.

Cholamandal Artists' Village

18km south of Chennai on ECR between Hotel Kailash Resort and VGP Temple of World Peace. ECR, Injambakkam, Chennai 600041. Open daily 9.30am–6.30pm. Entry free. (limited). *044 2449 0092/2449 4053. www.cholamandalartistsvillage.org.*
Cholamandal Artists' Village was established in 1965 by K.C.S. Panicker and nurtured by 30 of his students as a platform to help fellow artists and sculptors. Originally located in Egmore in a space provided by the Lalit Kala Akademi, the Artists' Village was relocated to this 4ha/10-acre plot. Founder and sculptor P.S. Nandan recalls how the campus started on a 186sq m/2,000sq ft patch. 'The sales of our canvas and batik work which was then in vogue went into making the artists' village, now home to 17 artists.'
Today, artworks and sculptures are displayed at the two galleries Indigo and Laburnum. Adjoining the complex is a shaded garden restaurant with a 30-seater air-conditioned Shiraz Art Café that offers Persian and Med cuisine *(open 11am–8pm)*. Two guesthouses are available for artists who apply for an 11-month studio-cum-residence programme.

DakshinaChitra★

21km south of Chennai on ECR after MGM Dizzee World. ECR, Muttukadu, Chennai 603118. Open Wed–Mon 10am–6pm. Rs.75, Rs.20 child 5–12yr (Rs.200 foreigner, Rs.90 festivals). . *044 2747 2603/2747 2783. www.dakshinachitra.net. Credit Cards accepted.*
This vibrant cultural space envisioned by Madras Craft Foundation and designed by architect Laurie Baker recreates the experience of rural life in the South through interactive encounters. Learn pottery, play the *chende* (drum), make block-printed handkerchiefs or try *kili jyotisam* (parrot astrology). Spread across an undulating sandswept ridge overlooking the Bay of Bengal, its 4ha/10 acres are demarcated into various zones. Among its 17 heritage houses is a Syrian Christian home from Kerala, a Chettinad merchant's house and an Ilkal weaver's home from Karnataka. The Gallery for Religious Art set in a Brahmin *agraharam* displays religious paraphernalia thematically arranged into Fire and Water (lamps and pots) and Artefacts. Short fun sessions in basket weaving, rice pounding, *kolam* drawing, *henna* designs and palm leaf decorations make it participatory for all ages. With a dedicated art gallery and space for folk arts, DakshinaChitra buzzes with seminars, school trips and hordes of tourists. A wide choice of mementos is for sale at the souvenir shop besides a craft bazaar where one can buy directly from the artisans. The restaurant Bekal serves excellent ethnic food of South India.

Covelong Beach

40km south from Chennai, on ECR en route to Mamallapuram. ***Beach Road, Covelong 603112, Kanchipuram District.*** P.

Kovalam, or Covelong, was a small fishing village before it was propelled to fame when Taj opened Fisherman's Cove, its luxury beach resort on the ramparts of Dansborg Fort (*see p177*). The beach offers the twin pleasures of sunbathing in a palm-fringed idyll with white sands and gentle sea or the adventures of windsurfing and other water sports at Muttukadu Backwaters nearby. Historically, Covelong was the ancient port established by the Nawab of Carnatic, Saadat Ali, which was taken over by the French in 1746 and destroyed by the British. The beach has other historical monuments in the vicinity like the old Catholic church.

Crocodile Bank★

44km south of Chennai, on ECR en route to Mammalapuram. ***Centre for Herpetology, Vanemmeli, Chengelpet District 606104. Open Tue–Sun 8.30am–5.30pm. Rs.35, Rs.10 child 3–10yr (Rs.20 camera, Rs.100 video). P Rs.10. Guided Tours: contact MCBT, feeding demos organised. 044 2747 2447. www.madrascrocodilebank.org.***

The Madras Crocodile Bank is the brainchild of well-known herpetologist **Romulus Whitaker**, the 'Snake Man of India'. Spanning 3.2ha/8 acres of lush vegetation, it is the largest crocodile breeding site in the country and a crowd magnet. Several species of African and Indian crocs and alligators are bred in captivity. Stony-eyed and rock-still at most times, with jaws open in an endless grin, they sometimes roll and attack each other when territories are encroached on. About 5,000 species are kept in their natural surroundings in open pools, enclosed by safety grilles and walls. Lazing in murky pools and on muddy banks are species like mugger (marsh crocodile), gharials, Morlet's crocodile from Mexico, American alligators, dwarf crocs from Africa and Siamese crocodiles. Information panels, labels and warning signs along the entire walkway give a fascinating insight into reptile behaviour. The park is a well-known reptile research station and was established with the objective of spreading awareness about the ecological role played by crocs. It also houses a snake farm where venom extraction demos are conducted. At the entrance, a little shop sells stuffed toys, curios and T-shirts, all with a reptile theme.

DakshinaChitra

ADDRESSES

STAY

Chennai has every conceivable form of accommodation – cheap lodges, boutique hotels, service apartments, beach resorts and business hotels to swanky 5-stars. The budget accommodations are concentrated to the north, around George Town, Egmore and Central railway stations. Upmarket hotels are located in Central and South Chennai, closer to the airport and main business and shopping hubs. Generally, the hotels listed are self-sufficient with speciality restaurants, bars/lounges, all-day dining, shopping arcades and night spots.

CENTRAL CHENNAI

The Accord Metropolitan – *35, GN Chetty Road, T Nagar, Chennai 600017. 044 2816 1000/4391 1000. www.theaccordmetropolitan.com. . 162 rooms.* . Grand stairways, lavish use of Italian marble and intricate gold-leaf work; not your average business hotel! Enjoy luxury high-altitude dining at Pergola, Chennai's highest open-to-sky restaurant, Season, an all-day multi-cuisine, besides a spa, swimming pool and fitness centre.

GRT Grand – *120, Sir Thyagaraya Road, T Nagar, Chennai 600017. 044 2815 0500/5500. www.grthotels.com. . 135 rooms.* . This smart business hotel was recently awarded the best 4-star hotel in India. GRT's grand high-rise offers many delights – the best Med cuisine in town at Azulia, 24hr multi-cuisine at Any Time, Indian specialities at Copper Point, as well as a three-level bar and therapy centre.

My Fortune – *Cathedral Road, Chennai 600086. 044 2811 0101. www.fortunehotels.in. . 92 rooms.* . A conveniently located luxury hotel (previously the Sheraton Chola) with an award-winning Indian restaurant, Peshawari, it also has a popular poolside bar/pub, Durrant's, with charming wood-panelled floors.

Sheraton Park Hotel & Towers – *T.T.K. Road, Chennai 600018. 044 2499 4101. www.itchotels.in. . 283 rooms.* . A luxury metropolitan hotel boasting five stellar restaurants including the ever-popular Dakshin (South Indian) with specialities like banana ***dosa***. The building and décor is a little dated, but rooms are spacious and comfortable. It's central location is ideal, but with an Irish-style pub (Dublin), the Westminster Bar, a nightclub (Gatsby 2000) and even a shopping arcade; who has time to step out?

Taj Club House – *2, Club House Road, Chennai 600002. 044 6631 3131. www.tajhotels.com. . 220 rooms.* . Located on a site where British bungalows and the historic Madras Club once stood, the hotel is fronted by a 4,180sq m/45,000sq ft blue glass façade. Traditional Indian artefacts adorn interiors of honey-toned wood. Beyond Indus serves outstanding Frontier cuisine from Punjab, Rawalpindi and Sindh and four-course business lunches. Kefi, the rooftop Med restaurant, recreates a rustic Greek country home. The 24hr Club House does great buffets, weekend BBQ dinners and Sunday brunches.

Taj Coromandel – *37, Mahatma Gandhi Road, Nungambakkam, Chennai 600034. 044 6600 2827. www.tajhotels.com. . 212 rooms.* . A 'Leading Hotel of the World', the Taj has hosted presidents from Carter to Clinton and royalty from across the globe. The recently renovated hotel has well appointed rooms with large bathrooms and attentive staff. It boasts a 24hr fitness room with an outdoor swimming pool surrounded by greenery. The aptly named restaurants, Southern Spice, Golden Dragon and Prego, serve speciality cuisine, besides Anise, an all-day diner.

Vivanta by Taj Connemara – *Binny Road, Chennai 600002. 044 6600 0000. www.vivantabytaj.com. . 150 rooms.* . Started in 1854 as the Imperial Hotel and re-established as The Connemara in 1890, this is Chennai's only heritage hotel. An Art Deco building with classy interiors, it offers pan-Asian cuisine at Hip Asia, Chettinad cuisine in an alfresco ambience at The Raintree, a poolside area for parties and Distil, a trendy bar/nightclub that specialises in fruit-based cocktails. The Sunday morning breakfast buffet at the Veranda is not to be missed.

⛁⛁⛁–⛁⛁⛁⛁ **Savera Hotel** – *146, Radhakrishnan Salai, Chennai 600004. ☏044 2811 4700. www.saverahotel.com. ♿. 230 rooms.* ☕ ▤. Rooms at this hotel in Gopalapuram have warm interiors and wood-toned flooring; some overlook the swimming pool. Enjoy Southern cuisine at Malgudi, try Awadhi and Mughlai fare at Minar rooftop restaurant, go for a buffet at The Piano or the all-day Lobby Café and Fondue and Baker's Basket for short eats.

⛁⛁⛁ **Courtyard Marriott** – *564, Anna Salai, Chennai 600018. ☏044 6676 4000. www.marriott.com. ♿. 231 rooms & 5 suites.* ☕ ▤. A glass-and-chrome fronted building with contrasting warm interiors. The 24hr coffee shop Paprika has a vibrant pepper theme, the purple and black Rhapsody (dinner only) serves authentic Italian, while Muffin Tree is a deli, bakery and gift shop rolled into one. Health club, spa and beauty salon also attached.

⛁⛁⛁ **The Park** – *601, Anna Salai, Chennai 600006. ☏044 4267 6000. www.theparkhotels.com. ♿. 214 rooms.* ☕ ▤. A trendy décor inspired by films, performances and screen sets, the Park comes with a 24hr diner (601), an 8th-floor Thai restaurant (Lotus), plush bar (Leather), spa (Aura), night-club (Pasha) and poolside Med lounge (Aqua) serving sunset cocktails.

⛁⛁⛁ **The Park Pod** – *23/13, Khader Nawaz Khan Road, Nungambakkam, Chennai 600006. ☏044 4295 5555. www.theparkhotels.com. ♿. 20 rooms.* ☕ ▤. A small boutique hotel with contemporary styling, it claims to have the first water bar in Asia – The Absolute Sky Bar – and a red-hot mosaic-tiled lap pool. Italia stirs up some good pasta and Continental fare.

⛁⛁⛁ **Quality Inn Sabari** – *29, Thirumalai Pillai Road, T Nagar, Chennai 600017. ☏044 2834 3030. www.sabarihotels.com. ♿. 72 rooms.* ☕ ▤. This comfortable hotel has all the usual facilities – music-themed bar (Grammy), all-day dining at Rendezvous, Cascade gourmet restaurant and Zero Bar.

⛁⛁⛁ **The Rain Tree** – *636, Anna Salai, Teynampet Chennai 600018. ☏044 2830 9999/2830 9977. www.tajhotels.com. ♿. 230 rooms.* ☕ ▤. A stylish, eco-sensitive business hotel, Rain Tree helps reduce your carbon footprint at every step – the George Fisher concealed cistern uses only 6 litres of water, a sewage treatment plant recycles water, and heat generated by the ACs heats water in the bathroom. Enjoy Punjabi cuisine at Up North, the rooftop restaurant and Chinese at Lemongrass at their 105-room branch on St Mary's Road, Alwarpet *(☏044 4225 2525)*.

⛁⛁⛁ **The Residency Towers** – *115, Thyagaraya Road, T Nagar, Chennai 600017. ☏044 2815 6363. www.theresidency.com. ♿. 174 rooms.* ☕ ▤. This luxury hotel has a grand reception area and spacious rooms. Crown (20th floor rooftop) has an alfresco deck and restaurant. At Bike and Barrel (an English pub), barrels double up as tables and a huge motorbike hangs from the ceiling. Southern Aromas offers good local cuisine; for round-the-clock dining head to Main Street. The management also runs The Residency *(☏044 28253434)* on GN Chetty Road, T Nagar.

⛁⛁–⛁⛁⛁ **Harrisons Hotel** – *315, Valluvar Kottam High Road, Nungambakkam, Chennai 600034. ☏044 4222 2777. www.harrisonshotels.com. ♿. 40 rooms.* ☕ ▤. An old name in Chennai, Harrisons was started in 1885, renovated many times and has finally evolved into an upscale boutique hotel. Dynasty, Meenam and Eden serve Chinese, Indian and Veg Conti fare.

⛁⛁ **Grand Orient** – *693, Anna Salai, (Near Anand Theatre), Chennai 600006. ☏044 2852 4111. www.empeehotels.com. 63 rooms.* ☕ ▤. A decent business hotel with multi-cuisine restaurant, coffee shop, business centre and Speed, a pub that hosts DJ nights on weekends *(6pm onwards)*. The same chain also runs the 50-room **Hotel Victoria** in Egmore *(☏044 2819 3638/1592)*.

SOUTH CHENNAI

⛁⛁⛁⛁ **Hilton Chennai** –*124/1 Jawaharlal Nehru Road, Ekkaduthangal, Chennai 600032. ☏044 2225 5555. www.hilton.com. ♿. 204 rooms.* ☕ ▤. A business hotel that blends contemporary and traditional Indian decor, its rooftop pool-cum-lounge bar offers great views of the city. Try *kadaloram* (coastal cuisine) at Ayla, all-day dining at Vasco's, wine and cheese at Vintage Bank, or the cafe in the spacious lobby. Located close to Olympia Tech Park.

Lemon Tree Hotel – *72 Sardar Patel Road, Guindy, Chennai 600032. 044 4423 2323. www.lemontreehotels.com. 108 rooms.* Upscale business hotel with award-winning accommodation, Lemon Tree has 15 hotels in 12 cities. Has a pool, 24hr multi-cuisine coffee shop (Citrus Café), hip bar (Slounge) and complimentary high-speed Wi-Fi access in the business center *(30min per day in room)*. Close to Tidel park, opp. Raj Bhavan.

Le Royal Meridien – *1 GST Road, St Thomas Mount, Chennai 600016. 044 2231 4343. www.leroyalmeridien-chennai.com. 240 rooms.* A white edifice spread over 1.4ha/3.5 acres with rooms in warm earthy tones overlooking a swimming pool, gardens and a fitness centre. Three restaurants – all-day International cuisine (Cilantro), speciality seafood (Kayal) and Royal Indian cuisine (Navaratna), besides two bars, a pub and a discotheque.

The Trident –*1/24, GST Road, St Thomas Mount, Chennai 600027. 044 2234 4747. www.tridenthotels.com. 167 rooms.* Set in a 2ha/5 acre-property landscaped by gardens, this low-rise red and white building is a refreshing break from the soaring 5-star edifices in Chennai. Samudra serves good coastal Indian cuisine, Cinnamon stirs up International fare all day long while Arcot is a swanky bar.

The Checkers – *30, Mount Road, Little Mount, Saidapet, Chennai 600015. 044 4399 4399. www.thecheckers hotel.com. 89 rooms.* Good-value hotel near Saidapet Church with two bars and three restaurants – Oriental cuisine at Crystal Jade, all day dining at Stimulation *(buffet Rs.700)* and 361 Degree rooftop grill and bistro. Hang out at Bartini Lounge Bar or catch Groove Nites *(every Sat 8.30pm)* at Wet, Sky Pool & Lounge – if you want a good night's sleep, request a room away from the revelry. Street-facing rooms on the upper floors have good views of the city.

Fortune Select Palms – *142, Rajiv Gandhi Salai (Old Mahabalipuram Road), Thoraipakkam, Chennai 600096. 044 3988 4444. www.fortunehotels.in. 129 rooms.* Part of a large pan-India chain, this business hotel comes equipped with a business centre, swimming pool, health club, a 24hr coffee shop, Zodiac, and Nostradamus Bar & Lounge. The Oriental Pavilion serves good Chinese.

Radisson Blu GRT Hotel – *531 GST Road, St Thomas Mount, Chennai 600016. 044 2231 0101/9789810101. www.radissonblu.com/hotel-chennai. 101 rooms.* A hotel renowned for its excellent service and modern rooms with wooden flooring. Enjoy extensive breakfasts at the poolside Garden Café, choose from 180 succulent kebabs at The Great Kabab Factory or canter into Gallop, the English polo club-inspired bar. Other perks include relaxing foot massages and free Internet access throughout the hotel.

Raj Palace Sundar – *12, Dr. Durgabai Deshmukh Road, Raja Annamalai Puram, Chennai 600028. 044 2493 8888/9566068888. www.hotelrajpalacesundar.com. 36 rooms.* An economy business hotel bang opposite Sathya Studios, with Durga Park restaurant serving *thali* meals *(Rs.99 onwards)* besides a rooftop café, Obul.

NORTH CHENNAI

Ambassador Pallava – *30, Montieth Road, Egmore, Chennai 600008. 044 2855 4476. www.ambassador india.com. 100 rooms.* High ceilings, teak furniture and hand-picked art imbue the hotel with an old-world charm. Besides one of the largest antique collections, it has a swimming pool, health club, squash facilities and a 24hr coffee shop. Serves Indian, Continental and Chinese cuisine.

The Pride Hotel – *216, EVR Periyar Salai, Poonamalee High Road, Kilpauk, Chennai 600010. 044 4398 9898. www.pridehotel.com. 115 rooms.* The clean and tidy rooms have a contemporary feel. The hotel has a rooftop restaurant, pool, Cafe Treat all-dining café, Casablanca multi-cuisine, Puran da Dhaba, Fuel Bar and Exhale, a fitness room, massage parlour and spa with jacuzzi and steam.

Comfort Inn Marina Towers – *2A, Ponniamman Koil Street, Egmore, Chennai 600008. 044 2858 5454. www.cimarinatowers.com. . 113 rooms.* . This decent business hotel with a lobby lounge has Stop cafe, Upper Deck bar and Seven restaurant.

Hotel Vestin Park – *39, Montieth Road, Egmore, Chennai 600008. 044 6642 3850/2852 7171. www.vestinpark.com. . 65 rooms & 5 suites.* . A typical value-for-money hotel, Splendour multi-cuisine serves an extensive buffet of over 30 items *(Rs.399)* and the rooftop restaurant Night Queen offers Malay & Arabic food.

Royal Regency – *26 & 27 Poonamallee High Road, Periamet, Chennai 600003. 044 2561 1777. www.regencygroupch.com. 103 rooms.* . Part of the Regency group, a local hotel chain that runs two more hotels near Egmore station (**Royal Paris**, **Royal Star**). All rooms are air-conditioned and Wi-Fi enabled and there is a multi-cuisine restaurant.

Chandra Park – *9, Gandhi Irwin Road, Egmore, Chennai 600008. 044 2819 1177/4050 6060. www.hotelchandrapark.com. 81 rooms.* . A reasonably priced business hotel near Egmore railway station, it has Taste Buds – a restaurant, Express coffee shop and 70mm, a bar.

WEST CHENNAI

Ambica Empire – *79, Jawaharlal Nehru Road, Vadapalani, Chennai 600026. 044 2362 1818/2362 1986. www.ambicaempire.com. . 100 rooms.* . Slightly pricey considering its location, however Ambica comes with an ayurvedic spa, Million Dollars pub and Green Chillies 24hr coffee shop, known for its Andhra delicacies and Midnight Biryani.

Radha Regent – *171, Jawaharlal Nehru Road, Arumbakkam, Chennai 600106. 044 6677 8899. www.radharegent.com. . 91 rooms.* . A smart-looking hotel with a high atrium lobby, which allows light to shimmer through the translucent roofing. The lobby-level Café in the Park, Aura Lounge Bar and Geoffrey's Pub are quite active. Oriental Blossom serves Szechwan and live teppanyaki grill while Sunday brunch *(12noon–4pm)* offers 99 delicacies and unlimited imported wine.

AROUND CHENNAI

Asiana Hotel – *1/238, Old Mahabalipuram Road (OMR), Semmencherry, Chennai 600119, 20km south of Adyar on OMR, after Infosys and TCS. 044 674 11000. www.asianahotels.com. . 114 rooms.* . Spread over 0.9ha/2.25 acres in the heart of the IT corridor, this stylish hotel offers great service and several dining options – Caramel, a 24hr multi-cuisine restaurant *(lunch buffets Rs.750)*, Silk, a Thai restaurant *(closed Mon)*, Wild Fire Speciality Grill *(closed Tue)*, iLounge Bar and Bytes, a 24hr Patisserie.

Vivanta by Taj Fisherman's Cove – *Covelong Beach, Kanchipuram District 603112, 40km south of Chennai Airport on ECR, turn left after Muttukadu Boating Point and ECR Dhaba. 044 6741 3333. www.vivantabytaj.com. . 138 rooms.* . Built on the ramparts of an old 18C Dutch fort, the 9ha/22-acre seaside hotel offers plush rooms, beachfront cottages and Scandinavian villas with views of the Bay of Bengal. The 929sq m/10,000sq ft swimming pool comes with its own plunge bar. With a choice of restaurants serving exotic seafood, Med and Continental fare (Bay View, Upper Deck, Seagull) and the signature Jiva Spa, this is luxury at its best.

Green Meadows Resort – *4/364-A, Anna Salai, Palavakkam, off ECR, Chennai 600041. On ECR turn left after Midway restaurant onto MGR Salai, turn right to Anna Salai. 044 2451 5555/5556/9840506986, 91761 48646. www.greenmeadowsresort.com. . 22 rooms.* . Just 100m from Palavakkam Beach and close to the theme parks on ECR is a piece of Kerala in Tamil Nadu. Lining the palm-fringed garden are unique heritage cottages, relocated piece by piece from Kerala and painstakingly reassembled. Stay in the century-old Era House built by Rajaraja Kaimal of the Thainadam Family or the Little Poovarani House once owned by an aristocratic Catholic plantation family. Kerala cuisine and seafood complete the picture.

EAT

Bustling with coffee shops, meal joints and popular veg chains, Chennai's eclectic eateries go beyond the South Indian stereotype. Tamilian cooks experiment with dynamic menus of mini fried ***idlis***, ***uthappams*** and ***dosas*** all with assorted fillings and spicy, tangy or sweet chutneys. Besides Dindigul Biryani, Madurai specialities, Chettinad cuisine and fusion food, Chennai's 5-star restaurants also stir up excellent Frontier and Continental fare while speciality restaurants serve Thai, Malaysian, Italian, American, Mexican and Mediterranean. Anna Nagar, T Nagar, Nungambakkam, Mylapore and Triplicane are packed with dining options, while seaside shacks at Elliot's Beach sell fresh fried seafood.

INDIAN

Anjappar Chettinad Restaurant – *J.P. Tower, 7/2, Nungambakkam High Road, Chennai 600034. 044 2821 7200/ 2825 6662/4214 4573. www.anjappar.com. . Open daily 11am–11pm.* For those who have had their fill of vegetarian fare. Established in 1964 and 25 outlets strong, Anjappur is known for its authentic Chettinad cuisine; besides mutton, chicken and seafood prepared in every possible ***masala*** and method, it flaunts exotic dishes like rabbit ***chukka*** (dry), ***kadai*** roast (quail) and ***kavuni arisi*** (black rice pudding).

Dindigul Thalappakatti Restaurant – *Venkatanarayana Road, T Nagar, Chennai 600042. 044 4550 6263. www.thalappakatti.com. . Open daily 11am–4pm, 6pm–12midnight.* Started in 1957 by Mr Nagasamy Naidu, it was the ***thalapa*** (traditional head dress) he wore that gave birth to the iconic brand 'Thalappakatti'. Its fame has inspired a slew of imitations. Besides various types of ***parotta*** (***Burma, adai kari, bunnu***), try the ***biryanis*** made of scented ***jeeragasamba*** rice and served with the signature ***dalcha*** (lentil mutton vegetable stew). Other outlets in Anna Nagar, Velachery and Nungambakkam ***(opp. Park Hotel)***.

Ente Keralam – *1, Kasturi Ranga Avenue 1st Street, Poes Garden, Kasturi Estate, Chennai 600018. 044 4232 8585. www.entekeralam.in. . Open daily 12.30–3.30pm, 7–11pm.* The taste of Kerala in the heart of Tamil Nadu. ***Lacy appams*** are passé; go for ***karimeen pollichathu*** (grilled Pearlspot in banana leaf), ***Thiruvananthapuram***-style ***kozhi varuthathu*** (deep-fried chicken), ***vazhapoo*** Cutlets (banana blossom patties), ***erachi ularthiyathu*** (beef fry Syrian Christian style) and other unpronounceable delights from God's Own Country. ***Biriyanis*** range from the mild ***moplah biriyani*** from Thalassery to the spicy ***kappa*** (tapioca) ***biriyani*** with beef.

Madurai Appu – *134/2, Triplicane High Road, Triplicane, Chennai 600005. 044 2858 0786/2859 1515/2859 2929. www.maduraiappu.com. . Open daily 12noon–11pm.* Run by a family of restaurateurs, Madurai Appu has five outlets in Chennai serving great Chettinad cuisine. Fluffy ***parottas*** are served with turkey, rabbit, quail and seafood and its signature dish is ***biryani*** cooked in firewood. Indian, Chinese and Tandoori are other options.

Ponnusamy Hotel – *55/1, Gowdia Mutt Road, Royapettah, Chennai 600014. 044 2813 0986/2813 3067. www.ponnusamyhotels.com. . Open daily 12noon–4pm, 7–11pm.* Started in 1954 as a small mess, Ponnusamy specialises in South Indian and Chettinad fare. Present in Chennai's leading malls, it has 11 outlets across India besides Dubai and Singapore. Fish ***varuval***, chicken ***varuval***, pepper chicken, chicken roast, chicken ***kozhambu*** and mutton fry are timeless classics, while fish ***poriyal***, ***kaadai*** (quail), pigeon, rabbit and crab provide variety.

Saravana Bhavan – *Y-209, 2nd Avenue, Anna Nagar, Chennai 600040. 044 2480 2577/2626 9721. www.saravanabhavan.com. . Open Mon–Sun, 6am–10.30pm.* Chennai's legendary pure-veg restaurant has 27 outlets in India and a global imprint in 10 countries from Europe to the Far East. Besides the staple ***dosa***, ***uthappam*** and ***idli***, there's more elaborate Indian and Chinese fare with ice cream and sundaes. Signature dishes are ***medhu vadai*** and ***kaima idli (spiced up leftover idli)*** served with ***raita***.

Murugan Idli Shop – *77-1/A GN Chetty Road, T Nagar, Chennai 600017. 044 2815 5462/4202 5076/9940238928. www.muruganidlishop.com.* *Open Mon–Sun, 9am–11pm.* There are ***idli*** shops and then there's Murugan Idli Shop. Soft steaming ***idlis*** of special ***ponni*** rice served on banana leaf with four types of chutney and ***sambar***. Oil and ***podi*** (chilli lentil powder) are charged separately. ***Vadai, dosai, uthappam*** and ***pongal*** are also on the menu. South Indian meals have recently been introduced across their 10 Chennai outlets.

Sangeetha Vegetarian Restaurant – *24, South Mada Street, near Mylapore Tank, Mylapore, Chennai 600004. 044 2464 3898. www.sangeethahotel.com.* *Open Mon–Sun, 6am–11pm.* Started as a tiny shack in 1984, Sangeetha is now a network of 21 vegetarian restaurants. Reasonably priced and very popular, it's known for its meals *(Rs.250)*, mini ***idlis*** and daily 'specials', exotic fare served at particular times – ***thuvarai adai dosai*** and ***kadubu idli (daily 4–11pm), vathakolambu satham*** and ***ela adai (Sat 5–10pm), rava vaangi bath*** and ***nendrapazham jamun (Sun 5–11pm)*** and ***gowni arisi idiappam*** with stew, ***arisi rava upma, palak bhatura***, sweet ***appam*** and ***chikku kesari*** on weekends. Wash it all down with South Indian filter coffee.

MULTI-CUISINE

Mainland China – *Sri Nivas Tower, Ground Floor, Cenotaph Road, Teynampet, Chennai. 044 4500 0236/ 2431 2168. www.mainlandchinaindia.com.* *Open daily 12noon–3.30pm, 7–11.30pm.* The largest chain of fine dining eateries in the country, Mainland China is satisfaction guaranteed. Crackling Spinach, Peking Duck, Sizzling Egg-plant with Spicy Tomato Garlic Sauce and Drunken Chicken in Shaoxiang wine are perennial favourites. There is another outlet in Hotel Tulip Aruna Complex in Nungambakkam.

Baan Thai – *10, Khader Nawaz Khan Road, Nungambakkam Chennai 600034. 044 2833 2611. www.baanthai.in.* *Open daily 12noon–3.30pm, 7–11.30pm.* If *'pee-pla-talay-gal-koong'* sounds like an oriental tune it's time to get a culinary education at Baan Thai. That's crab, fish, mixed seafood, chicken and prawn, available in a choice of fried and curried variants with noodles and rice. ***Por pir tod*** (spring rolls with glass noodles and ground chicken) and ***bai krapow kai*** (chicken with basil leaves) are great starters, served with dips.

Barbeque Nation – *Shri Devi Park Hotel, 1 Hanumantha Road, North Usman Road, T Nagar, Chennai 600017. 044 6060 0000/6453 0160/9381512199. www.barbeque-nation.com.* *Open daily 12.15–3.15pm, 7.15–11.30pm.* Live barbecue grills on the table and an 'all the meat you can eat' philosophy, Barbeque Nation is unlimited and unabashed in its approach. The daily menu consists of a choice of starters, soups and main courses, with ***roti*** and ***naan***, veg salads and desserts. To do justice to it, you need to fast for a day before going (and fast for a day after you return).

Benjarong – *146, T.T.K. Road, Chennai 600018. 044 2432 2640/4211 0061. www.benjarong.in.* *Open Mon–Sun, 12.15–2.45pm, 7.15–11.15pm.* Named after Thai painted porcelain in 'five colours', Benjarong is easily Chennai's top Thai restaurant. Excellent seafood, good ambience and classics including ***tom yum*** prawn soup and char-grilled duck. ***Phak vollappa*** (stir fry vegetables), ***gai hor baitey*** (chicken wrapped in pandanus leaves), ***pla rad prik*** (fish fillet in sweet basil sauce) and ***goong tod samunpai*** (crispy fried prawns in tamarind sauce).

Crimson Chakra/Cornucopia – *13, First Crescent Road, Gandhi Nagar, Adyar, Chennai 600020. 044 4211 5664, 9677277900. www.crimsonchakra.in.* *Open daily 12.30–3.30pm, 7.30–10.45pm.* A unique dining experience, this is fusion food at its best. ***Kheema biriyani***, crabmeat ***kulchas*** and Mom's Fish Curry to more unfamiliar fare like Drumstick Silk Curry, Roast Chilli Orange Duck Acapulco and Warm Prawn Beanthread Noodle Salad. Nibble on the complimentary hot bread before the food arrives. The Lebanese spread is equally impressive.

Sparkys Diner – *15, East Spurtank Road, Chetpet, Chennai 600031. 044 4263 4233. www.sparkysindia.com. . Open Mon–Fri, 12noon–11pm.* Authentic American dining from a rotund cook with a credo 'Never trust a skinny chef!' A menu inspired by his travels, Chef Thomas dishes out Hawaiian, Mexican, Australian and American classics like Philly Beef Steak Sandwich and Cajun Cola Chicken. In true Yankee style, the burgers are juicy and portions enormous.

Bella Ciao – *Lounge Beach Garden, 4, Shri Krishna Enclave, Kottivakkam, Chennai 600041. 044 2451 1130. www.bellaciao.in. . Open daily 11.30am–3.30pm, 6pm–11pm.* Started in 1998 by Italian chef Ciro Cattaneo, Bella Ciao is Chennai's first authentic Italian restaurant. The al fresco restaurant in a lovely bungalow near the beach serves famous wood-fired oven pizzas, home-made pastas, steaks and 18 organic salads. Pork chops and lamb in red wine come highly recommended.

Pelita Nasi Kandar – *17–18, Appaswamy Towers, Sir Thyagaraya Road, T Nagar, Chennai 600017. 044 2433 5759. www.pelita.com.my. . Open daily 10am–11pm.* A famous Malaysian restaurant chain with 27 outlets, their only overseas branch happens to be in Chennai. The name comes from Indian Muslim street food in Colonial Malaysia, where assorted meats and *nasi* (rice) would be hawked around on a yoke *(kandar)*. *Sambal udang* (tiger prawns in spicy curry) and *burung puyuh* (fried quail) are exemplary.

Texas Fiesta – *17/2, Shafee Mohammed Road, off Khader Nawaz Khan Road, Thousand Lights, Chennai 600006. 044 4308 7882. www.texasfiesta.in. . Open daily 11am–3.30pm, 7–11pm.* The best Tex Mex cuisine in town with traditional *quesadillas*, *enchiladas*, *tortillas* and *burritos*. Chicken Wings with Raging Buffalo Sauce and Grilled Tenderloin with Mexican Rice are hot favourites.

CAFES

Barista – *77, Rosy Towers, near MOP Vaishnav College, MG Road. 044 4214 4393. www.barista.co.in. Open daily 8am–11.30pm. Prices start at Rs.60.* Owned by Italy's largest coffee company, Lavazza, 200 espresso bars dot 30 cities in India, with nine in Chennai (Besant Nagar, T Nagar, Mylapore, etc). The barista (brewmaster) uses choicest Arabica beans and brews the Italian way. Good wraps, sandwiches, exclusive merchandise and classy ambience.

Café Coffee Day – *5, Rutland Gate, Khader Nawaz Khan Road, Nungambakkam. 044 6462 7082. www.cafecoffeeday.com. Open daily 10am–11pm. Prices start at Rs.40.* In malls, IT parks, colleges, offices to any available nook, India's largest coffee conglomerate has 70 outlets in Chennai alone. Fresh coffee beans are sourced from estates in Chickamagalur and tea and cold drinks are also available. Affordable prices and short eats makes it a popular youth hangout.

Qwiky's – *G7, Gee Gee Emerald, 151, Village Road, Nungambakkam, Chennai 600034. 044 8255 275, 8255 289. Open daily 11am–10.30pm. Prices start at Rs.40.* Chennai's own homegrown coffee pub with 70 outlets across India, Qwiky's has a strong presence in the South. Not perceived as hip and happening like its flashier counterparts, it is still the only chain to serve genuine South Indian filter coffee. You'll find Qwiky's coffee islands in large retail stores.

LEISURE

AKDR Golf Village – *3/381, Rajiv Gandhi Salai (OMR), Mettukuppam, Chennai 600 097. 044 2496 1617. www.akdrgolfvillage.com. Open Mon–Sun, 6am–9pm. Rs. 50 entrance, Rs.600–750/hr.* If the members-only Madras Golf Club or MGC is out of bounds, try AKDR! A nine-hole pitch and putt course, practice greens, 200m/220yd driving range with 15 sheltered bays, a pro shop, cafe; it's got the works. Courses for kids and beginners are available, as well as advanced lessons for pros and golf clubs and balls on hire.

Offroad Sports – *168/17 Pattipulam on ECR, 603104. 9840922122. www.offroadecr.com. Open Mon–Thu 10am–8.30pm, Friday 10am–9pm, Sat–Sun 9am–9pm. Rs. 500.* For an adrenaline rush, drop by at Offroad Sports, just 6km after Crocodile Bank and 8km before Mamallapuram on the ECR. Ride ATVs on the beach, on mud tracks or in the woods, camp in tents in casuarina groves, raft in the backwaters or play paintball.

Madras Boat Club – *2, 3rd Avenue, Boat Club Road, RA Puram, Chennai 600028. ☏044 2435 4751/2433 9289. www.madrasboatclub.in. Open Mon–Sun, 6am–10am and 3.30pm–6pm.* Established in 1867, MBC is one of the oldest rowing centres in India. Located on the Adyar River, this is where races, swimming and summer rowing camps are organised and temporary rowing memberships are allotted.

Muttukadu Boat House – *Muttukadu, East Coast Road. ☏044 2747 2369. www.tamilnadutoursim.org. Open Mon–Sun, 9am–5pm. Rs.130 (rowing boat 30min), Rs.300 (powerboat), Rs.450 (speedboat 10min).* Located 36km south of Chennai on the ECR, the boathouse in a TTDC-run complex offers boat rides and sailing in the serene backwaters of Muttukadu. The main thrill is taking the boat under a gently rocking bridge over the backwaters. Besides regular competitions and training camps, a windsurfing regatta is organised every year in Feb.

Royal Enfield – *Tiruvottiyur High Road, Tiruvottiyur, Chennai 600019. ☏044 4223 0361 (Rahul Shankhwar). www.royalenfield.com. Open 2nd & 4th Sat only, factory visit 10.30am. Rs. 600.* Peep into the factory of the world's oldest motorcycle manufacturers to see how a legend is born. Watch the fascinating manufacturing process of Bullet 350, the longest running model in constant production, made in India at this factory since 1955. Factory tours are organised on prior appointment. Pay visitor fees at the factory during the time of visit.

SHOPPING

SHOPPING MALLS

Ampa Skywalk – *1, Nelson Manickam Road, 627 Poonamalee High Road, Aminjikarai, Chennai 600029. ☏044 3024 9494/4218 6677/2374 2140. www.ampaskywalk.com. Open daily 10am–9pm.* Spread over 279sq m/300,000sq ft, SkyWalk is a spacious glass and aluminum structure with multi-level car parking of up to 12 floors. The 650-seater food court F3 (Food, Fun, Frolic) caters to 19 cuisines with five fine dining restaurants. Besides a 929sq m/10,000sq ft gaming zone, a four-row bowling alley and PVR Multiplex, Skywalk also boasts Chennai's first ice-skating rink Pandora *(Rs.200 for 30min, tutors provided)* and Tata Star Bazaar. On the 5th floor of the mall is Skywalk Hotel, a 20-room boutique hotel *(Rs.4,000)*.

Citi Centre – *10–11, Radhakrishnan Salai, Mylapore, Chennai 600004. ☏044 4351 8181/4351 8282. www.chennaiciticenter.com. Open daily 10am–9pm.* The only mall along Chennai's Beach Road stretch, Citi Centre is built in Neoclassical style, has an INOX Multiplex with seven screens, a LifeStyle outlet and Fun City for children. Besides familiar food joints like KFC, Subway, Pizza Hut and Barista, the mall also has local icons like Sangeetha, Ponnusamy and Gangotree. Limited parking is a problem.

Express Avenue – *Club House Road, Express Estate, Royapettah, Chennai. ☏044 43204040. www.expressavenue.in. Open daily 10am–10pm.* Another massive mall with top fashion and lifestyle brands and popular outlets like Big Bazaar, Westside, LifeStyle and Marks & Spencer. A busy food court, Fun City for kids and Escape Multiplex (a subsidiary of Sathyam Cinemas) dominate the top

Chennai Shopping

Shopping in Chennai can be rather hectic. A range of products entice an avid buyer; from Tanjore paintings and Chola bronzes to Kanjeevaram silks, cotton and other fabrics, gold jewellery, Auroville products, carvings in wood and stone, antique furniture, exquisite handicrafts, *deepams* (traditional lamps), *oonjals* (wrought iron swings)… the list is endless. Go pavement shopping at Pondy Bazaar, Cotton Market at Pantheon Road and Ranganathan Street at T Nagar, trawl the branded showrooms and malls on Anna Salai or stumble on treasures in quaint boutiques.

floor. There's also EMO, a non-alcoholic pub! The amount of available parking is decent, though expensive.

Spencer Plaza – *768–769, Anna Salai, Chennai 600002. ☏044 2849 1001. www.mangaltirth.com. Open daily 10am–11pm.* Reconstructed in 1985 on the site of India's first department store set up in 1863, Spencer is perhaps the oldest shopping mall in the country and was the only one in Chennai for decades. Spread over 11,600sq m/125,000sq ft and three phases, Spencer's has 400 shops including Cottage Emporium and Westside. Good for electronics and last-minute souvenir shopping.

MARKETS

Parry's Corner – *George Town, Chennai 600079.* Bustling colourful market with sweet shops, stores selling wedding cards, electronics stores and Empire Plaza, an entire building dedicated to optical products. Burma Bazaar nearby is great for imported goods while the century-old Evening Bazaar near Central Station sells vessels, furnishings and mats *(paayi)*, hence its popular name, Paayi Kadai.

Pondy Bazaar – *Near Panangal Park, T Nagar, Chennai 600017.* Large branded outlets, jewellery stores and cheek-by-jowl makeshift shops on the pavement selling footwear, bags, costume jewellery, watches, toys, crockery, kitchen appliances and everything else under the sun.

SPECIALITY SHOPS AND DESIGNER BOUTIQUES

Amethyst – *14, Jeypore Colony, Padmavathi Road, Gopalapuram, Chennai 600086. ☏044 2835 3581. www.amethystchennai.com. Open daily 10am–10pm.* A boutique and makeshift theatre space in an old Colonial-style house, Amethyst has exotic Indian jewellery, designer clothes, toiletries and a garden cafe that serves croissants and coffee.

Naturally Auroville Boutique – *30, Khader Nawaz Khan Road, Nungambakkam, Chennai 600006. ☏044 2821 7517/9840162008. www.auroville.org. Open Mon–Sat, 10.30am–8.30pm.* A great place to pick up Auroville's eclectic mix of products – pottery, bedspreads, scented candles, aromatherapy oils, organic coffees, breads and cheese. Also run an outlet in Besant Nagar.

Poompuhar Emporium – *818, Anna Salai, Chennai 600002. ☏044 8520 624/8550 157. www.poompuhar.org. Open Mon–Sat, 10am–8pm. Closed Sun.* A State-run emporium of the Tamil Nadu Handicrafts Development Corporation, it offers treasures the state is famous for – Tanjore art, Bronze sculptures, brass lamps, wooden craft, stone carvings, gems, artefacts and *kalamkari* and batik prints.

SIPA's Craftlink – *70, Kodambakkam High Road, Chennai 600034. ☏044 28257544/5. www.sipa-in. Open Mon–Sat, 9.30am-8pm. Closed Sun.* A fair trade federation of South India Producers Association, the collective work of over 7000 skilled artisans can be found here. Basketry, decorative candles, ceramic crockery, lampshades, lacquerware, kalamkari textiles, wooden products, stationery and more.

BOOKSHOPS

Crossword – *HPCL, new No. 47, old No. 82, TTK Road, Alwarpet, Chennai 600018. ☏044 4203 1705/4203 2096. www.crossword.in. Open daily 10.30am–9pm.* One of the most admired and awarded retail stores, Crossword has emerged as India's fastest growing chain of bookshops. 83 outlets at last count and only one in Chennai *(next to the flyover opp. Indian Oil petrol bunk)*, it has a wide range and serves as a platform for book launches, authors, poets and musicians.

Higginbotham's – *116, Anna Salai, Chennai. ☏044 2851 3519/2851 3520. www.higginbothamsstore.com. Open Mon–Sat 9am–7.30pm, Sun 10.30am–7.30pm.* Set up in 1844, Chennai's oldest bookshop and also the oldest in the country, Higginbotham's is an institution. Conspicuous at platform stalls of the Southern Railways, today it has 22 outlets in South India. Go to the Anna Salai store for old-world charm.

Landmark – *3, Apex Plaza, opp. Ispahani Centre, Nungambakkam High Road, Chennai 600034. ☏044 2822 1000/2823 9333. www.landmarkonthenet.com. Open daily 9am–9pm.* Books, movies, music, games, toys, regular quizzes, book-launches and music performances. Also Citi Centre, Spencer Plaza (Phase 2) and Ampa Skywalk.

Odyssey – *45–47, 1st Main Road, Gandhi Nagar, behind Adyar bus terminus, Chennai 600020. ✆044 2442 0393/2440 2264. www.odyssey.in. Open daily 10am–10pm.* A part of the Deccan Chronicle group, Odyssey runs 50 stores across 13 cities and 12 outlets in Chennai, selling music, movies, gifts, cards, toys, stationery, multimedia, et al. Adyar is the flagship store, though it's also present in Anna Nagar, ECR, SkyWalk and Express Avenue.

Oxford Bookstore – *Apeejay House, 39/12, Haddows Road, Chennai 600006. ✆044 2822 7711. www.oxfordbookstore.com. Open daily 9am–9pm.* Over 70,000 titles across 45 sections along with music and gifts, Oxford comes with a Cha Bar, a gallery/event space for readings, live music, theatre sessions and interactive discussions. Besides the usual fare, it has eclectic publishers like Kali, Tara, Katha and Zubaan.

PERFORMING ARTS

C.P. Ramaswami Aiyar Foundation – *The Grove, 1 Eldams Road, Chennai 600018. ✆044 2434 1778. www.cprfoundation.org. Open daily 9am–5pm.* A foundation that promotes India's cultural heritage, it is based in the ancestral home of noted jurist, administrator and statesman C.P. Ramaswami Aiyar. The C.P. Art Centre has three galleries where exhibitions, seminars, performances and lec-dems of contemporary and folk art and crafts are held. Besides art workshops and courses, a renovated ***vennirul*** (bathhouse) serves as an art gallery showcasing antique Tanjore paintings, Ravi Varma oleographs and prints and sketches of old Madras and Tamil Nadu.

Kalakshetra – *Kalakshetra Foundation, Thiruvanmiyur, Chennai 600041. ✆044 2452 4057/2452 0836. www.kalakshetra.net. Open daily 8.30am–11.30am. Closed 2nd & 4th Sat every month and Govt. holidays.* Founded in 1936 by Rukmini and George Arundale to revive Bharatanatyam, Kalakshetra moved from the Theosophical Society to a sprawling 40ha/100-acre campus in Adyar. Visitors are welcome to see the old ***gurukul*** system being followed to teach dance, drama and fine arts. Every month free cultural events, art exhibitions and dance performances are organised at the ***koothambalam*** (auditorium) while the annual festival season *(Dec–Feb)* is a ticketed event. Short-term courses and a winter dance camp are also organised.

Music Academy – *New No. 168 (Old No. 306), TTK Road, Royapettah, Chennai 600018. ✆044 2811 2231/2811 5162. www.musicacademymadras.in. Open daily 8am–9.30pm.* Another Chennai institution, the Music Academy was set up in 1928 to encourage the study of Carnatic music. Even today, the academy organises classical music and dance programmes, annual conferences, music competitions and workshops on rare compositions. It is the main venue for the annual Chennai Festival *(15 Dec–1 Jan)*, with hundreds of performances including the December Music Festival, a Dance Festival in January and Spirit of Youth festival.

Rasika Ranjani Sabha – *30/1, Sundareswarar Street, Mylapore, Chennai 600004. ✆044 2494 1767. Open Mon–Sat, 9.30am–6.30pm.* One of Chennai's oldest and most prominent ***sabhas*** (cultural organisations), it has been conducting ***kutcheries*** (Carnatic concerts) since the 1920s. Its location in the culturally rich locale of Mylapore makes it a great venue to watch regular performances.

NIGHTLIFE

10 Downing Street – *Kences Inn, 50, BN Road, T Nagar Chennai 600017. ✆044 2815 2152. Open daily 11am–11pm.* A popular nightclub with live bands on Saturday night.

Flame Le Club – *Le Royal Meridien, 1 GST Road, St Thomas Mount, Chennai 600016. ✆044 2231 4343. www.leroyalmeridien-chennai.com. Open daily 7–11pm.* Funky club with a specially designed long bar, curved bar, a dance floor and a podium for live performances. Plus, world-class Apogee Sound!

Pasha – *The Park Hotel, 601, Anna Salai, Chennai 600006. ✆044 42676000. www.theparkhotels.com. Open Wed–Sun, 8.30–1.30am.* A small nightclub with low seating, Pasha is a hip hangout. Indipop evenings (Wed) are a rage.

Pondicherry

Highlights

- Auroville, the City of Dawn *p136*
- Sri Aurobindo Ashram *p137*
- Excursion to the Red Mountain *p140*
- French Quarter Heritage Walk *p142*

On a balmy evening in Pondicherry (officially renamed Puducherry in 2006), the aroma of Creole cuisine hangs in the air, local policemen sport red *kepis* like French *gendarmes* and men hurl *boules* instead of marbles as they play *pétanque*. It's no surprise why Pondicherry is often called La Côte d'Azur de l'Est or the French Riviera of the East. Once the famed 'Poduke', a 2C Roman trading post, the 'Pudu-cheri' (new settlement) to the south became the heart of a powerful French enclave that stretched to Mahe (Kerala), Yanam (Andhra) and Karaikal further south. Much to the chagrin of the British just 160km north at Chennai, Pondicherry gave sanctuary to revolutionary ideologues like Sri Aurobindo and Subramanya Bharathi, who left their indelible mark here. Today Pondy is a delectable melange of villas, art cafes, institutions and all things French.

PONDICHERRY

Located in an oval grid, Pondicherry is a walker's delight with well-organised streets and quaint signboards displaying street names in French and Tamil, and quite often their renamed Indian versions. Goubert Avenue (Beach Road) and Anna Salai form the town's eastern and western edges, connected by two arterial roads, Lal Bahadur Shastri (Bussy) Street and Jawaharlal Nehru Street. South Boulevard (Subbaiah Salai) and

Sacred Heart Church

North Boulevard (SV Patel Road), connected by MG Road and Ambour Salai, complete the oblong.

Excursions and day trips from the city include **Auroville**★ *(10km)* **Gingee Fort**★ *(68km)* and **Tiruvannamalai** *(106km)*, where **Arunachaleswara Temple**★★ and **Sri Ramanasramam**★ can be visited.

French Quarter★★ and Tamil Quarter★

The cobblestoned paths of the French Quarter with its charming yellow and white buildings is towards the beachfront while a canal separates it from the Tamil Quarter, which lies inland. More congested with closely stacked homes displaying rich vernacular architecture, the Tamil Quarter is further demarcated into a Hindu Quarter in the north, the Christian Quarter in the centre (around the **Immaculate Conception Cathedral**) and the Muslim Quarter to the south. **Sri Aurobindo Ashram**★ is in the north of the French Quarter, whereas the Promenade, other key sights and most upmarket hotels, guesthouses, restaurants, cafes and boutiques are concentrated in the wide streets towards the south of this quarter.

Evenings and early mornings are pleasant for walkers and joggers as the Beach Road remains a vehicle-free zone between 6pm and 7.30am.

see Historical Sights, Religious and Spiritual Sights.

- **Population:** 675,000 (2011 India census).
- **Info:** Tourist Information Centre, Pondicherry Tourism, 40, Goubert Avenue, Pondicherry 605001. 0413 233 9497. www.tourism.pondicherry.gov.in.
- **Location:** On the Coromandel Coast, 20km north of Cuddalore and 162km south of Chennai.
- **Kids:** The aquarium, toy train and musical fountain *(weekends only)* at the Botanical Gardens.
- **Timing:** Jul–Feb is ideal as the monsoon and winter months provide respite from the tropical summer.
- **Guided Tours:** PTDC organises sightseeing tours – a full day *(9.30am–5pm)* includes veg lunch *(Rs.200 non-AC, Rs.250 AC)*. *See also Planning Your Trip.*

GETTING THERE AND AROUND

GETTING THERE

BY AIR – The closest airport to Pondicherry is Chennai International Airport, 160km north.

BY TRAIN – Pondicherry Railway Station, to the town's south side, has a computerised booking service for southern trains but connectivity is poor. All express trains run once a week via Villupuram *(36km)*, the nearest railhead. The Chennai–Pondicherry Passenger/56037 leaves daily at 6.35am from Egmore Station and takes 4.5hr to reach Pondicherry and does the return trip at 2.40pm. Puducherry Express/12255 from Bangalore's Yesvantpur Junction every Friday 11.15pm *(arr. Sat 9.40am)*, Puducherry Express/16044 from Mangalore Central every Monday 4.10pm *(arr. Tue 8am)* and Howrah-Puducherry Express/12867 every Sunday 11.30pm *(arr. Tue 8.30am)* bypass Chennai. The New Delhi-Puducherry Express/22404 every Sunday 11.50pm *(arr. Tue 6.45pm)* and Bhubaneswar–Puducherry Express/12898 every Tuesday 12noon *(arr. Wed 1.35pm)* are via Chennai's Egmore Station.

BY BUS – There's good bus connectivity of both state transport (PRTC, TNSRTC) and private buses (Volvo) to Pondicherry. Buses depart at regular intervals from CMBT Koyambedu Bus Terminus in Chennai *(every 15–30min, 3hr)*, Chidambaram *(every 20min, 2hr)*, Kanchipuram *(10 daily, 3–4hr)*, Tiruchirapalli *(every 30min, 5–6hr)*, Madurai *(hourly, 9–10hr)* and Bangalore *(10 daily, 9hr)*. All local and long-distance buses stop at the New Bus Stand, 0.5km away on the town's western edge.

BY CAR – Being connected from all sides by a good highway network, the most preferred mode of transport to Pondicherry is by road. From Chennai *(160km north, 3.5hr, cabs charge Rs.2,500)* one can drive via East Coast Road or take the Grand Southern Trunk Road *(NH-45)* via Tindivanam. From Bangalore *(320km, 5–6hr)*, take NH-7 till Krishnagiri and then NH-66 via Gingee Fort. Pondicherry is also well connected to Cuddalore, Chidambaram, Karaikal, Nagapattinam and Velankanni to the south by NH-45A.

GETTING AROUND

BY BUS – PTDC runs daily buses that cover most important tourist spots in town, making it a hassle-free and economical way to discover Pondicherry.

BY TAXI – The main taxi stand is outside the bus stand and a day's sightseeing can cost upward of Rs.1,200.

BY 2-WHEELER – The best way to experience Pondicherry and Auroville *(10km north)* is on two wheels. Besides several rental agencies on Mission Street and MG Road, most lodges arrange bicycles *(Rs.40)* and motorbikes/scooties *(Rs.180–200)* on hire.

ON FOOT – PTDC, Sri Aurobindo Ashram and INTACH organise guided walks in Pondicherry across the French and Tamil Quarters.

The French Connection

In the early 16C, the Portuguese were the first Europeans to return to India for trade in spice and textiles. By the 17C the Dutch and Danes followed, while the British established a trading post in Madras in 1639. Quite late to the Colonial party, La Compagnie (the French East India Company) was set up in 1664. The French arrived at Pondicherry in 1670 by invitation of the Sultan of Bijapur to create a commercial lodge, and Pondicherry soon became their Port of Call *(l'escale)*. After control went briefly to the Dutch in 1693, it was soon back in French hands and Pondicherry became a prominent fortified town under Governors François Martin and Joseph-François Dupleix.

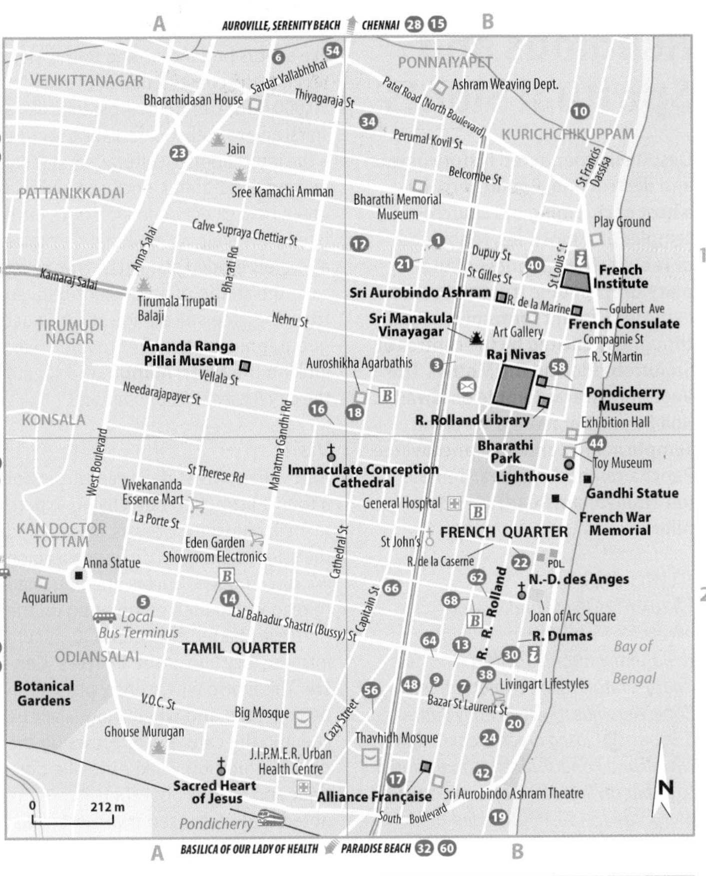

PONDICHERRY

WHERE TO STAY

Abi Krishna 2
Alps Residency (Hotel) 4
Anandha Inn 6
Annamalai International (Hotel) 8
Aurodhan 10
Calve 12
Clock Tower Hotel (The) 14
Coramandal Heritage (Hotel) 16
Corbelli (Hotel) 18
Dumas Guest House 20
Dupleix (Le) 22
Escale (L') 24
Europe (Hotel d') 26
Ginger 28
Gratitude 30
Maison Blanche (La) 32
Maison Perumal 34
Mass (Hotel) 36
Orient (Hotel de l') 38
Patricia Guest House 40
Pondicherry (Hotel de) 42
Promenade (The) 44
PR Pride Inn 46
Richmond (Hotel) 48
Sunway GRT Grand (The) 52
Surguru (Hotel) 54
Swades Guesthouse 56
Villa Bayoud 58
Villa Canelle 60
Villa Christophe 62
Villa Helena 64
Villa Indra 66
Villa Shanti 68

WHERE TO EAT

Aachiamma Chettinadu Restaurant 1
Adyar Ananda Bhavan 3
Anjappar Chettinad Restaurant 5
Bamboo Garden 7
Feu de Bois (Au) 9
Karai Chettinad Restaurant 11
Rendezvous Café Restaurant 13
Roma's Kitchen 15
Satsanga 17
Seagulls 19
Vietnam (Le) 21
West Boulevard Restaurant 23

Religious and Spiritual Sights

Despite its chequered history of war and destruction, Pondicherry has a host of charming old churches, temples and mosques, renovated or rebuilt. The openness of the place drew people from all over to explore different forms of spiritual thought as elicited by the centres of Sri Aurobindo and the Mother. The Vedapureswarar Temple on Iswaran Koil Street, Varadaraja Perumal Temple nearby and the Panchavatee Panchamukha Anjaneyar Temple (on Tindivanam Road) are other pilgrim sites.

AUROVILLE★

10km north of Pondicherry, accessible from ECR via Kuilapalayam or Bommayarpalayam (Old Auroville Road). Visitors' Centre, International Zone, Auroville. Open daily 9am–5.30pm. Closed lunch break 1–2pm, Diwali and Pongal. Matri Mandir closed to public on Sun afternoon. Entry free. Rs.5–50. Guided Tours: Contact Auroville Outreach Media. 0413 2622 204/2622 098. www.auroville.org. Credit cards accepted. For meditation inside Matri Mandir, book in person (10am–11am) or call 0413 2622268 (2–3pm), mmconcentration@auroville.org.in.

A Bit of History

Born out of the ideas of philosopher-yogi Sri Aurobindo to realise a new society through Divine Consciousness, Auroville was given concrete shape by his French-born disciple and life-long companion **Mirra Alfassa** (the Mother). Envisioned as a 'universal town where men and women of all countries live in peace and progressive harmony with a purpose to realise human unity', Auroville was formally established on 28 February, 1968. In a symbolic gesture, representatives of 124 countries and all Indian states placed a handful of earth from their homeland in an urn shaped like a lotus bud. According to the Master Plan, the construction of the city for 50,000 future residents is planned like a spiral galaxy with four radiating sectors – the international, cultural, residential and industrial zones, enclosed within a green belt. Over two million trees have been planted in an area that was once a severely eroded plateau with no cover save the shade of an ancient banyan tree. This tree still stands at the exact geographic centre of Auroville, overlooking the **Matri Mandir**, the soul of the city (*see sidebar opposite*).

Visit

Aurovillians insist their campus is not a tourist attraction but a living experiment in humanity. Flowers, incense and the usual trappings of organised religion are discouraged. Guests are requested to read wall panels elaborating on the Auroville Charter and watch a 10-minute introductory film at the **Visitors' Centre**. This is also where entry passes can be collected and where hours can be spent in the cafeteria or browsing the photo exhibition, Kalki Auroville boutique and Seagull bookshop. It must be noted that motorized transport is discouraged within the township.

Home to 2,200 residents from 45 nationalities living in small clusters over a 20sq km area, Auroville is a utopian concept. It can be approached from all sides as there are no compound walls to segregate it from the neighbouring villages. Nearly 125 commercial units operate in the commune and contribute a third of their revenue to maintain the self-sustaining campus.

Auroville's impressive product range includes handmade paper (Auroville Papers), indigo-dyed clothing (The Colours of Nature), incense (Encens d'Auroville), bodycare (Maroma Spa) to handicrafts, food products, metalwork, architecture and renewable energy. Every year a huge bonfire is organised at the Amphitheatre on 15 Aug, 21 Feb and 28 Feb in celebration of the birthdays of Sri Aurobindo, the Mother and Auroville itself.

© Anurag Mallick, Priya Ganapathy/MICHELaIN

Matri Mandir

Surrounded by beautiful gardens, the 29m/95ft-high high globe with a 36m/ 118ft diameter is the focal point of Auroville township and a place for quiet contemplation. Four access routes, named Mahakali, Maheshwari, Mahalakshmi and Mahasaraswati, lead into the Matri Mandir. Twelve petals in red sandstone enfold twelve meditation chambers, each named after the Mother's manifestations. In the core chamber, the White Room, a crystal orb placed at the centre taps a beam of sunlight as a symbol of future realisation. *Entry into the Matri Mandir is restricted and guests who obtain prior permission and passes to meditate inside are sent in two batches between 9.30–11am only.*

A shaded 1km footpath leads to the **Matri Mandir Viewing Point**, a raised garden area, south of the Park of Unity. An electric shuttle is available for people who find it difficult to walk. *For free passes to the Viewing Point contact Matri Mandir Info Centre; open Mon–Sat 9.45am–12.30pm, 1.45–4pm.*

SRI AUROBINDO ASHRAM★

At the intersection of Manakula Vinayagar Street and Rue de la Marine. Rue de la Marine, Pondicherry 605001. Open daily 8am–12noon, 2–6pm. Entry free. . Guided Tours: contact Bureau Central (0413 223 3604). 0413 222 4644/223 3644. www.sriaurobindoashram.org. Credit cards accepted. Children below 3yrs are not allowed. Camera, video, smoking and floral offerings are not allowed.

A Bit of History

Housed in a 150-year-old French building where Sri Aurobindo and the Mother lived for most of their lives, the Ashram is an oasis of serenity. When the Mother settled in Pondicherry in 1920 and the informal gathering of followers who flocked to learn Sri Aurobindo's Integral Yoga steadily increased, the Mother decided on collective organisation. With the vision of creating a space for followers to be free to pursue a spiritual path for the true actualisation of the Divine Self, the Ashram literally founded itself in 1926 and was moulded by the Mother over half a century. The Mother established Sri Aurobindo International Centre of Education (Ashram School) in 1952 and founded **Auroville**★ in 1968. In the central tree-shaded courtyard stands the flower-bedecked Samadhi enshrining the mortal remains of Sri Aurobindo and the Mother (who passed away in 1973). Visitors often sit around the Samadhi, with heads bowed in prayer.

Sri Aurobindo Ashram

© Anurag Mallick, Priya Ganapathy/MICHELIN

Visit

Behind its calm exterior, the Ashram buzzes with activity. The 1,500-strong community served by three generations of Ashramites work unselfishly, in the spirit of service with no hierarchy, successor or formula for life. Its 80 departments include farms, gardens, health care, guesthouses, engineering units, art studios and publications, among others. The complete works of Sri Aurobindo and the Mother are available at the SABDA bookshop in the main building and at Kripa, their outlet half a block away. Nearby is the **Bureau Central Office**, designed as an exhibition hall, which provides an introduction to the vision of Sri Aurobindo, the Mother and their method of spiritual practice, through permanent exhibits of photographs, videos and books. Daily tours are conducted for those interested in visiting the Ashram's various units. Accommodation is provided with prior booking in several Ashram guesthouses like The Retreat, Seaside and Park on Beach Road nearby. *(Bureau Central Information Centre: Cottage Complex, 3 Rangapillai Street, Pondicherry 605001; open 6am–8pm; 0413 223 3604; bureaucentral@sriaurobindoashram.org).*

SRI MANAKULA VINAYAGAR

2min walk south of Sri Aurobindo Ashram. Manakula Vinayagar Street. Open 5.45am–12.30pm, 4–9.30pm; Abhisheka 6.30am daily and 11am Mon–Thu. Temple closed festival days and holidays. Rs.10 (special entrance), child free. P. 0413 233 6544. www.manakulavinayagartemple.com. Dedicated to Lord Ganesha, the temple is believed to have been constructed five centuries ago. Legend has it that the old *kulam* (pond) on the west of the temple would get filled with *manal* (sand) since it was near the sea; hence it came to be known as 'Manakulam' Vinayagar. It is said that French missionaries tried in vain to pull the shrine down several times. One Frenchman threw the deity into the sea, but much to his amazement it miraculously returned to its place, and he eventually became a believer. Hence the deity is also referred as 'Vellakaran' (meaning white man or foreigner) Pillai. Various manifestations of Lord Ganesha adorn the inside walls. The 18-day **Brahmotsavam** and **Ganesh Chaturthi** are grand celebrations. Be sure to give a coin to the temple elephant Lakshmi in exchange for a friendly thump on the head from her trunk as blessing!

CHURCHES

Notre Dame des Anges

Parallel to Goubert Avenue, behind the Tourist Office. Access from Rue Surcouf. 3, Rue Dumas, Pondicherry 605001. Open daily 5.30am–7pm. P. 0413 233 4262.

Established by Capuchin friars who came from Chennai to Pondicherry in 1676, the Notre Dame des Anges (Church of Our Lady of Angels) was built in 1707 as an annexe to the St Louis Church inside the fort. Hence, its Tamil name Caps Kovil or 'Church of the Capuchins'. The church was destroyed in 1761 and rebuilt in 1855 in Greco-Roman style. Funds for its reconstruction came from Napoleon III, who also donated an oil painting of Our Lady of the Assumption, exhibited inside. The pastel peach exterior has given it another moniker, the Pink Church. Prayers are conducted here in French, making it the only church in Pondicherry that observes mass in three languages (English and Tamil being the other two). Don't miss **Marquis de Bussy's tomb** (1785) in an adjacent cemetery and a marble **statue of Joan of Arc** standing forlorn in an empty plot opposite the church.

Immaculate Conception Cathedral

Near VOC School. 204, Cathedral Street, Pondicherry 605001. Open daily. P. 0413 233 4262. www.pondicherryarchdiocese.org.

The story of Eglise de Notre Dame de la Conception Immaculée is one of resilience. First built by Jesuit fathers in 1692, the church was demolished within a year by the Dutch. Though hastily rebuilt in 1699, it soon collapsed. Shifted to its present site and reconstructed in 1728, the church was destroyed once more, this time by the British. But the church rose again; it was defiantly rebuilt a fourth time in 1791, and stands to this day. Structurally inspired by the Val-de-Grâce Church in Paris, the façade bears a statue of Our Lady with the infant Jesus in her arms. The church is also called Samba Kovil locally, a phonetic corruption of 'St Paul's Kovil'. The **Archbishop's House** next door, with its vaulted rooms and arcades, is worth a peep. The main festival, the Immaculate Conception of Blessed Virgin Mary, is celebrated on 8 December every year.

Sacred Heart of Jesus Church

At the junction of MG Road with South Boulevard opposite the railway station. 132, Sacred Heart Square, Subbiah Salai, Pondicherry 605001. Mass Mon–Sat 6am and 6pm, Sun 5.15pm. P. 0413 222 8916/222 5559. www.sacredheartpondy.com.

After the Archdiocese of Pondicherry was consecrated to the Sacred Heart of Jesus in 1895, a new church was commissioned on the town's southern side in 1902. Supported by 24 lofty columns, this neo-Gothic structure in red and white brick has an impressive entrance. The church's main attraction is its stained-glass windows of 28 saints and panels depicting scenes from the life of Jesus. The entrance door bears the Latin inscription *'sanctificavi locum istum, ut sit nomen meum ibi'* meaning 'I have consecrated this house, that my name be there forever. My eyes and my heart will be there forever'.

Recently renovated and elevated to the status of a basilica, the church has two grottos for Our Lady of Lourdes and the Sacred Heart of Jesus.

Basilica of Our Lady of Health

Located on a turn after Ariyankuppam Market en route to Chunnambar, 6km south of town on Cuddalore Road (NH-45A). Ariyankuppam, Pondicherry 605007. Open daily 6–9am, 4–9pm. P. 0413 260 0799.

In 1673, Armenians under the leadership of Bishop Adda Simon built the Church of Our Lady of Conception at Ariancoupam (Ariyankuppam), which was given to the Jesuits of the Carnatic Mission around 1700.

Under the new name of Our Lady of Health, the church became a popular pilgrim centre over the next three centuries. A 10-day feast is held every year in September between the first Friday

The Legend of Arunachala: Red Mountain

Arunachaleswar Temple is one of the five *pancha bhoota sthalams*, where Lord Shiva is worshipped as the sacred element fire. To put an end to the catastrophic fight between Vishnu and Brahma to prove who is greater, Shiva manifests himself as an *agni lingam* or column of fire and challenges them to find the top or bottom. Vishnu assumes the form of a boar and heads south to see the root while Brahma becomes a swan and flies heavenward. Vishnu soon gives up but Brahma encounters two *thazhambu* (ketaki) flowers that had been plummeting for ages, and entreats them to be false witnesses. However Brahma's lie is exposed and Shiva curses that Brahma would never be worshipped in temples, nor would the *ketaki* be used in Shiva worship. And thus the holy place where Shiva appeared as an inaccessible mountain *'annamalai'*, came to be known as Tiru-annamalai. To commemorate this event, every November during the 10-day Karthigai Deepam festival, priests on the summit of Arunachala light a massive sacred fire. It represents the fulfilment of Shiva's promise to reappear each year to remove the darkness of ignorance through light. The flame blazes for days and can be seen from 30km away. Thousands flock to see this marvel; when the fire is lit, many rush up the mountain to offer their libations, adding to the drama.

and the second Sunday when the church is at its festive best.

EXCURSION

Tiruvannamalai

Located north-west on NH-66 (Bangalore-Pondy Highway), 40km from Gingee and 106km from Pondicherry (2hr).

Arunachaleswara Temple★★

Arulmigu Arunachaleswara Temple, Tiruvannamalai 606601. 04175 252438. www.arunachaleswarar.com. Special entry Rs.20.

A mystical mountain that glints in the rays of the rising sun *(arun)*, where fiery skies form a blanket of red, the 818m/2,684ft-high **Mount Arunachala** or Annamalai *(See Sidebar, above)* is as holy as the Arunachaleswara Temple that lies at its base. Believed to be once an extinct volcano, in earlier *yugas* (Hindu eras) the hill was *agni* (fire), *manikkam* (emerald), *pon* (gold) and rock in the present age of Kaliyugam. There are eight *lingams* named after various gods marking the cardinal directions, giving an octagonal structure to the town – Agni Lingam, Yama Lingam, Niruthi Lingam, Varuna Lingam, Vayu Lingam, Kubera Lingam, Esanya Lingam and Indra Lingam, where the Arunachaleswara Temple is located.

Enter from the towering Raja Gopuram (East Tower) to reach the Kambattu Elayanar Murugan Temple, with the Shiva Ganga tank to the left and the 1,000-pillared *mandapam* to the right. Just ahead is the Patala *lingam* where Sri Ramana Maharishi is believed to have meditated while ants devoured his flesh. A large *nandi* statue stands to the front near the Sarva Siddhi Vinayak Temple. On the opposite side of Brahma *tirtham* (tank), is a shed where the temple elephant is housed. The *kili* (parrot) *gopuram* leads to an inner enclosure where the main temple stands. After worshipping Shiva at Arunachaleswara, devotees either ascend the holy mountain from the western tower (3–3.5hr) or do *girivalam* or *pradakshina*, a 14km circumambulation done barefoot (4hr). Besides the cave shrines of Skanda Asram, Guhe Namashivaya and Virupaksha, most of the 51 sights fall on the walking path dotted by ashrams, *mandapams*, *tirthas* (sacred spots) and *lingas*. Pavalakunnu (Coral Hill), en route to the bus stand, is ideal for a bird's eye view of the town and all the four temple towers. It's a 10min hike up 430 steps.

Sri Ramanasramam★

3km from the railway station and bus stand, 2km south-west of the temple at the town centre. Sri Ramanasramam

Arunachaleswara Temple with the Red Mountain in the background

© Anurag Mallick, Priya Ganapathy/MICHELIN

Post, Tiruvannamalai 606603. 04175 237200/9244937292. www.sriramanamaharishi.org. Open: office 7.30am–12.30pm, 2–6.30pm, bookshop 8–11am, 2–6pm.
Sri Ramana Maharishi, the legendary sage of Arunachala, first arrived here on 1 September 1886 as a 16-year-old boy. Attracted by its mystic air, this is where he realised his divine self. The Virupaksha cave where he stayed between 1899 and 1916 has a bench and a hill-shaped *lingam* carved by the saint himself. When followers thronged this tiny cave, he moved to a secluded spot further uphill. He lived in Skandasramam till 1922 before retiring to his spiritual retreat at the base of the hill.

The moment one enters the tranquil shaded grove of Sri Ramanasramam, a feeling of peace and calmness envelops every visitor. The air is charged by a divine vibration. Even the peacocks perched on the roof are meditative, occasionally letting out a plaintive call. The old hall where Sri Ramana Maharishi lived from 1928-49 is maintained as a meditation hall while the New Hall houses his Samadhi shrine. The adjoining Matrubhuteswara shrine contains the bodily remains of the saint's mother. Just opposite, in a leafy compound, stands the room where he attained Mahanirvana on 14 April, 1950. Important festivals and days marking the birth, advent and Mahanirvana of Sri Ramana Maharishi are celebrated with *pujas* and *abhishekams*.

The Ashram welcomes guests for quiet study, meditation or to find inner peace. By prior application *(write or email ashram@sriramanamaharishi.org)*, rooms are allotted for a maximum of 3 days in guesthouses around the Ashram (Ramana Vijayam, Chumma, Arul Ramana, Morvi and Achalam). A *gosala* (cattle farm) provides wholesome dairy products to the Ashram and *sattvik* (pure vegetarian) South Indian food, prepared in a spotless kitchen is served to guests at the dining hall.

Past the Samadhis of Ashram animals, a path leads to the cave shrines of Virupaksha and Skandasramam *(30–40min hike from here, 20min from the western tower of Arunachaleswara)*. Visitors can browse the library stocked with 30,000 books or buy Sri Ramana's literature, books on spirituality and philosophy and a large selection of photos, CDs/DVDs. Besides an active daily schedule, there's a Sri Chakra *puja* in the Matrubhuteswara Temple between 6pm–8.45pm every Friday, on full moon days and the first of every Tamil month. Oct–Feb is a busy season, so it's best to book early. There's no fee for boarding and lodging but voluntary donations are accepted.

WALKING TOUR

FRENCH QUARTER★★

The best place to begin a Heritage walk of the French Quarter is Beach Road (Goubert Avenue), lined by century-old buildings on one side and on the other, the Promenade, which comes alive with the chatter of French every evening.

Start from the Indian War Memorial at the northern end of Goubert Avenue and walk south.

French Consulate

Pass the yellow buildings of the **French Institute** *(see p145)* and Consulate General (earlier House of the Navy Admiral), Villa Bayoud (a heritage hotel), guesthouses of Aurobindo Ashram and the Promenade Hotel that housed a railway station built in 1878 for transporting goods.

Continue south on Goubert Avenue.

Gandhi Statue

This area served as a groundnut bags embankment till the 1920s. Gandhi's walking figure (believed to be Asia's tallest), replaced French Governor Dupleix, unceremoniously moved to a park at the end of the Promenade.

Face Bharathi Park opposite the Gandhi statue.

Lighthouse

Towering above the seascape is an 27m/88ft-tall lighthouse, the first on the Coromandel Coast, built in 1836. Its circular base currently serves as the Central Excise Officer's residence. Beyond it stands a statue of Nehru and **Bharathi Park**. The monolithic granite pillars around the Gandhi and Nehru statues were brought here from **Gingee** *(see p144)* after the French captured its fort in 1751.

Walk past the granite pillars further down Beach Road.

French War Memorial

Past the Custom House, French War Memorial dedicated to heroes of World War, Le Café (old porthouse in the 1930s), with stumps of the old pier visible in the sea, reach the Town Hall. The Ashram Press, Tourist Information Bureau and Ambedkar Manimandapam lie beyond.

Walk as far south on Beach Road and backtrack to the Town Hall.

Rue Dumas

Cutting in from the Town Hall, one enters Rue Dumas, the oldest street in the city, where the first French settlers lived. Walking past the pink-coloured **Notre Dame des Anges Church** and a Joan of Arc statue in front, cross Rue Bussy (LBS Street) junction to reach the Ecole Française d'Extreme Orient (School of Oriental Studies). A little ahead is Hotel de Pondicherry and the iconic Le Club, set in a 19C French villa.

Turn from Rue Dumas on to Bazar St Laurent Street and reach the parallel road, Romain Rolland.

Rue Romain Rolland

One of the best-maintained heritage buildings in the French Quarter is the Hôtel Lagrenée de Mézières (now a private embroidery house). Built in 1774 by a Councillor of Compagnie des Indes, the house has an exquisite entrance and a pillared verandah with lime plaster scrolls with floral motifs on the walls.

Taking the next parallel Rue Suffren, walk towards Bharathi Park.

Bharathi Park

(see opposite)

Historical Sights

For a tiny trading post coveted by Colonial powers and ancient dynasties, Pondicherry hides many histories in its folds. Much before the trade wars of the Portuguese, Danes, Dutch, British and French, it was once 'Poduke', a 2C Chola port with trade links as far as Rome and the Far East. Excavations at Arikamedu *(6km south)* **offer just beads and broken bits of amphora to string together its glorious past; now superimposed by its most recent influence – the French. Pondycherry's four main boulevards are strewn with over 1,200 heritage buildings, each chronicling a tale.**

FRENCH QUARTER★★

Stretching from Goubert Avenue to Gingee Salai (NSC Bose Street) between the North and South boulevard.

Built on sand dunes near the sea, the French Quarter developed along the seaboard and all of Pondicherry was enclosed within a fortified town by 1740. The Ville Blanche or White Town was separated from its Tamil half (Ville Noire or Black Town) by a storm-water canal. While the French Quarter was dominated by structures in classical European style, the **Tamil Quarter**★ had a traditional signature. Over the years, the two styles evolved into a Franco-Tamil idiom, a delightful blend seen in both parts of town.

When the British lost **Fort St George** (*see p70*) in Madras to Dupleix in 1746, they struck back by seizing Pondicherry in 1761 and destroying the town – save for a few structures. Almost the entire French Quarter, including the newly constructed Palace of Dupleix, was destroyed. Despite elaborate plans for reconstruction, it wasn't until the British departure in 1816 after the Treaty of Paris that Pondicherry was returned to the French. The new houses were built in the old style, with high walls, garden courts and ornate gateways, but better adapted to the climate. Pillared porticos offered better protection from the elements while pitched roofs gave way to flat terraces and high ceilings. The devastated fort area was used as a Place d'Armes or military parade ground (now **Bharathi Park**). Public buildings like Hôtel du Gouvernement and Palais de Justice were restored while hospitals and schools opened – Collège Royal (today Lycée Français), the Bibliothéque Publique in 1827 and Pharmacie du Gouvernement in 1829. For the growing Catholic community, the **Notre Dame des Anges church** was completed in 1855. A pier, *pont-debarcadère*, was inaugurated in 1866 and a railway line opened from Pondicherry to Villupuram in 1879. The French Quarter of today is the result of nearly a century of reconstruction.

BHARATHI PARK AND RAJ NIVAS

Located in the quadrilateral of Rue Labourdonnais, Rue Victor Simonel and Ananda Rangapillai Street. Entry is opposite the Jawaharlal Nehru statue. Rue Mahe de Labourdonnais, Pondicherry 605001. Park open 6am–9pm. Entry free.

At the very heart of the **French Quarter**★★, where Fort Louis once stood, lies the Government Park, renamed after Tamil poet-patriot Subramanya Bharathi (1882-1921). The landscaped gardens are laid out around the Aayi Mandapam or Park Monument at its centre. Built in 1863 in Greco-Roman style during the time of Napoleon III, the pavilion commemorates the provision of water to Pondicherry during his reign.

The park is the epicentre of all activity and the white *mandapam* has become an iconic representation of Pondicherry. Surrounding the Government Park are stately buildings like the Museum, Art Gallery, Legislative Assembly, Government Hospital and the 18C Palais du Gouverneur, which now serves as **Raj Nivas** *(closed to the public)*, the residence of the Lt Governor of Pondicherry.

BOTANICAL GARDENS

Off West Boulevard with an entrance south of the old city bus stand. Maraimalai Adigal Salai. Open 9am–5.30pm. Entry free, aquarium Rs.5, toy train Rs.2 (min. 20 passengers). P.

It was an experiment by French colonists that gave Pondicherry its largest green lung, the Botanical Garden. Spread over 36ha/89 acres, it was laid out in 1826 to analyse which crops were ideal for cultivation in the region. Flowerbeds, gravel-lined paths and fountains were added by C.S. Perrottet in 1831, transforming it to a full-fledged botanical garden. Besides 900 exotic plants from India and abroad, the park has an **aquarium** with ornamental fish, a **toy train** and a **musical fountain** that operates on weekends *(6.30pm and 7pm)*.

EXCURSION

Gingee Fort★

68km north-west of Pondicherry via Tindivanam. The fort is 2km west of town on the highway (buses from Pondicherry or Tiruvannamalai will drop off here if requested). Gingee, Tiruvannamalai–Pondicherry Road. Open 9am–5pm, no tickets issued after 4.30pm, hill climbing is restricted after 3pm. Rs.5, child below 15 yrs free (Rs.100 foreigner); ticket valid for both forts. Ideally visit on a weekday, as it's less crowded. Make sure to carry enough refreshments as there are no shops at the site.

Rising up from the yellow paddy fields like a colossus, the boulder-ridden Fort of Gingee dominates the landscape for miles around. The fort stretches across three precipitous hills – **Rajagiri** to the west, **Chakkilidurg** to the south-east and **Krishnagiri**, a small hill to the north (also called Rani Fort) – each capped by citadels. An 18m/60ft-thick wall connecting the hills encloses the fort within a rough triangle. Looking at the steep cliffs and high bastions, one would imagine the fort to be unconquerable, but it has been captured with alarming frequency. Founded by the Kone chiefs of Senjai in early 13C, the fort was improved upon by a succession of rulers who added most of its structures, walls and monuments between 1383-1760. Passed on from the Vijayanagar kings to the Adil Shahi dynasty of Bijapur, the Marathas and the Mughals, it finally came to the French in 1750, who were driven out by the British in 1761 after a 5-week siege. Their only significant contribution was to corrupt its traditional name Senjai to Gingee.

The fort can be accessed from the Tiruvannamalai–Pondicherry highway; a road south past the Sivan Temple leads to the main entrance. Dominating the Outer and Lower Fort to the left is the Saadathullah Khan Mosque, built in 1717 by the army commander of the Carnatic Nawabs. Delicate Persian inscriptions adorn its façade. Scattered around the crossroad are the Anjaneya Temple on the fort's southern side, a Kaliamman Temple and two outer gates – Pondicherry Gate and Vellore Gate. Entering from the main east gate, a circuitous path leads through an archway to the Inner Fort, dominated by a beautiful white pyramidal structure to the right, the Kalyana Mahal. Just ahead are the gymnasium, elephant tank, granary, magazine, palace site, Mohabbatkhan Mosque and a series of cells – the barracks and horse stables. Further west past a cluster of large banyan trees is the Venkatramana or Venugopalaswamy Temple, the fort's largest shrine.

Looming ahead is the 244m/800ft-high hill of Rajagiri. Walk up past the Kamalakanni Amman shrine to the main Rajagiri Citadel with two vaulted granaries, magazine, flagstaff, clock tower, audience hall, a treasury in Indo-Saracenic style and the Ranganatha Temple in Vijaynagar style. An arduous climb best done in early morning, Rajagiri offers great views. To the north-east one can see Krishnagiri, dotted by the Krishna Temple, Darbar Hall, Sri Ranganatha Temple, Kalyana Mantapa and oil wells.

Apart from its stunning locale and grand backdrop, another fascinating aspect of the fort is the ingenious hydraulic system that transported water to its upper precincts.

Museums and Art Galleries

Pondicherry has a buzzing art scene with regular exhibitions at Alliance Française, Touchwood, Aurodhan and cafes that double up as galleries. The French Institute and INTACH Heritage Centre have permanent exhibitions showcasing conservation efforts in the city. Revered Tamil poet Subramanya Bharathi's house on 20, Eswaran Dharamaraja Koil Street, and his protégé Bharathidasan's on 95 Perumal Koil Street, have been converted into small museums-cum-research centres that might interest enthusiasts.

PONDICHERRY MUSEUM

Just beyond Raj Nivas. St Louis Street, Pondicherry 605001. Open Tue–Sun 9.40am–5.20pm. Closed public holidays and 1–2pm on weekdays. Rs.5, child free. P. 0413 222 3950.

Established in 1983, the Pondicherry Museum is housed in a century-old double-storey structure. The museum's **Sculpture Gallery** has early specimens of Pallava and Chola sculptures from Karaikal. Also on display are seals, stone tools, Megalithic burial urns and Roman pottery from Arikamedu. The **Bronze Gallery** houses examples of Chola, Vijayanagar and Nayak periods while the **Transport Gallery** has many interesting modes of transport used in the 19C; some quaint attractions include horse-drawn coaches, palanquins, cattle carts and the Pousse Pousse, a vehicle pushed from the rear and steered by the rider. The Numismatics Section has coins from France, Britain and their colonies, including currency notes issued here during the French period.

French India Gallery

The main attraction of the museum is this gallery on the first floor with period furniture like consoles, settees, *tête-à-têtes* (S-shaped sofas), *comptoirs* (writing tables) and decorative pieces like lamps, clocks, porcelain vases, crockery, cutlery and liquor cabinets that embellished local French homes between 1673 and 1954. Don't miss the cot and replica of a chair used by French Governor Dupleix (1742-54), whose bust occupies a prominent place in the museum.

ROMAIN ROLLAND LIBRARY

Past Raj Nivas, next to Pondicherry Museum. Compagnie Street, Pondicherry 605001. Open Tue–Sun 7.30am–8.30pm, Mon (periodicals section only) 9am–5.30pm. P. 0413 233 6426.

One of the oldest in the country, the Romain Rolland Library was first established by French Governor Engene Desbaissyns de Richemont in 1827 as the Bibliotheque Publique. Earlier located at the Magasin General and then at the Mint Factory, it was renamed after the great French scholar during his birth centenary in 1966. Shifted to its current location in 1974, the library is a crash course in statistics – over 4 lakh books, 250 periodicals and a microfilm unit of 15,000 rare books for research scholars, the iconic library currently has 45,000 members and 7,500 student members. Nearly 1,000 people use its reading rooms daily. Its unique mobile library service carts books to nearby villages by bus to make them accessible to all.

FRENCH INSTITUTE

Between Rue St Gilles and Rue Dupuy and next to the French Consulate. 11, Saint Louis Street, Pondicherry 605001. Open daily 8am–12noon, 4–5.30pm. Library closed May and on holidays. Entry free. P. 0413 233 4168. www.ifpindia.org.

Housed in a handsome renovated 19C building, the Institut Francais de Pondicherry (IFP) was set up in 1954. It is the largest research institute dependent on the French Ministry of Foreign Affairs. A reservoir of knowledge, with three major departments dedicated to Indology, Social Sciences and Ecology, its prized collection includes tomes in Sanskrit and Tamil Sangam literature, 1,40,000 photographs of temples and

French Institute

edifices of South India and 8,500 palm-leaf manuscripts. Its collection of texts on Saiva Siddhanta, the largest in the world, finds a mention in UNESCO's 'Memory of the World' register. Research scholars and academics are welcome to use the well-stocked library.

ALLIANCE FRANÇAISE

Opposite Cre'art boutique. 58, Suffren Street, Pondicherry 605001. Office hours: Mon–Fri 8.30am–12.30pm, 2–6.50pm, library: Tue–Sat 8.30am–12.30pm, 3.30–7pm. Temporary 1-month membership Rs.250 (tourists). . 0413 233 8146/233 4351. www.alliancefrancaisepondichery.com.

Established in 1897, the Alliance Française de Pondichéry is among the first Alliances in the world after the one in Paris. Over the years, it has played an important role in cultural exchange between India and France. In Pondicherry'svibrant francophone climate, AFP keeps French alive through its ever-popular language courses. The centre hosts monthly cultural programmes like art exhibitions, movie screenings, jazz concerts, dance recitals, puppet shows and film shows on Sundays. 'Funny Saturdays' with cartoon film shows, storytelling and drawing, are dedicated exclusively to children.

The Maison Bellocq on Suffren Street houses the administrative block, auditorium, 12 classrooms and a multimedia library with a collection of 9,500 books, 30 magazines and 300 DVDs. The more informal Maison Colombani *(37, Dumas Street; 0413 222 5868; 8.30am–7pm)* has (for members only) a multimedia centre, art gallery and Café de Flore, a garden restaurant where special evenings and exclusive concerts are organised.

ANANDA RANGA PILLAI MUSEUM

From Mahatma Gandhi Street turn into Grand Bazaar lane onto Rangapillai Street; the mansion is on the left past Goubert Market. 109, Ananda Rangapillai Street. Entry permitted only as part of an INTACH walking tour. Guided Tours: INTACH Pondicherry. 0413 222 5991. www.intachpondicherry.org.

On a busy Tamil lane crammed with shops and trucks unloading cargo, it's hard to spot the house of the most important man in this part of town. Ananda Rangapillai was the chief *dubash* of the French (a local agent serving as a translator and interpreter between Indian and European merchants). His green-fronted mansion with contrasting red pillars stands out from the clutter but does little to announce its importance, hemmed in between P.V. Sundar Watch House and Anbu Store. Built in 1735, the house of Ananda Rangapillai is the oldest structure in the **Tamil Quarter**★. Left unscathed in the British sack of 1761, it is one of the best surviving examples of a Franco-Tamil house in Pondicherry.

On the Tamil-style ground floor elaborately carved wooden pillars surround an open central courtyard, while the European first floor has masonry pillars with Doric capitals supporting the terrace. Recently converted into a museum, the mansion contains exquisite pieces of furniture, rosewood cabinets with ivory inlay and Tanjore-style portraits of Ananda Rangapillai and his family.

Beaches

Pondicherry is the sort of place where people like to put their feet up and soak up the sun. There are four beaches to do just that. Bang opposite the 1.5km-long Goubert Avenue is Promenade Beach, the only one in town. The narrow strip of sand wedged against a rocky embankment is ideal for seaside walks and watching sunsets. While Serenity and Paradise Beaches (*see below***) are short drives north and south of town, Auro Beach is located opposite Auroville and is a peaceful place for a dip in its shallow waters.**

SERENITY BEACH

Just 5km north of Pondy off ECR road, look out for 7 Star Guest House and turn right for the beach. Thanthirayan Kuppam, Kottakuppam. P.

A 10-minute drive north of town, Serenity, like the name suggests, is a quiet beach for relaxation, a quick dip or sunbathing. The 1.5 km-long stretch of white sand is relatively empty on weekdays and serves as a welcome break from the tourist hum of the city. Kasha Ki Aasha, a handicraft store (*0413 222 2963/9791944182*) organises **Serenity Beach Bazaar**, a Saturday market (*open 10am–5pm*) behind Bodhi Café. Everything from textiles, jewellery, ceramics, handicrafts and products made of bamboo, coconut and paper are on offer, besides Auroville breads and organic produce.

PARADISE BEACH

Boat access from Chunnambar Boat House, 7km south on Dr Ambedkar and then Cuddalore Road. Chunnambar backwaters. Entry Rs.5, Rs.3 child (camera Rs.15, video Rs.40). Open 9am–6pm. Motorboat beach trip (Rs 75/head, 30min, minimum 10 persons, closes at 4pm), after 4pm only short trips (Rs.40/head, 15min). P.

Located near the mouth of the Chunnambar backwaters, it is the arduous and limited access by boat that has ensured this beach has clean sands and crystal-clear waters. Hence the name Plage Paradiso or Paradise Beach! Besides backwater jaunts by speedboat, motorboat, sailingboat, rowingboat and paddle boats, **Chunnambar Resort** also organises trekking, packed lunches and beach sports at Paradise. Sea cruises are also arranged for dolphin watching.

Promenade Beach in town

ADDRESSES

STAY

With roads and streets lined by heritage buildings, it is easy to stumble upon little gems and grand villas that have been renovated for hospitality. The sheer diversity of hotels catering to different wallets leaves one spoilt for choice. The unmistakable stamp of Sri Aurobindo is visible across Pondicherry with numerous seaside guesthouses and boutiques run by the Ashram.

HERITAGE

Le Dupleix – *5, Rue de la Caserne, Pondicherry 605001. 0413 222 6999/222 6001. www.ledupleix.com. 14 rooms.* . From heritage rooms heavy with the sweet smell of Burma teak to ultra-modern penthouses, every room of this designer heritage hotel is unique. Evocative of the regal life of François Dupleix, the Governor of Pondicherry, the refurbished 18C Colonial villa flaunts some of the most intricate woodwork seen in the French Quarter. Dine on Med or Pondicherry cuisine under an ancient mango tree in the Courtyard Gourmet Restaurant or slip into the bar, the Governor's Lounge, with a richly carved wooden ceiling commissioned by le Dupleix himself!

Villa Shanti – *14, Rue Suffren, Pondicherry 605001. 0413 4200028. www.lavillashanti.com. 15 rooms.* . Renovated French building with minimalist Greek-inspired interiors. Has a bar, cafe and rooftop garden restaurant.

Calve – *Old No. 36, Vysial Street, Pondicherry 605001. 0413 222 3738/222 4103. www.calve.in. 10 rooms.* . A 150-year-old Chettiar bungalow restored with Chettinad plaster and Athangudi tiles, Calve in its present form is a WelcomHeritage hotel. Its in-house restaurant Salle A Manger serves speciality French, Creole and Indian cuisine.

Maison Perumal – *58, Perumal Koil Street, Pondicherry 605001. 0413 222 7519/9442127519. www.cghearth.com. 10 rooms.* . Located in the Tamil quarter and lovingly restored by CGH Earth, this Chettiar bungalow with an ornate doorway ushers one into a sun-drenched courtyard with stained-glass balconies. Old pictures, large vats and antique furniture adorn the interiors. Like a home, the rooms are not numbered and the nameless restaurant stirs up a signature dish of the day and scrumptious seafood platters.

Hotel de l' Orient – *17, Rue Romain Rolland, Pondicherry 605001. 0413 234 3067/234 3068. www.neemranahotels.com. 16 rooms.* . An old Tamil home rebuilt by the French in the 1760s that once housed the Department of Education, the Neemrana hotel proudly retains the old name, Instruction Publique, at its entrance. Rooms overlook a leafy central courtyard with Carte Blanche restaurant specializing in Creole cuisine while antique wooden dolls add charm to the decor.

The Promenade – *23, Goubert Avenue, Pondicherry 605001. 0413 222 7750. www.sarovarhotels.com.* . *38 rooms.* . Located in the heart of the French quarter, this luxury boutique hotel on the oceanfront was once the old railway station building. Associated with one of India's top fashion brands, Hidesign, this stylish hotel has a French Colonial exterior with ultra-modern minimalist interiors. Rooms overlook Pondicherry's legendary beachfront with Risque, a lively bar, and Lighthouse, a romantic rooftop restaurant.

Aurodhan – *33, Rue François Martin, Kuruchikuppam, Pondicherry 605012. 0413 222 2795/222 2449. www.aurodhan.com. 25 rooms.* . One-stop integrated art gallery, heritage hotel and space for cultural events, especially known for its framing workshop and artist-in-residence programmes.

Gratitude – *52, Rue Romain Rolland, Pondicherry 605001. 0413 222 5029/9442177044. www.gratitudeheritage.in. 8 rooms.* . An ideal retreat for writers and artists looking for a tranquil getaway, the home was restored over 3 years in collaboration with INTACH. Decor is Anglo-French and the terrace has day beds and a yoga and massage room. The in-house boutique has limited edition vintage jewellery, clothing in natural fabrics and bags.

Dumas Guest House – *36, Rue Dumas, Pondicherry 605001. 0413 222 5726/9894172255. www.dumasguest house.com.* . *7 rooms.* . A late 17C Colonial guesthouse in the French Quarter just 20m/60ft from the beachfront, with rooms furnished in teak wood and a private terrace garden for guests.

L'escale – *31, Rue Dumas, Pondicherry 605001. 0413 222 2562/ 9500640845. www.lescale pondicherry.com. 7 rooms. Rs.190.* . A guesthouse in the heart of the French Quarter, the lofty L'escale has a terrace with a great ocean view. Continental breakfast served between 8am–12noon on the rooftop cafe, with free Wi-Fi.

La Maison Blanche – *14, Saradambal Mani Street, Dr Ambedkar Salai, Mudaliarpet, Pondicherry 605001. 979974762. www.lamaisonblanche.in. 6 rooms. Rs.150 (meals Rs.380).* . This French villa, painted white throughout, is the brainchild of Sylvain Labiche. Easy access to the beach promenade, 24hr check-in and check-out, and uncluttered living spaces make for a relaxed ambience.

Patricia Guest House – *20/28, Rue François Martin, Pondicherry 605001. 0413 233 5130. patriciaguesthouse. wordpress.com. 5 rooms.* . A lovely 200-year-old French villa near the sea with light and airy rooms, one street away from Aurobindo Ashram.

Hotel de Pondicherry – *38, Rue Dumas, Pondicherry 605001. 0413 222 7409. 12 rooms.* . A 170-year-old French warehouse, later converted into a boutique heritage hotel, has rooms named after former French governors and Tamil luminaries. The Dupleix suite aptly opens onto a private terrace. Antique teak beds, Thanjavur paintings and sepia-toned photographs add a wistful touch. Though no food is served, the French cuisine restaurant Le Club is located in the garden to the front.

Villa Bayoud – *5, Rue St Martin, Pondicherry 605001. 0413 222 7426. www.villabayoud.com.* . *10 rooms.* . A heritage hotel overlooking the Promenade near the Chief Secretariat; it doesn't get more posh than that! Plush four-posters and period furniture in rich brown tones lend a classy look while everything comes with a seaview – rooms, cafe and the rooftop garden restaurant.

Villa Christophe – *5, Surcouf Street, Pondicherry 605001. 9025817351. www.villachristophe.com. 3 rooms. Rs.250.* . A boutique guesthouse in a restored 19C villa with bathrooms as pretty as its rooms. Jasmine, hibiscus and frangipani seem right out of a brochure. Meals are not served but breakfast is arranged on request.

Villa Helena – *13, Lal Bahadur Shastri (Bussy) Street, Pondicherry 605001. 0413 222 6789/420 0377. villahelena@ sify.com. 7 rooms.* . What started out as an annexe where Roselyne Guitry, a perfumer from Burgundy, could store her collection of antiques soon transformed into a Colonial heritage hotel. The 130-year-old Villa Helena stands in a rainforest setting with a pebbled courtyard, an open-air lounge with planters' chairs, Satsangh restaurant and large rooms furnished in Colonial style.

Villa Indra – *43, Capitaine Marius Xavier Street, Pondicherry 605001. 0413 222 7979/9003531278. www.villaindra.in. 3 rooms. Rs.150.* . A small Colonial-style house with three comfortable rooms named Sakra (Powerful), Vajri (Thunderer) and Svargapati (Lord of Heaven) after the manifestations of Indra.

Villa Canelle – *3, Kasturibai Gandhi Street, Nethaji Nagar, Uppalam, Pondicherry 605001. 9791563787. www.lamaisonblanche.in/villa_canelle. 3 rooms.* . A French-run traditional Tamil guesthouse in a white and red colour theme located in a shaded compound, with a rooftop swimming pool-cum-canopy lounge.

Hotel Coramandal Heritage – *36, Needarajapayer Street, Pondicherry 605001. 0413 226 0269/9944338207. www.hotelcoramandal.in. 10 rooms.* . 150-year old Franco Tamil home with compact rooms, gallery of South Arcot paintings and a boutique. Coffee Door, its in-house cafe *(6.30am–10.30pm)*, serves sandwiches, coffee, juices, shakes and *lassis*.

Swades Guesthouse – *26, Chanda Sahib Street, Pondicherry 605001.*

℘9787728550. www.swades-guest house.com. 5 rooms. ☕ ▤. For a change, one of the few guesthouses not in the French or Tamil quarters, but in the charming Muslim Quarter. Rooms are small, the hosts are warm and the muezzin's call adds mood to the neighbourhood.

HOTELS & RESORTS

Anandha Inn – *154, S.V. Patel Road, Anna Salai, Thiruvalluvar Nagar, Pondicherry 605001. ℘0413 223 3000/233 0711. www.anandhainn.com. 70 rooms.* ☕ ▤. Well-appointed rooms with Wi-Fi connectivity, gymnasium, poolside lounge (Tantra), multi-cuisine restaurant (L'Heritage), Anandha spa with Ayurvedic rejuvenation packages.

Hotel Annamalai International – *479, Kamaraj Salai, Saram, Pondicherry 605013. ℘0413 224 7001. www.hotelannamalai.com. 70 rooms.* ☕ ▤. A popular hotel for business travellers as it boasts four conference halls. Large, clean rooms, a choice of three restaurants, a gym and a not so well maintained swimming pool.

Hotel Mass – *Maraimalai Adigal Salai, Pondicherry 605001. ℘0413 420 7001. www.hotelmass.com. 112 rooms.* ☕ ▤. This mid-range hotel near the bus station has a choice of rooms and suites, a multi-cuisine restaurant (Nanda), 24hr coffee shop, cake shop, bar and restaurant.

The Sunway GRT Grand – *155/D, 100 Feet Road, Pondicherry 605004. ℘0413 228 1608. www.grthotels.com. 61 rooms.* ☕ ▤. A luxurious GRT hotel with a full-fledged business centre and all amenities for a comfortable stay – pool, fitness centre, Wi-Fi connectivity and friendly staff. A great buffet, perhaps the most elaborate in the city, is served at Gardenia multi-cuisine restaurant. Open House, a 24hr restaurant is another option for a good bite.

Ginger – *Old Venus Theatre, Karuvadikuppam Main Road, Pondicherry 605008. ℘0413 666 3333. www.gingerhotels.com. 97 rooms.* ☕ ▤. One of the better budget hotels in the city with clean, basic rooms. The chain hotel has a gym, Wi-Fi, Appachi restaurant, bar and a Café Coffee Day outlet.

Hotel Alps Residency – *252/3, Main Road, Anandha Rangapillai Nagar, Pondicherry 605008. ℘0413 2243 666/224 5666/9655576888. www.hotelal psresidency.com. 14 rooms.* ☕ ▤. Fully furnished spacious and comfortable service apartments with functional kitchenettes. Rooftop lounge with a garden and Café Coffee Day outlet.

Hotel Richmond – *12, Labourdonnais Street, Pondicherry 605001. ℘0413 234 6363. www.the residency.com. 14 rooms.* ☕ ▤. Yellow and white fronted building with large windows and a small raised verandah lined with flowerpots. Bistro restaurant *(7am–11pm)* serves multi-cuisine while the bar stocks premium draught beers.

Hotel Surguru – *104, Sardar Vallabhai Patel Road, Pondicherry 605101. ℘0413 233 9022/222 7290. www.hotelsurguru.com.* 🚭 ♿. *57 rooms.* ☕ ▤. Luxurious rooms with Internet access, a separate business centre and multi-cuisine restaurant with live music.

Abi Krishna – *1–3, 1st Cross, Pon Nagar, Reddiyarpalayam, Pondicherry 605010. ℘0413 220 6969/9443257722. www.abikrishna.com. 30 rooms.* ☕ ▤. This hotel located near Indira Gandhi Square has well-furnished rooms with LED TV. Wi-Fi is available in the lobby.

The Clock Tower Hotel – *134, Lal Bahadur Shastri (Bussy) Street. ℘0413 222 7410/430 8410. www.theclocktowerhotel. com. 15 rooms.* ☕ ▤. Located at the junction of LBS/Bussy Street and MG Road, this functional hotel overlooks the clock tower after which it is named. Neat and tidy rooms.

Hotel Corbelli – *170, Mission Street, Pondicherry 605001. ℘0413 222 5301/450 0040/9791687722. www.hotelcorbelli.net. 28 rooms.* ☕ ▤. The location here is a big plus, and the rooms are well-furnished for a budget option. The rooftop restaurant, Don Giovanni, is renowned for its Italian pizzas.

Hotel D' Europe – *35, Ellapillaichavady Main Road, 100 Feet Road, Pondicherry 605005. ℘0413 220 0666/220 0699. www.hoteldeurope.com. 40 rooms.* ☕ ▤. Standard clean and spacious city hotel near Indira Gandhi statue on ECR, serves vegetarian South Indian cuisine.

PR Pride Inn – *183, Kamaraj Salai, Near Periyar Statue, Pondicherry 605013. 0413 224 4478/9. prprideinn@gmail.com. 12 rooms.* A modern budget hotel with a multi-cuisine restaurant and bar on the first floor.

AUROVILLE AND AROUND

The Dune EcoVillage & Spa – *Pudhukuppam, Keelputhupet (via Pondicherry University) 605014. 0413 265 5751/324 4040/9364455440. www.thedunehotel.com. 52 rooms.* Spread over 16ha/40 acres with its own beachfront, this luxury eco-friendly resort has aesthetically-designed villas and rooms, each one-of-a-kind. Using chairs from a ship-breaking yard, pillars from a dilapidated Chettinad house and recycled wine bottles for their Dynamised water, The Dune takes pride in its low carbon footprint. The seafood bar by the beach and gourmet restaurant uses farm-fresh organic vegetables to stir up amazing meals. Pamper yourself at Paradise Spa and discover *wat-su* (water shiatsu).

The Ashok Beach Resort – *ECR, Kalapet Beach, Pondicherry 605014. 0413 265 5160. www.ashokresort.com. 21 rooms & 2 cottages.* Spread over 26ha/65 acres, this palm-fringed ITDC-run beach resort has massive lawns and beachfront bar-cum-dining area, making it a good place for large groups. Sea cruises, cocktail dinners and beach parties are organised on request.

Ocean Spray – *7–9, ECR Main Road, Manjakuppam, Pondicherry 604303. 0413 265 0000/9600744554. www.oceanspray.in. 72 rooms & 34 villas.* A water-themed resort built around a 2ha/5-acre man-made lake with waterfront villas, open-to-sky jacuzzi rooms, tea lounge and Ska, a bar and disco.

Mango Hill – *Old Auroville Road, Bommayapalayam, Pondicherry 605104. 0413 265 5491-3. www.hotel-mangohill-pondicherry.com. 24 rooms.* Indian hotel with a French touch, on a hill planted with mango and cashew trees. Rooms with private terraces, overlook a pool.

The Neem Tree Hotel – *6 E, ECR, Sarukkupalam, Kottamedu, Kottakuppam 605104. 0413 2234 901/223 70003. www.theneemtree.in. 10 rooms.* Rooms overlook a lawn with a popular veg restaurant, Cinnamon Street.

Purple Resorts – *Auroville Main Road, Kuilapalayam, Auroville 605101. 0413 234 5694/9585554501. www.thepurple.in. 12 rooms.* Medium sized budget resort with neat rooms, garden, pool and three restaurants.

St James Court Beach Resort – *ECR, opp. Pondicherry Engg College, Chinna Kalapet, Pondicherry 605014. 0413 265 5275/265 5174. www.stjamescourtbeachresort.com. 72 rooms & 34 villas.* A beach resort just 50m/155yd from the seafront with open-air sea-facing restaurant, bar and swimming pool.

Hotel Bay Castle – *ECR, Periya Mudaliarchavadi, Pondicherry. 0413 262 3411/9025691010. www.hotelbaycastle.com. 13 rooms.* Simple, comfortable rooms with ink-blue bathrooms and rooftop dining overlooking coconut groves and the sea in the horizon. Close to Auroville.

TIRUVANNAMALAI

Sparsa Hotels & Resorts – *34, Athiyanthal Village, Chengam Road, Tiruvannamalai 606603. 04175 236 911/238 111/235 311. www.sparsaresorts.com. 28 rooms.* Set against the majestic backdrop of Mount Arunachala, Sparsa is an eco-friendly spiritual-themed resort with stone huts and thatched cottages in a landscaped garden. The Ecotel Resort follows a strict no smoking and no alcohol policy and Sathvam, the pure-veg restaurant, serves specialised *sattvik* food. A swimming pool, library, boutique and spa make it a relaxing retreat.

Arunai Anantha – *NH-66 (Pondy-Bangalore Road), Chengam Road, Aanaipirandaan Village, Tiruvannamalai 606603. 04175 237 275/238 726. www.arunaianantha.com. 44 rooms.* A 3-star resort with a serene atmosphere located on the town's quiet outskirts. Rooms open out to a view of Mount Arunachala, while luxury Swiss cottages face a beautiful garden. Swimming pool, yoga-cum-meditation hall, amphitheatre for live performances, spacious lawn for gatherings and a veg restaurant further enrich your stay.

Hotel Ashreya – *9, Ganapathy Nagar, Chengam Road (Near Girivala Paadhai), Tiruvannamalai 606603. 04175 322 444/323 331/9360013507. www.hotelashreya.com. 20 rooms.* A boutique hotel with studio and standard rooms, and a terrace with meditation benches overlooking Mount Arunachala. There's veg restaurant, Vaibhavam, and a separate bar and restaurant that serves non-veg.

Lakshmi Residency Inn – *69, Chengam Road, opp. Sri Ramana Asaramam, Tiruvannamalai 606603. 04175 236 099/235 245. www.lakshmi residency.com.* All rooms at this mid-range hotel are strictly no smoking and no alcohol.

EAT

With a lively culture of dining out, Pondicherry's restaurants rustle up everything from authentic French and Creole to spicy South Indian fare. Most hotels have attached restaurants and cafes open to the public. Leading the swish set in the French Quarter are The Courtyard at Le Dupleix, Carte Blanche at De l'Orient, Salle A Manger at Calve and Lighthouse at The Promenade. Don't miss the oven-fresh French breads, croissants and cakes from the city's patisseries and bakeries.

MULTI-CUISINE

Le Club – *38, Dumas Street, Pondicherry 605001. 0413 233 9745/421 0592. www.leclubraj.com. Open 9.30am–6.30pm.* Located in a garden of an old French villa with a spacious verandah, Le Club is actually a troika of exotic restaurants – Le Club Salon Dupleix (French), The Bistro (multi-cuisine garden restaurant) and Indochine (Vietnamese & South Asian restaurant, tapas & cocktail bar). Try seafood sizzlers, chicken in mustard sauce or authentic French dishes like ***salade de crabe a l'avocat*** (crab avocado salad), ***brochette de crevette au basilic*** (prawns in basil) or ***calmars au citron vert*** (squid) with Indian and French wines.

Bamboo Garden – *4, Bazar St Laurent Street, Pondicherry 605001. 0413 4201118.* Restaurant near the beach with bamboo huts serving Indian, Tandoori, Chinese and Italian food.

Rendezvous Café Restaurant – *30, Rue Suffren, Pondicherry 605001. 0413 233 0238/222 5558/233 9132/ 9443220737. Open Wed–Mon.* Busy terrace restaurant under a large thatched roof serving chilled beer, a wide choice of seafood and Continental cuisine.

Satsanga – *30–32, Labourdonnais Street, Pondicherry 605001. 0413 222 5867. www.satsanga. co.in. Open 8am–11.30pm.* Tucked into an old Colonial mansion, this popular joint rustles up Continental and Indian food. Steaks and sausages are good but locals claim the place is not what it used to be.

Seagulls – *8, Dumas Street, Near Port Office, Pondicherry 605001. 0413 233 8643. Open 11am–11pm.* A multi-cuisine restaurant-bar with a view of the backwaters specialising in Chinese and Tandoori food.

Le Vietnam – *35, Aurobindo Street, Mission Road Cutting, Pondicherry 605001. 0413 234 0111.* A unit of La Fiesta (a factory outlet for funky clothes), the restaurant dishes out Vietnamese and French cuisine, in a room full of pictures of Saigon and colourful paper lanterns.

Au Feu De Bois – *28, Lal Bahadur Shastri (Bussy) Street, Pondicherry 605001. 0413 234 1821. pierre_satsanga@ yahoo.co.in. Open Tue–Sun.* Pizzeria and Italian restaurant with roof garden serving authentic, wood-fired pizzas, pâtés, ravioli, salads and noodles.

West Boulevard Restaurant – *80A, Kandan Complex, Anna Salai, Pondicherry 605001. 9952614503. www.westboulevardmc.com.* Multi-cuisine with choice of Indian, Continental, Chinese and Mexican.

INDIAN

Aachiamma Chettinadu Restaurant – *18, Aurobindo Street, Pondicherry 605001. 0413 234 5678/ 645 7755. Open 10am–3.30pm, 6.30–10.30pm.* Multi-cuisine and spicy Chettinadu delicacies.

Anjappar Chettinad Restaurant – *239, Bussy Street, Pondicherry 605001. 0413 450 0301. www.anjappar.com.*

. *Open 11am–11pm.* A branch of a popular chain serving authentic Chettinad cuisine. Has another outlet in Vallalar Salai *(0413 420 7081).*

Karai Chettinad Restaurant – *100 Feet Road, near Indira Gandhi Square, Pondicherry 605005. 0413 2203066/8.* . *Open 12noon–11.30pm.* Another place that stirs the taste buds with Chettinad food.

Roma's Kitchen – *Auromodele, Auroville, Pondicherry 605001. 0413 262 2032. Open 12noon–2.30pm, 6.45–9.30pm. Open Tue–Sun.* . This popular hangout serves lip-smacking Indian cuisine from hot fish ***tikkas***, ***bhendi jalfrezi***, Hyderabadi ***biryani*** to spinach croquettes, pasta and other Western delights.

Adyar Ananda Bhavan – *25, Nehru Street, Pondicherry 605001. 0413 222 3333. www.aabsweets.in.* . *Open 9am –9pm.* Better known as A2B or AAB, the house of exclusive Indian sweets, savouries and snacks, the reputed confectioners started out in Adyar (Chennai) and now have 54 outlets.

CAFES & BAKERIES

Baker's Street – *123, Bussy Street, Pondicherry 605001. 0413 645 8888/ 9994427899. www. www.baker-street. in. Open daily 11am–10pm. Prices start at Rs.40.* A concept store designed around a diagonal street with French chefs stirring up delicacies. Ice cream, chocolate, bakery, cake shop, tea saloon and quiet corners for dining.

Banana Cafe – *Angle Rue Bazaar, St Laurent/Suffren, Pondicherry 605001. 9894308228, 9626561259. Prices start at Rs.120.* Small cafe in a white French villa whips up delicious pasta, pies, hibiscus soda and other French delights

Bodhi Beach Cafe – *Tandarayakuppam, opp. Neem Tree Hotel Cutting, off ECR, Pondicherry. 9944537666. bodhi_beach @yahoo.com. Open Tue–Sun 9am–7pm.* Beachside cafe at Serenity Beach serving only breakfast, lunch and coffee.

La Boulangerie – *Kuilapalayam, Auroville Road, off ECR . 0413 291 7949. Open daily 7am–5pm. Prices start at Rs.40.* Popular with Aurovillians. Serves oven-fresh croissants, quiche, baguettes and pastries at affordable prices.

Café Des Arts – *1, Labourdonnais Street, Pondicherry 605001. 0413 421 0540/9894910080. Open Wed–Mon 8.30am–7pm. Prices start at Rs.50.* Part of the Made in Gallery, this courtyard cafe and shop offers French coffee, breakfast, short eats and free Wi-Fi.

Le Café – *Goubert Avenue, near Gandhi Statue, Pondicherry 605001. 0413 291 7949. wowpondy@gmail.com. Prices start at Rs.35–100.* A top local hangout, the 24hr coffee lounge near the beach was once the old port building. Enjoy the view of the sea from its wind-swept verandah. Organic coffee, tea, pastries and snacks.

Cafe Flunch – *24, Bazar St Laurent Street, Pondicherry 605001.* Surprisingly good food, without the burden of ambience, the tiny no-frills cafe serves delicious French cuisine, steaks and pastas.

Choco-La – *319, Mission Street, Candappa Street Junction, Pondicherry 605001. 0413 222 1191. www.ebony foods.in. Open daily 9.30am–10pm. Prices start at Rs.60.* Pondicherry's first chocolate boutique is full of chocolate delights; truffles, fondant and hot cocoa with chocolate shavings.

Coffee.com – *236, Mission Street, south-west of Bharathi Park, Pondicherry 605001. 0413 233 9079. www.coffeedotcom.net. Open daily 10am–1pm. Prices start at Rs.45.* Cool place to hang out. Good coffee, pasta, baguettes, pastries and Internet.

Daily Bread – *54, Ambour Salai (upstairs), Pondicherry 605001. 0413 2226302, 2226268. www.dailybread pondicherry.com. Open daily 7.30am–10pm. Prices start at Rs.50.* A one-stop shop for assorted French breads, cakes, brownies and cookies. Another branch near the Indira Gandhi statue.

Farm Fresh – *Kuilapalayam, opp. La Boulangerie, Auroville Road. Open daily 8am–8pm. Prices start at Rs.45.* Wood-fired pizzas, pastas and salads, with free home delivery.

LEISURE

Ayurveda Holistic Healing Centre – *6, Senganiamman Kovil Street, Vazhaikulam, Pondicherry 605012. 0413 653 7651/9894468367. www.ayurojas.org.* A wide range of Ayurvedic treatments and short-term courses in yoga and Ayurvedic massage therapies.

Kalliyalay Surf Club – *Tandriankuppam, Pondicherry. ☏9442992874/9787306376. www.surfschooindia.com. Open daily 8–11.30am, 2–5.30pm. Rs.700 (single lesson), Rs.3,300 (5-day course) and Rs.5,600 (10-day course).* Located between Pondicherry and Auroville, the surf school conducts surfing lessons for the uninitiated from single lessons to 5–10 day courses. Duration 1hr30min. Handles groups of up to eight persons.

Red Earth Riding School – *Tindivanam-Pondicherry Road, next to Auroville Police Station. ☏9443237217. www.auroville.org /society/RERS.htm. Open Tue–Sun, 6–9am, 4–7pm. Rs. on request.* Interact with horses at a 9ha/22-acre riding school with Olympic-sized dressage and jumping arenas, two training rings, a tent pegging field and a cross-country course. Red Earth offers riding lessons for adults, guided walkouts for children and show jumping for competition riders. Minimum classes: 1 week.

Sandosham – *18, Diagou Moudaliar Street, Pondicherry 605001. ☏0413 235 4344/9790581490. www.sandosham.com.* An aesthetic healing centre in an old Tamil home, run by a French-Israeli couple who offer a mix of therapies from Ayurvedic massages and aromatherapy to gems and crystals. Yoga, vortex healing, Zen meditation also offered besides a boutique selling essential oils.

Temple Adventures Scuba – *Near Indira Gandhi Sports Complex. ☏9940219449. www.templeadventures.com. Rs.800/hr (snorkeling lessons), Rs.1,500 (trial dive), Rs.2,000–21,000 (PADI courses).* Scuba dive off Pondy's coast with PADI-certified instructors. Courses for beginners include sessions in the pool at the training and equipment display facility.

SHOPPING

MARKETS

Grand Bazaar – *Between MG Road & Bharathi Street.* Sandwiched between MG Road and Bharathi Street is this popular permanent daily market for vegetables, fruits, flowers, fish, spices, groceries and utensils.

Sunday Market – *Crossroads of Nehru Street and MG Road, Pondicherry.* The streets come alive with the famous Sunday Market where garments, old books, toys, crafts, household items, CDs and DVDs are sold for a good bargain.

SPECIALITY SHOPS AND DESIGNER BOUTIQUES

Artyzan – *The Dune Resort, 70, Pudhukuppam, Keelputhupet, via Pondy Univ. ☏0413 265 5528. www.artyzan.org. Open Mon–Sat, 9.30am–8.30pm.* A fair trade brand promoted by Children of the World–India Vocational Academy. Watch artisans at work at the Artyzan Design Shop and Studio that sells attractive beaded fashion accessories, key chains, pouches, etc.

La Boutique d'Auroville – *38, Jawaharlal Nehru Street, Pondicherry 605001. ☏0413 262 2150/233 7264. Open Mon–Sat, 9.30am–1pm and 3.30–8pm.* Auroville products, pottery, leather items, ***kalamkari*** work and garments.

Boutique D Auroshri – *18, Jawaharlal Nehru Street, Pondicherry 605001. ☏0413 222 2117. Open Mon–Sat, 9.30am–8.30pm.* Clothes and handicrafts from all over India and silver jewellery, paintings, bronzes, marble and sandalwood crafts.

Casablanca – *165, Mission Street, Pondicherry 605001. ☏0413 222 6495/233 6495. www.hidesign.com. Open daily 9am –10pm.* A Hidesign boutique spread across three floors with footwear, apparel, jewellery, toys and chocolates.

Cottonwood – *50, Needarajapayer Street, Pondicherry 605001. ☏0413 222 0634. Open Tue–Sun 10am–1pm, 4–8pm.* A colourful space for furniture, interior decor, antiques, textiles and handicrafts with art gallery showcasing works of local artists.

Cre'art – *53, Suffren Street. ☏0413 420 0258. Open Mon–Sat, 10am–7.30pm.* Concept boutique in the French Quarter selling eco-friendly clothes and handmade paper journals by Indian and European designers.

Diva Art – *64, Captain Marius Xavier Street, Pondicherry 605001. ☏98949 43386.* Mirrors and unusual vibrant papercraft accessories for interior decor and fashion.

Geethanjali Artifacts – *20, Rue Bussy, Pondicherry 605001. ✆0413 222 5920/420 0392. www.geethanjaliartifacts.com. Open daily 9am–8pm.* Colonial furniture and traditional artefacts like antique doors, pillars, bronzes, paintings and curios.

Kalki – *134, Mission Street, Pondicherry 605001. ✆0413 233 9166/222 1248. www.maroma.com. Open daily 10am–6pm.* Exclusive Auroville shopping with incense, aromatherapy, bodycare products, candles, jewellery, garments and gifts. Has a branch at Auroville Visitors' Centre *(✆0413 262 3450).*

Kasha Ki Aasha – *23, Surcouf Street, Pondicherry 605001. ✆0413 222 2963/ 222 2953. www.kasha-ki-aasha.com. Open Mon–Sat, 8am–7pm.* This craft shop-cum-cafe in an old Colonial home also organises Serenity Beach Bazaar on Sundays.

Living Art Lifestyles – *14, Bazar St Laurent Street, Pondicherry 605001. ✆0413 430 8773/9787748481. www.livingartindia.com. Open Wed–Mon 10am–8.30pm.* A place that fuses traditional art and contemporary style – *diyas*, antiques, candles, furnishings, art, garments and accessories handcrafted in India.

La Maison Rose – *8, Rue Romain Rolland. ✆0413 421 0806. Open Mon–Sun, 10am–7.30pm.* A lovely place with three boutiques, Oh la la! (Agathe Lazaro's creations for men, women, kids and home decor, Amethyst (Indian designer wear), and Domus (furniture).

The Red Courtyard – *2, Chetty Street, Pondicherry 605001. ✆0413 226 0310/ 9894340844/9994687978. theredcourtyard@yahoo.com. Open Mon–Sat, 10am–2pm and 4–7.30pm.* A little shop in a rock-garden courtyard selling designer dresses, accessories, handcrafted jewellery, antiques, home décor.

Touchwood – *44, Needarajapayer Street, Pondicherry 605001 (adjacent to Cottonwood, see opposite). ✆0413 421 0242. Open Tue–Sun 10am–2pm, 4–8pm.* More than just a vibrant handicraft boutique, it is a creative cultural centre with space for performing arts and exhibitions. Bindass Rooftop cafe is a cool hangout.

BOOKSHOPS

Focus Bookstore – *204, Mission Street, Pondicherry 605001. ✆0413 234 5513.* Run by Aurobindo Ashram with books on Indian culture and spirituality and a good collection of travel books.

Higginbotham's – *34, Ambour Salai (JVR Building), Pondicherry 605001. ✆0413 233 3836.* Part of the legendary chain of bookstores, the oldest in the country.

Kailash Librarie Française – *169, Lal Bahadur Shastri (Bussy) Street, Pondicherry 605001. ✆0413 222 8272.* A good selection of coffee-table and French books.

Landmark – *Ginger Hotel, Karuvadikuppam Main Road, Pondicherry 605008. ✆0413 223 4246. www.landmarkonthenet.com.* A tiny bookshop inside Ginger Hotel.

PERFORMING ARTS

Alliance Française – *38, Rue Suffren, Pondicherry 605001. ✆0413 233 8146. www.alliancefrancaisepondichery.com.* Jazz concerts, dance recitals, exhibitions and Sunday evening movies.

Aurodhan – *33, Rue François Martin, Kuruchikuppam, Pondicherry 605012. ✆0413 222 2795/222 2449. www.aurodhan.com. Open daily 9.30am–6.30pm.* Art gallery and exhibition space with dance performances, Indian classical shows and jazz and blues shows.

Jayalakshmi Fine Arts – *221, Mission Street. ✆0413 234 2036. Open daily 9.30am–1.30pm, 3.30–8.30pm, Sun 7am–12.30pm.* A reputed cultural academy with classes in classical dance, music – vocal, *veena* (Indian stringed instrument), *tabla* and other instruments. Private tuitions start at Rs.200/hr *(min 5hr).* Registration fee Rs.350.

NIGHTLIFE

Ska Discotheque – *Ocean Spray Resort, ECR. ✆0413 265 0000. www.oceanspray.in.* Pondy's most happening night spot with a neon dance floor, pool table and DJ. Ladies' night Fridays, DJ nights Saturdays and Desi nights Sundays.

Space Coffee & Arts – *2, Labourdonnais Street, Pondicherry. ✆0413 235 6253. Open 6am–11pm.* Semi open-air rooftop cafe with fairy lights and a lovely ambience to sip beer or cocktails. The gallery also has regular music shows.

Coromandel Coast

Highlights

- Pallava capitals of Kanchipuram and Mamallapuram *p157*
- Chidambaram Nataraja Temple *p168*
- Rama's trail in Rameswaram *p173*
- Danish legacy of Tranquebar *p177*

Dotted with holy shrines, pearl fisheries and ancient seaports, Tamil Nadu's Coromandel Coast has witnessed the ebb and flow of history and for centuries dictated the fortunes of many. While Mamallapuram prospered as a port under the Pallavas of Kanchi, it was succeeded by Nagapattinam of the Cholas, which flourished as a Buddhist centre from the 8C. Seeking to bypass the Arab traders who controlled maritime trade, European powers soon converged onto the coast, anglicising its name Cholamandalam or 'Realm of the Cholas' to Coromandel. By late 1530 the Portuguese had established a settlement at Mylapore (São Tomé). Soon, the Danes docked at Tranquebar (Tharangambadi) in 1620, the British moved from Masulipatnam to Madras in 1639, the Dutch shifted their headquarters from Pulicat to Nagapattinam by 1660 and the French established themselves at Pondicherry in 1671, acquiring Karaikal in 1737. All these delightful influences have shaped Coromandel's cultural, architectural and spiritual landscape. It was here that the first printing press in India and the oldest Tamil dictionary were conceived.

Fishermen and their boat sailing off from the Mamallpuram beach in the morning

COROMANDEL COAST

The Coromandel belt is a multi-hued palette of holy shrines, tranquil beaches, historic ports and stunning wildlife and bird sanctuaries. The great Pallava cities of **Mamallapuram**★★★ and **Kanchipuram**★★ are to the south and west of **Chennai**. **Cuddalore**, **Chidambaram**★ and **Tranquebar**★★ lie south of **Pondicherry**★ on a linear route along NH-45A, which runs parallel to the coast. Further south, beyond **Point Calimere Wildlife Sanctuary**, is the holy island of **Rameswaram**★, accessible via **Ramanathapuram**.

Mamallapuram★★★

Described as 'Kadal Malai', where the mountains meet the sea, the 7C Pallava port was named after Narasimhavarman I (630-68), hailed as Mahabali or Maha-malla, the great wrestler. Most of the historic monuments of Mamallapuram (or Mahabalipuram) were built during his reign and that of Narasimha Varman II (700-28). As the seaport flourished, it became a great centre for Pallava artists. Even today, the constant clink of chisel on stone echoes through its rock-cut caves and temples that have been accorded the status of a UNESCO World Heritage Site.

Exploring the Area – Branching off from ECR, the East Raja Street runs north

- **Population:** 478 per sq km.
- **Info:** Tourist Office, Beach Resort Complex, off ECR, Mamallapuram 603104. 044 27442232. www.tamilnadutourism.org.
- **Location:** South-eastern coast of Tamil Nadu from Pulicat to Kanyakumari (Cape Comorin). *See Chennai and Around and Pondicherry for sights north of Mamallapuram.*
- **Kids:** Mandapam Beach Park (Rameswaram).
- **Timing:** Keep a week aside for a road trip, preferably in the cooler months of Oct–Feb or during festivals.
- **Guided Tours:** TTDC organises a 1-day Kanchipuram–Mamallpuram coach tour that includes boating at Muttukadu *(see Chennai and Around).* They also organise a 3-day Rameswaram Tour by train (Rameswaram Express) from Chennai. Guided Boat Tours at Pichavaram's mangrove forests are available. *(See Planning Your Trip).*

to south of town and is the arterial road of Mamallapuram. It is intersected by three horizontal roads – Tirukkalkunram Road (leading to the hill shrine 15km west), Othavadai Street (a colourful lane with a concentration of budget lodges, shops and cafes) and Beach Road past the bus stand (leading to the **beach** and **Shore Temple**★★). West of the bus stand and running parallel to East Raja Street is Mada Koil Street, where **Arjuna's Penance**★★ and most of the rock-cut cave temples are located. The **Pancha Rathas**★★ lies to the southern end of the town while many of the major beach resorts lie north, off the ECR.
See Historical Sights, Beaches.

Kanchipuram★★

Ranked among the *saptapuris* or seven holy cities in ancient India, Kanchipuram is the only one south of the Vindhyas. Lauded in Tamil literature, dotted by 1,000 temples and home to learned scholars and saints, it was hailed as 'Nagareshu Kanchi' or the 'City of cities'. The capital of the Pallava kingdom and a vibrant centre of culture and trade for centuries, Kanchi controlled oil trade in the region. Every home had a *nadumuttram* or open courtyard where harvested rainwater was diverted into mills for oil extraction. The city's glorious weaving tradition of exquisite handwoven Kanjeevaram silks and cotton saris continues to this day in every street and alley.
Exploring the Area – When a city has 1,000 temples, it's important to know what to see. Kanchipuram is spread around two clusters – Big Kanchi (Shiva Kanchi), dominated by the **Kanchi Kamakshi Amman Temple**★ in the heart of town surrounded by 108 Shiva shrines, and Little Kanchi (Vishnu Kanchi) to the south-east that spreads around **Varadaraja Perumal Temple**★★. Kanchi also bears traces of two older quarters – Buddha Kanchi and Jain Kanchi, evident in the suburb of Tiruparuttikunram. Most shrines are located in and around the central quadrangle of Raja Street. 28km south is the temple town of **Uthiramerur**★.
See Religious and Spiritual Sights.

Chidambaram★

Once upon a time, the mangrove forests of **Pichavaram**★ stretched from the coast right up to Chidambaram. It was in this *thillai vanam* that Lord Shiva performed his Urddhva Tandava to defeat goddess Kali (*see sidebar p170*). It is thus no coincidence that the *thillai (Excoecaria agallocha)*, a mangrove species known for its sticky blinding sap, is the *sthala vriksha* (sacred tree) at the **Nataraja Temple**★★. Set aside half a day to do justice to the massive temple before exploring the world's second-largest mangrove forest at Pichavaram.
Exploring the Area – The **Nataraja Temple**★★ lies in the heart of Chidambaram in the central quadrangle of Car Street with access roads and temple towers on the north, south, east and west. The **Thillai Kali Amman Temple** is to the north of town while a 14km drive from Chidambaram off NH-45A leads to the unique ecological attraction of **Pichavaram**★.
See Religious and Spiritual Sights, National Parks and Wildlife Sanctuaries.

Tranquebar★★

Prior to becoming the only Danish outpost in India, Tranquebar was a small fishing village called Tharangambadi or Land of the Singing Waves. It was here missionary Bartolomeus Ziegenbalg established India's first printing press and did the first Tamil translation of the New Testament in 1715. The Danes built the Dansborg citadel and fortified *Trankebar* to assume complete control in 1777, eventually selling it to the British in 1845 for 12.5 lakh rupees. Apart from the Danish legacy, Tranquebar's beach is equally heady. Identified as one of the world's two ozone-rich beaches, the ozone breeze is believed to have a rejuvenating effect.
Exploring the Area – Most of Tranquebar's historic sights are within the walled precincts of the fortified town. A regal avenue called Kongensgade (King's Street) stretches from Landporten (Town Gate) in the west, past **New Jerusalem Church**★, **Zion's Church** and **Governor's Bungalow** to

GETTING THERE AND AROUND

(See also Planning Your Trip.)

GETTING THERE

BY PLANE – Chennai International Airport *(see p106)* is the perfect access point for exploring the Coromandel Coast from the north.

BY CAR – Kanchipuram *(75km south-west of Chennai)* is a 1.5hr drive on NH-4 via Sriperumbudur. Just 58km south of Chennai, Mamallapuram is accessible via the East Coast Road, which continues past Pondicherry all the way down the coast as NH-45A, linking Chidambaram, Tranquebar, Nagapattinam and Velankanni; all no more than 3hr drives from Trichy (Tiruchirappalli) International Airport *(about 160km to the west)*. Further south, Rameswaram is a 3.5hr drive from Madurai airport *(174km north-west)*.

BY BUS AND TRAIN – There are daily connections from Chennai to all destinations. From Chennai Egmore station the Rameswaram Express *(16701)* leaves every night at 9.40pm via Chidambaram, Sirkazhi and Mayiladuthurai to reach Rameswaram at noon the next day. The Nagore Express *(16175)* departs at 11.15pm to reach Nagore at 9.15am via Chidambaram and Nagapattinam.

GETTING AROUND

An excellent road network and good connectivity to major towns make it easy to explore the coast **by car**. The NH-45A *(ECR)* is a scenic drive *(see Driving Tour p160)*. Pre-paid cabs can be arranged in Chennai or Kanchipuram for Rs.2,500-3,000 per day for outstation trips.

Buses leave every 15min from Chennai to Kanchi between 4.30am and 10.30pm. Regular TNSTC day buses ply from Chennai to Nagapattinam via Mamallapuram, Pondicherry, Cuddalore, Chidambaram, Sirkazhi, Tranquebar, Karaikal and Nagore. Overnight SETC (State Express Transport Corporation) buses depart from Chennai Metropolitan Bus Terminus (CMBT) at Koyambedu *(044 24794705/9, www.tnstc.in)* to Nagapattinam and Velankanni. **Auto rickshaws** are ideal for local explorations, though **bicycles** and **two-wheelers** are also available on hire.

the Bungalow on the Beach, Neemrana's heritage hotel on the eastern seafront. To the right are **Ziegenbalg Memorial**, **Parade Ground** and **Dansborg Fort**★ while the **Masilamani Temple** stands to the left, constantly lashed by the sea. Other heritage buildings line Queen's Street, a road that cuts King's Street from north to south.

See Historical Sights.

Rameswaram★

One of the spiritual sites marking the four cardinal directions in India, the conch-shaped island of Rameswaram is a busy pilgrim centre. The **Ramanathaswami Temple** where Lord Rama worshipped Shiva after his conquest of (Sri) Lanka is the town's focal point. The 22 *theerthams* (holy tanks) within the temple and 31 sites scattered around the shrine form an important spiritual circuit for Hindus.

Exploring the Area – Rameswaram is an island surrounded by the Palk Strait and the Gulf of Mannar. Cut off from the mainland by the Pamban Channel, Rameswaram is connected to Mandapam (on the mainland) by the 2.3km Pamban Bridge.

A popular day trip from the island's main village (also called Rameswaram) is 18km south, to **Dhanushkodi**★, where the confluence of the Indian Ocean and the Bay of Bengal can be seen from the beach. Once connected by rail, Dhanushkodi is now accessible only by sandy tracks on four-wheel drive vans from Mukunduraya Chatiram, 14km from Rameswaram.

See Religious and Spiritual Sights.

DRIVING TOUR

COROMANDEL COAST

Though the 94km drive from Chidambaram to Velankanni via Nagore touches the holiest Hindu, Muslim and Christian shrines on the Coromandel Coast, NH-45A is more than a spiritual highway. With ancient Chola ports, Danish enclaves, French colonies and unique temples dotting the drive, it is a journey down history. The 2hr road trip may well stretch into 2 days, so start early.

From Chidambaram drive 10km south on NH-45A to Thaikkal, midway to Sirkazhi.

Thaikkal

A short 10km drive south of **Chidambaram**★, just across the Kollidam River is the charming village of Thaikkal, known for its weaving industry. A long line of thatched shops along the road flaunt striking *korai pai* (grass mats), cane swing chairs and baskets. It's a busy, narrow highway so park carefully for a quick buy.

Continue 10km on NH-45A to Sirkazhi.

Sirkali Bhramapureeswarar

An ancient three-tiered temple complex dedicated to three forms of Shiva. On the ground floor is the Brahmapureeswarar shrine where Brahma is believed to have worshipped Lord Shiva. The second level houses Shiva and Parvati on a *thoni* (boat). During the great deluge, Lord Shiva is said to have carried the 64 arts with him in a raft to this shrine, hence the name Thoniappar. On the third level Shiva is depicted as Sattanathar or Bhairavar, who quelled the arrogance of Trivikrama (Vishnu).

Drive 2km south of Sirkazhi on NH-45A and turn right at Sattanathapuram onto SH-64 for a 5km detour to Vaitheeswaran Temple at Pullirukkuvelur.

Vaitheeswaran Koil

One of the nine Navagraha temples (*see p236*) renowned for its Naadi astrologers, this is believed to be the spot where Angaraka (Mars) was cured of leprosy. Lord Shiva is worshipped as Vaitheeswaran or God of Medicine and his consort Thaiyalnayaki Ambal stands holding a bottle of medicinal oil to cure all diseases. Devotees offer *milagu* (pepper), salt and jaggery in the waters of the Siddhamritham tank and take a holy dip to cure their ailments.

Return to NH-45A and drive 10km south to Mudikandanallur (after Alangadu Junction) and turn left onto SH-22 for a 9km ride to the coast.

Poompuhar

The legendary port of Kaveripoompattinam, where the Cauvery meets the sea in poetic beauty (*poom* in Tamil) is the historic setting of the Tamil epic *Silappathikara* (Story of the Anklet). The namesake art gallery, a modern ostentatious building with an imposing makara thoranavayil (entrance) portrays the epic through stone sculptures carved by the students of Mamallapuram Art College. Statues of Kannagi and courtesan Madhavi adorn the gallery, though the *pièce de résistance* is the anklet-shaped tank. For history buffs, the **Marine Archaeology Museum** (*See p182*) is worth a visit.

Backtrack 9km from SH-22 onto NH-45A and turn left for the 10km drive to Thirukadaiyur.

Thirukadaiyur

Thirukadaiyur is known for its **Amrithakadeshwarar-Abirami Temple**, where the boy sage Markandeya prayed to Lord Shiva to save him from premature death at the hands of Yama. The temple is associated with longevity and couples observe significant landmarks in their life with special *pujas* like Shastiapthapoorthi (completing 60 years), Bheemaradha Shanthi (turning 70) and Sadabishegam (turning 80). Hotels like Abirami Residency, Vishwa, Sadabhighegam, Manivizha and Mookambikai Residency are overnight stay options. For *pujas*, contact: www.shastiapthapoorthi.com.

Continue 8km south on NH-45A to Tranquebar. Follow the Neemrana signboards to the left and enter through the Danish town gate.

Tranquebar★★

The Danish fortified town of Tranquebar (Tharangambadi) is the mid-point of this Coromandel coastal drive and an ideal stopover for the night. A walking tours will give you glimpses of its history (*see p178–9*). If in a hurry, take a quick drive down the historic King's Street to see **Dansborg Fort**★ (*see p177*), near the Bungalow on the Beach.

Exit from Landporten (Town Gate) back on to NH-45A and drive 14km south to Karaikal. You can't miss the church; its belfry is the tallest landmark in town.

Karaikal

Part of the Union Territory of Pondicherry, Karaikal's most arresting French monument is Our Lady of Angel's Church. Built a year after purchasing Karaikal from the King of Tanjore in 1739, the church was demolished by the British in 1760 but rebuilt by the French within a decade. After renovations in 1843, a 41m/133ft-tall belfry was added half a century later to house three huge clocks and five imported bells.

Drive 16km south of Karaikal on NH-45A for Nagore Dargah (see p171), before continuing 4km to Nagapattinam.

Nagapattinam

An ancient emporium in the Sangam period, Nagapattinam was an important Buddhist site in the 4–5C and at the centre of trading tussles between Colonial powers. St Anthony's Church, the CSI Christ Church, old Buddha Vihar, Custom House and Post Office are historic landmarks. The shoddy Government Museum can be overlooked as most of its exhibits were shifted to Madurai after the 2004 tsunami. A 12km drive further south leads to the holy pilgrim town of Velankanni.

Velankanni★

This old port town is famous for the **Basilica of Our Lady of Good Health**★ (*see p171*). Originally built in the 16C by Portuguese sailors, the Roman Catholic shrine has been renovated into a fine piece of Gothic architecture with tall white spires soaring to the sky.

Basilica of Our Lady of Good Health, Velankanni

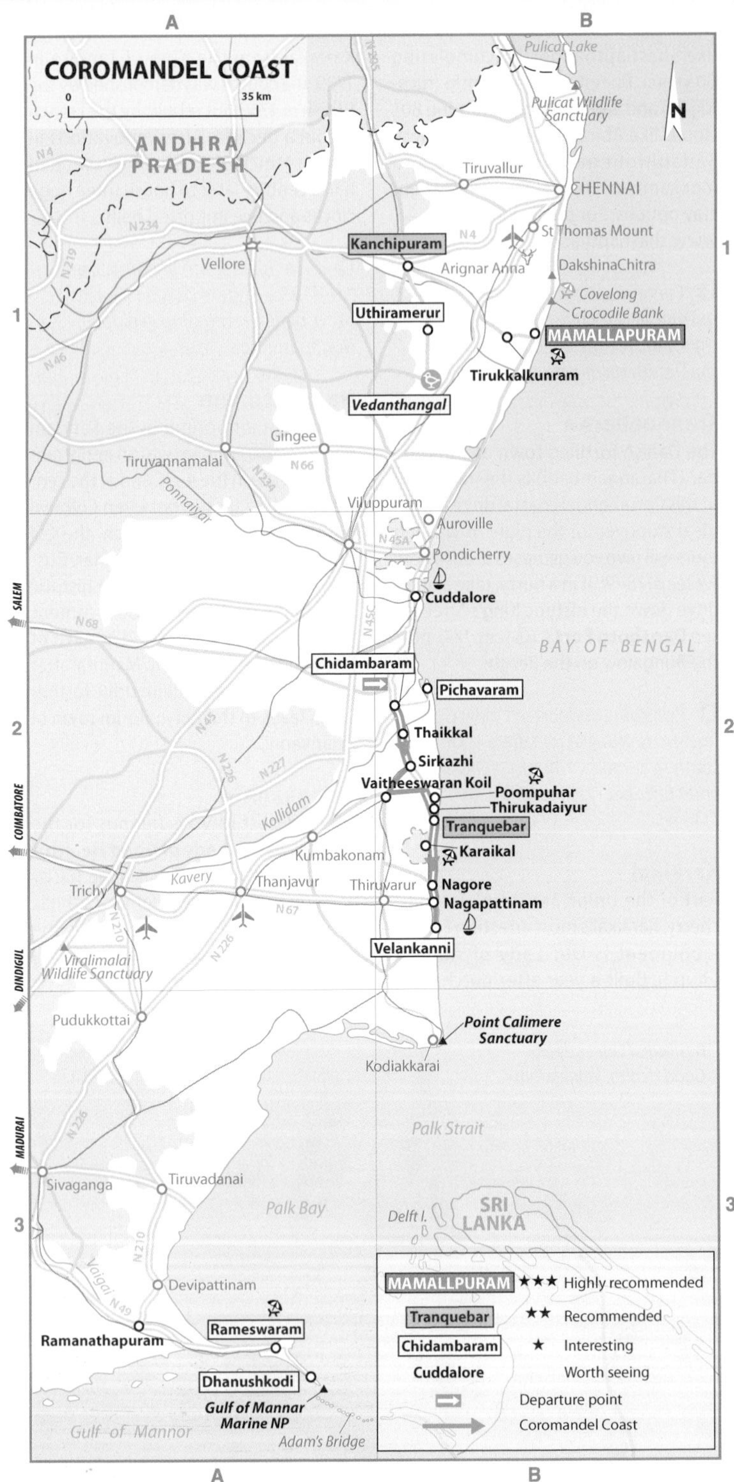

COROMANDEL COAST
0
35 km
A
B
1
2
3
N
ANDHRA PRADESH
Pulicat Lake
Pulicat Wildlife Sanctuary
Tiruvallur
CHENNAI
St Thomas Mount
Kanchipuram
Vellore
Arignar Anna
DakshinaChitra
Covelong
Crocodile Bank
Uthiramerur
MAMALLAPURAM
Tirukkalkunram
Vedanthangal
Gingee
Tiruvannamalai
Ponnaiyar
Viluppuram
Auroville
Pondicherry
Cuddalore
BAY OF BENGAL
SALEM
Chidambaram
Pichavaram
Thaikkal
Sirkazhi
Vaitheeswaran Koil
Poompuhar
Thirukadaiyur
Tranquebar
Karaikal
Kollidam
Kumbakonam
COIMBATORE
Kavery
Trichy
Thanjavur
Thiruvarur
Nagore
Nagapattinam
Velankanni
DINDIGUL
Viralimalai Wildlife Sanctuary
Pudukkottai
Point Calimere Sanctuary
Kodiakkarai
Palk Strait
MADURAI
Sivaganga
Tiruvadanai
Palk Bay
Delft I.
SRI LANKA
Vaigai
Devipattinam
Ramanathapuram
Rameswaram
Dhanushkodi
Gulf of Mannar Marine NP
Gulf of Mannor
Adam's Bridge
N4
N234
N219
N46
N205
N66
N45A
N45C
N68
N45
N226
N227
N210
N67
N49
MAMALLPURAM ★★★ Highly recommended
Tranquebar ★★ Recommended
Chidambaram ★ Interesting
Cuddalore Worth seeing
Departure point
Coromandel Coast

Religious and Spiritual Sights

Coromandel's celebrated shrines witness a steady flow of tourists all year round and multitudes of people in the festive season. The region is a rich brew of old Portuguese and Danish churches, Jain and Buddhist heritage, 16C Muslim *dargahs* and the dominating essence of Hindu temples built by the South's mightiest dynasties, marked by the triad of Kanchipuram, Chidambaram and Rameswaram.

TIRUKKALKUNRAM

15km west of Mamallapuram on SH-58 between Sadras and Chengalpattu (22km), about 70km south of Chennai. Bus 212A from Mamallapuram to Kanchi leaves every hour (Rs.5). *Vedagiriswarar Thirukovil, Tirukkalkunram, Kanchipuram District. Open daily 8.30am–1pm, 5–7pm. Entry Rs.2 (camera Rs.10, video Rs.25, Doli (palanquin) carrier Rs.150). Rs.15. 044 27447139.*

Reachable by a flight of 561 steps from an arched gateway, the temple of Vedagiriswarar and his consort Tripurasundari sits on Vedagiri Hill like a crown. The holy birds of Tirukkalkunram haven't been seen since 1998, but that does not diminish the sanctity of the unique Temple of Eagles. For centuries a pair of Egyptian vultures have visited the site around noon each day, to be fed an offering of rice, wheat, ghee and sugar prepared by the temple priests. To the untrained eye, the vultures appear as eagles (*kazhagu* in Tamil), hence the name *kazhagu koil* or *thiru-kazhagu-kundram*, meaning, Sacred Hill of the Eagles. According to legend, the birds represent eight heavenly sages who were punished by Lord Shiva to appear as pairs in each of the four *yugas* (eras). It is after these legendary birds that the temple is also called *Pakshi theertham*. The steep climb to the top offers a great view of the temple spires at the base of the hill where Lord Ganesha is enshrined, and Sangu Theertham (Conch Tank). Spread over 1,000 square yards, the raised rectangular pond has a shrine at its centre that houses over 1,000 conch shells. The shells miraculously emerge from the freshwater tank every 12 years. The Chitra Masam festival around March is a holy time to visit.

KANCHIPURAM★★

Ekambaranath Temple

Turn off from the Kanchipuram–Chengalpattu road into the temple street to access the shrine from South Mada Street in the northern part of town. The temple is 2km from the bus

Mango tree in Ekambaranath Temple

Ekambaranath and the Sacred Mango Tree

Kanchi is one of the *pancha-bhoota sthalams* where Lord Shiva is worshipped in the form of earth, one of the five elements. After Parvati playfully closed Lord Shiva's eyes and plunged the universe into darkness, she was sent to earth to expiate. As the love-lorn Kamakshi, the goddess performed great austerities and worshipped Lord Shiva by fashioning a *lingam* out of sand under a mango tree. In a divine test, Lord Shiva caused the neighbouring Vegavati River to overflow and flood the town. Not fearing for her own safety, Kamakshi embraced the *prithvi lingam* tightly, leaving the imprint of her bangles and breasts on it. Pleased by her devotion, Lord Shiva agreed to marry Kamakshi, who was united *(ekya)* with the Lord under the same mango *(amram)* tree. Thus the mud-*linga* of the Lord *(nath)* is worshipped as Ekambaranath, who is referred to as **Tazhuva Kuzhainthaar** in Tamil (He Who Melted in Her Embrace). The 3,500-year-old mango tree still stands in the temple compound. As a tribute, none of the temples in Kanchi have a separate shrine for Parvati, except the Kamakshi Temple, which is her divine abode.

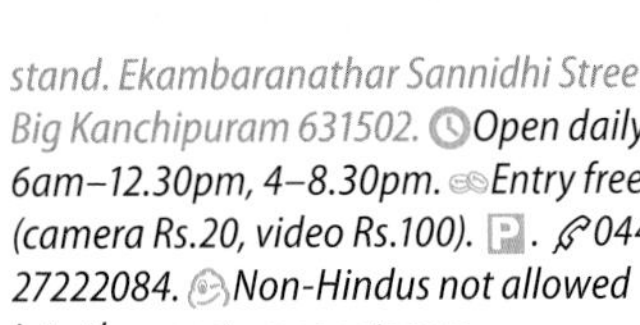

stand. Ekambaranathar Sannidhi Street, Big Kanchipuram 631502. Open daily 6am–12.30pm, 4–8.30pm. Entry free (camera Rs.20, video Rs.100). . 044 27222084. Non-Hindus not allowed into the sanctum sanctorum.

The largest and most popular Shiva temple in Kanchi, the 57m/187ft-high Rajagopuram of Ekambaranathar (or Ekambareswara) towers above the city's skyline. The sanctum sanctorum is believed to be 5,000 years old and the temple was renovated by several royal dynasties. The Pallavas built the shrine, the Cholas renovated it and the Vijayanagar kings added musical pillars, a *kalyana mantapa* and the nine-storey *gopuram*, erected by Krishnadevaraya in 1509. The outer sanctum is marked by a *makara thorana vayil*, a grand arched entrance shaped like a *makara*, a mythical sea creature with head and jaws of a crocodile, elephant trunk, scales of fish and a peacock tail. After *darshan* of the *prithvi lingam*, which has an unusual conical shape, it's customary to visit the sacred mango tree under whose shade Shiva and Parvati got married (*see sidebar opposite*). A stump of the 3,500-year-old tree is displayed at the entrance while a hallway past the temple *vahanas* (vehicles) leads to a courtyard where the original tree stands. It has four branches that bear fruits of four different shapes and tastes as an embodiment of the four *vedas*. Other highlights are the shrines of Bhadrakali Amman, Sahasra Lingam (a tall, beautiful *lingam* with 1,000 mini-*lingams* carved on it), the Vishnu shrine outside and the festive idols of the main deities. The large complex has five spacious corridors and a beautiful 1,000-pillared hall lined by granite columns capped with lions and lotus embellishments. During Navaratri, all the 108 Shiva *lingas* in the temple are lit up with lamps.

Kailasanatha Temple★★★

3km from the bus stand on the western edge of the city. 1.5km from Ekamberaswarar Temple, to the west of Putheri (SVN Pillai) Street at Big Kanchipuram. SVN Pillai Street, Kanchipuram 631501. Open 6am–6pm. Sanctum closes at 12noon. . Guided Tours: ASI employees double up as guides.

Set against sprawling lawns under the benign gaze of a massive Nandi, stands the squat sandstone temple complex of Kailasanatha. It is the oldest structure in Kanchi and represents early Dravidian architecture. Pallava king Rajasimha (Narasimhavarman II) constructed it as a royal shrine in the late 7C AD and his queens and son Mahendravarman III added the front portion in the 8C. About 58 small sub-shrines of Shiva, Parvati, Ganesha and Murugan surround the temple.

Once richly painted in vegetable dyes, sadly only a few alcoves with traces of

Pillars supported by standing lions, Kailasanatha Temple

© Anurag Mallick, Priya Ganapathy/MICHELIN

these ancient 8C murals remain. However, the profusion of carvings and detailed manifestations of Lord Shiva as Nataraja, Lingodbhava, Dakshinamoorthy and Ardhanarisvara can keep one enthralled for hours.

Kailasanatha was a worthy successor of the rock temples built earlier by the Pallavas at **Mamallapuram**★★★, where pillars were supported by seated lions. Interestingly, at Kanchipuram the grimacing lions stand on their hind legs, as if ready to pounce on anyone casting an evil eye on the empire.

Though the temple was spared any additions by the Chola and Vijayanagar kings, King Rajaraja Chola I did visit the temple and named it *Kachipettu Periya Thirukatrali* or 'Kanchi's Old Stone Temple'. Its splendid sanctum spire is believed to have inspired Rajaraja Chola I to build the **Brihadisvara Temple**★★★ at Thanjavur (*see p243*).

Perhaps the most intriguing feature of the temple is the small, narrow passage around the presiding deity of Rajasimheshwara. Devotees crawl into a hole to the left and emerge to the right, in an act of rebirth, which is believed to help them attain *moksha* or salvation.

Kanchi Kamakshi Amman Temple★

Accessed from Raja's Street or Kanchipuram Chengalpattu Road. New No. 6, Old No. 144/A, Kamakshi Amman Sannathi Street, Big Kanchipuram 631502. Open 5.30am–12noon, 4–8.30pm. Entry free. P. 044 27233433/27221214. www.kanchikamakshi.com. Non-Hindus not allowed into the sanctum sanctorum.

Of the 108 Shiva temples in Kanchi, Sri Kamakshi Amman is the only temple to have a separate *sanctorum* for the goddess. Besides Madurai Meenakshi and Vishalakshi in Varanasi, Kamakshi ranks among the three holiest shrines in India dedicated to Parvati. Kamakshi, or the Goddess of Love, who won Shiva's hand with her ardour, is the presiding deity of Kanchi. Built in the 14C by the Cholas, the temple is spread over 2ha/5 acres and has four entrances. Enter from the main *gopuram* flanked by statues of Kalabhairavar and Mahishasuramardini. Gayatri Mandapam, the place where the goddess resides, is marked by a golden *vimanam* (spire) crowning the sanctum. Kamakshi is seated in *padmasana* (lotus posture) displaying a meditative pose and is worshipped as Parabrahma Swaroopini. It is believed that Adi Sankaracharya installed a *sri chakra* (yantra) in front of the original *ugra swaroopini* (fierce form) to transform her into *shanta swaroopini* (beatific form). An image of Sankaracharya is also worshipped and the temple is closely connected to **Sri Kamakoti Peetam** nearby. Behind the

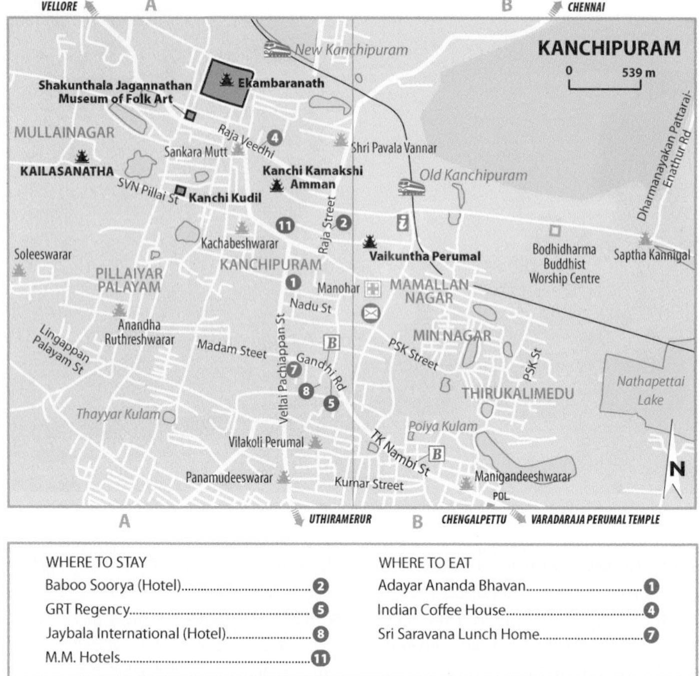

main shrine there is the temple tank and a tree where devotees offer wooden cradles. Fridays and full moon days are very auspicious. The Goddess Kamakshi is taken out on a procession within the temple precincts every Friday evening on a silver chariot while the temple is open for *darshan* at 11.30pm on all full moon days. Nearby, drop by at the **Ulagananda Perumal Temple** to see the large image of Lord Vishnu as Vamana stepping on the demon king Vali.

Vaikuntha Perumal Temple

Enter from East Raja Street diagonally opposite the flower market. Vaikuntha Perumal Koil Street, Big Kanchipuram 631502. Open 6am–12noon, 4–8pm. Entry free.

Built shortly after the construction of the **Kailasanath Temple** by Pallava King Paramesvara (Nandivarman II), Vaikuntha Perumal is a stone masonry temple dedicated to Lord Vishnu. Like the Sundara **Varadaraja Perumal temple**★★ at **Uthiramerur**★, the rare shrine is built on three different levels with Lord Vishnu worshipped in sitting, reclining and standing positions (*see p168–9*). The second tier is open on monthly Ekadasis (fasting days) while the temple's partially damaged third tier is opened once a year on the auspicious Vaikunta Ekadasi. The covered passages inside the temple's outer walls are supported by richly decorated sculptures depicting the life and times of King Paramesvara, the history of the temple, along with detailed explanations in an 8C script.

Varadaraja Perumal Temple★★

Continue on Gandhi Road past TK Nambi Street to reach the south-eastern edge of town. Where the Kanchipuram-Chengalpattu highway turns sharply to the left, enter from CV Rajagopal Street onto Sannathi Street. Varadaraja Perumal Sannathi Street, Little Kanchi, Kanchipuram 631501. Open 7am–12noon, 3.30–8pm. Rs.1 (100-Pillared Mandapam), Rs.2 (Darshan), (camera Rs.5, video Rs.100). Guided Tours: local guides are available. 044 27222773. www.kanchivaradarajartemple.com. Non-

Varadaraja Perumal, the Bestower of Boons

According to legend, after creating the universe, Lord Brahma desired to worship Lord Vishnu in his glorious form as Narayana. Despite his strict austerities, Brahma's desire was unfulfilled and a holy voice directed him to perform 1,000 Aswamedha Yaga (horse sacrifice), or he could go to Satyavrata Sthala (present-day Kanchi) and perform just one *yaga*. Hence the belief that a good deed done in **Kanchipuram★★** yields thousand-fold benefits. Brahma instructed the divine architect Vishwakarma to erect a city at Kanchi for the purpose. Since Brahma started performing the *yaga* without his consort Saraswathi, the angry goddess took the form of Vegavathi, a 'swift-flowing river' and threatened to destroy the sacrificial area. Brahma prayed to Lord Vishnu, who lay down in the path of the flowing river. As Saraswathi did not have the strength to cross Lord Vishnu, she entered the earth and disappeared. Saraswathi was later pacified and Brahma was able to perform his Aswamedha Yaga. As promised, Lord Narayana emerged from the holy fire in his resplendent form, which is why the face of the idol is riddled with dots. When the lord asked what Brahma wanted, he entreated him to reside permanently in this sacred place to bless all of humanity with his divine form. Narayana agreed and was henceforth known as Varada-raja Perumal, the royal bestower of boons.

Hindus are not permitted beyond the dhwajasthambam (flagstaff).

One of the holiest Vaishnava shrines in Kanchi, Varadaraja Perumal Temple, formerly known as Atthiiyurar, is perched on a slight elevation called the Hastagiri Hill. The number 40, symbolic of the four *vedas*, assumes particular significance here. Spread over 40 acres, the main shrine is reachable by 40 steps and there are 40 steps in the temple tank, **Anantha Saras teertha**, where the original deity of Atthi Varadar is housed. Every 40 years, the water is drained out and the 10m/32ft 9in-long wooden idol (carved from a fig tree) is taken out to mark the grand festival. The last time the spectacle took place was in 1979 and the next festival is scheduled to start at 6am on 2 July, 2019.

The palatial temple with four *prakaras* (compounds) was constructed across four centuries by various dynasties. The inside structure was built by the Pallavas, the main *gopuram* by Cholas while the Vijayanagar king Krishnadeva Raya built the magnificent 100-pillared **Kalyana Mandapam** in 16C out of a monolithic block of granite. Rearing horses serve as pillars and chains carved out of stone hang at the four corners to show the sculptor's mastery. Borne by a giant tortoise, the base of the *singhasanam* (throne) has stones that move and lace-like ornamentation through which toothpicks can be passed! When tapped, pillars emit distinct sounds of gold, silver and copper. The reliefs on the pillars depict sages, gods, courtesans and jesters; even European soldiers depicted as bearded men with striped trousers! Every inch of sculpted space is a statement. On either side of a mounted horse, a moustachioed figure depicts a North Indian soldier whereas on the other side he is turbanned like a South Indian.

Entering the inner courtyard, one climbs 10 steps, followed by 24 steps to the main shrine (representing the 24-syllable Gayatri mantra), before climbing the final six steps to the large statue of Varadaraja Perumal. The walls of the sanctum are decorated with ancient murals depicting Lord Krishna in Brindavan and expounding the Bhagwad Gita. Another highlight is the **golden lizard** in a side chamber. As per legend, Sage Bhrigu had two sons who were entrusted with the task of bringing holy water for worship every day. One day, the sage saw two dead lizards in the water with which *puja* had just been performed and cursed that his sons would be lizards in their next births. They were relieved of the curse only after praying to Vara-

Uthiramerur's Kudavolai System

Few know that the tiny village of **Uthiramerur★** is also heralded as the birthplace of democracy. A stone edict inscribed on the granite walls of the *grama sabha mandapa* (village assembly hall) at Vaikuntha Perumal Temple outlines the idealistic Kudavolai electoral system practised in the village. Dating to the reign of Parantaka Chola around AD 920, the Uthiramerur Kalvettu is an outstanding proof of local self-governance during the Chola period. The written constitution prescribes the mode of elections in the village administration, usually divided into 30 wards. Names of all contestants were written on chits of palm leaf, shuffled in a pot and drawn by a boy to choose elected representatives who looked after the garden, temple tanks and other committees. Unlike today's political scenario marred by crime and graft, the Kudavolai system was the Lokpal bill of its times. Contestants had to be between 35 to 70 years old, possess one *veli* land (ancient measure) and have a house built on taxable land on their own site. Knowledge of *vedas* and mantras was mandatory. Thieves, drunkards, people who had undergone punishments or those who had killed brahmins, women, cows or children were automatically disqualified.

daraja at Kanchi. The icons of two lizards and symbols of the sun and the moon on the ceiling hark back to this legend. Devotees climb a ladder to touch the motifs in order to rid themselves of any curse or ailments.

British general Robert Clive, a Vishnu devotee, is said to have presented an emerald necklace to the deity Varadaraja Perumal. The ornament is called **Clive makarakandi** and still used to decorate the idol on ceremonial occasions. The golden *utsava murti* is taken out after the daily morning *puja* around the main shrine.

Five main festivals are held every month to mark *amavasya* (new moon), *poornima* (full moon), *ekadasi* (11th day), *masa parab* (Tamil month) and *shravan nakshatra* (the deity's star). With 300 days earmarked for festivals in any given year, the chances of witnessing celebrations are high.

AROUND KANCHIPURAM

Uthiramerur★

Exit Kanchipuram town from Vallal Pachiappan Street, cross the Palar River and continue past the Vyakrapureeswarar Temple to reach Uthiramerur, 28km south. Sundara Varadarajan Street, Uthiramerur, Kanchipuram District 603406. Open daily 5am–12noon, 4–8pm. P. *044 27272693/94430 68382.*

Once known as Chaturvedhimangalam after King Nandivarma Pallavan donated the village to 1,200 Vedic scholars, Uthiramerur is a unique temple town. Beyond the Vaikuntha Perumal Temple in a landscaped garden, the white spire of the Sundara Varadaraja Perumal Temple lures passersby who are drawn by its antiquity. Built in AD 750 by the Pallavas, the unusual temple enshrines Perumal (Lord Vishnu) in all three postures – *ninraan* (standing), *irundhaan* (sitting) and *kidandhaan* (reclining). The sanctum is built in such a way that all three forms are set one above the other on three floors. Sri Sundara Varadaraja Perumal, the presiding deity, stands on the ground level accompanied by Sri Devi and Bhoodevi. Sri Vaikunda Varadhar is seen in the sitting posture on the next level while Sri Ranganathar rests on the snake Aadhisesha on the third floor. Exploring the maze of passages, inner sanctums and staircases without the usual rush of tourists or pilgrims makes the temple a delightful stopover.

CHIDAMBARAM★

Thillai Nataraja Temple★★

Enter town from the north by NH-45A onto North Car Street and turn right to reach East Car Street. East Car Street, Chidambaram 608001. Open 6am–12noon, 4.30–10.30pm. Entry free. P. *Guided Tours: Temple dikshi-*

tars often double up as guides though regular guides are also available. www.tillai.com.

Once a *thillai vana* (mangrove forest) where Lord Shiva performed his Ananda Tandava or Dance of Bliss, Chidambaram is the birthplace of the famous icon of Nataraja as the Cosmic Dancer (*see sidebar p170*). Here, Shiva propounded the theory and function of dance forms and 108 Bharatanatyam poses adorn the eastern and western towers. Chidambaram is also a *pancha bhoota sthalam* where Shiva is worshipped as **akash** or space, one of the five elements. Devotees focus their consciousness *(chitt)* on a formless space on a stage *(ambalam)*, from which the place derives its name. Spread over 21ha/51 acres, the Thillai Nataraja Temple is an architectural marvel where every space is nuanced with meaning and symbolism.

Built like a Kundalini *chakra* as per the Shaiva Siddhanta philosophy, the temple architecture is similar to the construction of the human body. The roof is made up of 21,600 gold tiles that represent the number of breaths the average human takes in a day. They are fixed by 72,000 nails, which symbolize the *nadis* (veins) in the body. The nine *kalasams* (finials) on the roof represent the nine energy centres and nine holes in the human body. The sandalwood frame of the sanctum sanctorum represents the skeletal system and where the Nataraj idol lies, is the heart. Four 41m/135ft-high towers with soaring 12m/40ft entrances lead to the magnificent temple, which has five *sabhas* (halls or stages). The **Nritta Sabha** or Dance Hall has magnificent sculptures of Shiva in Urddhva Tandava pose, and Kali marks the place where the dance competition was held. The **Deva Sabha** or Hall of the Gods is where the festival deities are kept, **Raja Sabha** is lined by the 1,000-pillared hall, **Kanaka Sabha** is the Golden Hall where the daily rituals are conducted and **Chit Sabha** is the Hall of Consciousness where Nataraja and Shivakami are housed.

It is reachable by a flight of five silver plated steps that represent the five syllables of the Panchakshara mantra *'Om Nama Shivaya'*. Here it is possible to worship god in both his formed and his *nirakaar* (formless) presence. Shiva and Parvati are embodied as Chidambaram Rahasya, an indecipherable *yantra* or geometric diagram on the wall of an empty space. Only a strand of 51 golden bilva leaves indicates the Lord's presence. A curtain, dark in the exterior indicating ignorance and bright red in the interior indicating wisdom, covers this space.

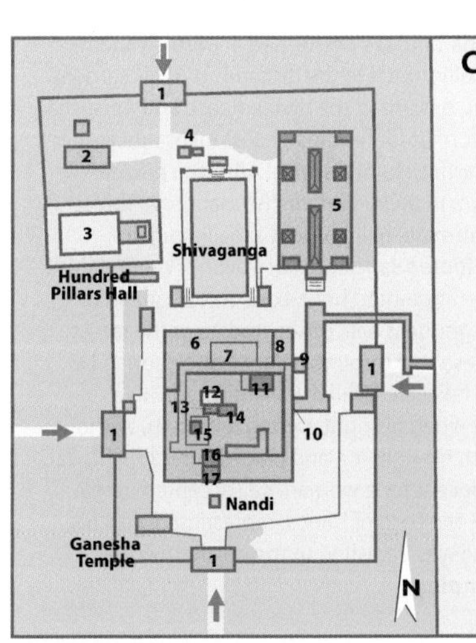

CHIDAMBARAM NATARAJA TEMPLE

1. The four Gopurams
2. Pandya Nayakam Temple
3. Devi Shivakamasundari Temple
4. Nine Lingas Temple
5. Thousand Pillars Hall or Raja Sabha
6. The 63 Nayanmars or Saints gallery
7. Shrine of the Mulasthana Lingam
8. The Kalyana Mandapam
9. The Yaga Shala
10. The 21 steps
11. Deva Sabha
12. Chit Sabha with the Golden Roof
13. Kanaka Sabha
14. Shrine of Brahma-Chandikeshvara
15. Shrine of the Navagrahas
16. The flagmast of the Nataraja Temple
17. Nritta Sabha

Paintings on the ceiling, Shivakami Amman Temple, Thillai Nataraja Temple

© Anurag Mallick, Priya Ganapathy/MICHELIN

Interestingly, the 1000-pillared hall has only 999 pillars. When the statue of Nataraja is brought out during festivals into the hall, his leg becomes the 1000th pillar. The outermost Prakaram also has the **Shivakami Amman Temple** with stunning paintings from the Nayaka period on the ceiling of the *mukhamantapam* or outer hall. The Shivaganga tank is where King Shveta Varman of Kashmir took a dip to cure his leprosy and shone like gold, earning the title Hiranya Varman. In gratitude, he started the construction of the temple's golden roof. Don't miss the **ruby abhisheka** every morning after the 10am *puja*, a manifestation of Nataraja from the red flames as Ratnasabhapati. While most temples close by 8pm, Chidambaram performs its closing ceremony at 10pm. It's believed all the other gods come here for the night and go the next morning. Hence the belief that a *puja* performed here goes to all the gods and Chidambaram's divine status as Kailash on Earth.

Nataraja, the Lord of Dance

Reminiscing about Lord Shiva's Ananda Tandava performed at Darukavanam, Lord Vishnu tapped his foot rhythmically, much to the discomfort of his serpent Adisesha. When asked about it, Vishnu described the divine dance and Adisesha yearned to witness it so he could perform it for his master. Vishnu grants that Adisesha would be reincarnated on Earth to fulfil his wish. Adisesha prayed to Lord Shiva who promised to perform in *thillai-vanam*, the mangrove forest of **Chidambaram★**. Reborn as the half-man, half-serpent sage Patanjali, Adisesha met Vyaghrapada the tiger-footed sage at *thillai-vanam*, where they worshipped a *swayambhulinga*. At the appointed hour, Lord Shiva appeared with 2,999 *dikshitars* (priests) but the goddess Kali, the custodian of the forest, refused them entry. The matter was resolved through a dance duel judged by Lord Vishnu where the winner would take over Thillai. Kali matched Shiva's every move, until the fateful moment when his right earring fell down. Without faltering, Shiva picked it up deftly with his right leg and placed it back on his ear. Since imitating the step would be indecent for a woman, Kali accepted defeat. Shiva remained in Thillai as **Nataraja**, the Lord of Dance, represented with his leg raised *(urddhva tandava)* while Kali was banished to the northern edge of the forest at **Thillai Kali Amman Temple**.

NAGORE

Nagore Dargah

16km south of Karaikal on NH-45A, 4km north of Nagapattinam. 19, Mohideen Palli Street, Nagore 611002, Nagapattinam District. Dargah is open at all times; the tomb doors open 4.20–7am, 6–9pm. Entry free. . 04365 250141/98424 41404. www.nagoredargah.com. Credit cards accepted.

A 16C saint from Manickkapur near Ayodhya, Hazrat Syed Shahul Hameed Qadir Vali came to the south after a successful tour of Lahore, Baluchistan, Afghanistan, Mecca and Sri Lanka. He performed many miracles along the way and when he arrived at the court of Thanjavur, he even cured the ailing Achuthuppa Naikan of a prolonged sickness. In gratitude, the ruler donated 12ha/30 acres of land near the seashore to the saint, who remained here for 28 years till his demise in 1559. The 500-year-old Nagore *dargah* where he is entombed spreads over 2ha/5 acres, topped by a golden dome surrounded by five lofty minarets.

The saint's miracles did not stop after his death and continue to this day, earning him the godly appellation 'Nagore Andavar'. The tomb of his wife Syed Sultan Beebi Amma Sahiba and son Hazarath Syed Mohamed Yoosuf Sahib flank the resting place of the saint. The 14-day Kanduri Urs festival, marked by the raising of pennants on the minarets, grand processions and firework displays, is celebrated with great fervour in May.

VELANKANNI★

Basilica of Our Lady of Good Health★

Drive 5km from Nagapattinam on NH-67 towards Tanjore till you reach Puththoor village, take a left and drive 10km to reach Velankanni Church entrance arch; the church is 3km from there. Velankanni Shrine Basilica, Velankanni 611111, Nagapattinam District. Open daily 5am–9pm. (snacks and drinks available in the car park). 04365 263423/263530/263584. www.vailankannishrine.org.

One of the most frequented Christian pilgrim centres in India, Velankanni (*see p61*) draws nearly two million visitors of all faiths each year. The historic church of the Virgin (*kanni* in Tamil) of Velai village owes its origins to three miraculous events that occurred within a span of a few years in the mid-16C – the apparition of Mary and the Christ Child to a slumbering cowherd, the curing of a lame buttermilk vendor and the rescue of Portuguese sailors from a violent cyclone. As a token of gratitude, the Portuguese replaced the original thatch structure by a 6x3m/24x12ft domed chapel. On subsequent visits they brought porcelain plates and a statue of Our Lady holding the Baby Jesus, standing on a globe. The church was dedicated on the feast of the Nativity of Mary (8 Sept), the day of their safe landing. More than 500 years later, the nine-day car festival still commemorates the event.

To accommodate the growing number of devotees, two chapels were added in the style of the basilica in France, earning the shrine the name 'Lourdes of the East'. The pristine white Gothic edifice with a tiled red roof stands at the centre of an imaginary cross with the **Naduthittu Church** and **Adoration Chapel** to the north and south forming its two arms. It was under a banyan tree at Naduthittu that the lame vendor offered buttermilk to the divine Lady and her child and ran to Nagapattinam with news of the miracle. On the far western end of the shrine, approachable by the Holy Path, is **Matha Kulam** or Our Lady's Tank where the cowherd rested and offered milk to the lady. On the seaward side of the church near the Shrine Offering Centre is a **Museum** *(open daily 6.30am–8pm)* that houses the offerings made by pilgrims to the Mother of Good Health for her magical cures. In 1962 His Holiness Pope John XXIII raised Velankanni Church to the status of basilica.

A new building, the Morning Star Church, is coming up on the northern side of the Holy Path. The 122m/400ft long, 42m/138ft wide, 12m/40ft high edifice will have no intermediate sup-

Dhanushkodi★ and Adam's Bridge

18km south of Rameswaram town and 10km off the road from Mukundarayar Chathiram, the ghost town of Dhanushkodi is a tiny strip of land that stitches together the wild Indian Ocean and the calmer Bay of Bengal. Formerly a busy fishing hamlet and pilgrim centre, it was mauled by a massive cyclone in 1964 and was since declared unfit for habitation.

A surreal landscape of half-eaten boats marooned in barren sandy expanses, marshes polka-dotted with birds, ruined rail tracks, shallow pools, shimmering crystal waters and laughing waves, prompts visitors to risk a bumpy ride from Mukundarayar Chathiram in shared mini-vans *(40min return trip, Rs.80)*. Like a crazy dune-bashing desert safari, the vans rattle along the ocean's shores cross-hatched with deep tyre trails to deposit tourists at Land's End, the eastern extremity of the Indian peninsula. From here is where Rama allegedly built his famous Adam's Bridge *(see opposite)* to Sri Lanka, 30km away. The series of reefs and sandbars can be clearly seen stretching into the distance. On the return trip, vans make a brief halt at the old village of Dhanushkodi. A small temple enshrines a floating stone (actually a coral) believed to be a relic of Rama's floating bridge to Sri Lanka.

port columns and will accommodate 15,000 worshippers. Several devotees visit Velankanni everyday to fulfil rites of passage for children (head tonsuring, ear piercing) and offer candles for prayer and healing.

RAMESWARAM★

Ramanathaswami Temple

Enter town from NH-49 which joins Middle Street, turn left on West Street and go around the temple, down North Street to reach the main entrance on East Street. East Street, Rameswaram 623526, Ramanathapuram District. Open daily 5am–1pm, 3–9pm. Entry free, holy bath of all 22 theerthams Rs.25. P. *04573 221223. www.rameswaramtemple.org.*

The sanctity of Rameswaram can be gauged by the fact that of the four *dhams* (holy pilgrim centres) in India, it is the only one dedicated to Shiva, and of the 12 *jyotirlingas* in the country, it is the only one in the South. Rameswaram reveals a mingling of faiths. Here, Lord Rama worshipped Lord Shiva, forever uniting Vaishnava and Shaiva beliefs. Devotees first have a ritual bath at **Agni Theertham** on the seashore, before entering the temple through the eastern gate. There are 22 holy *theerthams* inside the temple where various gods and kings got rid of curses and received boons. Pilgrims cover the sites in a pre-ordained circuit to be showered with holy water drawn from wells by nimble priests. The sweet water from each well is different and fortified with therapeutic properties. Walking the corridors is a slippery and damp affair and signboards desist pilgrims from entering the sanctum in wet clothes. Instead of the longer 22 holy dips, pilgrims can opt for a short-cut by going to the large *theertham* near the eastern gateway which has water collected from all the pools.

Originally a thatched shed looked after by a hermit, the temple was built and improved upon by a succession of kings. Ironically, it was a (Sri) Lankan king who built the sanctum sanctorum around the *moolalinga* of Lord Rama, Sri Ramanathaswami. The Sethupathi kings of Ramnad took over from 15C onwards and added stone *gopurams* (towers), a compound wall, *mandapams* and grand corridors. The famous third corridor on the outer wing, stretching 210m/690ft from east to west, is the longest temple corridor in the world. The 7m/22ft-high lofty corridor is lined by 1,212 granite pillars with statues of the king and ministers near the western entrance.

Rama's Trail

The sacred landscape of Rameswaram is littered with 31 *theerthams* (holy spots) stretching from Devipattinam and Tirupullani near Ramnad to Mandapam and Dhanushkodi. According to legend, when Lord Rama came to these southern Indian shores to rescue Sita from the clutches of Ravana, the demon king of Lanka, he first came to **Kodiakkarai** (Point Calimere) near Vedaranyam. This was where Hanuman allegedly met Lord Rama and informed him of Sita's plight at Ashoka-vanam. Since the spot faced the backyard of Ravana's palace, Lord Rama decided that a true warrior never attacked the enemy from behind and a frontal assault on Lanka would have to be launched. Coming south, Rama placed nine upright stones (Navapashanam) by the sea at **Devipattinam** *(14km northeast of Ramnad)* to propitiate the *navagrahas* (nine planets) so they would shed their auspicious light on him on the battlefield.

On arriving at Rameswaram, Lord Rama climbed **Gandhamadana Parvatam**, the highest point of the island, to reconnoitre Ravana's kingdom, 48km to the south. The place where Rama supposedly stood bears his footprint '**Ramar Padam**', enshrined at the Ramjharoka Temple. Seeing the vast expanse of water, Lord Rama prayed to Varuna, the Lord of the Seas to calm the waves. For 3 days and nights, he performed a rigorous penance. Lord Varuna finally agreed to aid Rama in building a rock bridge to Lanka and even to this day, the sea at Rameswaram remains calm with little or no waves. Meanwhile in Lanka, Ravana throws out his brother Vibheeshana for entreating him to return Sita and beg Rama's forgiveness. Abandoning the side of evil, Vibheeshana sought sanctuary under Lord Rama and the place where he surrendered is marked by the **Kothanda Ramaswamy Temple**. Located 12km from Rameswaram en route to Dhanushkodi, this was where Lakshmana performed his *pattabhishekam* (coronation). With help from the *Vanara Sena* (Monkey Army) and the engineers Nala and Neel, Rama soon built a floating bridge to Lanka (Adam's Bridge) at the narrowest point and launched an attack.

After his victorious return from Lanka, Lord Rama wanted to atone for *Brahmin-hatya* or the sin of killing Ravana, a grandson of Brahma. Lord Rama prayed to Iswara or Lord Shiva, hence the holy conch-shaped island came to be known as **Ram-Iswaram** (Rameswaram). Since the island had no Shiva shrine, Lord Rama instructed Hanuman to procure a *linga* from Kailash. When the auspicious hour drew near and the monkey god had not returned, Sita fashioned a *linga* out of mud to complete her Lord's worship. Hanuman soon arrived with the *linga* and was livid that the rituals were already over. He wrapped his tail around the mud linga and tried his best to dislodge it, to no avail. Due to his exertions, he lost his tail, and a rivulet of blood was formed, where the **Poonch-heen Hanuman Temple** stands today. To pacify Hanuman, Lord Rama installed his Vishwalingam next to the Ramalingam and ordained that henceforth prayers would have to be offered to Hanuman's *linga* first. Rama cleansed himself by washing his *jata* (matted locks) at **Jata Theertham** and took a holy dip at **Agnitheertham** before he performed his worship, a practice that continues to this day. A kilometre away, the ponds where Lakshmana and Sita got rid of their sins were called **Lakshmana Theertham** and **Sita Theertham** respectively. Dotting the entire area are other *mandapams* and sanctified spots, like **Jatayu Theertham** and **Sugreevar Theertham**, named after characters from the epic.

After the war, on Vibheeshana's request, Lord Rama broke the bridge with one end of his bow and marked the spot with it, hence the name **Dhanushkodi** (*dhanush* means bow, *kodi* is end).

Historical Sights

Witness to trade wars, dynastic feuds of great empires and a raging sea claiming its share, the Coromandel Coast has been an ever-changing playground of history. Standing on empty shores, one can only imagine the opulence of its once-glorious ports. Traces of British rule in Cuddalore, the barely visible French imprint at Karaikal and the Danish stamp on Tranquebar remain, and visitors have only a jigsaw of monuments, sculptures and stone relics to piece together history.

MAMALLAPURAM★★★

Shore Temple★★

Turn from East Raja Street onto Beach Road (Shore Temple Road). Shore Temple Road, Mamallapuram. Open daily 6.30am–6pm. Ticket counter closed 5.30pm onwards. Rs.10, child below 15yr free (foreigners Rs.250, video Rs.25). Same ticket is valid for 1-day visit to all monuments. . Guided Tours: local guides available. Contact Tourist Office, TTDC Beach Resort Complex, off ECR, Mamallapuram 603103. 044 27442232. www.tamilnadutourism.org.

One of the shining examples of Pallava legacy, the Shore Temple has been recognised as a UNESCO World Heritage site. Legend has it that seven such temples once dotted Mamallapuram's shores. Visible to ancient mariners from far at sea, the port was known in old times as the City of Seven Pagodas. Over time, six were reclaimed by the sea and just one pagoda now exists in the form of the twin spires of the Shore Temple. For over 1,200 years, this temple has braved an angry sea and erosive salt air. Though the external carvings have been

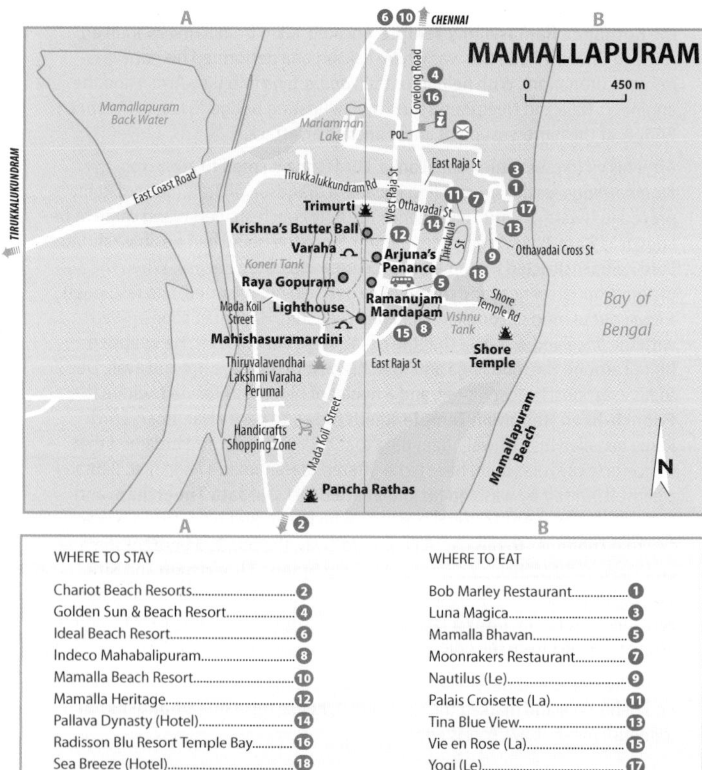

Boulder carving of Arjuna's Penance

extensively worn, the temple as a whole remains intact. One of the last temples to be built by the Pallavas, its construction began in early 8C during the reign of Narasimhavarman II (Rajasimha) (AD 695-722). Situated on the shore of the Bay of Bengal, it remains the earliest known example of a complete stone-built temple in layout and form of Dravidian architecture.

Approach from the west towards two low-walled enclosures bordered by *nandi* (bull) figures to enter the temple. The temple is dedicated to Lord Vishnu and Lord Shiva as indicated by the two *lingam* shrines, *(one towards the east and the other west)*, sandwiched by another shrine with a reclining image of Vishnu. Shiva the Destroyer faces dangers at sea, while Vishnu the Preserver watches over the town. The spires are tapered and it is said, in days of yore, it was also used as a lighthouse, with a fire burning at its apex. The Shore Temple influenced the architecture of the later Cholas, who succeeded the Pallavas. People sprawl on the manicured lawns to enjoy the beauty of this temple in the evening. At night, the temple acquires an unmistakable aura when it is illuminated.

Arjuna's Penance★★

North of the village centre, opp. the Sthalasayana Perumal Temple. Monument is on the main road and visible at all hours. Mada Koil Street, Mamallapuram. Same opening times and charges as Shore Temple (above).

Easily one of the most riveting features of Mamallapuram's rock art is the 6m/20ft-high and 24m/80ft-long boulder carving of Arjuna's Penance, the largest bas-relief in the world. Interestingly its shape is like the back of a whale and faces the sea. Some believe that Arjuna had undertaken a penance on the banks of the Ganges to appease Shiva so that the God would give him his powerful weapon, the Pashupatastra, hence the name 'Arjuna's Penance'. His image towards the west depicts him in a yogic pose on one leg with hands raised, meditating on Shiva. On the opposite side at the base near the elephants is a curious carving of a cat imitating Arjuna's pose on its hind legs, with a bevy of mice around it!

Another widely believed theory about the theme is that it's the 'Descent of the Ganges' onto Earth. There's a natural cleft in the middle of the bas-relief

WALKING TOUR

MAMALLAPURAM★★★

Barring the unusual Tiger's Cave amphitheatre and an ancient obelisk nearby that served as a lighthouse *(4km north of town)*, most of Mamallapuram's monuments are clustered around **Arjuna's Penance**★★ *(see p175)*.

A few steps north of it is a small gate with two paths – the left leads to the many rock-cut cave temples depicting scenes from mythology and the right goes towards Krishna's Butter Ball and Trimurti Cave.

Krishna's Butter Ball (Cat Stone)

A precariously perched boulder that seems it could roll down the sloping rock face any moment, Krishna's Butter Ball has defied all laws of physics for centuries. According to folklore, one day when Krishna returned from his bath he discovered that a cat had got to his butter Ball before him and turned the cat into stone. Tourists pour in daily to get photographed while trying to push it. Beyond the rock is Krishna's Swimming Pool.

A few paces further right is Bhima's Kitchen. Typically, anything huge is attributed to Bhima, the largest of the Pandava brothers. Three large monoliths lean against each other simulating a stone fireplace. About 20 steps ahead is the temple of the Holy Trinity.

Trimurti Temple

Dedicated to the divine trinity of Brahma-Vishnu-Maheshwara, the Trimurti Temple is a three-celled shrine with beautiful carvings. The middle shrine is occupied by Shiva. To the left is a stone with a circular hollow, full of green slimy water. This is called the Gopi's Churn, rumoured as the site where women used to churn butter for the divine cowherd, Krishna.

Return towards Krishna's Butter Ball and continue straight along the mud path behind Arjuna's Penance.

Varaha Cave★

Crossing the monolithic Ganesha Mandapam, an active temple, one reaches a small rock-cut *mandapam* to the right with remarkably carved horned lion pillars. Dedicated to the 'boar' avatar of Lord Vishnu, the striking cave is named after the beautiful representation of Varaha carrying Bhudevi (Earth Goddess) on the left. Opposite is a majestic bas-relief of Vishnu as Trivikrama overcoming Bali, the demon king.

Walk a little further up the incline.

Raya Gopuram

On a clearing to the left is the lofty unfinished Raya Gopuram (Temple Gateway). The door jambs display an intricate style of carving.

Continue along the main path.

Ramanujam Mandapam

Originally dedicated to Shiva, the pillared rock-cut temple was later converted into the Vaishnava Ramanujam Mandapam. The pathway between the rocks rises up slowly past a British-era **lighthouse**, with a red roof that commands a great view of Mamallapuram.

Walk just past the lighthouse.

Mahishasuramardini Cave★

A large rock-cut temple with two impressive panels on either side – Seshasayi Vishnu seen in cosmic repose to the left and in contrast, a panel on the right portraying goddess Durga as Mahishasurmardhini (slayer of the buffalo-headed demon Mahisha) denotes raw power, movement and energy. Come down the steps to reach a stone-carvers' colony on PWD Road.

that represents Ganga replete with rows of mythical creatures like *gandharvas, apsaras, ganas, nagas* and *naginis* (water spirits and snakes) to heighten the drama of the piece. From a cistern on top of the hillock, water used to be released on certain festive occasions for a hint of realism. Legend has it Sage Bhagirathi prayed to Lord Shiva to control the flow of the wild River Ganges, so Shiva knots Ganga in his dreadlocks and lets her cascade to nourish the earth. The bas-relief contains over 100 carvings of gods and goddesses, men and beasts, and episodes from the *Panchatantra*. Towards the right, an image of a herd of elephants with calves asleep under a great tusker call for attention. At the far right is an independent carving of a monkey grooming its young. Not surprisingly, the monument is used as a spectacular backdrop for the annual Dance Festival *(mid-Dec–late Jan)* held in Mamallapuram, which attracts the best cultural performers from across India.

Nearby

A little south of **Arjuna's Penance**★★ is the large **Krishna Mandapam** which displays a realistic portrayal of Krishna playing in the fields. The bas-relief also shows him lifting the Goverdhan Hill on his fingertip to protect his kinsmen from the anger of Indra.

Pancha Rathas★★

About 1.5km south of the village centre along Mada Koil Street, opposite the Handicrafts Shopping Zone.

Five Rathas Road (Mada Koil Street) Mamallapuram. Same opening times and charges as Shore Temple (above).

Mamallapuram's famous cluster of five chariot temples, the Pancha Rathas are among the most striking and oldest preserved specimens of *vimana* (pyramidal roof-tower) style architecture. Though they are named after the five Pandava princes from the epic *Mahabharata*, there is no apparent link with the heroes and it seems more a case of numerical coincidence. The temples are replicas of ancient wooden structures and represent the *rathas* or chariots of Dharmaraja Yudhishthira, Bhima, Arjuna, Draupadi and the twins Nakula-Sahadeva, who had to share a *ratha* between them.

Set in a sunken sandy compound, the free-standing chariots and the large monolithic animal carvings of an elephant and a lion are favourite landmarks for tourists. The carvings date back to the period of Narasimha Varman I *(AD 630-70)* and though work on the *rathas* was stopped after his death, they show few signs of being incomplete.

It is believed that four of these temples were carved out of one gigantic granite boulder. Dharmaraja Ratha, the southernmost and tallest one is perhaps the most ornate of the lot. It rests on a square base and has a tapering set of storeys with rows of pavilions. The wall panels depict carvings of Ardhanarishwara (Shiva-Shakti), Brahma, King Narasimha Varman I and Harihara (Shiva-Vishnu). The Bhima *ratha*, though the largest, is somewhat bereft of carvings but possesses pavilion-shaped embellishments and stands on an oblong base. The Arjuna and Draupadi chariots share a common base. The Arjuna chariot is nearly complete and has a fascinating unfinished sculpture of Shiva's bull behind it. The unusual Draupadi's chariot bears a roof akin to a thatched hut and has an image of Durga inside with a large standing lion outside. Beside the life-size elephant carving is the curved chariot of the twins Nakula and Sahadeva.

TRANQUEBAR★★

Dansborg Fort★

Enter from the ticket counter at the gate on the fort's north side, opposite the Bungalow on the Beach.

King's Street, Tranquebar 609313, Nagapattinam District. Open Sat–Thu 10am–5.45pm. Rs. 50, Rs.25 child (camera Rs.30, video Rs.100). P. Guided Tours: Contact INTACH office 04364 289299. www.tranquebar.in.

The first Danish expedition to India arrived at Tharangambadi in 1620. Governor Roland Crappé and Ove Gedde, Commander of the Danish Royal Navy,

WALKING TOUR

TRANQUEBAR★★

Walking down the Kongensgade (King's Street), a breezy avenue lined by majestic Danish Colonial buildings, is like a stroll into the hallways of Valhalla. Relive an era of trade and prosperity where German missionaries printed books in Tamil and Danish-Tamil houses lined the streets. Set aside half a day for a leisurely exploration.

Ziegenbalg Memorial

A cross on a memorial stone opposite **Dansborg Fort**★ *(see p177)* marks the arrival of the first Lutheran missionaries to India. Bartholomäus Ziegenbalg and Heinrich Plütschau landed at Tranquebar on 9 July, 1706 at the order of the Danish king Frederick IV to render spiritual and religious service in India.

Pass the Bungalow on the Beach (Collector's Bungalow) and continue straight on King's Street to reach the massive pillared edifice to the right.

Governor's Bungalow

Constructed as the private residence of Governor David Brown, it was made the official Governor's Bungalow after the Danish state purchased the building in 1784. It is currently being renovated into a museum. The adjacent Commander's House (Halkier's House) is now a Teacher Training Institute run by the Tamil Evangelical Lutheran Church.

Continue on King's Street to reach the junction of Queen's Street, opposite the Ziegenbalg statue.

Zion Church

Consecrated in 1701, Zion Church is the oldest Protestant Church in India. Built along with the fortification of Tranquebar, it marked the spread of the Danish population from Dansborg to surrounding areas. The first five Indian Protestant converts of the Danish Mission were baptised here in 1707.

Continue straight on King's Street; the church is on the left.

New Jerusalem Church★

When Zion Church couldn't accommodate the growing Christian population, Ziegenbalg and Plütschau built a new one in 1718. The magnificent church is a synthesis of German design and Indian architecture. Inside, the stained-glass windows throw prismatic patterns on the tomb of Ziegenbalg, who was buried in the church built by him. An old Danish cemetery on Kavalamettu Street behind the church can be accessed from the tiny lane, Church Street.

Diagonally opposite the church is Ziegenbalg Spiritual Centre, which houses a bookshop and library. Continue on King's Street past Van Theylingen's House.

Rehling's House

The early-18C building on King's Street with a white colonnaded façade served as the stately residence of two Danish Governor's Peter Hermanson and Johannes Rehling, and was named after the latter. To adapt to the tropical climate, the original pitched roof was replaced by a flat one and a first floor, verandahs and porches were added later.

Continue on King's Street past St Theresa Convent and the Gate House on the left.

Town Gate

Called Landporten in Danish, the first town gate was built in the 1660s. In 1791 Governor Peter Anker pulled down the original dilapidated gate and commissioned engineer Muhldorff to erect a new gate. After years of neglect, the gate was renovated to its former glory in 2002.

Turn back from the Town Gate and go around the Lady's Hostel onto Borgan Street, parallel to King's Street.

Gründler's House

The residence of Pastor Johann Ernst Gründler, who co-authored several books in Tamil with Ziegenbalg, Gründler's House later became a home for the aged and is currently a boys' hostel.

Turn left from Borgan Street onto Queen's Street, go past Tranquebar Maritime Museum and Perumal Kovil Street and take the second left onto Admiral Street.

Ziegenbalg Museum Complex

A small building on Admiral Street housed India's first printing press and later became the Dorothea Ziegenbalg Typewriting Centre, named after Ziegenbalg's wife. The property was acquired in the 18C to accommodate the growing Lutheran mission, which added a Church Hall, Grahl Hall, missionary buildings and living quarters. The complex has been converted into a school but has the Ziegenbalg Museum and his statue in the premises.

Return to Queen's Street, turn left and continue straight. Turn right onto Goldsmith Street to reach the seaward end.

INTACH Museum

A complex of five renovated Tamil houses, with exhibits and panels by Best Sellers Foundation, an INTACH museum *(open 9am–6pm; ☏04364 289299)* and a small art cafe. The Tranquebar Craft Resource Centre *(open 9am–5pm; ☏04364 289160)* sells cloth bags, terracotta figurines, coconut-shell curios and bracelets, key-chains, accessories and hand-woven baskets. The upper floor affords a good view of the Nayak House and Chinta Durai Sivan Kovil on one side and Vinayakar and Angalamman Kovil to the left.

Ziegenbalg's Legacy

A bronze life-size statue of German missionary Bartholomäus Ziegenbalg was erected in **Tranquebar★★** in commemoration of the Ter-Centenary of Tranquebar Mission (1706-2006). An interesting tablet encourages visitors to 'be always the first', listing out 21 pioneering efforts of Ziegenbalg. He was the first protestant missionary to India, the first royal missionary from Denmark, the first to introduce the printing press, the first to start a paper mill, the first to print a Tamil calendar and dictionary, the first to translate German hymns into Tamil and Tamil books into German, the first to introduce the Free Noon Meal Scheme and the first to preach a sermon in Tamil.

Take Post Office Street and turn left onto Masilamani Koil Street to end the walk at the seaside temple.

Masilamani Nathar Temple

One of the oldest surviving structures in town, the temple is dedicated to Mani Varneeswarar Masila Nathar. The temple's eastern wall had a stone inscription that recorded how 'King Maravarman Kulashekharan Pandian granted land for the construction of the temple in 1306' which is now exhibited at the Dansborg Museum. The shrine originally had three *mandapams*, but the raging sea claimed two, along with the beautiful Salangaikara Street that ran parallel to the beach.

Dansborg Fort

© Anurag Mallick, Priya Ganapathy/MICHELIN

established a trade treaty with King Raghunatha Nayak of Thanjavur at a monthly rent of Rs.3,111. For nearly 250 years, Tranquebar was the seat of power from where the Danes controlled their trade interests in India. The golden citadel of Dansborg, a superb example of Scandinavian defence architecture, was constructed in 1620 by Admiral Ove Gedde, who became Tranquebar's first Governor.

The fort was built on two levels – the upper level served as the residence of the Governor while rooms on the lower level adjoining the rampart wall were used as godowns, prisons and resting areas for soldiers. Besides rooms for security, gunpowder and ammunition, there were separate beer and wine rooms, horse stables and even rooms for pigeons! The **Parade Ground** adjacent to the fort was used for official parades and processions and was a bustling centre for trade.

A central chamber on the fort's upper level houses the **Danish Fort Museum**. On display are Danish artefacts, cannons, miniature ship models, panels outlining a detailed history of the fort, copies of imperial letters, lists of Danish Governors and ships that visited Tranquebar, even a whale bone that washed ashore. There's also a copy of the origianal trade agreement of the Danes with the King of Madurai.

In 2002, nearly 382 years after its inception, the historic fort was renovated by the Tranquebar Association of Denmark, the State Archaeology Department and the ASI.

Cuddalore

A 2,000-year-old trading port, Cuddalore is named after its location, *koodal oor* or 'place at the confluence' of three rivers, the Pennaiyar, Paravanar and Gedilam, which divides it into Old Town and New Town. Elihu Yale, a British officer bought a seafort from the rulers of Gingee in 1690 and called it **Fort St David** *(near River Gadilam, Devanampattinam)*. The deal was struck upon the strangest of clauses: the boundary of the British territory would be decided by random firing of cannonballs in all directions from the fort! Between 1746-52, it served as the British capital on the Coromandel Coast. The streets still retain old names of British officers like Clive Street, Wellington Street and Napier Road, while stray Colonial buildings hint at its glorious past. Garden House, earlier the official home of Robert Clive, Governor of Cuddalore, is now the District Collector's residence. However, the town is a pale shadow of its past with its tree-lined esplanades and charming homes with fruit orchards giving way to a busy, industrial township.

Museums and Art Galleries

Often, the temples of the Coromandel Coast serve as living museums, archiving a synthesis of art, history and mythology. Mamallapuram's open-air Rock Art and Sculpture Museum, the paintings on the ceiling at Chidambaram's Shivakami Amman Temple and the tragic remains of mural art at Kanchipuram's Kailasnatha Temple are hidden gems of Coromandel's heritage. The Dansborg Fort Museum at Tranquebar houses some fascinating relics while the art gallery at Kanchipuram's Kamakshi Temple documents the history of the renowned Shankaramadam.

KANCHIPURAM★★

Kanchi Kudil

On the road to Kanchi's Kailasanathar Temple. 53A, Sangeetha Vidwan Nayanar Pillai Street (Old Putheri Street), Kanchipuram. Open daily 9am–5pm. Rs.10, child free. (meals available on prior request, call 9941138703). P. Guided Tours: in-house guide available. 044 27227680/26211123/26264767. www.indiamart.com/kanchikudil.

The unassuming 90-year-old house with a tiled sloping roof seems to rebel against all the development around it, but once you step inside, it's as if time has stopped. Kanchi Kudil gives visitors a glimpse into the life of a typical agricultural family. The master's room, room for the women and children, *puja* room for the gods, open-to-sky courtyards, verandahs, kitchen and the backyard with agricultural implements have been well preserved. Traditional music in the background adds a touch of authenticity; informative write-ups outline the history of Kanchipuram while a small section has handicrafts for sale. Snacks and refreshments are provided from 9am to 5pm while home-cooked, traditional meals are served on prior request *(veg Rs.200, non-veg Rs.250).*

Shakunthala Jagannathan Museum of Folk Art★

Turn left from the 16-pillar mandapam on Ekambranathar Sannathi Street. C.P. Ramaswami Aiyar Foundation, Brahma Mandhiram, 6, Lingappan Street, Kanchipuram 631501. Open daily 9.30am–5pm. Closed public holidays and fortnight during Panguni Uttiram festival. Rs.20, child free (camera Rs.10, video Rs.25). P. Guided Tours: free guide service is available. 044 27230112/27260450. www.cprfoundation.org.

A hidden treasure trove near Ekambaranathar Temple, the 400-year-old ancestral home houses the personal collection of renowned educationist, administrator and social worker **C.P. Ramaswami Aiyar** (*see p131*). The *thinnai* (front veranda) serves as a craft shop while the *kalyana koodam* (main hall) is dominated by a large metal swing and life-size images of a Brahmin couple under a large *punkah* (traditional fan). Lining the walls are traditional furniture, ancient palm leaves and antique wooden dolls, once displayed for the *kolu* (festival of dolls) during Navaratri. A set of miniature dolls painted in gold called Puducherry Gilt is perhaps the most unique of the lot.

The history of Kanchipuram from 300 BC to the British period has been painted on

Puducherry Gilt dolls, Shakunthala Jagannathan Museum of Folk Art

the wall to the right. The Vadyashala is a repository of musical instruments used in folk and classical music, the *puja* room contains temple and ritualistic items in metal while Deepam is a collection of lamps, earlier used to illuminate the house. Lining the sunlit open courtyard are stone sculptures spanning a millennium, from 6C Pallava to 16C Vijayanagara periods. To the left, the Chitrashala, bearing traces of 200-year-old wall paintings, displays Tanjore art on glass and wood and cloth paintings in vegetable dyes.

The rooftop rooms, meant to capture the summer breeze, are also used as galleries. Pokkisham showcases copies of traditional jewellery while Vastralayam displays old silk saris, antique cottons and a hand loom, highlighting Kanchi's importance as an ancient cotton and silk weaving centre. The Zenana, a ladies' domain, aptly has traditional make-up cases, dresses, games and old puppets. The rooftop affords a great view of the **Ekambaranath Temple** spire. The museum is closed for 15 days during the Panguni Uttiram Festival *(Mar–Apr)* where the marriage of Kamakshi and Shiva is celebrated through *veda* chanting, an unbroken tradition in the house for the last few centuries.

POOMPUHAR

Marine Archaeology Museum

Located 24km from Mayiladuthurai on the seaward end of SH-22. While coming from NH-45A, take a diversion at Mudikandanallur (8 km), midway between Sirkazhi and Thirukadaiyur. Poompuhar Tourist Complex, Poompuhar 609105, Sirkazhi Taluk, Nagapattinam District. Open Sat–Thu 10am–5pm. Rs.5, child Rs.3 (foreigners Rs.50). P. 04364 260439/ 9176995843. www.tnarch.gov.in.

Ever since the historic port of Kaveripoompattinam or Poompuhar was ravaged by a tsunami centuries ago, people have only wondered how it would have been in its days of glory. Though early forays to piece together its history began in 1910, it wasn't until 1981 that the Archaeology Department conducted preliminary explorations. In 1997, antiquities recovered from excavations and offshore and onshore jaunts were archived in a special Marine Archaeology Museum, the only one of its kind in India. On display are shards of Roman pottery, Chinese vases and porcelain, British cooling jars, Buddha heads and *Buddhapadam* (feet imprints), large bricks, beads, wooden artefacts, terracotta figurines, lead ingots, stone sculptures and coins. The highlight of the excavations at Poompuhar is the ancient terracotta ring wells found at Vanagiri and Chinnavanagiri.

RAMANATHAPURAM

Ramalingavilasam Museum

Located on SH-34 in the northern part of town, 55km from Rameswaram. Palace Road, Aranmanai, Ramnad Taluk, Ramanathapuram 623501. Open Sat–Thu 10am–5pm. Rs.5, child Rs.3 (foreigners Rs.50). P. www.tnarch.gov.in.

The Ramalingavilasam Palace museum is a rare specimen where the building is perhaps more exquisite than the objects it houses. Built during the reign of Kizhavan or Raghunatha Sethupathi II (1674-1710) the most popular of the Sethupathi kings of Ramnad, the palace itself is a living museum with large murals, pillared halls lined with artefacts and ostentatious living spaces. The archaeological museum has a collection of iron spears, swords, daggers, guns and a *valari* (boomerang), besides antiquities excavated from Alagankulam. The richly painted ceiling and walls depict royal lifestyle, battle scenes with the Maratha kings of Thanjavur, colonial influences, gods and goddesses, erotic scenes, water sports and episodes from the Ramayana like Balakandam, the birth of Rama.

In the Darbar Hall, don't miss unusual exhibits like Abhisheka Peedam (anointment platform), Mugavai Thali (mud pot) used for burying the aged alive and a 1-tonne stone ball used to test the strength of prospective grooms.

National Parks and Wildlife Sanctuaries

Coromandel may not have the lush jungles of the hinterland but its rich tapestry of natural life holds many unusual encounters for a visitor. Watch blackbucks bound on saltpans off the coast, go boating in dense mangrove forests, see pelicans and flamingos liven up calm freshwater lakes or explore underwater marine life by glass-bottomed boats. The proximity of Kanchipuram and Mamallapuram to wildlife sites like Vandalur Zoo and Madras Crocodile Bank (*see Channai and Around*) **and Vedanthangal** (*see below*) **are a big bonus.**

VEDANTHANGAL BIRD SANCTUARY★

53km from Kanchipuram via Uthiramerur (22km) on SH-118 or Chengalpattu (26km) on NH-45. From Chennai (86km), take the first major right after Bukkathurai to drive 12km to the sanctuary. Vedanthangal, near Maduranthakam, Kanchipuram District. Open Wed–Mon 6am–6pm. Closed during monsoons. Rs.5, child free (camera Rs.25). P. 044 24321471 (Wildlife Warden, Chennai) or 044 22351471 (Children's Park, Guindy). www.forests.tn.nic.in/WildBiodiversity/bs_vedabs.html.

It was a crusade by the villagers that laid the foundation of India's oldest bird sanctuary in 1798. The Vedanthangal Bird Sanctuary, now managed by the Forest Department, spans only 200ha/494 acres of open water, yet at peak season it witnesses a great convergence of several species of birds (*see Nature p97*). Nov–Feb is the sanctuary's busiest period when waters are full and birds come to nest and settle till April, the start of the dry season. Dense clumps of trees in the water provide ample nesting sites that burst with hungry fledglings by Jan. Birders and tourists armed with binoculars and cameras stream in to capture the flutter of activity when openbill storks, spoonbills, pelicans, cormorants, herons and ibises unite at the waterfront. Migrant cuckoos, swallows, redshanks, sandpipers, paddy egrets and bee-eaters also abound at the site. The narrow tree-lined walking trail fringing the water's edge is interspersed with viewing platforms, park benches, watchtowers and eccentric avi-fauna sculpted water-taps

Grey herons at Vedanthangal Bird Sanctuary

and is bordered by a swathe of paddy fields on the other side. Parking spaces and snack stalls are available outside. The only stay option is the four-room Forest Rest House *(044 27598545; Rs.775/room)* near the bus stand on Velaiyaputhur Road, 0.5km from the sanctuary nearby.

PICHAVARAM★

14km east from Chidambaram. Arignar Anna Tourism Complex, Pichavaram 608102. Open 7am–6pm. Rs.5 forest entry fee, rowing boat and motorboat prices vary depending on duration of trips. (Ranging from Rs.110 for two people to Rs.2,000 for eight people). . Guided Tours: boatmen double up as guides. 04144 249399. www.pichavaram.co.in.

From Chidambaram to Pichavaram the road is a deeply rutted, potholed track with the occasional patch of tar. It is advisable to take the buses that ply hourly from Chidambaram.

An early morning boat ride in the backwaters of Pichavaram takes one into the deepest quiet of the mangrove forests (*see Nature p98*). Thousands of finger-like roots stretch achingly towards the marshy earth as slender boats negotiate the narrowest waterways through dark tunnels canopied by mangroves. Pichavaram's hypnotic charm has been captured by filmmakers who fancy its cinematic appeal. Tamil Nadu's film icon and former Chief Minister MGR shot his *Idaya Kani* film here in the 1970s, and recently film star Kamal Hasan's *Dasavatharam*, put Pichavaram back in focus by capturing it on celluloid.

Until recently, tourists had negligible options except to picnic briefly en route to or from Chidambaram. But now the **Saradharam Eco Resort** is a convenient perch for overnight stays. It has clean and decent rooms and great food served at their rooftop restaurant with the added bonus of superb views of the backwaters at dawn and dusk. The **TTDC Arignar Anna Tourist Complex** has a view tower *(Rs.5; 2min)* and a boat-house with several boats that tour the Pichavaram backwaters.

GULF OF MANNAR MARINE NATIONAL PARK

43km south-east of Ramanathapuram on NH49, just short of the Pamban Bridge. Gulf of Mannar Biosphere Reserve, Mandapam, Ramanathapuram District 623501. Open daily 7am–5.30pm. Glass-bottomed boats Rs.50/person, (eight persons/trip) from Mandapam Beach Park. . Guided Tours: Wildlife Warden, 76/1, Madurai Salai, Mandapam. 04567 230079. www.forests.tn.nic.in/wildbiodiversity/np_gmmnp.html.

One of world's richest marine biospheres, the Gulf of Mannar (or Sethusamudram) is home to about 3,600 rare species of marine flora and fauna. The Gulf of Mannar islands are located 8km from the hinterland and spread over 10,500sq km, with 560sq km forming the Gulf of Mannar Marine National Park. It is believed that the Mannar Reserve consists of 21 coral-rich islands that date back to 10,000 years including estuaries, mudflats, beaches, forests of the near shore environment, endemic mangroves, salt marshes etc. Several endangered species like dugongs have been sighted here besides dolphins, whales, sea cucumbers, sea turtles, sharks, pearl oysters, sprats, herrings, barracuda, sea horses and Gorgonian coral.

Tourists can take leisurely boat rides from **Thonithurai** *(8km from Mandapam)* or opt for glass-bottomed boats that provide exciting glimpses of underwater life around the coral reef. It takes 3 days to visit all the islands of the National Park. The best time is October to March and prior permission is needed from the Chief Conservator of Forests, Chennai or Chief Wildlife Warden, Mandapam.

Mandapam Beach Park

Open daily 7am–5.30pm. 9443112740. Rs.5, Rs.3 child, Rs.5 swimming pool.

A popular tourist site with fountains, park benches and recreation facilities for children. The Gulf of Mannar Biosphere Reserve Trust organises glass-bottomed boat rides from here. Though Mandapam is linked to **Rameswaram**★

via the 2km-long Indira Gandhi Bridge, it is the historic **Pamban Bridge** that steals the thunder as the country's first sea bridge, which linked Pamban Island to Mandapam on mainland India. Tourists often stop to see trains chug along over the sea and boats crossing under the cantilever rail bridge.

POINT CALIMERE SANCTUARY

55km south of Nagapattinam, 8km south of Vedaranyam on SH-63. Kodiakkarai, Nagapattinam District, 611011. Open 6am–6pm, all year round. Rs.10, child free. P. Guided Tours: Wildlife Warden, Collectorate Building, Nagapattinam 611002. 04365 253091/253092. www.pointcalimere.org.

On the swollen tip of Tamil Nadu's central coast past the sweeping acres of salt pans around Vedaranyam, is the swampy wetland of Point Calimere, where hordes of blackbuck roam free. Located just across the Palk Strait from Sri Lanka, this jutting piece of land is also known as **Kodiakkarai Bird Sanctuary** and is a mixed habitat of dry evergreen forest and swampland. The best time for animal sighting is from Mar–Aug while Oct–Jan is ideal for birdwatching. From Nov–Feb, the sanctuary becomes the winter retreat for over 250 species including rare migratories arriving from faraway Poland, Russia and Iran – bar-headed geese, eastern steppe eagles, black bitterns, Indian black-crested bazas and Ruddy shelducks. The main highlight takes place in Dec–Feb, when the swamps are rouged pink with the endless ballet of flamingos descending in thousands to feast on shrimps and prawns. Spot-billed pelicans and teals also frequent the place. In the dense forests one discovers other animals and birds, including the vibrantly winged Indian pitta.

Thamppuswamy Illam Forest Rest House *(04365 252724)* and **Veliman Illam** are the only overnight options. Booking can also be done via the Wildlife Warden in Nagapattinam *(04365 253092; wlife_kmb@sancharnet.in)*. Only tea stalls can be found near the sanctuary, but vegetarian meals are available in Vedaranyam at Karaivani *(near the bus stand)*.

VALLANADU WILDLIFE SANCTUARY

16km east of Tirunelveli on the Tirunelveli–Thoothukudi Road. Vallanadu Village, Srivaikundam Taluk, Thoothukudi District 628252. P. Guided Tours: District Forest Officer, Collectorate Complex, Tirunelveli, Kokirakulam, 8. 0462 2500778. www.forests.tn.nic.in/wildbiodiversity/ws_vbs.html.

In the 19C, hordes of blackbuck could be found all over the plains of Tamil Nadu, but human development, poaching and extensive agriculture had pushed the blackbuck to four main regions; **Guindy** (Chennai), **Mudumalai** (near Masinagudi), **Point Calimere** (Nagapattinam District) and **Vallanadu**, its southern-most extent. The Vallanadu Wildlife Sanctuary was created to protect these endangered wild antelope from extinction by providing a conducive environment for them to grow and breed. Spread across 16sq km on a hillock, the scrub forest of the sanctuary is a well-known haven for about 20 to 40 blackbuck along with various wild animals and birds. Both evergreen and deciduous trees can be found in this sanctuary, but the dry heat and drought-like conditions have stunted tree growth, making it easier for blackbuck to graze. A **peacock farm** has been included among other simulated natural habitats in the park. Apart from blackbuck there are jungle cats, mongoose, spotted deer, hares and over 120 species of birds. During winter, the park is visited by several migratory bird species from other countries. The untamed splendour of the forest attracts a large number of tourists every year, who usually drive down to the sanctuary. While Tirunelveli town has more hotel options, there is a Government Circuit House and Tamil Nadu Tourist House at Thoothukudi and Tirunelveli. Contact the District Forest Officer *(see above)*.

Beaches

The dazzling beauty of the 644km stretch of the Coromandel Coast, strung together by maritime trade centres, forts and temple towns has been immortalised in books and poetry since eternity. While several beach towns were ravaged by the tsunami of 2004, many lesser-known beaches still exist, though some strips of golden sand edged by swaying palms and casuarina groves are more mesmeric than others.

MAMALLAPURAM BEACH

On ECR 58km south of Chennai. Shore Temple Road, Mamallapuram 603104, Kanchipuram District. *. Tourist Office: 044 27442232/9176995869.*

Picture 20km of sandy shores facing the wide blue rolling sea with a backdrop of an ancient port scattered with sublime stone temples, rock-cut caves and monoliths chiselled to perfection (*see Historical Sights*). **Mamallapuram★★★** (or Mahabalipuram) is a walk into the dreamtime stories of Pallava artistry, a place where natural beauty and history collide marvellously. A warren of stalls selling food, shell curios and souvenirs leads to the beach. Towards the left, is the legendary **Shore Temple★★** (*see p174*) majestically poised in a grassy compound lined by a wall with stoic seated *nandi* (bulls). Tourists throng the beach, but given its special aura, it is easy to find one's bliss.

POOMPUHAR BEACH

40km from Chidambaram. Poompuhar 609105, Nagapattinam District. .

Tall palms sway in the wind as the waves break over Poompuhar's beach, awash with greyish sand. Located in the delta of the sacred Cauvery River as she pours into the sea, **Poompuhar** was the sunken port town of **Kaveripoompattinam** ruled by the Cholas. Post the 2004 tsunami, a rocky levee has been added for protection and the beach is now a favourite picnic site. A few grandiose monuments including one carved with a bathing scene form a bizarre backdrop against the raw wonder of the sea. The seven-storeyed **Silappathikara Art Gallery** inspired by the Tamil epic showcases the region's history.

The TTDC-run **Poompuhar Tourist Complex** (*04364 260439, 9176995843*) offers economical shell-shaped cottage stays.

Mamallapuram Beach, the Shore Temple in the background

ADDRESSES

STAY

A trip to the Coromandel Coast stirs up a range of accommodation options to suit every pocket. Mamallapuram is hot on the tourist circuit and has several luxury beach resorts and vibrant guesthouses with rooftop cafes. For a quiet retreat away from the crowds, head further down the coast to Tranquebar's heritage bungalows. Busy spiritual towns like Kanchipuram and Rameswaram have a number of decent hotels besides a cluster of ***dharamshalas***, ashrams and ***chathirams/choultries*** (rest houses) with lodging and food at minimal cost. Off-beat adventure camps give visitors a chance to camp in tents by the beach or basic rooms near wildlife sanctuaries.

MAMALLAPURAM

Radisson Blu Resort Temple Bay – *57, Covelong Road, Mamallapuram 603104. 044 274 43636. www.radissonblu.com. . 144 rooms.* . Spread around one of the largest swimming pools in south Asia, the resort is a 19ha/46-acre oasis on a quiet bay overlooking the Shore Temple. Elegant chalets and villas face the pool, the garden or the bay while exclusive pool chalets come with private plunge pools. The Wharf, an award-winning seaside speciality restaurant, serves excellent platters, grills and pastas. There's also a 24hr multi-cuisine restaurant, fitness centre, nine-hole golf course and spa. Wake up early for a catamaran ride into the Bay of Bengal to see the Shore Temple from the sea.

Chariot Beach Resorts – *Five Rathas Road, Mamallapuram 603104. 044 274 25000/274 43002/944499272. www.chariotbeachresorts.com. 70 rooms.* . A resort to the south of town near the Pancha Rathas, rooms face the garden or the pool while independent cottages have a sea view and open-to-sky showers. Kapi all-day dining does good evening grills and there's a bake house, spa, olympic-size pool and 12ha/30-acre sports activity area.

Ideal Beach Resort – *Kovalam Road (ECR), Mamallapuram 603104. 044 274 42240/274 42443. www.idealresort.com. 88 rooms.* . Close to Tiger's Cave, the resort has a beachside restaurant, swimming pool, Ayurvedic health centre, gift shop and cycles on hire. Dine under palm trees, in beachside huts or at poolside barbecues while enjoying cultural programmes. They also have an orchid farm 3km from the resort.

Indeco Mahabalipuram – *Shore Temple Road, Mamallapuram 603104. 044 274 43914/274 42287/ 9444410398. www.indecohotels.com. . 30 rooms.* . Right opposite the Shore Temple parking, yet away from the din, this heritage hotel is located on an 1820s British camping site. Earlier Sterling Beach Resorts, it was taken over by Indeco Hotels and renovated into a piece of art that features a fascinating collection of antiques. The restaurant Pongamiya is named after the pongam tree around which it's built. An alfresco extension spills over to the swimming pool and ornate lampposts dot the pathway to rooms that overlook a garden. Drop in for a drink at Clive Bar or get pampered with some Ayurveda.

Golden Sun & Beach Resort – *59, Covelong Road, Mamallapuram 603104. 044 274 42245/274 42946. www.hotelgoldensun.com. 60 rooms.* . Located 3km before town, the beach resort has a lively tavern overlooking a pool with sunbeds strewn around. A short stroll from the lawn leads to the sandy beach 200m/220yd away.

Hotel Pallava Dynasty – *37, East Raja Street, Mamallapuram 603104. 044 374 11422/274 42400, 9092696669. www.hotelpallavadynasty.com. 13 rooms.* . Tucked away in a quiet nook off the main road with comfortable cottages in a tropical patch with a lovely garden courtyard.

Hotel Sea Breeze – *18, Othavadai Street, Mamallapuram 603104. 044 274 43035/274 43065/9244992111. www.hotelseabreeze.net. 68 rooms.* . One of the few beach hotels located within town, the reasonably priced star 3-star hotel has a pool, Ayurvedic massage parlour and is close to the action on Othavadai Street.

Mamalla Beach Resort – *108, Kovalam Road (ECR), Mamallapuram 603104. 044 274 42375/274 42475/9442646875. www.mamallaresort.com. 50 rooms.* Just north of town near Pallava Beach, the resort is set against a casuarina grove with a pool and lawns. Lounge by the sea or dine at Seagull, an open-to-sea restaurant. The weekend breakfast and vegetarian lunch buffet on Sundays are quite popular.

Mamalla Heritage – *104, East Raja Street, Mamallapuram 603104. 044 274 42060/260/360. www.hotelmamallaheritage.com. 43 rooms.* One of the older hotels in town on the main road with decent rooms, poolside dining at Waves, a rooftop seafood restaurant and Golden Palate, a popular restaurant that serves vegetarian fare and great *thalis*.

KANCHIPURAM

GRT Regency – *487, Gandhi Road, Kanchipuram 631502. 044 272 25250. www.grthotels.com. 35 rooms.* Kanchipuram's best hotel with a big name to back it, GRT Regency has excellent rooms, well-informed staff who can guide one to the temples or procure the elusive Kanjivaram *idlis*, Cellar, a nice Colonial-style bar and Dakshin, a 24hr multi-cuisine restaurant that serves buffet lunch on weekends. Great location to buy Kanjeevaram saris from the numerous co-operative stores on Gandhi Road.

M.M. Hotels – *65–66, Nellukara Street, Kanchipuram 631502. 044 2722 7250. www.mmhotels.com. 48 rooms.* Centrally located close to the Kachhabeshwar Temple and the shrines around Raja Street with value-for-money rooms. **Saravana Bhavan** has a restaurant located here (*see p191*).

Hotel Baboo Soorya – *85, East Raja Street, Kanchipuram 631501. 044 272 22555/372 16082. www.hotelbaboosoorya.com. 38 rooms.* One of the older names in town, the recently renovated hotel has decent rooms and the popular Anjappar Chettinad restaurant.

Hotel Jaybala International – *504, Gandhi Road, Kanchipuram 631501. 044 272 24348/4453/9728. www.hoteljaybala.com. 30 rooms.* Another old hotel that has been given a facelift, Jaybala has neat rooms and a small swimming pool. **Saravana Bhavan** has a branch on the ground floor (*see p191*).

CHIDAMBARAM

Lakshmi Vilas – *Near Sivan Kovil, Neduncheri t. Puthur Village, Chidambaram District. 04144 221336. www.lakshmivilas.co.in. 20 rooms.* 2km east of the famous Veeranam Lake and a 12km drive from Chidambaram, Lakshmi Vilas is the only heritage hotel in the area. Built in 1927, the traditional landlord's bungalow was recently renovated by the Saradharam group. Spread on a sprawling 1.8ha/4.5-acre campus overlooking a Shiva temple, the boutique hotel has a Chola architectural theme, Heritage bar and restaurant and Coconut Grove cafe.

Eco Cottage Pichavaram – *Pichavaram, Cuddalore District 608002. 04144 221336/9442591466. www.hotelsaradharam.co.in. 10 rooms & 10 cottages.* Earlier a TTDC hotel, it is currently on lease to Saradharam who revamped the dingy rooms into comfortable air-conditioned chambers and are adding 10 cottages nearby. The restaurant dishes out fresh fish and prawns caught in the backwaters served in a terrace restaurant overlooking the mangroves. A refreshing alternative to the noise of Chidambaram and the perfect overnight base for an early morning boat ride.

Grand Palace Stay – *12, Railway Feeder Road, Chidambaram 608001. 04144 239977/239777. www.grandpalacestay.com. 21 rooms.* Conveniently located diagonally opposite the railway station, GPS is a no-frills hotel with both a multi-cuisine restaurant, Kings Kitchen, and Raj Bhavan, a pure veg restaurant.

Hotel Saradharam – *19, VGP Street, Chidambaram 608001, Cuddalore District. 04144 221336/9. www.hotelsaradharam.co.in. 45 rooms.* Bang opposite the bus stand, this mid-range hotel is the obvious choice for a comfortable stay in town with clean, furnished rooms, good service and efficient staff to manage the show. Besides a conference hall and a cocktail lounge, the hotel has a choice of theree restaurants – Anupallavi serves oriental and continental cuisine in a Tanjore ambience, Pallavi is the non-AC vegetarian restaurant while Geethanjali is its air-conditioned equivalent.

Hotel Akshaya – *17–18, East Car Street, Chidambaram 608001. 04144 220191/220192. www. hotel-akshaya.com. 35 rooms.* . A value-for-money hotel, Akshaya's biggest plus is its location. Right next to the Nataraja temple, its terrace garden offers a view of all four towers making it an ideal perch to witness the grand temple car procession during the annual festival. Aswini, the multi-cuisine restaurant, serves South Indian, Chinese and tandoori fare.

TRANQUEBAR

The Bungalow on the Beach *– 24, King's Street, Tranquebar 609313, Nagapattinam District. 04364 288065/ 289034/9750816034. www.neemrana-hotels.com. 8 rooms.* . Once the British Collector's Office, Neemrana's heritage property is a grand edifice with a spacious wraparound verandah that offers unparalleled views. The Masilamani Nathar Temple to the left, the Dansborg Fort to the right and the beach of singing waves to the front complete the panorama. The spacious rooms are named after Danish ships that docked at Tranquebar. Colonial furniture, antique dolls and rare collectibles give the bungalow a touch of the old. Dine indoors or on the verandah.

Nayak House – *Goldsmith Street, Tranquebar 609313, Nagapattinam District. 04364 288065/289034/ 9750816034. www.neemranahotels.com. 4 rooms.* . Named after Raghunatha Nayak, the ruler of Madurai who granted trading rights to the Danes, Nayak House is a sea-facing Tamil house better suited for the budget traveller. Besides three rooms (Silver, Gold and Platinum), it also boasts the tallest room in Tranquebar (Bronze), ideal for honeymooners.

NAGAPATTINAM

Mangala Heritage Home – *Meda Mada Villagam Street, Thirupugalur Village, Nagapattinam District. 9840215765. www.mangalaheritage home.co.in. 5 rooms.* . Tucked away from the coast 23km from Nagore on SH-67 to Kumbakonam, Mangala is indeed a hidden gem. The traditional heritage home, painted in vivid yellow and blue, overlooks the vast tank of Thirupugalur's famous Agneeswara Temple. Red oxide floors, terracotta tiles, hand beaten brass washbasins and wooden pillars around a sunlit courtyard go perfectly with the home-cooked vegetarian food served on banana leaves.

VELANKANNI

Clinton Park Inn – *Church Main Road, Velankanni 611111, Nagapattinam District. 04365 264990/98. www.clinton parkinn.com. 58 rooms.* . It was the lack of proper hotels in Velankanni that prompted the launch of Clinton Park Inn. A 3-star property and definitely the most luxurious one in Velankanni, it offers squeaky clean rooms, Esprido Liquido bar and Caravela multi-cuisine restaurant.

Hotel Seagate Country Club – *Main Road, Vailankanni 611111, Nagapattinam District. 04365 263910/ 9842456109. www.hotelseagate.co.in. . 60 rooms & 8 cottages.* . Part of a three-hotel chain, Seagate offers good views of the church from most rooms. It also runs the budget 50-room **Hotel Picnic** and the more luxurious **Seagate Resorts** with a pool. All offer free stay for drivers.

MGM Vailankanni Residency – *64/F 2, Nagapattinam Main Road, Vailankanni 611111. 04365 263900/263979/263 336/9940662772. www.mgm-hotels.com. 27 rooms & 8 cottages.* . Part of the same chain that runs the MGM Beach Resort at Muttukadu, the hotel is 1km from the shrine near the Velankanni arch as one enters town. Enjoy the quiet atmosphere, lounge in the pool or dine on multi-cuisine fare at Lotus.

RAMESWARAM

Hotel Queen Palace – *Near bus stand, NH Road, Rameswaram 623526. 04573 221013/221131/9442100704. www.hotelqueenpalace.com. . 40 rooms.* . A value-for-money star hotel near the bus stand with a vegetarian restaurant. One of the few hotels that thoughtfully allows pets; though why one would bring them to the pilgrim town of Rameswaram is the question.

Hotel Royal Park – *Semma Madam, Ramnad Highway, Rameswaram 623526. 04573 221680/221321/9443159722. www.hotelroyalpark.in. . 40 rooms.* . One of the first budget luxury hotels in town, Royal Park is 2km from the main temple. The reception area is kitschy but the rooms are decent, while Bhojan serves pure veg food.

Hotel Vinayaga – *5, Kumaran Road (Railway Feeder Road), Rameswaram 623526. 04573 222361/9500722288. www.poppyshotel.com. . 45 rooms.* . Part of the Poppy Group with six hotels in South India, Vinayaga is located near Rameswaram railway station. Rooms are comfortable but have a distant view of the sea. The veg restaurant serves decent Indian food.

Hotel Sunrise View – *1/3G, East Car Street, Rameswaram 623526. 04573 223434/222453. www.hotelsunrise view.com. 31 rooms.* . The closest stay near the temple offering reasonable luxury is just a few steps from the eastern tower. Besides rooms with views – the temple, the sea or sunrise, the hotel can arrange *pujas* at the shrine.

EAT

If global flavours, seafood specialities and a laid-back ambience lend a characteristic charm to Mamallapuram's rooftop cafes on Othavadai Street and Tranquebar's heritage resorts, the rest of the Coromandel Coast has a distinctly South Indian touch. Budget restaurants in the heart of temple towns like Kanchipuram (Gandhi Road, Nellukara Street), Rameswaram and Chidambaram (Car Streets) lure customers with steaming *idlis* and hot *dosas* or sumptuous veg and spicy non-veg food served on a banana leaf.

MAMALLAPURAM

Luna Magica – *Bajanai Koil Street, Fisherman's Colony, Mamallapuram 603104. 044 274 42767/27242521. Open daily 7am–10pm.* 100m/110yd north of Othavadai Street right on the beach is this old favourite. Crabs, lobsters, tiger prawns and the day's catch are usually kept live in a tank to hard sell the freshness, though just the name is guarantee enough. Food is good, though sizzlers are more reasonably priced.

Moonrakers Restaurant – *34, Othavadai Street, Mamallapuram 603104. 044 272 42115/9444184060. www.moon rakersrestaurants.com. Open daily 10am–10.30pm.* Mamallapuram's iconic restaurant and favourite hangout started as a small shack in 1994. The atmosphere and music is still better than the food, though the mixed grill seafood platter is the best in town.

Bob Marley Restaurant – *182, Bajanai Koil Street, Fisherman's Colony, Mamallapuram 603104. 9840098260/ 9940050060/9840439363. Open 7am–12midnight.* A popular terrace restaurant with floor-seating offers freshly prepared seafood, good views and a lazy breeze… or maybe that's just the reggae.

Mamalla Bhavan – *212, South Madha Street, Mamallapuram 603104. 044 274 42250. www.mamallahotels.com. Open daily for breakfast and lunch.* Popular South Indian joint opposite the bus stand, serving *idli, dosa, vada* and other tiffin items, besides *thalis* at lunch.

Le Nautilus – *Othavadai Cross Street, Mamallapuram 603104.* Just down the street from Moonrakers, Nautilus is a French-run cafe-restaurant known for its soups, French fare and generous portions.

La Vie en Rose – *9, College Road, Mamallapuram 603104. 044 274 42522.* Small unobtrusive restaurant with few rooms on the southern part of town near the Sculpture Museum. It's not just the name that's French, there's genuinely good spaghetti and salad on offer.

Le Yogi – *10, Othavadai Street, Fisherman's Colony, Mamallapuram 603104. 044 274 42571. Open daily 7.30am–11pm.* Run by a friendly Franco-Indian couple, Fabienne and Muji, Le Yogi offers genuine filter coffee, yummy Nutella coconut pancakes and all kinds of seafood, besides 'Tibetan Moms' and 'Spring Rool'. Spellings may be questionable, but the crab in lemon butter is mind-blowing.

La Palais Croisette – *8A, Othavadai Street, Mamallapuram 603104. ✆044 274 42331. Open daily 7am–11pm. www.hotelramakrishna.com.* Rooftop restaurant at Ramakrishna Hotel serving good music besides pasta, salad and pancakes. The set breakfast is great, as are the croissants, cinnamon rolls and chocolate cakes.

Tina Blue View – *1, Othavadai Cross Street, Mamallapuram 603104. ✆044 274 42319/9840727270. Open 11am–3pm, 7–11pm.* Rooftop restaurant-cum-lodge with a breezy terrace, great views and really fresh fish.

KANCHIPURAM

Adyar Ananda Bhavan – *68B, Nellukara Street, Big Kanchipuram, 631502 ✆044 272 33295. www.aabsweets.in. Open Mon–Sat 9.30am–6.30pm.* More of a snack joint with fast food items, sweets, juices and more.

Indian Coffee House – *434, Gandhi Road, Little Kanchipuram. ✆044 272 25644. Open daily 6.30am–9pm.* It's not just the coffee or the ***dosas***, it is the buzz of conversation, clatter of spoons and slurps of tea that make Coffee House a delightful institution.

Saravana Bhavan – *66, Nellukara Street, Kanchipuram 631502. ✆044 2722 6877. www.saravanbhavan.com.* . *Open daily 6am–10pm.* The best place in Kanchi for pure vegetarian and South Indian fare. Part of a well known chain, this branch is attached to the M.M. Hotels complex *(see p188)* and there is a second excellent outlet in Hotel Jaybala *(see p188)*.

Sri Saravana Lunch Home – *38–40, Gandhi Road, Kanchipuram 631501. ✆044 2722 6043. Open 24hr.* Located near the bus stand, this is a popular eatery serving great South Indian ***thalis*** and breakfast items at a reasonable price.

RAMESWARAM

Chola Hotel – *North Street, Rameswaram 623526. ✆04573 221307. Open 24hr.* Had enough of vegetarian food? Try the carnivorous delights at Chola non-veg with ***biryanis***, chicken ***masala*** and goat-head curry.

Hotel Vasantha Bhavan – *34A, East Car Street, Rameswaram, Ramanathapuram 623526. ✆04573 221587/9443131101. Open daily 5am–11pm.* Located near the State Bus Stand close to the temple's eastern entrance; great for a quick meal.

Ganesh Mess – *3, Middle Street, Rameswaram 623526. ✆04573 222947/ 9994063984. Open daily 7am–10pm.* Really economical eatery near Hotel Maharaja serving veg South Indian fare, including delicious ***pongal, vada sambar*** and meals.

Gujarat Bhavan – *516, Sannidhi Street, Rameswaram 623526. ✆04573 221301/221159. Open 24hr.* For a change of palate from the glut of South Indian eateries, try the Gujarati ***thalis***.

CAFES

Buddha Café – *46/3, Othavadai Street, Mamallapuram 603104. ✆9962905712/9840771801. Prices start at Rs.60.* A thatched rooftop café overlooking the main street that stirs up Crepe Nutella, Muesli Fruit Curd Honey and Ayurvedic juices, besides usual sea fare.

Café Coffee Day – *1, NGO Layout, opp. Sriperumbudur Arch, Highway, Kanchipuram District. ✆9047106788. www.cafecoffeeday.com. Open daily 10am–11pm. Prices start at Rs.50.* The perfect answer for sudden cravings for latte, cappuccino, calzones or spinach corn sandwich. They also run an outlet on ECR near Mamallapuram.

Gecko Café – *14, Othavadai Cross Street, Mamallapuram 603104. ✆9840734229. www.gecko-web.com. Open daily 7am–10pm. Prices start at Rs.70.* An airy rooftop cafe overlooking a lake serving great pancakes, omelettes and seafood, best washed down with fresh juices and banana ***lassis***.

LEISURE

Adventure Zone – *37, Cheyyur Road, Zamin Endathur village, Taluk Madhurantankam 603311, Kanchipuram District. ✆044 2754 0178/9786536584. www.adventurezone.8k.com/index.html. Open year-round. Rs.1,800–6,905 (stay and adventure package), Rs.350–650* *(only activities).* Located 11km from Madhurantankam, the place whips up a taste of adventure *(1–2 days)* at reasonable prices. Activities include rapelling, obstacle course, shooting and seasonal activities like parasailing, scuba and jeeping/off-roading besides scenic tours to villages, saltpans and birding sites. Stay in AC Swiss cottages with bunk beds. ***(Booking:** New 5, 3rd East Street, Kamaraj Nagar, Thiruvanmiyur, Chennai 600041; ☏9444384608 Mon–Fri, 10am–6pm).*

Serena Spa – *Radisson Blu Resort Temple Bay, 57, Covelong Road, Mamallapuram 603104. ☏044 274 43636. www.serena spa.com. Open 8am–8pm. Prices start at Rs.500 yoga, Rs.1,400 massage (30min), mini spa packages (2hr) Rs.3,700 and upwards.* Tucked away in a far corner of the resort surrounded by water pools and grassy lawns is this exclusive spa. There are gender-separated wet areas, a large relaxation deck, hairdressing and beauty treatments, steam–sauna–jacuzzi, and even a boutique. The spa offers a range of local and international treatments.

Sri Durga Kerala Ayurvedic Massage & Yoga – *143/1, Othavadai Street, Fisherman Colony, Mamallapuram 603104. ☏9840288280/9600125189. www.aboutmahabalipuram.com/ sridurga.html. Open 7am–8pm. Prices start at Rs.350.* One of the many massage and yoga parlours in Mamallapuram, though quite professionally run. Yoga classes are organised in the morning and evening and for women, female masseuse are available.

Temple Adventures – *Covelong Road, Mamallapuram 603104. ☏9789844191/ 9940219449. www.templeadventures.com. Bodyboards Rs.50–200/hr, surfboards Rs.200–500/2hr, lessons Rs.800/3hr, boat trips Rs.3,000–4,000/hr, guide Rs.1,000/ hr.* Learn surfing with experienced adventure operators; those who know the ropes can get equipment on hire. Boating is arranged for groups, with a choice of sunrise, sunset or full moon tours.

SHOPPING

SHOWROOMS

Arignar Anna Silk Handloom Weavers – *15, Vazhakarutheeswarar Koil Street, Kanchipuram 631501. ☏044 27222148/27229019/27231373. www. annasociety.com.* One of the largest weaving societies in Kanchi with 2,000 weavers, offering a wide range of saris from elegant casual wear to heavy jacquard designs for weddings.

Kamatchi Co-optex Showroom – *182, Gandhi Road, Kanchipuram 631501. ☏044 272 28892. www.cooptex.com.* Established in 1935, the Tamil Nadu Handloom Weavers' Co-operative Society currently has 202 showrooms across the state, of which this is a Presidents' Award-winning store.

Pachaiyappa's Silks – *167, Gandhi Road, opp. Theradi, Kanchipuram 631501. ☏044 2722 7695/3465/0742/0865. www.pachaiyappas.in.* An old name in the business since 1926, promising good quality at fixed, value-for-money prices. The three-storey outlet, hard-to-miss on Gandhi Street, has a range of flashy silks and modern designs in an air-conditioned environment.

Dravidian Handicrafts – *17 & 18, Hotel Akshaya, East Car Street, Chidambaram 608001. ☏04144 395977. www.dravidian sculptures.com.* Chidambaram's leading manufacturers and sellers of bronzes and wood carvings of gods and goddesses.

Kalam Sea Shell Mart – *27-A, Muslim Street, Rameswaram 623 526, Ramnad Dist, Chidambaram 608001. ☏04573 221294/222194/9443122196. www.kalamseashells.com.* Wholesalers of seashell handicrafts like shell lampshades, beaded curtains, pen holders, wall hangers, shell mirrors, gift items, key chains, jewellery and rare seashells.

Mayan Handicrafts – *38, Five Rathas Road, Mamallapuram 603104. ☏044 27442206/9500119387. www.mayan handicrafts.in.* Specialists in stone sculpture of all sizes including Buddha, Ganesha, Hanuman and other Hindu deities, *deepa sthambas* (stone lamps), stone fountains, pillars and decorative pieces. Drop by at their factory *(☏044 27443706)* on ECR.

Poompuhar – *Shore Temple Road, Mamallapuram 603104. ℘044 274 42224. www.poompuhar.org.* The State-run handicraft store is a pool of artefacts sourced from the various manufacturing hubs of Tamil Nadu Handicrafts Corporation. Besides stone sculpture from Mamallapuram, there are bronze icons from Swamimalai, ***kuthu vilakku*** (standing lamps) or hanging oil lamps from Madurai and Tirunelveli, Thanjavur art plates and sandalwood carvings.

Southern Arts & Crafts – *72, East Raja Street, Mamallapuram 603104. ℘044 274 43675. www.southernarts.in.* Bronzes, stone and wooden sculptures, Raja Ravi Verma's oliographs, Colonial furniture in teak or rosewood, Tanjore art on wood or glass, door panels, decorative lamps, figurines, wall hangings, flower vases and *uralis* (metal vessels).

MARKETS

Gandhi Road Market – *Kanchipuram.* With nearly a dozen major Weaver's Co-operative Society shops located here, Gandhi Road is a good place to pick up hand loom kanjeevaram silks and cottons.

Pancha Rathas Shopping Complex – *Five Rathas Road, Mamallapuram.* A shopping zone near the Pancha Rathas parking with a complex of shops selling ethnic handicrafts, dolls, small stone sculptures, shell crafts and touristy knick-knacks.

SPECIALITY SHOPS AND DESIGNER BOUTIQUES

The Boutique – *Shore Temple Road, Mamallapuram 603104. ℘044 274 42127. theboutique@sancharnet.* A shop opposite the Shore Temple selling jewellery, statues, carpets, paintings, handicrafts from Kashmir and Tibetan masks from Ladakh.

Queen Art Emporium – *41, Othavadai Street, Mamallapuram 603104. ℘044 274 42742/9444160724. www.queenart emporium.com.* A good collection of sculptures in various stones and shades.

Tranquebar Resource Craft Centre – *Goldsmith's Street, Tranquebar 609313. ℘044 274 42742/9444160724. http://tranquebar.in/. Open daily 9am–5pm.* Small outlet selling cloth bags, terracotta figurines, coconut-shell curios, bowls and jewellery, key chains, accessories and hand-woven baskets made of palm. There is a good cafe onsite. Proceeds go towards tsunami benefit programmes.

BOOKSHOPS

Guru Book Centre – *16, Nellukkara Street, Kanchipuram 631502. ℘044 272 60256/9842316661.* Bang opposite Sangeetha Hotel is this sweet little bookshop stocking novels, books, maps etc.

JK Bookshop – *144, Othavadai Street, Mamallapuram 603104. ℘9840442853. Open daily 8.30am–9pm.* A small store with a collection of books in English, French and German that can be bought or swapped; proceeds go to fund schools for village children.

PERFORMING ARTS

Kattaikkuttu Sangam – *36 Punjarasantankal Village, Aiyankarkulam 631502, Kanchipuram District. ℘044 272 42044/9944369600. www.kattaikkuttu.org. Open daily 7am–5pm.* 8km from Kanchipuram is the shaded 2.8ha/7-acre campus of Kuttu Kalai Kudam Centre for performing arts. Here, young students are taught ***kattaikkuttu***, a rural form of theatre from Tamil Nadu's northern districts that uses song, music, dance, make-up, costumes, drama and ritual. All-night plays are frequently organised. Guests are welcome to visit the Gurukulam and the centre also hosts 45min performances.

Kanchi Kamakoti Peetham – *Srimatam Samsthanam, 1, Salai Street, Big Kanchipuram 631502. ℘044 2722 2115. www.kamakoti.org.* Besides a lot of work in social health care, education, spiritualism and charity, the Peetham also conducts several music festivals, especially during holy periods like Navratri *(Aug–Sep)* and Chaturmasya vrata *(Jul–Nov).*

NIGHTLIFE

Butterball Bed & Breakfast – *Main Road, Mamallapuram 603104. ℘044 274 42850/9840793902.* A small bed and breakfast place behind Nilgiri's, on weekends it transforms into a live music platform with occasional blues and jazz gigs.

Chettinad

Highlights

- Delicious Chettinad cuisine *p59*
- Kanadukathan heritage town *p200*
- Learn about Athangudi tiles *p201*
- Stay in a Chettiar mansion *p202*

Chettinad is the land of an enterprising Tamil trading community called Nagarathars (townsfolk). Using riches from across the seas and teak shipped from Burma, they built palatial mansions between the 19C and 20C, earning the title Nattu-kottai Chettiars, those who built fortresses on land. Integral pillars of the Chola Empire and forerunners of the banking system in India, Chettiars were also masters of town planning. By cleverly harvesting rain water through *eri* (reservoirs) and *urani* (tanks), they transformed an arid wasteland into an oasis of plenty. Their grand homes, delectable cuisine and gracious hospitality is what makes Chettinad an unparalleled heritage region.

KARAIKUDI

Karaikudi, the largest and most populous town in Chettinad, is a nucleus for the 74 adjoining Chettiar settlements and clan temples strewn between **Pudukkottai** and Chettinad's second-largest town, **Devakottai** *(18km south of Karaikudi).*

Besides acting as the main hub for transport, accommodation and eating out, Karaikudi is also home to architectural gems like Aayiram Jannal or the House of 1,000 Windows. Don't bother counting, the term is purely figurative.

Chidambara Vilas, Ramachandrapuram, Kadiapatti

KANADUKATHAN★★

The heritage town of Kanadukathan *(14km north of Karaikudi)* perhaps has the highest density of large mansions anywhere in Chettinad.

Besides two heritage hotels, Chettinadu Mansion and Visalam, the **Chettinad/ Raja Palace★** is worth a look. So is the Chettinad railway station *(4km from the palace)*, with the Raja's private waiting room furnished with divans, recliners and bidets.

- **Population:** 1.5 lakhs (Karaikudi).
- **Info:** M.Rm.Rm. Cultural Foundation. 044 24612578. chettinadculture@yahoo.com.
- **Location:** A tiny landlocked region in south central Tamil Nadu at the junction of Pudukkottai and Sivaganga districts.
- **Timing:** Summers are hot, so visit between November and March or in the monsoon months of July and August.
- **Guided Tours:** Most heritage hotels arrange guided tours for visits to heritage homes, weaving units and tile-making factories.

THE CHETTIARS

As ship chandlers of the Cholas, the Chettiars traded rice from the Kaveri Delta and salt from the Coromandel Coast and followed trade routes to far-off lands. After the destruction of their settlement at Kaveripoompattinam (Poompuhar) by a tsunami (some contend they were wronged by a Chola king), the Chettiars sought refuge in the favourable Pandya lands to the south. They came to this barren hinterland in the 8C and settled in four villages around the temple at **Ilyathangudi** *(25km west of Karaikudi,* *see p198**).* They were soon granted nine temples, around which the first clans grew and eventually became 96 settlements in a 1,500sq km area between **Pudukkottai** and **Sivaganga**.

They rebuilt their fortunes and soon become moneylenders to farmers, *zamindars*, *palaykaras* (petty chieftains) and kings alike. Their good relations with the Rajas of Pudukkottai, Sivaganga and Ramanathapuram brought them to the attention of the British East India Company. British expansionism led

GETTING THERE AND AROUND

GETTING THERE

BY PLANE – The nearest airports are Madurai (domestic) and Trichy (Tiruchirappalli) (international).

BY TRAIN – Daily passenger and express trains from Chennai to Rameswaram via Trichy stop at Kanadukathan *(Chettinad station)* and Karaikudi *(℘04565 222341)*. The most convenient option is the overnight Rameswaram Express *(16701)* from Chennai Egmore station at 9.40pm, which reaches Karaikudi next morning at 7.10am. The return train *(16702)* at 8.30pm reaches Chennai at 6.25am.

BY BUS – There are regular bus services to Karaikudi from Chennai, Madurai, Thanjavur, Trichy, Rameswaram and Palani. Overnight buses start from Chennai between 6.30–10pm and take 9–10hr to reach Karaikudi next morning *(Rs.360–600)*.

BY CAR – Strategically located on NH-210 and equidistant from Madurai *(80km west, 2hr)* and Trichy *(90km north, 2hr)*, Karaikudi is well connected to Thanjavur *(130km, 2.5hr)* and Rameswaram *(150km, 3hr)*. Chennai *(425km)* and Bangalore *(433km)* are 7hr drives.

GETTING AROUND

All State Transport buses from Karaikudi to nearby villages and towns of Devakottai, Tirupattur, Rayavaram and Tirumayam start from Old Bus Stand to the south *(10min walk, Rs.40 by auto)*. Mofussil buses terminate at the New Bus Terminus to the north. Local taxis are available at the centre of town. Walk around the streetscapes to appreciate the rich architecture of Chettinad mansions.

them to Ceylon in 1796 and Burma in 1824. Their business acumen helped them expand their trade to Mauritius, Africa and across the Far East. Such was the power they wielded that they financed the creation of entire countries and returned to build grand mansions with their fortune. As moneylenders, the Chettiars offered every possible service promised by a modern bank. Between 1875 and 1925, they practically controlled the Indian economy.

Greatly affected by World War II and political upheavals across the Far East, many returned bankrupt and were forced to sell off their mansions bit by bit. With families scattered across the globe, caretakers keep house, and it is only during weddings and family gatherings that the empty halls of Chettiar homes ring out with stories, laughter and the clangor of the kitchen.

Tirumayam Fort

DRIVING TOUR

TRICHY TO KARAIKUDI

The drive to Chettinad down the Trichy–Pudukkottai–Ramanathapuram Road, or NH-210, is littered with ancient cave temples, Ayyanar shrines, forts and museums. It's best to leave early for the 89km drive to Karaikudi as the diversions off the highway are bound to slow you down.

Keeranur Ayyanar

25km south of Trichy make a quick stop just short of Keeranur town to see a striking Ayyanar shrine (folk deity) with offerings of tall terracotta horses. Look out for the temple arch opposite the HP petrol pump.

Continue 11km south of Keeranur (about 17km before Pudukkottai) and turn right from NH-210. Go past the Periyar memorial at Samathuvapuram to reach a gravel road to the hill 1.5km from the highway.

Narthamalai Cave Temples★

Surrounded by a chain of hills with ancient caves and some of India's longest rock-cut edificies, Narthamalai's western hill has two cave temples, an old Jain shrine and the other dedicated to Vishnu.

Head west on Oorapatti Road and turn onto Sittanavasal Road to reach the Sittanavasal cave 14km away.

Sittanavasal Cave Paintings★

The rock-cut Jain monastery with remnants of frescoes from the 7C ranks among the best after Ajanta Caves. Arduously painted on the ceiling of the Arival *koil*, the exquisite 'lotus pond' is a detailed collage of overlapping fish, ducks, animals and two monks gathering lotuses.

From Sittanavasal turn onto the Kulithalai–Manapparai Road and continue onto Pudukkottai, 15km away.

Pudukkottai

The seat of the erstwhile Thondaiman kings, Pudukkottai meaning 'new fort', has a noteworthy museum. Started in 1910 by Marthanda Bhairava Thondaiman, the **Government Museum**★ (*℘04322 22247*) at Thirugokarnam, on the town's outskirts, is the second-largest in Tamil Nadu and a hidden treasure sadly overlooked by many travellers. The fascinating collection houses art objects, wood carvings, sculptures, bronzes, coins, textiles, weapons, ornaments, paintings, musical instruments, prehistoric tools and historical records.

Continue 8km south of Pudukkottai and after crossing the railway track, turn right from the arch at Namunasamudram

Ilyangudi Ayyanar★

Stop by at the Ayyanar Shrine in this small hamlet known for its exceptionally large collection of terracotta horses in a sacred grove. As protector of the village, the Ayyanar uses the terracotta horses and elephants as transport to guard the village at night.

Drive 12km south to Tirumayam.

Tirumayam

Visit Tirumayam for its impressive hill **fort**★ and the two rock-cut temples at its base (*see p200*). A 5km diversion towards **Ramachandrapuram** leads to Chidambara Vilas, Chettinad's most plush heritage hotel (*see Addresses*).

At Tirumayam, the road forks and the right-hand road, the NH-226, goes on via **Tirupattur** to **Sivaganga**, with its dilapidated 1730 palace (*see p200*).

The left-hand road continues 10km to heritage town **Kanadukathan**★★, from where it's 14km to **Karaikudi**, the heart of Chettinad.

Karaikudi

(*See p194, 198*).

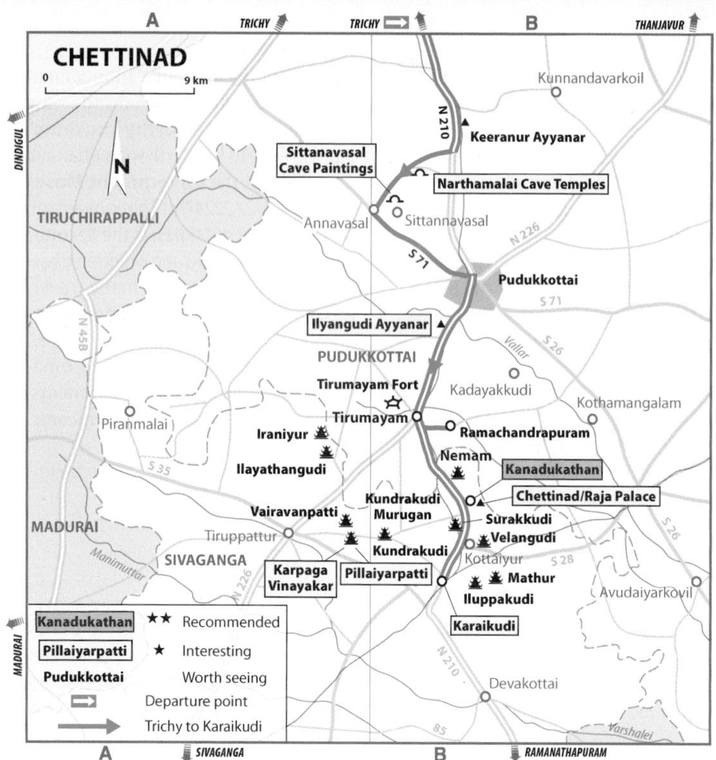

Religious and Spiritual Sights

The spiritual landscape of Chettinad is dotted by Ayyanar clusters, Jain cave shrines, rock-cut temples at Narthamalai and Sittanavasal (*see Driving Tour*) and important shrines like the Murugan Temple at Kundrakudi, the Ganesha Temple at Pillaiyarpatti and the Vishnu Temple at Tirumayam Fort (*see Historical Sights*). Every Chettiar owes allegiance to one of the nine clan temples adopted and renovated by his forefathers.

AROUND KARAIKUDI

Chettiar Clan Temples

Head 3km SW of Karaikudi to Iluppakudi and continue 2km NE on Karaikudi Rd to Mathur. Backtrack to Karaikudi railway station and go 6.5km N to Velangudi near Kottaiyur. Continue 10km N via Pallathur and Kanadukathan to Nemam. Return via Kanadukathan to Surakkudi, 5.5km S on NH-536. Take the Palavangudi Rd via Kundrakudi to Pillaiyarpatti 13km SW and Vairavanpatti, 1.5km NW. Continue N towards NH-36 and drive 11.5km to Ilayathangudi and Iraniyur. Return to Karaikudi, 27km SE via Koviloor-Tirupathur Rd. Most temples are closed 12noon–4pm.

Located within a 25km radius of Karaikudi, each of the exceptional nine Chettiar clan temples is architecturally unique. **Iluppakudi**, named after the *iluppai* or Indian Butter tree, has a naturally formed *lingam*. Nearby, the shrine of Ainootheswarar at **Mathur** boasts a 70ft-tall *rajagopuram* and lion sculptures holding stone-carved balls in their jaws that can be rotated. The shrine at **Velangudi**, dedicated to Kandeswarar, is still surrounded by the *vela* trees after which it's named. **Nemam**, built as per strict rules of sculpture or *'niyamam'*, has musical pillars, an intricate *vimanam* and two large sculpted elephants near the shrine of Soundaranayagi. The Desikanathar Temple at **Surakkudi** has seven painted *vimanams* and a 16-pillared *mandapam* resting on stone lions. The Karpaga Vinayakar Temple at **Pillaiyarpatti**★ (see below) is a major tourist attraction.

Nearby, **Vairavanpatti** has several wall paintings dating back to 1864. **Ilayathangudi** is believed to be the place where the deities Kailasnathar and his consort Nithyakalani rested, hence the name (*ilaippu* – tiredness, *attru* – removal, *gudi* – place). The Arkondanathar temple at **Iraniyur** houses 50 bronzes, including a 12C Nataraja statue and beautiful wall paintings.

PILLAIYARPATTI★

Karpaga Vinayakar Temple★

13km north-west of Karaikudi towards Tirupattur on Madurai Road. Karpaga Vinayakar Thirukovil Street, Pillayarpatti 630207. Closed 1–4pm. Entry free. 04577 264240/264241. www.pillayarpattitrust.com.

Easily the most popular shrine in Chettinad, this rock-cut temple (the most important of the nine clan temples) is dedicated to Valampuri Vinayakar, a large Ganesha seated in *padmasana* (lotus position) with a gold-fronted trunk bent to the right. Carved from the rocks, it is the idol's black appearance that gives the temple its popular name, Karpaga Vinayakar. Believed to be 1,600 years old, the temple's northern tower was erected by the Pandya kings while the Nagarathar community, who renovated it in 1284, added the eastern tower and an adjoining *mandapam*.

The ceiling of the hall is painted in vegetable dyes and bears old inscriptions while ornate sculptures adorn the pillars.

KUNDRAKUDI

Kundrakudi Murugan Temple

10km north-west of Karaikudi towards Tirupattur, just 3km short of Pillaiyarpatti. Open 6am–11am, 4pm–8pm. Entry free. 04577 264227/9790583820.

Lord Murugan's temple is built on a peacock-shaped hill and a beautiful legend. On hearing from a demon that Lord Brahma's swan and Lord Vishnu's eagle were boasting they could fly faster than him, the peacock swallowed them, only to be punished by Lord Murugan for his vanity. It was on this very rock that the peacock undertook a penance and found atonement. Steps snake up the 60m/200ft hillock, which lies at the exact centre of Chettinad.

Temples dedicated to Murugan's elder brother **Ganesha** dot the hill while excavated cave shrines lie on its western side. In most temples, the *navagraha* (Lords of the Nine Planets) are oriented towards their respective directions; at Kundrakudi, all planets face the main statue of Lord Murugan, deified here as **Shanmuganathar** (the six-faced one).

Karpaga Vinayakar Temple Tank

Historical Sights

Besides the outstanding treasures of Raja Palace and Tirumayam Fort, other colossal edifices lie scattered in the dustbowl of Chettinad. Of particular note are Sri Letchmi Vilas at Athangudi (Athangudi Palace), the Periya Minor Veedu at Devakottai and the residence of philanthropist Alagappa Chettiar in Kottaiyur, who gifted his palatial mansion to start the Women's College. Don't miss Tamil Nadu's oldest district museum at Pudukkottai (*see Driving Tour*).

KANADUKATHAN★★

Chettinad/Raja Palace★

Located in front of the Chidamabara Vinayagar temple tank in the heart of Kanadukathan town. Raja Front Street, Kanadukathan, Via Karaikudi. Entry free (by prior appointment). Guided Tours: a caretaker shows around visitors. Guests of the Bangala and Chettinadu Mansion have privileged access.

The 110-year-old Chettinad Palace, the oldest surviving building of its style and size, was built by Dr S.Rm.M. Annamalai Chettiar, founder of the Indian Bank and the Annamalai University in **Chidambaram** (*see Coromadel Coast*). Honoured as Diwan Bahadur by the British, conferred with knighthood and finally given the hereditary title of Raja of Chettinad by the King of England in 1929, his palatial mansion was henceforth known as Raja Palace. His portrait dominates the meeting hall decorated with 2.5m/8ft-long tusks shipped from South Africa. Gleaming pillars of Burma teak lead to a series of pillared courtyards and halls inside.

An adjoining building, run as a private **museum** by Visalakshi Ramaswamy, is a treasure trove of Chettinad culture. On show is traditional jewellery, clothing, copper vessels, large troughs for water and grain and a quaint Chettiar travelling kit – a mobile basket full of *masala dabbas*, choppers, rice bins and ladles! Visalakshi's M.Rm.Rm. Cultural Foundation works towards reviving Chettinad's languishing traditions like *kottans* (woven baskets), Athangudi tiles, Madras plaster (egg-lime mix that gives walls a white mirror finish) and Chettinad saris.

Just one lane away, in a small workshop, five looms clatter away in the quietness of Kanadukathan as artisans weave these nine yards of wonder.

TIRUMAYAM

Tirumayam Fort

10km north of Kanadukathan on the Karaikudi–Pudukkottai Road towards Trichy (NH-210). Tirumayam Hill, Pudukkottai District. Open daily 9am–5.30pm. Rs.5 (Rs.100 foreigners, video Rs.25). Guided Tours: arranged on request by Chidambara Vilas.

Built in 1687 by Sethupati Vijaya Raghunatha Tevan of Ramanathapuram, the fort once stretched around the massive rock at Tirumayam in seven concentric rings, of which only four remain. Gateways marking the cardinal directions dot the base of the hill. Halfway to the top on the right is an old magazine and a chamber on the opposite side enshrines a *linga* placed on an unusual *yonipitha*. Though largely degraded, the fort has a bastion at its highest point mounted by a British cannon, which gives a good view of the surrounding landscape.

On the southern slope at the boulder's base are two ancient **rock-cut temples** dedicated to Shiva and Vishnu with voluptuous larger-than-life sculptures of dancers and divine beings on the pillars. The Vishnu shrine overlooks a serene temple tank and the main shrine has an unusual reclining image of Vishnu hewn out of rock.

SIVAGANGA

Sivaganga Palace

58km south-west of Karaikudi.

Built in 1730, the palace at Sivaganga, or Gowri Vilasam, is beautiful even in ruin. Thankfully, the temple of Sri Rajarajeshwari, the royal family's tutelary deity, is largely intact. Nearby, **Nadai Kinaru** is a miniature swimming pool reserved for royal baths.

Athangudi Tiles

© Anurag Mallick, Priya Ganapathy/MICHELIN

It's a small nondescript village near **Karaikudi** that's responsible for the riveting floor spaces found in Chettinad homes. The tradition of Athangudi tiles started over 100 years ago as tile companies opened up to feed the construction frenzy of mansions. Unlike mass-produced ceramic tiles, Athangudi tiles are cast by hand using local sand, fine gravel and cement. Available mostly in dark earthy hues with geometric, floral designs, the tiles are locally called *poo kallu* (floral stones). Black and white assemblage and motifs for creating borders or relief is a Chettinad speciality. A visit to Athangudi is essential to understand how the tile is made and one of the best places to see it is the **Ganapathy Tile Factory**.

First, white cement, ordinary cement and oxide powder are mixed by hand and added to finely sieved sand. Only oxides of red, yellow, green and off-white are used. An outer wooden frame is placed on a square sheet of glass and an inner metal design frame is placed into which the dye is poured. The frame is gently shaken to level the paint and removed. A variation of this is the freehand style, done with deft artistic strokes without a frame. A mix of mud and cement (3:1) is then sprinkled onto it and the excess is shaken off, before being packed with cement. The cement is scraped off and re-dusted a few times, before being levelled with a final coat. The outer frame is carefully removed and the tile left to dry. After curing in rainwater tanks for 2 days, the tiles are sun-dried for a week, before the glass is removed to reveal a gleaming Athangudi tile. A group of three artisans can churn out 250 tiles a day.

The process of laying Athangudi tiles is perhaps as important as manufacturing them and only masons trained in the art can make the precise calculations to fit them correctly. Since the average tile is 2cm wide and quite heavy, the cement layer on the floor should be 4cm thick for the tile to sit properly. It has to be uniformly packed and the tile should not make a hollow sound when tapped. The beauty of Athangudi tiles is that they require no polishing and get a natural shine with regular use.

Be it imported tiles from Italy and Japan in the old days or the modern era of designer floor tiles in ceramic, vitrified materials, marble and granite, the earthy Athangudi tile seems to be holding its own. The renovation of heritage houses, growth in tourism and demand from independent buyers and architects has ensured that Athangudi stays in business. Today, 40 units operate in Athangudi, employing 400 people. Tiles can be bought in Athangudi at Rs.33/sq ft and some companies will deliver the cargo to your doorstep and do the complete fitting, for a cost.

Selva Industries; Athangudi; www.athanguditiles.com.
Tile Kraft; near New Bus Stand, Karaikudi; www.thetilekraft.com.

ADDRESSES

STAY

There are several hotels and lodges in the three important towns of Devakottai, Sivaganga and Karaikudi, which has decent options like **Subhalakshmi Palace** *(℘04565 235200/235203/405200)*, **Nachiappa Palace** *(℘04565 230077/9487556587)* and **Hotel Jagan** *(℘04565 227273/ 225446/9444290310)*.

Budget lodges like **Malar** *(℘04565 239601/9443123771)*, **Udhayam** *(℘04565 234068/236331)*, **Anand** *(℘04565 238468)* and **Sugam International** *(℘04565 237051)* are centred around the two bus stands. However, for those who can afford it, staying in a **Chettinad mansion** is the ideal way to experience the region's charms:

Chidambara Vilas – *TSK House, Ramachandrapuram, Kadiapatti, off Tirumayam Fort. ℘0433 3267070/9843348531. www.chidambaravilas.com. 24 heritage rooms.* This opulent mansion was built over 100 years ago and is Chettinad's latest and most luxurious heritage hotel. An exquisite doorway leads to inner courtyards with pillars made of teak, rosewood and granite. The restaurant, a renovated *Bomma Kottai* (Hall of Dolls) serves authentic Chettinad meals on banana leaves. Great rooftop views, a swimming pool, spa and cultural performances.

Visalam – *LF Road, Kanadukathan 630103. ℘04565 273301/273354. www.cghearth.com. 15 rooms.* Built as a father's gift for his daughter, the Art Deco building has lavish rooms. Teak beds, antique furniture and black and white snapshots of the Chettiar family add a warm homely touch. Besides three dining areas (one for each meal), a swimming pool, library and an interactive kitchen, bullock cart rides and cultural programmes like *nadaswaram* recitals are also arranged.

The Bangala – *Devakottai Road, Senjai, Karaikudi 630001. ℘04565 220221/250221. www.thebangala.com. 25 rooms. Rs.300.* A 1910 Colonial family home, the Senjai Bangala was a fashionable venue for tea parties and tennis tournaments for VIPs. The furniture, cutlery and crockery used by the Governor of Madras, Sir Athur Hope, who visited in the 1940s is still in use. Rooms overlook a central garden with a swimming pool and spa. Chettinad meals *(Rs.600)* are served on banana leaves with cooking demos and kitchen tours. Mrs. Meyyappan, the *grande dame* running the show, co-authored *The Chettiar Heritage*.

Chettinadu Mansion – *SARM House, Behind Raja's Palace, TKR Street, Kanadukathan. ℘04565 273080/9443495598. www.chettinadumansion.com. 12 rooms.* Sprawled over 3,700sq m/40,000sq ft, this century-old mansion is run as a B&B heritage hotel by the genial Mr Chandramouli. The mansion's succession of courtyards with ornate pillars, balconies and 100 rooms are a delight. Pamper yourself with Ayurvedic massages and enjoy authentic Chettinad meals *(Rs.600)* in the regal front hall.

Saratha Vilas – *832, Main Road, Kothamangalam 630105. ℘9884203175/9884936158. www.sarathavilas.com. 8 rooms.* Built by a wealthy Chettiar merchant and painstakingly restored by two French architects, Michel Adment and Bernard Dragon, a century later, every room is unique. Retaining the essence of Chettinad architecture, the duo infused it with French minimalist sensibility. Enjoy Franco-Tamil cuisine, besides Ayurvedic massages and a garden at the back.

Chettinadu Court – *Near Rajah's Palace, Rajah's Street, Kanadukathan. ℘04565 273080/9846344305. www.deshadan.com. 8 rooms.* Run by Chettinadu Mansion two streets away, the newly constructed village resort has thatched roofs, a restaurant and a bullock cart for village tours to see ancient mansions, pot making, basket weaving, sari weaving and tile making. *(Meals Rs.290.)*

Chettinaadu Narayanaa Inn – *Near Raja Palace, Raja Street, Kanadukathan. ℘94426 36124. www.chettinaaduinn.com. 8 rooms.* Run by Rm.N. Karuppiah and his wife

Mrs K. Muthayee, this Chettinad house organises cycle tours and bullock cart rides of adjoining villages on request.

EAT

For a region synonymous with master chefs who have made Chettinad cuisine a household name, it is ironic that the area possesses woefully few dining choices. Humble shacks are low on ambience but serve tasty signature dishes like chicken Chettinad, mutton ***chukka***, ***kaada*** fry and ***nandu masala***. While most eateries are clustered in Karaikudi, the best way to enjoy a lavish Chettinad spread is in the comfort of luxurious heritage hotels.

Saranya Restaurant – *Behind New Bus Stand, Karaikudi. 04565 227273. www.hoteljagan.com.* Non-veg restaurant in the lobby of Hotel Jagan serving Chettinad, Tandoori and Chinese fare. A separate veg restaurant dishes out South Indian cuisine.

Shree Naarayanaas Coffee House – *Raja Street, Kanadukathan. 04565 283199/9486824017. www.chettinaaduinn.com.* Well-furnished air-conditioned restaurant and a rooftop restaurant serving Chettinad specialities and multi-cuisine.

Hotel Annapoorna – *45/1, Koviloor Road, Karaikudi. 04565 238467. www.hotelannapoorna.net.* The oldest vegetarian restaurant in Karaikudi, serving a wide repertoire of Indian, Tandoori, Chinese dishes and South Indian snacks.

Friends Restaurant – *100 Feet Road, TT Nagar, Karaikudi. 04565 236622.* Cute little garden restaurant serving non-veg Chettinad meals and side dishes like mutton ***chukka***, ***nandu*** (crab) ***masala*** and ***kaada*** (quail) fry.

Saffron Restaurant – *1, Church, 1st Street, Sekkalai Road, Karaikudi. 04565 235277. www.hotelsubhalakshmi palace.com.* Popular veg restaurant at Hotel Subhalakshmi Palace serving delicious South Indian dishes and Chettinad specialities.

BAKERIES

Karaikudi is dotted with bakeries that are widely patronised for the assortment of biscuits, buns, macaroons, rusks, salted snacks and cakes they offer. **Sekkalai Bakery** and **The Best Bangalore Iyannkar Bakery** on Sekkalai Road, **British Biscuit Company** in Senjai and **Corner Bakery** on 100 Feet Road are local favourites.

British Bakery & Sweets – *opp. Periyar Statue Bus Stop. Karaikudi. 9715173741. Prices start at Rs.30.* A wide variety of snacks as well as Madurai's famous coolant ***Jigar Thanda***, an intriguing concoction of ***badam*** milk, ***nannari*** sherbet (sarsaparilla extract), ***kalpasi*** (spice), ***Boost*** (malt-based chocolate drink) and ice cream.

LEISURE

Saratha Vilas – *832, Main Road, Kothamangalam 630105. 98842 03175, 98849 36158. www.sarathavilas.com.* Ayurvedic massages, besides guided thematic trails on Architecture, Town Planning, Temples and Handicrafts.

SHOPPING

Though Chettinad has no glitzy malls or fancy boutiques to flaunt, the sheer diversity of goods on offer is surprising. From hand-woven saris, handcrafted Athangudi tiles (*see p201*), furniture to diamonds, Karaikudi's busy streets are full of bargains.

Antique shops on **Muneesvaran Kovil Street** sell everything from sepia photographs, old advertising posters, religious paintings to brass vessels, temple lamps, Belgian enamelware and Czech pewter jars. For gold and diamond jewellery in modern and traditional designs, browse **MKS Jewellers** on Amman Sannathi and **Karaikudi Maganlal Mehta** in Welcome Lodge Complex.

Karaikudi is famous for its ***kandanki*** or Chettinad saris, woven out of coarse cotton, ideal for the hot clime. Brightly hued with bold checks, stripes and large borders, some come with ***gopura karai*** (temple tower) design. Saris are available in shops on Karaikudi's **MM Street** and the **Co-Optex Showroom** on Sekkalai Road. **M.Rm. House** at Kanadukathan sells loom-fresh saris under their brand 'Kandangi'.

Also ask about the weekly ***sandai*** (shandy), a colourful rural market where fresh vegetables and cattle accessories are sold.

Southern Tamil Nadu

Highlights

- Land's End at Kanyakumari *p206*
- Madurai Meenakshi Temple *p210*
- Kalakad-Mundanthurai Tiger Reserve *p223*
- Courtallam Falls healing waters *p224*

Historic temples set in abodes chosen by gods, fairytale palaces built by powerful dynasties, exquisite stone sculptures and nature's bounteous waterfalls, rivers and forests tied with a ribbon-like coastline; the eight districts of Southern Tamil Nadu hold many attractions. With Madurai Meenakshi Temple as the crowning glory, a virgin deity Kanyakumari guarding the cape, and a dense network of sacred centres like Tenkasi, Tirunelveli, Suchindram and Tiruchendur sprinkled across it, the spiritual weight of the region clearly belies its size. Every visitor to Southern Tamil Nadu experiences something special in the awe-inspiring shrines, the frenzy of festivals, the grandeur of old palaces, the healing waters at Courtallam, the crack and boom of fireworks at Sivakasi or the peaceful meditative air of Vivekananda Rock. The stories of the land are woven inextricably with myth and reality; this is where the great Tamil poet Thiruvalluvar wrote his epic, where Swami Vivekananda attained enlightenment, and where Mahatma Gandhi shunned his urban attire, donned a loin cloth and shawl and led the country to freedom.

Original painted panel at Meenakshi Sundareshwarar Temple, Madurai

SOUTHERN TAMIL NADU

The region south of the Vagai River extending from **Madurai**★★★ in the north to **Tirunelveli** and **Kanyakumari**★, the southern-most point of the Indian mainland has been considered sacred for centuries. From **Tenkasi** and **Courtallam**★ in the Western Ghats to **Tiruchendur**★ on the eastern coast, the region is intersected by holy rivers, forests, mountains, waterfalls, caves and shrines. Not surprisingly, most nodal cities and towns are built around enchanting temples with stunning palaces nearby.

Madurai★★★

The legendary Kadambavanam where Lord Shiva showered *madhuram* or sweet nectar from his matted locks as blessing, Madurai was the historic seat of the Pandyas. With the **Meenakshi Sundareswar Temple**★★★ as its spiritual core and the Vaigai River as its lifeline, the city flowered as the cultural capital of ancient Tamil Nadu and was hailed as the Athens of the East. It hosted the last Tamil Sangam, a literary conclave that produced the Tamil epic *Silappathikaaram*. Praised in song, literature and historic travelogues, Madurai was the celebrated 'Methora' of Megasthenes, the Greek envoy who

- **Population:** Madurai dist. (3,041,038), Tirunelveli dist. (3,072,880), Kanyakumari dist. (1,863,174) (2011 Census).
- **Info:** Tourist Office, 180 West Veli Street, Madurai. ☎0452 2334757. Open Mon–Fri 10am–5pm, Sat 11am–1pm. www.tamilnadutourism.org.
- **Location:** Spread over eight districts of southern Tamil Nadu from Madurai to Kanyakumari.
- **Kids:** Athisayam Theme Park, go-karting at Hawa Valley, Eco Park (Madurai), Baywatch Water Amusement Park (Kanyakumari).
- **Timing:** Keep 2 days aside for Madurai and around and a day each for Tirunelveli, Tiruchendur, Courtallam and Kanyakumari.
- **Guided Tours:** The Tourist Office organises half-day *(5hr)* sightseeing tours at 7am and 3pm to Thirumalai Nayak Palace and Gandhi Museum, ending at Meenakshi Temple *(Rs.125 per head)*.

visited India in the 3C BC. Changing hands from the Cholas to the Madurai Nayaks and eventually the British, it has grown into the third-largest city in Tamil Nadu. Its busy streets are abuzz night and day – from early morning prayers to late-night looms weaving Sungundi saris and round-the-clock eateries and the daily drill of shipping out loads of heady Madurai *malli* (jasmine). Madurai is indeed *thoonga nagaram*, the city that never sleeps.

Exploring the Area – It may not seem apparent when one negotiates its busy streets, but Madurai's original plan was in the shape of a lotus, symbolising the structure of the cosmos. The city spreads around the **Meenakshi Temple**★★★, surrounded by concentric rectangular streets named after Tamil months like Chittirai, Aadi, Aavani Moola and Maasi. The largely dry Vaigai River cuts across Madurai diagonally from north-west to south-east, running parallel to the NH-85 to its south. **Thirumalai Nayak Palace**★★ and **St Mary's Cathedral** are 1.5km south-east of the temple. **Gandhi Memorial** and the **Government Museum** are north of the Vaigai, off Alagar Kovil Road en route to **Pazhamudhir Cholai Temple. Thirupparankundram Temple** is 8km south-west on Thirumangalam Road.

The railway station is 2km west of the temple, the airport is 12km south of the city and Mattuthavani Integrated Bus Stand on Kurivikaran Road is to the north on the Madurai–Melur route.

See Religious and Spiritual Sights, Historical Sights, Art Galleries and Museums.

Tirunelveli

As per Tamil literature Tirunelveli is the quintessential perfect land blessed with all five geographical landscapes – *kurinji* (mountains) or Western Ghats, *mullai* (forests) of Kalakkad and Mundanthurai, *marudham* (paddy fields) irrigated by the Tamiraparani and its tributaries, *neidhal* (coastal region) of Radhapuram and *palai* (desert) of *teri* lands. Which is why each dynasty claimed the land as their own – 'Pandiyanadu' under the early Pandyas, 'Mudikonda Cholamandalam' of the Imperial Cholas, 'Tirunelveli Seemai' of the Madurai Nayaks and Nawabs of Arcot and 'Tinnevelly' under the British, who acquired the region in 1801. Under the benign gaze of **Nellaiappar Temple**★, Shiva's largest in Tamil Nadu, the city continues to prosper, attracting visitors with its many charms.

Exploring the Area – Located on the southern-most tip of the Deccan Plateau, Tirunelveli forms an important junction on NH-7. The city caresses the western side of the perennial Tamiraparani River, whereas its twin municipal city Palayamkottai lies on the eastern side, across the 12-arched Sulochana Mudaliar Bridge. The New Bus Stand *(Puthiya Perunthu Nilayam)* in Veinthaankulam serves as the main bus station. NH-7A links Tirunelveli to **Thoothukudi** (also known as Tuticorin) *(54km east)* while SH-40 goes 59km south-east via Krishnapuram to **Tiruchendur**★ and 53km north-west to **Tenkasi**, 5km short of **Courtallam**★. The **Kalakad-Mundanthurai Tiger Reserve** is 54km east of Tirunelveli on SH-39 via Ambasamudram.

See Religious and Spiritual Sights, National Parks and Wildlife Sanctuaries.

Tirunelveli Halwa

A soft glutinous sweet made of wheat, sugar and copious quantities of ghee, *tirunelveli halwa* is a melt-in-your-mouth delicacy that is Tirunelveli's most famous export. Slightly brown, translucent and sold at Rs.100/kg, the *halwa* is available at several shops around the railway station on Madurai Road. Santhi Sweets in the Central Bus Stand building is the best place to buy, though half a dozen shops bear the famous name. The genuine shop is the one always thronged by crowds!

Kanyakumari★

India's legendary Land's End, Kanyakumari is a dynamic landscape where the Eastern and Western Ghats collide and

Kanyakumari in the morning, with a view to Vivekananda Rock Memorial and the statue of Thiruvalluvar

Official seal of Tamil Nadu

Srivilliputhur, the birthplace of Vaishnava saints Periyazhvar and Andal, is home to the Vatapatrasayee or Vadapathrasayanar Temple. It is the magnificent 11-tiered *gopuram* rising to a height of 59m/192ft that serves as the official symbol of the Tamil Nadu Government.

three giant water bodies merge. Kumari, the unmarried goddess and protector of the land, inspired the British to name the place Cape Comorin. The region came under the Southern Travancore kingdom of King Marthanda Varma (1706-58), who defeated the Dutch East India Company in 1741 in the historic Battle of Colachel *(40km north-west)*, marking the end of Dutch power in India. The captured Flemish admiral Eustachius De Lannoy joined Marthanda Varma and helped modernise the Travancore army. The **Padmanabhapuram Palace**★★ and Captain Lennoy's tomb at **Udayagiri Fort** are reminders of Kanyakumari's rich legacy.

Exploring the Area – On two rocky islets just off the shore, south-east of the **Kumari Amman Temple**, are **Vivekananda Rock Memorial** and the gigantic 41m/133ft-tall **statue** of Tamil poet-saint Thiruvalluvar, accessible by a boat ride *(Rs.20)* from the Poompuhar Shipping Corporation jetty. The sights, shops, motels and eateries on the lanes along the beach form the town's main hub. The jagged edges of the Western Ghats rise up from paddy fields as gusty winds sweep the highway. In one linear stretch northwest from Kanyakumari on NH-47 are **Suchindram** *(12km)*, **Nagercoil** *(18km)* and **Padmanabhapuram Palace**★★ *(35km)* and **Udayagiri Fort** close to Thuckalay.

See Religious and Spiritual Sights and Historical Sights,

Courtallam★

The Agasthiyar Malai Hills, from whose lofty heights the Chittar River dashes down through roots and herbs as **Courtallam Falls**★ (*see p224*), is a mystical Eden dotted by shrines. The hill retreat of Sage Agastya and one of the five *sabhas* or Dancing Halls of Lord Nataraja, it was immortalised in *Kutrala Kuravanji* by Tamil poet Thirukuda Rasappa Kavirayar, who sang an ode to Kutralam's (Courtallam) divine beauty while standing at its highest point. After the Poligar Wars (1799-1802), Courtallam became a favourite of British officers who were drawn by its restorative waters. When the first Collector of Tirunelveli, J.D. Lushington set up residence, Courtallam became a *cutchery*, a sanatorium and an orchard. Exotic cash crops like mangosteen introduced at Courtallam by the Company's resident Lord Casamajor continue to thrive and the village of Kasimejapuram still bears his name.

Exploring the Area – Courtallam is 5km south-west of **Tenkasi**, home to the **Sri Kasi Vishwanatha Temple**★.

GETTING THERE AND AROUND

Also see Planning Your Trip.

GETTING THERE

BY PLANE – Madurai's central location makes in an excellent travel hub. The nearest international airport is Trichy *(134km north-east)*, a 2.5hr drive on NH-45B. Madurai Airport, 12km south of the city, is connected by daily flights to Chennai and Bangalore, though Tuticorin Airport *(at Vaagaikulam, 15km south-west of Thoothukudi and 22km east of Tirunelveli)* is the quickest way to access the southern tip. Kingfisher Red *(IT 4915, 2.20pm)* flies daily from Chennai and takes 1.5hr. The closest airport to Kanyakumari is Trivandrum, 86km north-west in Kerala.

BY TRAIN – Madurai Junction is one of the busiest and most well-maintained railway stations in the country. From Chennai Egmore, Madurai is 8–9hr by train *(Rs.260 sleeper)*. Vaigai Express *(12635, 12.45pm)* is a good day train while Pandian Express *(12637, 9.15pm)* is the best overnight option, besides Nellai and Pothigai Express, which reach Madurai early morning. The Himsagar Express *(16318, 70hr)* from Jammu Tawi in Kashmir to Kanyakumari touches 70 destinations across nine states and is the longest train journey in the country.

BY ROAD – NH-7 cuts north to south from Salem and Dindigul to Tirunelveli and Kanyakumari while NH-49 heads west to east from Cochin and Theni to Rameswaram. NH-45B from Trichy to Thoothukudi passes through Madurai. There are regular day and overnight buses from Chennai to Madurai *(8–10hr, Rs.500–700)*.

GETTING AROUND

Most **trains** from Chennai to Madurai continue southward to other destinations. From Chennai Egmore, Nellai Express *(12631, 8.50pm)* and Tiruchendur Express *(16735, 4.05pm)* go via Madurai and Tirunelveli, Pothigai Express *(12661, 8.05pm)* goes to Tenkasi via Madurai and Srivilliputtur while Kanyakumari Express *(12633, 5.30pm)* goes via Madurai, Tirunelveli and Nagercoil. Three daily passenger trains run between Tirunelveli and Tiruchendur *(62km, 2.5hr)*.

Regular **buses** depart from Tirunelveli New Bus Stand *(8km from railway station, Rs.80 by auto)* to Tiruchendur, taking 1.5hr. NH-7 connects Madurai to Tirunelveli *(154km south, 2hr40min)* and Kanyakumari *(245km, 4hr)*, 90km further south. NH-45B connects Madurai to Thoothukudi *(142km south, 2.5hr)* and NH-49 to Theni and Munnar *(156km west, 3 hr)*. Since Madurai is a large congested city, it has several bus stands. Arapalayam *(4km north of the railway station*) on Puttuthoppu Road has mostly north- and westbound buses to Theni, Salem, Dindigul and Kodaikanal. The new Madurai Integrated Bus Terminus (MIBT) at Mattu Thavani *(0452 4219938)* in the north connects to destinations north and east. Periyar Bus Stand in the centre *(200m/220yd from railway station)* has buses for the airport and Alagar Kovil whereas Palanganatham has southbound buses for Tirunelveli, Nagercoil and Kanyakumari.

Within the destinations, it's best to engage an **auto rickshaw** or a **taxi** to cover the sights.

A short distance from Courtallam's centre is Main Falls and Sri Kutralanathar Temple. Puckle's Path, named after the District Collector who laid it in the 1860s, leads to Thenaruvi and beyond to the natural cavern of Paradesi Pudai. 4km from town is Five Falls (past the boathouse on Five Falls Main Road). 7km south-east of town and a short diversion off the Tirunelveli–Shenkottai Road is Old Courtallam Falls. From Courtallam, Shenkottai is 7km north-west on the Tamil Nadu–Kerala border.

See Religious and Spiritual Sights.

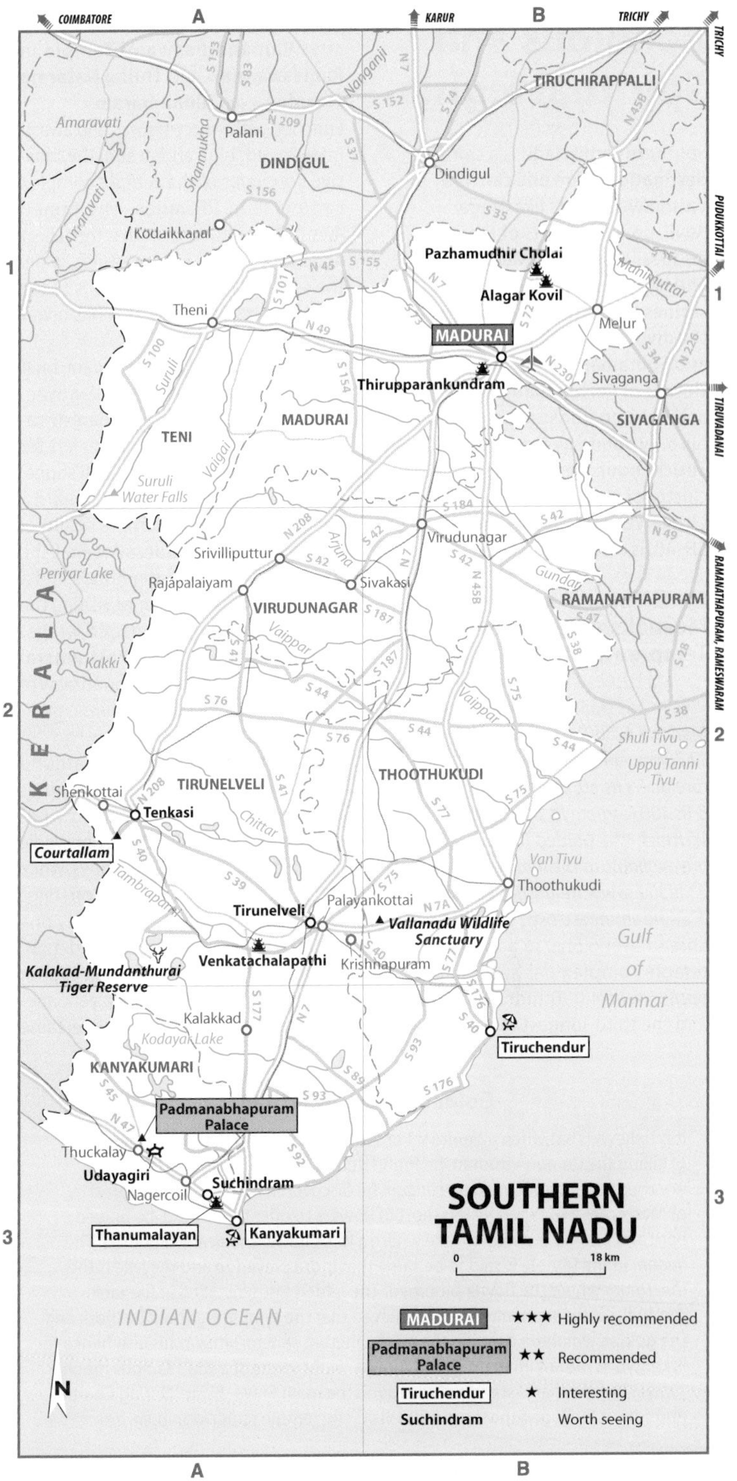
SOUTHERN TAMIL NADU
0 18 km
MADURAI ★★★ Highly recommended
Padmanabhapuram Palace ★★ Recommended
Tiruchendur ★ Interesting
Suchindram Worth seeing
COIMBATORE
KARUR
TRICHY
PUDUKKOTTAI
TIRUVADANAI
RAMANATHAPURAM, RAMESWARAM
TIRUCHIRAPPALLI
DINDIGUL
Palani
Dindigul
Kodaikkanal
Pazhamudhir Cholai
Alagar Kovil
Theni
Melur
MADURAI
Thirupparankundram
Sivaganga
SIVAGANGA
TENI
Suruli Water Falls
Periyar Lake
Virudunagar
Srivilliputtur
Rajapalaiyam
Sivakasi
VIRUDUNAGAR
RAMANATHAPURAM
KERALA
Kakki
Shuli Tivu
Uppu Tanni Tivu
THOOTHUKUDI
TIRUNELVELI
Shenkottai
Tenkasi
Courtallam
Van Tivu
Thoothukudi
Tirunelveli
Palayankottai
Vallanadu Wildlife Sanctuary
Venkatachalapathi
Krishnapuram
Kalakad-Mundanthurai Tiger Reserve
Gulf of Mannar
Kalakkad
Kodayar Lake
Tiruchendur
KANYAKUMARI
Padmanabhapuram Palace
Thuckalay
Udayagiri
Suchindram
Nagercoil
Thanumalayan
Kanyakumari
INDIAN OCEAN
N

Religious and Spiritual Sights

Southern Tamil Nadu is a spiritual destination. Here one can find Vaishnava shrines like Alagar Kovil, powerful seats of the goddess at Madurai Meenakshi and Kanyakumari, sacred Shiva shrines at Tenkasi and Tirunelveli, the divine trinity at Suchindram and Subramanya's legendary hill shrines of Pazhamudhir Cholai and Thirupparankunram, besides his only abode by the sea at Tiruchendur. Nava-tirupathis, a cluster of nine shrines between Tirunelveli and Tiruchendur on SH-40, is also interesting.

MADURAI★★★
Meenakshi Sundareshwarar Temple★★★

1km east from railway station and Periyar bus stand. East Chitrai Street, Madurai 625001. Open daily 5am–12.30pm, 4pm–10pm. Entry free, foreigners Rs.50, special entrance Rs.15 & Rs.100 (camera Rs.50, video Rs.250). Rs.25. Guided Tours: guides are available at the temple. 0452 2344360. www.maduraimeenakshi.org. Main shrine is closed to non-Hindus.

Spread over 6.5ha/16 acres, this huge temple complex has several *mandapams*, over 4,000 monolithic pillars and the third-longest temple corridor after **Ramanathaswami Temple** in **Rameswaram**★ and **Thillai Nataraja Temple**★★ in **Chidambaram**★.

Enriched with stucco figures and awash in deep red, blue and green, the massive *gopurams* of the temple complex can be seen for miles. The famed 49m/160ft south gopuram is the tallest and heaves with 1,511 sculptures, while the 46m/152ft north entrance is called Motta (bald) Gopuram as it has fewer sculptures.

The 47m/153ft-high Rajagopuram, built in the 13C by Maravarman Pandyan, for Swamy Sannidhi or Sundareshwarar shrine and a gateway to its left for Amman Sannidhi or Meenakshi shrine, mark the eastern side. Customarily, devotees offer prayers to the beautiful emerald idol of Goddess Meenakshi, bedecked with gold, diamonds and a sparkling nose-ring prior to visiting the Shiva shrine. The colonnaded wraparound passage around the **Pottramarai** (golden lotus) tank offers a good view of the gleaming golden *vimanams* crowning the two sanctums.

Ash-smeared *swamis* bustle around the labyrinth of corridors and shrines performing *pujas*, solemnising weddings and conducting classes on Vedic chanting for young Brahmin boys, while devotees hurry with their floral offerings for a *darshan*. Amidst this activity one can easily miss the fascinating details. Around Pottramarai tank, devotees pour sacred ash over Vibhuthi Pullaiyar Ganesha in a ritual reminder that we came

Golden Lotus Theertham

It is believed that when a penitent Lord Indra came to Earth to wash the sins of killing the demon Virudran, he found deliverance only after performing rigorous penance and *puja* to a *lingam* he discovered in the kadamba forest of **Madurai**★★★. When he ran short of flowers to offer to the Lord, he prayed hard and bathed at a nearby lake where a lotus flower magically bloomed. The *lingam* in the temple is said to be same that Indra prayed to and the lake is the *theertham* where the flower bloomed. The gilded lotus installed in the tank symbolises this incident. It is also believed that the temple was built by Indra and the golden *vimanam* capping the main sanctum sanctorum was his gift, hence it is known as Indra Vimanam. Ashta Airavat (eight forms of Indra's famous mount, Airavat the elephant) stand guard around the main Shiva shrine. During Chaitra Purnima, it is alleged that Lord Indra visits the temple to perform *puja*.

Gopurams of Meenakshi Sundareshwarar Temple

© Christophe Boisvieux/age fotostock

from dust and will return to dust. Etched on marble slabs along the southern corridor wall are 1,330 verses of the epic poem *Thirukurral*, penned by poet-saint Thiruvalluvar and dedicated to the temple. The 400-year-old murals in vegetable dyes and mounted wooden panels depicting the Thiruvilayadal (64 miracles performed by Shiva) were whitewashed in 2002, though the all-important central ceiling panel portraying Lord Shiva's marriage with Meenakshi is untouched. Life-like sculptures on the pillars depict characters from the *Ramayana* and *Mahabharata*, mythical creatures and gypsy dancers. A massive grindstone symbolises the fantastic tale of Murthy Naayanaar, an ardent Shiva devotee who decided to grind his own hand to make sandalwood paste to anoint the *linga*! Lord Shiva blessed that he would be king and ironically, since the Pandya king had no heirs, Murthy Naayanaar became the ruler who never wore a crown because of his dreadlocks!

The monolithic Nandi Mandapam and two gold and copper plated *dhwajasthambas* (flagstaffs) herald the entrance to the main shrine. Towards the north are images of Shiva and Kali in the throes of their dance competition. Devotees fling butter balls, sold at a stall, to placate the fuming Kali, who lost the divine test. Nearby, the pillars in Kambathadi Mandapam bear sculptures of the 64 forms of Shiva and a rare image of Vyagra Shakti Ganesha, with the torso of Parvati and a tiger from the waist downwards. Below the Indra Vimanam stands the handsome *linga* of Sundareswarar flanked by a five-faced Sadashiva Murthy and Gayatri Devi at the entrance. The Velli Mandapam houses a fabulous Nataraja dancing with his right leg raised instead of the left. The unusual aspect is attributed to a dream of King Rajasimha Pandyan, who felt that the Lord must have been tired of dancing on his right leg all the time and requested him to dance on his left leg!

The 110 pillars in Meenakshi Nayakkar Mandapam bear *yalis* and the stunning votive lamp-holder with 1,008 lamps is lit on festive occasions. Meenakshi depicted with a parrot in her hand, symbolising wisdom, has the Kilikuttu Mandapam or Parrot Cage Hall outside her shrine where parrots offered by devotees were housed. In the 16C Oonjal Mandapam festive idols of Lord Shiva and Meenakshi are placed on a swing as *oduvars* (chanters) extol their praises in song. At 9pm, the idols and Shiva's slippers are carried in a palanquin to the bedchamber, where priests perform *lalipuja* (lullabies). The silver doors of the bedroom are opened only for the unique night ceremony and morning hymn to wake up the divine pair.

The 1,000-pillared Ayiramkal Mandapam actually has 984 pillars and serves as the **Temple Art Museum** *(open 7am–7.30pm, Rs.5, Rs.2 child)*.

While a line of 64 Pandya kings built most of the temple complex, some sections are attributed to an earlier period.

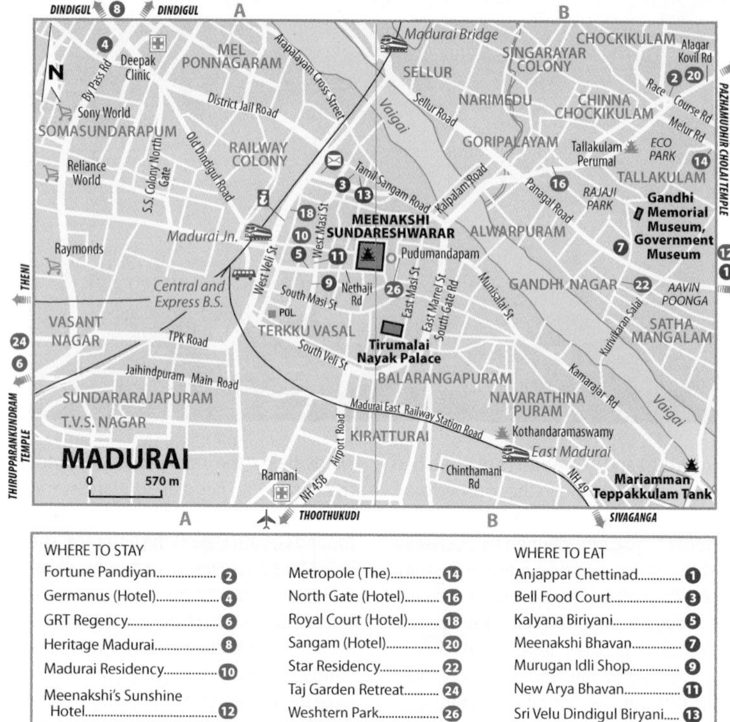

Though several statues and musical pillars were desecrated in the 14C by Malik Kafur's invading army, the main shrines were spared. The Madurai Nayaks subsequently renovated the temple to its former glory. Thirumalai Nayak was a particularly influential ruler who made huge contributions to the temple in the 17C. Befittingly, statues of him and his wives stand in the main sanctum. The **Ashta Shakti Mandapam** (eight forms of the goddess), built by the queens, was where free food was served to visiting devotees; today it is used to sell religious paraphernalia! The sculptures on the pillars recount Lord Shiva's miracles, the story of Meenakshi's birth and her royal life as the princess of Madurai.

AROUND MADURAI

Thirupparankundram Temple

8km south-west of Madurai on NH-7. Thirupparankundram, Madurai South Taluk 625005. Open daily 5.30am–1pm, 4pm–9pm. Entry free (phone camera Rs.20, camera Rs.100, video Rs.500). . 0452 2482248,2484359. http://thirupparankundramtemple.org. Set against an imposing hilly backdrop, the temple's vibrant façade heralds one of the famed *aru padai veedu* or six sacred abodes of Lord Murugan (*see p13*). Here, he was married to Devasena, the beautiful daughter of Lord Indra, who had been performing severe austerities to win his love. For centuries, devotees have thronged Thirupparankundram as an auspicious venue for marriages and even today the chants of *vetrivel muruganukku arohara* (hail to the lance-wielding Lord) resound in the air as pilgrims ascend the steps to the cave shrine. At the entrance, devotees fling butter balls to soothe the fierce image of Kali for removal of *dhristi* or the malefic evil eye. Shiva as Nataraja performing for Parvati reclined against Nandi and Shiva as a mother pig suckling piglets are interesting sculptures. Nearby, lamps are offered to Goddess Durga by women on Tuesday evenings and Friday morning. Another lamp-lit

Thirupparankundram Temple

enclosure has the beautiful stone sculpture portraying the divine marriage ceremony being solemnised by Indra. Built in the 8C, the massive 48-pillared entrance hall and lofty stone doorway lead past an array of stalls selling religious souvenirs. Devotees take a holy dip in Saravana Poigai, Mahalakshmi Theertham or any of the 11 *theerthams* before climbing to a cluster of cave shrines dedicated to Ganesha, Shiva and Vishnu and the main shrine atop the hillock. Each of the five cells within the sanctum sanctorum enshrines a different deity. The Dargah of Sekundar, the Islamic saint Hazrat Sultan Sikander Badshah Shaheed Razi who meditated in the caves of Thirupparankundram, is also nearby.

Alagar Kovil

21km north-east of Madurai on Alagar Kovil Road at the foothills of Pazhamudhir Cholai. Alagar Kovil Road, Madurai District. Open daily 7am–12noon, 4–7.30pm. P. 0452 2470228. www.madurai.com/azhagar.htm.

The stunning Alagar Kovil Complex with its vibrant *gopuram* and profusely carved pillared *mandapams* is comparable to the Nayak Mandapams of Madurai (*see p210*). Regarded among the 108 Sacred Abodes of Vishnu and praised in early literary works, the temple was built at an ancient site and is dedicated to Lord Vishnu as Sundarajar or Alagar, the brother of Meenakshi who solemnised her marriage to Lord Shiva. The festive idol made of pure gold reflects the finesse of ancient craftsmanship. In the vicinity are subsidiary shrines like Kalyana Sundaravalli in the south, Andal in the north, and Sudarshanar. A flight of 18 richly decorated steps leads to the shrine of Karuppanna Swamy, the guardian deity whose doors are usually kept closed. A 3km trek takes one to the Raakayi Amman shrine atop the hillock, which is closely linked to this temple. During the famous Chitharai festival *(Apr–May)*, the Alagar idol is carried to **Madurai**★★★ amidst much fanfare to attend the divine wedding of Meenakshi and Lord Sundareshwarar. Don't miss the unusual offering of crispy *alagar kovil dosai*, prepared from rice and black gram given as *prasada* to visitors. Around the temple site are remains of a fortified township of a bygone era. A short drive leads to the unusual shrine of the fierce Jwala (angry) Narasimha or Yoga Narasimha at Yaanaimalai (Elephant Hill). The idol is apparently soothed with libations of milk and curd and the vent in the roof lets his raging fumes escape.

Pazhamudhir Cholai Temple

24km north-east of Madurai, 3km uphill from Alagar Kovil. Alagar Malai Hills, Madurai District. Open daily 6am–6pm. Entry free, special entry

The Legend of Avvaiyar

A legend associated with Pazhamudhir Cholai is the battle of wits between a young boy and Avvaiyar, the great Tamil poet-saint and devotee of Murugan. When Avvaiyar came to these hills, a little boy pestered her with a flurry of questions which she answered cleverly until she got tired and rested under a tree. The boy climbed the tree and asked if she wanted a hot or cold fruit. Bewildered by the odd query and convinced that it was a foolish one, she asked for a cold fruit. The young boy shook the branch and some berries fell to the ground, which she picked up, blew gently to remove the dust and popped into her mouth. The boy promptly countered her gesture and asked why she 'blew' the fruit as if it was hot. Astonished by his smartness, she realised that he was the all-knowing Lord Murugan. She begged his forgiveness and asked him to grant her with his wisdom. The place was thus called *Pazham* (fruit) *-udhir* (shaken) *-cholai* (dense garden), or the Garden where the Lord shook the fruit. En route to the temple, a small board near a tiny Ganesha idol points out the ancient berry tree that Avvaiyar rested under.

Rs.20 gives a close view of the deity. P. *0452 2470228. www.lordmurugan.com. There are lots of monkeys along the ghat road. Avoid carrying food openly.*

A short drive from **Madurai**★★★ to Pazhamudhir Cholai, another famous *aru padai veedu* or six sacred abodes of Lord Murugan takes one into the cool environs of dense *solai* (forests) of Vrishabhadri, where Murugan is deified as Kurinji Nilakkizhavan, the Lord of the Hills. His idol in the sanctum is flanked by his two consorts Devasena and her younger sister Sundara Valli. Legend has it that Valli, reborn as sage Shivamuni's daughter, was brought up in these forests by a tribal headman, Nambi Raja. She met Lord Subramanya and quenched his thirst when he came to these woods disguised as an old hunter. Despite being a small temple, several people foot the distance, savouring the pleasant surroundings that abound with fruit trees, medicinal plants and hums of nature. Fruit-sellers sell local fresh fruits and juice along the way.

On the top of the hill *(1km walk)* lies the perennial spring Noopura Ganga, which supposedly gushed from Vishnu's anklet, with a **shrine** consecrated to Raakkayi Amman *(7am–12noon, 4–7.30pm)* worshipped by the local tribal community.

TENKASI

Sri Kasi Vishwanatha Temple★

53km from Tirunelveli via SH-40 and 5km north-east of Courtallam. Tenkasi Taluk, Tirunelveli District 627811. Open daily 6am–12pm, 4pm–9pm. P. *Guided Tours: local guides and priests offer to show the highlights of the temple for a small fee. 04633 222373, 222133. www.tenkasitemple.org.*

When the *linga* brought from Kasi (Varanasi) by Madurai's ruler Jatilavarman Harikesari Parakkirama Pandiyan took root in a *bilva* grove in Sivakasi, the king took it as god's will. However, a divine dream led him to a self-manifest *linga* and a large Nandi statue in the Chitra River and the king erected a grand temple in AD 1445. The place was hailed as Tenkasi or Dakshina Kasi, the Kashi of the South. Pilgrims who cannot travel to the north find solace in visiting the holy Kasi Vishwanatha temple, the town's epicentre. Massive twin sculptures of Virabhadra, Nataraja, Venugopala, Manmatha and his graceful companion Rathi, and damsels gaze down from the chiselled pillars in the entrance hall. The main shrine of Shiva as Kasi Vishwanatha is towards the left while his consort Lokanayaki is on the right with the shrine of Bala Subramanian in the middle. There are several shrines in the outer and inner precincts dedicated to major deities from the Hindu pantheon, *mandapams* with marvellously carved musical pillars, festival idols and holy tanks including the Kasi Theertham. The Thiruvolakka Mandapam carved from a single rock houses a *sahasra lingam* with 1,008 tiny *lingams* carved into a single stone. Cool winds from the surrounding hills and the spiritual vibe of the place coax people to linger and absorb its beauty. It is believed that the original entrance tower was hit by lightning in 1924 and the nine-storey *gopuram* was rebuilt in the 1990s. At 55m/180ft, the tower's walkway provides great views of Tenkasi. The main festivals are Aipasi Thirukalyanam in October and Masi Magam in February.

TIRUNELVELI

Nellaiappar Temple★

2km south-west of River Tambraparni. Chepparai Nataraja Temple, Chepparai, Tirunelveli District. Open daily 6am–11am, 4pm–8pm. P. *0462 2339910.*

A towering 13C edifice built by the Pandyas for Lord Shiva as Nellaiappar and Parvati as Kanthimati, the temple belies its older history that traces back to AD 700. Famed for its musical pillars, impressive sculptures and ancient inscriptions, the temple's mythological and historical importance is almost palpable. It is rumoured that the holy town got its name from the miraculous *nel-veli* (paddy fence) that protected the food grains meant for worship during the floods. The architectural excellence showcased in the colonnaded halls is indeed admirable – Mani Mandapam's monoliths wrapped with 48 small musical pillars producing a range of notes, Somavara Mandapam's larger-than-life carvings, the 1,000-pillared hall and garden setting of Vasantha Mandapam and the glorious Sangili Mandapam added in the 17C connecting the twin shrines of the main deities. Don't miss the legendary dance hall, Tamra Sabha (Copper Hall) a true wonder in woodwork with a copper roof, set deep inside the temple. During the Margazhi Arudra Darisanam *(15 Dec–15 Jan)*, the idols of Nataraja and Sivakami are placed here for elaborate rituals during the enactment of Shiva's divine dance. Behind the Tamra Sabha, the shrine of Chandana Sabhapati, smeared with sandal paste casts a golden glow along the hall. The Periya Sabhapati shrine house houses a permanent image of Nataraja. The temple also has a beautiful shrine for Nellai Govindar, the reclining idol of Vishnu. Navaratri, Thirukalyanam (Oct–Nov) and Bhrahmostavam *(Jun–Jul)* are other important festivals here.

Murugan's Emblem

Legend has it that **Tiruchendur★** or 'The sacred town of victory' was where the great battle between Lord Murugan and the demon Surapadma took place. The Lord split Surapadma into two using his *vel*, or spear. One half became his emblematic rooster and the other a peacock, which became his *vahana* (vehicle). After the war, Murugan's troops came to the shore to quench their thirst. On finding the water in the Nazhi Kinaru well to be brackish, Murugan planted his *vel* or spear causing freshwater to gush out. Even today, the 1.3sq m/14sq ft brackish well has a smaller well within it with sweet water.

KRISHNAPURAM

Venkatachalapathi Temple

13km from Tirunelveli en route to Tiruchendur. Krishnapuram, Tirunelveli District. Open daily 7–9.30am, 6.30–9.30pm. Entry free. P.

The Krishnapuram Venkatachalapathi Temple is one among the nine Alwar Nava Tirupatis sacred to Vaishnavaites. The main deity is Vishnu as Venkatachalapathi or Venkateshwara accompanied by his two consorts, Sri Devi and Bhoo Devi. The *mandapam* built during the reign of Veerappa Nayak displays a pair of stone-cut elephants at the entrance and beautiful scenes from the Puranas and great epics on its six central pillars. The dazzling genius of the sculptors is apparent when one listens to the bell-like tinkling sound emitted when the pillars are tapped gently or sees the intricacy of the stone carvings and sculptures. The theatre of arts or Ranga Mandapam has sculptures which provide valuable insights into the social life and times of the past. The temple festivities during Vaikunta Ekadasi (Dec–Jan) and the 11-day Brahmotsavam *(Sep–Oct)* attract lakhs of people.

TIRUCHENDUR★

Subramanya/Murugan Temple

60km south-east of Tirunelveli by SH-40 or 90km north-east of Kanyakumari by SH-176 (Thoothukudi–Tiruchendur–Kanyakumari Road). Arulmigu Subramanya Swami Temple, Tiruchendur 628215. Open daily 5am–9pm. P. Guided Tours: local guides are available. 04639 242221/242270. www.tiruchendur.org.

Located near the sandy beaches of the Gulf of Mannar, Tiruchendur's most famous landmark is the Subramanya Temple, another of the six sacred abodes of Lord Murugan *(see p13)*. With an imposing nine-storeyed 42m/137ft *gopuram* signalling its entrance to the west, a long 1.5km closed corridor leads towards the main shrine. Several stalls selling religious souvenirs line the corridor and tired travellers rest under its shade. Originally built on sandstone reefs and extended by the Chera and Pandya rulers, the temple's majestic tower was first erected 300 years ago. With time, the temple crumbled under the brunt of the sea and three ascetics rebuilt it over 72 years till 1941. The elevated Ananda Vilas Mandapam has black granite pillars while the pillared Vasantha Mandapam was added recently. The main shrine possesses a standing image of Subramanya and a Shiva *linga*. Behind it is a set of five *lingas* (*pancha lingas*) in a cave worshipped by Lord Subramanya himself. In the corridor around the main shrine, a monolithic image depicts Lord Murugan astride a peacock fighting the demon Surapadma *(see sidebar, above)*. Two separate shrines are dedicated to his consorts Devasena and Valli. Outside the temple, devotees wash their feet or bathe in the sea or a small sacred tank called Nazhi Kinaru. The nearby small cave, Valli Guhai, has a few idols and gives veracity to the story of how Lord Murugan conspired with his brother Ganesha to win Valli's heart. It is said that Ganesha appeared as a rogue elephant and frightened Valli in the forest, so she ran and hid in the cave until rescued by Lord Murugan. Allegedly several idols were looted from the main temple when the Dutch occupied Tiruchendur briefly in the 17C. About 2km away, the ancient **Shiva Kolundeeshwarar Temple** is worth a look.

KANYAKUMARI★

Kumari Amman Temple

Located at the end of Beach Road on the oceanfront; entry to the temple is through the northern gate. Beach Road, Kanyakumari. Open daily 4.30–12.30am, 4–8.15pm. Entry free. P. 04652 246223. Men must remove their shirts and vests before entering the temple. Non-Hindus are not permitted inside. Cameras and mobile phones are not allowed and have to be deposited at the entrance.

Located at the tip of the Indian peninsula, the small temple of Kumari Amman in Kanyakumari has been a spiritual magnet for centuries. It is believed that as the confluence of the Arabian Sea, the Indian Ocean and the Bay of Bengal, the *theerthams* and bathing *ghats* of Kanyakumari are among the most sacred in the country. The passageway along the outer wall is unexceptional but the rolling sea, **Vivekananda Rock Memorial** *(see p219)* and the Thiruvalluvar statue command attention. Astrologers, shopkeepers and hawkers peddle their wares on the way to the northern entrance. The temple is reached by a dark passageway with a gaggle of pushy priests who intercept visitors for money, though *darshan* is free. Standing in the sanctum sanctorum is the black idol of Kanyakumari, bedecked in bridal finery and a beautiful garland, her nose-ring glinting in the lamplight. She holds a double row of prayer beads in her hand. According to folklore, the brilliance of her diamond nose-ring acted like a beacon for passing ships. Drawn by it, some

Kanyakumari, the Virgin Goddess

Created as the invincible *parashakti* who emerged from the sacred fire, the 'virgin goddess' Kanyakumari was sent to Earth to vanquish the dreadful demon Banasura who had terrorised the southern region. She grew up with a desire of marrying Shiva and performed a severe penance to win his love. Impressed by her tantalising beauty and devotion, Lord Shiva agreed to marry her at midnight on an auspicious day. Since only an unmarried girl could kill the demon, Sage Narada feared that Shiva's marriage would ruin the cosmic plan. On the fateful night, the groom's party set out in merriment from Suchindram, but Narada disguised himself as a rooster and signalled daybreak before midnight. Tricked into believing that he was late for the wedding, Shiva's procession returned from Vazhukkumpaarai to Suchindram, leaving Kanyakumari heartbroken and livid. Jilted by Shiva, Kanyakumari vowed to remain unmarried. Meanwhile Banasura decided to take her by force and in the bitter fight that ensued, Kanyakumari slew him and restored peace in the region.

vessels unwittingly crashed against the rocky shoreline, prompting the closure of the sea-facing eastern door! The main festivals are held in Vaikasi *(May–Jun)* and Navaratri *(Sept–Oct)*.

SUCHINDRAM

Thanumalayan Temple★

13km north-west of Kanyakumari, on the banks of the Palayar River. Arulmigu Sthanumalayan Temple, Suchindram. Open daily 4am–1pm, 5–8.30pm. Entry free. P. *Guided Tours: local guides and priests offer to show the highlights of the temple for a small fee. 04652 241421, 241270. www.suchindram.com. Phones, cameras and video cameras not allowed inside the temple. They have to be deposited for a small fee at the entrance. Men must remove their shirts before entering the shrine.*

At the curve of a busy road in the hamlet of Suchindram, the snow-white 45m/148ft *gopuram* of the Thanumalayan Temple hovers like a cloud against the blue sky. With its coating of seashell powder, it seems like a bleached version of the typical Dravidian temple towers loaded with stucco figures. It took three kings from different dynasties to build the temple – the Chera King Marthanda Varma, Chola King of Thanjavur and Pandya King Thirumalai Nayak of Madurai. A row of 1,008 stone maidens holding lamps lines the long corridor leading to the shrine. The temple's unique feature is the three-headed idol of Trimurthi under an ancient *champaka* tree and the *lingam* in the main shrine, marked by 16 crescent moons and placed under the hood of a silver snake. Three *alankaras* or *pujas* are performed to the *lingam*, which represents Shiva *(sthanu)* at the top, Vishnu *(mal)* in the middle and Brahma *(aya)* at the base, hence the name Thanumalayan.

The temple also has its share of architectural delights – the musical pillars of Chutaprakar Mandapam reproduce sounds of drums, bells and musical notes, while stone loops at Chenabhagaraman Mandapam mimic the *jaltarang* (musical water bowls), the stone *dwarapala* at the entrance allows a twig to pass from one ear to the other and a large white Nandi stands near the sanctum. People flock to the 6m/18ft Anjaneya statue and offer butter or garlands made of lentils to seek his blessings. Other charming sculptures like the unusual Vigneswari (a fusion of Ganesha and Parvathi), Lord Krishna advising Arjuna before the Mahabharatha War and an ancient boulder with 3C epigraphical carvings merit a closer look.

Historical Sights

As a major hub of powerful dynasties like the Pandyas and Cheras and later the Nayaks and the British, South Tamil Nadu has witnessed several milestones in history. Here, chieftains like Veerapandiyan Kattabomman took on the might of the British Empire and Travancore king Marthanda Varma subjugated the Dutch navy. The most lasting historical monuments remain Thirumalai Nayak Palace in Madurai, Padmanabhapuram Palace and the memorials of Mahatma Gandhi and Swami Vivekananda in Kanyakumari.

MADURAI★★★

Thirumalai Nayak Palace★★

About 1.5km south-east of Meenakshi Temple. Palace Road, Madurai, 625001. Open daily 9am–5pm. Rs.10, child Rs.5 (foreigners Rs.50, camera Rs.30, video Rs.100). P. *Guided Tours: local guides available. 0452 2332945, 2338992.*

Built in 1636 by Thirumalai Nayak, the king of Madurai, the grand palace is a quarter of its original size. Earlier the royal quarters, theatre, temple, living quarters, arsenal chamber, palanquin, bandstand, pond and garden were all contained within the two main portions – Swargavilasa or Celestial Pavilion and Rangavilasa or Entertainment Pavilion. Today, only the **Swargavilasa** with its **Darbar Hall** and **Nataka Sala** survive and offer glimpses into the artistic brilliance of the time. Superb stuccowork embellishes the domes and impressive scalloped arches of this colonnaded palace. The large open-to-sky quadrangle offers a dramatic view of the splendid Indo-Saracenic architectural marvel made with brick and mortar. The **Darbar Hall** is an arcaded octagon capped by a 21m/70ft dome which houses the ornamental royal throne. Colossal white pillars with magnificent arches border the corridor and run along the courtyard. Each pillar soars to about 13m/42ft in height and has a girth of 4m/13ft capped by foliated brick arches that extend the height to 20m/66ft! The pillars and walls coated with a paste made of shell, lime and egg white display an unmatched smoothness and glossy sheen that is still intact. Sadly, the sculpted stone horsemen flanking the steps near the hall are badly damaged and many pillars are vandalised with graffiti.

Mariamman Teppakkulam Tank

Named after the Vandiyur Mariamman Temple to its north, the gigantic Teppakulam tank *(4km east of the centre of Madurai on NH-49)* is one of South India's largest man-made temple tanks. It is also the setting for one of Madurai's biggest events, the Float Festival, celebrated in the month of Thai *(Jan–Feb)*. This unique ritual was started in the 17C by King Thirumalai Nayaka as part his birthday celebrations. The 335x290m/1,100ftx950ft area was excavated to make bricks for building the **Thirumalai Nayak Palace★★** and was later converted into a stepped tank fed by the Vaigai River through a network of underground channels. Twelve rows of granite steps lead to the tank, which has an island pavilion in the centre with a garden shrine dedicated to Lord Vinayaka.

The legendary Float Festival sees thousands of people gathering to take Madurai's presiding deities, Lord Sundareshwarar and Goddess Meenakshi, on a royal boat ride around the tank. The procession idols are brought in a palanquin at dawn, placed on a bedecked *theppa* (float or raft) and slowly tugged in circles round a specially built pavilion in the *kulam* (tank). The deities are placed in the central shrine until evening and ferryboats take people to and fro for *darshan*. At dusk, oil lamps, garlands, festoons and fairy lights illuminate the place and on the final day, a dazzling display of fireworks marks the end of the festivity.

Vast sections of ceilings and domes are rendered with vibrantly hued delicate paintings, giving it a bejewelled appearance studded with pristine stucco details. The multiplicity of the levels and arches magnifies the splendour of the inner pavilions. The adjoining hall **Nataka Sala**, the venue for dance and music shows, used to be a lamp-lit daily spectacle for royalty. An epigraphy section leads out of the building to a **Sculpture Garden** where exhibits are lined up like troops, as if awaiting a royal inspection. Records suggest that the palace was demolished by the king's grandson Chokkanatha Nayak who transplanted a portion of this palace to Thiruchirapalli. The quadrangle serves as a seating area for the daily sound and light show *(6.45–7.35pm, Rs.50, Rs.25 child 5–12yr)* which narrates the glorious saga of this palace. About 200m/220yd from here is one of the oldest Roman Catholic churches in the region. **St Mary's Cathedral Church**, with its elegant Roman-style bell towers, is the seat of the Roman Catholic Archdiocese of Madurai.

KANYAKUMARI★

Gandhi Mandapam

200m south-west of Kumari Amman Temple by the seafront. Gandhi Mandapam Road, near Kanyakumari Beach. Open daily 7am–7pm. Entry free. P.

Overlooking the waters of the Indian Ocean, the Gandhi Memorial or Gandhi Mandapam is a bright pink lotus-like structure with tapering domes. Built like a temple, the place enshrines the urn which held the ashes of Mahatma Gandhi before it was immersed in the sea. People came here to pay their last respects to the Father of the Nation on 12 Feb 1948 and continue to do so to this day. The shrine has Gandhiji's ubiquitous *charkha* or spinning wheel, the symbol of India's struggle for Independence, emblazoned on its façade and bell-shaped niches in its domes. The central dome is 24m/79ft high, marking Gandhiji's age when he was assassinated. A unique architectural aspect allows the rays of the sun to fall directly on the urn every year at noon on Gandhi Jayanthi *(2 Oct)*, the anniversary of his birth.

Vivekananda Rock Memorial and Exhibition

Off Kanyakumari Beach. Boat Jetty, Kanyakumari. Open Wed–Mon 7–11am, 2–5pm. Rs.20 ferry (8am–4pm), Rs.10 entry, child below 5yr free. P. *Guided Tours: contact Vivekananda Kendra. 04652 247012. www.vkendra.org/vrm, www.vivekanandakendra.org.*

Perched upon a large rock about 488m/1,600ft from the shore, the Vivekananda Rock Memorial is dedicated to one of India's greatest philosopher-saints, Swami Vivekananda. It is believed Swamiji swam to **Sripadam Parai** (the isolated boulder where Goddess Kanyakumari performed penance and awaited Shiva) and meditated for three days in December 1892. A few weeks later he left for Chicago for the World Religious Conference where he made his most famous speech. A steady train of pilgrims and tourists alight on this windy outcrop that is perhaps the best vantage point to absorb the dramatic meeting of three mighty waters at the southern tip of the Indian peninsula. Others seek the peaceful silence of the large **Dhyana Mandapam** or Meditation Hall to pay their tribute to the spiritual master.

The memorial was built in 1970 across an area of 1.6ha/4 acres under the guidance of Eknath Ranade and the Vivekananda Rock Memorial Committee. Sthapathi S.K. Achari, the chief architect and engineer, created this edifice by blending various architectural styles and using red and blue granite. Swami Vivekananda's statue in the **Sabha Mandapam** or Assembly Hall faces the smaller rock which allegedly bears the brownish foot imprint 'Sripadam' of Goddess Kanyakumari enshrined in the Sripadam Mandapam. A few stalls sell books on religion, yoga, philosophy and Swamiji's teachings besides small souvenirs.

On the return trip, the ferry makes a stop at the imposing 41m/133ft-high statue of **Thiruvalluvar**, the legendary poet-saint of Tamil Nadu (*see Literature* *p83*). The rock pedestal is 38ft high and represents the 38 chapters of virtue in the saint's epic poem *Thirukkural*. The statue symbolises wealth and love resting on a foundation of virtue. Ten sculpted elephants line the base of the *mandapam* and 140 steps lead to the saint's holy feet as he surveys the Kanyakumari Coast.

Back on shore, near the main road, is the **Wandering Monk Exhibition** *(open daily 8am–12noon, 4pm–8pm, Rs.2, www.vkendra.org)* housed in a neat building fronted by a garden. An inspiring virtual tour in pictures and words, it chronicles Swami Vivekananda's travels around the subcontinent. Forty-one information panels in English, Hindi and Tamil, murals and photos enliven the whole experience. At the Vivekananda Kendra Campus in Vivekanandapuram *(2km from Kanyakumari)*, visit the **Vivekananda Pictorial Exhibition** *(open daily 9am–1pm, 5–9pm, Rs.2)* which traces India's journey from the past to the present with Swamiji's inspiring messages.

AROUND KANYAKUMARI

Padmanabhapuram Palace★★

35km from Kanyakumari on the road to Tiruvananthapuram. Drive via Puliyoorkuruchi and turn right from Thuckalay; the palace is 1.5km away. Thuckalay Village, Kalkulam Taluk, Kanyakumari District. Open Tue–Sun 9am–4.30pm. Closed national holidays, tickets counter closed 1–2pm. Rs.25, Rs.10 child 5–12yrs (camera Rs.25, video Rs.1,500). P. Guided Tours: local guides are at the venue. 04651 250255.

Set in the erstwhile capital of Travancore, Padmanabhapuram Palace is a wonder in wood and stone that served as the royal seat from 1555 to the late 18C. Earlier within the 75ha/186-acre Kalkulam Fort, it was Raja Marthanda Varma, the founder of modern Travancore, who transformed it into a living heritage of art. When he took charge and consolidated his kingdom, he resurrected its crumbling image with a complete makeover. He erected temples, razed the 14C mud fort and Kalkulam Palace and replaced it with a granite fortress with four bastions and a stunning palace. In 1744, it was renamed Padmanabhapuram Fort and Palace after the supreme deity of Travancore. The complex comprises 14 palaces with 127 royal rooms located in clean well-maintained grounds. The Manimalika (Clock Tower) with its 200-year-old clock ticking silently is visible from afar and entering the grand Padipara, or main gate is like turning back the hands of time. The façade of the palace exemplifies typical traditional Kerala architecture, marked by exquisite woodwork, sloping tiled roofs and a series of open courtyards. The intricately carved gabled roof of the Poomukham leads into the exclusive royal guest area. Its polished interiors and profusely carved floral wooden ceiling grab instant attention–the latter is a masterpiece that captures 90 varieties of flowers and pendants. A solid granite cot, a Chinese-style throne and ceremonial painted bows *(ona villu)* are the accents here. The Mantrasala or King's Council Chamber on the upper floor has a stunning Gajalakshmi carving as a backdrop to the ornamental throne and seats for ministers. Graceful curved wooden louvres filter light from the sides and add a warm glow around, while lotus carvings embellish the ceiling.

The oldest building is the Thaikottaram or Mother Palace which served as a place for worship during the Bhadrakali festival. A small chamber called Ekantha Mandapam or Chamber of Solitude has a stunning array of gleaming woodwork, of which the pillar carved from a solid jackfruit tree with intricate floral designs is the main focus. This building once had a 1km-long secret passage that the Royal Family and their entourage could use in an emergency. Long corridors, open courtyards and coloured windows overlook the exterior gardens. The fabulous Navaratri Mandapam with superbly carved stone pillars and black polished floor was used to stage performances. The chamber hidden by a wooden screen with peep-holes ensured privacy for royalty viewing dance, drama and music performances! The Uppirikka Malika or Perumal Kottaram is a four-storeyed structure with the royal treasury, sleeping chambers and study rooms. The fantastic Mural Pagoda on the third floor houses some of the best preserved vividly painted murals. The 300-year-old Royal Bed of Raja Marthanda Varma is a massive four-poster created from 64 varieties of medicinal (Ayurvedic) wood. Its lace-like carvings and a ceremonial crest was presented by the Dutch East India Company to the king. The ceiling here exhibits Indo-Chinese teak wood carvings.

A closer look at the extraordinary paintings adorning the walls of the royal rooms makes one aware of the artistic wealth that has been so scrupulously preserved.

Also in town, the **Archaeological Museum** is worth a visit for its precious collection of wooden sculptures, stone images, inscriptions, copper plates, old coins, weapons, rare tools of torture, mural art and ancient metal vessels and utensils.

Padmanabhapuram Palace

Udayagiri Fort *(2km away)* is where Marthanda Varma's Dutch General De Lannoy's Tomb is situated. Being a Christian, De Lannoy was barred from entering Raja Marthanda Varma's palace at Padmanabhapuram, so he stayed at Udayagiri. Over time, the fort gained fame as De Lannoy Kotta and the loyal general was hailed as 'Valiya Kappithaan' or, 'the great Captain'.

Museums and Art Galleries

The region's rich legacy finds an excellent showcase in its many museums. At Madurai, get a glimpse into the life and times of Mahatma Gandhi and learn about the 'Wandering Monk' Swami Vivekananda at Kanyakumari. Besides Madurai and Kanyakumari, Government museums are also located at Tirunelveli and Virudunagar. Several art galleries thrive in the streets around the Madurai Meenakshi Sundareshwarar Temple. Sri Lakshmi Art Gallery near Swami Sannidhi, Athavan Art Studio on West Masi Street, Raji Arts & Crafts and Cottage Expo Crafts on North Chithrai Street are well-loved.

MADURAI★★★

Gandhi Memorial Museum★

3km from Periyar Bus Stand, 4km from Mattu Thavani Bus Stand. Gandhi Museum Campus, Tamukkam, Madurai 625020. Open Tue–Sun 10am–1pm, 2–5.45pm. Closed Govt. holidays. Entry free (camera Rs.50). P. Guided Tours: guides are available at venue. 0452 2522822/2531060. www.gandhimmm.org.

One of the only seven museums in the country dedicated to the legacy of Mahatma Gandhi, the museum is set in the beautiful Tamukkam Summer Palace of Rani Mangammal of the Nayak dynasty. Built in 1670, the domed palace was taken over by the Nawabs of Carnatic and the British East India Company. It served as the official residence of British Judges and District Magistrates of Madurai. In 1955, the 5ha/13-acre palace complex was gifted by the state to Gandhi Smarak Nidhi and renovated into a museum. Opened on 15 April 1959, the Gandhi Memorial Museum offers fascinating insights about the man who steered India to freedom. Little do people know of Madurai's impact on Gandhiji's life. In his 20 visits to the state, he came here five times. It was during his second visit to Madurai in 1921 that Gandhiji, moved by the poverty of the peasants, forsook his long coat and *topi* and adopted his trademark loincloth and shawl. Even the momentous 'Temple Entry Movement' for *harijans* (considered untouchables) took place after his visit in 1934. On learning that lower caste members were banned inside temples, Gandhiji refused to enter **Madurai Meenakshi Temple**★★★. His campaign against untouchability bore fruit when the doors of Madurai's temple were opened to all in 1939; Gandhi stepped inside the shrine in 1946.

The **Darbar Hall** has 265 pictures and panels documenting the Freedom Struggle and turning points of the last 300 years. Other sections include a gallery on South Indian handicrafts and the biographical tour of Gandhiji's life through rare photos, quotes, murals, paintings and letters. Unusual letters reveal Gandhiji's knowledge of Tamil – his signature to a friend in Devakottai and a few lines he penned when the famous Tamil poet Subramanya Bharathi passed away. The **Hall of Relics and Replicas** contains 14 original artefacts used by Mahatma Gandhi including a shawl, spectacles and yarn spun by him. A macabre highlight is the bloodstained cloth worn by him when he was assassinated. The **Philately section** has envelopes, postcards and stamps released in Gandhi's honour across the globe. The library, added in 1947, archives 36,000 books, photocopies of Gandhiji's 27,000 letters and 22 reels of microfilm. **Bapu Kutir**, a replica of Gandhiji's hut in Sevagram, and the amphitheatre which can seat 8,000 people lie south of the museum. The memorial pillar enshrines a portion of Gandhiji's ashes.

Government Museum

3km from Periyar Bus Stand, 4km from Mattu Thavani Bus Stand. Gandhi Museum Campus, Tamukkam, Madurai 625020. Open Sat–Thu 9.30am–5pm. Closed 2nd Saturdays and national holidays. Rs.5, child Rs.3 (foreigners Rs.100). P. Guided Tours: guides are available. 0452 650298.

Established in 1980-1 during the 5th World Tamil Conference, the museum has a good collection of bronzes, sculptures, musical instruments, megalithic pottery, wood carvings, ancient paintings, folk and tribal objects on display. One can browse through interesting specimens in sections devoted to Anthropology, Geology, Botany and Zoology. The Numismatics gallery traces the evolution of Indian coins. As an extension of its role in promoting traditional art and culture, the museum organises training programmes on Tanjore painting, batik art, taxidermy and screen printing besides special summer camps on Tamil music, Bharathanatyam, yoga and Varmakkalai.

KANYAKUMARI★

Government Museum

Just off the main road on the left after the Wandering Monk Museum. Gandhi Mandapam Road, Kanyakumari 629702. Open 9.30am–5pm. Closed Fri, 2nd Saturdays and national holidays. Rs.5, child Rs.3 (foreigners Rs.100). P.

Opened in 1991, the museum has a small collection of objects and photographs on various themes from Archaeology to Biology. A detailed set of wood carved panels that were part of the 6m/18ft temple chariot from Ramanathapuram are on display. Tribal crafts and baskets, artefacts from Karaikudi like betel-leaf boxes, incense holders, ancient lamps and brassware and a selection of beautifully carved musical instruments act as a great window to the region's culture. The Travancore Gallery documents the history of the erstwhile rulers of Kanyakumari and the art section displays Raja Ravi Varma prints besides works of other Indian and Western artists.

National Parks and Wildlife Sanctuaries

The stretch from Nilgiris to Kanyakumari along the Western Ghats accounts for most of Tamil Nadu's forests. Yet the area around Agasthiarmalai has an enviable diversity of fauna. Conservationists record it as a natural greenhouse for 2,000 varieties of medicinal plants and a habitat of several rare, endemic and endangered species. The natural wealth of the ecologically fragile region has prompted the Government to earmark it as a Biosphere Reserve.

KALAKAD-MUNDANTHURAI TIGER RESERVE

45km south of Tenkasi or 54km east of Tirunelveli. Amabasamudram, Papanasam Upper Dam Road, Tirunelveli District. Open daily 6am–6pm. Rs.15, Rs.10 child 5–13yr (child under 5 free, Rs.25 camera, Rs.150 video). Rs.15 (car). Guided Tours: FRH can arrange a local guide for birding and treks. 0462 2552663 (Tirunelveli), 04635 261100 (Kalakad). http://projecttiger.nic.in/kalakad.htm. For prior permission to stay at Mundanthurai Rest House, contact Deputy Director, Project Tiger Office, Ambasamudram (opp. Marriage Hall) or Field Director, Kalakad-Mundanthurai Tiger Reserve, NGO 'A' Colony, Tirunelveli. Avoid Mar–May as temperatures average 38–44°C. Sept–Mar is the best time to visit.

Straddling the Tamil Nadu–Kerala border, the Kalakad-Mundanthurai Tiger Reserve is an 895sq km tract of undulating land with metamorphic rocks draped by evergreen forests, scrub and grasslands. The park's biodiversity matches its rich and varied terrain. Located at the southern end of the Western Ghats, one of the 18 Biodiversity Hotspots in the World, the reserve stretches along the 288km border, hemmed in between Kerala to the west and Tirunelveli District to the north and east. The sagely peak of Agasthiarmalai (1,868m/6,129ft), the third highest in South India, lies in Kerala, but trekking trails marked out by forest officials, over 250 bird species, waterfalls and scenic vistas make KMTR a haven for wildlife enthusiasts.

Historically the Pandyas, Madurai Nayakas and the British ruled the area and it was R.K. Puckle, the District Collector of Tirunelveli who organised the Forest Department in 1864. Almost a century later, Mundanthurai was declared a Tiger Sanctuary in 1962 and the entire Kalakad Reserve Forest was notified as a sanctuary to protect the endangered lion-tailed macaque in 1976. By 1989, KMTR became the 17th Tiger Reserve in India and the only one its kind in Tamil Nadu. There is a sizeable population of its apex species, the tiger and the leopard (panther), but they are elusive. Herds of elephants frolic in the watering holes and it is easy to see sambar, spotted deer and the occasional mouse deer, barking deer or gaur. Nilgiri tahrs are seen in higher regions. The woods are home to sloth bears, brown mongoose, brown palm civets, Indian pangolins, Malabar spiny dormouses, Nilgiri langurs, slender lorises, bonnet macaque and wild dogs. The forest also crawls with king cobras, pythons and green pit vipers. Apart from the Agamid lizard (rediscovered in Kakachi forest) and the rare arboreal skink, the crocodiles released into the reservoirs in the 1970s are thriving! For birders, highlights include Ceylon frogmouth, grey-headed bulbul, great black woodpecker, great pied hornbill, great Indian hornbill, Malabar grey hornbill, Oriental bay owl and broad-tailed grass warbler.

Nourished by two monsoons a year *(Jun–Aug and Oct–Dec)*, the reserve is a watershed for 14 major rivers and streams. The scenic sights Agasthiar Falls, Karayar Dam and Papanasam Dam are a must do. Boating options at the dam allow a ride to Banatheertham Falls for a 1hr stop to have an indulgent shower.

Courtallam Falls★

Tenkasi–Shenkottai Road, Tirunelveli District 627802. Located 167km south-west of Madurai by NH-208 via Srivilliputhur and Rajapalayam, 142km north-west of Kanyakumari, take NH-7 to Tirunelveli (58km) and SH-40 to Tenkasi (6km north-east). Vehicle entry Main Falls Rs.30, Old Courtallam Rs.40, Five Falls Rs.30.

Aintharuvi-Five Falls

© Anurag Mallick, Priya Ganapathy/MICHELIN

Tagged as the Natural Spa of the South, Courtallam (or Kuttralam) Falls is the collective name for the many waterfalls and cascades made by River Chittar thundering down the rocky cliffs of the Western Ghats. Unlike the early artworks of British artist Thomas Daniell which depict it as a virtually unknown spot of wilderness filled with raw beauty, today the place is crammed with tourists who come to bathe under its therapeutic waterfalls. Since the river flows through forests of medicinal herbs, roots and minerals before its descent, it is believed to be fortified with tremendous healing properties. The cool climate coupled with gusty winds and the characteristic gentle drizzles invigorate the mind and body, making it a popular hub.

Located on the Kerala–Tamil Nadu border, Courtallam has nine major falls and the key ones have convenient road access. Near the car park, shops sell towels, shorts and toiletries as rows of crazy billboards featuring WWE wrestlers and muscled superstars 'model' for local massage parlours offering special oil and therapeutic body massages! **Peraruvi (Main Falls)**, the biggest draw, plummets from a height of 60m/120ft and has people of all ages jostling for a good shower. In what appears like a mega community bathroom, fully clothed women cluster to the right, the elderly and children troop to the left and well-oiled men of all shapes and sizes bear the full force of the central torrent. The best season is June to September and between November and January during north-eastern monsoons.

The gentler **Chittaruvi Falls** is close by. Spreading like the hood of a five-headed serpent spitting from the crags is **Aintharuvi (Five Falls)** 5km/3mi from the Main Falls with a nearby shrine dedicated to Ayyanar Shastha. 6.5km/4mi from the Main Falls is **Pazhaya Courtallam (Old Courtallam Falls)** with an ancient shrine of Thirukoortalanatheeshwara (Lord of the Peaks) at the foothills. The conch-shaped temple is noted for its stunning Chitra Sabha (one of the famous Pancha Sabhas) with beautiful mural paintings and medicinal wood carvings housing a Nataraja deity. Boating in the nearby lake, an aquarium and children's park are the other attractions.

A mile-long trek from Main Falls up the mountain leads to **Shenbaga Devi Falls**, named after an old temple nearby. The quieter, dream-like **Tenaruvi (Honey Falls)** is 5km/3mi further, evidently labelled after the honeycombs garlanding the rocky overhang. The small **Puliaruvi (Tiger Falls)** once considered the watering hole of the big cats has bathing *ghats* for pilgrims visiting the Pashupathi Shashta Temple in the vicinity. **Pazhathota Aruvi (Fruit Garden Falls)** near the Government Horticulture Park above Five Falls is off-limits to the public. About an hour's drive from Courtallam past Shenkottai on the state border, **Palaruvi (Milk Falls)** plunges from the lofty forests of Ariyankavu and offers a panoramic valley view.

Beaches

Though the long Tamil Nadu coastline has many pristine beaches, they haven't been exploited to their tourism potential and often languish in obscurity. The lack of proper infrastructure, rough waters, presence of temples and pilgrim crowds with traditional outlook, have ensured beaches like Tiruchendur and Kanyakumari remain spiritual escapes. Around Kanyakumari, Vattakottai *(6km north-east)* **with its sea fort, Sothavillai** *(12km west on NH-44)*, **Sanguthurai** *(15km east on Periyakadu Road Seaway)* **and Muttom** *(33km via Nagercoil on SH-46)* **are great places for sunsets, picnics and watching local fishermen at work.**

Tale of the Seven Sands

The three different waters bring in heaps of mineral-rich sand which gives Kanyakumari's beaches their unusual seven-coloured sands. However, the legend of the town's virgin deity is far more poetic. It is said that when Kanyakumari was left at the altar by Lord Shiva, the distraught goddess flung her wedding feast to the ground and vowed that she would never marry. The elaborate food preparations of rice and lentils went to waste and turned into the multi-tinted sand found on the beach.

KANYAKUMARI BEACH

Accessible from NH-7 to Beach Road, south of Gandhi Mandapam and Kanyakumari Temple. Beach Road, Kanyakumari. ✕ P.

The intriguing southern-most point of the Indian peninsula, **Kanyakumari★** or Cape Comorin is at the confluence of the grand trio of water masses – the Bay of Bengal, Arabian Sea and Indian Ocean. With key sights located nearby, the beach is easily the busier side of town, crammed with eateries, hotels and shops. People flock to Kanyakumari Beach to capture its kaleidoscopic sunrise and sunset, sometimes climbing up the lighthouse for a better view. The unusual sight of the sun and moon facing each other on the same horizon occurs during Chitra Poornima (full moon in April). On other full moon days, it's a treat to watch the sunset and moonrise happen almost simultaneously. Despite its scenic views, the treacherous rocks and unpredictable waters around the beach means that tourists should not venture too deep– a protective wall has been built to avoid accidents. A unique aspect of Kanyakumari is its multi-coloured sand (*see sidebar, above*), sold as a souvenir at beachside stalls. Other collectibles, trinkets and handicrafts made of seashells, woven palm leaves and coconut can be bought at bargain prices in the bazaar fringing the beach.

Kanyakumari Beach

ADDRESSES

STAY

Despite Madurai, Kanyakumari and Tiruchendur being pilgrim centres, the accommodation options vary from heritage hotels, beach resorts, boutique properties to luxurious city hotels. In Madurai, most of the budget lodges are clustered around West Perumal Maistry Street while the more luxurious options are away from the city centre.

MADURAI

Heritage Madurai – *11, Melakkal Main Road, Kochadai, Madurai 625016. 0452 2385455/ 3244185. www.heritagemadurai.com. . 35 villas, 32 rooms.* . Spread over 7ha/17 acres, Heritage Madurai is a green oasis in the heart of the city. Originally a British Gentlemen's Club, it was refurbished by architect Geoffrey Bawa using materials from around Madurai. The 134-year-old granite floor is sourced from a mill while the restaurant is set around a large banyan tree, lit by a searchlight from a British warship. Spacious villas come with plunge pools and the common large swimming pool is styled after the Teppakulam Tank. Guests can learn garland making, pottery and weaving in the small recreated Chettinad village. A golf simulator, bar, Svasti spa for Ayurvedic and Thai massages and delicious South Indian and Sri Lankan cuisine make the stay thoroughly enjoyable.

Taj Garden Retreat – *40, TPK Road, Pasumalai Hills, Madurai 625004. 0452 2371601. www.thegatewayhotels.com. . 63 rooms.* . Located 7km from town en route to Thirupparankunram, the heritage hotel is contoured across 25ha/63 acres of the Pasumalai Hills. The Colonial flavour is maintained with period rooms, wooden floors and well-laid-out gardens. The restaurant offers a great view of the city, and the large pool, tennis court and lounge bar make it the perfect escape.

Fortune Pandiyan – *Race Course Road, Chokkikulam, Madurai 625002. 0452 2537090/4356789. www.fortunepandiyanhotel.com. . 42 rooms.* . Slightly away from the hustle and bustle north of Vaigai River, the hotel has large comfortable rooms and a good restaurant and bar attached. Entry is from Alagar Kovil Road.

GRT Regency – *38, Madakkulam Main Road (TPK Road), NH-7, Palanganatham Signal Junction, Madurai 625003. 0452 2371155. www.grtregency.com. . 57 rooms.* . Coming from the GRT stable, this is a stylish city hotel located near Palanganatham Bus Stand in the southern part of town. It has a multi-gym, swimming pool, boutique, bar and Ayush Ayurvedic therapy centre offering authentic Kerala oil massages. Breakfast is an elaborate multi-cuisine buffet. Round-the-clock foreign exchange and free Wi-Fi.

Hotel Sangam – *Alagar Kovil Road, Madurai 625002. 0452 4244555/ 2537531. www.sangamhotels.com. . 60 rooms.* . Located next to Pandiyan Hotel, Sangam is a good hotel with a bar, small pool, shopping arcade and a restaurant that serves excellent Indian, Continental and Chinese cuisine to the accompaniment of classical performances, ***veena*** recitals and folk dances.

Hotel Germanus – *28, By Pass Road, Madurai 625010. 0452 4356999. www.hotelgermanus.org. . 84 rooms.* . The largest business and leisure hotel in town, all rooms are centrally air-conditioned and Wi-Fi enabled. Besides Utsav multi-cuisine, Cloud Seven bar, a health club and a 24hr coffee shop, there's a good rooftop restaurant with night views of the temple and the city. Driver's accommodation is provided.

Hotel North Gate – *Palam Station Road, Goripalayam, Madurai 625002. 0452 2523030/4383030. www.hotelnorthgate.co.in. 36 rooms.* . Opposite the American College on the main road north of the Vaigai, North Gate is close to Gandhi Museum road. Gourmet restaurant on the ground floor and roof garden restaurant.

Hotel Royal Court – *4, West Veli Street, Madurai 625001. 0452 4356666. www.royalcourtinfo.com. 69 rooms.* . A business hotel within walking distance of the railway station. The multi-cuisine restaurant serves North and South Indian food, while the

rooftop restaurant offers great views and barbecue dinners.

Madurai Residency – *14–15, West Marret Street, Madurai 625001. 0452 4380000/4380647. www.madurairesidency.com. 77 rooms.* . Earlier Classic Residency, it is a 15min walk from the western tower of Madurai Meenakshi Temple. Rooms have been renovated but Wi-Fi is limited to the lobby. It has a bar and AC multi-cuisine restaurant on the 2nd floor besides another on the rooftop.

Meenakshi's Sunshine Hotel – *14, Meenakshi Mission Road, Lake Area, Madurai 625107. 0452 4524444. www.hotelsunshine.co.in. . 40 rooms.* . A brand new hotel with a balcony in all rooms, Wi-Fi enabled, solar-heated hot water and 24x7 room service. Sunny Platter serves good Continental, Chinese and South Indian dishes like Malabar fish curry, Madurai mutton *chukka* and char-grilled kebabs and *tikkas*.

The Metropole – *17A, Melur Road, Vinayaga Nagar, Madurai 625020. 0452 4222222/4352222. www.the-metropolehotel.com. 28 rooms.* . Opposite the District Courts near Raja Muthaiah Mandram and Eco Park, this swish hotel has a multi-cuisine terrace restaurant with great views.

Star Residency – *43–44, Kuruvikkaran Salai, Madurai 625020. 0452 4343999/9842162466. www.starresidencyhotels.com. 65 rooms.* . Located near Anna Bus Stand en route to the Collectorate and Gandhi Museum, this is a good business hotel popular with foreign tourists. Refurbished rooms, Wi-Fi connectivity and a restaurant and coffee shop.

Weshtern Park – *4, TB Road, Mahaboopalayam, Madurai 625010. 0452 4202137. www.weshternpark.com 48 rooms.* . The spelling may be off, but the hotel isn't. Located west of the railway station on Old Dindigul Road, it offers complimentary Wi-Fi, hot water from 5am–9am and buffet dinners for Rs.300 at West Gate, its multi-cuisine restaurant.

KANYAKUMARI

Hotel Sea View – *East Car Street, Kanyakumari 629702. 04652 247841. www.hotelseaview.in. 56 rooms.* . Overlooking the boat jetty, Sea View's deluxe rooms offer a good view of sunrise and the harbour. It has a reasonably priced multi-cuisine restaurant and bar.

Hotel Sparsa – *6/112B, Beach Road, Kanyakumari 629702. 04652 247041. www.sparsaresorts.com. . 46 rooms and 2 suites.* . Set against green lawns near Sunset Point with a good view of the sea, Sparsa is one of the best places to stay in Kanyakumari. Auroma multi-cuisine restaurant, Lands End bar, swimming pool, health club.

Hotel Sun World – *6/81-B, Kovalam Road, Kanyakumari 629702. 04652 247899/9442057000. www.hotelsunworld.com. 46 rooms.* . This large, new mid-range hotel has a great location overlooking Vivekananda Rock and the Thiruvalluvar statue. However, sea-view rooms with balconies are quite expensive. Ayurvedic massage and a pool are also available on site.

Indien Hermitage – *Marungoor Village, Kanyakumari 629402. 04652 254405. www.indienhermitage.com. 12 rooms.* . The perfect hideaway away from the crowded beachside *(14km from town)*. Set in a 5ha/12-acre plot situated against the stunning backdrop of Marutha Malai (Hill of Medicinal Herbs), it is run by the affable 'German' Raju, an interesting tour guide from Chennai who set up the resort in 2006 with help of his German friends. Homely food, excellent views from the water tank and a gigantic 550sq m/6,000sq ft swimming pool!

Hotel Sangam – *2–18 A6, South Car Street, Kanyakumari 629702. 04652 246161/246262. www.sangamgrouphotels.com. 25 rooms.* . Leading hotel chain in Kanyakumari with several options around the beach – **Hotel Samudra** on Sannathi Street *(41 rooms)*, **Gopi Nivas Grand**, their first hotel *(63 rooms)*, **Triveni Tourist Home**, their largest *(133 rooms)*, **Lakshmi Tourist Home** *(39 rooms)*, **Hotel Seaface** *(31 rooms)* and the more premium Kerala-style **Parvathi Nivas**.

Hotel Singaar International – *5/22, Main Road, Kanyakumari 629702. 04652 247992/9443312147. 102 rooms.* . A lovely mid-range hotel, Singaar is located near the railway station. Spread over 2.5ha/6 acres, it has a business centre, swimming pool with lawns, children's park, Ayurvedic massage, Internet cafe and two good restaurants – King Flower multi-cuisine and the open-air Orchard.

Hotel Siva Murugan – *2/93, North Car Street, Kanyakumari 629702. 04652 246862/9842150255/9698888888. www.hotelsivamurugan.com. 48 rooms.* Newly renovated hotel with spacious, tidy rooms and attached balconies. Good value for the price you pay.

Hotel Tri Sea – *Near Seashore, Kovalam Road, Kanyakumari 629702. 04652 246586/9487817474. www.triseahotel.com. 50 rooms.* Large hotel with sea-facing rooms, multi-cuisine restaurant and a rooftop swimming pool.

TIRUNELVELI

Hotel Sri Bharani – *29-A, Madurai Road, Tirunelveli 627001. 0462 2333234/9843359555. www.sribharanihotels.com. 57 rooms.* Reasonably priced hotel opposite the Old Bus Stand with neat rooms and complimentary Wi-Fi. The Nellai Saravana Bhavan restaurant on the ground floor is excellent.

Hotel Sri Janakiram – *30, Madurai Road, Tirunelveli 627011. 0462 2331941. www.srijanakiramhotels.com. 70 rooms.* An old hotel located close to the railway station, it has a rooftop garden and an AC restaurant, Maruthi, that serves decent North Indian, Chinese and South Indian cuisine.

COURTALLAM

Esakki High View Resorts – *Five Falls Main Road, Courtallam 627802. 04633 283773. http://courtallamesakkihighviewresorts.yolasite.com. 33 rooms.* Located en route to Five Falls Esakki offers individual cottages with attached car park, Farm Garden Restaurant, Barringan Pub and a go-kart area for children.

The Kuttalam Heritage – *Shenkottai-Kuttalam Main Road, Ilanji 625805. 04633 233022/236051. www.thekuttalamheritage.com. 19 rooms and 10 cottages.* Located on the main road towards Shenkottai and cut away from the busy town centre, it is one of the best places to stay in Courtallam. Rooms and cottages with sit-out are laid out in a shaded mango orchard with a nice pool, Ayurvedic massages, bar and a restaurant that serves great South Indian and Kerala cuisine.

Saaral Resort – *42/42A, Shenkottai Road, Courtallam, Tenkasi 627802. 04633 283601. www.saaralresort.com. 40 rooms.* Sitting pretty against green lawns, the white Kerala-style structures with red tiled roofs offer a wide choice of rooms – cottages, deluxe rooms, penthouses to heritage rooms. With three bars, Srineedhi multi-cuisine restaurant, play area for children, gym and therapy centre, Saaral is a great base.

TIRUCHENDUR

Hotel Chitra Park – *367, Travellers Bungalow Road, Tiruchendur 628215. 04639 243766/9486380900/9965472812. hotelchitrapark.com. 60 rooms.* Located near the domestic airport and railway station, the hotel offers free pick-up service and even has a communication centre with net browsing and laser printouts.

Hotel Udhayam International – *Travellers Bungalow Road, Tiruchendur, Thoothukudi District. 04639 242566/9884404292. www.hoteludhayaminternational.com. 41 rooms.* Situated between Murugan Temple and the railway station. Besides a choice of rooms and suites, it has a separate veg restaurant and Bell multi-cuisine serving good non veg.

Chendur Residency – *370/142-C, TB Road, Tiruchendur 628215. 04639 245384. www.chendurresidency.com. 10 rooms.* Small reasonably priced hotel that handles local tour packages and travel arrangements.

THOOTHUKUDI (TUTICORIN)

GRT Regency Tuticorin – *3/187, Periyanayagapuram Road, Palayamkottai Road (NH-7A), Thoothukudi 628101. 0461 2340777/7708733377. www.grthotels.com. 51 rooms.* Located opposite the New District Collectorate, this budget luxury hotel has a fitness centre, great restaurant and Wi-Fi in all rooms, besides more luxurious studio rooms and penthouses.

Bell Harbour – *23, South Beach Road, Thoothukudi 628001. 0461 2323456. www.bellhotels.in. 6 cottages.* Close to the old harbour,

Madurai's Mocktail

When in Madurai, try a glass of refreshing *jigar thanda*, the city's signature mocktail. This chilled concoction is a bizarre yet delicious mix of reduced milk, almond milk, *kadal paasi* (China grass), *sago* and *nannari* sherbet (herbal drink made of Sarsaparilla roots) topped with a dollop of ice-cream and chocolate malt!

the small theme hotel offers unique luxury cottages made out of specially fabricated shipping containers. The 200-cover restaurant, decorated with motifs of ocean life, specialises in fresh sea-food, multi-cuisine and Indian delicacies.

SIVAKASI

Hotel Bell Sivakasi – *Nehru Road, Sivakasi 626123. 04562 225180. www.bellhotels.in. 42 rooms.* Easily the best address in town, the hotel was started by Standard Fireworks as there was no decent place to stay or eat for visitors to India's Cracker Capital. Unexpected luxury, a nice pool and a restaurant that serves an amazing spread of pizzas, pastas and Indian fare.

EAT

Beyond the clichéd *idli–dosa–vada–sambar* realm, some places in Southern Tamil Nadu enhance the palate with quirky local tiffins, snacks, and desserts. For a local speciality, try *dindigul biryani* prepared with *serakasamba* rice or the famous fish fry at Shankar Vilas aka Sevadan Kadai at Kanyakumari. All the major hotels have in-house dining including rooftop restaurants which are great places to relax in the evenings with superb city views.

MADURAI

Anjappar Chettinad – *Hotel Annamalai International, 120 Feet Road, Madurai 625001. 0452 4520006. www.anjappar.com. Open daily 11am–11pm.* The best place in this temple town to indulge your carnivorous cravings. A great dining ambience and the best of Chettinad cuisine.

Bell Food Court – *55, Tamil Sangam Road, Madurai 625001. 0452 2350832. www.bellhotels.in. Open daily 7.30am–3.30pm, 4.30pm–11pm.* A 400-cover restaurant offering a wide choice of delicious Indian and Continental fare, with ample car parking and play area for children.

Sri Velu Dindigul Biryani – *56, Grace Tower, near Simmakal, Tamil Sangam Road, Madurai. 0452 4510010/9150341301. Open daily 11am–4.30pm, 6–10.30pm.* Three types of ***biryani*** served on banana leaf with onion ***raita*** and ***dalcha*** for lunch besides steamed rice with ***rasam*** and side dishes like crab gravy, quail fry, prawn ***masala***, mutton ***chukka***, ***thala kari***, mutton chops and liver roast. In the evening, ***idli***, ***idiappam***, ***kari dosai*** and ***paaya*** are served.

Kalyana Biriyani – *10, Nethaji Road, Madurai. 9894145555. Open Mon–Sat 11am–11pm.* Conveniently located near Periyar Bus Stand, this is Madurai's most popular ***biriyani*** joint serving excellent chicken, mutton, egg and fish *biriyanis*.

Meenakshi Bhavan – *141, Collector Office Road, Anna Bus Stand, Madurai. 0452 4391588/2529052. www.meenakshibhavan.com. Open daily 6am–11pm.* Popular chain of veg restaurants, it has South Indian meals, snacks, sweets and weekly special menus. They also run an outlet near Madurai Railway Station on the main road.

Murugan Idli Shop – *196, West Masi Street, Madurai 625001. 0452 2341379. www.muruganidlishop.com. Open daily 7am–11pm.* Located opposite Pothys Textiles, this iconic shop opened in 1966. Their trademark soft ***idlis*** served with four chutneys are sold alongside tiffin items like ***dosas*** and ***uthappams*** *(not available between 11am–4pm; rice dishes are served instead).* They also run outlets on 46, Thalavoy Street and on platform 4/5 at Madurai railway station.

New Arya Bhavan – *268, West Masi Street, diagonally opp. Dandayudhapani Temple, Madurai 625001. 0452 3299104/3299107. www.newaryabhavan.com. Open daily 9am–10pm.* This Iconic eatery that started in 1947 sells sweets and snacks.

TENKASI

Bell Monkey – *391–393, Courtallam–Madurai Main Road, Ilanji, Tenkasi 627805. 04633 225280. www.bellhotels.in. . Open 7.30–3.30pm, 4.30pm–11pm.* Named after the monkeys in the surrounding forests, the restaurant is located on the town's quiet outskirts. The menu is predominantly South Indian. A dorm and 2 cottages are available for an overnight stay.

KANYAKUMARI

Archana – *East Car Street, Kanyakumari 629702. 04652 246787/ 246887. www.hotelmaadhini.com. . Open daily 7–10.30am, 12noon–3.30pm, 7–10.30pm.* Located in the Maadhini Hotel and one of the better places to eat in Kanyakumari. Primarily serving Indian fare, the AC restaurant serves both veg and non-veg dishes while the evening garden restaurant serves tandoori.

CAFES

Café Coffee Day – *HIG 24, Near Colcha Complex, 80 Feet Road, Annanagar, Madurai 625020. 0452 5390336. www.cafecoffeeday.com. Open daily 9am–9pm. Prices start at Rs.50.* Part of the famous CCD chain, the menu offers a range of hot and cold coffees, teas and fruit-based drinks, besides *samosas*, sandwiches and short eats.

Café T's – *HIG 18, Kamarajar 4th Street, Chinna Chokkikulam, Madurai 625002. 8903030303. Open daily 10.30am–10.30pm. Prices start at Rs.50.* A revamped version of Tornado Café serving coffee, tea and cold beverages like shakes, sundaes, sodas, slush and ice-cream, besides pizzas, burgers, sandwiches, frankies and rolls.

Hot Breads – *KK Nagar Arch, 1, Vinayagar Nagar, Madurai 625020. 9344151600. www.hotbreads.in. Open daily 7am–10pm. Prices start at Rs.50.* Popular bakery-cum-café near Court Bus Stop serving cakes, breads and doughnuts, besides fast food snacks like sandwiches, burgers and pizzas.

Saravana Coffee Bar – *67, Tamil Sangam Road, Madurai 625001. 9940990105. Open daily 6am–10pm. Prices start at Rs.15.* Located north of the Meenakshi Temple near Indian Pharmacy, this traditional joint serves good filter coffee.

LEISURE

Athisayam Theme Park – *Paravai, NH-7 (Madurai–Dindigul Main Road), Madurai 625002. 0452 2463848-50. www.athisayampark.com. Open daily 10am–6.30pm. Rs.400, Rs.250 child.* 12km from Madurai, Athisayam has separate dry and wet parks with games and rides, boating, restaurant and a recreated waterfall.

Baywatch Water Amusement Park – *Sunset Point, Kanyakumari 629702. 04652 246565/246375/9048000222. www.baywatch.co.in. Open daily 9.30am–6.30pm. Rs.220, Rs.190 child.* Touted as 'India's first seaside amusement park', Baywatch comes with dry and wet rides, ice-cream kiosks and a restaurant. Ticket includes entry to the nearby Wax Museum.

Hawa Valley – *Natham Main Road, Kadavur, near Indian Overseas Bank, Madurai District 625107. 0452 2478365.* Located 20km from Madurai and popular for go-karting. Restaurant set amidst landscaped gardens.

Madurai Eco Park – *Behind Corporation, Madurai 625020. 8903030303. Open 10.30am–10.30pm. Rs.2, Rs.1 child.* Spread over 0.8ha/2 acres, the Eco Park is a good place to relax within the city. A musical fountain, mini boating centre, ornamental trees, soft grassy lawns with well-laid-out paths and a children's play area are the main highlights.

Sivananda Yoga Vedanta Meenakshi Ashram – *New Natham Road, Saramthangi Village, Vellayampatti, Madurai District 625503. 0452 2912950, 9865155335. www.sivananda.org. Yoga camps Rs.400/day.* The Ashram organises year-round 2-week yoga breaks for beginners, as well as teacher training courses. Fee includes meals, yoga and shared stay in dorms. The campus, a 5min walk from Pavanna Vilakku junction *(22km from Madurai)* has a boutique, library and health hut.

SHOPPING

SHOPPING MALLS

Majesty Cine Mall – *144, Lake View Road, KK Nagar, Madurai 625020. 0452 4392786. Open daily.* A good place to catch a movie, this multiplex is run by Big Cinemas and has food outlets including *Marry Brown*.

Milan'em Mall – *100 Feet Road, KK Nagar, Madurai 650020. ✆0452 4347000, 9843080383. www.milanem.com. Open daily 10am–11pm.* Madurai's first shopping mall, Milan'em is spread over 8,300sq m/90,000sq ft with lots of shopping options under one roof – clothes, shoes, music, gifts, home needs.

MARKETS

Tailor's Market – *Pudhu Mandapam, East Chitrai Street, Chinnakadai area, Madurai 625001. Open daily.* Crammed with garment and tailor shops, this is Madurai's best place to get a custom-made outfit in a wide range of materials for men, women and kids.

Flower Market – *Nelpettai, Mattuthavani, Madurai 625007. Open daily.* The market is these days adjacent to Mattuthavani Bus Stand. A great place to see the unloading and vending of flowers like marigolds and the eponymous ***Madurai malligai*** (jasmine).

SPECIALITY SHOPS AND DESIGNER BOUTIQUES

APN Shell Craft – *Opp. Government Bus Stand, Kanyakumari 629702. ✆04652 246368/247627. www.apnshells.com. Open daily.* Largest wholesalers and exporters since 1974 of over 200 varieties of Indian seashells; they also sell palm leaf articles and handicrafts.

Cottage Arts Emporium – *36, North Chitrai Street, Madurai 625001. ✆0452 2623614/2622491. www.cottagearts emporium.com. Open Mon–Sat, 10.30am–8pm.* Jewellery, shawls, carpets, paintings and decorative pieces sourced from across India – painted furniture and ***jharokhas*** (windows) from Rajasthan, Tibetan ***thankas***, inlay work from Agra and more.

Cottage Industries Exposition Ltd – *30, North Chitrai Street, Madurai 625001. ✆0452 2630240. www.cieworld.com. Open Mon–Sat, 10.30am–7.30pm.* A good showcase of furnishings, jewellery, shawls, carpets, art and statues sourced from CIE's vast network of craftsmen.

Handloom House – *154, East Veli Street, Madurai 625001. ✆0452 2335753. Open daily 9am–9pm. Price Rs.350–2,000.* Buy a range of affordable saris – from Madurai's famous cotton ***sungundi*** with batik, block and dot prints to Sankaran Kovil saris, checked plain weaves and Kanchi cottons.

Nalli Silks Sales Depot – *85–86, South Masi Street, Madurai 625001. ✆0452 2345126. www.nalli.com. Open daily, 9am–9pm.* The premiere address for exquisite silk saris since 1928, Nalli also stocks Banarasi silks, hand looms and fancy designs. They run another outlet on Jadamuni Koil Street *(✆0452 2625884/2626352).*

BOOKSHOPS

Grahish Book World – *156, 2nd Floor, Vakil New Street, Madurai 625001. ✆9047034271. Open daily.* Shop opposite Amman Temple selling books, mags and other publications.

Liberty Book Centre – *3, West Veli Street, Madurai 625001. ✆0452 2342819.* Popular bookshop located opposite the railway junction.

Turning Point Books – *Town Hall Road, 75, Venkatesh Towers, Madurai 625001. ✆0452 2347398. Open Mon–Sat 10am–9pm.* A 3rd-floor bookshop opposite New College House.

PERFORMING ARTS

Kadambavanam – *Natham Road, Parali, Dindigul District 624401. ✆04544 220322/9003926209/9500954090. www.kadambavanam.in. Open 5pm onwards. Daily cultural programme starts at 6pm.* A 25km drive from Madurai, Kadambavanam Cultural Centre features a live showcase of Tamil Nadu's traditions through dance, music, arts and crafts, rural games and food. Vibrant Tamil folk arts like ***karagam***, ***kavadi***, ***oyilattam***, ***thappattam*** and ***poikkal kudhirai*** are performed, interspersed with stories and explanations. The show ends with a traditional buffet dinner *(Rs.450)* in a rustic setting.

Sri Sadguru Sangeetha Samajam – *15A, Gokhale Road, Chinna Chockikulam, Madurai. ✆0452 2530858, 2531036.* Madurai's premiere venue for regular music, dance and cultural performances, held in the Lakshmi Sundaram Hall. The annual festival in Jan and Meenakshi Kalyanam festival in April are also held here.

Central Tamil Nadu

Highlights

- The temple town, Kumbakonam *p238*
- Brihadisvara Temple, Thanjavur *p243*
- Srirangam, the world's largest temple complex *p247*
- The British hill retreat of Yercaud *p251*

Criss-crossed by rivers like the Kaveri and Kollidam and irrigated by 33 river basins, Central Tamil Nadu is not just the rice bowl of the state, but also its heart and soul. History reveals that arts have flourished only when the stomach is fed and the mind nourished. The Cholas, who held sway over the region for nearly 500 years, patronised music, dance, painting, sculpture and literature. The troika of royal shrines at Thanjavur, Gangaikondacholapuram and Darasuram built between the 11C and 12C marked the zenith of an empire that stretched from coast to coast and spread across islands from the Maldives to China. In recognition of their cultural value, UNESCO inscribed the three World Heritage Sites as the Great Living Chola Temples in 2004. The region's charm lies in its diversity and plurality, where Thanjavur's Nayak kings wrote treatises in Telugu and Sanskrit and the Bhonsle rulers inscribed their history in Marathi. Be it the weaving of a sari, the crafting of a bronze or the soulful rendition of poems by Thygaraja, Syama Sastri and Muthuswami Dikshitar, every act was an invocation to the divine.

Brihadisvara Temple, Thanjavur in the evening

CENTRAL TAMIL NADU

Many of Central Tamil Nadu's most famous sights are clustered around the cities of **Kumbakonam**★★, **Thanjavur** ★★★ and **Trichy**★★★ and innumerable shrines dot the banks of the Kaveri (*see sidebar p234*). Around Kumbakonam, metal-casters in **Swamimalai** and **Nachiyar Kovil** churn out exquisite bronze idols while every lane and alley from **Darasuram** to **Tirubhuvanam** resounds with the clatter of looms as weavers produce vibrant silks. Sacred spots in this area include some of the 108 divya desams (sacred sights dedicated to Lord Vishnu) and Navargraha temples dedicated to the nine planets.

Kumbakonam★★

Spread out between the Kaveri and Arasalar rivers, Kumbakonam is dotted with no less than a hundred temples in and around town – most of which are dedicated to Shiva or Vishnu. Kumbakonam is where Lord Shiva dispersed the seeds of life that took the shape of *lingams* across the countryside; today the busy streets of this junction town are rich with the aroma of its legendary degree coffee.

Exploring the Area – NH-45C enters Kumbakonam from the north-east, via **Gangaikondacholapuram Tem-**

- **Population:** Trichy 700,000; Thanjavur 220,000; Kumbakonam 150,000.
- **Info:** Tourist Office, Hotel Tamil Nadu, Williams Road, opp. Central Bus Stand, Trichy 620001. Open daily 10.30am–5.45pm. ✆0431 2460136. www.tamilnadutourism.org.
- **Location:** Along the southern bank of the Kaveri in the central delta region.
- **Kids:** Boating on Yercaud Lake and ATVs/Kids Battery Car rides (*see Addresses, Grange Resort*).
- **Timing:** 1 week – 2 days for Yercaud and 5 days between Kumbakonam, Thanjavur and Trichy.
- **Guided Tours:** The Tourist Office at Jawan Bhavan opp. GPO organises a temple tour of Thanjavur (*✆04362 230984, Mon–Fri 10am–5.30pm*). Several tour operators in Kumbakonam arrange Navagraha temple trips.

Kaveri (Cauvery) River

Dashing down from its perch at Hogenakkal Falls on the state's north-western border, the Kaveri is dammed at Mettur and Bhavani, before it sashays into a broad river. At Upper Anicut, 14km west of **Trichy★★★**, it splits into the northern branch, Kollidam, and the southern branch, Kaveri, which join to form the islet of **Srirangam★**, before continuing eastward past **Thanjavur★★★** and **Kumbakonam★★** to reach the Bay of Bengal.

ple★★★ 33km away, merges with the State Highway and exits Kumbakonam to the west towards the UNESCO World Heritage site **Airavatesvara Temple★★** at Darasuram, and the hill sanctum of **Swamimalai Murugan** nearby. Most of the shrines are clustered around the NH-45C that bisects the town. The **Kumbeswara Temple★★** and adjoining **Sarangapani Temple★**, separated by the Potramarai Tank, lie to the immediate north of the highway, while Ramaswamy Temple and **Nageswara Temple** lie south. **Chakrapani Temple** is located to the north near P Shanmugham Road. *See Driving Tour, Religious and Spiritual Sights.*

Thanjavur★★★ (Tanjore)

Named Thanjanapuram after the demon who died and attained salvation here, the historic city was once Kuberapuri; the old Kubera Temple in Palia Agraharam is its only reminder. In AD 846, Vijayalaya Chola laid the foundation of the Imperial Cholas at Thanjavur until Rajaraja's son Rajendra Chola moved the capital to Gangaikondacholapuram in 1025. Under the long prosperous reign of the Cholas, great temples were built and culture flourished. After their decline in the 13C, the Telugu Nayaks (1535-1675) and Marathas (1676-1855) ruled Thanjavur, renovating shrines, patronising the arts and treasuring libraries as sanctuaries of knowledge. Proof of the city's cultural importance is evident from the products created here – Tanjore painting (*see Art p81*), Thanjavur *veena*, Tanjore art plate and the ubiquitous *thalai atti bommai* or bobble-head Thanjavur dolls.

Exploring the Area – The Grand Anicut Canal halves Thanjavur into north and south. The **Brihadisvara Temple★★★** is located by the canal in the south-west part of the old city within Chinna Kottai (Little Fort), part of the 16C Sivaganga Fort built by the Nayaks. Just north of the temple is Sivaganga Tank with the Schwarz Mission Church on the east. The church was founded in 1779 by noted German missionary Christian Friedrich Schwartz, the teacher of Maharaja Serfoji II. North of the bus stand by the canal, the **Thanjavur Palace★★** occupies the old city centre in Periya Kottai (Big Fort). The railway station is 0.5km south of the canal at the southern end of Gandhiji Road where most hotels, shops and the tourist office *(open 9am–4pm)* are located. *See Religious and Spiritual Sights, Historical Sights.*

Trichy★★★ (Tiruchirappalli)

Urayur, the old settlement of Trichy, served as the capital of the early Cholas. It was in 270 BC, about 10 miles from Urayur, that Karikala Chola built a stone *bund* or *Kallanai* to divert the mighty Kaveri and irrigate the fertile delta region. Two millennia later, it remains the oldest man-made dam in the world still in use! Dominating the city's skyline and rivalled only by the spire of Our Lady of Lourdes Church is the 83m/272ft hill-shrine of **Rock Fort★**. Believed to be 3,500 million years old, the rock bears the imprint of the Pallavas, later Cholas and the Nayaks who switched their capital from Madurai to Tiruchirapalli several times. The British conquest of 'Trichnopoly' in the Carnatic Wars (1746-63) consolidated the empire in India. Today, churches built by them co-exist alongside centuries-old temples, an old mosque built by the Nawab of Arcot and the Dargah of Natharvalli.

Exploring the Area – Bordered by the Kaveri River to the north, **Rock Fort★** is about half a kilometre from it, towering over the busy city centre. There are two bus stations – Chatram Bus Stand is 0.5km west of Rock Fort in the northern part of town while Central Bus Stand, the railway station, tourist office and most hotels are 2.5km south in the Cantonment (Junction Road) area. About 2km north of Rock Fort, on the large **Srirangam**★ island, is **Sri Ranganathaswamy Temple**★★★ and **Sri Jambukeshwara Temple**★ 2km east of it.

See Religious and Spiritual Sights.

Yercaud★

The term 'Poor Man's Ooty' sometimes used to describe Yercaud is ironic, as the first plantations were introduced here in the 1820s, before they spread to the Nilgiris in 1843. Its invigorating climate, a welcome break from the hot plains of Salem, soon attracted missionaries and educationists as it developed into a European sanatorium where Afghan princes and weary British troops revived their spirits and French missions and Danish chapels co-existed alongside German-run estates. Boating, countryside hikes, a clutch of viewpoints and an unhurried pace not seen in most hill stations makes Yercaud a charming getaway.

Exploring the Area – Perched at 1,372m/4,500ft in the Shevaroy Hill range of the Eastern Ghats, Yercaud is named after the *yeri* (lake) amidst a *kaad* (forest) that lies in the heart of town. About 32km north of **Salem**, the nearest town, the hill retreat is reachable by 20 winding hairpin bends. Once the ascent is complete, visitors can lose themselves in the swathes of coffee, pepper and orange plantations.

Most sights are scattered around the lake – **Pagoda Point** is to the east and **Lady's Seat** to the south, and **Killiyur waterfalls**, **Botanical Garden**★ and **Shevaroyan Temple** to the north. Public transport is limited, so it's best to drive or hire a car to explore the sights.

See Hill Stations.

GETTING THERE AND AROUND

(*Also see Planning Your Trip.*)

GETTING THERE

BY PLANE – There are daily flights from Chennai and other destinations to Trichy International Airport *(8km south of the city centre, ℘0431 2340551)*. From Trichy, Thanjavur is an hour's drive *(57km east)* on NH-67 while a 45min drive from Thanjavur on NH-45C leads to Kumbakonam *(40km further east)*.

BY TRAIN – The overnight Rockfort Express *(16177)* departs daily from Chennai Egmore Station at 10.30pm and reaches Trichy and Thanjavur the next morning, terminating at Kumbakonam at 7.40am. Trichy Express *(16853)* leaves Egmore daily at 8.30am and reaches Trichy at 4.30pm via Kumbakonam and Thanjavur. Yercaud Express departs at 10.30pm from Chennai and reaches Salem at 5.15am. Catch a cab *(Rs.900)* or bus for a 1hr drive 32km north to Yercaud.

BY BUS – There are regular day buses and night coaches from CMBT, Koyambedu in Chennai to Thanjavur Bus Stand and Trichy.

GETTING AROUND

Trichy, Thanjavur and Kumbakonam lie along a linear route and are 1hr drives from each other. Daily **trains** like Rock Fort Express and Trichy Express link all three destinations. Regular **buses** depart from Thanjavur's Municipal Bus Stand south of town to Kumbakonam *(1hr)* and Trichy *(1hr30min)*.

From Kumbakonam bus station north of Mahamaham Tank, buses leave every few minutes for Thanjavur via Darasuram. Some buses also go via Gangaikondacholapuram *(33km north)*.

Most sights are scattered in and around town so a pre-arranged **taxi** is convenient. However, **auto rickshaws** are more economical and practical for negotiating the busy streets. **Bicycles** are also available on hire.

 DRIVING TOUR

NAVAGRAHA TEMPLE CIRCUIT

Located within a 60km radius around **Kumbakonam**★★ from Sirkazhi and Karaikal in the east, the Navagraha temples are dedicated to the nine celestial bodies. People offer worship for the removal of *doshas* (ill effects of planets) and to fulfil their wishes. One can do a leisurely drive over 2–3 days or opt for a guided 1-day tour (*See Planning Your Trip*).

Start the tour from the temple of the sun god, 15km from Kumbakonam near Aduthurai, 3km off the Poompuhar Main Road.

Suryanarkoil

While most other Navagraha temples are Shiva shrines with a separate sanctum for one of the planets, **Suryanar Temple** (*open 6am–12.30pm, 4–8pm; 0435 2472349; www.suriyanarkoil.com*) is devoted exclusively to the sun god. Outside the 15.5m/518ft-high Rajagopuram to the north is a holy tank called Surya Pushkarni. The temple faces west and Surya stands with his consorts Usha and Chhaya Devi.

Drive 3km north-east from Suryanar Kovil on the Kathiramangalam–Panthanellur Road to Kanchanur.

Kanchanur

The **Agnishwaraswamy Temple** (*open 7am–12.30pm, 4–8pm; 0435 2470155/2473737*) is the place where Agni, the fire god, worshipped Shiva. The temple also houses a shrine for Shukran (Venus). Fridays are favourable to the goddess and white cloth is offered for decoration to get rid of evil effects.

From Kanchanur drive 20km to Mayiladuthurai and continue 14km north-east on SH-64 to reach Vaithiswaran Temple.

Pullirukkuvelur

The fiery red Chevai (Mars or Mangal) is appeased by offering red flowers at **Vaithiswaran Temple** (*open 6am–1pm, 4–9pm; 04364 279423*). Tuesdays are best suited for worship and the bronze image of Angaraka placed in the shrine is taken out in a procession.

Drive 7km on Vaithiswaran Koil Road to NH-45A, cross Jamia Masjid and turn left at Talikattha Mariamman Temple to reach Thiruvenkadu, 6km off the highway.

Thiruvenkadu

The temple of Buddh (Mercury), en route to Poompuhar, is located within the large **Shiva temple of Swetaranyeswarar** (*open 6am–12noon, 4–9pm; 04364 256424*). The colour green and the white *kanthal* flower (gloriosa lily) are sacred to him and he is usually worshipped on Wednesdays.

Drive 3.5km south to Melaiyur, turn left on SH-22 towards Poompuhar and take a right at Dharmakulam, for another 3.5km to the temple at Keezhaperumpallam.

Keezhaperumpallam

Quite close to Thiruvenkadu and about 20km from Sirkazhi, the **Naganathar Temple of Shiva** (*open 6am–1pm, 4–8pm; 04364 275222*) is where Ketu (south lunar node) is worshipped, usually on Tuesdays, and fasting is recommended. Take sweet potato and fruit juice once a day and avoid salt and spices.

Return to NH-45A and drive 28km via Thirukkadaiyur and Tranquebar to Karaikal from where Thirunallar is about 5km west on the SH-147 or Kumbakonam–Karaikal Road.

Thirunallar

The large complex of the **Dharbaranyeshwarar Shiva Temple** (*open 6am–1pm, 4–9pm; 04368 236530*) also houses the shrine of the powerful Shani (Saturn), and Shanivar

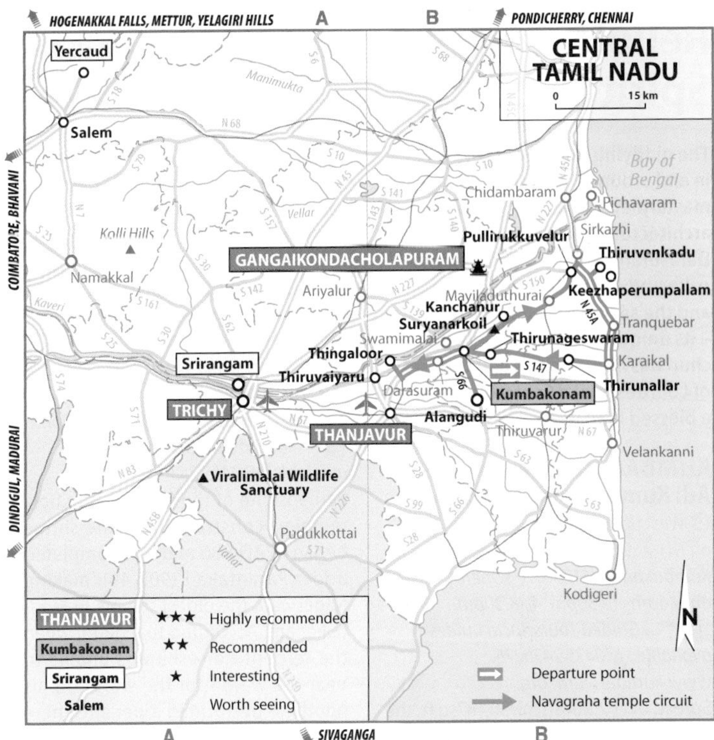

(Saturday) is the most appropriate day for worshipping him with black cloth. The sacred Nala Theertham where King Nala took a holy dip to get rid of a curse lies north-west.

Drive 47km on SH-147 to reach Thirunageswaram, just 5km short of Kumbakonam.

Thirunageswaram

The **Naganathar** or **Nageswara Temple of Shiva** (*open 6am–1pm, 4pm–8.30pm; 0435 2463354*) is a large complex with a shrine dedicated to Rahu (north lunar node) and his consorts in the outer corridor of the southern corner. The unique Uppiliappan Temple of Lord Vishnu (where offerings are made without salt) is just 0.5km away.

If it's been a long day, break the journey at Kumbakonam (see p233) before covering the remaining shrines, which lie in different directions.

Alangudi

17km south of Kumbakonam via Sakkottai and Velangaiman on SH-66.

Prime benevolent among the nine planets, Guru (Jupiter) is enshrined at the **Aabhatsakay Eswarar Temple** (*open 6am–1pm, 4–9pm; 04374 269407*). Guruvaar (Thursday) is Guru's chosen day and white jasmine is offered for worship. Devotees observe a fast, wear yellow and give away yellow clothes as charity besides offering 24 lamps and walking 24 times around his shrine.

Thingaloor

33km west of Kumbakonam via Papanasam on SH-22, Thingaloor is located 15km north of Thanjavur via Thiruvaiyaru.

Tingal ooru, or village of the Moon, is named after the shrine of Chandra in the **Kailasanathar Shiva temple** (*open 7am–8pm; 04362 2360936/262499*) on the banks of the Kaveri. Only the southern entrance is used.

Religious and Spiritual Sights

The giddying number of shrines in and around Kumbakonam, the masterpieces of Chola temple architecture from Thanjavur to Darasuram, India's largest temple spire and complex at Srirangam and the sacred hot spots of Trichy – its unique temples, *dargahs* and churches like St John's and Our Lady of Lourdes, make Central Tamil Nadu a blessed land indeed.

KUMBAKONAM★★

Adi Kumbeswara Temple★★

West of the Pottramarai Tank, off NH-45C. NH-45C, Mutt Street, Kumbakonam 612001. Open daily 6am–12.30pm, 4–8.30pm. P. Guided Tours: local guides available. 0435 2420276. www.kumbeswarar.org.

Spread over 2,804sq mi/30,187sq ft, the legendary shrine of Kumbeswara is the largest Shiva temple in Kumbakonam and lies in the middle of town facing east. Four big towers mark the outer *prakara* – Kailasa Gopuram, Katta Gopuram, Mulavar Gopuram and the 39m/128ft-high eastern gateway Rajagopuram. A covered market selling trinkets and religious paraphernalia signals the approach to the multi-coloured nine-terraced tower. An early morning visit lets one see the 40-year-old temple elephant Mangalamba being bathed in a compound to the right. Past the flag-staff and the silver mounts, in the main sanctum, is the original mud *linga* made by Lord Shiva (*see sidebar opposite*). No *abhishekams* or liquid oblations are performed; instead the *linga* is coated with *punugu* (dark, perfumed secretion of the civet cat!).

In the northern circumambulatory path to the west is the resting chamber of the Lord and his consort Mangal Ambigai. To the east stands the principal deity Sri Kiratamurti holding a bow and arrow flanked by Somaskanda to his left, and Nataraja on the right. The temple also has a sub-shrine for Adi Vinayaka. The six-headed idol of Lord Subrahmanya nearby is unique. He has six hands instead of 12, each holding a different weapon.

Don't miss the Navarathri Mandapam, carved from a single block of stone, displaying 27 stars and 12 zodiac signs.

Sri Nageswara Temple

Diagonally opposite Sarangapani Temple, south of NH-45C, accessible from S. Madhappa Street. Near Old Bus Stand, Kumbakonam 612001. Open daily 6.30am–12noon, 4–9pm. P. Guided Tours: local guides available. 0435 2430386.

Perhaps one of the finest early Chola temples, construction of the shrine began in AD 886 and was completed under Parantaka I (907-40), making Nageswara the oldest temple in Kumbakonam. According to legend, when the serpent Adisesha was unable to bear the weight of the world on his hood, he performed a penance here and was blessed with strength by Shiva and Parvati. The temple well he bathed in was called Naga Theertham and the shrine was named Nageswara. Pause under the main gateway for a moment to see old paintings of Nataraja on the ceiling. In an inner courtyard stands the Nataraja shrine. Bearing 12 zodiac signs, four mammoth elephants, two rearing horses and wheels with tiny figures for spokes, the grand *mandapam* gives the appearance of a giant chariot and is believed to have descended from the heavens. Climb up the steps to see the stunning bronze images of Nataraja in the throes of his Tandava dance and Sivakami keeping *tala* (beat).

Equally noteworthy is the outer wall of the sanctum, with exquisite statues of Brahma and Ardhanariswara and slender figures in niches depicting the temple's wealthy patrons. In a divine event, every year on the 11th, 12th and 13th days of Chithrai *(Apr/May)*, the sun's rays fall on the *lingam* through an opening in the eastern tower.

Sri Sarangapani Temple★

East of Pottramarai Tank. NH-45C, Kumbakonam 612001. Open daily 6am–12noon, 4–8pm. P. *0435 2430349. www.srisarangapanitemple.org.*

After the temples in Tirupathi and Srirangam, the Sarangapani Temple ranks third in the list of 108 divya desams or sacred sights dedicated to Lord Vishnu. Once when Sage Shaunaka was performing a sacrifice, he asked Sage Bhrigu which God was the greatest. After visiting the holy trinity, Bhrigu replied that Lord Vishnu was the greatest as he didn't react even after being kicked on the chest, though his consort Goddess Lakshmi was upset and stormed off. To atone for his misdemeanour, Bhrigu was reborn as Sage Hema and while performing a penance at Kumbakonam, Goddess Lakshmi appeared as a young girl on a thousand-petalled lotus. She prayed to be reunited with Lord Vishnu after she had abandoned him earlier. Bhrigu adopted the girl, named her Kamalavalli and eventually gave her hand in marriage to Lord Vishnu, who arrived in a chariot as *Saranga-pani* (bearer of the bow, Saranga). The legend is mirrored across the temple. The main shrine, which is shaped like a chariot drawn by horses and elephants, is believed to have descended from heaven. The lake where the sage found the divine lotus became Pottramarai Tank. And since the goddess came here before the Lord, she is worshipped first. The temple has two gateways, one to the north (Uttarayana) open from 14 January to 15 July and the other to the south (Dakshinayana) open from 15 July to 14 January.

The towering 46m/150ft Rajagopuram to the east, rich with manifestations of Lord Vishnu and disrobed *gopis*, was raised by Lakshmi Narayana Swami, an ardent devotee who has a separate shrine.

Since he died a bachelor during Deepavali, it is said that the Lord himself performed his funeral rites. Even now, on every Deepavali, the temple priests perform *shraddha* for him on behalf of the Lord.

Sri Chakrapani Temple

2km north-west of the railway station, on the bus route to Swamimalai from the Town Bus Stand. From Sarangapani Temple continue north on Bazaar Street. Kumbakonam 612001, Thanjavur District. Open daily 6.15am –12.30pm, 4.30–9.15pm. P.

Town of the Celestial Pot

Before the advent of the present era of Kaliyuga, Brahma prayed to Lord Shiva to save the world from destruction in anticipation of the Great Deluge. Lord Shiva instructed Brahma to worship the *kumbha* (pot) containing *amritha* (nectar) and the seeds of creation. At the time of the deluge, the pot was placed atop *Maha Meru* (Himalayas) and the floodwaters carried it south. Lord Shiva appeared as a *kirata* (hunter) and shot an arrow at the pot. The spilt *amritha* from the broken pot formed the sacred Mahamagam Tank while some collected in the Pottramarai Tank. Lord Shiva mixed the *amritha* with the pieces of the broken pot, fashioned it into a *lingam* and merged into it. Hence, he is worshipped as Kirata Murti, Amrudeswara or Adi Kumbeswara and the place was called **Kumbakonam★★** or the Town of the Celestial Pot.

The seeds of creation were dispersed. The place where the *bilva* leaf from the pot came to rest became a *bilva-vanam* at the present-day Nageswarar Temple. The site where the sacred thread fell became Gautameswarar or Yagnopaveeteswarar. The area where the coconut from the pot came to rest was Abimugeswarar. The string securing the pot formed the *linga* at Someswarar while the place where Shiva shot the arrow *(baanam)* became Banapureeswarar. The legend explains the many temples in and around Kumbakonam.

The Sacred Mahamaham Tank (Mahamagam Kulam)

Holier than the holiest rivers, the Mahamaham Tank is where the nectar from the celestial *kumbha* fell. Spread over 2.5ha/6.2 acres in the heart of town near the Abimukeshwar Temple and surrounded by 16 small *mandapams*, the tank is an irregular rectangle though the devout believe it's shaped like a pot. Every 12 years in the Tamil month of Masi *(Feb–Mar)*, when the sun is in Aquarius *(kumbha)*, Jupiter transits Leo and moon is in conjunction with the constellation Maham, the **Mahamaham festival** is held. Its waters are so sacred that the nine river goddesses Ganga, Yamuna, Saraswati, Sarayu, Sindhu, Narmada, Godavari, Krishna and Kaveri choose precisely this auspicious occasion to converge for a holy bath and cleanse themselves of the sins accumulated from devotees who bathed in their waters. Pilgrims turn out in lakhs during the festival. The last time this spectacle was organised was 6 Mar 2004 so the year to watch out for is 2016. The tank attracts its share of pilgrims all year round, who bathe, dip their feet or offer prayers. A shrine to the nine rivers, the Nava Kannika Temple, is located on the tank's eastern side.

0435 2403284. www.srichakrapanitemple.org.
After Lord Vishnu killed the demon Jalandhara, his divine discus Sri Chakra lodged itself on the banks of the Kaveri and Lord Brahma consecrated it. Jealous of its dazzling luminosity, Surya the sun god increased his brightness, leading to catastrophic results. When the discus withdrew its brightness, the sun realised his folly and begged forgiveness. The merciful Lord Vishnu appeared from the Sri Chakra and ordained that the place would henceforth be called Bhaskar Kshetra, after the sun. In gratitude, Surya built a temple in honour of Sri Chakrapani Swami, God of the Discus. Since the sun is the head of all planets, offering prayers to the eight-armed deity of Chakrapani is believed to remove malefic effects of the *navagrahas*. A bronze image of Thanjavur King Serfoji II graces the shrine, as he was cured of an illness here. Don't miss the exquisite pillars, the Amirtha Pushkarani tank to the north, and a *Pancha mukha* (five-faced) Hanuman in the outer *prakaram*.

AROUND KUMBAKONAM

Airavatesvara Temple★★

4km west of Kumbakonam, a short deviation south of NH-45C before it meets the Chennai Bypass Road. Darasuram, Thanjavur District 612702. Open daily 6.30am–8.30pm. Entry free. P. Guided Tours: Superintending Archaeologist, ASI, Chennai 9. (Guide Dorai 9944312150). 044 25670396, 25670397. http://asi.nic.in/asi_monu_whs_cholabt.asp.
Though much smaller than the other UNESCO World Heritage Sites of **Thanjavur** (*see p243*) and **Gangaikondacholapuram** (*see p242*) built earlier, the Darasuram Temple is an architectural gem. Conceived by Chola king Rajaraja II (1143-73), the superstructure with stucco images and vegetable dye paintings was added later by the Nayaks in 17C. The Rajagambhiran Mandapam in front is built like a chariot with wheels drawn by horses and elephants. A small image of Lord Buddha has been carved in a panel under a rearing horse. Lining the steps like a railing is the sculpture of a lion devouring an elephant, which tourist guides interpret as Hinduism overpowering Buddhism! Each of the 108 pillars in the *mandapam* are different and depict Shiva and Parvati's marriage, Parvati in various Bharatanatyam poses and Lord Murugan's marriage to Valli. The black stone sculpture of Annapurna is an exquisite specimen, with the skill of the Chola sculptor evident in the details of the nails, the smile and fine ornaments. The small shrine of Daivanayaki Amman is guarded by female *dwarapalikas*. The exterior walls are rich with sculpture – a Trimurti of Ardhanarishwar, Vishnu and Brahma, a portly Kubera, *siddha gurus* (eminent

sages), the fierce Kala Bhairava and Veerabhadra, a three-eyed Saraswati in lotus position and a stunning Lingodbhavamurti on the western wall. Some empty recesses belong to sculptures that were taken to Thanjavur 30 years ago. The architecture is so rich it's easy to miss the subtle details. A sculpture of the sun god indicates east and west; on the eastern side the lotus is blooming, on the west, it is closed. Wall friezes depict interesting scenes like a four-in-one acrobat, jugglers, a woman in labour and a monkey pestering a lady, besides episodes from the *Periya Purana*.

Don't miss the five different designs of the trellis screens in the Alankara Mandapam in the north-east corner. It's hard to imagine the temple at the height of its glory, when lotus blooms decorated the base and *diyas* (lamps) lit up its exterior. The adjoining shrine of **Periya Nayaki Amman** and the weaving village of **Darasuram** are worth a look.

Airavata and the *Linga* at Darasuram

When Sage Durvasa gifted a celestial garland to Lord Indra who was passing by, the god placed the wreath on the head of his royal mount, the white elephant Airavata. Irked by the bees attracted by its heady aroma, Airavata trampled upon the garland, thus incurring the sage's curse that he would lose his pristine white colour. It was only after Airavata prayed to Lord Shiva at this site that he regained his former glory and the *lingam* worshipped by him was known as **Airavateswara**. Lord Yama too is believed to have prayed here to rid himself of an affliction and the tank is called **Yama Theertham**. Yama's image adorns a *mandapam* in the south-west corner of the temple.

Swamimalai Murugan

8km west of Kumbakonam via SH-22, near the bus stand. Off SH-22, Bazaar Street, Swamimalai 612302. Open daily 6am–1pm, 4.30–9pm. P. 0435 254421. http://murugan.org/temples/swamimalai.htm.

Built like a citadel, Swamimalai is fourth among the *aru padai veedu* or six sacred shrines dedicated to Lord Murugan (*see p13*). It was here that Murugan took on the role of a *swami* (teacher) to expound the meaning of the *pranava mantra* to his own father, Lord Shiva (*see sidebar, above*). As the shrine of the six-headed god, the number six is a recurrent theme. The temple is built on an artificial 60ft high hillock reachable by 60 steps that supposedly represent the average Hindu lifespan of 60 years leading to the Lord. The upper temple of

Lingodbhava-murti, Airavatesvara Temple

Swamimalai, where a son taught his father

Once Sage Bhrigu performed a severe penance where a sacred fire emanated from his head and rose up to the heavens. The frightened *devas* (gods) prayed to Lord Shiva, who put out the fire by covering the saint's head with his hands. Since the sage had a boon that anybody disturbing his mediation would forget all his knowledge, Lord Shiva suffered a similar fate. Later, when Lord Brahma visited Mount Kailasa, the playful child Lord Murugan asked him the meaning of *Om*, the *pranava mantra*. When Brahma admitted his ignorance, Murugan imprisoned him and all creation came to a standstill. The gods begged Lord Shiva to get Brahma released but Murugan justified his punishment. Bound by his curse, Lord Shiva too had no answer and Murugan expounded the lesson to his father who played student. Since Lord Shiva accepted Murugan as his *swami* (teacher) on this *malai* (hill), the place was called Swamimalai and the deity Swaminathan.

Lord Murugan, called *mel koil*, has a 6ft-high statue of Swaminatha holding the *dandayutham* (staff) while the *kizh koil*, or lower temple, is dedicated to Lord Sundareswarar and goddess Meenakshi.

Nachiyar Koil

Exit Kumbakonam by Needamangalam Main Road and drive south onto SH-65, turn left at Sakkottai onto Kodavasal–Thiruvarur road to reach the temple (a total of 10km from the town). SH-65, Nachiyar Koil, Thirunaraiyur, Kumbakonam Taluk. Open daily 7.30am–12.30pm, 4.30–9pm. Entry free. P. *0435 2467167, 2466459. http://kalkarudabhagavan.com.*

One of the 108 divya desams or sacred sites of Lord Vishnu, it is however his consort, Goddess Lakshmi, who enjoys right of way. Found by Rishi Chyavana's son Sage Medhavi under a *vanjula* (ashoka) tree, the goddess in her earthly manifestation was called Vanjulavalli. Lord Vishnu traced her with the help of Garuda and married her as a commoner, but not before the sage extracted a promise that his daughter would get due prominence. The Nachiyar (Goddess) Temple, dedicated to Lakshmi, was built at the site where she married Lord Vishnu and their idols depict them in wedding posture. Customary offerings are first made to the goddess and then the Lord. The Lord's posture, bent in deference towards Nachiyar, reinforces the fascinating tale.

Besides the serene image of Garuda, Lord Vishnu's idol is noteworthy, surrounded by Sankarshana, Pradyumna, Anirudha, Purushottama and Vasudeva, collectively called Pancha Vyuha, who have temple tanks dedicated to them.

Kal Garuda Sevai

During temple festivals a mysterious thing happens during the *purapaadu* or procession. As four people carry the stone image of Kal Garudan out of the sanctum, its weight steadily increases and the number keeps doubling as the procession goes along. So, eight, 16, 32 and finally 64 devotees are required to lift Garuda! The divine occurrence happens so that the *utsava murti of* Nachiyar remains in front at all times and is not overtaken by the swift Garuda. On the return journey, he starts getting proportionately lighter, as finally four devotees can carry him back to his shrine.

Gangaikondacholapuram Temple★★★

Head 33km north of Kumbakonam by NH-45C on the Chennai route via Thirupannadal to Jayankondam, then turn left onto NH-227 for the 2km drive to the temple. NH-227, Jayankondam taluk, Ariyalur District 621802. Open daily 6.30am–8.30pm. Entry free.

P. *Guided Tours: Superintending Archaeologist, ASI, Chennai 9. 044 25670396, 25670397. http://asi.nic.in/asi_monu_whs_cholabt.asp.*

After his conquest over northern territories, Rajendra I (1012-44), the illustrious son and successor of the great Chola king Rajaraja I (985-1014) adopted the title of Gangaikonda or 'One who conquered the Ganga'. To commemorate his victory, he built a new capital city for the Chola Empire at a strategic location 72km north-east of Thanjavur and named it Gangaikondacholapuram. For nearly 250 years from AD 1025, it remained the Chola capital and most of Rajendra's successors were crowned here. The sacred Ganga water brought back by the king was poured into a well for the worship of the *linga* housed in the city's central showpiece, the new Brihadisvara Temple. The imperial crest of the Cholas was shaped into a lion figure of plaster brickwork over the well, called **Simha Kinaru**.

Though the complex and the 55m/182ft *vimanam* are smaller than the temple at Thanjavur (*see right*), this Brihadisvara Temple is often referred to as a refined mirror image of the original. A small shrine of Shiva's loyal guard Chandikesvarar is located near the steps to the north and a shrine of Durga as Mahishasuramardini in the north-east. Shiva's mount Nandi guards the eastern entrance. Sculptures line the temple's wall and niches all around, notably Dakshinamurthi *(south)*, Vishnu-anugrahmurthi *(west wall)* and Kalanthakamurthi *(north)* but the most exquisite specimens lie tucked away in niches by the side of the northern entrance steps to the sanctum, those of Sarasvati and Chandesanugrahamurti.

The site suffered greatly during English rule as in 1896 the surrounding fort-like wall was pulled down and the granite blocks reused to construct the Lower Anicut Dam over the Kollidam River. A British officer even ordered the demolition of the temple to harvest the stones as building material, but local protest and outrage ensured the temple was preserved. A small **museum** housing Chola artefacts excavated from the site is a 2min walk from the temple.

THANJAVUR★★★

Brihadisvara Temple★★★

Located by the Grand Anicut Canal in the south-west part of the old city, it is accessible from Hospital Road. Park opposite the eastern entrance on Vallam Road. Vallam Road, Chinna Kottai, Thanjavur 613004. Open daily 6.30am–8.30pm. Amman Temple closed 12.30–4pm. Entry free. P. Guided Tours: local guides charge Rs.250–300 for a 2hr tour (try K.T. Raja on 9442714563). 04362

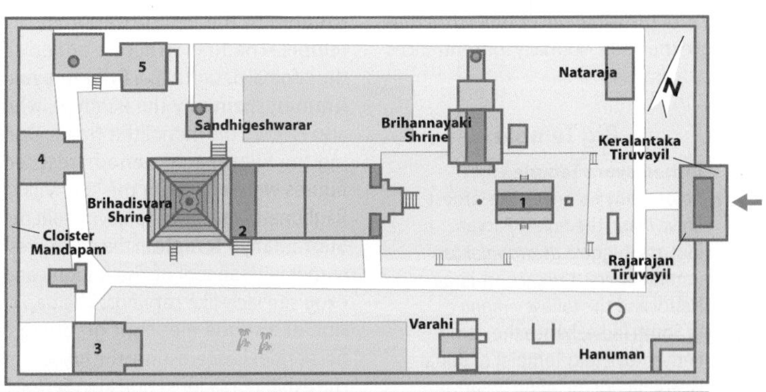

BRIHADISVARA TEMPLE

1. Nandi Mandapam
2. Dakshinamoorthy
3. Ganesha Shrine
4. Karuvurar Shrine
5. Murugan Shrine

274476. www.thanjavurpalace devasthanam.com.

The Brihadisvara Temple at Thanjavur is a landmark in many ways. Built on a monumental scale, the likes of which had never been seen, the grand temple was a symbol of Chola power (*See History p63*) and marked the rise of Thanjavur as a bastion of Tamil culture. Commissioned by emperor Rajaraja I (985-1012) in 1004 and the most ambitious building project of the Cholas, it took just six years to complete. The king inaugurated it in his 25th year of reign and named it after himself as Rajarajesvara Peruvudaiyar. Built out of 1,30,000 tonnes of granite, unavailable in the delta region of the Kaveri, the stones were carted all the way from **Pudukottai** and **Trichy**★★★, 75km away. Black granite for the 4m/13ft-tall *maha linga* was sourced from the Narmada Hills while a river was channelled to make a moat around the outer walls of the fort-like complex.

Visit

Located within a spacious inner *prakara* running 240m/787ft from east to west and 120m/394ft from north to south, the temple is built as per 27 *agamas* of *shilpa shastra*, or traditional rules of architecture. The Chola stamp is unmistakable. Unlike other shrines, the entrance *gopuram* is a squat structure much smaller than the inside spires, reserving all the glory for the *vimanam* or superstructure above the gods. Normally four entrances

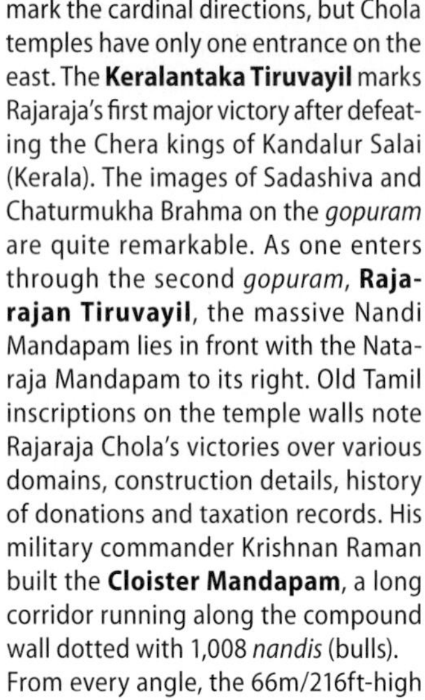

mark the cardinal directions, but Chola temples have only one entrance on the east. The **Keralantaka Tiruvayil** marks Rajaraja's first major victory after defeating the Chera kings of Kandalur Salai (Kerala). The images of Sadashiva and Chaturmukha Brahma on the *gopuram* are quite remarkable. As one enters through the second *gopuram*, **Rajarajan Tiruvayil**, the massive Nandi Mandapam lies in front with the Nataraja Mandapam to its right. Old Tamil inscriptions on the temple walls note Rajaraja Chola's victories over various domains, construction details, history of donations and taxation records. His military commander Krishnan Raman built the **Cloister Mandapam**, a long corridor running along the compound wall dotted with 1,008 *nandis* (bulls).

From every angle, the 66m/216ft-high *vimana* with 13 receding tiers towers majestically like Mount Mahameru, Lord Shiva's abode. Its crowning glory, an 81-tonne *shikhara* (cupola), was fixed in place by pushing it up an incline that started 6km away! The ornate temple spire is hollow from the inside and creates a *sookshm* (subtle) *lingam* that represents the formless form of Adavallan (Nataraja), the tutelary deity of the Cholas. The cavernous sanctum sanctorum also has stunning Chola fresco paintings (*a torch is required to see them).*

Despite the decline of the Cholas by 1279, each succeeding dynasty contributed to the beautification of the temple. The first structure added to the original design was a **Brihannayaki Amman shrine** by the Pandyas, who also erected the monolithic Nandi. During the Vijayanagar period, frescoed figures were added. In the 16C, Vijaya Raghunath Nayak of Thanjavur built the **Subramanya Temple** in the north-west corner with an idol of Shanmugha and exquisite lace-like carvings. The depiction of a rogue elephant grabbing a horse rider is interesting; the horse stirrup exhibits a sailor's knot! King Serfoji II added the **Ganesha Temple** in the 18C and the Marathas embellished the Amman shrine with the Devi Mahatmya story, the Subramanya Temple with regal

Big Temple

Brihadisvara Temple★★★ holds many records – the largest Shiva *linga*, the tallest Parvati idol, the biggest *dwarapalakas* (doorkeepers), the second-largest Nandi and the tallest *vimana* in South India, hence the name Periya Kovil (Big Temple) or Brihat-Isvara (*brihat* meaning great). It even boasts the largest temple elephant who greets visitors at the arched gate!

Pilgrims climbing the steps of the Rock Fort Temple

© travelib india/Alamy

portraits and the pillared corridors with paintings from Shiva Purana and miracles from *Tiruvilaiyadal*. It is uncanny to see wall-to-wall Marathi inscriptions in the heart of Tamil Nadu. The history of the ruling Bhonsle dynasty inscribed on the temple's south-western wall is believed to be the lengthiest inscription in the world. But the bigger spectacle is the fortnightly *abhisheka* for Nandi with 1,500 litres of milk to the sounds of Panchakshara mantras.

TRICHY★★★

Rock Fort Temple★

Located east of the Teppakulam, the entrance is from the Manikka Vinayakar Temple on NSB Road in Chinna Bazaar. Off NSB Road, Trichy 620002. Open daily 6am–8pm. Rs.3 entry to Ucchimalai (camera Rs.20, video Rs.100). P. 0431 2704621. www.thiruchyrockfort.org.

The *malaikottai* or hill fort of the Cholas served as a military outpost of the Vijayanagar kings and the Madurai Nayaks but it was during the Carnatic wars in the mid-18C that the British gave it the name Rock Fort and anglicised the city's name from Thiruchirapalli to Trichnopoly or Trichy. However, the 83m/272ft-high rocky outcrop towering above the flat tracts has a much older history. The hill is hailed as Dakshina Kailasam, as it is said to be one of the three fragments that flew off the Himalayas in a fierce tussle between Vayu the wind god and Lord Vishnu's serpent Adisesha. Geologically the rock is said to be one of the oldest in the world and remained untouched for over 3.5 billion years until the Pallavas became the first to put chisel to rock. Mahendra Varman (AD 580-600) carved the beautiful rock-cut cave temple of Lallitanpura Pallaveswara Griham and added a Shiva temple, the Cholas built

Rock Fort, Lord Ganesha's Hideaway

After killing Ravana and retrieving Sita from Lanka, Lord Rama gifted Vibhishana an idol of Lord Ranganatha, a form of Vishnu, cautioning him that it would take root wherever it was placed. On his way back to Lanka, Vibhishana passed through **Trichy★★★** and wished to take a holy dip and perform his daily rituals in the Kaveri River. Lord Ganesha appeared in the guise of a young cowherd and offered to hold the idol. But the moment Vibhishana went into the water, Vinayaka planted the idol on the sandy banks of the Kaveri. An angry Vibhishana chased the boy up a hill (Rock Fort) to punish him but the boy revealed his divine form and Vibhishana apologised and left empty-handed. **Ucchi Pillayar Temple** or 'Lord Vinayaga on the hilltop' was created, and the place where the idol took root became the **Sri Ranganatha Swamy Temple** at **Srirangam★**.

Thiruvanaikkaval: The Spider and the Elephant

Two Shiva *ganas* (attendants), Malyavan and Pushpadanta, were at loggerheads about who was more devoted to Lord Shiva. They cursed each other to become an elephant and a spider and came to Jambukeshwara to continue their worship on Earth. Every morning, the elephant poured holy water from the Kaveri as a libation over the *lingam* under the jambu tree. The little spider diligently spun a web over the *lingam* to shade it from falling leaves and harsh sunlight. Though the elephant's morning rituals would destroy the spider's web, it would painstakingly rebuild it everyday. One day, the spider got angry and crawled into the elephant's trunk and bit it to death, killing itself in the bargain. Moved by their devotion, Lord Shiva relieved them of their curse. The temple was called Thiru Aanai Koil after the sacred elephant and a sculpture in the shrine portrays the legend. It is believed that the spider was reborn as **Ko Chen Kannan**, the red-eyed Chola king who built 70 temples on either side of the Kaveri, including the one at Thiruvanaikkaval. In cognisance of his old enmity in his previous life, all temples built by him were *yanai yera koils*, or temples where elephants cannot enter. The gates were so tiny, even baby elephants cannot squeeze through while the *mada koils,* or storeyed temples, had the sanctum on the upper floor, ensuring that they couldn't be viewed from afar by the tallest elephant!

the hill fort and the Nayaks of Madurai built the Ganesha shrines.

Visit

The temple is built at three levels – the **Manikka Vinayakar** temple at the foothill, the **Thayumanaswamy Shiva** temple in the middle and the **Ucchi Pillayar** temple (*see sidebar p245*) on the summit. The two-storeyed Shiva temple is the biggest shrine, housing a massive stone *linga* and a separate sanctum for Parvati. According to a legend, Lord Shiva took the form of a mother to help a woman in labour and is thus worshipped as Matrubhuteswarar or Thayum-Anna-Swamy (The Lord who acted like a Mother). The paintings on the ceiling and the granite chain with nine loops of the Chittira Mandapam are worth a look. Steps tunnelled through the hillock and carved on the steep rock face lead to the small Ganesha temple on top, which offers a panoramic view of Trichy, **Srirangam**★ and the rivers Kaveri and Kollidam.

Sri Jambukeshwara Temple★

Located 3km north of Rock Fort en route to Srirangam, turn right from the Trichy–Chennai Trunk Road onto Sannathi Street, opp. Rama Theertham. Thiruvanaikkaval, Trichy 620005. Open daily 6am–1pm, 4–9.30pm. Entry free (camera Rs.30, video Rs.200). P. 0431 2230257. www.thiruvanaikavaltemple.org.

One of the five *pancha sthalas*, this is where Lord Shiva is worshipped as the element, water. The story goes that Parvati once mocked Lord Shiva's penance and was sent to Earth to expiate. As instructed, she came to the mystical *venn naaval* tree sprouting from Sage Jambu's head and worshipped Shiva by fashioning a *lingam* out of the holy waters of the Kaveri. Lord Shiva appeared before her, imparted *Shiva gnana* (Divine knowledge) and took abode under the white jamun tree. The place was called Jambukeshwaram and the *appu* (water) *lingam*, enshrined under the tree, still oozes water. Parvati took lessons from Shiva as a student facing east, so the temple idols are similarly installed and she is hailed as Akhilandeswari or the goddess who gained knowledge of the entire cosmos. Since Lord Shiva acted as her guru, no *thiru kalyanam* (marriage) is conducted for the deities. The noon *puja* is not to be missed when the priest dresses up like a woman to worship Lord Jambukeshwara, in a symbolic recrea-

Sri Ranganathaswamy Temple

tion of goddess Akhilandeswari's *puja*. Another peculiarity is the unusually small entrance of the sanctum, measuring only 1.2m/4ft by 0.75m/2.5ft (*see sidebar p248*).

SRIRANGAM★

Sri Ranganathaswamy Temple★★★

5km north of Rock Fort, cross the Kaveri bridge by the Trichy–Chennai Trunk road and turn left on Ammamandapam Road to reach the temple's southern gate. North Uthrai Street, Srirangam, Trichy 620006. Open daily 7am–1pm, 2–6pm. Sanctum is closed for 1hr rituals between 8–9am, 1–2pm, 6–7pm. Entry free (viewpoint Rs.10, camera Rs.50, video Rs.100. Art Museum: Rs.5 (open daily 9am–1pm, 2–6pm). Guided Tours: local guides are available. 0431 2432246. www.srirangam.org. Non-Hindus not allowed into main sanctums.

Located on a sacred islet formed between the Kaveri and Kollidam (Coleroon) rivers, the Srirangam Temple is spread over 156sq km, making it the world's largest temple complex. The foremost of the 108 divya desams, or sacred sights dedicated to Lord Vishnu, the one-of-a-kind temple is enclosed in seven concentric rectangular enclosures. The *saptha prakarams* represent the seven *chakras* or nodal energy centres of the human body at the centre of which dwells the soul – the 6.4m/21ft statue of Ananthashayana or Lord Vishnu reclining on the snake Anantha. Of the seven *prakarams*, four are located inside the temple while three – Uthra Street, Chitra Street and Adayavalanjan Street – are outside, lined with houses and shops. Three entrances mark the north, east and south, dominated by the 72m/236ft-high **Rajagopuram**, the highest temple tower in the world. The massive complex has 21 *gopurams* and 53 *upa-sannathis* (sub-shrines). The fourth *prakaram* is dominated by the white Vellai *gopura* in the east and the Sesharayar Mandapam to the south; its eight monolithic pillars bear the famous sculptures of warriors astride rearing horses. On either side are the Thousand-Pillar Mandapam with 953 surviving pillars and the Ramanujar Mandapam. The **Art Museum** with old ivory tusks and antique specimens of Tanjore art is worth a peek. The Karthikai Gopura in the third enclosure leads to the Garuda Mandapam which houses an exceptional gigantic **statue** of Vishnu's mount that leaves one awestruck. The sacred tank, Chandrapushkarni, is to the east. From southern Aryabhattal in the second enclosure one enters the first enclosure, Rajamahendran Prakaram, through Nazhikettan Gopura. The Tondaiman Mandapam with painted ceiling stands to the north-west and the Arjuna Mandapam and Kili Mandapam in the east.

Historical Sights

The sprawling palace complex found in the old town of Thanjavur is a historical highlight of Central Tamil Nadu. The royal family still reside here in the Huzur Mahadi Palace. Sri S. Babaji Rajah Bhonsle, the 6th descendant of Serfoji II *(see below)*, **is the hereditary trustee of 88 temples and two heritage monuments and the local convener for INTACH. Elsewhere in Thanjavur, in the Manimandapam basement, the Rajaraja Chola Museum** *(2km south-west of town on Trichy Road, open 10am–1pm, 2–5.30pm, Rs.2)*, **houses the relics excavated at Gangaikondacholapuram.**

THANJAVUR★★★

Thanjavur Palace★★

The entrance to the palace complex is from East Main Street, opposite the handicraft shops Kandiya Heritage and Tanjore Collections. East Main Street, Periya Kottai, Thanjavur 613009. P. *Guided Tours: INTACH (04362 235268/231486, secy@tnjpalace.com). 04362 223384.*

Located in the heart of the old city and surrounded by a huge fort wall, the Aranmanai or Thanjavur Palace was built by the Telugu Nayaks and the Marathas who succeeded them (*see History p68*). From 1674 to 1855, it served as the official residence of the ruling Bhonsle family of Thanjavur. It was under Raja Serfoji II (1798-1832) that Thanjavur reached the glorious heights once attained under Rajaraja Chola. Besides promoting arts like painting, music and theatre, the philanthropist king also set up South India's first Devanagari printing press within the palace!

The 4ha/10-acre complex is a maze of interesting sights that keeps one engaged for hours. A narrow approach through an arch leads to the main square, with the bright-coloured façade of **Sarasvathi Mahal Library** in front (*see below*). To its east, approachable by a path, lie the **Maratha Darbar Hall and Royal Museum** (*see below*). In an adjoining enclosure west of the library is the famed **Art Gallery** (*see below*) with the conical spire of the 58m/190ft Arsenal Tower reaching towards the sky. To the right of the enclosure is the **Nayak Darbar Hall** where the famed Chola bronzes are housed. West of it is the music hall Sangeetha Mahal, with the **Government Handicraft Empo-**

Sarasvathi Mahal Library Museum, Thanjavur Palace

rium *(open 10am–6pm; ✆04362 271586, 239293)* located on its first floor. Facing the empty ground is the seven-storeyed **Bell Tower**, reminiscent of the architectural style of the Gingee Nayaks. The tower earlier had more levels, which were destroyed by lightning. The **Sarjah Mahadi** on the edge of the palace complex is another beautiful building with ornate windows. At the eastern gate of the fort at Beerangi Medu, don't miss the massive Rajagopala Beerangi (cannon). The old palace store is used as a **Palace Gallery** where artefacts and handicrafts are on sale *(✆04362 235268; tnjpalace@rediffmail.com)*.

Art Gallery

Open daily 10am–1pm, 3–6pm. Ticket counter closes at 5.45pm, admission to tower closes at 5.30pm. Art Gallery: Rs.20 (foreigner Rs.50, camera Rs.30). Tower Rs. 50 (camera Rs.30, video Rs.100).

The birth of Thanjavur's Art Gallery was by accident. When an archaeologist from Calcutta spotted a neglected idol by the riverside and wished to take it back to Calcutta Museum, locals demanded that it should stay within the district. The idol was brought and placed in the empty corridor of the palace building. The Collector decreed that all such derelict sculptures should be stored here and thus, the Art Gallery came into existence in 1951.

The high domed hall at the entrance called **Pooja Mahal** showcases stone sculptures, notably a Muruga idol from Sirkazhi and 12C sculptures from Darasuram – Gajasamhara Siva and Bhikshatanar. On the western side of the quadrangle is **Rama Chowdham**, the private audience hall of the Nayaks. Built in 1600, its massive pillars are capped with stucco figures and a white statue of Maharaja Serfoji with folded arms greets every visitor. The upper walls are so richly decorated with black and white floral designs, imperial crests, lions and angels, one might miss the real show below – glass cases full of exquisite Chola bronzes. Rishabhavahana Devar or Lord Shiva as a peasant with Parvati, Subramanya holding bow and arrow, several Natarajas and Kalyanasundarar, or Lord Shiva's marriage, are outstanding pieces. North of the courtyard, the hall at the base of Indira Mandir or the conical Arsenal Tower houses additional sculptures, bronzes and a millennium-edition gilded statue of Rajaraja Chola. A stairway leads to the upper floors of the **Arsenal Tower**, which offers a bird's eye view of the palace complex and the city. Also on display is a 28m/92ft-long whale bone that washed ashore in Tranquebar on 26 Feb 1955.

Maratha Darbar Hall and Royal Museum

Open daily 9am–6pm. Rs.2 (camera Rs.30, video Rs.150). ✆04362 273623. Same ticket is valid for Maratha Darbar Hall, Bell Tower and Sarjah Mahadi.

Situated on the eastern side of Sarasvathi Mahal Library is a small compound reachable through a narrow passageway. On the far side of the grassy courtyard with a Nandi and well in the centre is Maharaja Serfoji's Memorial Hall Museum or Royal Museum, a white edifice with sculptures lining an arched corridor. A cursory glance to the left reveals a sloping tiled roof that seems like an annexe. But a step inside dispels all notions of simplicity. The Maratha Darbar Hall, remodelled by Shahaji in 1684, is a grand edifice made up of two *mandapams* – the front sloping roof supported by wooden pillars and a raised *mandapam* to the rear. Massive granite pillars plastered with brick and lime and dramatically painted in vertical stripes of blue, yellow and red support the vaulted roof. Stucco figures occupy niches on top of the pillars while the ceiling and walls are rich with murals. The portrait paintings on the east wall and hunting scenes depicted on the north wall are masterpieces. On a rectangular granite pedestal in the centre stands the *darbar* seat of the Maratha kings of Thanjavur. Inlaid with mirrors and supported by wooden pillars, it served as the royal seat of the king, who gave audience to his assembled subjects.

Sarasvathi Mahal Library Museum
Open Thu–Tue 10am–1pm, 1.30–5.30pm. Closed Wed, 2nd Saturdays, Govt. holidays. Entry free. 04362 234107.

One of the few medieval libraries to have survived the vagaries of time, Sarasvathi Mahal is the oldest in Asia. Conceived as the Royal Palace Library by the Thanjavur Nayaks (1535-1675) and developed by their Marathas successors, it blossomed into a treasure house of knowledge under Serfoji II. Its priceless collection includes nearly 50,000 palm leaf and paper manuscripts in Sanskrit, Tamil, Marathi and Telugu, 5,000 folios of illustrated paper paintings and 1,300 bundles of Maratha Raj records. All 65,000 books in English, French, German and Danish have been signed by the king. To highlight the library's significance, a small fraction is on display at the Sarasvathi Mahal Library Museum. Under the benign gaze of a massive oil painting of the Maharaja astride a horse, one can marvel at Thanjavur paintings on wood, glass and canvas and treatises like *Gajasastra* and *Aswasastra* (studies of elephants and horses).

The small museum brims with interesting exhibits – rare atlases, physiognomy charts of Charles le Brun's comparison of human faces with birds and beasts, portraits of Thanjavur Maratha kings, old prints by Daniel and Frasier, illustrations of Chinese torture, microscopic writing and sketches of the 64 bathing *ghats* in Benares, commissioned during the king's famous pilgrimage to Kasi in 1820-1.

AROUND THANJAVUR

Visit the birthplace of poet-saint Thyagaraja at **Thiruvaiyaru** *(13km north on the SH-27)*. Every year in January, thousands congregate at his memorial for the Thyagaraja Aradhana festival, when the banks of the Kaveri resound once again with the strains of Carnatic music.

National Parks and Wildlife Sanctuaries

The region is not known for its wildlife, yet nature divulges its secrets in the unlikeliest of places. Near Thanjavur, water birds congregate at Kallaperambur Lake west of town, recently notified as a bird sanctuary. Yercaud, which teemed with bears, elephants and big cats until the 19C, is good for birdwatching and even boasts a small Deer Park, while Viralimalai is a haven for peacocks.

VIRALIMALAI

30km south-west of Trichy on NH-45B (the Trichy–Madurai Highway). Off NH-45B, Viralimalai Taluk, Pudukkottai District 621316. Open daily 8am–5pm. Ticket counter closes at 2.30pm. Entry free. P. 0431 2414265 (DFO, Trichy)

The Offering of Cheroots

Legend has it that Karuppamuthu Pillai, minister of a Kumaravadi chief and devotee of Subramanya, was stranded by heavy rains at the Viralimalai Temple. Lord Murugan appeared as a passerby, offered a cigar and led him to the temple. In gratitude, the minister decreed that cheroots would be offered to god at the last puja, a practice that continues to this day.

Viralimalai Wildlife Sanctuary is a protected area, although it does not have park boundaries. A temple dedicated to Lord Murugan was built here in the 9C. Reachable by a flight of 207 steps, it's possible to spot the beautiful peacocks (India's national bird) on the surrounding scrubland during the climb. The highlight of the temple is the six-headed idol of Lord Shanmuganathar. Best time to visit is October to April.

Hill Stations

A discontinuous range of mountains running parallel to the east coast of South India, the Eastern Ghats are not as well-known or explored as the Western Ghats. Dotted by waterfalls, lakes, viewpoints and ancient shrines, the quaint hill-retreats are devoid of the usual tourist trappings of Ooty or Kodaikanal – perhaps adding to their appeal. Criss-crossed by winding roads and perfect for gentle treks, the Ghats stretch from Yelagiri and the Javadi Hills to the north and Sirumalai and Karandamalai near Dindigul to the south. In the middle lie the Pachaimalai Hills in Trichy District, the Kolli Hills in Namakkal District, and Yercaud, the pride of the Shevaroy Hills.

YERCAUD★

Access is through Salem; drive north on Yercaud Road and continue on SH-188 to reach the Salem–Yercaud Ghat Road; it's a 22km climb from the tollgate at the base of Shevaroy Hills. A lesser-used route from the eastern side is via SH-18 (Tirupathur Road); cross Paruthickadu and turn left at Kuppanur onto the Yercaud Ghat Road (closes 6pm). 32km north of Salem in the Shevaroy Hills of the Eastern Ghats.

A good reason why more people don't come to Yercaud is that they must deal with the urban sprawl of **Salem** to get here. But once the busy town slips away, the 20 hairpin bends slowly climb up the Shevaroy Hills, which have been offering respite from the hot plains for centuries (*see sidebar, below*). The highest point is the **Servarayan Temple**, at a height of 1,623m/5,326ft, which gives the hill range its anglicised name, Shevaroy. The tribal cave shrine is dedicated to Servarayan and his consort Kaveriamman, who supposedly got water to this hill tract as part of her dowry.

The lake occupies the heart of town but the forest that surrounded it was cleared for coffee, pepper and orange and the Tamil name *yeri-kaad* was spruced up to Yercaud. From the lake, roads radiate towards Yercaud's various viewpoints.

Past Lake Forest, a Colonial heritage hotel in an old coffee estate, the road leads 4km east to **Pagoda Viewpoint** (often misspelt as Pakoda Point), the best place to catch a sunrise. The viewing tower overlooks a Rama temple and a tribal village in the valley below. It was earlier called Pyramid Point by the British after the stone cairns that dot the area. Stone implements found here indicate the existence of an older culture. While returning, stop by at the **Grange Resort** (*see sidebar and Addresses*) to

A Colonial Getaway

Yercaud★ owes its origin as a hill station to Scottish planter M.D. Cockburn, the District Collector of Salem (1820-9) who introduced coffee here in 1820. It was at the Grange Estate that the first Arabica coffee plantations and fruit orchards took root. Cockburn built a small bungalow called The Grange and undertook the first survey of the Shevaroy Hills in 1827. By 1836, a German planter, G.F. Fisher, purchased the Salem Zamindari to become the first and only European Zamindar in the Presidency. The British took complete control of the Shevaroy Hills in 1842 and a year later Cockburn planted the first coffee estate in the Nilgiris at Kotagiri. During the 1857 Sepoy Mutiny, The Grange was fortified and ramparts built for cannons and an underground cellar was added to store food to last a 6-month siege. The castle-like structure is now part of the private property of Grange Resorts. In 1866 David Arbuthnot, Collector of Salem, granted land for coffee cultivation to English planters. One of the first to settle here was Ms. Henrietta Charlotte Rosario, who invested a fortune from her coffee nurseries in Brazil. The Lake Forest Hotel (*see p256*) is built around her historic estate, the East Lynne Farm Coffee Estate.

Yercaud landscape

© Anurag Mallick, Priya Ganapathy/MICHELIN

explore Yercaud's stunning scenery in quad bikes and ATV rides.

Just south of the lake past Hotel Shevaroys, a 2km hop near Sterling Resorts, is **Lady Seat** or **Suicide Point**. It is an ideal perch for sunsets when the waters of Mettur Dam shimmer in the far distance to the right. On a slightly higher elevation is Gent's Seat with Children's Seat nearby completing the happy family with a view of the lake and Yercaud town. Nearby is the small Ornamental Lake and Montfort School, one of the many schools set up in the hills by the British.

North of the lake past Anna Park, the road branches with the left turn going to **Kiliyur Waterfalls**. The straight road continues 2.5km north to a **Botanical Garden**★ *(open daily 10am–1pm, 2–4pm; Rs.3, (camera Rs.10, video Rs.300)* that houses the third-largest orchidarium in India after Kolkata and Shillong. The Orchid Trail, a 260m/284yd walk around 25,000 sets of plants, can take half an hour or half a day, depending on one's interest. The pitcher plant and *kurinji* flower are prime attractions, though the real surprise lies a short climb up a hill. Perched on some boulders is the unusual **Bell Rock**, which emits a soft tinkle when struck hard by a stone.

Continuing on the main road, 0.5km away on a sharp bend is the **Rajarajeshwari Temple** *(open daily 7am–12noon, 4–7pm, ℘04281 222354)*. A small Ashta Maha Shakti shrine dedicated to eight gods, it has unusual sacred objects like crystal rosaries, mercury *lingams* and *yantras*. The temple trust also runs Srimath Perfumery with herbal therapeutic oils, precious stones, *malas* and spices for sale. A few minutes away, turn right off the main road for the winding ascent to the **Shevaroyan Temple**. Just ahead are Bear's Cave and Norton Bungalow in the middle of a plantation.

AROUND YERCAUD

Bright yellow signboards advertise 'the world's largest *sri chakra*' at **Maha Meru Temple** though the 12km drive is likely to end in disappointment. Located in a landscaped garden in a coffee estate, the modern temple has a cement roof in the shape of a *sri chakra*, and is at best a personal whim with delusions of grandeur. The Loop Road continues to **Kaveri Peak** and returns via small villages back to the lake. And if so much activity seems too much effort for a hill station, just prop your feet up in a planter's chair and relax.

ADDRESSES

STAY

Most pilgrim towns are crammed with budget lodges and hotels of a similar standard, however, it is possible to find some pockets of luxury that make a pleasant change. From riverside villas with pastoral ambience to heritage bungalows in the hills, modern resorts and business hotels, Central Tamil Nadu has quite a few surprises in store. While fancier hotels have great restaurants attached, street-side eateries have more character.

KUMBAKONAM

Mantra Veppathur – *1, Bagavathapuram Main Road Extn, 536/537A Sri Sailapathipuram Village, Veppathur 612103, Kumbakonam. 0435 2462261, 2460141. www.mantraveppathur.com. . 30 rooms.* . Situated in a coconut grove near Suryankovil, Mantra Veppathur is a an eco-friendly resort with a traditional touch. Every visitor is welcomed with a drink of ***panakam*** (jaggery and ginger) or ***nannari*** sherbet and a soothing foot massage. Agraharam-style cottages are decorated with Kanjeevaram silks, Athangudi tiles and Tanjore dolls while veg cuisine is served at Annaprakshana. An Ayurvedic spa, swimming pool, cultural performances and bullock cart rides to old Chola temples make it a holistic experience.

Paradise Resort – *3/1216, Tanjore Main Road, Darasuram, Ammapet, Kumbakonam 612103. 0435 2416469, 3291354, 9943311354. www.paradiseresortindia.com. . 43 rooms.* . Just off the busy main road between Darasuram and Swamimalai is an enchanted world where geese and guinea fowl roam the lawns as the River Arasalar swiftly rustles by. The charms of rustic life in a traditional South Indian resort can be enjoyed in a renovated townhouse, pool-view heritage room or river-view heritage row house. The South Indian restaurant serves great Chettinad food or one can dine in thatched tree huts in the woods. There is a pottery making and bronze crafting centre, as well as an Ayurvedic spa and oxen carts for village rides.

OVM Resorts – *Asoor Bypass, Kumbakonam 612501. 0435 2442196. www.ovmresorts.com. 10 rooms.* . Cut off from the busy town in a quiet suburb to the north, this small resort is the only one in the area to offer lake boating. Twin cottages stand in a coconut grove with a swimming pool, a multi-cuisine restaurant and a play area for children overlooking a picturesque lake. Nature walks are organised.

Hotel Riverside Resort & Spa – *32–33, College Road, Kumbakonam 612002. 0435 2443555/2443666, 9600002474. www.pgphotelriverside.com. . 10 rooms & 4 cottages.* . A resort set in a landscaped garden with independent clusters of rooms and Kumbakonam's only poolside bar. Mayuri multi-cuisine, an exclusive veg restaurant, swimming pool, health club and spa and warm attentive staff make the stay special.

Hotel Le Garden – *Naal Road, Kumbakonam 612001. 0435 2402526. www.hotellegarden.com. 50 rooms.* . The first star hotel in Kumbakonam with a bar, spa, Ayurvedic massage centre, 24hr coffee shop, rooftop restaurant (Spice Garden) and a multi-cuisine restaurant (Le Tanjore). Rooms for Rs.999 available at their budget properties – **Le Garden Inn** on Gandhi Adigal Salai *(0435 2427977)* and **Iyyangar Guest House** on Pachayappa Agraharam Street *(0435 2427677)*.

Hotel Habib Towers – *122, Kamaraj Road, Kumbakonam 612001. 0435 2403181, 9442553400. www.hotelhabibtowers.com. 49 rooms.* . Located opposite the railway station, a decent hotel with 10 categories of rooms and suites to choose from, free Wi-Fi, tour packages and car rentals.

Hotel Rayas – *18, Head Post Office Road, Kumbakonam 612001. 0435 2423170/2001712/2422545/9842923170. www.hotelrayas.com. 54 rooms.* . Located between Nageswara Temple and Mahamaham Tank, Rayas comes with warm interiors in honey and brown and Sathars pure-veg and non-veg restaurants. Cars/drivers are arranged on request.

Hotel Athityaa – *48, (11–12), Thanjavur Road, Kumbakonam 612001. 0435 2403794, 2401795. www.kumbakonamhotelathityaa.com. 23 rooms.* . Good value-for-money hotel opposite Sarangapani Temple with a pure-veg restaurant. Cabs are arranged for sightseeing tours.

Sivamurugan Hotel – *60 Feet Main Road, Kumbakonam 612001. 0435 2424276, 5276, 6276, 7276. www.sivamurugan.in. 30 rooms.* . An economy hotel within walking distance of New Bus Stand, Sivamurugan offers a view of the Kumbeswara, Sarangapani and Nageswara temples from the terrace.

SWAMIMALAI

Indeco Swamimalai – *6/30B, Agraharam, Thimmakudy Village, Baburajapuram Post, Kumbakonam 612302. 0435 2480044/2480385/ 9444410396. www.indecohotels.com. . 28 rooms.* . Spread over 2,2ha/5.5 acres on the site of an old 1896 ***agraharam*** or Brahmin village, Indeco Swamimalai (earlier Sterling Anandham) is a themed heritage resort. Entering a reception decorated with antique fans, guests are welcomed with a foot massage. Besides heritage rooms, an Ayurveda centre, a temple tank-shaped pool and elaborate ***thalis*** served at the Annaiya Adapu restaurant, the resort has its own farm, cowshed, deer park and units for bronze casting and pottery. Every evening the Noor Deepam Mantapam is lit up with 100 lamps and the ***oppoor maiyyam*** or village centre thrums with cultural programmes.

Hotel Namaskar – *67, Thirumanchana Street, Swamimalai 612302. 0435 3208087, 2454087, 93616 37444. www.hotelnamaskar.com. 25 rooms.* . Budget hotel just 10m/30ft from the Swamimalai Murugan Temple.

VG Tower Deluxe Lodge – *2/16, North Street, Swamimalai 612302. 0435 2455229, 2455088, 94431 30257. www.swamimalai.in. 19 rooms.* . Close to the entrance of the Murugan Temple, the hotel runs a popular pure-veg restaurant called Mami Mess (not to be confused with the one in Kumbakonam).

THANJAVUR (TANJORE)

Hotel Parisutham – *55, GA Canal Road, Thanjavur 613001. 04362 231801/231844. www.hotelparisutham.com. . 50 rooms.* . A top-notch hotel with Wi-Fi, large swimming pool in a small garden, massages at Ayurvedic therapy centre and a multi-cuisine restaurant with regular live music and folk performances.

Ideal River View Resort – *Vennar Bank, Pali Agraharam, Thanjavur 613003. 04362 250533/250633. www.idealresort.com. . 20 rooms.* . Cut away from the busy city, the resort is 7km north of town just off NH-45C to Thiruvaiyaru. Clusters of cottage-type rooms with balconies open out to views of the river or the garden where rice, vegetables and fruits are grown organically. Dine at the restaurant, under palm trees or in an open deck by the riverbank while enjoying classical performances. The resort comes with a mini golf course, pool, Ayurvedic massage and money exchange. Bicycles on hire and regular shuttles to Thanjavur are provided.

Hotel Gnanam – *Anna Salai, Market Road, Thanjavur 613001. 04362 278501. www.hotelgnanam.com. 40 rooms.* . Just across the bus stand close to the Big Temple and shopping areas, Gnanam's USP is its excellent location. There's an exclusive vegetarian restaurant, Sahana, while Diana, the bar-cum-multi-cuisine restaurant serves decent kebabs, North Indian fare and chilled beer.

Hotel Oriental Towers – *2889, Srinivasam Pillai Road, Thanjavur 613001. 04362 230724, 231467, 231950. www.hotelorientaltowers.com. 163 rooms.* . A mid-range hotel overlooking a busy noisy street, it has a pool, bar, garden restaurant, supermarket, Internet centre and an attached mall, though rooms are a trifle ill-maintained. Marutham serves veg South Indian fare while Mullai does multi-cuisine.

Hotel Sangam – *Trichy Road, Thanjavur 613007. 04362 239451. www.hotelsangam.com. . 54 rooms & 3 suites.* . Tucked away in a patch of green in the southern part of town, Sangam is an unmissable white edifice on Trichy Road. It's the perfect oasis to come back to after a long day of sightseeing. Warm, attentive staff, a palm-fringed pool with gym and an excellent restaurant, done in regal red and gold, serves Chettinad, Continental and Indian cuisine. In the evenings, watch cultural programmes like ***veena*** recitals and classical and folk dances.

Star Residency – *20/1A, SM Road, Thanjavur 613007. 04362 276333/ 276334. www.starresidencyhotels.com. 65 rooms.* A relatively new hotel, the white five-storey building has a wide choice of rooms and a good multi-cuisine restaurant that serves Continental breakfast and sumptuous buffets.

Pandiyar Residency – *14, Cutchery Road, Thanjavur 613001. 04362 231295, 231604, 93448 90612. www.pandiyar residency.com. 20 rooms.* Small hotel located opposite the Brihadisvara Temple near the flyover, with a bar, curio shop and an air-conditioned multi-cuisine restaurant.

PLA Residency – *2886, Srinivasam Pillai Road, Thanjavur 613001. 04362 278391/9965551175. www.plaresidency. com. 27 rooms.* Small executive business-class hotel with a glitzy façade and Rice Bowl restaurant that serves decent Chinese cuisine.

TRICHY

Hotel Sangam – *Collector's Office Road, Trichy 620001. 0431 2414700/ 4244555. www.hotelsangam.com. 60 rooms.* Part of the Sangam chain, the hotel is in a quieter part of the city. Rooms have been recently refurbished and a new wing added. The restaurant serves multi-cuisine, besides an Egyptian-themed bar, a 24hr coffee shop, pool, gym and money exchange.

SRM Hotel – *Race Course Road, Kajamalai Colony, Edamalaipatti Pudur, Trichy 620023. 0431 2421303. www.srm hotels.com. 79 rooms.* This 2.2ha/5.5 acre hotel (earlier Royal Southern) close to the airport and NH-210 to Chettinad has independent villas and a new tower block with rooms and suites. Besides a good restaurant called Spice of India, bar, gym, pool, business centre and Ayurvedic massages, SRM also offers sightseeing tours and complimentary transfers from the bus stand, railway station or airport.

Breeze Residency – *3/14, Mc Donald's Road, Trichy 620001. 0431 2414414/4045333. www.breezeresidency. com. 123 rooms.* The newly renovated hotel (earlier Jenny's Residency) boasts a good pool, cosy rooms and decent food. There is a 24hr coffee shop serving salads, sandwiches, soups, desserts and cappuccinos and Madras, which dishes out multi-cuisine, besides a poolside snack counter and a 'Wild West' themed bar.

Femina Hotel – *109, Williams Road, Cantonment, Trichy 620001. 0431 2414501. www.feminahotels.in. 200 rooms.* Pretty close to the main bus stand, Femina is an old hotel that has been given a facelift. Hi-speed broadband, pool, fitness centre, men's salon, a restaurant with separate veg and non-veg kitchens and an arcade nearby with shopping and dining options.

Grand Gardenia – *22–25, Mannarpuram Junction, Trichy 620020. 0431 4045000/9585644000. www.grandgardenia.com. 38 rooms.* Located just south of Trichy railway station, the hotel's unassuming frontage belies its inviting interiors. Spacious rooms have wooden flooring and Wi-Fi, with two good restaurants to choose from – Kannappa for Chettinad cuisine and the rooftop Golden Palm.

Hotel Mayas – *Karur Bypass Road, Chinthamani, Trichy 620002. 0431 2705712. www.hotelmayas.com. 57 rooms.* Located to the north near Chatram Bus Stand, Mayas is a good base to cover Rock Fort and Srirangam. Geethanjali is the vegetarian restaurant and Pushapanjali, the bar.

Hotel Sonas – *75/E, Salai Road, Thillai Nagar, Trichy 620018. 0431 2763656/454229. www.hotelsonas.in. 36 rooms.* This business-class hotel is located quite close to Rock Fort, the shopping areas and food joints. Also boasts its own multi-cuisine restaurant.

Ramyas Hotel – *13-D/2, Williams Road, Trichy 620001. 0431 4000400/ 2414646/2414747. www.ramyas.com.*

110 rooms. ☕ ▤. Very close to the bus stand and a 10min walk from the railway station, Ramyas has two wings. Rooms in the new wing are remarkably better than the shabby old section so ask accordingly. The ground-floor veg restaurant Amirthan serves South Indian while the non-veg Meridian, and Chola Bar, are on the lower level.

⊖–⊖⊖ **Guru Hotel** – *13-A, Royal Road, Cantonment, Trichy 620001. ℘0431 2415881/4200666. www.guruhotel.in. 69 rooms.* ☕ ▤. Located near the bus stand, Guru is a no-frills hotel where the food is better then the rooms – Kurunji is a busy non-AC veg restaurant with an air-conditioned dining hall in the basement, serving *dosas* and South Indian meals on banana leaves.

⊖ **Hotel Shaans** – *19, Tennur High Road, Trichy 620 017. ℘0431 4026161/2742655/9597742311. www.hotelshaans.com. 70 rooms.* ☕ ▤. A value-for-money hotel with renovated rooms, a bar and shopping arcade, though its main highlight is the excellent restaurant, Thaai.

YERCAUD

⊖⊖⊖ **GRT Nature Trails** – *SkyRocca Yercaud, 20th hairpin bend, Salem–Yercaud Main Road, Yercaud 636602. ℘04281 225100/9442700260. www.grthotels.com.* ♿. *41 rooms.* ☕ ▤. Perched on rugged green hills overlooking a valley and coffee plantations, each room at this boutique hotel comes with its own balcony and faces the valley or the pool. The skywalk, activity centre, trekking trips, bicycle rides and adventure zone keep guests busy. Besides a kebab kitchen on the lawns and Baker's Basket for cakes and pastries, it has a great bar and multi-cuisine restaurant. A business centre, Wi-Fi access throughout and three banquet halls with wide terrace lawns also make it a great corporate getaway.

⊖⊖⊖ **The Lake Forest Hotel** – *Near Anna Park, Ondikadai Post, Yercaud 636602. ℘04281 223217/9444001438. www.yercaud.indecohotels.com.* ♿. *60 rooms.* ☕ ▤. Just north of Yercaud Lake, a cobbled path leads to this charming Colonial resort. Once the East Lynne Farm Coffee Estate, the resort is built around Rosar Villa, an 1840s bungalow named after its former Portuguese owner. The front lobby doubles up as a restaurant and museum, adorned with rare memorabilia. Each room is unique; all bear an imperial touch and some offer panoramic views of the Shevaroy Hills. Friendly, attentive staff and excellent food served indoors or in the sun-dappled courtyard.

⊖⊖⊖ **Fairholme Bungalow** – *Tipperary Road, near the Retreat, Yercaud 636601. ℘4281 226767/9442146266. www.stayatyercaud.com. Bungalow with 3 rooms.* Tucked away behind the Montfort School south of the lake, this Colonial bungalow overlooks a garden. Ideal for a group of up to 15, Fairholme has three quaint rooms with red oxide floors and fireplaces, a dining area, private sit-out and complimentary campfire. Food must be ordered from outside. Treks and plantation walks into coffee estates are organised.

⊖⊖⊖ **The Regent Hill Side Resort** – *Hospital Road, Yercaud 636601. ℘94 43700000/9442800000/9443341245. www.enjoyyercaud.com. 4 rooms and 11 cottages.* ☕ ▤. A small, intimate boutique resort-cum-museum set in an 1860 coffee estate with old-world luxury suites named after Colonial bungalows (Constantia, Belmont and Sunny Side). The resort has designer bathrooms, red oxide or broken mosaic floors, quirky signboards leading you to it and an avid host who loves sharing Yercaud's heritage. Home-style food, made on prior demand, is served in the restaurant or on the green lawns.

⊖⊖⊖ **Grand Palace Hotel & Spa** – *Killiyur Falls Road, Yercaud 636602. ℘04281 223481/9865256255. www. grandpalaceyercaud.com. 43 rooms.* ☕. Spread over 3.2ha/8 acres about 2km from the centre of town, this luxury hill resort offers great views of the lake and the mist-covered hills. Attentive staff, a decent restaurant and vehicles arranged on hire make it a great hideaway.

⊖⊖⊖ **Sterling Resorts** – *11, Lady's Seat, Yercaud 636601. ℘044 33573300/ 33553300. www.sterlingresort.co.in. 65 rooms.* ☕ ▤. Built on the edge of a rock perch overlooking a mountain slope and the Salem city below, the resort's location is unbeatable, although it is in need of maintenance. Every room has a decent view and there's a play area for a kids and a restaurant. Monkeys are a menace, so keep doors and windows locked.

Grange Resort – *Cockburn Road, Five Roads, Yercaud 636601. 04281 222180/316055. www.grangeresort.com. 17 cottages.* A boutique plantation resort set in a 40ha/100 acre coffee plantation clothed in pepper and orange, the independent cottages exude an air of tranquillity. Fresh hand-picked vegetables grown in private organic farmlands are served at the restaurant. A boutique shop stocks Gujarati dresses, bags, saris, handicrafts and home-made chocolates but the main attraction is the fleet of ATVs for adventure rides through Yercaud's scenic terrain.

Hotel Shevaroys – *Yercaud Hills, Salem 636601. 04281 222288/222383/ 9944999599. www.shevaroysgroup.com. 77 rooms and 11 cottages.* For years Yercaud's iconic establishment, Shevaroys opened its doors in 1971, though its original charm of wooden floors and quaint cottages has been replaced by a renovated cement structure. With a fitness centre, spa, beauty parlour, Ayurvedic massages and a games centre for kids, it's a good place for families. Besides an ice-cream parlour and a bakery, it has several dining options – Silver Oak multi-cuisine, Red Dragon for Chinese, Malar pure-veg restaurant and a cocktail lounge called Bear's Cave.

EAT

The region's proximity to Chettinad has spawned far more hotels and restaurants serving Chettinad cuisine than in its place of origin. Trichy's bus stand area is a major hub of eateries. Besides typical vegetarian restaurants, Kumbakonam is famous for the roasting technique that produces its degree coffee, and interestingly, the origin of the South Indian *sambar* as an accompaniment to rice preparations can be traced to Thanjavur.

KUMBAKONAM

Hotel Chela – *9, Ayekulam Road, Kumbakonam 612001. 0435 6499060/ 2430336/9944304657. www.hotelchela.com. Open daily 5.30am–9.30pm.* Though the hotel has rooms *(Rs.990–1,045)*, the real surprise is a decent North Indian restaurant in the southern heartland, which serves excellent tandoori dishes.

Mami's Mess – *Off Big Street (Periya Theru), Kumbakonam 612001. Open Mon–Sat.* A small iconic shack serving home-made veg South Indian food. The taste of the affordable, wholesome food makes up for the lack of ambience. ***Idli***, ***dosa***, ***upma***, ***puri***, ***vada***, ***pongal***, tea, coffee and milk for breakfast and full meals for lunch served on a plantain leaf.

Meenakshi Bhavan – *23, Nageswaran North Street, Kumbakonam 612001. 0435 2430749. Open daily.* Serves traditional South Indian staples of *dosas*, *uthappams* and *appams*, besides unusual fare like *paal paniyaram*, *veetu dosa*, *idiappams* (string hoppers) with coconut milk and milk *periyada* (mildly sweet ball of black gram bean flour).

Hotel Venkatramana – *40, Gandhi Park North, Kumbakonam 612001. 0435 2400736/2400836. www.kumbakonamhotelvenkataramana.com. Open daily.* Run on the ground floor of Sri Venkkatramana's Residency, this busy eatery has been serving traditional South Indian food for over 60 years. All dishes are without garlic. Try local specialities like ***rava dosa*** with ***gosthu*** (spiced lentil-eggplant gravy, like *sambar*), ***thirumal vadai***, ***kadappa*** (potato-*moong dal kurma*), ***kothumai*** or cracked wheat ***halwa***.

THANJAVUR (TANJORE)

Sathars Restaurant – *167, Gandhiji Road, Thanjavur 613001. 04362 231041. Open daily 12noon–4pm, 6.30–11pm.* Busy eatery that serves a wide array of Mughlai, tandoori and Chinese cuisine. Their *ceylon parathas* are quite good and they have an AC section upstairs.

Raja's Curry – *Court Road, Thanjavur 613001. Open daily.* A halal restaurant that serves both Indian and

Chinese veg and non-veg dishes. The *thali* is pretty decent and comes for Rs.40.

Thevar's Biryani – *Gandhiji Road, Thanjavur 613001. 04362 270979. . Open daily 11.30am–3.30pm, 6.30–10.30pm.* The best place to grab a *biryani* in Thanjavur, besides a wider choice of non-veg dishes.

Vasantha Bhavan – *Old Bus Stand, Thanjavur 613001. 9944216666. . Open daily 8am–10pm.* Very good traditional vegetarian restaurant with crispy *dosas* and fluffy *idlis* served in the morning till 11am and lunch *thalis* for Rs.35, served on banana leaves from noon.

TRICHY

Kannappa Restaurant – *22–25, Mannarpuram Junction, Trichy 620020. 0431 4045005. . Open daily 11.30am–11.30pm.* Located in Thillai Nagar near Woraiyur, it serves great Chettinad food, including specialities like *kola oorandai* (mutton meatballs), *kada* fry (quail) and *naatukoli* fry (country chicken). Their fish fry and *biriyanis* are excellent.

Sri Lakshmi Nivas – *15, NSB Road, Trichy 620002. 0431 2714242. . Open daily 6.30am–10.30pm.* Located in the main shopping hub near the Rock Fort temple, decent Indian food with an AC hall upstairs.

Sri Saravana Bhavan – *3B, Mega Complex, Rockins Road, Trichy 620001. 0431 2463636. . Open daily 6am–11pm.* Located opposite the Central Bus Stand near Hotel Ramyas, very good *thalis* for lunch and South Indian vegetarian fare at other times.

YERCAUD

Salem Heights – *20th hairpin Bend, Salem–Yercaud Main Road, Yercaud 636602. 04281 225100, 9442700260/2. www.grthotels.com. . Open daily 7am–11pm.* Fourth-floor restaurant at GRT Nature Trails SkyRocca with views of the valley and Salem town. Serves excellent multi-cuisine.

Karuppaiah Chettinad Mess – *Nagaloor Road, Yercaud. . Open daily 8am–10pm.* Local eatery at the main junction near Yercaud Lake serving South Indian snacks, *parathas*, *biryanis* and meals for Rs.35, besides Chettinad specialities like *kadai* fry, mutton *sukka* and other non-veg dishes.

CAFES

Sri Murugan Café – *73, Mutt Street, Kumbakonam 612001. 0435 2403766/ 9487731641. www.kumbakonamhotels.in. Open daily. Prices start at Rs.20.* Located near Kanchi Shankara Mutt, Murugan also has rooms, though it's the food that's the big draw. The pure-veg restaurant serves great meals and there's a separate AC family restaurant.

Sri Saraswathy Café – *4H, Rockins Road, Trichy 620001. 0431 2410022. Open daily 5.30am–10.45pm. Prices start at Rs. 20.* Located opposite the Trichy railway junction, the busy cafe serves South Indian snacks, tea and filter coffee.

LEISURE

ATV Quad India – *Grange Resort, Five Roads, Cockburn Road, Yercaud. 9786022611/9994022611. www.atv quadindia.com. Open daily 10am–6pm. Prices start at Rs.100 (350m) to Rs.1,500 (5km).* A wide range of all-inclusive guided ATV adventures in quad and dirt bikes and dune buggies in a 40ha/100-acre site. Choose from short 100m/110yd laps, 1.5km trails or 6km forest trails as per one's degree of skill. The Moonlight Trail and Bison Trail are for the truly adventurous.

SHOPPING

SHOPPING MALLS

Philomena Shopping Mall – *1, Arulananda Nagar, Trichy Road, Thanjavur 613007.* It has outlets like Appar Books, Spencer's Store, Vasantha Bhavan restaurant and a few sari and garment shops.

MARKETS

Gandhi Market – *East Boulevard Road, Trichy 600010. 9894562424.* The 128-year-old Gandhi market in the heart of the city is one of the biggest and oldest in Tamil Nadu and teems with shops and trucks unloading fresh fruits and vegetables.

SPECIALITY SHOPS AND DESIGNER BOUTIQUES

Heritage Arts Emporium – *5, Ammamandapam Road, Srirangam, Trichy*

620006. *2432299/2432113.* Located just north of the Kaveri River and selling bronzes, wooden carvings, gems, silver tribal jewellery, statues in wood and ***panchaloha***, antique sculptures, cotton embroidery and carpets.

Kandiya Heritage – *97/618, East Main Street, Thanjavur 613001.* *04362 278773/232682.* A double storey arts and crafts store opposite the entrance to the Palace Complex. Handicrafts, statues, ornate wall friezes and garments.

Poompuhar – *West Boulevard Road, near Main Guard Gate, Singarathope, Trichy.* *0431 2704895. Open Mon–Sat 10am–8pm.* Tanjore paintings, art plates, bronzes, statues, dolls and all the handicrafts you want to buy, without the hassle of bargaining. The fixed price Government shop is also located at Kumbakonam *(TSR Big Street, 0435 2425199)* and Thanjavur *(Railway Station Road, 04362 230060).*

Rajan Industries – *107, Main Road, Thimmakudi, Swamimalai 612302.* *0435 2480886. www.rajanbronzearts.com.* Leading manufacturers of bronze and ***panchaloha*** icons, ornamental lamps, Tanjore Paintings and wood carvings.

T. Venkatesaraja Arts & Crafts – *646, Kondirajapalayam, East Main Street, Thanjavur 613001.* *04362 239109.* State and National Award winner selling Thanjavur paintings and traditional arts.

S. Devasenapathy Sthapathy Sons – *19/9, Raja Veethi, Swamimalai 612302.* *0435 2454429. www.sthapathi.com.* National Award-winning bronze casters who have crafted idols for ISKCON Bangalore and Hindu temples across the world.

S. Sundaravadivel & Co. – *10/29, Pettai K.V. West Street, Kumbakonam 612001.* *0435 2420683. www.southindian handicrafts.co.in.* One-stop shop since 1964 for Indian handicrafts, bronze statues, brass lamps, ***panchaloha*** statues and Tanjore paintings.

V. Swaminatha Iyer & Co. – *55, TSR Big Street, Kumbakonam.* *0435 2420209/ 24244840/9442611478.* Started in 1935, specialists in traditional silk saris with ***butta, samudrika*** (conch designs), temple borders to designer saris from Rs.3,000–7,000, besides children's ***pavda*** or set *(Rs.650–5,000)* and silk ***dhotis*** *(Rs.1,750–20,000).*

Sri Meenatchi Vilas Patthira Maligai – *29–30, Potramarai South Street, Kumbakonam 612001.* *0435 2402797.* Popular brass, copper and steel vessel shop that also sells furniture and templeware items like ***panchaloha*** (five-metal) statues, bells, ***kalasam*** and lamps.

Vathina Silk Centre – *15, Old Agraharam, Darasuram.* *9443849791/ 9894282961. www.vathinasilk@gmail.com.* Browse through vivid silks in weaver Kamsan's house with a loom on the first floor and great view of Darasuram Amman Temple from the terrace. If the saris are too pricey, pick up silk scarves *(small Rs.750, large Rs.1,100)* and explore the weaver's lane

BOOKSHOPS

Higginbotham's – *25, Nandhi Koil Street, Teppakulam, Trichy 620002.* *0431 2704418.* Legendary bookshop with fiction, non-fiction and educational books on medicine and engineering, besides CDs and magazines. They also run an outlet at Thanjavur railway station.

New Century Book House – *12, Raja Raja Cholan Shopping Complex, South Rampart, Thanjavur 613001.* *04362 231371.* A popular chain with a good collection of books.

PERFORMING ARTS

Kalai Kaviri College of Fine Arts – *18, Benwells Road, Cantonment, Trichy 620001.* *0431 2460678/2412340. www.kalaikavirifinearts.com.* A dance troupe established in 1978 that performs Indian classical and folk dances with a message of love and peace. The group has performed in India and abroad.

Rasika Ranjana Sabha – *146, West Boulevard Road, Main Guard Gate, Trichy 620002.* *0431 2704736.* Established in 1914, the centre conducts regular music competitions and vocal and instrumental performances.

South Zone Cultural Centre – *Ministry of Tourism and Culture, Dept. of Culture, Medical College Road, Thanjavur 613004.* *04362 241726. www.ezccindia.org.* Dedicated to fine arts, dance, drama, music, theatre and research into dying art forms, the SZCC organises cultural and collaborative programmes.

Western Ghats

Highlights

- Palani, Lord Murugan's hill shrine *p265*
- Wildlife safari at Mudumalai *p267*
- Misty haven of Kodaikanal *p277*
- Nilgiri Mountain Railway to Ooty *p278*

One of the 10 richest biodiversity hotspots in the world, the Western Ghats are a rich mosaic of wildlife parks teeming with endemic species and hill stations dotted by lakes, waterfalls and plantations.
For centuries, the hills were home to tribes like the Todas, Kurumbas, Irulas, Paniyas and Badagas, before the British 'discovered' the invigorating hill stations as an escape from the scorching plains of Madurai and Chennai. The rich aromatic Nilgiri tea was blended in the plantations of Kotagiri and Coonoor, a military sanatorium was established at Wellington and the rules of snooker were formulated in 'Snooty Ooty', which became the summer capital of Madras Presidency.
From intrepid planters, European missionaries, Indian princes, *burra sahibs* **and English ladies, the hills later attracted film crews and families seeking recreation and rest. Be it hikes through pine-scented forests, driving holidays of the hills, golfing at Kodaikanal, Nilgiris and Coimbatore or wildlife adventures at Mudumalai and Top Slip, the Western Ghats are nature at its very best.**

View from Pillar Rock, Kodaikanal

WESTERN GHATS

In Tamil Nadu, the ghats stretch from Nilgiri Biosphere Reserve in the north with **Mudumalai**★, **Ooty**★★, **Coonoor**★★ and **Kotagiri** as the key destinations. Mettupalayam at the foot of the hills is the nearest rail link. South of **Coimbatore**, Pollachi is the closest base for **Anamalai** (Elephant Hills) to cover Top Slip and Parambikulam.

Kodaikanal★★ has two access points from Palani and Theni and is easily reachable from **Madurai**★★★. Note that **Courtallam**★ and the **Kalakad-Mundanthurai Tiger Reserve** lie south of the Palakkad Gap and are accessible from **Tirunelveli** in Southern Tamil Nadu *(see p223–224)*.

- **Population:** The Nilgiris (735,071), Kodaikanal (32,391), Coimbatore District (3,472,578).
- **Info:** Tourist Information Centre, Charing Cross, Ooty 643001. 0423 2443837. www.tamilnadutourism.org.
- **Location:** Western Tamil Nadu, bordering Kerala.
- **Kids:** Black Thunder Theme Park at Mettupalayam, Jolly World and lake in Ooty, Boating and pony rides at Kodai.
- **Timing:** 5 days to 1 week for the Nilgiris, 2 days for Kodai and 1 day for Top Slip.
- **Guided Tours:** TTDC organises 3-day weekend tours of Kodaikanal and Ooty for Rs.2,500/person *(all-inclusive return trip by road from Chennai, with non-AC transport/stay)*.

Mudumalai★

The first wildlife sanctuary to be established in South India, the park was created in 1940 spanning 6,000ha/14,800 acres. The region was so wild that during World War II it served as a training camp from 1943 to 1947 for soldiers off to fight in the jungles of Burma. Gradually enlarged to over five times its original size, the park is part of the Nilgiri Biosphere Reserve and forms an important migratory corridor for elephants. Surrounded by adjoining reserves like Bandipur *(87,400ha/216,000 acres)* in Karnataka and Wayanad *(34,400ha/85,000 acres)* in Kerala, the forests are a passage for nearly 2,000 elephants. The undulating highway chases the Moyar

River through the park as Malabar giant squirrels nimbly run overhead on bamboo thickets. Roadside encounters with elephants and bison are common and nature camps around Masinagudi are great bases for birdwatching.

Exploring the Area – Located on the north-western part of Nilgiris in the north-west corner of the state, Mudumalai lies on the tri-junction of Karnataka, Kerala and Tamil Nadu. The Mysore–Ooty highway running through the park follows the course of the Moyar River, which separates Mudumalai from the adjoining Bandipur Tiger Reserve. Elephant rides into the jungle are booked at the visitors' centre at Theppekadu and feeding and bathing rituals can be observed at the Elephant Training Camp nearby (*see p268)*. While jeep safaris are not allowed inside the park, private drives around the periphery are as rewarding. Most of the wildlife lodges are located around Bokkapuram at Masinagudi, 7km away on the shortcut to **Ooty**★★. *See National Parks and Wildlife Sanctuaries.*

Ooty★★ (Ootacamund)

The ancestral homeland of the Todas, the Nilgiris, or Blue Mountains, received their first European visitor in 1603 when Rev. Jacome Forico documented its tribes. The hills lay forgotten for two centuries until the British acquired them from Tipu Sultan after the Treaty of Srirangapatnam in 1799. Preliminary surveys raved about its 'English climate' and in 1819, John Sullivan, the Governor of Coimbatore, trail-blazed up the hills. A Toda burial site was acquired, the first stone cottage was built and coffee (introduced by M.D. Cockburn at Kotagiri) was replaced by tea, *cinchona* and teak.

Ootacamund's transformation from Toda village to Snooty Ooty was complete. The Colonial stamp is palpable in the lovely estate bungalows turned homestays and hotels, the aromatic whiff of Nilgiri tea and the spectacular **Nilgiri Mountain Railway**★★★ that chugs from Mettupalayam to Ooty, rightfully called the 'Queen of Hill Stations'.

Exploring the Area – The heart of Nilgiris District, Ooty is well connected to several destinations – **Mudumalai National Park**★ via **Kalhatty Falls** and Singur Ghat, **Coonoor**★★ via Ketti and Wellington and **Kotagiri** via **Doddabetta**★ *(2,637m/8,650ft)*, the highest peak in the Nilgiris. The town's main hub is Charing Cross, a busy junction on Commercial Road, which heads south to Big Bazaar and the racecourse. The bus stand and railway station are nearby, and further west is the lake. *See Hill Stations.*

Coimbatore

Coimbatore was once an important stopover on the Roman trail that stretched from Muziris (Kodungallur in Kerala) to Arikamedu (near Pondicherry). Lying in the shadows of the Western Ghats, the region is legendary for the purity of its water, mildness of its climate, nuances of its cuisine and sweetness of its language. The second-largest city in Tamil Nadu and a hub for textiles, automobiles, education and health care, Coimbatore's many industries have earned it the epithet 'Manchester of South India'.

Exploring the Area – While the city itself has not much to offer to a tourist, Kovai (as residents call it) is an ideal base for excursions to the scenic hideaways of **Pollachi**, **Valparai** and **Top Slip** and dams like Siruvani, Aaliyar and Sholayar. The airport is 11km east of the city and there are daily flights from Chennai and other cities. Coimbatore has many bus stands: Gandhipuram has buses going east and north-east to Erode, Tirupur, Salem and Sathyamangalam; Singanallur has buses to Madurai and Trichy; Ukkadam has buses to Palakkad, Palani and Pollachi; Mettupalayam Road Bus Stand has Ooty-bound buses; while long-distance Express buses leave from Thiruvalluvar or SETC Bus Stand.

Kodaikanal★★

Set up as a European sanatorium in 1845 by the American Madura Mission, Kodaikanal's main hub is an artificial lake, created in 1863. Boat clubs, walking paths, churches, parks and a golf course

soon followed and in 1901 an American boarding school for the children of missionaries was started.
The British set up Fort Hamilton, a military outpost at Beri Jam, a marsh 21km from Kodai and built a road to Top Station in 1925. Fearing a possible Japanese invasion of South India in 1942, the British hastily repaved the 81km stretch as an escape route from the hills to the harbour at Cochin. With a maximum elevation of 2,481m/8,140ft, the Kodaikanal–Munnar Road *(old SH-18)* was among the highest motorable roads in India south of the Himalayas until closed to traffic in 1990. The historic 3-day trek requires written permits and is one of 17 scenic walks that showcase the area's natural splendour – thick shola rainforests enveloped in mist, the smell of eucalyptus and pine and the fabled kurinji that flowers every 12 years.
Exploring the Area – Situated on a 2,133m/6,998ft-high plateau in the upper **Palani Hills**★, Kodai is reachable from the north via **Murugan's Temple**★ at Palani or from the south-east via Bathalagundu. The two *ghat* roads meet 12km from Kodai at Perumalmalai (2,440m/8,005ft), the highest peak in the Palani Hills. The road climbs via **Silver Cascade Falls** and **Shembaganur** *(with a Natural History Museum)* to the bus stand in the heart of town.
See Religious and Spiritual Sights, Hill Stations.

GETTING THERE AND AROUND

(Also see Planning Your Trip).

GETTING THERE

For the Nilgiris, Mettupalayam is the nearest railhead connected by the overnight Nilagiri Express *(12671)*, which runs daily from Chennai Central at 9pm and reaches Mettupalayam at 6.15am via Coimbatore, the closest airport *(80km/1hr away)*. Several buses ply from Chennai, Mysore, Bangalore and Coimbatore to Ooty. From Koyambedu bus stand in Chennai, TNSETC has overnight buses and KPN Travels *(044 24796688)* has AC sleeper and non-AC semi-sleeper buses *(13hr, Rs.580–775)* that reach Ooty at 8.30am. Buses take 7–8hrs from Coimbatore and 9hr from Bangalore. Kodaikanal is 165km south-east of Coimbatore Airport, though Madurai is the closest airport *(122km, 3.5hr)*. Kodai Road *(80km, 2.5hr)* is the nearest railhead connected by Nagercoil Kurla Express. By road, Kodai is reachable from Theni or Dindigul *(94km, 3hr)* via Batalagundu or Palani *(64km north)*.

GETTING AROUND

Mettupalayam, at the base of the Nilgiris, is 38km from Coimbatore by NH-67, which continues up the *ghat* road to Coonoor and Ooty *(46km)*. SH-15, a fork to the right, goes to Ooty via Kotagiri *(33km)*. At Thalaikundha, NH-67 forks again – the Ooty–Mysore shortcut via Kalhatty Falls leads to Masinagudi *(6km from Theppakadu)*, where most jungle resorts of Mudumalai are located. NH-67 continues left via Pykara skirting Mukurthi National Park to Gudalur and joins the other road at the Information Centre/Range Office at Theppakadu, before continuing to Bandipur and Gundulpet. The Nilgiri Mountain Railway is a leisurely way to explore the hills. The 7.10am train from Mettupalayam reaches Coonoor at 10.30am and Ooty at 12noon. The return train leaves Ooty at 3pm *(3.5hr)* *(see p278)*.
From Coimbatore, NH-209 heads 44km south to Pollachi and continues 66km south-east to Palani, 65km north of Kodaikanal, a 2hr climb by Palani Ghat Road. The southern access is by Kodai Ghat Road from Batalagundu on NH-45 *(Dindigul–Theni Road)*. The two *ghat* roads meet at Perumalmalai *(12km from Kodai)*. From Pollachi, Top Slip is accessible via Anamalai and Sethumadai and the same highway continues to Parambikulam Wildlife Sanctuary in Kerala.

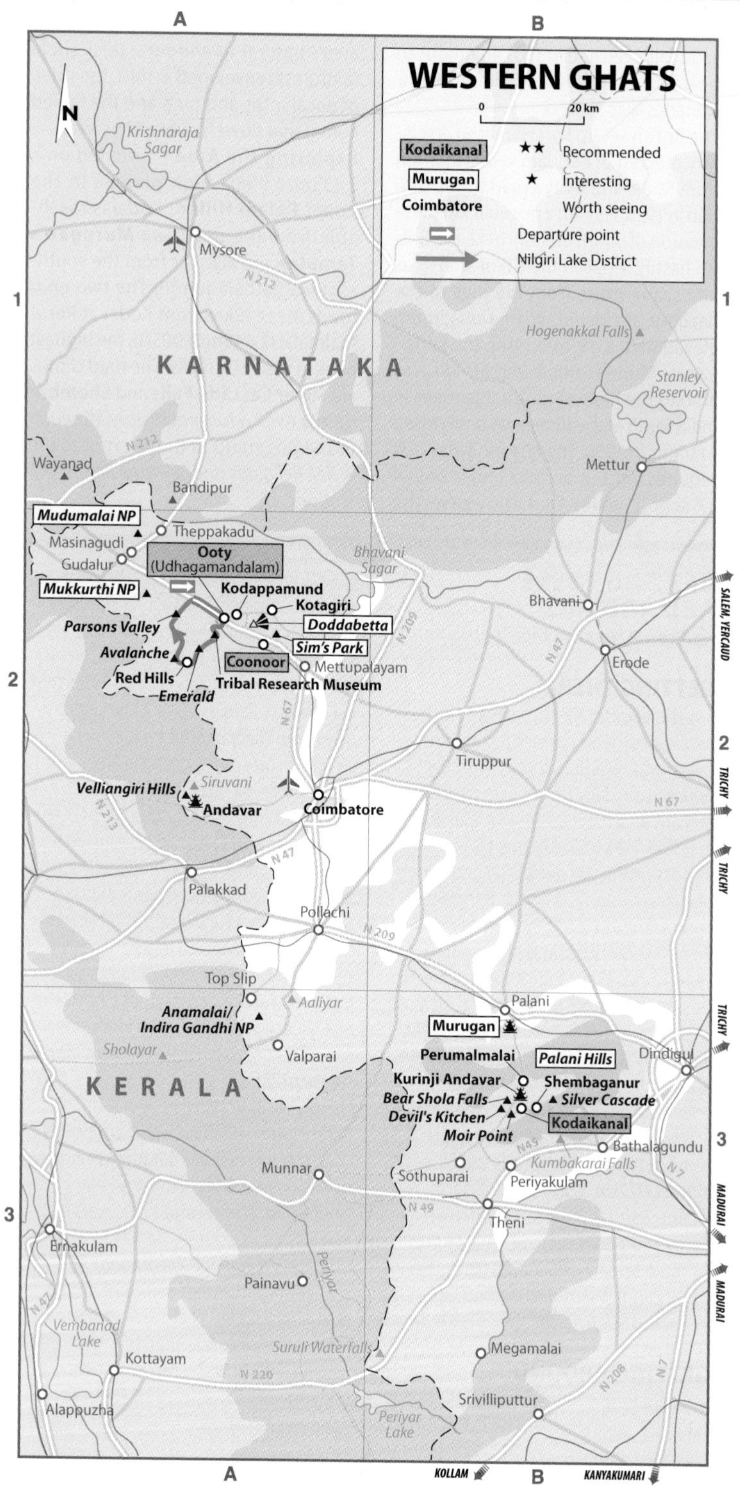

WESTERN GHATS
0
20 km
Kodaikanal
Murugan
Coimbatore
★★ Recommended
★ Interesting
Worth seeing
Departure point
Nilgiri Lake District
A
B
1
2
3
N
Krishnaraja Sagar
Mysore
N 212
Hogenakkal Falls
KARNATAKA
Stanley Reservoir
Mettur
Wayanad
Bandipur
Mudumalai NP
Theppakadu
Masinagudi
Gudalur
Ooty (Udhagamandalam)
Bhavani Sagar
Mukkurthi NP
Kodappamund
Kotagiri
Doddabetta
Parsons Valley
Avalanche
Sim's Park
Coonoor
Mettupalayam
Red Hills
Emerald
Tribal Research Museum
Bhavani
Erode
N 209
N 47
N 67
SALEM, YERCAUD
Tiruppur
Siruvani
Velliangiri Hills
Andavar
Coimbatore
N 213
TRICHY
Palakkad
Pollachi
N 209
Top Slip
Anamalai/ Indira Gandhi NP
Aaliyar
Sholayar
Valparai
Palani
Murugan
Perumalmalai
Palani Hills
Dindigul
KERALA
Kurinji Andavar
Shembaganur
Bear Shola Falls
Silver Cascade
Devil's Kitchen
Kodaikanal
Moir Point
Bathalagundu
Kumbakarai Falls
Munnar
Sothuparai
Periyakulam
N 49
Theni
MADURAI
Ernakulam
Painavu
Periyar
Vembanad Lake
Suruli Waterfalls
Megamalai
Kottayam
N 220
Alappuzha
Srivilliputtur
Periyar Lake
N 208
N 7
KOLLAM
KANYAKUMARI

Religious and Spiritual Sights

The sacred mystique of mountains have been extolled down the ages in mythology and epics. Gods, demons and sages have been linked to hilly abodes for centuries and the Western Ghats has its fair share of stories and shrines. The inexplicable peace, energy and meditative air that these hills exude prompt people to undertake arduous treks and pilgrimages and build shrines and ashrams in holy places like Palani and Velliangiri. Ancient tribal cultures with folk and animist deities thrive in the deep forests while hill stations like Ooty and Coonoor in the Nilgiris and Kodaikanal have lovely churches set up by early missionaries.

PALANI HILLS★

Murugan Temple★

65 km from Kodaikanal. Dandayudhapani Swami Devasthanam, Adivaram Palani 624601. Open daily 6am–7.30pm. Entry free, electric winch Rs.10 or Rs.50 (one way), rope car Rs.15 (normal day) Rs.50 (festival/special day). Guided Tours: contact Joint Commissioner/Executive Officer, Temple Office. 04545 242236. www.palanimurugantemple.org/palani/index.aspx.

One of the six abodes of Lord Murugan, Palani traces its origins to sibling rivalry. Once, Lord Ganesha and Murugan had an argument as to who was greater. To resolve the dispute between his sons, Lord Shiva offered a divine pomegranate as a prize to whoever went around the world quicker. Murugan scoffed at Ganesh, who had a mouse for a vehicle, and set off from Mount Kailash on his swift peacock. The wily Lord Ganesha merely circled his parents thrice as he considered them his universe. Lord Shiva smiled and adjudged him the winner. When Lord Murugan returned from his world tour, he came to know what transpired and in a huff, left Kailash for the South. Shiva pacified him by saying that Murugan himself *(nee-you)* was the fruit *(pazham)* of all wisdom and knowledge. Hence the place where Murugan settled down was called *'Pazham Nee'* or Palani. But a miffed Murugan was not appeased and moved to the top of the hill. Around 650 steps lead up to the 9C hill-temple perched at 457m/1,500ft, built by Cheraman Perumal, which offers spectacular views of paddy fields, rivers and the Palani Hill range. The famous temple

Palani's Kavadi tradition

The whole universe had congregated at Mount Kailash to attend Lord Shiva's wedding, causing the earth to tilt. Lord Shiva asked Sage Agastya to go southwards to set right the balance. Shiva also gifted him two divine hillocks, Sakthigiri and Shivagiri and instructed Agastya to install them in South India. Unable to bear his heavy burden, the sage abandoned the hills in a forest and journeyed on. Later, Agastya ordered his disciple Idumban to trace the two hillocks and bring them further south. Idumban pondered about this impossible task until divinity intervened – a *Brahma-danda* (Brahma's staff) appeared and celestial snakes fastened the hillocks like ropes. Idumban slung the hillocks over his shoulders like two baskets and headed southward. When he set down his burden, or *kavadi*, near Palani to rest a while, the hillocks took root at the spot. Murugan, the Lord of the Hill, appeared as a boy in a loincloth with a baton. When Idumban asked him for help to lift the *kavadi*, the impudent boy said that it belonged to him. An altercation ensued and Idumban was killed. However, Lord Shiva restored him to life and granted a boon that those who carry *kavadis* to Murugan temples for the fulfilment of vows will be blessed. Lord Murugan is worshipped at Palani as Dandayuthapani (Lord with the Wooden Staff in His hand), and the tradition of carrying *kavadis* continues to this day.

Isha Yoga Centre

The famous spiritual retreat run by Sadhguru Jaggi Vasudev's Isha Foundation on 61ha/150 acres of forested land at the foothills of the sacred Velliangiri, offers people the opportunity to travel inward on a journey towards physical and emotional well-being through yoga, meditation and public service. The non-religious centre imparts all four forms of yoga: *gyan* (knowledge), *karma* (action), *kriya* (energy) and *bhakti* (devotion) through residential courses, retreats and *sathsangs* (group meditation). The beautiful architecture of the massive Dhyanalinga Temple and meditation hall, and the Linga Bhairava and Theerthakund at the centre have created the perfect ambience for spiritual retreat. *For details on programmes, retreats and registration contact Isha Yoga Centre, Velliangiri Foothills, Semmedu, Coimbatore 641114; open daily 6am–8pm; ☏0422 2515345/2515346; www.ishafoundation.org.*

houses a unique *Navapashanam* idol of Murugan as Dandayudhapani Swami, or 'Lord with the Wooden Staff in His Hand' made combining nine poisonous herbs. The *abhishekam* water and overnight sandal paste are considered a sure cure for even the most uncurable diseases. A good time to visit Palani is the Thaipusam festival in January, when nearly 2 lakh pilgrims flock to Palani, carrying *kavadis* or wooden baskets to recreate the age-old legend.

VELLIANGIRI HILLS

Andavar Temple

40km from Coimbatore to Poondi at the base of the hill. Arulmigu Velliangiri Andavar Temple, Poondi. Open daily 7am–1pm, 2–5.45pm. Guided Tours: local guides are available mainly in festive season for a price. Besides this the Thenkailaya Bhakthi Peravai (a non-profitable charitable trust) created by devotees of the Velliangiri Mountains organises the 2-day Thenkailaya Yatra or trek to the Seventh Hill. Contact Thenkailaya Bhakti Peravai, Kastuba, Narayanan Avenue, 1st Street, Krishna Colony, Behind Naveen Hospital, Singanallur Post, Coimbatore 641005. ☏9443145660/9443117660.

Though swathed in a blanket of green forests, Velliangiri, or White Mountain, got its name because of the ethereal mist and cloud cover crowning its peak. After the virgin goddess Kumari's marriage to Lord Shiva was stalled so that she could fulfil her divine purpose of killing Banasura, Lord Shiva walked in dejection till he reached the Velliangiri Hills. He climbed the mountain and sat on the peak in quiet meditation until the very mountains imbibed his spiritual energy. The place was called *Then-kailasam* or Kailash of the South and Lord Shiva is worshipped in his *swayambu* or self-manifest form in a cave temple. The swayambu *linga* is surrounded by four other *lingas*, hence it is also called Panchalinga. Over centuries, many ascetics practised severe austerities and attained self-realisation in the caves and crannies, adding to the holiness of these mountains. It is also said that Sage Agastya came here and taught a different form of yoga in these environs. The seven-crested hill is believed to represent the seven *chakras* or energy centres of the human body and pilgrims can meditate here to receive enlightenment in all the seven basic dimensions of life. The arduous trek from the Poondi Temple at the base to the cave temple of Shiva at Velliangiri, atop the peak at 1,829m/6,000ft, takes about 3–5hr one way depending on one's fitness and goes past a Vinayaka shrine, a Naga statue by a spring, a small sacred pond and some minor shrines. One may discover mendicants and *babas* meditating amidst the precariously perched rocks even to this date and if it is a clear day, one can admire the scenic views of the Valparai Mountain, Attapadi in Kerala and the Siruvani Dam and lake! The main pilgrim season is January to March. Other holy sites nearby like Pambatti Siddhar Guhai, Ottar Samadhi and Sadhguru Shri Brahma's Samadhi are worth a visit.

National Parks and Wildlife Sanctuaries

Mudumalai *(321sq km)* **forms part of an important migratory corridor for elephants. South of the Palakkad Gap, Indira Gandhi National Park in the Anamalai Hills extends into Parambikulam and Eravikulam. Further south still is the Kalakad-Mundanthurai Tiger Reserve** *(see p223)*. **The region has a high number of endemic species like the Nilgiri tahr, an endangered mountain goat and the state animal of Tamil Nadu, as well as numerous birds like Nilgiri laughing thrush, Nilgiri pipit, Nilgiri flycatcher and Kodai white-bellied shortwing.**

MUDUMALAI NATIONAL PARK★

NH-67 runs through the park and buses plying from Mysore (91km) to Ooty stop at the Reception Centre at Theppakkadu. Mudumalai is reachable from Ooty via Pykara and Gudalur or via Kalhatty (36km from Ooty).
NH-67, Theppakkadu, the Nilgiris. Traffic from Bandipur and Mysore is restricted after 6pm. Rs.15. P. *Guided elephant rides (7am–9am, 3pm–6.30pm, 45min) can be booked at Theppakkadu Visitor Centre (open daily 6.30am–6pm). For stay in FRH, contact Range Officer, Theppakkadu, 0423 526235 or Wildlife Warden, Mount Stuart Hill, Ooty 643001. www.forests.tn.nic.in/wildbiodiversity/ws_mws.html.*

Once a renowned game reserve of the Madras Presidency, Mudumalai, Tamil Nadu's most famous National Park was established as far back as 1940. Mudumalai, meaning 'ancient hills', occupies pristine tropical hill forests and is located at the meeting point of Karnataka, Tamil Nadu and Kerala. Contiguous to Karnataka's Bandipur Tiger Reserve in the north separated by the river Moyar and Kerala's Wynad Wildlife Sanctuary on the west, the park is part of the Nilgiri Biosphere Reserve. The Reception Centre, located at Theppakadu (*theppam* means tank, *kadu* is forest), is the gateway to the National Park.

Bestowed with enviable and abundant biodiversity, Mudumalai draws naturalists, birdwatchers, wildlife buffs and anthropologists from near and afar. Easily accessible from Ooty, Mysore and Calicut, the region is a wildlife magnet packed with resorts and forest lodges. The vegetation is dense with tropical deciduous trees towards the west, owing to the south-west monsoons and gradually changes to dry deciduous and thorny scrub towards the east, which receives the gentler north-east monsoons. Its variable terrain of hills, valleys, ravines, flats, streams and swamps enables it to maintain varied wildlife.

Herd of elephants in Mudumalai National Park

Elephant Training Camp, Theppakadu

A big hit with visitors, the Elephant Camp at Theppakadu (*see Mudumalai National Park*) is a conservation and training centre where wild elephants are tamed, including the notorious inmate Loki, a crop-raiding elephant who killed 14 people across two states. Usually a killer is terminated, but the programme here meant he could be trained and used as a symbolic messenger to the world about the plight of Asian elephants. More elephants have been born in captivity here than anywhere else in the world and they are engaged in eco-tourism, patrolling for poachers and, as with Loki, to control man–elephant conflict outside India's wildlife sanctuaries. Every year, thousands of tourists flock to see the morning and evening feeding activity or watch the elephants' bathtime. Elephant rides and entertainment like dancing, football and other antics are also part of this unique interactive programme. Two elephants even perform a daily *puja* at 6pm in a small Ganesha temple close by and do a reverential circumambulation around it! *Open daily 6.30am–9am and 4pm–6pm.*

The forests teem with wildlife – from herbivores like elephants, gaurs, sambars, spotted deer, Indian muntjacs and wild boars, primates like langurs and bonnet macaques to carnivores like tigers, sloth bears and striped hyenas. Dholes or Asiatic wild dogs are sighted in Masinagudi and Theppakkadu while leopards are in the Kargudi area. Fruit-bearing trees and the rich vegetation of tall elephant grass, bamboo, teak, rosewood, mathi, vengai and the vibrant flame of the forest attract over 300 bird species including mynas, barbets, babblers, parakeets and several raptors. Notable species include the Malabar grey hornbill, Malabar trogon, great black woodpecker with its vibrant scarlet crest, tiny-eared owl, scops owl, changeable hawk eagle, crested serpent eagle and the endangered black-and-orange flycatcher.

The rivers Moyar, Biden Halla and Benne Hole drain the western part of the sanctuary. The Moyar Gorge, carved by the force of the river as it plunges 100m/300ft down into the Moyar Falls is a scenic spot while other viewpoints include upper Kargudi Hill and the lake swamp of Ombetta Vayal where herds of gaurs and elephants can be seen. February to May and September to October is the best time to visit. April nights are magical when the park is aglow with waves of fireflies.

MUKKURTHI NATIONAL PARK★

Located 45km from Ooty, there are four access points to the park. From the north, it can be reached from Anumapuram near Pykara (24km from Ooty on NH-67). The route via Parsons Valley and Hodgson's Camp heads to Western Catchment II and III. A 25km drive from Red Hills/Avalanchi (30km from Ooty) leads to Upper Bhavani Dam, towards the south of the sanctuary bordering Silent Valley National Park. This point can also be reached from Ooty (60km) via Manjoor. South-east corner of Nilgiris Plateau, Nilgiris District. Guided Tours: apply for trekking permits in advance from Range Officer, Office of Wildlife Warden, Mount Stuart Hill, Ooty 643001, the Nilgiris. 0423 2444098, 24445971. www.forests.tn.nic.in/wildbiodiversity/np_muknp.html.

India's equivalent to the Appalachian Blue Ridge Mountains, Mukkurthi National Park *(2,556m/8,386ft)* in the Nilgiris forms one the safest havens for the Nilgiri tahr in the world. Spread across 78.46sq km, the cool and misty reaches of the National Park have an average elevation of over 2,400m/8,000ft. Much of the region's pristine nature is retained due to the daunting territory and limitations of road access; thus making it ideal trekking terrain.

The high altitude ensures winter nights *(Dec–Feb)* are freezing and the monsoons *(Apr–Aug)* bring in 2,500mm of rainfall, accompanied by strong gusty winds. Unlike anywhere else in the subcontinent, the vegetation in Mukkurthi is akin to Himalayan flora with rhododendrons, berries and orchids exhibiting a high degree of endemism. The fauna includes animals of the plains and mountains like Nilgiri tahrs, sambars, barking deer, elephants, black-naped hares, jungle cats, civet, dholes (wild dogs), jackals, stripe-necked mongoose, Nilgiri martens, otters and giant squirrels. Birdwatchers have a field day with several hill species, raptors like kestrels, black eagles, black-winged kites and endemics besides grey jungle fowls, flycatchers and thrushes. Many reptile species and butterflies are abundant here. To preserve the rich biodiversity, the forest department does not encourage casual tourism. However, camps for special-interest groups like trekkers and students are allowed. Prior permission has to be obtained from the Forest Department to enter the park and for stay at Forest Rest Houses in Bangi Tapal, Upper Bhavani (EB), Mukkurthi Fishing Hut, Parson's Valley or to camp at the basic trekking sheds.

ANAMALAI/INDIRA GANDHI NATIONAL PARK

34km west of Pollachi and 65km south-west of Coimbatore. Frequent buses operate from Pollachi to Top Slip (35km) while buses plying from Palani and Coimbatore stop at Pollachi. Private vehicles also run from Pollachi and Parambikulam. Visitors' Centre, Top Slip, Coimbatore District. Open daily 6am–6pm. Top Slip Park Centre Rs.50 (camera Rs.10, video Rs.50), Rs.750/25 people 1hr forest bus safari, Rs.400/4 people 30min elephant safari, Rs.140/ head van safari to Parambikulam (3hr). . Guided trek (2.5hr) Rs.500/ up to 5 persons. For trekking permits contact Forest Range Officer, Top Slip or Wildlife Warden, 178, Meenkarai Road, Pollachi 642001 (Mon–Fri 9am–5pm). 04259 238360. www.forests.tn.nic.in/ wildbiodiversity/ws_igws.html.

In the old days, the British had established teak forests in the region and used to harvest timber by 'slipping' it down a narrow canal to the plains, giving the place its name, **Top Slip**. In 1854, D. Hamiliton, an Englishman visited the Anamalai region and noted it as 'surpassingly grand and incomparably beautiful'. Over a century and a half later, the area continues to lure people with its profound beauty. The Anamalais (also spelt Anaimalai and Annamalai), or Elephant Hills, were probably named after the huge population of pachyderms inhabiting its forests. In 1976, an area of 578sq km was recognised as the Anamalai Wildlife Sanctuary for its rich birdlife and species like the gaur (Indian bison), tiger, panther, wild boar, porcupine, spotted deer, sambar, mouse deer, barking deer and wild dog. Unique habitats like Karianshola, Grasshills and Manjampatty were added to the sanctuary, which was renamed after Indira Gandhi and made into a National Park in 1989. The endless undulating hills blanketed by a mixed vegetation of groves, forests of evergreen and tropical trees, teak and rosewood, valleys, waterfalls and vast reservoirs like Parambikulam, Aliyar, Thirumurthi, Upper Aliyar, Kadambarai, Sholayar and Amaravathi are breathtaking. Nearly 300 species of birds inhabit the park including its flagship species the Great Pied Hornbill, the rare Ceylon Frogmouth and Red-winged crested cuckoo. Nilgiri langurs and lion-tailed macaques which aren't found in **Mudumalai**★, can be seen here. Anamalai also has a rich cache of over 2,000 floral species; orchids, palms, ferns, cane and reeds. Karianshola's vast collection of medicinal plants prompted the creation of a Medicinal Plant Conservation Area and Interpretation Centre there. Tourists opt for forest jeeps or elephant safaris to observe wildlife at close quarters. The adventurous choose guided treks across the changing topography to Pandaravara *(8km)*, Kozhikamuthi *(12km)* or the exacting hike to Perunkundru peak *(32km)*. Bookings must be made in advance from the Office of the Wildlife Warden in Pollachi to stay in forest rest houses or lodges. Best season to visit is December to April – September to March as the favoured time for treks.

Hill Stations

Named Blue Mountains after its blue-tinged hills covered in grey mist, the Nilgiris boasts three hill stations. Ooty, Coonoor and Kotagiri form a golden Colonial triangle, accessible by scenic *ghat* roads and heritage mountain railway. Further south in the Palani Hills, sacred to Lord Murugan, Kodaikanal is surrounded by clusters of scenic villages like Perumalmalai, Poombarai, Mannavanur and Kavunji. Around Coimbatore and Pollachi, high-altitude dams like Aliyar, Sholayar and Siruvani are ideal as day trips.

OOTY★★

89km from Coimbatore via Mettupalayam (54km south-east) and Coonoor (19km) by NH-181, which continues to Gudalur, Mudumalai and Bandipur en route to Mysore (160km).

Guided Tours: seasoned guides of the Tourist Guides Association (0423 2444449) at Reflections lake near the bus stand organise sightseeing trips and half- or full-day treks to tea estates and Toda villages (Rs.250–500). Contact Tourist Information Centre, Hoteliers' Association, Charing Cross, Ooty 643001, 0423 2443837 or Tourist Office, Wenlock Road, Ooty 643001. 0423 2443977.

John Sullivan (1788-1855)

Though no memorials or statues mark Ooty's founder, Sullivan's legacy is everywhere. His Stone House, built on land acquired from the Todas for Rs.100, was the first modern house in Ooty. The oak planted by Sullivan in front of his house in 1823 still stands. By 1825 Sullivan created a lake for irrigation and promoted the growth of plantations. Thanks to his tireless efforts, Ooty was made a military sanatorium in 1828. St Stephen's Church, consecrated in 1834, became the first church in the Nilgiris and it was here Sullivan laid his wife and daughter to rest. Tragically, they died within weeks of each other in 1841.

Sent to investigate the 'fabulous tales' surrounding the Blue Mountains or 'Neilgherries', **John Sullivan** (*see sidebar, above*), the Collector of Coimbatore set up a bungalow at Kotagiri in 1819 and came to Ooty in 1822. After his departure, the Commandant of Ooty moved into Sullivan's house in 1846, which was later occupied by three European schools (including Lawrence, which shifted to Lovedale). The large patch of green set up to grow 'English vegetables at reasonable cost' was converted into a Botanical Garden in 1848. The Stone

Ooty Lake

House served as the Summer Secretariat of the Governor of Madras Presidency till 1937 and Ooty eventually became what Sullivan had envisioned it to be – the Queen of Hill Stations, Scotland of the East. The 'sweet half-English air of Neilgherry' drew poet Lord Alfred Tennyson while Lord Lytton, Viceroy of India, raved about Ooty's 'Hertfordshire lanes, Devonshire downs, Westmoreland lakes, Scotch trout streams and Lusitanian views'.

Sadly, much of Ooty's original charm has been overrun by mass tourism. Whilst the town is heavily built up, some remnants of Old Ooty can still be enjoyed, particularly if you choose to stay on the quiet outskirts of the town.

Sights

Located in an amphitheatre of hills stretching over 3km in a north-westerly direction, one of the hill station's most famous sights, the artificial **Ooty Lake**★, can be found to the south-west of town. The **Boat House** *(open 9am–5.30pm, Rs.10, child Rs.5, camera Rs.100)* is the hub of all activities with boating, horse rides, gardens, eateries and touristy amusement parks. Motorboats are available for 20min at Rs.485 *(10-seater)* and pedal boats for 30min at Rs.90 *(2-seater, Rs.100 deposit)*. Besides horse riding *(Rs.50 for a full round, double for a white horse!)*, ornamental plants and seeds are also available near the lake exit.

Nearby **Thread Garden** *(open daily 8.30am–7.30pm, Rs.10, camera Rs.30, ✆0423 2445145, www.threadgarden.com)* is a bizarre collection of 150 species of plants recreated out of thread. On the road back towards town, the TTDC run **Jolly World Lake Park** *(Rs.10, child Rs.5, camera Rs.100)* has slides and go-karting and is popular with families.

To the south is Fern Hill while east of the lake beyond the race course is Elk Hill on whose lower north-western slope lies India's largest rose garden. Set up in 1995 to commemorate the Centenary Flower Festival, the **Rose Garden** *(open daily 9am–6.30pm, Rs.20, camera*

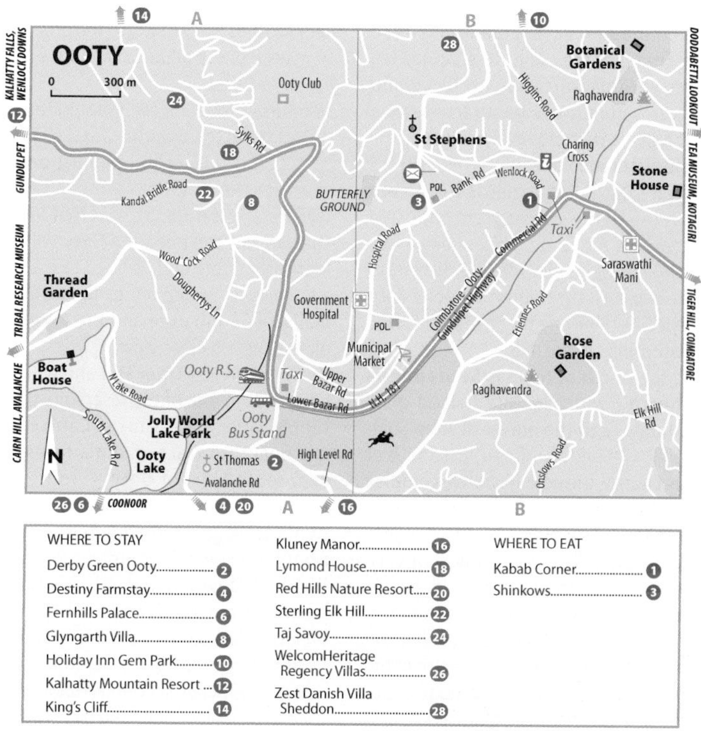

Rs.30) is spread over 4 ha/10 acres in five terraces and boasts 2,241 rose varieties (best enjoyed in early summer). In 2006, it was rated the best rose garden in South Asia, winning the Garden of Excellence Award at Osaka.

Etiennes Road, which skirts north of the garden, joins **Charing Cross**, Ooty's main junction. Due east and spreading around Sullivan's original **Stone House** is the Government Arts College. Just across the busy SH-15 is **Lawley Institute**, a club formed in 1911 for upper-class Indians in response to the snobbish attitude of the Ooty and Gymkhana clubs. Ironically, Sir Arthur Lawley, Governor of Madras laid the foundation stone.

North of it, opposite the Tibetan Market off Woodhouse Road, is another famous sight of Ooty, the **Botanical Gardens**★ *(open daily 8am–6.30pm, Rs.10, child Rs.3, camera Rs.10, video Rs.100, ℘0423 2442545)*, occupying a deep ravine below Raj Bhavan, the summer residence of the Governor. Designed in 1848 with the help of W.G. McIvor from the Kew Royal Botanical Garden in England, the 26ha/65-acre garden has various nurseries, terraces and conservatories. Its chief attractions are a 20 million-year-old fossil tree trunk, the unusual dragon tree, a Toda *mund* (tribal village), an Italian garden laid by Italian POWs and the kikuyu grass imported from East Africa, on which many a film song has been picturised. Adjacent to the garden is the Hebron School, established in 1899, one of the many historic institutions in the hills.

To the north of town is **St Stephens Church**★ with exquisite stained-glass windows and the graves of John Sullivan's wife and daughter. Just south of the church, the administrative complex is a clutch of Colonial buildings – the District Court, Head Post Office and Collector's Office, with iconic shops like Mohans and Higginbotham's in the Oriental Building nearby. Breeks Memorial School, named after James Wilkinson Breeks, the first District Collector of the Nilgiris, was started in a heritage building (now part of the Nilgiris District Court complex), until it was relocated to Charing Cross near Adams Fountain in 1886. It was here Lord Macaulay coined the syllabus of the modern education system for India. South of Hospital Road, half-hidden in a grove of eucalyptus, is another institution, **Nilgiri Library**, built in 1858. On an adjoining 1.6ha/4-acre plot is the main branch of the State Bank of India, opened in 1866 as the Bank of Madras.

Around Town

A great way to escape Ooty's tourist jumble is to head out to the many excursions around town. The **Tea Factory and Museum** *(open daily 8.30am–6.30pm, Rs.10, child Rs.5, ℘0423 2231679, 94430 55529)*, 4km on State Highway 15 at Kil Kodappamund is a must-visit for a crash course in tea. The museum documents the history of tea in three sections – across the world, in India and in the Nilgiris, with brilliant tidbits like how the British employed Chinese prisoners in the early tea plantations. A souvenir shop sells mementoes and assorted tea varieties and one can watch the process from bush to cup at the Doddabetta Tea Factory nearby.

10km from town on the Kotagiri Road is **Doddabetta Lookout**★. At 2,633m/8,640ft it is the second-highest peak south of the Vindhyas. As per local folklore, it was from this spot that John Sullivan saw the beautiful Ooty Valley for the first time and decided to found a town. A telescope brings the distant plains of Coimbatore and the Mysore plateau within close view.

East of town lies **Tiger Hill** and a 3km hike leads to one of the reservoirs that supply water to Ooty town. **Cairn Hill** is a beautiful tract of shola forests, 3km south-west of Ooty en route to the **Tribal Research Museum** and **Avalanche** *(see Driving Tour p274)*. About 8km away on Gudalur Road is **Wenlock Downs**★, named after Governor of Madras Beilby Lawley, 3rd Baron Wenlock. The 8,000ha/20,000 acres of undulating grassland stretching for miles was where the famous Ooty Hunt used to take place. Initiated by the 74th

Filmy Chakkar

The 'Filmy Chakkar' is a popular sightseeing tour of Ooty's legendary filming locales. Besides Ooty Lake, Botanical Gardens and Wenlock Downs, cinema crews have explored every single frame worth capturing on celluloid, from Pine Forest to School Mundh Toda Hamlet.

Most of the sights are on the Old Mysore Road via Gudalur – Sixth Mile *(10km)*, Sandy Nullah or Kamaraj Sagar Dam, Pei Mund or Devils Down and Pykara Dam and Boat House *(19km)*. Eager tourist guides will rattle off film names, songs, maybe even the colour of the dresses the Bollywood stars wore. Cult films like *Karz* and *Maine Pyar Kiya* were shot here extensively. *Poochho Zara Poochho* from Raja Hindustani was shot at 9th Mile, dubbed Shooting Medu. It was on these grassy hills that Madhuri Dixit pranced to songs like *Kehdo ki tum (Tezaab), Mujhe neend na aaye (Dil)* and *Koyal si teri boli (Beta)*. Director Inder Kumar even had a lucky tree in the Botanical Garden that he featured in every film. St Michael's Convent at Ketti and the tea gardens of Coonoor were the backdrop for *Mera dil bhi (Saajan). Chhaiyya Chhaiyya (Dil Se)* was shot on the Nilgiri Mountain Railway.

Tinseltown's fascination with the Nilgiris reached new heights when Mithun Chakraborty shifted base from Mumbai in the 1990s to set up a film studio in Ooty (Mithun's Dream Factory) and a hotel for film units (now Howard Johnson The Monarch). He even had a clause that he would only star in films shot in the area!

Highland Regiment in 1835 to chase sambar, bison and wild boar, the Wenlock Downs today accommodates the Ooty Gymkhana Club and Golf Course, besides the Government Sheep Farm and Hindustan Photo Films Factory.

13km north of Ooty on the road to Masinagudi via Sigur Ghat is **Kalhatty Falls**, a 40m/120ft cataract that's a 3.2km hike from Kalhatty village. 5km further on the Ooty–Mysore short-cut is Bellikal with the Silver Stone Estate.

COONOOR★★

26km north-west of Mettupalayam by NH-181, a ghat road with 14 hairpin bends and 19km south of Ooty via Ketti, Aruvankadu and Wellington.

Guided Tours: Tranquilitea organises 'Cups that Cheer', a 1hr tea tasting tour for Rs.250.

Contact Tranquilitea, Tenerife Hill, Rosery Gardens, Pittapuram Palace Compound, Coonoor 643101.

9443841572. www.tranquilitea.in.

Perched along an 1,800m/5,900ft-high ridge, Coonoor is the second-largest town in the Nilgiris. An anglicised form of the old Badaga name *kunna-ooru* (small gathering site), Coonoor's quieter charms and ideal climate made it the chosen retreat of British planters and Indian royalty.

The town is roughly divided into two halves. Lower Coonoor is where the Municipal Bus Stand, market and railway station are located. Mount Road, Coonoor's main street, climbs up past the Government Hospital at the hairpin bend, with St Anthony's Church (1876) on the left and St John's Church (1893) on the right, next to the dilapidated Coronation Gate opened by Lord Erskine, Governor of Madras, to commemorate the coronation of King George VI and Queen Elizabeth in 1937. Mount Road ends at Bedford Circle, a busy junction from where Upper Coonoor begins.

Sights

Although Coonoor is known mostly for hiking, there are a few sights of interest in and around town. Near Bedford are old Colonial hangouts like **Coonoor Club** and the iconic **Glenview Hotel** (1847), which now houses the office of United Planters' Association of Southern India (UPASI), an apex body of planters formed in 1893.

Tucked away on an elevation in a grove of cypresses beyond Taj Gateway Hotel is the historic **All Saints' Church**★ *(open*

 DRIVING TOUR

NILGIRI LAKE DISTRICT

60km/1day.

Start from Ooty, past Fernhill Palace junction onto Muthorai Road towards Avalanche.

A short drive is all it takes to escape the busy tourist melee of Ooty. The roads are rough and the scenery can literally be to die for, so try this only in an off-road vehicle. Eight stunning lakes dot a 25km radius – Emerald, Avalanche, Upper Bhavani, Parson's Valley, Porthimund and Western Catchment 1, 2 and 3 *(inside Mukurthi National Park)*. One can drive up to the forest checkpost at the Avalanche Orchidarium and Trout Fishery but to go beyond, permits are issued at the DFO office *(℘0423 2444083)* near the District Collectorate, Ooty.

Tribal Research Museum

Stop by at Cairn Hill shola, a popular birding spot 3km south-west of town, before continuing 7km to Muthorai-Palada for a glimpse of the region's rich and endangered tribal culture. Situated on two hillocks is the **Tribal Research Centre and Museum** *(10km south-west of town centre; open Mon–Fri 10am–1pm, 2–5pm, entry free, ℘0423 2550340)*. See open-air tribal houses of the Todas, Kotas, Paniyas and Kurumbas besides life-size models of various tribes and info in the museum.

Continue past Good Shepherd International School and the Potato Research Station via Nanjanad and Ithalar to Emerald, 10km south-west.

Emerald

One look at the shimmering blue and you know why it's called Emerald. The lake has a hydroelectric power station built sometime in the 1950s. Technically, the Surukipalayam Bridge separates Emerald from Avalanche, but the road access is more roundabout.

Backtrack to the main road and after a few kilometres turn right on Avalanche Road. Continue past Indiranagar village and Red Hills turn-off (on the right) to reach Avalanche, 13km from Emerald.

Avalanche

Vast farmlands of potato, carrot and cabbage line the drive to Avalanche, named after the famous calamity that struck the valley in 1823. Permits are required to go past the forest checkpost to the powerhouse and the scenic inner shortcut to Upper Bhavani. A diversion on this road leads to Lakkidi, a lakeshore site near the earthen dam. With prior bookings, Destiny Farm Stay near Avalanche is ideal for those looking to overstay.

The road continues south-east to Kundah Dam but backtrack 7km from Avalanche to Red Hills.

Red Hills

Set in a century-old British estate, Red Hills Nature Resort is a great perch to enjoy a farmstay and a view of the beautiful Emerald Lake.

Drive past old Colonial cottages of Emerald Valley Estate as fields give way to forests till you reach a tri-junction – one road goes to the Western Catchment lakes, one to Mukurthi Lake and the third continues straight via Porthimund to Parsons Valley, 14km north of Red Hills.

Parsons Valley

Stop by at Porthimund Lake to see the two peaks of Nilgiri and Mukurthy *(to its right)* on the far side. Surrounded by forests of pine, the Parsons Valley Dam was where the last scene of Mani Ratnam's film *Roja* was shot. A 2km hike leads to Hodgson's Camp, a good base to explore Mukurthi National Park.

Drive 14km east to return to Ooty.

Fri–Sun). Established in 1854 by Sir Robert Stanes, founder of United Nilgiri Tea Estates in Coimbatore, the church celebrated its 150th anniversary in 2004, when a special postage stamp was released depicting its lovely stained-glass windows. Stanes and his wife Harriet Huntingdon Harris lie buried in the shadow of the lofty steeple in a small garden cemetery. A stone tablet remembers their son James Robert Stanes, who established Coonoor's Runnymede Coffee Estate and tragically drowned at Kalhatty Falls in 1852. Also buried here is General Brackley Kennet, on whose land the church was built, who was killed at Coonoor in 1857. The ancient organ, a stunning piece of craftsmanship, can still be played, though there are few who know how to play it!

Coonoor's botanical highlight is **Sim's Park**★, 3km from town on Kotagiri Road *(Rs.20, children Rs.10, camera Rs.30, video Rs.75)*. Established in 1874 by J.D. Sim, secretary of the Madras Club, the 12ha/30-acre garden occupies a deep ravine. Spread over an elevation of 1,768–98m/5,801–98ft, the terraced park has eight sections with rose beds, grassy terraces and undulating pathways. Nearly 1,000 species of plants thrive here, including several ferns that cannot grow in the cold climes of **Ooty**★★. Look out for the rudraksh tree *(Elaeocarpus ganitrus)*, monkey puzzle *(Araucaria bidwillii)*, Queensland kauri pine *(Agathis robusta)* and other specimens brought from as far as the Cape of Good Hope in 1895. A small pond at the bottom offers the charms of boating. The annual fruit and vegetable show, held over 2 days in the last week of May, attracts large crowds.

To learn how tea is processed, visit **Highfield Tea Factory** *(Swamy & Swamy Plantations; ☏0423 2230023/9443042266)*, a 1km hike down Walker's Hill Road adjacent to **Sim's Park**★.

Around Town

The road from Coonoor to Kotagiri is dotted with beautiful sights and viewpoints. Just above **Sim's Park**★ is a Badaga shrine of Mahalingaswami, a Shiva temple that's opened just once a year for worship on 1 June. About 5km from the park is **Lamb's Rock** named after Captain Lamb who served in the East India Company fleet and created a path to the cliff overlooking the Burliar ravine. A few kilometres away is **Lady Canning's Seat**, where Charlotte Canning spent time painting and sketching while her husband Charles Canning, the Governor General of India, was occupied with the 1857 Sepoy Mutiny (after which he was made India's first Viceroy). 4km from Lamb's Rock is **Dolphin's Nose**, named after its distinctly shaped viewpoint that juts out dramatically. **Catherine Falls** shimmers in the distance with Badaga *hattis* (huts) perched above the chasm.

Law's Falls is 5km below Coonoor on Mettupalayam Road off Wenlock Bridge. The scenic spot is named after Colonel Law, who constructed a new *ghat* road from Mettupalayam to Coonoor in 1871. From Katteri Junction, 3km short of Coonoor at the last hairpin bend, the road leads past Glendale, Parkside and Nonsuch Tea Estates to the **Droog Fort**. Situated on the spur of Hulikallu Durg or Tiger Rock Fort, Droog is a British corruption of *durg* (fort). Known to locals as Pakkasuran Kote, it served as an outpost for Tipu Sultan. **Pakkasuran Viewpoint** is a 4km hike from the Nonsuch Estate bungalow, which is also a great base for Karamadai and Eagles Nest viewpoints, as well as Ripple Vale Falls.

10km from Coonoor on Kundha Road is the 60m/180ft **Katteri Falls**, the third-highest waterfall in the Nilgiris. In 1903, India's first hydel power plant was established to here to run the cordite factory at Aruvankadu.

KOTAGIRI

30km east of Ooty, 20km from Coonoor and 33 km from Mettupalayam via four hairpin bends. Guided Tours: KWEA (Kotagiri Wildlife and Environment Association) organises guided walks like the 3-day John Sullivan Trail. Contact KWEA 5/112, Jackanarai, Aravenu, Kotagiri. ☏04266 371345/374510.

Once the domain of the Kota tribes, the unassuming Kotagiri has many firsts to its credit. It was the first hill station to be set up by the British in the Nilgiris, the first stop on the *ghat* road and the first place where tea, coffee and other spices were planted. Today Kotagiri is a serene alternative to the overdevelopment of **Ooty**★★.

Lying on an open terrace massif at 1,982m/6,503ft in the shadow of the Doddabetta range, its sunny climate was not too cold or damp like Ooty and Coonoor and was ideal for both the sick and the homesick. After initial surveys in 1812 and 1818 reported 'a tableland of European climate', John Sullivan *(see sidebar p270)* ascended the Nilgiris in January 1819. He camped at Dimbhatti, literally 'soft as a pillow', a valley north of Kotagiri. Sullivan returned in May and began constructing a bungalow at Dimbhatti and became the first European resident of the Nilgiris. The path from Sirumugai near Mettupalayam to Dimbhatti was completed in May 1823 until a new route to Coonoor was laid in 1830-2. After promising results at Yercaud, M.D. Cockburn, the Collector of Salem, planted the first coffee estate at Kotagiri in 1843. On finding the climate not suited for coffee, the first tea plantation was set up by Cockburn's daughter in 1863. With the Catherine Falls named after his wife, the imprint of the Cockburns is hard to miss.

Sights

No trip to Kotagiri is complete without paying a visit to **John Sullivan's Bungalow** *(open daily 10am–5pm; Rs.10; 9942545085; www.thenilgiris.org)*, 1km from town at Kannerimukku Village. Called Pethakal Bungalow by the local Badagas after a sacred stone that existed there, the lone surviving two-storey dwelling has had a tumultuous past. First bought by Governor Lushington, who let them out for free to English soldiers, it was later acquired by a Parsi firm and a British officer until the bungalow and the 2ha/5-acre land went back to the Badagas in 1880. It was used as a village school, a cattle shed, a godown for storing potatoes and hay and eventually fell into disuse. In 2002, the International Year of the Mountains, it was restored to its original glory and now houses the **Nilgiris Documentation Centre** run by the Save Nilgiris Campaign. The library and resource centre has everything you want to know about the Nilgiris. Rare books, archived pictures, British-period prints, CDs and DVDs, artefacts and info on the indigenous tribes and the life and times of the man who fought for their rights, John Sullivan.

To buy wild honey, beeswax balms and candles, incense, spices, stationery, Kurumba paintings, Toda shawls and agro-ecological products, drop by at **Green Shop** *(open daily 10am–6pm; 04266 273887; www.lastforest.in)* at Johnstone/Kamaraj Square, run by Last Forest and supported by a local NGO, the Keystone Foundation *(www.keystone-foundation.org)*.

Around Town

Kotagiri is one of the best places for plantation stays, tea estate walks, forest hikes and treks or drives to various falls and viewpoints. A good place to start is **Longwood Shola**★, the only surviving patch of pristine forest around Kotagiri. Located 3km from town on the eastern side of Kairbetta village, the 116ha/287-acre forest is an ideal spot for birdwatchers. With an impressive checklist of 80 species, it boasts 10 of the 16 birds endemic to the Western Ghats.

5km from Kotagiri on Mettupalayam Road at Aravenu, the road branches off 3km to Geddhehaada Halla or **Catherine Falls**. At 76m/250ft, the two-stepped waterfall is the second highest in the Nilgiris. About 7km from Kotagiri near Uliyatti village is **Elk Falls**.

Kodanand viewpoint is 18km from Kotagiri on the eastern-most ridge of the Nilgiris. On a clear day, it offers a panoramic **view**★★★ of Gajalahatti Pass, Moyar River, Mysore Plateau, the 405ha/1,000-acre Kodanad Tea Estate and the meeting point of the Eastern and Western Ghats.

20km from town via the villages of Kil Kotagiri, Sholurmattam, Karagodu-

View from Kodanand viewpoint

mattam and Kadasholai is the sacred **Rangaswamy Peak** *(1,785m/5,855ft)* where the Irulas perform a temple ceremony in September or October. North-west of the peak beyond Denad is **Rangaswamy Pillar**, a stunning pillar of rock rising above the mist to 122m/400ft, associated with a Kota folk hero.

KODAIKANAL★★

64km south of Palani and 60km from Batalagundu (20km from Kodai Road railway station) on Dindigul Theni Road. Guided Tours: TTDC has a 3-day weekend tour to Kodai from Chennai at Rs.2,500/person (all-inclusive, non-AC), local tour operators, taxis and guides organise a 16-Sights Tour of Kodai. Contact Tourist Office, Municipal Bus Stand, Kodaikanal. 04542 241675. (Closed Sunday).

Once home to the Paliyan and Pulaiyan tribes and scattered remains of the Stone Age, the **Palani Hills**★ thrum to ancient vibrations. Sacred to Lord Murugan, his temple at Palani (*see sidebar p265*) inspired a European lady to set up the Kurunji Andavar Shrine here.

Western fascination with the 'Pulney Hills' is not new. The American Madura Mission introduced coffee plantations here in the 1800s while British surveyor Lt. B.S. Ward was the first European visitor in 1821. He camped at Vellagavi Village *(south of Kodai)* and presented a favourable report about its invigorating climate. Access from Madurai soon drew eminent collectors, judges, doctors and missionaries who built houses and offices around present-day Lake Road and St Mary's Road. By 1845 American missionaries moved into Sunnyside and Shelton, two bungalows on the plateau's southern end. The Anglican Church was set up jointly in 1860 while the American Madura Mission built Union Church in 1895. La Providence, a bungalow on Upper Shola Road, became a residence for Roman Catholic fathers. The Collector of Madurai Sir Vere Henry Levenge, who lived in Pambar House after his retirement, created a lake in 1863 by damming three streams. He introduced boating on the lake, developed access roads and planted exotic plants like pine and pear. In 1867, Major J.M. Partridge brought wattle and Australian bluegum trees, which accounts for Kodai's eucalyptus oil and the wonderful smell in the air.

Walking paths, gardens, boat clubs and a golf course (*see Addresses)* were laid down while an international school was opened exclusively for European children. With the opening of the motorable Law's Ghat Road in 1916, Kodaikanal's tryst with tourism was assured. The summer festival of music and dance is held in May, marked by boat races, flower shows, pageants and dog shows.

Nilgiri Mountain Railway near Ooty

Nilgiri Mountain Railway★★★

The climb to Ooty from the plains used to be a treacherous journey on a *ghat* road in bullock carts, ponies and palanquins aided by the Nilgiri Carrying Company's Mail and Express Tonga Service. British engineers proposed a mountain railway as early as 1854 but it wasn't until 1891 that Lord Wenlock, the Governor of Madras, laid the foundation of the Nilgiri Mountain Railway. In 1899, the first train chugged up the slopes from **Mettupalayam** *(326m/1,069ft)* to **Coonoor**★★ *(1,712m/5,617ft)*, before the rail link was extended to **Ooty**★★ *(2,203m/7,228ft)* in 1903.

Though not as old or lengthy as the other mountain railways at Darjeeling and Shimla, the 46km train journey is the steepest in Asia, with a maximum gradient of 1:12 (8.33 percent). The railway link was not just an engineering marvel, it also revolutionised the Nilgiri tea industry with swift transportation from the estates to the plains and back to Britain. Using a rack and pinion Alternate Biting Teeth (ABT) system, it takes nearly 5hr for the ascent with the engine pushing the train from behind. The scenic terrain past hills, valleys, forests and plantations changes with every mile as the train negotiates 16 tunnels, 27 viaducts and 208 curves. From Mettupalaiyam station, the train climbs 7km past betelnut, palm and coconut plantations to Kallar, an elevation of 405m/1,329ft. The train crosses Kallar Bridge over the Bhavani River, Adderley Viaduct, Burliar Bridge and 14 tunnels as it crosses tropical jungles via Hill Grove to Coonoor *(Adderley, Runnymede and Kateri are no longer stops).*

Long before Shah Rukh Khan and Malaika Arora danced to *Chhaiyya Chhaiyya* on a moving train, the Nilgiri Mountain Railway was depicted in David Lean's 1984 film *A Passage to India*. Coonoor railway station, a beautiful Colonial structure built in 1897, was one of the scenic locales. A steam locomotive, X 37390, constructed by Swiss Locomotive Works in 1922 and retired after chugging 7.5 lakh km, stands outside! From Coonoor, the train climbs via Wellington, Aruvankadu, Ketti, Lovedale and Fernhill (the highest point) to Ooty. The train leaves daily from Mettupalayam at 7.10am to Ooty and returns at 3pm, completing the downhill journey in 3.5hr. There are also four daily trains each way between Ooty and Coonoor. In 2005, the Nilgiri Mountain Railway was added by UNESCO to its list of World Heritage Sites. Despite having computerised ticketing systems, the NMR still issues manually stamped Edmondson railway tickets, retaining its old-world charm.

Sights

The starfish-shaped **Kodaikanal Lake**★ forms the nucleus of this compact town. Surrounded by eateries and carts selling hot *bajjis* and tea, the lake's 5km perimeter is ideal for walks *(45min)*, cycling or horse rides. Boats are available at the TTDC Boat House or Kodaikanal Boat and Rowing Club and anglers can cast a line for carp and trout with prior permission from the Inspector of Fisheries in Kodaikanal.

East of the lake is the busy Seven Road Junction, surrounded by hotels, restaurants, curio shops and stores advertising Kodai's home-made chocolates, marshmallows, incense and aromatic oils.

South-east of the lake is **Bryant Park** *(open daily 7am–7pm; Rs.20, camera Rs.30)*, laid in 1908 by H.D. Bryant, a forest officer from Madurai. The 8.3ha/20.5-acre botanical garden is a storehouse of 325 species of trees, with a separate section for 740 rose varieties and ornamental plants on sale at the nursery.

Just across the road, beyond **St Peter's Church** (Church of South India), is the legendary **Coaker's Walk** *(open 7am–7pm; Rs.5)*, cut into the hill's south-eastern ridge by Lt Coaker in 1872. Hemmed in between Villa Retreat and Greenland's Youth Hostel, the 1km paved path offers scenic views. Dolphin's Nose, Pambar River and Madurai can be seen more clearly through the telescope in the small **observatory** *(Rs.3)*.

For more long-distance viewing, drop by at the **Kodaikanal Observatory**, perched atop the town's highest point north of the lake on Observatory Road. Started in 1898, it is one of the oldest observatories in the world and India's only Solar Physical Laboratory. One of the oldest extant telescopes in the world and rare solar photographs are also on showcase. The exclusive precincts are open to visitors only on Friday between 10am–12.30pm and 7–9pm.

North of Observatory Road, 1.6km from the lake is **Bear Shola Falls**, a watering hole for bears in the past. Convent Road heads north of **Kodai Lake**★, to **Kurinji Andavar Temple** 3km away, with spectacular **views**★★★ of the **Palani Hills**★ and Vaigai Dam. Dedicated to Lord Murugan, Lord of the Hills, the temple slopes are carpeted with kurinji, whose purple-blue flowers blossom every 12 years (watch out for 2016).

From Bryant Park, the road splits into St Mary's Road, which ends in Pambarpuram at St Salette, the oldest church in Kodaikanal. The right of the fork Club Road merges into Upper Shola Road. Upper Lake Road offers a panoramic **view**★★ of the lake while Fairy Falls Road leads to the wispy waterfall near the Horticultural Research Station. The Upper Shola Road meanders south-west of the lake to **Green Valley View** (Suicide Point) and a clutch of shops.

Around Town

The standard 16-Sights Tour covers most of the spots around town *(Rs.800–1,000 by car/jeep, Rs.150/person by 17-seater mini-van)*. Cycles, hired mostly for rides around the lake, are a little impractical for sightseeing as the mountain roads are steep and the sights are far apart.

Shembaganur, 6km on the Kodai Ghat Road, has a Natural History Museum founded in 1895 and maintained by the Sacred Heart College. Stuffed specimens, rare butterflies of the **Palani Hills**★ and a 300-strong orchid collection are on display in an old-world atmosphere. Just ahead, about 8km outside town on the approach route from Palani is Kodai's most popular waterfall, **Silver Cascade**, formed by the backwaters of the Kodai Lake. 12km from Kodai is **Perumalmalai** *(2,400m/7,874ft)*, the highest peak in the Kodai Hills. It's a 3km hike from the village, which is just one of the 17 routes outlined in a pamphlet available at the District Forest Office.

The road past Kodai Golf Club *(see Addresses)* continues to **Pillar Rock**, a 122m/400ft vertical column of three rocks, 7km from town. Nearby is **Devil's Kitchen**, dubbed 'Guna' Caves after Kamal Hassan's hit film. About 9.5km from town **Moir Point** *(2,310m/7,580ft)* marks a fork in the road with the left going past a forest barrier to **Beri Jam**, a beautiful reservoir 23km from Kodai amid dense forests of acacia and pine.

ADDRESSES

STAY

The diversity of stay options in the Western Ghats is amazing. Delightful resorts and bungalows in and around the plantation towns of Ooty, Coonoor and Kotagiri in the Nilgiris, the European charms of Kodaikanal and Kamarajar Valley in the Palani Hills and wildlife getaways at Mudumalai near Bandipur and Top Slip near Pollachi are some of the region's spectacular highlights.

OOTY

Taj Savoy – *77, Sylks Road, Ooty 643001. 0423 2225500. www.tajhotels.com. . 40 rooms.* . Spread over 2.4ha/6 acres of landscaped gardens and colourful flowerbeds, the Colonial-style cottages of the Savoy were built between 1829-65. Most rooms come with fireplaces and despite being equipped with modern luxuries they exude an old-world charm. Canterbury Bar is a classic English-style bar, the Tea Lounge with a quaint fireplace overlooks lush green lawns, while the Dining Room offers a delightful dining ambience with live piano in the evenings (except Tue). Wi-Fi, a 24hr fitness centre and an Ayurvedic centre, as well as cultural programmes and excursions organised on request.

Fernhills Palace – *Selbourne Road, Fernhill Post, Fernhill, Ooty 643004. 0423 2442555/2443910/ 9443249470. www.fernhillspalace.co.in. 19 suites.* . Originally built in 1844, this property later became Ooty's legendary club Hotel Moonisami. Curry n Rice serves Anglo-Indian and Western cuisine besides 600-year-old recipes of the Wadiyar dynasty. Plush rooms, a lounge and a bar with red mahogany decor complete the royal rendezvous. Fitness centre, salon, conference facilities and play area for kids.

Sterling Elk Hill – *25, Ramakrishna Mutt Road, RK Puram, Elk Hill, Ooty 643004. 0423 2452634/ 2441395. www.sterlingresort.co.in. 116 rooms.* . This 1.8ha/4.4 acre resort with sloping roofs and terracotta tiles offers a choice of rooms from a studio to a two-bedroom apartment with a balcony. Magnolia, the multi-cuisine restaurant serves good Indian, Chinese and Continental cuisine besides local delicacies of the Nilgiri tribes. There's a 24hr coffee shop, business centre, clubhouse, Internet cafe, gift shop and play area for children. Daily treks are organised to Lovedale and Cairn Hill.

Zest Danish Villa Sheddon – *30, Sheddon Road, Ooty 643001. 0423 2442880. www.zestbreaks.com. 15 rooms.* . Located on a 0.9ha/2.3-acre patch of peace and quiet north of St Stephen's Church, the 180-year-old Danish villa has been with the Mahindra family since 1947. Hamlet-styled interiors with a cosy wooden touch and earthy furnishings open out to breathtaking views of the hills or the garden. Leslige restaurant serves sumptuous multi-cuisine and buffet meals for Rs.450. Soft adventure sports like rock climbing, rapelling, downhill bicycle tours, treks and camping are organised, besides barbecues and bonfires at night.

Derby Green Ooty – *29–49, Baikey Road, off Etiennes Road, Ooty 643001. 0423 2441700/9159784784. www.clubmahindra.com. 91 rooms.* . A heritage resort run by Club Mahindra on 2.2ha/5.5 acres of beautifully landscaped gardens, Derby Green overlooks the racecourse in the heart of town. The old Colonial structure has been painstakingly refurbished and is an exquisite combination of modern amenities and British decor. Ascot serves great multi-cuisine and Svaastha spa offers rejuvenation packages.

Lymond House – *78, Sylks Road, Ooty, The Nilgiris 643001. 9739447562. www.serendipityo.com/ lymondhouse.html. 6 rooms.* . Adjacent to the Savoy Hotel and set amidst flowering trees and sprawling lawns, this 1856 Victorian bungalow comes with two large Victorian drawing rooms with open log fires, three suites (named Isis, Grace and Flora) and three luxury double rooms, replete with antique four-poster beds, dressers and open fireplaces.

Holiday Inn Gem Park – *Sheddon Road, Ooty 643001. 0423 2442955. www.holidayinn.com. . 95 rooms.* .

This contemporary hotel in the northern part of town offers comfort at a reasonable price. Rooms and luxurious suites on seven levels face the Doddabetta peak and valley with breathtaking views of the landscape. Toda Cafe on the fifth floor serves multi-cuisine and barbecue grills while Jade Garden next to Valley Bar at the lobby does excellent Chinese. The hotel comes with a business centre, health clubband spa with steam, sauna, Ayurvedic and traditional massages, a sports court, pool and play areas for children.

Glyngarth Villa – *Golf Club Road, Finger Post, Ooty 643005. 0423 2445754/2445115/9843570095. www.glyngarthvilla.com. 5 rooms.* . A heritage home built in 1850 by Sir Walter Mounde, Glyngarth has played host to many distinguished visitors, including India's first PM Jawaharlal Nehru. Heritage rooms, suites and cottages have polished wooden floors and period furniture. Read Colonial accounts and other titles from the mini library or snuggle up by a log fire.

Kluney Manor – *196/197, Patna House, RK Puram, Mount Pleasant, Ooty 643001. 0423 2447336. www.kluneymanor.chobs.in. 25 rooms.* . In 1828, Capt. McPherson of the British Army built the Kluney Manor and later, the Maharaja of Patna made it his summer retreat. Sitting pretty on stately lawns overlooking a valley with a view of the Nilgiri Hills and cut off from the hubbub south of the lake, this charming villa offers the Colonial comfort of log fires, massive four posters and great food.

King's Cliff – *Havelock Road, Ooty 643001. 0423 2452888/9487000111. www.kingscliff-ooty.com. 9 rooms.* . This 1850s Colonial bungalow is on a sprawling campus a little away from the centre of Ooty, on a hill overlooking the valley. Each room comes with a working fireplace and modern amenities like satellite TV and telephone. Earl's Secret serves excellent Western, Continental and Indian fare and there is also a reading room. Have a cup of tea on the lawns, explore the estate, go horse riding, fishing, for open jeep jungle rides or trek uphill.

WelcomHeritage Regency Villas – *Fernhill Palace, Ooty 643004. 0423 2443098/2442555. www.welcomheritagehotels.com. 19 rooms.* . Spread over 6ha/15 acres within the Fernhills Palace complex, the red and white Colonial villas come with massive windows, old wooden floors and period furniture. Meals Rs.300–400

AROUND OOTY

Destiny Farmstay – *Muligoor Village, Avalanche, Ooty 643001. 0423 2224545/9487000111. www.destinyfarmstay.com. 25 rooms.* . Fancy staying in a farm with horses, cows, geese, rams and dogs for company? Want to pick farm-fresh vegetables and herbs for your meals? Or wish to wake up to a breathtaking view of mist rising up over the valley? This farmstay, 25km from Ooty, is the perfect answer. The access is so wild, it requires the farm's 4x4 army truck to ferry guests over the last 2km. The ranch-house-styled building has four blocks – Wild West, Great Explorers, Men of Nature and Planet Savers – furnished with warm wooden flooring, country furniture and fireplaces. Visit the dairy, drop a line at the small fishing pond, camp by the lake, go horse riding or improve your golf at the small putting area.

Red Hills Nature Resort – *Emerald, Nilgiris 643209. 0423 2595755/9442254755/9842259544. www.redhill-india.com. . 7 rooms.* . Perched atop a 2,134m/7,000ft hillock overlooking the Emerald Lake, this 1875 white-washed gabled bungalow sits pretty amidst a 100ha/250-acre tea garden and a lawn with colourful flower beds. Located 27km from Ooty, the nature resort is run by Bhanu and Vijay Kumar, who are an excellent resource on local trails. Go fishing, trekking and sightseeing, while enjoying homely food and local delicacies like Badaga chicken with beans.

Kalhatty Mountain Resort – *Kalhatty Village, Ooty 643101. 9443053800. www.kalhattymountainresort.com. . 21 rooms.* . Located 14km north of Ooty on the Sigur Ghat road, the estate is located in 20ha/50 acres of tea and 10ha/25 acres of coffee abutting a patch of wilderness. The showpiece is a heritage stone structure or castle with nine suites surrounded by lawns and a large flowery garden. A 2km complimentary 4-wheel drive leads to a jungle camp offering six riverside cottages with two rooms each and six tents (five-man) ideal for large adventure groups. Treks, campfires, barbecues, hikes to waterfalls and wildlife safaris are organised *(Rs.2000/ jeep)*. Tariff includes all meals.

COONOOR

The Tryst – *Carolina Tea Estate, PO Box 6, Coonoor 643102. 0423 2207057. www.trystindia.com. . 6 rooms. . Closed May–Aug.* A quirky homestay run by an equally interesting couple, your hosts are Dr Sathya Rao, a holistic medical practitioner/writer and Ann, a Yorkshire lady. Located 2.5km from town near Moores Garden on Mount Pleasant side, the Tryst has nice lawns, gazebos with ponds, secluded sit-outs in the garden and a billiards room and library. Rooms are crowded with artefacts and done up in Indian, Italian, Egyptian and Victorian themes. Much of the ingredients for the European and Indian cuisine on offer come from the in-house fruit, vegetable and herb gardens. Tariff includes breakfast and dinner.

The Gateway Hotel – *Church Road, Coonoor 643101. 0423 2225400. www.thegatewayhotels.com. . 32 rooms.* . A stone's throw from All Saints Church in Upper Coonoor, the heritage Colonial retreat is surrounded by manicured lawns and great views that imbue it with a sense of space. Most rooms have fireplaces and high ceilings with private gardens. Also boasts an Ayurveda centre for massages, fitness centre, library, Hampton bar and Wi-Fi across the hotel. The Dining Hall restaurant serves excellent Chettinad cuisine and local dishes like Nilgiri Korma, Chicken Ball Curry and *Gassu Dhotti*.

– **180°McIver** – *McIver Villa, 1–4, Orange Grove Road, Coonoor 643101. 0423 2233323/9715033011/9486414830. www.serendipityo.com/mciver.html. . 6 rooms.* . A 120-year-old Colonial hotel named after the stunning 180-degree view of Coonoor and the surrounding hills. La Belle Vie, the multi-cuisine restaurant serves excellent organic food. They also run Amberina, a tea-planter's bungalow at Devala near Gudalur and The Wilds at Northern Hay near Mudumalai with four-rooms in a renovated coffee warehouse surrounded by a 40ha/98-acre patch.

Acres Wild – *571, Upper Meanjee Estate, Kannimariamman Kovil Street, Coonoor 643101. 0423 2232621/ 9443232621. www.acres-wild.com. . 5 rooms.* . A 9ha/22 acre-family-run organic cheese-making farm 3km from town, Acres Wild comes with three cottages. The hosts Tina and Mansoor encourage guests to participate in farm activities and learn how to make jam, bread or soap besides courses on cheese making. Farm-fresh bread, cheese and vegetables are rustled into fixed meals *(Rs.350)* while 2hr guided tours are provided on weekends *(Rs.100)*.

Wallwood Garden – *Blair Athol, Kotagiri Road, Coonoor 643101. 0423 2230584. http://wallwood-garden.neemranahotels.com. 10 rooms.* . Barely a 2-minute walk from Sim's Park in Upper Coonoor, Blair Athol was built a century ago by a Scottish Major General who sold it after World War I to a British couple who ran it as a boarding house. The mansion has been converted into a heritage hotel run by Neemrana. With classy rooms named after trees, an award-winning pomological garden and fixed meals *(Rs.350–450)*, get ready to be transported back in time.

Bella Vista – *71, Shanthi Vijaya School Road, Mount Pleasant, Coonoor 643102. 044 28545777/9884077710. www.bellavistastay.com. . 6 rooms.* . A boutique bungalow with rooms named after flowers surrounded by landscaped lawns and lush gardens with fruit trees like peach and guava. Two separate dining areas serve a mix of Continental, Chinese, North and South Indian cuisine with bonfire and grills arranged on request.

AROUND COONOOR

Kurumba Village Resort – *Ooty Mettupalayam Road, Hill Grove Post, Kurumbadi 643102. 0423 2103002/ 2237222/9443998886. www.kurumbavillageresort.com. 70 rooms.* .

Located in a forest patch between the fourth and fifth hairpin bends on the *ghat* road to Coonoor, Kurumba Village is set in an old British spice plantation of nutmeg, cloves, pepper and lofty trees of jackfruit and rosewood. Named after one of the five ancient tribes of the Nilgiris, its tribal-styled cottages in earthy tones and thatched roofs are decorated with Kurumba artefacts. French windows and balconies offer an unhindered view of the Nilgiri Hills while the dining area is perched above a murmuring brook. Walking tours of the spice plantation and hikes are also organised. Tariff includes all meals.

Devashola Homestay – *Kollacombay Post, Coonoor 643101. 0423 2230406. www.devashola.com. . 12 rooms.* . 24km from Coonoor beyond Musapuri Village, the award-winning Devashola Estate offers magical stays in early-1900s bungalows amidst endless tea plantations stretching over 260ha/650 acres. Choose from Mango Tree Bungalow, Sultana Bungalow, Palaniappa Bungalow, row houses in Bison Valley Cottage or Mupargad Dormitory, each done up in British decor and lots of wood. With no phone signal or TV to keep one occupied, guests automatically turn to the bountiful nature all around. Complimentary trekking and jeep safaris to viewpoints are organised. With sumptuous vegetarian meals prepared by experienced caretakers *(included)* and the warm hospitality of the estate managers, it's a plantation stay at its best.

NoneSuch Retreat – *Nonsuch Estate & Post, Via Coonoor 643238. 0423 2281200/2281501. www.nonesuchretreat.com. . 3 rooms.* . Located 10km from Coonoor, this 1872 tea plantation bungalow overlooks the plains of Karamadai to the south and Coonoor town to the north. Surrounding it at 1,676m/5,500ft are 427ha/1,055 acres of tea plantations and the area is packed with stunning views. The bungalow itself is located on manicured lawns, which are regularly awarded 'best-maintained garden'. Besides factory and estate visits, several hikes are arranged *(Rs.500/couple)*.

De ROCK-Jungle Living – *Lambs Rock, Guernsey, Coonoor 643101. 0423 2103030/9488482303. www.de-rock.com. . 16 rooms.* . A stunning location 7km from town, De Rock is a boutique homestay with four cottages flanked by shola forests and tea estates. Cliff View cottages of exposed brick and wood have sit-out verandahs overlooking Lamb's Rock, Rainforest View with private balconies have large windows that frame the greenery, Plains View cottages offer a spectacular sunrise and the twinkling lights of Coimbatore at night, while Silver View *(glass house)* has great views all around. Home-cooked food is served in a picturesque outdoor dining area.

Adderley Guest House – *Via Dolphin's Nose Viewpoint, Coonoor 643102. 0423 2206779/94449 93176. www.glendalestays.in. . 5 rooms.* . Once part of the vast estates of the Stanes family in the mid-1800s, Glendale offers luxury plantation stays at various estate bungalows. The 135-year-old Adderley Guest House is an original planter's bungalow while Runnymede Guest House is a three-bedroom bungalow 6km from Coonoor on the Mettupalayam Highway.

KOTAGIRI

La Maison – *Hadathorai Tea Estate, Kotagiri. 9047589252/9585857732. www.lamaison.in. . 4 rooms.* . This French-run boutique heritage homestay was built in 1897 on top of a hill. The original coffee and orange plantations were replaced by tea and the tigers, panthers and bison hunted by the Kays still adorn the house as trophies. Large bay windows, varnished floors, antique doors of Burma teak, high ceilings with original teak carpentry, fireplaces with rosewood frames and verandas of Rajasthan sandstone smack of elegant class. Traditional saris hang over beds and windows while antiques, bronzes, potteries, lamps and modern pieces of art litter the house (some of which are for sale). There's a jacuzzi, kids' pool, French *petanque* and Wi-Fi, though no TV. Tariff includes all meals.

Nahar's Retreat & Wellness Spa – *Near Mount Don Bosco, Kota Hall Road, Kotagiri 643217. 04266 273300/274400/ 9443053548. www.naharhotels.com.* *11 rooms.* . Part of the same group that runs the Nahar's Nilgiris Hotel and Residency in Ooty, the Stone House Retreat is synonymous with Kotagiri. Though the hotel is old and cosy, the premium rooms in the new building are quite swanky. Prana offers only veg fare but the highlight is the authentic Ayurvedic treatment and massages by Kairali. A spa, steam and heated swimming pool are rare luxuries in a hill town. Pick-up and drop-off organised to various destinations.

Sunshine Bungalow – *Club Road, Kotagiri 643217. 04266 271214/94865 53104/94870 69047. www.thesunshinebungalow.com.* *4 rooms.* . One of the oldest bungalows in Kotagiri, the 225-year-old property's sun-dappled verandah, long porches and quintessential British décor transport every visitor to another era. All rooms come with original 17C four-poster beds while the stylish living room and lounges with wood-panelled flooring offer a stunning view of the garden and the hills.

Twin Tree Mountain Resorts – *5/39-A Corsley Estate Road, Kotagiri 643217. 04266 275333/9443477559/ 9444073237. www.twintreekotagiri.com. 8 rooms.* . A small new resort opposite River Side Public School, Twin Tree's two blocks Pipal and Banyan have swanky rooms in contemporary style overlooking a manicured lawn and a stunning peak view.

Moonshadow Cottage – *5/43 T, Corsley Road, Kotagiri 643217. 04266 271080/9443960539/9786036728. www. moonshadowcottage.in.* . *5 rooms.* . Well-furnished rooms with wooden floors and stylish bathrooms in lush landscaped gardens with amazing views and multi-cuisine dining.

MUDUMALAI

Jungle Retreat – *Bokkapuram, Masinagudi 643223. 0423 2526459/2526469. www.jungleretreat.com. 13 rooms.* . This 14ha/35-acre resort wrapped around the foothills of the Nilgiris is Mudumalai's top getaway. Rohan Mathias offers warm hospitality; there is a stunning rockpool against a mountain backdrop; mind-blowing continental food ***(Rs.1,470/ person)***; and convivial barbecue fires. Beautifully landscaped trees like laburnum and cherry attract sunbirds to your doorstep. The adjoining forest houses India's smallest woodpecker, the speckled piculet to the great black woodpecker, among the largest in Asia. Choose from treehouses, cottages, dorms ***(Rs.2,024/bed)*** and double-bedroom suites ***(Rs.13,000)***. Take the forest trail to a 2ha/5-acre plot up the mountainside to camp at night or trek to the misty village of Sholur. Plantation visits and full- or half-day tours are organised to silk farms, tribal villages, Ooty, Coonoor and Gopalaswamy Betta.

Jungle Hut – *Bokkapuram, Masinagudi 643223. 0423 2526463. www.junglehut.in.* *16 rooms.* . This 8ha/20-acre property located in a thicket of trees has ponds for fishing, a scenic swimming pool and deluxe cottages with private verandahs. Vegetables, herbs and spices freshly hand picked from the backyard farm are rustled into delicious meals served in a cosy candle lit dining area overlooking the pool. There's no music, TV or phone in the rooms; the only sounds are the chirp of birds and occasional alarm calls. Nature hikes and birdwatching trails are organised into the adjoining forests. Tariff includes meals.

Creek n Crag – *Wild Canopy Reserve, Kunjapanai, near Tottalingi village. 0423 2526034/94432 80658. www.creekncrag.com.* . *4 rooms.* Situated 8km from Masinagudi in one corner of a 121ha/300-acre coffee estate surrounded by a natural scrub forest, this 150-year-old property was originally a hunting lodge for a British soldier stationed in Ooty in 1869. The massive coffee storage rooms have been converted into two mega-deluxe rooms while two deluxe treehouses add a bit of novelty. Enjoy luxurious meals ***(Rs.1,000/day)*** as you savour the breathtaking view of mist-clad mountains.

Inn the Wild – *Northern Hay Estate, Singara Post, Masinagudi 643229. 8526181386. www.innthewild.com.* . *14 rooms.* Set amidst 23ha/65 acres of tropical wilderness, the luxurious options range from traditional cottages, thatched-roof jungle shacks, tribal homes, treetop rooms with sit-out and a stand-alone mini tree house with a great view of the lake on the property. Jeep safaris are organised at Rs.600/person and meals cost Rs.850/day.

De ROCK-Jungle Living – *Bokkapuram, Masinagudi 643223. 9442525003/9626905665. www.de-rock.com. 15 rooms.* An eco-sensitive resort at the base of the Nilgiris, the cottages have built-in furniture and huge French windows that maximise the stupendous mountain view. Bamboo huts, tents and tree house offer some variety and delicious home-cooked meals are served buffet-style. Do a 1.5hr trek to the mountaintop, opt for jeep rides to Vibudi Malai Temple, Moyar Temple and Chemanatha Temple ***(Rs.250/head)*** or go fishing with bamboo rods.

Glenview Resorts – *Bokkapuram, Masinagudi 643223. 0423 2526666. www.glenviewresorts.com. 8 cottages.* Located in a dense clump of vegetation, Glenview comes with a wide choice of stay options. From log huts, stone huts, mud huts, Swiss tents, tribal huts inspired by the Paniya, Kurumba and Irula tribes to rugged bamboo tree houses, each of the cottages are unique. Meals are served in a rustic-style restaurant at Rs.700/day and there's a separate bonfire and recreation area.

Blue Valley Jungle Resorts – *Bokkapuram, Masinagudi 643223. 0423 2526244/344. www.bluevalleyjungleresorts.com. 13 rooms.* A luxury resort designed by a German architect and built with black stones, each cottage has independent views of the mountains and bamboo groves. Besides a 6-bed bungalow, tents and tree house, it has a mini gym and conference room. In the morning, trek to a temple on the mountain or Bison Valley viewpoint and go for evening and night-time safaris.

Tamarind Tree – *Mudumalai, Masinagudi 643223. 9845044322/9843277177. www.thetamarindtree.in. 8 rooms.* Named after the large tamarind tree on the property, the deluxe rooms, ***machans*** and studio apartments made of wood, thatch and brick blend nicely into the surroundings. Meals are arranged for Rs.700/person, besides campfires, mountain biking, rock climbing, trekking ***(Rs.200)*** and visits to tribal villages.

KODAIKANAL

The Carlton – *Lake Road, Kodaikanal 624101. 04542 240056. www.krahejahospitality.com. 91 rooms.* One of Kodai's most famous and premium resorts, Carlton is centrally located near the lake. There are several in-house eating options – Hearth 24hr coffee shop, Silver Oak multi-cuisine, End of the Road Bar and The Lawns on the upper terrace with pasta counters and barbecues. Besides a games and recreation area, bookshop, handicraft store, foreign exchange and Internet cafe, the Carlton Boathouse offers rides in ***shikharas*** and rowing boats.

Fairway Inn – *Brooklyn, Convent Road, Kodaikanal 624103. 9442328446. www.fairwayinn.co/. 1 cottage.* A luxury homestay within walking distance of the lake, with deep-tissue and relaxing massages on offer and access to the Kodai Golf Club nearby. A beautiful garden and gazebo, a snug room heated by an antique wood stove and a fully-equipped kitchen with fridge and microwave for those fond of cooking. Locally grown organic veggies are available at 25 percent discount, besides Kodai cheese and 20 flavours of home-made chocolate.

The Fern Creek – *212/118, Fern Hill Road, Kodaikanal 624101. 04542 243486/9345690524. www.theferncreek.com. 7 tents.* Stay in Swiss luxury tents spread across 0.6ha/1.5 acres with exotic Eastern furniture in teak and water hyacinth and world-class fittings. Enjoy boutique hospitality and Oriental therapies at Aura Balinese Spa. A multi-cuisine cafe, garden gazebo, recreation room equipped with home theatre, a wide collection of books and movies and a fireplace guarantee a holiday well spent.

Zest Coaker's Villa – *Noyce Road, Near Coaker's Walk, Kodaikanal 624103. 04542 246225/241365. www.zestbreaks.com. 11 rooms.* 'Solheim' House (Danish for House of the Sun), is a large Colonial villa on a stone-paved campus perched on a sunny hillside overlooking a valley. Run as a small boutique hotel by Club Mahindra, the stone cottage with a gabled roof has contrasting interiors that bear a more contemporary look. There's a small play area for children while soft adventure sports, downhill cycling and treks are also organised.

Cinnabar – *Chettiar Road, Kodaikanal 624101. 04542 240220/ 9842145220. www.cinnabar.in. 2 rooms.* This homestay is run by a warm and friendly couple, Vasu and Bala; the farm guesthouse is located in a serene campus of gardens and fruit trees. Detached from the main house are two immaculate guest rooms with hardwood floors, pine ceilings and Colonial bric-à-brac with a chef, master gardener, baker, cheese maker and even a jam lady at your service. Cinnabar's outstanding food is the highlight with varied menus each night ranging from Italian, Middle Eastern, Asian, Continental and Indian. Home-made granola, fresh-baked bread, home-cured cheese, gourmet coffee and tomato juice and salads from the organic garden are real highlights. Opt for a 3-day organic farming stay and you can learn bread baking, cheese making and vegetable harvesting, besides two complete menus and a take-home recipe booklet.

Misty Cove – *Lake Road, opp. Claverack Dorm, Kodaikanal 624101. 9841025076/9381272480. www.misty cove.net. 5 cottages.* An exclusive Colonial-style homestay by the lakefront, Misty Cove's central location is hard to beat. Set in a quiet nook amidst beautiful award-winning gardens, the property has 150m/500ft frontage of the lake. All cottages come with a large and small bedroom, a living room with a fireplace, a bathroom with hot water and a kitchen. You won't even notice the absence of a TV. Being a 100 pecent vegetarian homestay, no outside non-veg food, alcohol or tobacco is allowed. Meals are Rs.175–250 and a self-cooking option is available for Rs.350/day.

Kodai International – *Laws Ghat Road, Kodaikanal 624101. 04542 245190. www.kodaiinternational.com. 76 rooms.* A prominent hotel popular with families because of the facilities on offer – a small amusement park for kids, an in-house golf range, cute little bird zoo, Ayurveda massage centre, sports parlour, health club and bar. The Orchard restaurant serves decent Indian food. Local tours and treks are also organised.

Kodai Resort Hotel – *Coaker's Walk, Kodaikanal 624101. 04542 240632/241301. www.kodai resorthotel.com. 50 cottages.* Located less than a kilometre from town, set in a fruit orchard of pears and plums, this hotel has comfortable rooms with great views, plush executive suites with mini-gardens and an Ayurvedic spa. Guinea fowl and geese waddle in the sprawling garden. The restaurant built on the site of Overdane, an old English cottage, retains its original name and churns out mouthwatering fare. Open barbecue, health club, beauty parlour, children's park and a shop are added frills.

Hotel Villa Retreat – *Coaker's Walk, Kodaikanal 624101. 04542 240940. www.villaretreat.com. 14 rooms.* A charming Colonial retreat in a beautiful garden with ivies climbing up the stone walls, the retreat is on the eastern end of Coaker's Walk. The Victorian-style chalets and villas offer excellent views, snug fireplaces, home-cooked food and free Wi-Fi. Trekking tours organised.

Dalethorpe – *Convent Road, Kodaikanal. 04542 240656/9443322710. www.dalethorpe.com. 6 rooms.* Set in 0.6ha/1.5-acres, this charming homestay is a 1930s English bungalow. Standing in a grove of pine, beautiful lawns and gardens with exotic flowers and ornamental plants, it is a short walk from the lake. Dalethorpe has a kitchen that guests can use, although breakfast on the lawns and home-style food is also available on prior order.

AROUND KODAIKANAL

⊖⊖-⊖⊖⊖ **Elephant Valley** – *Ganesh Puram, Pethuparai (via), Perumalmalai, Kodaikanal 624104. ℘0454 2230399. www.elephantvalley hotel.com. 20 villas.* ☕. A 22km drive from Kodai and an 8km diversion off Palani Road, this 40ha/100-acre organic farm doubles up as a nature reserve with tree house, tents and cottages overlooking a coffee plantation and Gangavaar River. Local granite and reclaimed doors, windows and wood have been used in the eco-friendly construction with Colonial and Art Deco furniture. Freshly picked produce from the veg garden and orchard are served up in a thatched gourmet restaurant. The gourmet coffee, processed, roasted and packed at the plantation, has been awarded India's Best Organic Arabica in France and Italy in 2004. Nature walks and horse riding make up the activity quotient.

⊖⊖⊖ **Double Dutch Resort** – *Holland House, Athoor, Dindigul District 624701. ℘0454 3294499, 0451 2556763, 9443828742. www.doubledutchresort.com.* ⊭*. 6 rooms.* Located on the spurs of Palani Hills, this 3.2ha/8-acre Dutch-run resort is in a scenic valley bordered by Kamarajar Lake to the south and a reserve forest to the north. Food is an eclectic mix of Indian, European, Indonesian and Mexican dishes *(Rs.900/ person)* and dinner is usually served on the rooftop. Homemade jams, marmalades and bread go with a rich bounty from the farm – fresh fruits, vegetables, eggs, milk, cheese and curd, besides Dutch coffee. A small library and a grassy lakeside with shaded hammocks to read them in, or birdwatch from the verandah covered with bougainvillea. Get pampered at the in-house beauty parlour and massage or go on walks *(30min to 1 day)* to the lake, cave temple, waterfall, rice fields, peanut gardens and palm groves.

⊖⊖⊖ **Wild Rock** – *Kannivadi Hills, Sadayandi Kovil Road, Athoor Village, Dindigul District 624701. ℘0451 2471572/ 2470454. www.wildrock.asia.* ⊭*. 5 rooms.* ☕ ▤. Built in local granite, stone and marble, the country house comes with a swimming pool overlooking the lake. A restaurant, barbecue counter and fruit and salad kiosk serve delicious Indian fare *(Rs.950/person)*. Adventure sports like rock climbing, river crossing, trekking and mountaineering are organised, besides angling, horse riding, trips to villages and visits to cattle fields and farms.

EAT

The region's culinary landscape is a delectable mix of influences – from traditional South Indian eateries serving ***dosas*** and ***parottas***, the Kongu-naad cuisine typical of Coimbatore and Pollachi, the tribal influence of the Badagas and Todas to the Colonial touch of bakes and grills in the Nilgiris and Kodaikanal. Besides local cheese and home-made chocolates, several farmstays and boutique hotels serve excellent farm-fresh organic food. The Bus Stand and Poet Thyagarajar (PT) Road (near Seven Roads Junction) in Kodai and Charing Cross in Ooty are the main hubs for eating out.

OOTY

⊖⊖ **Kabab Corner** – *Commercial Road, Ooty 643001. ℘0423 2447321.* ⊭*. Open lunch and dinner.* A good place for North Indian non-veg cuisine with succulent kebabs, ***tandoori*** items and delicious butter chicken.

⊖⊖ **Shinkows** – *38/83, Commissioners Road, Ooty 643001. ℘0423 2442811.* ⊭ ♿*. Open daily 12.30–3.45pm, 6.30–9.45pm.* Down the road from Higginbotham's and St. Stephen's Church, Shinkows is an old Ooty institution serving good 'Indian Chinese' in a dim-lit ambience. Locals swear it's lost a bit of its original charm, however the Chilli Beef, Chilli Chicken and Young Chow Fried Noodles are still great.

KODAIKANAL

⊖⊖ **Tava Restaurant** – *PT Road, Seven Roads Junction, Kodaikanal 624101.* ⊭ ▤*. Open Thu–Tue 12noon–4pm, 5–10pm.* Located opposite New Hotel Punjab, this small, popular joint serves good veg food at reasonable prices. The North Indian ***thali*** is recommended.

Tibetan Brothers – *PT Road, Kodaikanal 624101. 04542 244638. Open daily 12noon–10.30pm.* One of Kodai's several Tibetan establishments, it serves yummy *momos*, *thukpas* and *fuyong* (Tibetan omelette) with *amdo* bread, a refreshing change from the South Indian/Tandoori staple. Enjoy Tibetan food amid portraits of the Potala Palace, Dalai Lama, *thangkas* and a sign 'Please do not use wine or drugs. Regardless of your status and position!'

COIMBATORE

That's Y Food – *24/49, TV Swamy Road (East), RS Puram, Coimbatore 641002 0422 4365117. www.thatsyfood.com. Open daily 1pm–3pm, 7pm–11pm.* A popular fusion restaurant/cafe serving delicious North Indian fare, including *biryanis*, *tikkas* and *dals* (Panchratni or Jaipuri are great). Equally adept at salads, pastas and Continental specialities. The desserts are divine – try hazelnut cakes, chocolate and apple tarts, sizzling brownies or mud soufflés.

Sree Annapoorna – *75, East Arokiasamy Road, RS Puram, Coimbatore 641002. 0422 4367373/4367474. www.sreeannapoorna.com. Open daily 11am–3pm, 5–10pm.* Coimbatore's iconic South Indian eatery with 13 branches all over the city serving excellent South Indian tiffin items, besides North Indian and Chinese. The coffee and *sambar* are legendary, as are the mushroom *biryani, upma khichdi*, curd *vada, sambar vada* and lunchtime *thalis*.

CAFES

Fay's Confectionery – *PT Road, Seven Road Junction, Kodaikanal 624101. 04542 241209. Open Wed–Mon 10am–8pm. Prices start at Rs.65.* Kodai's legendary bakery/cafe known for its home-made pastries, chocolates and cakes, besides short eats.

Sidewalk Café – *Commercial Road, near Charing Cross, Ooty 643001. 0423 2442173/2443685. www.naharhotels.com. Open daily 10.30am–9.30pm. Prices start at Rs.80–250.* A cosy Italian cafe at Nahar Hotels with bright cheerful interiors serving excellent pizzas, soups, sandwiches, cakes and assorted juices. The potato and leek soup and Popeye Pizza (with spinach) are legendary.

Tranquilitea Tea Lounge – *Off Kattabettu–Kotagiri Road, Coonoor 643101. 9443841572. www.tranquilitea.in. Open daily 11am–8pm. Prices start at Rs. 100.* Set in a 19C Colonial bungalow, sip world's finest teas accompanied by gourmet delicacies. Pick up gift teas of your choice, packed in Toda embroidered bags, crocheted pouches, teak boxes and charming gift packs.

LEISURE

Black Thunder – *Ooty Main Road, Mettupalayam, Coimbatore District 641305. 04254 226632-40. www.btpark.org. Open Mon–Sun, 9.30am–5.30pm. Entry Rs.400, Rs.350 children.* 26ha/65-acre theme park at the base of the Nilgiris with rollercoasters, water rides and other amusement avenues. They also run snack counters, veg and non-veg restaurants and a 40-room resort.

Jacaranda Spa & Salon – *Coral Gables Inn, Coonoor Club Road, Coonoor 643101. 0423 2232561/9442289565. Open Tue –Sun 9am–7pm. Rs.450–900 (50min).* Pamper yourself with a wide range of spa facials and body treatments, besides head and shoulder massages, manicures, pedicures and reflexology.

Kodaikanal Golf Club – *Golflinks Road, Kodaikanal 624103. 04542 240323. http://www.kodaigolf.com/home.htm.* This century-old 18-hole course undulating over 46ha/114 acres is thickly wooded and bison on the green add to the challenge. Temporary memberships are given to golfing enthusiasts and golf tournaments are held in January, April and May.

Palms Day Spa – *Palms Palace, Minerva House, Welbeck Road, Ooty 643001. 0423 2223232/2223179. www.palmsworld.in. Open daily 7am–7.30pm. Rs.1,000 for 1hr massage.* Set up in 1958 this beauty, health and rejuvenation centre is run by a Dutch-based company that specialises in plant-based herbal remedies and spa treatments.

SHOPPING

MARKETS

Coonoor Market – *Market Road, Lower Coonoor. Some sections closed on Friday.* A quaint market bustling with shops selling Nilgiri tea, jewellery, provisions and clothes, meat and fish stalls and a colourful vegetable section with fresh fruits and vegetables stacked in piles or spilling out of blue plastic troughs.

SPECIALITY SHOPS AND DESIGNER BOUTIQUES

Cottage Crafts – *PT Road, Kodaikanal 624101. ✆04542 240160. Open daily 10am–8pm. Closed Govt. hols.* Run by CORSOCK (Co-ordinating Council for Social Concerns in Kodai), a self-help society set up in 1970, the store sells eco-friendly crafts, warm clothing and gift items made by local disadvantaged groups.

Eco Nut – *PT Road, Kodaikanal 624101. ✆04542 243296. www.eco-nut.com. Open Mon–Sat 10.30am–5.30pm.* Perhaps the first organic and health food shop in South India, Eco Nut is a small shop with a mind-boggling range of products – organic tea, coffee, hand-pounded brown rice, breakfast cereals, pure honey, organic dried fruits, herbal drinks, Ayurvedic and Siddha medicines, natural perfumes, essential oils, shampoos and books on health and nutrition. Also on sale are ready-to-eat fresh breads, cheese, muffins, jams, peanut butter and chocolates.

Green Shop – *Sargun Villa, Club Road, opp. Hill Bunk Petrol Pump, Ooty 643001. ✆0423 2441340. www.lastforest.in. Open Mon–Sat 9.30am–1.30pm, 3–7pm.* Run by Keystone Foundation near the Ooty Club, the shop has wild honey, eco-conscious personal care products and indigenous handicrafts, bags and shawls made by local Nilgiri tribes. They also run outlets in Kotagiri at Johnston/ Kamarajar Square *(✆04266 273887)* and Bedford Circle, Upper Coonoor *(✆0423 2238412)* selling organic food, local handicrafts, essential oils, incense, clothes, books, CDs and toys.

Mohans – *Opp. Collector's Office, Commercial Street, Ooty 643001. ✆0423 2442376. Open Fri–Wed 10am–1pm and 3pm–8pm.* Ooty's iconic department store since 1947 that stocks clothes like Toda embroidered shawls and linen, art and crafts as well as home-made chocolates. Their affiliate store Rose and Teak on Mysore Road sells exquisite antiques, though the real treasures can be found in their warehouse.

Needle Craft – *Erin Villa, Singara Estate Road, Coonoor 643101. ✆0423 2230788. Open daily 10.30am–5.30pm.* A short scenic drive from Bedford leads to a beautiful Colonial villa surrounded by the Singara Tea Estate and a garden with an explosion of flowers. Run by Naaz Jaffer, Needle Craft has beautiful lace, embroidery and cross-stitch linen on sale. Choose from a range of bedspreads, doilies, tablecloths, towels, cocktail napkins or embroidered handkerchiefs.

Vriksh – *Primrose, Church Road, Bedford, Coonoor 643101. ✆0423 2221730. www. vrikshfurnitureantiques.com. Open daily 9.30am–6.30pm, Sun only Apr–May.* Run by Mrs Kirat Rajpal Singh, this antique-cum-furniture store has exquisite period furniture lovingly restored. Besides beds, chairs, chests and tables made of rosewood and teak, you can buy clocks, lights, paintings, prints, enamelware, porcelain and other bric-à-brac for the house.

BOOKSHOPS

Higginbotham's – *Commissioner's Road, Ooty 643001. ✆0423 2443736, 2442546. www.higginbothamsstore.com. Open Mon–Sat 9am–1pm, 2pm–5.30pm.* Housed in the beautiful Oriental Building, Higginbotham's has a good collection of fiction and non-fiction titles, maps and books on the Nilgiris. It also has a small outlet near the Tourist Office at Charing Cross.

PERFORMING ARTS

Upasana Academy of Fine Arts – *35, Nehru Stadium, Coimbatore 641018. ✆0422 230696.* Monthly music and dance performances are held in the Nani Palkiwala Auditorium.

NIGHTLIFE

Corniche Inn Resort – *11/10, Jambukandy Thadagam Road, Anaikatty, Coimbatore 641108. ✆0422 2657022. www.pearlscorniche.com.* Located on the outskirts of Coimbatore, the resort has a swanky bar with an excellent wine and liquor collection from across the world. It provides the perfect ambience to savour delicious finger food.

INDEX

A

Accessibility .30
Adam's Bridge .172
Adi Kumbeswara Temple 238
Airavatesvara Temple 240
Airlines .31
Alagar Kovil .212
Alangudi 237
Alwars, The .84
Anamalai National Park 269
Andavar Temple, Velliangiri Hills 266
Annadurai, C.N. 69, 71
Architecture .72
Arignar Anna Zoological Park .117
Arjuna's Penance .175
Art .78
Arunachala Legend 140
Arunachala, Mount 140
Arunachaleswara Temple 140
Arupadai Veedu .13
Athangudi Tiles 201
ATMS .41
Auroville .136
Auto Rickshaws .35
Avalanche .274
Avvaiyar Legend .214

B

Baksheesh .42
Banks .41
Bartering .39
Basic Information .39
Basilica of Our Lady of Good Health, Velankanni .171
Beaches
- Chennai and Around 119
- Coromandel Coast 186
- Pondicherry 147
- Southern Tamil Nadu 225

Bharata Natyam .92
Bharathi, Subramanya 69, 86
Birdwatching .16
Boat, By .32
Books .22
Books and Films .22
Brihadisvara Temple .243
Bronzes .80
Bus, By .34
Business Hours .39

C

Cafes and Bakeries
- Central Tamil Nadu 258
- Chennai and Around 128
- Chettinad 203
- Coromandel Coast 191
- Pondicherry 153
- Southern Tamil Nadu 230
- Western Ghats 288

Calendar of Events .24
Car, By .34
Carnatic Music .89
Cauvery River 234
Ceiling Paintings .80
Central Chennai .103
Central Tamil Nadu 7, 232
Chennai .103
- Armenian Church 110
- Children's Park, Guindy National Park 117
- Clive House 112
- Elliot's Beach 119
- Fort Museum 112
- Government Museum 115
- Guindy National Park 116
- Kapaleeswarar Temple 108
- Little Mount 110
- Luz Church 108
- Marina Beach 119
- Marina, The 103, 119
- San Thome Basilica 108
- Snake Park, Guindy National Park 117
- Sri Ramakrishna Math 109
- St Mary's Church 112
- St Thomas Mount 110
- Theosophical Society 109
- Thousand Lights Mosque 110
- Valluvar Kottam 111
- Vivekanandar House 116
- Wellesley House 112

Chennai and Around 6, 102
Chennai Wall Art .53
Chettiar Clan Temples .198
Chettiars, The .195
Chettinad 7, 194
Chettinad Cuisine .59
Chettinad Mansions .76
Chettinad/Raja Palace 200
Chidambaram 158, 168
Children, Activities for .18
Cholamandal Artists' Village .120
Chola Temples .74
Christianity .51
Cinema .86
Climate .10
Coach, By .34
Coffee .20
Cogan, Andrew .69
Coimbatore 262, 288

Colonial Period, The 68
Colonial Rule 71
Column Sculptures 79
Communications 39
Consulates 29
Cookery 17
Coonoor 273
Coromandel Coast 6, 97, 156
Courses 17
Courtallam 207
Courtallam Falls 224
Covelong Beach 121
Crafts 19
Credit and Debit Cards 41
Crocodile Bank 121
Cuddalore 180
Cuisine 58
Currency 41
Customs Regulations 30
Cycling 14

D

DakshinaChitra 120
Dance 92
Dansborg Fort 177
Day, Francis 69
Dhanushkodi 172
Discounts 40
Divya Desams 13
Driving 34
Driving Tours
Central Tamil Nadu 236
Coromandel Coast 160
Chettinad 197
Western Ghats 274

E

Early Stone Reliefs 78
East Coast Road (ECR) 120
East India Company, The 68
Economy 54
Economy Chain Hotels 36
Egmore, Chennai 104
Ekambaranath and the Sacred Mango Tree 164
Ekambaranath Temple 163
Electricity 40
Embassies 29
Emerald 274
Emergency Numbers 39
Emporiums 21
Energy Sources 55
Entry Requirements 29

F

Festivals 24
Films 23
Filmy Chakkar 273
Fishing 14
Flights 31
Folk Dances 93
Folk Music 90
Fort St George 103, 111
French Quarter, Pondicherry 133, 143

G

Gandhi Mandapam, Kanyakumari 219
Gandhi Memorial Museum, Madurai 221
Gangaikondacholapuram Temple 242
George Town 103
Getting Around 31
Getting There 31
Getting There and Around
Chennai and Around 106
Chettinad 196
Coromandel Coast 159
Pondicherry 134
Southern Tamil Nadu 208
Western Ghats 263
Gingee Fort 144
Golf 14
Government 54
Government Museum, Kanyakumari 222
Government Museum, Madurai 222
Governor's Bungalow, Tranquebar ...178
Gründler's House 179
Gulf of Mannar Marine National Park 184

H

Health 30
Heritage Hotels 37
Hiking 15
Hill Stations
Central Tamil Nadu 251
Western Ghats 270
Hinduism 51
Historical Sights
Central Tamil Nadu 248
Chennai and Around 111
Chettinad 200
Coromandel Coast 174
Pondicherry 143
Southern Tamil Nadu 218
History 61
Homestays 37
Horse Riding 15
Hostels 36
Hotel Booking 36

INDEX

I

Ilayathangudi 199
Ilyangudi Ayyanar 197
Iluppakudi 198
Independence 71
Indira Gandhi National Park. 269
Insurance 30
INTACH Museum, Tranquebar 179
International Calls 39
International Visitors 29
Internet. 40
Isha Yoga Centre 266
Islam 52
Iyer, U.V. Swaminatha 86

J

Jewellery 20

K

Kailasanatha Temple 164
Kalakad-Mundanthurai Tiger Reserve223
Kambar 84
Kanadukathan 195, 200
Kanchanur 236
Kanchi Kamakshi Amman Temple 165
Kanchi Kudil 181
Kanchipuram 158, 163, 181
Kanyakumari. 206, 216, 219, 222
Kanyakumari Beach 225
Kanyakumari, the Virgin Goddess 217
Karaikal. 161
Karaikudi 194
Karpaga Vinayakar Temple. 199
Kattabomman, Veerapandya. 65, 69
Kavadi 93
Kaveri River 234
Keeranur Ayyanar 197
Keezhaperumpallam 237
Know Before You Go. 28
Kodaikanal. .262, 277
Kolam 49
Kolattam. 93
Kollywood 87
Kotagiri. 275
Krishnapuram. 215
Krishna's Butter Ball 176
Kumari Amman Temple. 216
Kumbakonam. 233, 238
Kummi. 93
Kundrakudi 199
Kundrakudi Murugan Temple 199
Kurinji 94

L

Language. 52
Laundry 40
Leatherwork 19
Leisure
Central Tamil Nadu 258
Chennai and Around 128
Chettinad. 203
Coromandel Coast 191
Pondicherry 153
Southern Tamil Nadu. 230
Western Ghats 288
Lifestyle 48
Light Music 91
Liquor Law. 40
Literature 82

M

Madurai 205, 210, 218, 221
Magazines 42
Mahamagam Kulam 240
Mahamaham Tank. 240
Mahishasuramardini Cave 176
Mail 40
Mamallapuram. 157, 174, 176, 186
Mamallapuram Beach 186
Mandapam Beach Park 184
Marathas, The. 68
Mariamman Teppakkulam Tank 218
Marine Archaeology Museum, Poompuhar 182
Marudham. 96
Masilamani Nathar Temple. 179
Mathur 198
Matri Mandir 137
Media 56
Meditation. 17
Meenakshi Sundareshwarar Temple. .210
Mobile Phones 39
Money. 41
Motorcycle, By 34
Mudumalai 261
Mudumalai National Park 267
Mukkurthi National Park 268
Mullai. 95
Murugan's Emblem. 215
Murugan Temple, Palani Hills 265
Museums and Art Galleries
Chennai and Around 115
Coromandel Coast 181
Pondicherry 145
Southern Tamil Nadu. 221
Music. 89
Musical Instruments. 20

Music Season of Chennai, The.........90
Mylapore, Chennai 104

N

Nachiyar Koil.........................242
Nagapattinam 161
Nagore 171
Nagore Dargah.......................171
Narthamalai Cave Temples...........197
Nataraja, the Lord of Dance 81, 170
National Calls 39
National Parks and Wildlife Sanctuaries
- Central Tamil Nadu.....................250
- Chennai and Around 116
- Coromandel Coast 183
- Southern Tamil Nadu................... 223
- Western Ghats 267

Nature...............................94
Nature Lodges 37
Navagraha Temple Circuit 236
Navagraha Temples 13
Nayaka Strongholds and Palaces 75
Nayaka Temples......................75
Nayaks, The..........................67
Nayanmars, The......................84
Neidhal..............................97
Nellaiappar Temple..................214
Nemam..............................198
New Jerusalem Church 178
Newspapers 42

Nightlife
- Chennai and Around 131
- Coromandel Coast 193
- Pondicherry 155
- Western Ghats 289

Nilgiri Lake District 274
Nilgiri Mountain Railway............ 278
Nilgiris, The..........................94

O

Ootacamund, *see Ooty*
Ooty..........................262, 270
Opening Hours................... 19, 39
Organised Sightseeing Tours..........16

P

Paadal Petra Sthalam 13
Padmanabhapuram Palace 220
Palai.................................99
Palani Hills.....................265, 277
Pallava Temples......................73
Pancha Bhoota Sthalams 13
Pancha Rathas 177
Parsons Valley.......................274
Passport.............................29
Pazhamudhir Cholai Temple 214

Performing Arts
- Central Tamil Nadu..................... 259
- Chennai and Around 131
- Coromandel Coast 193
- Pondicherry 155
- Southern Tamil Nadu................... 231
- Western Ghats 289

Pichavaram 98, 184
Pillaiyarpatti 199
Plane, By.............................31
Point Calimere Sanctuary............185

Pondicherry...................6, 132
- Alliance Française...................... 146
- Ananda Ranga Pillai Museum........... 146
- Basilica of Our Lady of Health........... 139
- Bharathi Park 143
- Botanical Gardens...................... 144
- French Consulate....................... 142
- French Institute 145
- French War Memorial................... 142
- Gandhi Statue.......................... 142
- Immaculate Conception Cathedral...... 139
- Lighthouse 142
- Notre Dame des Anges 139
- Paradise Beach......................... 147
- Pondicherry Museum 145
- Raj Nivas............................... 143
- Romain Rolland Library................. 145
- Rue Dumas 142
- Rue Romain Rolland.................... 142
- Sacred Heart of Jesus Church 139
- Serenity Beach......................... 147
- Sri Aurobindo Ashram.................. 137
- Sri Manakula Vinayagar................. 138
- Sri Ramanasramam..................... 140

Poompuhar 160, 182, 186
Poompuhar Beach.................. 186
Population...........................48
Ports 32
Post 40
Public Holidays................... 24, 42
Pudukkottai.........................197
Pulicat Lake Bird Sanctuary 118
Pullirukkuvelur...................... 237
Puravai Attam.........................93

R

Railway..............................32
Railway Retiring Rooms...............37
Rajagopalachari, C................ 69, 71
Ramalingavilasam Museum..........182
Ramanathapuram...................182

INDEX

Ramanathaswami Temple 172
Ramanujam Mandapam, Mamallapuram 176
Ramasamy, E.V. (Periyar) 69, 71
Rama's Trail 173
Rameswaram 159, 172
Raya Gopuram, Mamallapuram 176
Red Hills 274
Rehling's House 178
Religion.............................50
Religious and Spiritual Sights
Central Tamil Nadu 238
Chennai and Around 108
Chettinad............................ 198
Coromandel Coast 163
Pondicherry 136
Southern Tamil Nadu.................. 210
Western Ghats 265
Religious Festivals...................25
Restaurants...........................38
Rock Fort Temple, Trichy............ 245

S

Seasons..............................10
Serfoji II............................69
Shakunthala Jagannathan Museum of Folk Art 181
Shola Forests.........................95
Shopping 19
Central Tamil Nadu 258
Chennai and Around 129
Chettinad............................ 203
Coromandel Coast 192
Pondicherry 154
Southern Tamil Nadu.................. 230
Western Ghats 288
Shore Temple 174
Sightseeing 16
Silappathikaram.......................83
Sirkali Bhramapureeswarar 160
Sittanavasal Cave Paintings..........197
Sivaganga 200
Sivaganga Palace..................... 200
Smoking...............................42
South Chennai 104
Southern Tamil Nadu 7, 204
Spas 17
Spices 21
Spiritual Circuits.....................13
Sport 57
Sri Chakrapani Temple............... 239
Sri Jambukeshwara Temple 246
Sri Kasi Vishwanatha Temple.........214
Sri Nageswara Temple 238
Srirangam 247
Sri Ranganathaswamy Temple 247
Sri Sarangapani Temple............. 239
Street and Railway Platform Food 38
Subramanya/Murugan Temple.......216
Suchindram...........................217
Sullivan, John 270
Surakkudi........................... 199
Suryanarkoil 236
Swamimalai Murugan 241

T

Tamil 43
Tamil Quarter, Pondicherry 133
Tanjore Painting.......................81
Tanjore, *see Thanjavur*
Tea 20
Tenkasi 214
Textiles 20, 80
Thaikkal 160
Thanjavur................. 234, 243, 248
Thanjavur Palace 248
Thanumalayan Temple 217
Themed Tours..........................11
Theppakadu 268
Thillai Nataraja Temple 168
Thingaloor.......................... 237
Thirukadaiyur....................... 160
Thirukkural 83
Thirumalai Nayak Palace............218
Thirunageswaram................... 237
Thirunallar.......................... 237
Thirupparankundram Temple........212
Thiruvaiyaru 250
Thiruvanaikkaval.................... 246
Thiruvenkadu 237
Tholkappiam...........................82
Time...................................42
Tipping 42
Tiruchendur..........................216
Tiruchirappalli, see Trichy........... 234
Tirukkalkunram 163
Tirumayam 197, 200
Tirumayam Fort 200
Tirunelveli 206, 214
Tirunelveli Halwa.................... 206
Tiruvannamalai 140
Tourist Offices........................28
Tourist Offices Abroad 29
Town Gate, Tranquebar..............178
Train, By 32
Tranquebar 158, 161, 177, 178
Transport 35
Traveller's Cheques....................41

Tribal Research Museum............274
Trichy........................234, 245
Trimurti Temple....................176
Tuticorin Airport 208

U

Useful Words and Phrases 43
Uthiramerur 168

V

Vaccinations 30
Vaikuntha Perumal Temple 166
Vairavanpatti 199
Vaitheeswaran Koil................ 160
Vallanadu Wildlife Sanctuary.........185
Varadaraja Perumal Temple......... 166
Varaha Cave.........................176
VAT..................................42
Vedanthangal Bird Sanctuary 183
Velangudi...........................198
Velankanni.................... 161, 171
Velliangiri Hills 266
Vellore Fort 114
Venkatachalapathi Temple...........215
Viralimalai 250
Visa..................................29
Vivekananda Rock Memorial.........219
Volunteering.........................18

W

Walking Tours
Around Fort St George 112
Chennai Guided Tours.................. 113
French Quarter, Pondicherry............ 142
Mamallapuram.......................... 176
Tranquebar 178
Wall Carvings 79
Water Sports..........................16
Websites..............................28
Weekend Breaks 10
Western Ghats 7, 94, 260
What to See and Do 14
When and Where to Go...............10
Where to Stay and Eat 36

Y

Yercaud........................235, 251
Yoga..................................18
Yogis 83

Z

Ziegenbalg Memorial................178
Ziegenbalg Museum Complex 179
Zion Church, Tranquebar 178

STAY

Around Coonoor 282
Around Kodaikanal.....................287
Around Ooty...........................281
Chennai and Around 122
Chettinad.............................202
Chidambaram..........................188
Coonoor 282
Courtallam........................... 228
Kanchipuram 188
Kanyakumari..........................227
Kodaikanal........................... 285
Kotagiri............................. 283
Kumbakonam..........................253
Madurai 226
Mamallapuram.........................187
Mudumalai 284
Nagapattinam 189
Ooty................................. 280
Pondicherry 148
Rameswaram 189, 191
Sivakasi............................. 229
Swamimalai........................... 254
Thanjavur............................ 254
Thoothukudi.......................... 228
Tiruchendur 228
Tirunelvell 228
Tranquebar 189
Trichy................................255
Velankanni............................189
Yercaud.............................. 256

EAT

Chennai and Around 126
Chettinad.............................203
Kanchipuram 191
Kanyakumari.......................... 230
Kodaikanal............................287
Kumbakonam.......................... 257
Madurai 229
Mamallapuram.........................190
Ooty..................................287
Pondicherry 152
Tenkasi 230
Thanjavur............................ 257
Trichy............................... 258
Yercaud.............................. 258

MAPS AND PLANS

THEMATIC MAPS

Principal Sights........Inside front cover
Chennai ....Inside back cover

MAPS AND PLANS

Chennai and Around
Chennai 107

Pondicherry
Pondicherry......................... 135

Coromandel Coast
Coromandel Coast.................. 162
Kanchipuram 166
Chidambaram Nataraja Temple 169
Mamallapuram..................... 174

Chettinad
Chettinad.......................... 198

Southern Tamil Nadu
Southern Tamil Nadu 209
Madurai 212

Central Tamil Nadu
Central Tamil Nadu 237
Brihadisvara Temple................. 243

Western Ghats
Western Ghats 264
Ooty................................ 271

MAP LEGEND

	Sight	Seaside resort	Winter sports resort	Spa
Highly recommended	★★★			
Recommended	★★			
Interesting	★			

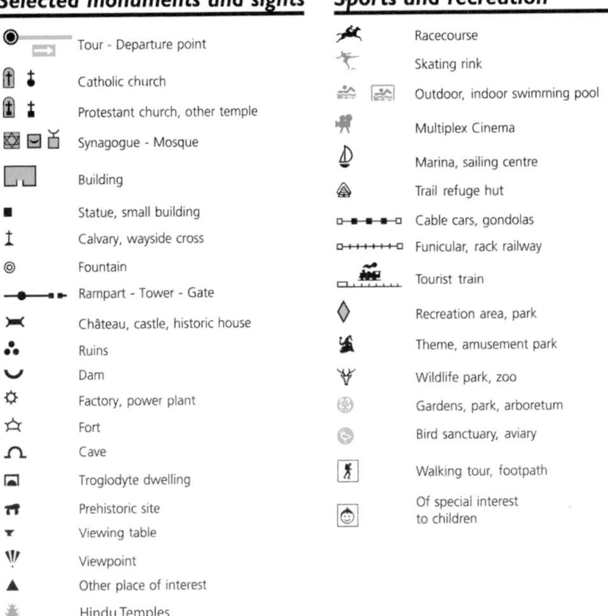

Selected monuments and sights

- Tour - Departure point
- Catholic church
- Protestant church, other temple
- Synagogue - Mosque
- Building
- Statue, small building
- Calvary, wayside cross
- Fountain
- Rampart - Tower - Gate
- Château, castle, historic house
- Ruins
- Dam
- Factory, power plant
- Fort
- Cave
- Troglodyte dwelling
- Prehistoric site
- Viewing table
- Viewpoint
- Other place of interest
- Hindu Temples

Sports and recreation

- Racecourse
- Skating rink
- Outdoor, indoor swimming pool
- Multiplex Cinema
- Marina, sailing centre
- Trail refuge hut
- Cable cars, gondolas
- Funicular, rack railway
- Tourist train
- Recreation area, park
- Theme, amusement park
- Wildlife park, zoo
- Gardens, park, arboretum
- Bird sanctuary, aviary
- Walking tour, footpath
- Of special interest to children

Abbreviations

G, POL	Police (Federale Politie)
H	Town hall (Hôtel de ville ou maison communale)
J	Law courts (Palais de justice)
M	Museum (Musée)
P	Local government offices (Gouvernement provincial)
P	Provincial capital (Chef-lieu de provincial)
T	Theatre (Théatrè)
U	University (Université)

Additional symbols

- Tourist information
- Motorway or other primary route
- Junction: complete, limited
- Pedestrian street
- Unsuitable for traffic, street subject to restrictions
- Steps – Footpath
- Train station – Auto-train station
- Coach (bus) station
- Tram
- Metro, underground
- Park-and-Ride
- Access for the disabled
- Post office
- Telephone
- Covered market
- Barracks
- Drawbridge
- Quarry
- Mine
- B F Car ferry (river or lake)
- Ferry service: cars and passengers
- Foot passengers only
- ③ Access route number common to Michelin maps and town plans
- Bert (R.)... Main shopping street
- AZ B Map co-ordinates

The Michelin Adventure

It all started with rubber balls! This was the product made by a small company based in Clermont-Ferrand that André and Edouard Michelin inherited, back in 1880. The brothers quickly saw the potential for a new means of transport and their first success was the invention of detachable pneumatic tires for bicycles. However, the automobile was to provide the greatest scope for their creative talents. Throughout the 20th century, Michelin never ceased developing and creating ever more reliable and high-performance tires, not only for vehicles ranging from trucks to F1 but also for underground transit systems and airplanes.

From early on, Michelin provided its customers with tools and services to facilitate mobility and make traveling a more pleasurable and more frequent experience. As early as 1900, the Michelin Guide supplied motorists with a host of useful information related to vehicle maintenance, accommodation and restaurants, and was to become a benchmark for good food. At the same time, the Travel Information Bureau offered travelers personalised tips and itineraries.

The publication of the first collection of roadmaps, in 1910, was an instant hit! In 1926, the first regional guide to France was published, devoted to the principal sites of Brittany, and before long each region of France had its own Green Guide. The collection was later extended to more far-flung destinations, including New York in 1968 and Taiwan in 2011.

In the 21st century, with the growth of digital technology, the challenge for Michelin maps and guides is to continue to develop alongside the company's tire activities. Now, as before, Michelin is committed to improving the mobility of travelers.

MICHELIN TODAY

WORLD NUMBER ONE TIRE MANUFACTURER

- 70 production sites in 18 countries
- 111,000 employees from all cultures and on every continent
- 6,000 people employed in research and development

Moving
for a world

Moving forward means developing tires with better road grip and shorter braking distances, whatever the state of the road.

CORRECT TIRE PRESSURE

RIGHT PRESSURE

- Safety
- Longevity
- Optimum fuel consumption

-0,5 bar

- Durability reduced by 20% (- 8,000 km)

- Risk of blowouts
- Increased fuel consumption
- Longer braking distances on wet surfaces

forward together
where mobility is safer

It also involves helping motorists take care of their safety and their tires. To do so, Michelin organises "Fill Up With Air" campaigns all over the world to remind us that correct tire pressure is vital.

WEAR

DETECTING TIRE WEAR

The legal minimum depth of tire tread is 1.6mm. Tire manufacturers equip their tires with tread wear indicators, which are small blocks of rubber moulded into the base of the main grooves at a depth of 1.6mm.

Tires are the only point of contact between the vehicle and road.

The photo below shows the actual contact zone.

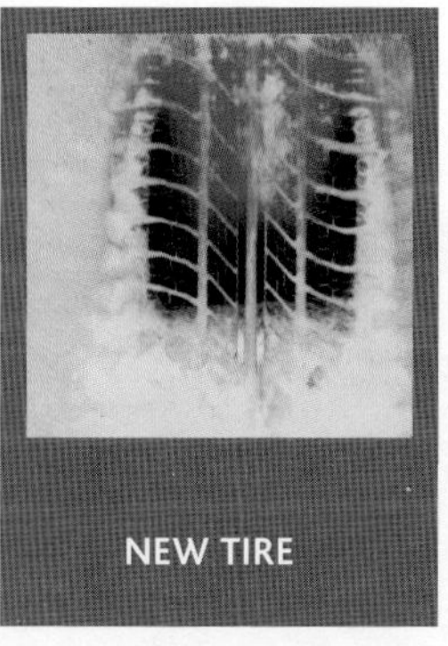

NEW TIRE

WORN TIRE
(1,6 mm tread)

If the tread depth is less than 1.6mm, tires are considered to be worn and dangerous on wet surfaces.

Moving forward
means sustainable mobility

INNOVATION AND THE ENVIRONMENT

By 2050, Michelin aims to cut the quantity of raw materials used in its tire manufacturing process by half and to have developed renewable energy in its facilities. The design of MICHELIN tires has already saved billions of litres of fuel and, by extension, billions of tons of CO2.

Similarly, Michelin prints its maps and guides on paper produced from sustainably managed forests and is diversifying its publishing media by offering digital solutions to make traveling easier, more fuel efficient and more enjoyable!

The group's whole-hearted commitment to eco-design on a daily basis is demonstrated by ISO 14001 certification.

Like you, Michelin is committed to preserving our planet.

Chat with Bibendum

Go to
www.michelin.com/corporate/en
Find out more about
Michelin's history and the
latest news.

QUIZ

Michelin develops tires for all types of vehicles.
See if you can match the right tire with the right vehicle…

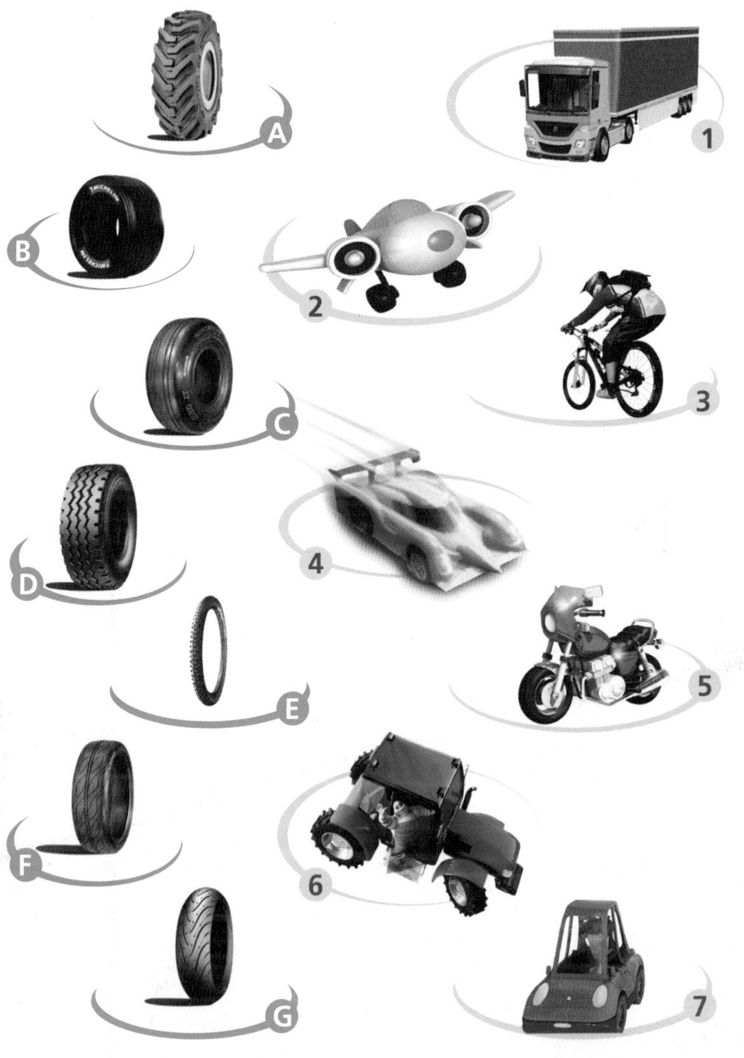

Solution : A-6 / B-4 / C-2 / D-1 / E-3 / F-7 / G-5

Michelin Travel Partner

Société par actions simplifiées au capital de 11 629 590 EUR
27 cours de l'Ile Seguin - 92100 Boulogne Billancourt (France)
R.C.S. Nanterre 433 677 721

ISBN 978-2-067188-47-1
Printed: February 2013
Printed and bound in India